Stanley Gibbon
Stamp Catalogu

Poland

2nd edition 2023

STANLEY GIBBONS
THE HOME OF STAMP COLLECTING

By Appointment to
Her Majesty The Queen
Philatelists
Stanley Gibbons Ltd,
London

1st Edition – 2015
2nd Edition – 2023

Published by Stanley Gibbons Ltd
Editorial, Publications Sales Offices
and Distribution Centre:
7 Parkside, Christchurch Road, Ringwood,
Hants BH24 3SH

British Library Cataloguing in
Publication Data.
A catalogue record for this book is available
from the British Library.

Errors and omissions excepted. The colour reproduction of stamps is only as accurate as the printing process will allow.

ISBN-13 978-1-73986-965-6

Item No. R1425-23

Printed by
Sterling, Kettering

Stanley Gibbons Foreign Catalogue Parts 2–22

ABOUT THIS EDITION

The Stanley Gibbons Poland catalogue contains all the stamps of Poland from the very earliest issues to mid-2022. Here you will find up-to-date lists for all the stamps from the earliest issues of Poland; all major varieties are included, notably perforation, watermark and shade variations, overprint types and major errors.

Apart from the stamps of the current issuing country, this catalogue also covers German Occupation of Poland, Polish Military Posts, Polish Occupation of Central Lithuania, Polish Post Offices Abroad (Constantinople, Danzig, Odessa), Allenstein, Danzig, Marienwerder and Upper Silesia.

- Prices checked and updated throughout
- Poland new issues updated to June 2022

The first supplement to this edition appeared in *Gibbons Stamp Monthly* for March 2023.

Clare de la Feuillade, Editor
Shelley Day, Advertising Sales
Sue Price, New Issues Listings
Barbara Hawkins, Pricing Assistant
Leslie Fuller, Proof Reader

SPECIALIST SOCIETIES

Society for Polish Philately in Great Britain
Email: jkorzeniowski@talktalk.net

Polonus Philatelic Society
1510 Los Altos Drive
Burlingame CA
94010 USA

Website: www.polonus.org

STAMPS ADDED

121a
122a

NUMBERS ALTERED

OLD	NEW	OLD	NEW
3975a	3976	3977	3978i
3975b	3977	3977a	3978j
3975c	3978	3977b	3978k
3975d	3978a	3977c	3978l
3975e	3978b	3977d	3978m
3975ea	3978c	3978	3978n
3975eb	3978d	3978a	3978o
3975ec	3978e	3978b	3978p
3975h	3978f	3978ba	3978q
3975i	3978g	3978bc	3978r
3976	3978h	3978bd	3978s

Stamp

Contents

Stanley Gibbons Holdings Plc

Stanley Gibbons Limited, Stanley Gibbons Auctions
399 Strand, London, WC2R 0LX
Tel: +44 (0)207 836 8444
E-mail: support@stanleygibbons.com
Website: www.stanleygibbons.com
for all departments, Auction and Specialist Stamp Departments.

Open Monday–Friday 9.30 a.m. to 6 p.m.
Shop. Open Monday–Saturday 9.30 a.m. to 6 p.m.

Stanley Gibbons Publications, Mail Order and Gibbons Stamp Monthly
7 Parkside, Christchurch Road, Ringwood, Hampshire, BH24 3SH
Tel: +44 (0)1425 472363
E-mail: support@stanleygibbons.com

Monday–Friday 8.30 a.m. to 5 p.m.

Stanley Gibbons Publications Overseas Representation
Stanley Gibbons Publications are represented overseas by the following:

Australia
Renniks Publications PTY LTD
Unit 6, 30 Perry St, Matraville,
NSW 2036, Australia
Tel: +612 9695 7055
Website: www.renniks.com

Canada
Unitrade Associates
99 Floral Parkway, Toronto,
Ontario M6L 2C4, Canada
Tel: +1 416 242 5900
Website: www.unitradeassoc.com

Canada
F.v.H. Stamps
102-340 West Cordova Street,
Vancouver, BC, V6B 1E8, Canada
Tel: +1 604 684 8408
Website: www.fvhstamps.com

Canada
Armstrong's
PO Box 261
Bright's Grove
Ontario, Canada, N0N 1C0
Tel: +519 464 2688
Website: www.armstrongsstamps.ca

Denmark
Nordfrim A/S
Kvindevadet 42,
Otterup DK-5450, Denmark
Tel: +45 64 82 1256
Website: www.nordfrim.com

Italy
Ernesto Marini S.R.L.
V. Struppa, 300, Genova, 16165, Italy
Tel: +39 010 802 186
Website: www.ernestomarini.it

Japan
Japan Philatelic
PO Box 2, Suginami-Minami,
Tokyo 168-8081, Japan
Tel: +81 3330 41641
Website: www.yushu.co.jp

Netherlands
Uitgeverij Davo BV
PO Box 411, Ak Deventer, 7400
Netherlands
Tel: +3188 0284300
Website: www.davo.nl

New Zealand
House of Stamps
PO Box 12, Paraparaumu,
New Zealand
Tel: +61 6364 8270
Website: www.houseofstamps.co.nz

New Zealand
Philatelic Distributors
PO Box 863
15 Mount Edgecumbe Street
New Plymouth 4615, New Zealand
Tel: +6 46 758 65 68
Website: www.stampcollecta.com

Singapore
C S Philatelic Agency
Peninsula Shopping Centre #04-29
3 Coleman Street, 179804, Singapore
Tel: +65 6337-1859
Website: www.cs.com.sg

USA
Vidiforms Company Inc
115 North Route 9W, Congers,
New York NY 10920, United States
Tel: +1 845 268 4005
Website: www.showgard.com

USA
Amos Media Company
1660 Campbell Road,
Suite A, Door #9,
Sidney OH 453652480,
United States
Tel: +1 937 498 2111
Website: www.amosmedia.com

General Philatelic Information and Guidelines to the Scope of Stanley Gibbons Foreign Catalogues

These notes reflect current practice in compiling the Foreign Catalogue.

The *Stanley Gibbons Stamp Catalogue* has a very long history and the vast quantity of information it contains has been carefully built up by successive generations through the work of countless individuals. Philately itself is never static and the Catalogue has evolved and developed during this long time-span. These notes apply to current policy – some of the older listings were prepared using slightly different criteria – and we hope you find them useful in using the catalogue.

THE CATALOGUE IN GENERAL

Contents. The Catalogue is confined to adhesive postage stamps, including miniature sheets. For particular categories the rules are:

(a) Revenue (fiscal) stamps or telegraph stamps are listed only where they have been expressly authorised for postal duty.
(b) Stamps issued only precancelled are included, but normally issued stamps available additionally with precancel have no separate precancel listing unless the face value is changed.
(c) Stamps prepared for use but not issued, hitherto accorded full listing, are nowadays footnoted with a price (where possible).
(d) Bisects (trisects, etc.) are only listed where such usage was officially authorised.
(e) Stamps issued only on first day covers and not available separately are not listed but priced (on the cover) in a footnote.
(f) New printings, as such, are not listed, though stamps from them may qualify under another category, e.g. when a prominent new shade results.
(g) Official and unofficial reprints are dealt with by footnote.
(h) Stamps from imperforate printings of modern issues which also occur perforated are covered by footnotes or general notes, but are listed where widely available for postal use.

Exclusions. The following are excluded:

(a) non-postal revenue or fiscal stamps;
(b) postage stamps used fiscally;
(c) local carriage labels and private local issues;
(d) telegraph stamps;
(e) bogus or phantom stamps;
(f) railway or airline letter fee stamps, bus or road transport company labels;
(g) cut-outs;
(h) all types of non-postal labels;
(i) documentary labels for the postal service, e.g. registration, recorded delivery, airmail etiquettes, etc.;
(j) privately applied embellishments to official issues and privately commissioned items generally;
(k) stamps for training postal officers;
(l) specimen stamps (except those distributed by the UPU).

Full listing. 'Full listing' confers our recognition and implies allotting a catalogue number and (wherever possible) a price quotation.

In judging status for inclusion in the catalogue broad considerations are applied to stamps. They must be issued by a legitimate postal authority, recognised by the government concerned, and must be adhesives valid for proper postal use in the class of service for which they are inscribed. Stamps, with the exception of such categories as postage dues and officials, must be available to the general public, at face value, in reasonable quantities without any artificial restrictions being imposed on their distribution.

We record as abbreviated Appendix entries, without catalogue numbers or prices, stamps from countries which either persist in having far more issues than can be justified by postal need or have failed to maintain control over their distribution so that they have not been available to the public in reasonable quantities at face value. Miniature sheets and imperforate stamps are not mentioned in these entries.

The publishers of this catalogue have observed, with concern, the proliferation of 'artificial' stamp-issuing territories. On several occasions this has resulted in separately inscribed issues for various component parts of otherwise united states or territories.

Stanley Gibbons Publications have decided that where such circumstances occur, they will not, in the future, list these items in the Stanley Gibbons catalogue without first satisfying themselves that the stamps represent a genuine political, historical or postal division within the country concerned. Any such issues which do not fulfil this stipulation will be recorded in the Catalogue Appendix only.

For errors and varieties the criterion is legitimate (albeit inadvertent) sale over a post office counter in the normal course of business. Details of provenance are always important; printers' waste and fraudulently manufactured material are excluded.

Certificates. In assessing unlisted items due weight is given to Certificates from recognised Expert Committees and, where appropriate, we will usually ask to see them.

New issues. New issues are listed regularly in the Catalogue Supplement in *Gibbons Stamp Monthly*, then consolidated into the next available edition of the Catalogue.

Date of issue. Where local issue dates differ from dates of release by agencies, 'date of issue' is the local date. Fortuitous stray usage before the officially intended date is disregarded in listing.

Catalogue numbers. Stamps of each country are catalogued chronologically by date of issue. Subsidiary classes (e.g. postage due stamps) are integrated into one list with postage and commemorative stamps and distinguished by a letter prefix to the catalogue number.

The catalogue number appears in the extreme left column. The boldface type numbers in the next column are merely cross-references to illustrations. Catalogue numbers in the *Gibbons Stamp Monthly* Supplement are provisional only and may need to be altered when the lists are consolidated. Miniature sheets only purchasable intact at a post office have a single MS number; sheetlets – individual stamps available – number each stamp separately. The catalogue no longer gives full listing to designs originally issued in normal sheets, which subsequently appear in sheetlets showing changes of colour, perforation, printing process or face value. Such stamps will be covered by footnotes.

Once published in the Catalogue, numbers are changed as little as possible; really serious renumbering is reserved for the occasions when a complete country or an entire issue is being rewritten. The edition first affected includes cross-reference tables of old and new numbers.

Our catalogue numbers are universally recognised in specifying stamps and as a hallmark of status.

Illustrations. Stamps are illustrated at three-quarters linear size. Stamps not illustrated are the same size and format as the value shown unless otherwise indicated. Stamps issued only as miniature sheets have the stamp alone illustrated but sheet size is also quoted. Overprints, surcharges, watermarks and postmarks are normally actual size. Illustrations of varieties are often enlarged to show the detail.

CONTACTING THE CATALOGUE EDITOR

The editor is always interested in hearing from people who have new information which will improve or correct the Catalogue. As a general rule she must see and examine the actual stamps before they can be considered for listing; photographs or photocopies are insufficient evidence. Neither she nor her staff give opinions as to the genuineness of stamps.

Submissions should be made in writing to the Catalogue Editor, Stanley Gibbons Publications, 7 Parkside, Christchurch Road, Ringwood, Hants BH24 3SH. The cost of return postage for items submitted is appreciated, and this should include the registration fee if required.

Where information is solicited purely for the benefit of the enquirer, the editor cannot undertake to reply if the answer is already contained in these published notes or if return postage is omitted. Written or email communications are greatly preferred to enquiries by telephone and the editor regrets that she or her staff cannot see personal callers without a prior appointment being made.

The editor welcomes close contact with study circles and is interested, too, in finding local correspondents who will verify and supplement official information in overseas countries where this is deficient.

We regret we do not give opinions as to the genuineness of stamps, nor do we identify stamps or number them by our Catalogue.

TECHNICAL MATTERS

The meanings of the technical terms used in the Catalogue will be found in *Philatelic Terms Illustrated*, published by Stanley Gibbons.

1. Printing

Printing errors. Errors in printing are of major interest to the Catalogue. Authenticated items meriting consideration would include background, centre or frame inverted or omitted; centre or subject transposed; error of colour; error or omission of value; double prints and impressions; printed both sides; and so on. Designs *tête-bêche*, whether intentionally or by accident, are listable. *Se-tenant* arrangements of stamps are recognised in the listings or footnotes. Gutter pairs (a pair of stamps separated by blank margin) are excluded unless they have some philatelic importance. Colours only partially omitted are not listed, neither are stamps printed on the gummed side.

Printing varieties. Listing is accorded to major changes in the printing base which lead to completely new types. In recess-printing this could be a design re-engraved, in photogravure or photolithography a screen altered in whole or in part. It can also encompass flat-bed and rotary printing if the results are readily distinguishable.

To be considered at all, varieties must be constant.

Early stamps, produced by primitive methods, were prone to numerous imperfections; the lists reflect this, recognising re-entries, retouches, broken frames, misshapen letters, and so on. Printing technology has, however, radically improved over the years, during which time photogravure and lithography have become predominant. Varieties nowadays are more in the nature of flaws and these, being too specialised for a general catalogue, are almost always outside the scope. We therefore do not list such items as dry prints, kiss prints, doctor-blade flaws, blanket set-offs, doubling through blanket stretch, plate cracks and scratches, registration flaws (leading to colour shifts), lithographic ring flaws, and so on. Neither do we recognise fortuitous happenings like paper creases or confetti flaws.

Overprints (and surcharges). Overprints of different types qualify for separate listing. These include overprints in different colours; overprints from different printing processes such as litho and typo; overprints in totally different typefaces, etc.

Overprint errors and varieties. Major errors in machine-printed overprints are important and listable. They include overprint inverted or omitted; overprint double (treble, etc.); overprint diagonal; overprint double, one inverted; pairs with one overprint omitted, e.g. from a radical shift to an adjoining stamp; error of colour; error of type fount; letters inverted or omitted, etc. If the overprint is handstamped, few of these would qualify and a distinction is drawn.

Varieties occurring in overprints will often take the form of broken letters, slight differences in spacing, rising spacers, etc. Only the most important

would be considered for footnote mention.
Sheet positions. If space permits we quote sheet positions of listed varieties and authenticated data is solicited for this purpose.

2. Paper

All stamps listed are deemed to be on 'ordinary' paper of the wove type and white in colour; only departures from this are mentioned.
Types. Where classification so requires we distinguish such other types of paper as, for example, vertically and horizontally laid; wove and laid bâtonné; card(board); carton; cartridge, enamelled; glazed; GC (Grande Consommation); granite; native; pelure; porous; quadrillé; ribbed; rice; and silk thread.

The 'traditional' method of indentifying chalk-surfaced papers has been that, when touched with a silver wire, a black mark is left on the paper, and the listings in this catalogue are based on that test. However, the test itself is now largely discredited, for, although the mark can be removed by a soft rubber, some damage to the stamp will result from its use.

The difference between chalk-surfaced and pre-war ordinary papers is fairly clear: chalk-surfaced papers being smoother to the touch and showing a characteristic sheen when light is reflected off their surface. Under good magnification tiny bubbles or pock marks can be seen on the surface of the stamp and at the tips of the perforations the surfacing appears 'broken'. Traces of paper fibres are evident on the surface of ordinary paper and the ink shows a degree of absorption into it.

The various makeshifts for normal paper are listed as appropriate. They include printing on: unfinished banknotes, war maps, ruled paper, Post Office forms, and the unprinted side of glossy magazines. The varieties of double paper and joined paper are recognised.
Descriptive terms. The fact that a paper is hand-made (and thus probably of uneven thickness) is mentioned where necessary. Such descriptive terms as 'hard' and 'soft'; 'smooth' and 'rough'; 'thick', 'medium' and 'thin' are applied where there is philatelic merit in classifying papers.
Coloured, very white and toned papers. A coloured paper is one that is coloured right through (front and back of the stamp). In the Catalogue the colour of the paper is given in italics, thus

black/*rose* = black design on rose paper.

Papers have been made specially white in recent years by, for example, a very heavy coating of chalk. We do not classify shades of whiteness of paper as distinct varieties. There does exist, however, a type of paper from early days called toned. This is off-white, often brownish or buffish, but it cannot be assigned a definite colour. A toning effect brought on by climate, incorrect storage or gum staining is disregarded here, as this was not the state of the paper when issued.
Safety devices. The Catalogue takes account of such safety devices as varnish lines, grills, burelage or imprinted patterns on the front or moiré on the back of stamps.
Modern developments. Two modern developments also affect the listings, printing on self-adhesive paper and the tendency, philatelic in origin, for conventional paper to be reinforced or replaced by different materials. Some examples are the use of foils in gold, silver, aluminium, palladium and steel; application of an imitation wood veneer; printing on plastic moulded in relief; and use of a plastic laminate to give a three-dimensional effect. Examples also occur of stamps impregnated with scent; printed on silk; and incorporating miniature gramophone records.

3. Perforation and Rouletting

Perforation gauge. The gauge of a perforation is the number of holes in a length of 2 cm. For correct classification the size of the holes (large or small) may need to be distinguished; in a few cases the actual number of holes on each edge of the stamp needs to be quoted.
Measurement. The Gibbons Instanta gauge is the standard for measuring perforations. The stamp is viewed against a dark background with the transparent gauge put on top of it. Though the gauge measures to decimal accuracy, perforations read from it are generally quoted in the Catalogue to the nearest half. For example:

Just over perf.
12¾ to just under perf. 13¼ = perf 13
Perf. 13¼ exactly, rounded up = perf 13½
Just over perf.
13¼ to just under perf. 13¾ = perf 13½
Perf. 13¾ exactly, rounded up = perf 14

However, where classification depends on it, actual quarter-perforations are quoted.
Notation. Where no perforation is quoted for an issue it is imperforate. Perforations are usually abbreviated (and spoken) as follows, though sometimes they may be spelled out for clarity. This notation for rectangular stamps (the majority) applies to diamond shapes if 'top' is read as the edge to the top right.

P 14: perforated alike on all sides (read: 'perf 14').

P 14×15: the first figure refers to top and bottom, the second to left and right sides (read: 'perf 14 by 15'). This is a compound perforation. For an upright triangular stamp the first figure refers to the two sloping sides and the second to the base. In inverted triangulars the base is first and the second figure refers to the sloping sides.

P 14–15: perforation measuring anything between 14 and 15: the holes are irregularly spaced, thus the gauge may vary along a single line or even along a single edge of the stamp (read: 'perf 14 to 15').

P 14 irregular. perforated 14 from a worn perforator, giving badly aligned holes irregular spaced (read 'irregular perf 14').

P *comp(ound)* 14×15: two gauges in use but not

necessarily on opposite sides of the stamp. It could be one side in one gauge and three in the other, or two adjacent sides with the same gauge (Read: 'perf compound of 14 and 15'). For three gauges or more, abbreviated as 'P 14, 14½, 15 or compound' for example.

P 14, 14½: perforated approximately 14¼ (read: 'perf 14 or 14½'). It does not mean two stamps, one perf 14 and the other perf 14½. This obsolescent notation is gradually being replaced in the Catalogue.

Imperf: imperforate (not perforated).

Imperf × P 14: imperforate at top and bottom and perf 14 at sides.

P 14×imperf = perf 14 at top and bottom and imperforate at sides.

Such headings as 'P 13 × 14 (vert) and P 14 × 13 (horiz)' indicate which perforations apply to which stamp format – vertical or horizontal.

Some stamps are additionally perforated so that a label or tab is detachable; others have been perforated suitably for use as two halves. Listings are normally for whole stamps, unless stated otherwise.

Other terms. Perforation almost always gives circular holes; where other shapes have been used they are specified, e.g. square holes; lozenge perf. Interrupted perfs are brought about by the omission of pins at regular intervals. Perforations have occasionally been simulated by being printed as part of the design. With few exceptions, privately applied perforations are not listed.

Perforation errors and varieties. Authenticated errors, where a stamp normally perforated is accidentally issued imperforate, are listed provided no traces of perforation (blind holes or indentations) remain. They must be provided as pairs, both stamps wholly imperforate, and are only priced in that form.

Stamps merely imperforate between stamp and margin (fantails) are not listed.

Imperforate-between varieties are recognised, where one row of perfs has been missed. They are listed and priced in pairs:

Imperf between (horiz pair): a horizontal pair of stamps with perfs all around the edges but none between the stamps.

Imperf between (vert pair): a vertical pair of stamps with perfs all around the edges but none between the stamps.

Where several of the rows have escaped perforation the resulting varieties are listable. Thus:

Imperf vert (horiz pair): a horizontal pair of stamps perforated top and bottom; all three vertical directions are imperf – the two outer edges and between the stamps.

Imperf horiz (vert pair): a vertical pair perforated at left and right edges; all three horizontal directions are imperf – the top, bottom and between the stamps.

Straight edges. Large sheets cut up before issue to post offices can cause stamps with straight edges, i.e. imperf on one side or on two sides at right angles. They are not usually listable in this condition and are worth less than corresponding stamps properly perforated all round. This does not, however, apply to certain stamps, mainly from coils and booklets, where straight edges on various sides are the manufacturing norm affecting every stamp. The listings and notes make clear which sides are correctly imperf.

Malfunction. Varieties of double, misplaced or partial perforation caused by error or machine malfunction are not listable, neither are freaks, such as perforations placed diagonally from paper folds. Likewise disregarded are missing holes caused by broken pins, and perforations 'fading out' down a sheet, the machinery progressively disengaging to leave blind perfs and indentations to the paper.

Centering. Well-centred stamps have designs surrounded by equal opposite margins. Where this condition affects the price the fact is stated.

Type of perforating. Where necessary for classification, perforation types are distinguished. These include:

Line perforation from one line of pins punching single rows of holes at a time.

Comb perforation from pins disposed across the sheet in comb formation, punching out holes at three sides of the stamp a row at a time.

Harrow perforation applied to a whole pane or sheet at one stroke.

Rotary perforation from the toothed wheels operating across a sheet, then crosswise.

Sewing-machine perforation. The resultant condition, clean-cut or rough, is distinguished where required.

Pin-perforation is the commonly applied term for pin-roulette in which, instead of being punched out, round holes are pricked by sharp-pointed pins and no paper is removed.

Punctured stamps. Perforation holes can be punched into the face of the stamp. Patterns of small holes, often in the shape of initial letters, are privately applied devices against pilferage. These 'perfins' are outside the scope. Identification devices, when officially inspired, are listed or noted; they can be shapes, or letters or words formed from holes, sometimes converting one class of stamp into another.

Rouletting. In rouletting the paper is cut, for ease of separation, but none is removed. The gauge is measured, when needed, as for perforations. Traditional French terms descriptive of the type of cut are often used and types include:

Arc roulette (percé en arc). Cuts are minute, spaced arcs, each roughly a semicircle.

Cross roulette (percé en croix). Cuts are tiny diagonal crosses.

Line roulette (parcé en ligne or en ligne droite). Short straight cuts parallel to the frame of the stamp. The commonest basic roulette. Where not further described, 'roulette' means this type.

Rouletted in colour or coloured roulette (percé en lignes colorees or en lignes de coleur). Cuts with coloured edges, arising from notched rule inked simultaneously with the printing plate.

Saw-tooth roulette (percé en scie). Cuts applied zigzag fashion to resemble the teeth of a saw.

Serpentine roulette (percé en serpentin). Cuts as sharply wavy lines.

Zigzag roulettes (percé en zigzags). Short straight cuts at angles in alternate directions, producing sharp points on separation. US usage favours 'serrate(d) roulette' for this type.

Pin-roulette (originally *percé en points* and now *perforés trous d'epingle)* is commonly called pin-perforation in English.

4. Gum

All stamps listed are assumed to have gum of some kind; if they were issued without gum this is stated. Original gum (o.g.) means that which was present on the stamp as issued to the public. Deleterious climates and the presence of certain chemicals can cause gum to crack and, with early stamps, even make the paper deteriorate. Unscrupulous fakers are adept in removing it and regumming the stamp to meet the unreasoning demand often made for 'full o.g.' in cases where such a thing is virtually impossible.

Until recent times the gum used for stamps has been gum arabic, but various synthetic adhesives – tinted or invisible-looking – have been in use since the 1960s. Stamps existing with more than one type of gum are not normally listed separately, though the fact is noted where it is of philatelic significance, e.g. in distinguishing reprints or new printings.

The distinct variety of grilled gum is, however, recognised. In this the paper is passed through a gum breaker prior to printing to prevent subsequent curling. As the patterned rollers were sufficient to impress a grill into the paper beneath the gum we can quote prices for both unused and used examples.

Self-adhesive stamps are issued on backing paper from which they are peeled before affixing to mail. Unused examples are priced as for backing paper intact. Used examples are best kept *on cover* or *on piece*.

5. Watermarks

Stamps are on unwatermarked paper except where the heading to the set says otherwise.

Detection. Watermarks are detected for Catalogue description by one of four methods:

(1) holding stamps to the light;
(2) laying stamps face down on a dark background;
(3) adding a few drops of petroleum ether 40/60 to the stamp laid face down in a watermark tray; or
(4) by use of the Stanley Gibbons Detectamark, or other equipment, which works by revealing the thinning of the paper at the watermark. (Note that petroleum ether is highly inflammable in use and can damage photogravure stamps.)

Listable types. Stamps occurring on both watermarked and unwatermarked papers are different types and both receive full listing.

Single watermarks (devices occurring once on every stamp) can be modified in size and shape as between different issues; the types are noted but not usually separately listed. Fortuitous absence of watermark from a single stamp or its gross displacement would not be listable.

To overcome registration difficulties the device may be repeated at close intervals (a **multiple watermark**), single stamps thus showing parts of several devices. Similarly a large **sheet watermark** (or all-over watermark) covering numerous stamps can be used. We give informative notes and illustrations for them. The designs may be such that numbers of stamps in the sheet automatically lack watermark; this is not a listable variety. Multiple and all-over watermarks sometimes undergo modifications, but if the various types are difficult to distinguish from single stamps notes are given but not separate listings.

Papermakers' watermarks are noted where known but not listed separately, since most stamps in the sheet will lack them. Sheet watermarks which are nothing more than officially adopted papermakers' watermarks are, however, given normal listing.

Marginal watermarks, falling outside the pane of stamps, are ignored except where misplacement causes the adjoining row to be affected, in which case they may be footnoted.

Watermark errors and varieties. Watermark errors are recognised as of major importance. They comprise stamps intended to be on unwatermarked paper but issued watermarked by mistake, or stamps printed on paper with the wrong watermark. Watermark varieties, on the other hand, such as broken or deformed bits on the dandy roll, are not listable.

Watermark positions. Paper has a side intended for printing and watermarks are usually impressed so that they read normally when looked through from that printed side.

Illustrations in the Catalogue are of watermarks in normal positions (from the front of the stamps) and are actual size where possible.

Differences in watermark position are collectable as distinct varieties. In this Catalogue, however, only normal sideways watermarks are listed (and 'sideways inverted' is treated as 'sideways'). Inverted and reversed watermarks have always been outside its scope: in the early days of flat-bed printing, sheets of watermarked paper were fed indiscriminately through the press and the resulting watermark positions had no particular philatelic significance. Similarly, the special make-up of sheets for booklets can in some cases give equal quantities of normal and inverted watermarks.

6. Colours

Stamps in two or three colours have these named in order of appearance, from the centre moving outwards. Four colours or more are usually listed as multicoloured.

In compound colour names the second is the

predominant one, thus:
orange-red = a red tending towards orange;
red-orange = an orange containing more red than usual.

Standard colours used. The 200 colours most used for stamp identification are given in the Stanley Gibbons Colour Key. The Catalogue has used the Key as a standard for describing new issues for some years. The names are also introduced as lists are rewritten, though exceptions are made for those early issues where traditional names have become universally established.

Determining colours. When comparing actual stamps with colour samples in the Key, view in a good north daylight (or its best substitute: fluorescent 'colour-matching' light). Sunshine is not recommended. Choose a solid portion of the stamp design; if available, marginal markings such as solid bars of colour or colour check dots are helpful. Shading lines in the design can be misleading as they appear lighter than solid colour. Postmarked portions of a stamp appear darker than normal. If more than one colour is present, mask off the extraneous ones as the eye tends to mix them.

Errors of colour. Major colour errors in stamps or overprints which qualify for listing are: wrong colours; one colour inverted in relation to the rest; albinos (colourless impressions), where these have Expert Committee certificates; colours completely omitted, but only on unused stamps (if found on used stamps the information is footnoted).

Colours only partially omitted are not recognised.

Colour shifts, however spectacular, are not listed.

Shades. Shades in philately refer to variations in the intensity of a colour or the presence of differing amounts of other colours. They are particularly significant when they can be linked to specific printings. In general, shades need to be quite marked to fall within the scope of this Catalogue; it does not favour nowadays listing the often numerous shades of a stamp, but chooses a single applicable colour name which will indicate particular groups of outstanding shades. Furthermore, the listings refer to colours as issued: they may deteriorate into something different through the passage of time.

Modern colour printing by lithography is prone to marked differences of shade, even within a single run, and variations can occur within the same sheet. Such shades are not listed.

Aniline colours. An aniline colour meant originally one derived from coal-tar; it now refers more widely to colour of a particular brightness suffused on the surface of a stamp and showing through clearly on the back.

Colours of overprints and surcharges. All overprints and surcharges are in black unless otherwise in the heading or after the description of the stamp.

7. Luminescence

Machines which sort mail electronically have been introduced in recent years. In consequence some countries have issued stamps on fluorescent or phosphorescent papers, while others have marked their stamps with phosphor bands.

The various papers can only be distinguished by ultraviolet lamps emitting particular wavelengths. They are separately listed only when the stamps have some other means of distinguishing them, visible without the use of these lamps. Where this is not so, the papers are recorded in footnotes or headings. (Collectors using the lamps should exercise great care in their use as exposure to their light is extremely dangerous to the eyes).

Phosphor bands are listable, since they are visible to the naked eye (by holding stamps at an angle to the light and looking along them, the bands appear dark). Stamps existing with and without phosphor bands or with differing numbers of bands are given separate listings. Varieties such as double bands, misplaced or omitted bands, bands printed on the wrong side, are not listed.

8. Coil Stamps

Stamps issued only in coil form are given full listing. If stamps are issued in both sheets and coils the coil stamps are listed separately only where there is some feature (e.g. perforation) by which singles can be distinguished. Coil strips containing different stamps *se-tenant* are also listed.

Coil join pairs are too random and too easily faked to permit of listing; similarly ignored are coil stamps which have accidentally suffered an extra row of perforations from the claw mechanism in a malfunctioning vending machine.

9. Booklet Stamps

Single stamps from booklets are listed if they are distinguishable in some way (such as watermark or perforation) from similar sheet stamps. Booklet panes, provided they are distinguishable from blocks of sheet stamps, are listed for most countries; booklet panes containing more than one value *se-tenant* are listed under the lowest of the values concerned.

Lists of stamp booklets are given for certain countries and it is intended to extend this generally.

10. Forgeries and Fakes

Forgeries. Where space permits, notes are considered if they can give a concise description that will permit unequivocal detection of a forgery. Generalised warnings, lacking detail, are not nowadays inserted since their value to the collector is problematic.

Fakes. Unwitting fakes are numerous, particularly 'new shades' which are colour changelings brought about by exposure to sunlight, soaking in water contaminated with dyes from adherent paper, contact with oil and dirt from a pocketbook, and so on. Fraudulent operators, in addition, can offer to arrange: removal of hinge marks; repairs of thins on white or coloured papers; replacement of missing margins or perforations; reperforating in true or false gauges; removal of fiscal cancellations; rejoining of severed pairs, strips and blocks; and (a major hazard) regumming. Collectors can only be urged to purchase from reputable sources and to insist upon Expert Committee certification where there is any doubt.

The Catalogue can consider footnotes about fakes where these are specific enough to assist in detection.

PRICES

Prices quoted in this Catalogue are the selling prices of Stanley Gibbons Ltd at the time when the book went to press. They are for stamps in fine condition for the issue concerned; in issues where condition varies they may ask more for the superb and less for the sub-standard.

All prices are subject to change without prior notice and Stanley Gibbons Ltd may from time to time offer stamps at other than catalogue prices in consequence of special purchases or particular promotions.

No guarantee is given to supply all stamps priced, since it is not possible to keep every catalogued item in stock. Commemorative issues may, at times, only be available in complete sets and not as individual values.

Quotations of prices. The prices in the left-hand column are for unused stamps and those in the right-hand column are for used.

Prices are expressed in pounds and pence sterling. One pound comprises 100 pence (£1 = 100p.).

The method of notation is as follows: pence in numerals (e.g. 10 denotes ten pence); pounds and pence up to £100, in numerals (e.g. 4.25 denotes four pounds and twenty-five pence); prices above £100 expressed in whole pounds with the '£' sign shown.

Unused stamps. Prices for stamps issued up to the end of the Second World War (1945) are for lightly hinged examples and more may be asked if they are in unmounted mint condition. Prices for all later unused stamps are for unmounted mint. Where not available in this condition, lightly hinged stamps are often available at a lower price.

Used stamps. The used prices are normally for stamps postally used but may be for stamps cancelled-to-order where this practice exists.

A pen-cancellation on early issues can sometimes correctly denote postal use. Instances are individually noted in the Catalogue in explanation of the used price given.

Prices quoted for bisects on cover or *on large piece* are for those dated during the period officially authorised.

Stamps not sold unused to the public but affixed by postal officials before use (e.g. some parcel post stamps) are priced used only.

Minimum price. The minimum catalogue price quoted is 10p. For individual stamps prices between 10p. and 95p. are provided as a guide for catalogue users. The lowest price charged for individual stamps purchased from Stanley Gibbons Ltd. is £1.

Set prices. Set prices are generally for one of each value, excluding shades and varieties, but including major colour changes. Where there are alternative shades, etc, the cheapest is usually included. The number of stamps in the set is always stated for clarity.

Where prices are given for *se-tenant* blocks or strips, any mint price quoted is for the complete *se-tenant* strip or block. Mint and used set prices are always for a set of single stamps.

Repricing. Collectors will be aware that the market factors of supply and demand directly influence the prices quoted in this Catalogue. Whatever the scarcity of a particular stamp, if there is no one in the market who wishes to buy it it cannot be expected to achieve a high price. Conversely, the same item actively sought by numerous potential buyers may cause the price to rise.

All the prices in this Catalogue are examined during the preparation of each new edition by expert staff of Stanley Gibbons and repriced as necessary. They take many factors into account, including supply and demand, and are in close touch with the international stamp market and the auction world.

GUARANTEE

All stamps are guaranteed genuine originals in the following terms:

If not as described, and returned by the purchaser, we undertake to refund the price paid to us in the original transaction. If any stamp is certified as genuine by the Expert Committee of the Royal Philatelic Society, London, or by B.P.A. Expertising Ltd, the purchaser shall not be entitled to make claim against us for any error, omission or mistake in such certificate. Consumers' statutory rights are not affected by this guarantee.

The establishment Expert Committees in this country are those of the Royal Philatelic Society, 15 Abchurch Lane, London, EC4 7BW and BPA Expertising Ltd, PO Box 1141, Guildford, Surrey, GU5 0WR. They do not undertake valuations under any circumstances and fees are payable for their services.

Abbreviations

Printers

A.B.N. Co.	American Bank Note Co, New York.
B.A.B.N.	British American Bank Note Co. Ottawa
B.D.T.	B.D.T. International Security Printing Ltd, Dublin, Ireland
B.W.	Bradbury Wilkinson & Co, Ltd.
Cartor	Cartor S.A., La Loupe, France
C.B.N.	Canadian Bank Note Co, Ottawa.
Continental	Continental Bank Note Co. B.N. Co.
Courvoisier	Imprimerie Courvoisier S.A., La-Chaux-de-Fonds, Switzerland.
D.L.R.	De La Rue & Co, Ltd, London.
Enschedé	Joh. Enschedé en Zonen, Haarlem, Netherlands.
Format	Format International Security Printers Ltd., London
Harrison	Harrison & Sons, Ltd. London
J.W.	John Waddington Security Print Ltd., Leeds
P.B.	Perkins Bacon Ltd, London.
Questa	Questa Colour Security Printers Ltd, London
Walsall	Walsall Security Printers Ltd
Waterlow	Waterlow & Sons, Ltd, London.

General Abbreviations

Alph	Alphabet
Anniv	Anniversary
Comp	Compound (perforation)
Des	Designer; designed
Diag	Diagonal; diagonally
Eng	Engraver; engraved
f.c.	Fiscal Cancellation
H/S	Handstamped
Horiz	Horizontal; horizontally
Imp, Imperf	Imperforate
Inscr	Inscribed
L	Left
Litho	Lithographed
mm	Millimetres
MS	Miniature sheet
NY	New York
Opt(d)	Overprint(ed)
P or P-c	Pen-cancelled
P, Pf or Perf	Perforated
Photo	Photogravure
Pl	Plate
Pr	Pair
Ptd	Printed
Ptg	Printing
R	Right
R.	Row
Recess	Recess-printed
Roto	Rotogravure
Roul	Rouletted
S	Specimen (overprint)
Surch	Surcharge(d)
T.C.	Telegraph Cancellation
T	Type
Typo	Typographed
Un	Unused
Us	Used
Vert	Vertical; vertically
W or wmk	Watermark
Wmk s	Watermark sideways

(†) = Does not exist

(–) (or blank price column) = Exists, or may exist, but no market price is known.

/ between colours means 'on' and the colour following is that of the paper on which the stamp is printed.

Colours of Stamps

Bl (blue); blk (black); brn (brown); car, carm (carmine); choc (chocolate); clar (claret); emer (emerald); grn (green); ind (indigo); mag (magenta); mar (maroon); mult (multicoloured); mve (mauve); ol (olive); orge (orange); pk (pink); pur (purple); scar (scarlet); sep (sepia); turq (turquoise); ultram (ultramarine); verm (vermilion); vio (violet); yell (yellow).

Colour of Overprints and Surcharges

(B.) = blue, (Blk.) = black, (Br.) = brown, (C.) = carmine, (G.) = green, (Mag.) = magenta, (Mve.) = mauve, (Ol.) = olive, (O.) = orange, (P.) = purple, (Pk.) = pink, (R.) = red, (Sil.) = silver, (V.) = violet, (Vm.) or (Verm.) = vermilion, (W.) = white, (Y.) = yellow.

Arabic Numerals

As in the case of European figures, the details of the Arabic numerals vary in different stamp designs, but they should be readily recognised with the aid of this illustration.

٠	١	٢	٣	٤	٥	٦	٧	٨	٩
0	1	2	3	4	5	6	7	8	9

International Philatelic Glossary

English	*French*	*German*	*Spanish*	*Italian*
Agate	Agate	Achat	Agata	Agata
Air stamp	Timbre de la poste aérienne	Flugpostmarke	Sello de correo aéreo	Francobollo per posta aerea
Apple Green	Vert-pomme	Apfelgrün	Verde manzana	Verde mela
Barred	Annulé par barres	Balkenentwertung	Anulado con barras	Sbarrato
Bisected	Timbre coupé	Halbiert	Partido en dos	Frazionato
Bistre	Bistre	Bister	Bistre	Bistro
Bistre-brown	Brun-bistre	Bisterbraun	Castaño bistre	Bruno-bistro
Black	Noir	Schwarz	Negro	Nero
Blackish Brown	Brun-noir	Schwärzlichbraun	Castaño negruzco	Bruno nerastro
Blackish Green	Vert foncé	Schwärzlichgrün	Verde negruzco	Verde nerastro
Blackish Olive	Olive foncé	Schwärzlicholiv	Oliva negruzco	Oliva nerastro
Block of four	Bloc de quatre	Viererblock	Bloque de cuatro	Bloco di quattro
Blue	Bleu	Blau	Azul	Azzurro
Blue-green	Vert-bleu	Blaugrün	Verde azul	Verde azzuro
Bluish Violet	Violet bleuâtre	Bläulichviolett	Violeta azulado	Violtto azzurrastro
Booklet	Carnet	Heft	Cuadernillo	Libretto
Bright Blue	Bleu vif	Lebhaftblau	Azul vivo	Azzurro vivo
Bright Green	Vert vif	Lebhaftgrün	Verde vivo	Verde vivo
Bright Purple	Mauve vif	Lebhaftpurpur	Púrpura vivo	Porpora vivo
Bronze Green	Vert-bronze	Bronzegrün	Verde bronce	Verde bronzo
Brown	Brun	Braun	Castaño	Bruno
Brown-lake	Carmin-brun	Braunlack	Laca castaño	Lacca bruno
Brown-purple	Pourpre-brun	Braunpurpur	Púrpura castaño	Porpora bruno
Brown-red	Rouge-brun	Braunrot	Rojo castaño	Rosso bruno
Buff	Chamois	Sämisch	Anteado	Camoscio
Cancellation	Oblitération	Entwertung	Cancelación	Annullamento
Cancelled	Annulé	Gestempelt	Cancelado	Annullato
Carmine	Carmin	Karmin	Carmín	Carminio
Carmine-red	Rouge-carmin	Karminrot	Rojo carmín	Rosso carminio
Centred	Centré	Zentriert	Centrado	Centrato
Cerise	Rouge-cerise	Kirschrot	Color de ceresa	Color Ciliegia
Chalk-surfaced paper	Papier couché	Kreidepapier	Papel estucado	Carta gessata
Chalky Blue	Bleu terne	Kreideblau	Azul turbio	Azzurro smorto
Charity stamp	Timbre de bienfaisance	Wohltätigkeitsmarke	Sello de beneficenza	Francobollo di beneficenza
Chestnut	Marron	Kastanienbraun	Castaño rojo	Marrone
Chocolate	Chocolat	Schokolade	Chocolate	Cioccolato
Cinnamon	Cannelle	Zimtbraun	Canela	Cannella
Claret	Grenat	Weinrot	Rojo vinoso	Vinaccia
Cobalt	Cobalt	Kobalt	Cobalto	Cobalto
Colour	Couleur	Farbe	Color	Colore
Comb-perforation	Dentelure en peigne	Kammzähnung, Reihenzähnung	Dentado de peine	Dentellatura e pettine
Commemorative stamp	Timbre commémoratif	Gedenkmarke	Sello conmemorativo	Francobollo commemorativo
Crimson	Cramoisi	Karmesin	Carmesí	Cremisi
Deep Blue	Blue foncé	Dunkelblau	Azul oscuro	Azzurro scuro
Deep bluish Green	Vert-bleu foncé	Dunkelbläulichgrün	Verde azulado oscuro	Verde azzurro scuro
Design	Dessin	Markenbild	Diseño	Disegno

English	French	German	Spanish	Italian
Die	Matrice	Urstempel. Type, Platte	Cuño	Conio, Matrice
Double	Double	Doppelt	Doble	Doppio
Drab	Olive terne	Trüboliv	Oliva turbio	Oliva smorto
Dull Green	Vert terne	Trübgrün	Verde turbio	Verde smorto
Dull purple	Mauve terne	Trübpurpur	Púrpura turbio	Porpora smorto
Embossing	Impression en relief	Prägedruck	Impresión en relieve	Impressione a relievo
Emerald	Vert-eméraude	Smaragdgrün	Esmeralda	Smeraldo
Engraved	Gravé	Graviert	Grabado	Inciso
Error	Erreur	Fehler, Fehldruck	Error	Errore
Essay	Essai	Probedruck	Ensayo	Saggio
Express letter stamp	Timbre pour lettres par exprès	Eilmarke	Sello de urgencia	Francobollo per espresso
Fiscal stamp	Timbre fiscal	Stempelmarke	Sello fiscal	Francobollo fiscale
Flesh	Chair	Fleischfarben	Carne	Carnicino
Forgery	Faux, Falsification	Fälschung	Falsificación	Falso, Falsificazione
Frame	Cadre	Rahmen	Marco	Cornice
Granite paper	Papier avec fragments de fils de soie	Faserpapier	Papel con filamentos	Carto con fili di seta
Green	Vert	Grün	Verde	Verde
Greenish Blue	Bleu verdâtre	Grünlichblau	Azul verdoso	Azzurro verdastro
Greenish Yellow	Jaune-vert	Grünlichgelb	Amarillo verdoso	Giallo verdastro
Grey	Gris	Grau	Gris	Grigio
Grey-blue	Bleu-gris	Graublau	Azul gris	Azzurro grigio
Grey-green	Vert gris	Graugrün	Verde gris	Verde grigio
Gum	Gomme	Gummi	Goma	Gomma
Gutter	Interpanneau	Zwischensteg	Espacio blanco entre dos grupos	Ponte
Imperforate	Non-dentelé	Geschnitten	Sin dentar	Non dentellato
Indigo	Indigo	Indigo	Azul indigo	Indaco
Inscription	Inscription	Inschrift	Inscripción	Dicitura
Inverted	Renversé	Kopfstehend	Invertido	Capovolto
Issue	Émission	Ausgabe	Emisión	Emissione
Laid	Vergé	Gestreift	Listado	Vergato
Lake	Lie de vin	Lackfarbe	Laca	Lacca
Lake-brown	Brun-carmin	Lackbraun	Castaño laca	Bruno lacca
Lavender	Bleu-lavande	Lavendel	Color de alhucema	Lavanda
Lemon	Jaune-citron	Zitrongelb	Limón	Limone
Light Blue	Bleu clair	Hellblau	Azul claro	Azzurro chiaro
Lilac	Lilas	Lila	Lila	Lilla
Line perforation	Dentelure en lignes	Linienzähnung	Dentado en linea	Dentellatura lineare
Lithography	Lithographie	Steindruck	Litografía	Litografia
Local	Timbre de poste locale	Lokalpostmarke	Emisión local	Emissione locale
Lozenge roulette	Percé en losanges	Rautenförmiger Durchstich	Picadura en rombos	Perforazione a losanghe
Magenta	Magenta	Magentarot	Magenta	Magenta
Margin	Marge	Rand	Borde	Margine
Maroon	Marron pourpré	Dunkelrotpurpur	Púrpura rojo oscuro	Marrone rossastro
Mauve	Mauve	Malvenfarbe	Malva	Malva
Multicoloured	Polychrome	Mehrfarbig	Multicolores	Policromo
Myrtle Green	Vert myrte	Myrtengrün	Verde mirto	Verde mirto
New Blue	Bleu ciel vif	Neublau	Azul nuevo	Azzurro nuovo
Newspaper stamp	Timbre pour journaux	Zeitungsmarke	Sello para periódicos	Francobollo per giornali
Obliteration	Oblitération	Abstempelung	Matasello	Annullamento
Obsolete	Hors (de) cours	Ausser Kurs	Fuera de curso	Fuori corso

English	French	German	Spanish	Italian
Ochre	Ocre	Ocker	Ocre	Ocra
Official stamp	Timbre de service	Dienstmarke	Sello de servicio	Francobollo di
Olive-brown	Brun-olive	Olivbraun	Castaño oliva	Bruno oliva
Olive-green	Vert-olive	Olivgrün	Verde oliva	Verde oliva
Olive-grey	Gris-olive	Olivgrau	Gris oliva	Grigio oliva
Olive-yellow	Jaune-olive	Olivgelb	Amarillo oliva	Giallo oliva
Orange	Orange	Orange	Naranja	Arancio
Orange-brown	Brun-orange	Orangebraun	Castaño naranja	Bruno arancio
Orange-red	Rouge-orange	Orangerot	Rojo naranja	Rosso arancio
Orange-yellow	Jaune-orange	Orangegelb	Amarillo naranja	Giallo arancio
Overprint	Surcharge	Aufdruck	Sobrecarga	Soprastampa
Pair	Paire	Paar	Pareja	Coppia
Pale	Pâle	Blass	Pálido	Pallido
Pane	Panneau	Gruppe	Grupo	Gruppo
Paper	Papier	Papier	Papel	Carta
Parcel post stamp	Timbre pour colis postaux	Paketmarke	Sello para paquete postal	Francobollo per pacchi postali
Pen-cancelled	Oblitéré à plume	Federzugentwertung	Cancelado a pluma	Annullato a penna
Percé en arc	Percé en arc	Bogenförmiger Durchstich	Picadura en forma de arco	Perforazione ad arco
Percé en scie	Percé en scie	Bogenförmiger Durchstich	Picado en sierra	Foratura a sega
Perforated	Dentelé	Gezähnt	Dentado	Dentellato
Perforation	Dentelure	Zähnung	Dentar	Dentellatura
Photogravure	Photogravure, Heliogravure	Rastertiefdruck	Fotograbado	Rotocalco
Pin perforation	Percé en points	In Punkten durchstochen	Horadado con alfileres	Perforato a punti
Plate	Planche	Platte	Plancha	Lastra, Tavola
Plum	Prune	Pflaumenfarbe	Color de ciruela	Prugna
Postage Due stamp	Timbre-taxe	Portomarke	Sello de tasa	Segnatasse
Postage stamp	Timbre-poste	Briefmarke, Freimarke, Postmarke	Sello de correos	Francobollo postale
Postal fiscal stamp	Timbre fiscal-postal	Stempelmarke als Postmarke verwendet	Sello fiscal-postal	Fiscale postale
Postmark	Oblitération postale	Poststempel	Matasello	Bollo
Printing	Impression, Tirage	Druck	Impresión	Stampa, Tiratura
Proof	Épreuve	Druckprobe	Prueba de impresión	Prova
Provisionals	Timbres provisoires	Provisorische Marken. Provisorien	Provisionales	Provvisori
Prussian Blue	Bleu de Prusse	Preussischblau	Azul de Prusia	Azzurro di Prussia
Purple	Pourpre	Purpur	Púrpura	Porpora
Purple-brown	Brun-pourpre	Purpurbraun	Castaño púrpura	Bruno porpora
Recess-printing	Impression en taille douce	Tiefdruck	Grabado	Incisione
Red	Rouge	Rot	Rojo	Rosso
Red-brown	Brun-rouge	Rotbraun	Castaño rojizo	Bruno rosso
Reddish Lilac	Lilas rougeâtre	Rötlichlila	Lila rojizo	Lilla rossastro
Reddish Purple	Poupre-rouge	Rötlichpurpur	Púrpura rojizo	Porpora rossastro
Reddish Violet	Violet rougeâtre	Rötlichviolett	Violeta rojizo	Violetto rossastro
Red-orange	Orange rougeâtre	Rotorange	Naranja rojizo	Arancio rosso
Registration stamp	Timbre pour lettre chargée (recommandée)	Einschreibemarke	Sello de certificado lettere	Francobollo per raccomandate
Reprint	Réimpression	Neudruck	Reimpresión	Ristampa
Reversed	Retourné	Umgekehrt	Invertido	Rovesciato
Rose	Rose	Rosa	Rosa	Rosa
Rose-red	Rouge rosé	Rosarot	Rojo rosado	Rosso rosa
Rosine	Rose vif	Lebhaftrosa	Rosa vivo	Rosa vivo
Roulette	Percage	Durchstich	Picadura	Foratura
Rouletted	Percé	Durchstochen	Picado	Forato
Royal Blue	Bleu-roi	Königblau	Azul real	Azzurro reale

English	French	German	Spanish	Italian
Sage green	Vert-sauge	Salbeigrün	Verde salvia	Verde salvia
Salmon	Saumon	Lachs	Salmón	Salmone
Scarlet	Écarlate	Scharlach	Escarlata	Scarlatto
Sepia	Sépia	Sepia	Sepia	Seppia
Serpentine roulette	Percé en serpentin	Schlangenliniger Durchstich	Picado a serpentina	Perforazione a serpentina
Shade	Nuance	Tönung	Tono	Gradazione de colore
Sheet	Feuille	Bogen	Hoja	Foglio
Slate	Ardoise	Schiefer	Pizarra	Ardesia
Slate-blue	Bleu-ardoise	Schieferblau	Azul pizarra	Azzurro ardesia
Slate-green	Vert-ardoise	Schiefergrün	Verde pizarra	Verde ardesia
Slate-lilac	Lilas-gris	Schierferlila	Lila pizarra	Lilla ardesia
Slate-purple	Mauve-gris	Schieferpurpur	Púrpura pizarra	Porpora ardesia
Slate-violet	Violet-gris	Schieferviolett	Violeta pizarra	Violetto ardesia
Special delivery stamp	Timbre pour exprès	Eilmarke	Sello de urgencia	Francobollo per espressi
Specimen	Spécimen	Muster	Muestra	Saggio
Steel Blue	Bleu acier	Stahlblau	Azul acero	Azzurro acciaio
Strip	Bande	Streifen	Tira	Striscia
Surcharge	Surcharge	Aufdruck	Sobrecarga	Soprastampa
Tête-bêche	Tête-bêche	Kehrdruck	Tête-bêche	Tête-bêche
Tinted paper	Papier teinté	Getöntes Papier	Papel coloreado	Carta tinta
Too-late stamp	Timbre pour lettres en retard	Verspätungsmarke	Sello para cartas retardadas	Francobollo per le lettere in ritardo
Turquoise-blue	Bleu-turquoise	Türkisblau	Azul turquesa	Azzurro turchese
Turquoise-green	Vert-turquoise	Türkisgrün	Verde turquesa	Verde turchese
Typography	Typographie	Buchdruck	Tipografia	Tipografia
Ultramarine	Outremer	Ultramarin	Ultramar	Oltremare
Unused	Neuf	Ungebraucht	Nuevo	Nuovo
Used	Oblitéré, Usé	Gebraucht	Usado	Usato
Venetian Red	Rouge-brun terne	Venezianischrot	Rojo veneciano	Rosso veneziano
Vermilion	Vermillon	Zinnober	Cinabrio	Vermiglione
Violet	Violet	Violett	Violeta	Violetto
Violet-blue	Bleu-violet	Violettblau	Azul violeta	Azzurro violetto
Watermark	Filigrane	Wasserzeichen	Filigrana	Filigrana
Watermark sideways	Filigrane couché	Wasserzeichen liegend	Filigrana acostado	Filigrana coricata
Wove paper	Papier ordinaire, Papier uni	Einfaches Papier	Papel avitelado	Carta unita
Yellow	Jaune	Gelb	Amarillo	Giallo
Yellow-brown	Brun-jaune	Gelbbraun	Castaño amarillo	Bruno giallo
Yellow-green	Vert-jaune	Gelbgrün	Verde amarillo	Verde giallo
Yellow-olive	Olive-jaunâtre	Gelboliv	Oliva amarillo	Oliva giallastro
Yellow-orange	Orange jaunâtre	Gelborange	Naranja amarillo	Arancio giallastro
Zig-zag roulette	Percé en zigzag	Sägezahnartiger Durchstich	Picado en zigzag	Perforazione a zigzag

Guide to Entries

A **Country of Issue** – When a country changes its name, the catalogue listing changes to reflect the name change, for example Cambodia was formerly known as Kampuchea, the stamps in South East Asia are all listed under Cambodia, but spilt into Kampuchea and then Cambodia. When a country spilts, for example Czechoslovakia split into Czech Republic and Slovakia, there will be a listing for Czechoslovakia and then separate sections for Czech Republic and Slovakia.

B **Currency** – Details of the currency, and dates of earliest use where applicable, on the face value of the stamps.

C **Country Information** – Brief geographical and historical details for the issuing country.

D **Illustration** – Generally, the first stamp in the set. Stamp illustrations are reduced to 75%, with overprints and surcharges shown actual size.

E **Illustration or Type Number** – These numbers are used to help identify stamps, either in the listing, type column, design line or footnote, usually the first value in a set. These type numbers are in a bold type face – **123**; when bracketed **(123)** an overprint or a surcharge is indicated. Some type numbers include a lower-case letter – **123a**, this indicates they have been added to an existing set. New cross references are also shown in bold.

F **Date of issue** – This is the date that the stamp/set of stamps was issued by the post office and was available for purchase. When a set of definitive stamps has been issued over several years the Year Date given is for the earliest issue. Commemorative sets are listed in chronological order. Stamps of the same design, or issue are usually grouped together, for example one of the French Marianne definitive series' was first issued in 2002 but includes stamps issued to the end of 2004.

G **Number Prefix** – Stamps other than definitives and commemoratives have a prefix letter before the catalogue number.
Their use is explained in the text: some examples are A for airmail, E for East Germany or Express Delivery stamps.

H **Footnote** – Further information on background or key facts on issues.

I **Stanley Gibbons Catalogue number** – This is a unique number for each stamp to help the collector identify stamps in the listing. The Stanley Gibbons numbering system is universally recognised as definitive.
Where insufficient numbers have been left to provide for additional stamps to a listing, some stamps will have a suffix letter after the catalogue number (for example 214*a*). If numbers have been left for additions to a set and not used they will be left vacant.
The separate type numbers (in bold) refer to illustrations (see **E**).

J **Colour** – If a stamp is printed in three or fewer colours then the colours are listed, working from the centre of the stamp outwards (see **R**).

K **Design line** – Further details on design variations

L **Key Type** – Indicates a design type on which the stamp is based. These are the bold figures found below each illustration, for example listed in Cameroun, in the Germany catalogue is the Key type A and B showing the ex-Kaiser's yacht *Hohenzollern*. The type numbers are also given in bold in the second column of figures alongside the stamp description to indicate the design of each stamp. Where an issue comprises stamps of similar design, the corresponding type number should be taken as indicating the general design. Where there are blanks in the type number column it means that the type of the corresponding stamp is that shown by the number in the type column of the same issue. A dash (–) in the type column means that the stamp is not illustrated. Where type numbers refer to stamps of another country, e.g. where stamps of one country are overprinted for use in another, this is always made clear in the text.

M **Coloured Papers** – Stamps printed on coloured paper are shown – e.g. 'brown/*yellow*' indicates brown printed on yellow paper.

N **Surcharges and Overprints** – Usually described in the headings. Any actual wordings are shown in bold type. Descriptions clarify words and figures used in the overprint. Stamps with the same overprints in different colours are not listed separately. Numbers in brackets after the descriptions are the catalogue numbers of the non-overprinted stamps. The words 'inscribed' or 'inscription' refer to the wording incorporated in the design of a stamp and not surcharges or overprints.

O **Face value** – This refers to the value of each stamp and is the price it was sold for at the Post Office when issued. Some modern stamps do not have their values in figures but instead shown as a letter, for example Great Britain use 1st or 2nd on their stamps as apposed to the actual value.

P **Catalogue Value** – Mint/Unused. Prices quoted for pre-1945 stamps are for lightly hinged examples.

Q **Catalogue Value** – Used. Prices generally refer to fine postally used examples. For certain issues they are for cancelled-to-order.

Prices
Prices are given in pence and pounds. Stamps worth £100 and over are shown in whole pounds:

Shown in Catalogue as	Explanation
10	10 pence
1·75	£1·75
15·00	£15
£150	£150
£2300	£2300

Prices assume stamps are in 'fine condition'; we may ask more for superb and less for those of lower quality. The minimum catalogue price quoted is 10p. and is intended as a guide for catalogue users. The lowest price for individual stamps purchased from Stanley Gibbons is £1.
Prices quoted are for the cheapest variety of that particular stamp. Differences of watermark, perforation, or other details, often increase the value. Prices quoted for mint issues are for single examples. Those in *se-tenant* pairs, strips, blocks or sheets may be worth more. Where no prices are listed it is either because the stamps are not known to exist (usually shown by a †) in that particular condition, or, more usually, because there is no reliable information on which to base their value.
All prices are subject to change without prior notice and we cannot guarantee to supply all stamps as priced. Prices quoted in advertisements are also subject to change without prior notice.

R **Multicoloured** – Nearly all modern stamps are multicoloured (more than three colours); this is indicated in the heading, with a description of the stamp given in the listing.

S **Perforations** – Please see page x for a detailed explanation of perforations.

A Country of issue

Ethiopia

B Currency

100 Centesimi = 1 Lira

Italian military operations against Ethiopia began on 3 October 1935 and Addis Ababa, from which the Emperor had departed for Europe, was captured on 5 May 1936. Ethiopia was annexed by Italy on 9 May 1936 and the King of Italy was proclaimed Emperor.

C Country Information

D Illustration

E Illustration or Type number

631 Sir Rowland Hill and Penny Black

632 Christmas Landscape

F Date of issue

G Number prefix

1918 (July). POSTAGE DUE. Surch as T **3**.

D28	**D12**	4c. on 10c. magenta and orange	£86000	£70000
D29		8c. on 20c. magenta and orange	27·00	55·00
D30		12c. on 30c. magenta and orange	85·00	£140
D31		16c. on 40c. magenta and orange	£325	£600

A set of four postage due stamps (as **D12** of Italy), are known. The values are cancelled with four horizontal bars, overprinted - Pechino - and surcharged with new values. However these stamps were not issued.

H Footnote

(Des R. Garrasi. Photo)

I Stanley Gibbons Catalogue number

1947 (1 Sept). AIR. 50th Anniv of Radio. As T **202/203**. W **191** (sideways). Perf 14.

688	**202**	6l. bluish violet	20	15
689	**203**	10l. deep carmine-red	20	15
690	–	20l. reddish orange	1·30	1·10
691	**202**	25l. turquoise-blue	1·90	1·30
692	**203**	35l. deep dull blue	3·00	2·40
693	–	50l. bright purple	4·00	3·25
688/693 *Set of 6*			9·75	7·50

J Colour

K Design line

Designs: 20l., 50l. Heinkel He 70 Blitz wireless-equipped airplane.

(Des E. Federici. T **1** recess with background typo, T **2** photo)

1929 (1 Aug). T **1** (with a repetition of minute white letters reading 'POSTEVATICANE' in horizontal rows on a tinted background) and T **2**. Perf 14.

L Key Type column

1	**1**	5c. brown/*rose*	25	30
2		10c. grey-green/*green*	55	60
3		20c. violet/*lilac*	1·10	85

M Coloured Papers

XXI
Congresso
Idrologico
(3)

1930 (25 Sept). 21st Hydrological Congress. Nos. 17A/25A optd with T **3**.

N Surcharges and Overprints

O Face value

26	5c. claret	20·00	19·00
27	10c. sepia	22·00	19·00
28	20c. scarlet	37·00	19·00
29	25c. green	46·00	19·00
30	30c. deep blue	22·00	19·00
31	50c. chocolate	£700	65·00
32	1l.25 deep blue	£475	95·00
33	5l. claret	£250	£400
34	10l. olive-green	£250	£450
26/34 *Set of 9*		£1600	£1000

P Catalogue Value – Mint

Q Catalogue Value – Used

(Des Rita Moreno (800l.), M. Temo (900l.). Photo)

1998 (5 Sept). First Death Anniversary of Mother Teresa (founder of Missionaries of Charity). T **1036** and similar multicoloured design. Perf 14×13½ (800l.) or 13½×14 (900l.).

R Multicoloured Stamp

S Perforations

2513	800l. Type **1036**	1·80	35
2514	900l. Mother Teresa *(vert)*	2·10	45

Engraving is a matter of light and shadow

By Adrian Keppel

Over his long career, Master engraver Czeslaw Slania, born in Poland in 1921, created more than 1000 stamps for numerous postal authorities around the world. To mark the centenary of his birth, Adrian Keppel picks out just a few of his significant creations.

Ask any stamp collector to name a stamp engraver and I bet you ten to one they will come up with the name of Slania. Such was his worldwide fame that even after more than 15 years since his passing, Czeslaw Slania (1921–2005) is still a household name.

A SIGNIFICANT ANNIVERSARY

This year marks the centenary of the master engraver's birth, and, as if to corroborate the above, quite a few postal administrations have taken the opportunity to mark this anniversary with a stamp issue. So far, we have seen a very stylish portrait, engraved by Martin Mörck, issued in Monaco (*Fig 1*), and a triplet of miniature sheets issued by some Nordic countries, again based on an engraved stamp by Mörck. Others are bound to follow, with Swedish and Polish issues expected in October.

Fig 1 *Monaco was the first country to commemorate Slania's birth centenary with a stamp issue*

It is the perfect time, then, to take a look back at the career, which lasted over half a century, of an engraver who created more than 1000 stamps, attracting at least as many superlatives!

ORIGINS OF THE MASTER ENGRAVER

Born near Katowice, Poland, on 22 October 1921, it was clear from an early age that Slania had a special talent for drawing, although it must be said he had some trouble finding a proper outlet for it. Slania started out young by selling his drawings to fellow pupils at school so they could get good marks. He later got found out for having perfectly forged the headmaster's signature. As early as then, it was generally thought Slania would become an important artist. But that was not before he executed his forging techniques in World War II by copying identity cards and other documents for the Polish underground forces.

After the war, Slania attended the Krakow Academy of Fine Arts, specialising in graphic techniques, such as etching and copper engraving. The Albertina Museum in Vienna, Austria, which probably holds the world's largest collection of engravings, became a shrine for him. For a while, he worked for the Naradowa Printers where, among other things, he worked on anatomy handbooks for medical students.

Slania's diploma engraving was a small format interpretation of Matejko's painting *Grunwald*, depicting the 1410 battle of Tannenberg. Slania was so fascinated by the painting and the challenge of recreating it as an engraving that soon after he embarked on another, much larger, version, which took him two years to complete.

In 1950, he was employed by the Government Printing Works in Poland, thanks to efforts from the stamp engraver Marian Polak. Slania's first effort, engraved just after the printers' move from Lodz to Warsaw, still in 1950, was a stamp depicting Joseph Stalin. It was never issued. But from March 1951, Slania's designs and engravings did start gracing the philatelic catalogues (*Fig 2*).

Fig 2 *Among Slania's earliest stamp engravings is this 1951 Six Year Plan (Mining) issue of Poland*

TO SWEDEN

The year 1956 was a tumultuous one in Polish politics and the threat of a repeat performance of the Hungarian Revolution in Poland made many Poles flee their country, among them Czeslaw Slania. He decided to settle in Sweden, where he hoped he would be able to get work as an engraver.

Soon after arriving in Sweden, Slania visited Sven Ewert; the master engraver of the Swedish Post. Slania's erstwhile tutor, Marian Polak, had spoken highly of Ewert's engraving talents. In fact, the two had both been students of the famous Austrian engraver Ferdinand Schirnböck. While Ewert saw Slania's potential, there was no place for him at the Swedish Post at that time.

And so, Slania started his Swedish career washing dishes at the post office railway depot restaurant in Stockholm. He also got a job as a retoucher, and was given the odd engraving job, such as for savings bank stamps and radio licence labels.

To hone his skills even more, Slania started engraving his famous boxer labels in the late 1950s. He created a sheet of 23 non-postal labels of all the boxing world champions from John L Sullivan 1889 onwards (*Fig 3*).

Fig 3 *One of the 23 boxer labels Slania engraved in the 1950s to hone his skills*

His final portrait was that of Cassius Clay who became a world champion in 1964. He initially had hoped to do many more labels, but as he disagreed strongly with the split of the World Boxing Federation, he stopped working on them. Much later, after Slania's passing, his colleague and compatriot Piotr Naszarkowski created a 24th label in the same style but depicting Slania as the World Champion engraver (*Fig 4*).

Fig 4 *After Slania's death, Piotr Naszarkowski adapted the boxer label format to honour his late colleague and compatriot*

After some years, Slania decided not to waste his time any longer and move to Canada. He had been given a good job offer from the Canadian Bank Note Company and was about to leave Sweden when the Swedish post got in touch with him. Ewert was ill and needed an assistant, and would Slania be interested? Slania said yes, and that was the beginning of an illustrious career at the Swedish Post.

Right from the very start, Slania impressed with his work. His first two engravings made were the portraits of the painter Anders Zorn and the poet Gustaf Fröding, issued in 1960. That of Fröding especially was amazing. Slania managed to take the rather basic design by Asberg and turn it into a powerful yet affectionate engraved portrait (*Fig 5*).

Fig 5 *Even from early in his career Slania managed to impress with his portrait stamps, such as this one from 1960 featuring the poet Gustav Fröding*

Another of Slania's early excellent portraits was that of King Gustav VI Adolf, for a new definitive set introduced in 1972 (*Fig 6*). Unfortunately, the death of the king soon after meant the set was cut short and only two values were ever issued, but the portrait was used again in 1973 as part of a memorial issue.

Fig 6 *Slania's 1972 definitive portrait of King Gustav VI Adolf, which would also be used for the king's 1973 memorial issue*

A MASTER OF DIFFERENT TECHNIQUES

While most of his work exists of traditional line engravings, Slania wasn't averse to trying out different engraving methods. His 1962 Skokloster Castle stamp and his 1968 Haverud Aquaduct stamps, for example, are both a combination of line engraving and etched foliage.

Slania's Prince Eugen stamp of 1965 was engraved using the time-consuming stipple engraving (*Fig 7*). Rather than using lines, a large number of dots are engraved to create the image. Slania used this stipple technique again for such stamps as his arctic hare and golden eagle stamps from 1968. Slania's Bo Bergman stamp from 1969 shows a combination of dots and dashes, but unfortunately the applied technique was too refined to print well.

Fig 7 *Slania applied the stipple technique on his 1965 portrait stamp of Prince Eugen*

When Sweden's stamp printing office acquired a new three-colour stamp printing press in 1964 from Goebel AG, they produced test stamps, engraved by Slania, to test the new machine. The test stamps depicted the interior of Uppsala Cathedral and had no denomination. Much later, these test stamps inadvertently ended up on the philatelic market, usually advertised as proof material for the 1967 stamp of the same design.

To avoid these test stamps becoming unjustifiably expensive philatelic items purporting to be what they're not, the Swedish Post went on a promotional campaign in 1974, producing the test stamps in large quantities and handing them out during Stockholmia 1974. The exercise was repeated two years later, when multicoloured test stamps were used for similar booklets handed out during Hafnia 1976 (*Fig 8*).

Fig 8 *Slania's 1964 Swedish test stamp would be reprinted frequently as promotional material in the 1970s*

Multi-colour rotary printing presses were still a fairly new thing at the time, which is why Slania got the chance to engrave another test stamp for such presses. This time it was to be used in Denmark, for their multi-colour intaglio M3 press. The design depicts Grundtvig Church and was introduced in 1968 (*Fig 9*).

Fig 9 *Slania test engraving for Denmark's new rotary press in 1968, depicting Grundtvig Church*

A third test stamp was created by Slania for the new printing press M4, which the Danish stamp printers acquired in 1980. This time an equestrian statue of King Frederik VII was the subject. So many different types exist, in pure recess or in combination with offset or photogravure printing, that it is easy to miss that there are actually two different engraved dies.

EXAMPLES OF PHILATELIC HUMOUR

Slania is known for his philatelic humour in that he often managed to include some personal or funny detail in his engravings. The earliest example of that is on the 1g.40 value from the 1954 set marking the tenth anniversary of the Second Republic in Poland. The scene is a bookshop and Slania managed to incorporate the names of at least six people on a number of book covers: his mother, sister, cousin, niece, ex-wife and the Chief of the Ministry of Post.

The 1973 'Tourism in Dalecarlia' issue includes a stamp depicting the Vasa Ski Race. The skier in the bottom left-hand corner is a self-portrait of Slania (*Fig 10*).

Fig 10 *In 1973, Slania secretly included his self-portrait in a Swedish stamp, disguised as a skier*

SLANIA AROUND THE WORLD

Through the many decades of Slania's career, his fame became more widespread and he ended up engraving stamps for many countries around the world. He had by then learned that in order to maximise the impact of his engravings, it was important to work closely together with staff at the printers. He would even stipulate this in his contracts with those countries that did not make use of the printing facilities in Sweden.

It is obvious from his work that Slania remained a keen student of the art of engraving. Within philately, he was known to be especially interested in the works of Austrian engravers such as Ferdinand Schirnböck, Hans Ranzoni and Rudolf Toth.

In his early days, the stamp engravings of the Czechoslovakian engravers, especially, caught Slania's eye; more than, for example, those of the well-known French engravers. Slania appreciated the dynamic interpretive style of those Czechoslovakian engravers, such as Schmidt and Svengsbir, especially compared to the contemporary Polish style of engraving, which could be described as slightly provincial.

Slania also studied the great master engravers of the art world. The works of Rembrandt, especially, were the subject of his studies, and he was even able to disprove theories from experts at the Louvre in Paris with regards to the chronological order of progressive proofs from Rembrandt's etchings. No wonder then that one of his many 'titles' was the 'Dürer of the Twentieth Century'.

Slania's reputation was such that he became the official Court Engraver not only of Sweden, but of Monaco as well. For many of the Scandinavian countries, in particular Denmark and Greenland, he was the sole engraver of their many recess-printed stamps for years on end.

For these countries, as well as for many others, he produced many wonderful portrait stamps, earning him the unofficial title of 'Master of Portrait Engraving'. His portrait work may also be admired on the 1995 Great Britain set, portraying Sir Rowland Hill and Guglielmo Marconi (*Fig 11*).

Fig 11 *For Great Britain, Slania engraved portraits of both Guglielmo Marconi and Sir Rowland Hill in 1995*

Even though his portrait work undoubtedly forms the highlight of his oeuvre, Slania was an experienced engraver of all subjects. Turning again to his work for Great Britain, we may admire his ships on the 1982 Maritime Heritage set and his 2002 pillar boxes stamps, which were his final work for Royal Mail.

The 1984 Bicentenary of the First Mail Coach Run issue is particularly special. After Slania had engraved the stamps, someone at the printers' dropped one of the dies, rendering it unusable. They told Slania, but by the time they had sent the original artwork back to him, Slania had already re-engraved the die from memory!

Another stamp Slania had to start again from scratch was the 1986 Stamp Day issue for Iceland. Halfway through the engraving process, Slania took a break, only to see his daughter pick up his burin and the steel plate and starting to mimic her father's actions, thereby scratching the plate irreparably!

The 1999 small-format, high-value Machin definitives of Great Britain were printed by Enschedé and De la Rue. The work of the two printers may be distinguished by minor varieties in the engraving of the values. This, however, is not attributable to Slania's work. He engraved a single die which had a square blank space, where the printers' own engravers could insert the values needed for the stamps.

Earlier that year, Slania's large-format Machin stamp had already been issued in a prestige booklet (*Fig 12*).

Fig 12 *Slania also engraved several Machin stamps in 1999*

These were not his first portraits of Queen Elizabeth II, though. In the 1980s, Slania was involved in a project to replace the Machin design by something with a more updated portrait. He engraved a Lord Snowdon portrait. The project was eventually shelved, but Slania's portrait was translated to offset and used on postal orders.

When communism in Poland came to an end in the late 1980s/early 1990s, Slania was able to visit Poland again, and he started engraving stamps for his native country once more. Among his favourites is the 1999 stamp he engraved for the National Stamp Exhibition 'Walbrzych '99', depicting Ksiaz Castle (*Fig 13*). Another major work for Poland was the 1993 miniature sheet for 'Polska '93', depicting Lech's Encounter with the White Eagle.

Fig 13 *This 1999 miniature sheet (Reduced) was one of Slania's favourite Polish engravings*

More and more, various postal authorities turned to Slania for their major issues. Slania became known as the 'King of the Burin'. His stamp engravings received many accolades, such as the 1978 engraving of the old library building on a Faröe Islands stamp, which was pronounced the most beautiful stamp in the world (*Fig 14*). Slania's 1975 ballet stamp from Sweden and his 1983 Monaco stamp depicting Café de Paris from his Belle Epoque series enjoyed a similar fate. His Swedish Fiddler stamp, an engraving of Zorn's painting, also issued in 1983, was given the Robert Stolz Award for being the most beautiful music stamp of the year (*Fig 15*). China's 1997 Pheasants stamps, engraved by Slania, were the first Chinese Republic stamps engraved outside of China.

Fig 14 *This 1978 stamp engraving for the Faröe Islands was declared the 'most beautiful stamp in the world' at the time*

Fig 15 *Slania's fiddler stamp was pronounced 'most beautiful music stamp' of 1983*

Slania himself increasingly became part of the stamp issuing programme. In 1991, he engraved an incredibly detailed booklet pane for Sweden, depicting the Coronation of King Gustav III. The booklet was issued to honour the 70th birthday of Slania, with a non-postal label included in the pane referring to this fact (*Fig 16*).

Fig 16 *In 1991, the Swedish Post marked Slania's 70th birthday with a special issue (Reduced)*

This was followed by an even more magnificent tour de force in the year 2000: the engraving of Ehrenstrahl's famous painting *The Great Deeds of Swedish Kings*, part of a miniature sheet that had no other function than to mark the fact that it was Slania's 1000th stamp (*Fig 17*)! Besides that, it also turned out to be the largest stamp ever engraved, and as such, it was given a mention in the Guinness Book of World Records.

Fig 17 *Slania's 1000th stamp engraving was a miniature sheet issued solely to mark that very milestone (Reduced)*

Another of Slania's records had occurred some years earlier. In 1986, he engraved the stamp design commemorating the recently assassinated Swedish Prime Minister Olof Palme in a record time of five and half days (*Fig 18*)!

Fig 18 *Slania engraved his 1986 Olof Palme stamp in the record time of only five and a half days!*

HIS 1000TH STAMP!

Ever since the mid 1990s, Slania had made it a personal goal to reach this milestone of 1000 stamps. However, there is a theory that Slania's 1000th stamp may actually be his 1001st! In 1985, the United States issued two similar 'Veteran' stamps, one honouring Korean War veterans and the other honouring World War I veterans. After it became known that a non-American had engraved the World War I stamp, political pressure was brought to bear, for it was deemed that such patriotic stamps should not have been engraved by a foreigner.

Slania was, therefore, pressured into signing a letter in which he denied having engraved the Korean War stamp, and the credits were given to the American engraver Thomas Hipschen. After Slania's death, his logbook proved that he had most certainly engraved that stamp as well, which proved the many Slania followers right, who had always believed he had engraved the Korean War stamp too (*Fig 19*).

Fig 19 *Slania was forced to deny having engraved the USA Korean war veterans stamp in 1985*

Whether his 1000th or 1001st, Slania declared this particular stamp to be his favourite. It followed a rather long list of stamps he was wont to call his favourite at some point in time. Among those is the 1979 Ram definitive of the Faroe Islands (*Fig 20*). Slania even inquired after his subject on a subsequent visit to the islands, only to find out it had been eaten!

Fig 20 *Slania's 1979 Faröe Islands stamp was amongst one of his favourite designs*

FAILING HEALTH

At the end of his career, failing health started to hamper the by then octogenarian Czeslaw Slania in his work, and his colleague Piotr Naszarkowski had to step in and finish some of the jobs given to Slania. Most famous of those is the Elvis Presley stamp, issued in Sweden in 2004 (*Fig 21*). This was a stamp for which Slania had already started the engraving. He had worked on the background but was not able to finish his engraving. So, the actual portrait was done by Naszarkowski, who also tried to tidy up the background as much as possible. This proved rather difficult, so the end result still looks a bit like a badly woven fabric but is still an improvement on the original.

Fig 21 *Due to his declining health, Slania was unable to finish the 2004 Elvis Presley stamp, so his colleague, Naszarkowski, had to step in and complete the engraving*

Other consignments given to Slania but eventually engraved by Naszarkowski are the 2005 Greta Garbo issue for both Sweden and the United States, and the 2005 US Duck Stamp. For this issue, Slania had already produced some intaglio artwork, but Naszarkowski started the project again from scratch, not making use of Slania's work.

One of Slania's final stamps was the portrait of Princess Grace for a Monaco stamp, part of the 2004 MonacoPhil sheetlet paying homage to the princess (*Fig 22*). Slania was ill but did manage to finish the engraving. He asked Naszarkowski to send the plate on to Monaco, who felt he had to comply, even though he could clearly see the engraving was done with shaky hands.

Fig 22 *While the 2004 Princess Grace of*

Monaco stamp is still beautiful, experts may note how Slania's final engravings were done in a shaky hand

Slania remained highly active until his dying days, with his final work, the engraving of a United Nations set marking the 60th anniversary of that organisation being issued just a month before his death in 2005.

Slania left behind a legacy of artistic splendour and dazzling records, which will probably never be emulated. The still active engraver Martin Mörck comes closest to achieving a similarly amazing portfolio but dwindling worldwide demand for hand-engraved stamps means that he probably won't be able to overtake his predecessor. And so, we will forever hold that 'There will never be another Czeslaw Slania'!

This article first appeared in *Gibbons Stamp Monthly*, November 2021.

Poland

1860. 100 Kopeks = 1 Rouble
1918. 100 Pfennig = 1 Mark
1918. 100 Halerzy = 1 Korona (South Poland)
1918. 100 Fenigów = 1 Marka (North Poland and throughout the country in 1919)
1924. 100 Groszy = 1 Zloty

I. RUSSIAN PROVINCE

The ancient Kingdom of Poland was partitioned between Russia, Austria and Prussia in 1772–1795. Napoléon created a Grand Duchy of Warsaw and in 1815 most of this became a new Kingdom of Poland, with the Tsar of Russia as king. Following a revolt in 1803–1831, Poland beame a Russian province in 1832.

1 Russian Arms

(Eng H. Mejer. Type Govt Ptg Office, Warsaw)

1860 (1 Jan). Wove paper. Perf 11½ to 12½.

1	1	10k. deep blue and carmine	£3750	£475
		a. Blue and rose	£3000	£375
		b. Pale blue and pale rose	£2500	£325
		c. Frame of oval ptd twice, in rose and in blue	£8000	£1400
		d. Imperf		£21000

As 1 January 1860 was a Sunday when post offices were closed, No. 1 was not available until 2 January (local Gregorian calendar). Letters to Russia had to have town postmark in Russian; as Russia still used the Julian calendar at this time the corresponding date was 20 December 1859.

Another Polish revolt in 1863–1864 led to the incorporation of Poland in the Russian postal system on 13 February 1865 and the replacement of Polish stamps by Russian stamps. No. 1 was demonetised 13 April 1865 (Gregorian calendar).

II. REPUBLIC

From 1915 to 1918, Poland was in German and Austro-Hungarian occupation. Overprinted German stamps were used in the German Zone (see German Occupation issues at the end of this list) and Austro-Hungarian Military Post stamps in the Austro-Hungarian Zone. On 3 November 1918 a Polish Republic was proclaimed; during 1919–1921 Poland acquired large areas from surrounding states. Western Galicia, part of the Austrian Empire, was awarded to Poland by the Powers on 8 May 1919. On 20 November 1919 the Powers agreed that Eastern Galicia (which in 1918–1919 had been the West Ukrainian Republic) should be under Polish protection for 25 years; on 14 March 1923 this decision was repealed, and the area was integrated with Poland. The German province of Posen (Poznań) and parts of West Prussia and Lower Silesia were awarded to Poland by the Treaty of Versailles, 28 June 1919, and part of Upper Silesia was awarded to her after plebiscite in 1921. After almost continual warfare between Poland and Russia from 1918 to 1920, the Treaty of Riga, 18 March 1921, gave Poland large parts of White Russia and Volhynia. Central Lithuania was acquired on 8 April 1922.

A. REGIONAL ISSUES

2 Sigismund III Vasa Column, Warsaw

3 Arms of Warsaw

4 Polish Eagle

5 Jan III Sobieski Monument, Warsaw

(Des E. Trojanowski. Litho)

1918 (17 Nov). Warsaw issue. Stamps prepared for use by Warsaw Citizens' Post, surch and optd 'Poczta Polska' as in Types **2/5**. Background of central design in buff. Wmk Horiz Wavy Lines. Perf 11½.

2	**2**	5f. on 2g. brown	1·80	1·30
		a. Surch inverted	£225	£250
		b. Surch double		
3	**3**	10f. on 6g. green	1·30	1·30
		a. Surch inverted	19·00	19·00
		b. Surch double		
		c. Watermark omitted		
4	**4**	25f. on 10g. carmine	12·50	3·25
		a. Surch inverted	34·00	34·00
		b. Error. '52' instead of '25'	£10000	
5	**5**	50f. on 20g. blue	10·50	8·25
		a. Surch inverted	£450	£450
		b. Surch double		

(6a)

(6b)

T **6**: Distance between 2nd and 3rd bars:

6a: 3¼ mm (1st printing, 5.12.18)

6b: 4 mm (2nd printing, 15.1.19)

1918 (5 Dec)–**19**. Issue for former area of German Occupation. Nos. 6 etc. of German Occupation of Poland (German stamps optd 'Gen, Gouv Warschau').

*A. Surch or overprinted as T **6a**.*

7A	**17**	5pf. green	2·20	90
8A	**24**	5 on 2½pf. grey	65	40
9A	**17**	5 on 3pf. brown	12·50	5·25
10A		10pf. carmine	1·00	40
11A	**24**	15pf. slate-violet	65	40
12A	**17**	20pf. deep blue	65	65
		c. Violet-blue	75	40
13A	**24**	25 on 7½pf. orange	1·30	40
14A	**17**	30pf. black and orange/*buff*	65	40
15A		40pf. black and carmine	1·90	1·90
16A		60pf. magenta	1·30	1·30
7A/16A *Set of* 10			21·00	11·00

*B. Surch as T **6b** (15.1.19).*

6B	**17**	3pf. brown	44·00	34·00
7B		5pf. green	3·75	1·30
8B	**24**	5 on 2½pf. grey	1·30	50
9B	**17**	5 on 3pf. brown	£130	£110
10B		10pf. carmine	1·30	65
11B	**24**	15pf. slate-violet	65	50
12B	**17**	20pf. deep blue	65	65
		c. Violet-blue	65	65
		d. Ultramarine	£1900	£3500
13B	**24**	25 on 7½pf. orange	19·00	7·50
14B	**17**	30pf. black and orange/*buff*	1·30	40
15B		40pf. black and carmine	12·50	12·50
16B		60pf. magenta	2·50	1·30
6B/16B *Set of* 11			£200	£150

Many of the above exist with inverted or double overprint, with 'Pocata' or 'Poczto' for 'Poczta', or with various letters omitted or inverted.

7

(8)

1918 (5 Dec). Issue for former zone of Austro-Hungarian occupation. Imperial Welfare Fund stamps of Austro-Hungarian Military Post, optd as in T **7**, at Lublin.

17	**6**	10h. green	12·50	12·50
		a. Opt inverted	£100	90·00
		b. Opt double	£2250	£900
		c. Opt double, one inverted	£2750	£1100
18	**7**	20h. claret	9·50	12·50
		a. Opt inverted	65·00	65·00
		b. Opt double, one inverted	£2250	£650
19	**6**	45h. blue	9·50	14·00
		a. Opt inverted	65·00	65·00
		b. Opt double, one inverted	£2250	£650

1918 (19–21 Dec). Second issue for former Austro-Hungarian zone. Emperor Charles stamps of Austro-Hungarian Military Post Surch as in T **8**, at Lublin. Perf 12½.

(a) With stars.

20	**4**	3h. on 3h. olive-green	38·00	31·00
		a. Surch inverted	£4250	£4250
		b. Perf 11½	70·00	44·00
		ba. Surch inverted	£4250	£4250
		c. Perf 11½×12½	38·00	34·00
21		3h. on 15h. rose-pink	8·75	8·75
		a. Surch inverted	31·00	38·00
22		10h. on 30h. deep green	8·75	8·75
		a. Surch inverted	31·00	38·00
		b. Surch in violet	£130	£100
		ba. Surch inverted		
23		25h. on 40h. olive	19·00	15·00
		a. Surch inverted	47·00	55·00
		b. Perf 11½	65·00	39·00
		ba. Surch inverted	£225	£225
24		45h. on 60h. carmine	8·75	8·75
		a. Surch inverted	36·00	34·00
25		45h. on 80h. blue	10·50	10·50
		a. Surch inverted	44·00	44·00
26		50h. on 60h. carmine	23·00	19·00
		a. Surch inverted	65·00	44·00

On Nos. 22/27 'HAL.' is in capital letters.

Most of the above exist with left-hand star omitted. In such cases it is often replaced by a vertical smudge running right across the stamp.

Stamps with cancellations before the date of issue are forged surcharges made on genuine stamps.

(b) With two bars instead of stars.

27	**4**	45h. on 80h. blue	15·00	12·50
		a. Surch inverted	50·00	44·00
		b. Surch double, one inverted	£1700	

(c) Optd only (21 December).

28	**4**	50h. green	38·00	38·00
		a. Opt inverted	£130	£130
29		90h. violet	9·50	7·50
		a. Opt inverted	£140	£130

1h., 2h., 5h., 6h. and 12h. values with overprint only are private productions.

(9)

(10)

11

1919 (10 Jan). Issue for Western Galicia. Austrian stamps of 1916 optd at Cracow.

*(a) Optd with T **9** (Nos. 45/48) or similar type (others).*

30	**49**	3h. violet (Imperial Crown)	£500	£550
31		5h. yellow-green	£600	£550
32		6h. orange	70·00	65·00
		a. Opt inverted	£63000	
33		10h. claret	£500	£500
34		12h. greenish blue	£110	80·00
35	**60**	15h. Venetian red (Charles I)	90·00	40·00
36		20h. deep green	£300	£160
37		25h. blue	£2500	£2000
38		30h. dull violet	£750	£425
39	**51**	40h. olive (Arms)	50·00	31·00
		a. Opt inverted	£500	
		b. Opt double	£2250	
40		50h. deep green	22·00	19·00
		a. Opt inverted		£39000
41		60h. deep blue	12·50	14·00
		a. Opt inverted	£425	
42		80h. red-brown	15·00	15·00
		a. Opt inverted	£375	£300
		b. Opt double	£2250	
43		90h. claret	£1600	£1300
44		1k. red/*yellow*	35·00	31·00
45	**52**	2k. deep blue (Arms)	20·00	17·00
46		3k. carmine	£250	£225
47		4k. green	£275	£225
48		10k. deep violet	£14000	£15000
		a. Violet	£22000	£25000

*(b) Surch with T **10**.*

49	**51**	25 on 80h. red-brown	12·50	11·50
		a. Surch inverted	£275	£160

On Nos. 30/44 the overprint has a diamond shape between 'POCZTA' and 'POLSKA'.

The 3k. with inverted overprint is a forgery.

Stamps of Austria

N53 Mercury

1919 (10 Jan). NEWSPAPER. Newspaper stamps of Austria (Mercury) optd at Cracow similar to T **9** but with diamond shape between 'POCZTA' and 'POLSKA'.

N50	**N53**	2h. brown	29·00	24·00
N51		4h. green	16·00	14·50
N52		6h. blue	14·50	14·00
N53		10h. orange	£300	£250
N54		30h. claret	16·00	18·00
N50/N54 *Set of 5*			£325	£300

1919 (10 Jan). POSTAGE DUE. Postage Due stamps of Austria (Numerals) optd at Cracow with T **9** (Nos. D57/D59) or similar type (others).

D50	**D55**	5h. carmine	19·00	21·00
D51		10h. carmine	£4750	£8000
D52		15h. carmine	13·00	14·00
		a. Opt inverted	£4500	£3500
D53		20h. carmine	£800	£650
D54		25h. carmine	55·00	50·00
D55		30h. carmine	£2250	£2000
D56		40h. carmine	£500	£500
D57	**D56**	1k. blue (R.)	£5500	£6500
D58		5k. blue (R.)	£5500	£6500
D59		10k. blue (R.)	£22000	£25000
		a. Black opt	£82000	£97000

On Nos. D50/D56 the overprint has a diamond shape between 'POCZTA' and 'POLSKA'.

1919 (Jan). POSTAGE DUE. Nos. D287 and D289 of Austria (Francis Joseph I) optd at Cracow similar to T **9** but with diamond shape between 'POCZTA' and 'POLSKA'.

D60	**50**	15 on 36h. violet	£600	£600
D61		50 on 42h. brown	80·00	75·00
		a. Opt double	£3500	£5500

(Des J. Michalski. Litho at Cracow)

1919 (25 Feb). Issue for Western Galicia. Stout wove paper. No gum. Imperf.

50	**11**	2h. grey	1·90	1·40
51		3h. dull violet	1·30	1·30
52		5h. green	1·30	70
53		6h. orange	29·00	35·00
54		10h. lake	1·30	70
55		15h. brown	1·30	70
56		20h. olive-green	1·30	90
57		25h. carmine	1·10	70
58		50h. indigo	1·30	85
59		70h. blue	1·90	1·40
60		1k. carmine and grey	1·90	1·90
50/60 *Set of 11*			39·00	41·00

On the 2h. and 3h. the currency is inscribed as 'halerze'. Stamps printed by typography are forgeries; the 2h. and 3h. can be also identified by the inscription 'halerzy'.

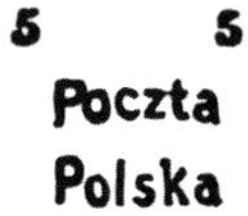

(12)

(13)

(14)

1919 (5 Aug). Poznań provisional issue. Stamps of Germany ('Germania') surch as T **12**.

61	**17**	5 on 2pf. grey	44·00	27·00
62	**24**	5 on 7½pf. orange	3·25	2·50
		a. Surch double	£1300	£1200
63	**17**	5 on 20pf. blue	3·25	1·90
64		10 on 25pf. black and red/*yellow*	9·50	6·25
65		10 on 40pf. black and carmine	5·00	3·25
61/65 *Set of* 5			60·00	37·00

A 10 on 80pf. stamp was prepared for use but was never issued.

KOWEL LOCAL ISSUES. During August 1919 a number of Ukrainian postage stamps were overprinted and placed on sale in Eastern Galicia, notably Kowel. The stamps were only on sale between the 20th and 24th of August. They were withdrawn when the Polish Ministry of Posts and Telegraphs took over the area. There is some doubt as to whether the Civilian Commissioner had permission to issue such stamps. Forgeries are also known.

1919 (15 Sept). Gniezno provisional issue. Stamps of Germany ('Germania') surch with T **13** or T **14**.

66	**24**	5 on 2pf. yellowish grey (R.)	£375	£325
		a. Surch inverted	£32000	
67		10 on 7½pf. orange (G.)	£350	£190

Forgeries of these surcharges exist, including inverts of the '10'.

B. ISSUES FOR SOUTHERN POLAND

Austrian Currency

15

16

17 Agriculture

18 Ploughing in Peace

19 Polish Uhlan

D20

(Des E. Trojanowski (T **15**) and E. Bartlomiejczyk (Types **18/19**). Typo)

1919 (27 Jan). Value in halerzy or korony.

(a) Imperf.

68	**15**	3h. brown	35	35
		a. Ribbed paper	50	50
69		5h. bright green	35	35
		a. Ribbed paper	50	50
70		10h. orange	35	35
		a. Ribbed paper	50	50
71		15h. scarlet	35	35
		a. Ribbed paper	50	50
72	**16**	20h. grey-brown	35	35
		a. Ribbed paper	50	50
73		25h. pale blue	35	35
		a. Ribbed paper	50	50
74		50h. red-brown	35	35
		a. Ribbed paper	50	50
75	**17**	1k. green	65	40
		a. Ribbed paper	90	65
76		1k.50 brown	7·50	4·25
77		2k. deep blue	3·25	3·75
		a. Ribbed paper	9·50	6·25
78	**18**	2k.50 purple	20·00	11·50
		a. Ribbed paper	25·00	15·00
79	**19**	5k. grey-blue	23·00	17·00
68/79 *Set of* 12			50·00	35·00

(b) Perf 10-11½ and compound.

80	**15**	3h. brown	35	35
		a. Ribbed paper	1·30	65
81		5h. bright green	35	35
		a. Ribbed paper	40	40
82		10h. orange	35	35
		a. Ribbed paper	40	40
83		15h. scarlet	35	35
		a. Ribbed paper	40	40
84	**16**	20h. grey-brown	35	35
		a. Ribbed paper	40	40
85		25h. pale blue	35	35
		a. Ribbed paper	40	40
86		50h. red-brown	35	35
		a. Ribbed paper	50	40
87	**17**	1k. green	35	35
		a. Ribbed paper	40	40
88		1k.50 brown	90	40
		a. Ribbed paper	5·00	2·75
89		2k. deep blue	1·30	55
		a. Ribbed paper	5·00	2·50
90	**18**	2k.50 purple	1·90	80
		a. Ribbed paper	5·00	2·50
91	**19**	5k. grey-blue	2·20	1·20
		a. Ribbed paper	5·00	2·50
80/91 *Set of* 12			8·25	5·25

1919 (9 Sept). POSTAGE DUE. Value in halerzy. Typo. Wove paper. Perf 11½.

D92	**D20**	2h. deep blue	30	20
D93		4h. deep blue	30	20
D94		5h. deep blue	30	20
D95		10h. deep blue	30	20
D96		20h. deep blue	30	20
D97		30h. deep blue	30	20
D98		50h. deep blue	40	20
D99		100h. deep blue	75	1·80
D100		500h. deep blue	3·00	4·00
D92/100 *Set of* 9			5·25	6·50

These stamps were originally issued for use as Postage Dues in former Austrian territory, until superseded by Nos. D126/D136. The stock on hand was used for ordinary postage for a time, from February, 1920.

Stamps perforated 11 are forgeries.

See also Nos. D128/D136 and D144/D147.

C. ISSUES FOR NORTHERN POLAND

Polish Currency

1919 (27 Jan). Value in fenigów or marka. Medium wove paper. Clear impression.

(a) Imperf.

92	**15**	3f. brown	50	40
		a. Ribbed paper	2·50	1·90
93		5f. green	50	40
		a. Ribbed paper	65	40
94		10f. purple	50	40
		a. Ribbed paper	50	40
95		15f. lake	50	40
		a. Ribbed paper	50	40
96	**16**	20f. blue	50	40
		a. Ribbed paper	50	40
97		25f. olive	50	40
		a. Ribbed paper	50	40
98		50f. green	50	40
		a. Ribbed paper	65	40
99	**17**	1m. violet	3·75	3·50
		a. Ribbed paper	4·50	4·25
100		1m.50 green	7·50	7·00
		a. Ribbed paper	15·00	12·50
101		2m. brown	7·00	7·50
102	**18**	2m.50 red-brown	31·00	22·00
		a. Ribbed paper	38·00	25·00
103	**19**	5m. purple	38·00	44·00
92/103 *Set of* 12			80·00	80·00

(b) Perf 11½.

104	**15**	3f. brown	40	30
		a. Ribbed paper	50	40
105		5f. yellow-green	35	30
		a. Ribbed paper	40	40
106		10f. purple	30	30
		a. Ribbed paper	40	40
107		15f. scarlet	40	30
		a. *Carmine*	40	30
		b. Ribbed paper	65	40
108	**16**	20f. blue	30	30
		a. Ribbed paper	50	40
109		25f. olive	30	30
		a. Ribbed paper	40	40
110		50f. green	40	35
		a. Ribbed paper	50	40
111	**17**	1m. violet	70	40
		a. Ribbed paper	65	65
112		1m.50 green	90	40
		a. Ribbed paper	1·30	90
113		2m. brown	1·50	55
114	**18**	2m.50 red-brown	1·90	65
115	**19**	5m. violet	1·90	1·20
104/115 *Set of* 12			8·50	4·75

From 1 February 1920, this series could be used throughout Poland.

See also Nos. 128/143, 146 and 179 etc.

(19a)

(19b)

20

21 Prime Minister Paderewski

22 W. Trąmpczyński

23 Eagle and Sailing Ship

1919 (3 May). First Polish Philatelic Exhibition and Polish White Cross Fund. Surch as T **19a** (Nos. 116/118) T **19b** (Nos. 119/120), in violet. Imperf.

116	**15**	5+5f. yellow-green	65	45
		b. Perf 11½	65	50
117		10+5f. purple	1·90	3·75
		a. Ribbed paper	9·50	7·50
		b. Perf 11½	1·30	50
		ba. Ribbed paper	7·50	6·25
118		15+5f. lake	1·30	65
		a. Ribbed paper	7·50	6·25
		b. Perf 11½	65	50
		ba. Ribbed paper	7·50	6·25
119	**16**	25+5f. olive	1·30	65
		b. Perf 11½	1·30	50
		ba. Ribbed paper	7·50	6·25
120		50+5f. green	1·30	1·30
		a. Ribbed paper	7·50	6·25
		b. Perf 11½	2·50	1·90
		ba. Ribbed paper	7·50	6·25
116/120 *Set of 5*			5·75	6·00
116b/120b *Set of 5*			5·75	3·50

No. 120 is also known with overprint T **19a** (*price* £1300 *imperf unused*, £950 *perf 11½ used*).

(Des E. Bartłomiejczyk (10f., 50f., 1m.), E. Trojanowski (15f., 25f.), F. Polkowski (20f.). Typo)

1919 (15 June)–**20**. Opening of First Session of Parliament. Inscr 'SEJM 1919'. Perf 11½.

121	**20**	10f. mauve	45	35
		a. Imperf pair		
122	**21**	15f. red	45	35
		a. Imperf pair		
123	**22**	20f. brown (21×25 mm)	1·10	65
124		20f. brown (17×20 mm) (1920)	6·25	8·75
125	–	25f. sage-green	75	40
126	**23**	50f. greenish blue	75	40
127	–	1m. violet	1·40	90
121/127 *Set of 7*			10·00	10·50

Designs: Horiz as T **21**—25f. General Piłsudski. As T **23**—1m. Griffin and fasces.

1919 (9 Sept). POSTAGE DUE. Value in fenigów. Typo. Wove paper. Perf 11½.

D128	**D20**	2f. vermilion	1·10	1·10
D129		4f. vermilion	50	50
D130		5f. vermilion	40	40
D131		10f. vermilion	40	40
D132		20f. vermilion	40	40
D133		30f. vermilion	40	40
D134		50f. vermilion	40	40
D135		100f. vermilion	2·50	1·30
D136		500f. vermilion	4·75	2·75
D128/D136 *Set of 9*			9·75	7·00

See also Nos. D144/D147.

D. ISSUES FOR THE WHOLE OF POLAND

1 February 1920

O24

(O24a) A

(O24b) B

(Des E. Bartłomiejczyk. Typo)

1920 (Feb–Nov). OFFICIAL.

(a) Stars as in A on 3 to 50f. Medium wove paper. Perf 11½, 10 or compound (1 February).

O128	**O24**	3f. scarlet	30	50
O129		5f. scarlet	35	50
O130		10f. scarlet	35	50
O131		15f. scarlet	35	50
O132		25f. scarlet	45	50
O133		50f. scarlet	35	50
O134		100f. scarlet	35	50
O135		150f. scarlet	45	50
O136		200f. scarlet	1·90	55
O137		300f. scarlet	2·50	55
O138		600f. scarlet	3·75	1·30
O128/O138 *Set of 11*			10·00	5·75

Some stamps in this issue are known imperforate.

(b) Stars as B. Thin laid paper. Perf 11½ (20 November).

O139	**O24**	5f. scarlet	40	35
O140		10f. scarlet	40	40
O141		15f. scarlet	45	55
O142		25f. scarlet	1·60	55
O143		50f. scarlet	85	65
O139/O143 *Set of 5*			3·25	2·30

The stamps on thin paper are printed from new plates in which the stars are inclined outwards instead of inwards, and the figures are larger.

1920. (Feb)

Thin wove paper. Coarse impression. Perf 10-11½ and compound.

128	**15**	5f. green	40	30
129		10f. chocolate	40	30
130		15f. scarlet	40	30
131	**16**	20f. blue	40	30
132		25f. olive	40	30
133		50f. green	40	30
134	**17**	1m. slate-violet	40	30
128/134 *Set of 7*			2·50	1·90

Thin horizontally or vertically laid paper. Coarse impression. Perf 9 to 11½ and compound.

135	**16**	25f. dull olive	40	30
136		50f. dull blue-green	40	30
137	**17**	1m. slate-violet	40	30
138		2m. brown	40	30
139	**18**	3m. red-brown	4·50	40
140	**19**	5m. purple	1·30	40
141		6m. rose-carmine	2·10	40
142		10m. vermilion	65	40
143		20m. green	4·75	50
135/143 *Set of 9*			13·50	3·00

Examples of the 20m. in *téte-bêche* pairs are postal forgeries.

Nos. 144/145 are vacant.

1920 (1 May). POSTAGE DUE. As Nos. D132, etc. but on thin laid paper. Perf 9 to 11½.

D144	**D20**	20f. deep blue	35	40
D145		100f. deep blue	35	40
D146		200f. deep blue	1·60	40
D147		500f. deep blue	1·60	40
D144/D147 *Set of 4*			3·50	1·40

Though T **D20** in blue was originally sold for Austrian currency, this re-issue on thin paper was taken at face value in fenigów.

24

25

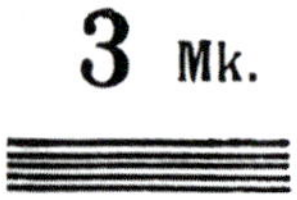

(26)

(Des E. Bartłomiejczyk. Typo)

1920 (1 May). Redrawn value tablet. Thick wove paper. Perf 10 to 11½ and compounds.

146	**24**	40f. bright violet	50	40

See also Nos. 182 and 184.

(Des E. Trojanowski. Typo)

1920–21. Thin laid or wove paper. Perf 9 to 14½ and compounds.

147	**25**	1m. carmine	30	45
148		2m. green	30	45
149		3m. pale blue	65	55
150		4m. rose	30	45
151		5m. brown-purple	30	45

152		8m. bistre-brown (1921)	65	65
147/152 *Set of* 6			2·30	2·75

The 3m. comes on laid paper (vertical or horizontal) only; the other values exist both on laid paper (8m. horiz only; others vert or horiz) and on wove paper.

1921 (25 Jan). Surch with T **26**.

153	**24**	3m. on 40f. bright violet	55	40
		a. Surch inverted		
		b. Surch double	31·00	

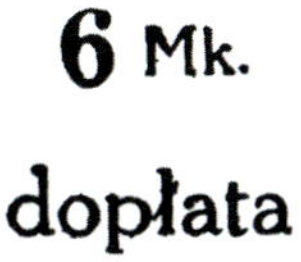

(D27)

(27)

D28

1921 (25 Jan). POSTAGE DUE. Surch as T **D27**.

D154	**11**	6m. on 15h. brown	75	3·50
		a. Surch double		
D155		6m. on 25h. carmine	75	3·00
		a. Surch inverted		
D156		20m. on 10h. lake	4·75	10·50
		a. Surch inverted		
D157		20m. on 50h. indigo	3·75	6·50
D158		35m. on 70h. blue	8·00	25·00
D154/D158 *Set of* 5			16·00	44·00

1921 (5 Mar). Red Cross Fund. Surch with T **27**, in red. Perf 9.

154	**19**	5m.+30m. purple	2·20	11·50
155		6m.+30m. rose-carmine	2·20	11·50
156		10m.+30m. vermilion	6·25	24·00
157		20m.+30m. green	75·00	£160
		a. Opt in carmine	£950	£2000
154/157 *Set of* 4			75·00	£190

(Des E. Trojanowski. Typo)

1921 (15 Apr). POSTAGE DUE. Wove or laid paper. Size 17×21–22 mm. Perf 9 to 14½ and compound.

D159	**D28**	1m. indigo	30	40
D160		2m. indigo	30	40
D161		4m. indigo	30	40
D162		6m. indigo	55	40
D163		8m. indigo	55	40
D164		20m. indigo	55	40
D165		50m. indigo	55	40
D166		100m. indigo	90	50
D159/D166 *Set of* 8			4·50	3·00

Nos. D159/D166 exist on a range of different papers in varying shades.
For stamps size 19×24 mm, see Nos. D199/D215.

28

29

30

(Des E. Bartłomiejczyk and W. Huzarski (T **30**). Typo)

1921 (2 May). New Constitution. Perf 11–11½.

158	**28**	2m. green	1·60	9·75
159		3m. blue	4·50	10·50
160		4m. scarlet	95	90
		a. Error. Carmine	£650	
161	**29**	6m. carmine	95	1·70
162		10m. slate-green	1·10	95
163	**30**	25m. violet	5·00	1·30
164		50m. myrtle green and buff	2·30	90
158/164 *Set of* 7			15·00	23·00

The large labels issued 29 May 1921 (25m. and 100m.) inscribed 'AERO-TARG: POZNAN 1921', with 'T.A.B.R.O.M.I.K.' at foot are not a Government issue.

31 Sower

32

(Des B. Wisniewski. Typo)

1921–22. Peace Treaty with Russia. Laid (No. 165) or wove (all) paper. Perf 9 to 14½ and compounds.

(a) Size 28×22 mm (May–August 1921).

165	**31**	10m. deep turquoise (*shades*)	1·30	40
166		15m. orange-brown	80	40
167		20m. red	1·90	40

(b) Size 27¼×21½ mm (10m.) or 25½×21 mm (20m.) (February 1922).

168	**31**	10m. blue-green	1·90	40
169		20m. brown-red	1·60	50
165/169 *Set of* 5			6·75	1·90

(Des E. Trojanowski. Typo)

1921–23.

(a) Thick wove paper. Perf 9 to 14½ and compounds (June 1921).

170	**32**	25m. violet and buff	80	50
171		50m. carmine and buff	1·10	50
172		100m. black-brown and orange	1·10	50
173		200m. pink and black	1·10	50
170/173 *Set of* 4			3·75	1·80

(b) Thin wove paper. Perf 10½ to 14½ and compounds (February–April 1923).

174	**32**	300m. yellow-green	40	40
175		400m. chocolate	80	40
176		500m. plum	90	40
177		1000m. orange	2·30	40
178		2000m. indigo-violet	70	40
174/178 *Set of* 5			4·50	1·80

33 Silesian Miner

34 Copernicus

35 Konarski

(T **33** des E. Bartłomiejczyk. Typo)

1922 (19 June)–**23**. Issue for districts of Upper Silesia.

(a). Perf 9 to 14½ and compound.

179	**15**	5f. blue	2·30	1·40
180		10f. mauve	2·30	1·40
181	**16**	20f. red	2·30	1·90
182	**24**	40f. purple-brown	2·30	1·90
183	**16**	50f. red-orange	2·30	1·90
184	**24**	75f. blue-green (7.22)	2·30	2·30
185	**33**	1m. slate (7.22)	2·30	1·90
186		1.25m. deep green (7.22)	2·30	3·50
187		2m. carmine (7.22)	2·30	1·90
188		3m. emerald (7.22)	2·30	1·90
189		4m. deep ultramarine (7.22)	2·30	3·25
190		5m. yellow-brown (7.22)	2·30	1·90
191		6m. red-orange (7.22)	3·25	8·50
192		10m. pale chocolate (7.22)	3·25	2·50
193		20m. deep purple (7.22)	3·25	2·75
194		50m. olive (7.22)	3·25	6·75

(b) Thicker paper. Perf 10 to 13½.

195	**33**	80m. red (3.23)	8·75	27·00
196		100m. bright violet (3.23)	8·75	20·00
197		200m. dull orange (3.23)	13·50	37·00
198		300m. pale blue (15.4.23)	23·00	80·00
179/198 *Set of* 20			85·00	£190

Upper Silesia was divided between Germany and Poland after a plebiscite held on 20 March 1921.

1923 (Mar)–**24**. POSTAGE DUE. Wove paper. Size 19×24 mm. Perf 12½.

D199	**D28**	50m. indigo	30	30
D200		100m. indigo	30	30
D201		200m. indigo	30	30
D202		500m. indigo	55	30
D203		1000m. indigo	40	30
D204		2000m. indigo	40	35
D205		10000m. indigo	25	30
D206		20000m. indigo	30	30
D207		30000m. indigo	30	30
D208		50000m. indigo	65	35
D209		100000m. indigo	35	40
D210		200000m. indigo	65	40
D211		300000m. indigo	6·25	65
D212		500000m. indigo	3·25	90
D213		1000000m. indigo	1·90	1·30

D214		2000000m. indigo	3·25	2·10
D215		3000000m. indigo	4·50	3·50
D199/D215		*Set of* 17	22·00	11·00

Nos. D205/D215 were issued in the period from January to March 1924.

1923 (June–Nov). 450th Birth Anniversary of Copernicus (astronomer) and 150th Death Anniversary of Konarski (educationist). Typo. Perf 10½–12½ and compounds.

199	**34**	1000m. slate	95	90
200	**35**	3000m. red-brown	75	1·00
		a. Error 'KONAPSKI'	23·00	31·00
201	**34**	5000m. carmine	1·30	1·30
199/201		*Set of* 3	2·75	3·00

No. 200a occurs in positions 5 and 15.

(36)

(37)

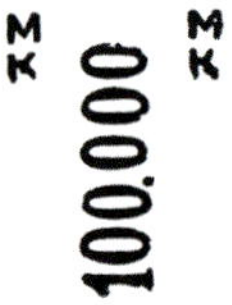

(38)

39

1923–24. Various stamps surch.

(a) With T ***36***.

202	**32**	10,000m. on 25m. violet and buff	6·25	35

(b) As T ***37***.

203	**31**	25,000m. on 20m. red (No. 167)	5·25	4·25
204		25,000m. on 20m. brown-red (169)	2·75	35
205		50,000m. on 10m. deep turquoise (No. 165)	9·50	40
205*a*		50,000m. on 10m. blue-green (No. 168)	2·50	35

On No. 204 the surcharge is smaller.

(c) As T ***38*** *(1924)*.

206	**25**	20,000m.on 2m. green	2·20	90
207		100,000m.on 5m. brown-purple	2·10	65
202/207		*Set of* 7	27·00	6·50

All the above exist with surcharge inverted and surcharge double.
Nos. 206/207 exist on both laid and wove paper.
No. 205 only the wove paper printing was surcharged.

1923 (Nov). POSTAGE DUE. Surch in figures.

D216	**D28**	'10000' on 8m. indigo	45	40
D217		'20000' on 20m. indigo	55	60
D218		'50000' on 2m. indigo	75	70
D216/D218		*Set of* 3	1·60	1·50

1924 (Jan–Mar). Typo. Perf 10 to 13½.

208	**39**	10,000m. brown-purple	3·25	65
209		20,000m. sage-green	1·90	40
210		30,000m. scarlet	2·50	65
211		50,000m. apple-green	7·50	65
212		100,000m. chestnut	2·50	65
213		200,000m. light blue	2·50	40
214		300,000m. magenta	6·25	70
215		500,000m. brown	6·25	3·00
216		1,000,000m. pink	65	65·00
217		2,000,000m. deep green	1·10	£500
208/217		*Set of* 10	31·00	£525

40

41 President Wojciechowski

42

(Typo State Graphic Institution)

1924 (1 May). New Currency. Perf 10½ to 13½ and compound.

218	**40**	1g. yellow-brown	1·30	1·10
219		2g. grey-brown	1·30	80
220		3g. orange	1·30	80
221		5g. sage-green	1·30	80
222		10g. blue-green	3·75	1·30
223		15g. scarlet	3·75	2·00
224		20g. light blue	16·00	45
225		25g. claret	28·00	45
		a. Error. Slate	£10000	£11000
226		30g. bright violet	34·00	65
		a. Grey-blue	£275	£200
227		40g. slate	13·00	80
228		50g. magenta	3·25	65
218/228		*Set of* 11	95·00	8·75

No. 225a came from a cliché of the 25g. in the plate of the 40g.

1924–26. POSTAGE DUE. New Currency. Typo. Size 20×25½ mm. Perf 10½ to 13½ and compound.

D229	**D28**	1g. brown	25	35
D230		2g. brown	25	35
D231		4g. brown	30	35
D232		6g. brown	30	35
D233		10g. brown	3·25	35
D234		15g. brown	9·50	35
D235		20g. brown	6·25	35
D236		25g. brown	11·50	35
D237		30g. brown	90	35
D238		40g. brown	1·20	35
D239		50g. brown	1·20	35
D240		1z. brown	80	35
D241		2z. brown	80	35
D242		3z. brown	1·10	1·20
D243		5z. brown (1926)	1·10	55
D229/D243		*Set of* 15	35·00	5·75

See also Nos. D290/D295.

(Des F. Aumiller. Litho)

1924 (1 Oct). Perf 12×11½.

229	**41**	1z. scarlet	50·00	3·75
		a. Imperf	£450	

1925 (1 Jan). National Fund. Typo. Perf 12½.

230	**42**	1g.+50g. yellow-brown	9·50	35·00
231		2g.+50g. grey-brown	9·50	35·00
232		3g.+50g. orange	9·50	35·00
233		5g.+50g. sage-green	9·50	35·00
234		10g.+50g. blue-green	9·50	35·00
235		15g.+50g. scarlet	9·50	35·00
236		20g.+50g. light blue	9·50	35·00
237		25g.+50g. claret	9·50	35·00
238		30g.+50g. bright violet	9·50	35·00
239		40g.+50g. slate	£140	44·00
240		50g.+50g. magenta	9·50	35·00
230/240		*Set of* 11	£210	£350

43 Holy Gate, Vilna

44 Town Hall, Poznań

45 King Sigismund Vasa Column, Warsaw

46 Wawel Castle, Cracow

47 Jan III Sobieski Statue, Lwòw

48 Galleon

I.

II.

Nos. 243/246:

I. Coarse printing; background lines touch the figures.

II. Redrawn, clearer design; white surround to figures.

Two types of No. 247:

a. Ornament finishes with 2 points

b. No points

III.

IV.

Nos. 249:

III. Background lines continue through 'GR'.

IV. Background lines shortened to give white surround to 'GR'.

V.

VI.

Nos. 250/251:

V. '40' small, 6 mm across.

VI. '40' larger, 6½ mm, nearer to spire.

1925–27. Typo. Perf 10½×11, 11½×12½, 11½, 12½×13 (13×12½ on 15g. and 40g.).

241	**43**	1g. brown	50	45
242	**47**	2g. brown-olive	65	65
243	**45**	3g. pale blue (Type I)	2·00	35
		a. Type II	2·75	35
244	**44**	5g. green (Type I)	2·20	35
		a. Type II	3·25	35
245	**45**	10g. violet (I)	1·70	35
		a. Type II	2·75	35
246	**46**	15g. carmine (Type I)	2·30	35
		a. Type II	3·25	35
247	**48**	20g. carmine-red (Type a)	9·00	35
		a. Type b	28·00	40
248	**43**	24g. grey-blue	23·00	2·50
249	**47**	30g. dull blue (Type III)	3·25	40
		a. Type IV	8·75	40
250	**46**	40g. light blue (Type V) (1927)	2·50	40
		a. Type VI	85·00	40
251	**48**	45g. mauve	65·00	1·90
241/251 *Set of* 11 (*cheapest*)			£100	7·25

Use of the 1g. was obligatory on all internal correspondence in payment of a special tax.

The 20g. printed by lithography is a postal forgery.

49 LVG Schneider Biplane

50 Chopin

51 Marshal Piłsudski

(Des L. Sowiński. Typo)

1925 (10 Sept). AIR. Perf 12½.

252	**49**	1g. pale blue	1·30	9·50
253		2g. orange	1·30	9·50
254		3g. yellow-brown	1·30	9·50
255		5g. brown	1·30	1·30
256		10g. blue-green	1·30	1·30
257		15g. bright magenta	6·25	1·90
258		20g. olive-green	16·00	9·50
259		30g. carmine	8·50	3·25
260		45g. deep lilac	16·00	6·25
252/260 *Set of* 9			48·00	47·00

Stamps perforated 11½ are forgeries.

Some stamps are known imperforate.

(Des Z. Kamiński. Litho)

1927 (1 Mar). Perf 11½.

261	**50**	40g. deep ultramarine	19·00	5·00

1927–28. Typo. Perf 12½×13.

262	**51**	20g. carmine (*shades*) (19.3.27)	7·50	65
262*a*		25g. yellow-brown (*shades*) (1.2.28)	9·50	65
		b. Perf 11½	9·50	65

No. 262 has the shading of the central portrait and background formed of dots (*price* £190).

No. 262*a*, the shading is made up of lines (*price* £325).

52 President Mościcki

53

54 Dr K. Kaczkowski

1927 (3 May). Perf 12×11½.

263	**52**	20g. vermilion	7·50	1·50

(Des B. Kamiński. Typo)

1927 (3 May). Educational Funds. Background of coloured wavy lines. Perf 11½.

264	**53**	10g.+5g. purple/*green*	16·00	15·00
265		20g.+5g. indigo/*straw*	18·00	18·00

1927 (27 May). Fourth International Military Medical Congress, Warsaw. Litho (10g.) or typo (others). Perf 11½ or 12½ (40g.).

266	**54**	10g. grey-green	7·50	5·00
267		25g. carmine	11·50	5·75
268		40g. blue	19·00	4·50
266/268 *Set of* 3			34·00	13·50

55 J. Słowacki (poet)

56 Marshal Piłsudski

57 President Mościcki

1927 (28 June). Transference of Słowacki's remains to Cracow. Typo. Perf 12½ or 12½×13.

269	**55**	20g. claret	8·75	1·90

(Des Z. Kamiński. Eng F. Schirnböck. Recess)

1928 (3 May). Warsaw Philatelic Exhibition. Sheet 117×88 mm. Types **56/57** in deep sepia. Perf 12½.

MS270	50g. and 1z.(+1z.50)	£375	£475

This miniature sheet was sold to those who purchased a 1z.50 entry ticket to the Warsaw Philatelic Exhibition.

See also Nos. 272/273, 328 and **MS**332*b*/**MS**332*c*.

58 General Joseph Bem

59 H. Sienkiewicz

60 The ancient Slav God, Świętowit

1928 (May). Typo. Perf 12½×13.

271	**58**	25g. bright rose	7·00	65

1928 (May)–**31**. T **56** (wove paper) and **57** (vertically laid paper). Various perfs, 10½ to 13½ and compounds.

272	**56**	50g. bluish slate	7·25	35
272*a*		50g. blue-green (5.31)	14·50	65
273	**57**	1z. slate-black/*cream*	19·00	90
		a. Horiz laid paper (1930)	65·00	7·75
272/272*a*/273 *Set of* 3			37·00	1·70

(Des E. Gaspé. Typo)

1928 (Oct). Henryk Sienkiewicz (author). Perf 12×12½.

274	**59**	15g. bright blue	3·25	65

(Des Z. Kamiński. Typo)

1928 (15 Dec). National Exhibition, Poznań. Perf 12½×12.

275	**60**	25g. red-brown	3·75	65

61

62 King Jan III Sobieski

D63

(Des Z. Kamiński. Typo)

1928 (15 Dec). Perf 12×12½.

276	**61**	5g. violet	55	35
277		10g. green	1·00	35
278		25g. red-brown	1·10	50
276/278 *Set of* 3			2·40	1·10

Stamps printed by lithography and the 25g. with vertical edges imperforate are postal forgeries.

(Des F. Schirnböck. Typo)

1930 (July). Birth Tercentenary of King Jan III Sobieski. Perf 12×12½.

279	**62**	75g. purple	6·25	45

1930 (July). POSTAGE DUE. Typo. Perf 12½×13.

D280	**D63**	5g. brown	60	40

63

64 Kościuszko, Washington and Pulaski

(Des T. Gronowski. Typo)

1930 (1 Nov). Centenary of November Rising (29 November, 1830). Perf 12½×13.

280	**63**	5g. purple	65	40
281		15g. blue	4·75	75
282		25g. red-brown	95	40
283		30g. rosine	12·50	6·25
280/283 *Set of* 4			17·00	7·00

The 25g. perf 11 is a postal forgery.

(Des R. Kleczewski. Eng W. Vacek. Recess)

1932 (3 May). Birth Bicentenary of George Washington. Vert laid paper. Perf 11½.

284	**64**	30g. chocolate/*cream*	3·25	65

65

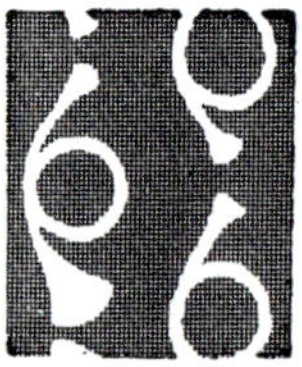

66

1932–33. Typo. W **66**. Perf 12×12½.

284*a*	**65**	5g. violet (1933)	1·30	35
285		10g. green	1·30	35
285*a*		15g. claret (1933)	1·30	35
286		20g. grey	1·30	35
287		25g. bistre	1·30	35
288		30g. scarlet	3·25	35
289		60g. cobalt	9·50	50
284*a*/289 *Set of* 7			17·00	3·00

The 25g. and 30g. on unwatermarked paper are postal forgeries; the 25g. is line perf 12½, the 30g. perf 13.

1932. POSTAGE DUE. Size 19×24 mm. Typo. Perf 12½.

D290	**D28**	1g. brown	30	35
D291		2g. brown	30	35
D292		10g. brown	1·30	35
D293		15g. brown	1·40	35
D294		20g. brown	12·50	35
D295		25g. brown	31·00	35
D290/D295 *Set of* 6			42·00	1·90

PRINTER. The letters 'P.W.P.W.' below the designs of some stamps from 1933 onwards stand for 'Panstwowa-Wytwornia Papierów. Wartosciowych' (the Government Printing Works).

67 Town Hall, Toruń

68 Franciszek Żwirko (airman), Stanislaw Wigura (aircraft designer) and RWD-6 SP-AHN

1933 (2 Jan). Seventh Centenary of Toruń. Recess. W **66**. Perf 11½.

290	**67**	60g. blue/*cream*	55·00	3·25

No. 291 is vacant.

(Des R. Kleczewski. Eng W. Vacek. Recess)

1933 (15 Apr). Victory in Flight round Europe Air Race, 1932. W **66**. Perf 11½ or 12½.

292	**68**	30g. grey-green	31·00	3·75

1933 (21 May). Toruń Philatelic Exhibition. Recess. W **66**. Perf 11½.

293	**67**	60g. scarlet/*cream*	19·00	26·00

No. 293 was sold at 1z., at the Exhibition.

69 Altar piece, St Mary's Church, Cracow

O70

(Des R. Kleczewski. Eng W. Vacek. Recess)

1933 (10 July). Fourth Death Centenary of Veit Stoss (sculptor). Vert laid paper. Perf 11½.

294	**69**	80g. red-brown/*cream*	25·00	3·25

1933 (1 Aug). OFFICIAL. T **O70** (and similar type). Typo. W **66**. Perf 12×12½.

(a) Inscr 'ZWYCZAJNA' (Ordinary).

O295	(30g.) mauve	55	50

(b) Inscr 'POLECONA' (Registered).

O296	(80g.) scarlet	55	50

See also Nos. O306/O307.

70 *The Liberation of Vienna*, by J. Matejko

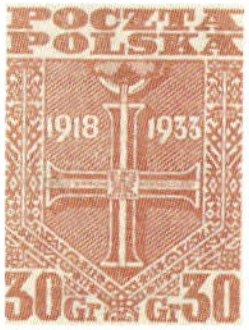

71 Cross of Independence

(Des R. Kleczewski. Eng W. Vacek. Recess)

1933 (12 Sept). 250th Anniversary of Relief of Vienna. Vert laid paper. Perf 12×11½ or 11½.

295	**70**	1z.20 blue/*cream*	50·00	19·00

1933 (11 Nov). 15th Anniversary of Proclamation of Republic. Typo. W **66**. Perf 12½×13.

296	**71**	30g. scarlet	9·50	90

Wyst. Filat.
1934
Katowice

(72)

73 Piłsudski and Legion of Fusiliers' Badge

20
groszy

(D74)

1934 (5 May). Katowice Philatelic Exhibition. Optd with T **72**. W **66**. Perf 12×12½.

297	**65**	20g. grey (R.)	55·00	50·00
298		30g. scarlet	55·00	50·00

Overprints reading '1934 r.' in the centre are proofs.

(Des R. Kleczewski. Eng W. Vacek. Recess)

1934. 20th Anniversary of Formation of Polish Legion. Perf 11½.

299	**73**	25g. blue (1.10)	5·00	75
300		30g. sepia (6.8)	6·00	75

1934–38. POSTAGE DUE. Postage Due stamps of 1924–1926 surch as T **D74**.

D301	**D28**	10g. on 2z. brown (1938)	30	35
D302		15g. on 2z. brown (30.11.36)	30	35
D303		20g. on 1z. brown (30.11.36)	40	35
D304		20g. on 5z. brown (6.8.34)	9·50	35
D305		25g. on 40g. brown (7.37)	90	35
D306		30g. on 40g. brown (7.37)	1·50	35
D307		50g. on 40g. brown (7.37)	1·50	50
D308		50g. on 3z. brown (1935)	2·40	45
D301/D308 *Set of* 8			15·00	2·75

Challenge
1934
(74)

55 gr.
(75)

1 zł.
(76)

DOPŁATA **10 GR.**
(D77)

1934 (28 Aug). International Air Tournament. Optd in red with T **74** or larger overprint (18½×8½ mm).

301	**49**	20g. olive-green	9·75	19·00
302	**68**	30g. grey-green	22·00	6·25

1934 (1 Oct)–**35**. Surch as T **75** (Nos. 303/304) or T **76**.

303	**69**	25g. on 80g. red-brown/*cream*	9·50	1·30
		a. 'gr.' lower than '25'	£250	50·00
304	**65**	55g. on 60g. cobalt	6·25	65
		a. Comma instead of full point after 'gr'	38·00	38·00
		b. Full point missing after 'gr'	47·00	38·00
305	**70**	1z. on 1z.20 blue/*cream* (R.)	31·00	9·50
		a. 'l' 4½ mm (1935)	31·00	9·50
303/305 *Set of* 3			42·00	10·50

No. 303. Surcharge in each of the upper corners over original value.
No. 305. Surcharge in the centre at the foot with bars in upper corners obliterating original value. Figure '1' of surcharge measures 5½ mm.

1934–36. POSTAGE DUE. No. 273a surch as T **D77** (differing in size and detail for each value). Horiz laid paper.

D309	**57**	10g. on 1z. black/*cream* (R.) (1.6.36)	95	65
		a. Vert laid paper	47·00	55·00
D310		20g. on 1z. black/*cream* (Br.) (15.2.36)	1·90	65
D311		25g. on 1z. black/*cream* (B.) (1.10.34)	95	65
		a. Vert laid paper	47·00	50·00
		b. Error. '23' instead of '25'	6·25	12·50
D309/D311 *Set of* 3			4·50	1·80

1935 (1 Apr). OFFICIAL. Redrawn types resembling Nos. O295/O296.

O306	(30g.) violet-blue ('ZWYCZAJNA')	30	50
O307	(80g.) brown red ('POLECONA')	40	50

77 Marshal Piłsudski

Kopiec
Marszałka
Piłsudskiego
(78)

(Des M. R. Polak. Litho (Nos. 308, 309/310) or typo (others))

1935 (May–July). Mourning for Marshal Piłsudski. Perf 11½×13 (No. 308) or 11 (others).

306	**77**	5g. black (7.35)	95	40
307		15g. black (7.35)	95	75
308		25g. black (*litho*) (16.5.35)	1·60	40
308*a*		25g. black (*typo*) (7.35)	11·50	40
309		45g. black (28.5.35)	6·25	3·75
310		1z. black (28.5.35)	12·50	7·50
		Nos. 285a and 299 optd with T ***78***.		
311	**65**	15g. claret (B.) (31.5.35)	2·20	1·00
312	**73**	25g. blue (R.) (31.5.35)	5·25	4·00

See also No. **MS**358*a*.

79 Pieskowa Skala (Dog's Rock)

80 President Mościcki

(Des R. Kleczewski (Nos. 313/315, 324), L. Sowiński (Nos. 316, 321/323, 325/326), W. Borowski (Nos. 317/320). Eng W. L. Vacek (Nos. 313, 315, 322, 324/325, 327), M. R. Polak (Nos. 314, 316, 317/319, 321, 323, 326), J. Piwczyk (No. 320))

1935–37. As T **79** (various views, ship and buildings) and T **80**.

	(a) Typo. Perf 13×12½.		
313	5g. violet-blue (16.8.35)	75	30
314	10g. yellow-green (1.12.35)	65	30
315	15g. greenish blue (5.8.35)	4·50	35
316	20g. violet-black (1.12.35)	2·75	35
	(b) Recess. Perf 13×12½ (5g. to 20g., 25g. (Plate II), 45g., 50g. (Plate II)) or 13 (others). Plate I 28.3×21.3 mm, Plate II 28.5×22 mm.		
317	5g. violet (1.4.37)	65	30
318	10g. yellow-green (1.4.37)	1·00	30
319	15g. brown-lake (1.4.37)	80	40
320	20g. brown-orange (1.4.37)	1·30	65
321	25g. deep blue-green (Plate I) (1.12.35)	1·60	40
	a. Plate II (1937)	75	30
322	30g. scarlet (1.12.35)	2·00	30
323	45g. magenta (Plate I) (16.1.36)	95	30
	a. Plate II (1937)	65	30
324	50g. black (Plate I) (16.1.36)	4·50	40
	a. Plate II (1937)	1·30	40
325	55g. blue (Plate I) (16.1.36)	6·25	75
	a. Plate II (1937)	6·25	75
326	1z. sepia (16.1.36)	8·50	1·50
327	3z. sepia (15.9.35)	3·25	12·50
313/327 *Set of* 15 (*cheapest*)		32·00	17·00

Designs: As T **79**—No. 314, Lake Morskie Oko; No. 315, *Piłsudski* (liner); No. 316, Pieniny-Czorsztyn; No. 317, Monastery of Jasna Góra, Czestochowa; No. 318, *Batory* (liner) and Sea passenger terminal, Gdynia; No. 319, University, Lwòw; No. 320, Administrative Buildings, Katowice; 25g. Belvedere Palace, Warsaw; 30g. Castle at Mir; 45g. Castle at Podhorce; 50g. Cloth Hall, Cracow; 55g. Raczynski Library, Poznań; 1z. Vilna Cathedral.

1936 (3 June). Tenth Anniversary of Mościcki Presidency. As T **57** but inscr '1926. 3. VI. 1936' below design. Perf 12½.

328	**57**	1z. bright blue	8·75	12·50

GORDON-BENNETT 30.VIII.
1936
(81)

1936 (15 Aug). Gordon-Bennett International Balloon Race. Optd with T **81**.

329	30g. scarlet (B.) (No. 322)	7·50	10·00
330	55g. blue (R.) (No. 325)	11·50	8·75

82 Marshal Śmigly-Rydz

83 President Mościcki

(Des S. Chrostowski. Eng M. R. Polak. Recess)

1937 (July–Aug). Perf 12½.

331	**82**	25g. slate-blue (1.7)	45	40
332		55g. blue (8.37)	65	65

See also No. **MS**358*a*.

1937 (1 Sept). Visit of King of Romania. Three sheets each 102×125 mm each containing a block of four of earlier types in new colours. Perf 12½.

MS332*a* 25g.×4, sepia	34·00	44·00
MS332*b* 50g.×4, slate-blue	34·00	44·00
MS332*c* 1z.×4, black	34·00	44·00

(Eng J. Piwczyk. Recess)

1938 (1 Feb). President's 70th Birthday. Perf 12½.

333	**83**	15g. greenish slate	1·10	35
334		30g. purple	1·30	40

84 Kościuszko, Paine and Washington

84a Postal Coach

(Des W. Boratyński. Eng W. Vacek. Recess)

1938 (17 Mar). 150th Anniversary of US Constitution. Perf 12×12½.

335	**84**	1z. deep blue	2·50	2·50

(Des W. Boratyński. Eng W. Vacek. Recess)

1938 (3 May). Fifth Philatelic Exhibition, Warsaw. Sheet 130×103 mm. Perf 12×12½ or imperf.

MS335*a* **84a** 45g.×2 green; 55g.×2 blue	80·00	£140

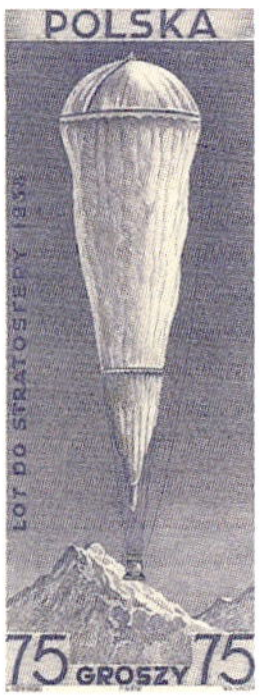

84b Stratosphere Balloon

85 Boleslaw the Brave

85a King Wladislaw Jagiello and Queen Jadwiga

86 Marshal Piłsudski

87 Teschen comes to Poland

D88

(Des L. Sowiński. Eng W. Vacek. Recess)

1938 (15 Sept). Proposed Polish Stratosphere Flight. Sheet 75×125 mm. Perf 12½×12.

MS335*b* 75g.(+1z.25) violet	70·00	90·00

(Des W. Boratyński (5g. to 1z.), M. Watorek (2z.) and Z. Rozwadowski (3z.). Eng H. Dutczyński (5g., 45g., 50g., 1z.), J. Piwczyk (10g., 30g., 55g., 75g.) and M. R. Polak (others). Recess)

1938 (11 Nov). 20th Anniversary of Independence.

*(a) Designs as Types **85** and **85a** (5g. to 2z.) and T **86**. Perf 12½×13 or 13×12½ (3z.).*

336	5g. red-orange	25	30
337	10g. green	25	30
338	15g. red-brown	25	30
339	20g. greenish blue	65	90
340	25g. purple	40	30
341	30g. rose-red	65	30
342	45g. black	95	1·90
343	50g. magenta	95	40
344	55g. bright blue	65	30
345	75g. blue-green	4·50	1·90
346	1z. orange	4·50	2·00
347	2z. carmine	16·00	22·00
348	3z. slate-blue	10·50	19·00
336/348 *Set of* 13		36·00	45·00

*(b) Sheet 102×125 mm containing four portraits as T **83** but with value and inscr transposed, all in purple. Recess. Perf 12½.*

MS348*a* 25g. Marshal Piłsudski; 25g. President Narutowicz; 25g. President Mościcki; 25g. Marshal Śmigly-Rydz	25·00	38·00

Designs: 10g. Casimir the Great; 20g. Casimir Jagiellon; 25g. Sigismund August; 30g. Stefan Batory; 45g. Chodkiewicz and Żółkiewski; 50g. Jan III Sobieski; 55g. Symbol of Constitution of 3 May, 1791; 75g. Kościuszko, Poniatowski and Dąbrowski; 1z. November Uprising, 1830–1831; 2z. Romuald Traugutt.

For stamp as No. 338, but without crossed swords in foreground; see No. 357.

(Des W. Boratyński. Eng W. Vacek. Recess)

1938 (1 Nov). Acquisition of Teschen. Perf 12½×13.

349	**87**	25g. purple	3·25	70

1938 (25 Nov)–**39**. POSTAGE DUE. Typo. Perf 12½×12.

D350	**D88**	5g. blue-green	25	35
D351		10g. blue-green	25	35
D352		15g. blue-green (1939)	25	35
D353		20g. blue-green (1939)	70	35
D354		25g. blue-green (1939)	45	35
D355		30g. blue-green (1939)	75	35
D356		50g. blue-green (1939)	1·20	75
D357		1z. blue-green (1939)	5·00	4·50
D350/D357 *Set of* 8			8·00	6·50

88 Warmth

89 Tatra Mountaineer

89a (No. 357)

(Des W. Boratyński. Eng J. Piwczyk. Recess)

1938–39. Winter Relief Fund. Perf 13×12½.

350	**88**	5g.+5g. red-orange (21.12.38)	60	1·30
351		25g.+10g. purple (10.1.39)	1·50	3·75
352		55g.+15g. bright blue (15.3.39)	2·50	7·50
350/352 *Set of* 3			4·25	11·50

(Des W. Boratyński. Eng M. Dutczyński. Recess)

1939 (6 Feb). International Ski Championships, Zakopane. Perf 12½×13.

353	**89**	15g. red-brown	1·30	1·30
354		25g. purple	1·90	2·20
355		30g. carmine	3·25	2·50
356		55g. bright blue	9·50	6·25
353/356 *Set of* 4			14·50	11·00

1939 (2 Mar). As No. 338, but crossed swords in foreground replaced by ornamental dais.

357	**89a**	15g. red-brown	65	40

90 Marshal Piłsudski and Polish Legionaries

(Des W. Boratyński. Eng J. Piwczyk. Recess)

1939 (1 Aug). 25th Anniversary of Battles of First Polish Legions.

(a). Perf 12½×13.

358	**90**	25g. purple	95	65

(b) Sheet 103×125 mm comprising former types printed in violet-grey. Recess. Perf 12½.

MS358*a*	25g. Type **90**; 25g. Type **77**; 25g. Type **82** (*sold for* 1z.75)	28·00	55·00

III. GERMAN OCCUPATION

1939–1945

German armies invaded Poland on 1 September 1939 and on 17 September Russian troops invaded from the east. On 28 September Poland was divided between Russia and Germany; Germany annexed the territory she had lost in 1919–1921 and also parts of the provinces of Łódź, Warsaw, Cracow and Bialystok; on 12 October the rest of the area seized by Germany became a protectorate called the General-Government. Russian stamps were used in the area to the east of River Bug, annexed by the Soviet Union.

(91)

(92)

1939 (1–4 Dec). T **94** of Germany (Hindenburg) surch as T **91**. Wmk Swastikas. Perf 14×14½.

359	6g. on 3pf. bistre-brown	40	65
360	8g. on 4pf. slate-blue	40	65
361	12g. on 6pf. deep green	40	65
362	16g. on 8pf. orange-red (4.12)	90	2·00
363	20g. on 10pf. chocolate (4.12)	40	65
364	24g. on 12pf. carmine	40	65
365	30g. on 15pf. claret (4.12)	90	2·00
366	40g. on 20pf. light blue (4.12)	90	65
367	50g. on 25pf. ultramarine	90	1·30
368	60g. on 30pf. bronze-green	90	65
369	80g. on 40pf. magenta (4.12)	90	1·30
370	1z. on 50pf. black and green	2·00	2·50
371	2z. on 100pf. black and yellow	4·00	4·50
359/371	*Set of* 13	12·00	16·00

1940 (Feb–Mar). Stamps of Poland, 1937–1939, optd as T **92**, at State Printing Works, Vienna.

372	2g. on 5g. red-orange (No. 336)	40	50
373	4g. on 5g. red-orange (No. 336)	40	50
374	6g. on 10g. green (No. 337)	40	50
375	8g. on 10g. green (No. 337)	40	50
376	10g. on 10g. green (No. 337)	40	50
377	12g. on 15g. red-brown (Type I) (No. 357)	40	50
	a. Type II	1·60	4·00
378	16g. on 15g. red-brown (No. 357)	40	50
379	24g. on 25g. slate-blue (No. 331)	2·00	4·00
380	24g. on 25g. purple (No. 340)	40	50
381	30g. on 30g. rose-red (No. 341)	40	50
382	30g. on 5g.+5g. red-orange (No. 350)	40	90
383	40g. on 30g. purple (No. 334)	65	2·00
384	40g. on 25g.+10g. purple (No. 351)	40	90
385	50g. on 50g. magenta (Type I) (No. 343)	40	90
	a. Type II	5·25	12·50
386	50g. on 55g. blue (No. 332)	50	1·30
387	60g. on 55g. bright blue (No. 344)	10·50	23·00
388	80g. on 75g. blue-green (No. 345)	10·50	23·00
388*a*	1z. on 55g.+15g. blue (No. 352)	5·75	14·50
389	1z. on 1z. orange (No. 346)	11·00	23·00
390	2z. on 2z. carmine (No. 347)	4·00	9·00
391	3z. on 3z. slate-blue (No. 348)	5·25	13·00
372/391	*Set of* 26	49·00	£110

Two types of 12g. and 50g. Type I is as in T **92**. In Type II the figures of value are very close to the 'G' and 'I' of 'General'.

1940 (Feb–Mar). Nos. D353/D356 optd with T **92**, at State Printing Works, Vienna.

391*a*	50g. on 20g. blue-green (No. D353)	1·80	5·25
391*b*	50g. on 25g. blue-green (No. D354)	7·75	21·00
391*c*	50g. on 30g. blue-green (No. D355)	23·00	46·00
391*d*	50g. on 50g. blue-green (No. D356)	1·30	4·00
391*e*	50g. on 1z. blue-green (No. D357)	2·50	5·25
391*a*/391*e*	*Set of* 5	33·00	75·00

PRINTER. All stamps from Nos. O392 to 477 were printed at the State Printing Works, Vienna.

O93

93 Copernicus Memorial, Cracow

(94)

(Des Kreb. Design photo; figures of value typo)

1940 (5 Apr–5 Aug). OFFICIAL. As T **O93**.

(a) 31×23 mm. Perf 12½ (5 April).

O392	6g. pale brown	1·10	3·75
O393	8g. grey	1·10	3·75
O394	10g. pale green	1·10	3·75
O395	12g. deep green	1·10	2·50
O396	20g. deep brown	1·10	4·00
O397	24g. brown-red	15·00	2·50
O398	30g. crimson-lake	1·30	4·00
O399	40g. deep violet	1·30	7·75
O400	48g. pale olive	5·00	7·75
O401	50g. blue	1·30	4·00
O402	60g. deep olive	1·10	3·25
O403	80g. purple	1·10	3·75

(b) 35×26 mm. Perf 13½×14 (5 April).

O404	1z. purple and grey	3·00	7·75
O405	3z. red-brown and grey	3·00	7·75
O406	5z. orange and grey	3·50	9·50
O392/O406	*Set of* 15	38·00	70·00

(c) Size 21×16 mm.

O407	6g. brown (5.8)	1·00	2·00
O408	8g. grey (5.8)	1·00	2·30
O409	10g. blue-green (5.8)	1·30	2·50
O410	12g. deep green (5.8)	1·00	2·30
O411	20g. deep brown (22.7)	1·00	2·00
O412	24g. brown-red (5.8)	1·00	2·00
O413	30g. crimson-lake (22.7)	1·30	2·50
O414	40g. deep violet (22.7)	1·30	2·50
O415	50g. blue (22.7)	1·30	2·50
O407/O415	*Set of* 9	9·25	19·00

(Des Professor Puchinger. Photo)

1940 (5 Aug)–**41**. Views as T **93**. Perf 14.

392	6g. brown	40	1·00
393	8g. chestnut	40	1·00
394	8g. blue-black (8.9.41)	90	90
395	10g. emerald	35	40
396	12g. deep green	3·50	1·20
397	12g. violet (8.9.41)	60	50
398	20g. deep brown	35	40
399	24g. lake	35	40
400	30g. reddish violet	35	40
401	30g. purple (8.9.41)	60	90
402	40g. blue-black	35	40
403	48g. red-brown (8.9.41)	1·00	1·60
404	50g. blue	35	40
405	60g. deep olive	35	40
406	80g. deep violet	80	65
407	1z. reddish purple (9.9.40)	3·50	2·00
408	1z. blue-green (8.9.41)	90	1·60
392/408	*Set of* 17	13·50	13·00

Designs: 6g. Florian Gate, Cracow; 8g. Castle Keep, Cracow; 10g. Cracow Gate, Lublin; 20g. Church of the Dominicans, Cracow; 24g. Wawel Castle, Cracow; 30g. Old Church in Lublin; 40g. Arcade, Cloth Hall, Cracow; 48g. Town Hall, Sandomir; 50g. Town Hall, Cracow; 60g. Courtyard of Wawel Castle, Cracow; 80g. St Mary's Church, Cracow; 1z. Bruhl Palace, Warsaw.

1940 (17 Aug). Red Cross Fund. Pictorial types of 1940–1941 (colours changed), surch as T **94**, in red.

409	12g.+8g. greyish olive	2·50	5·25
410	24g.+16g. greyish olive	2·50	5·25
411	50g.+50g. greyish olive	3·25	7·50
412	80g.+80g. greyish olive	3·25	9·75
409/412	*Set of* 4	10·50	25·00

95

96

(Nos. 413/419. Des O. Engelhardt-Kyffhäuser. Eng F. Lorber. Recess)

1940 (26 Oct). First Anniversary of German Occupation. T **95** and similar types. Thick straw-coloured paper. Perf 14½.

413		12g.+38g. deep green	2·00	4·50
414		24g.+26g. red	2·00	4·50
415		30g.+20g. deep violet	3·00	7·75
413/415 *Set of* 3			6·25	15·00

Designs: 24g. Woman with scarf; 30g. Fur-capped peasant (as T **96**).

1940 (1 Dec). Winter Relief Fund. Perf 12½.

416	**96**	12g.+8g. deep green	1·00	2·50
417		24g.+16g. red	1·00	3·25
418		30g.+30g. purple-brown	2·00	4·00
419		50g.+50g. blue	2·00	4·50
416/419 *Set of* 4			5·50	13·00

D97

97 Cracow

1940 (1 Dec). DELIVERY. Photo. Perf 14.

D420	**D97**	10g. red-orange	80	2·00
D421		20g. red-orange	80	2·00
D422		30g. red-orange	80	2·50
D423		50g. red-orange	1·90	3·75
D420/D423 *Set of* 4			3·75	9·25

Ordinary postage stamps only paid for delivery to the nearest sub-office and the above were applied in addition to pay for delivery to the addressee.

(Des Gessner and W. Kreb. Eng F. Lorber. Recess)

1941 (20 Apr). Perf 14½.

420	**97**	10z. grey and red	1·80	4·00

Issued in sheets of eight.

98 The Barbican, Cracow

99 Adolf Hitler

(Des Fahringer and Gessner. Eng F. Lorber. Recess)

1941. T **98** and similar horiz design. Perf 13½×14.

421	**98**	2z. blue (22.5)	1·20	1·30
422	-	4z. green (10.7)	1·20	2·50

Design: 4z. Tyniec Monastery.
See also Nos. 465/468.

(Des W. Dachauer. Eng F. Lorber)

1941 (26 Oct)–**44**.

(a) Photo. Perf 14.

423	**99**	2g. grey	25	50
424		6g. yellow-brown	25	50
425		8g. deep grey-blue	25	50
426		10g. yellow-green	25	50
427		12g. deep violet	25	50
428		16g. red-orange	2·10	3·25
429		20g. deep brown	25	50
430		24g. lake	25	50
431		30g. purple	25	50
432		32g. deep blue-green	35	65
433		40g. blue	25	50
434		48g. chocolate	1·80	1·30
435		50g. deep blue (7.43)	35	1·20
436		60g. olive (7.43)	35	1·20
437		80g. deep purple (7.4.3)	35	1·20
423/437 *Set of* 15			6·75	12·00

(b) Recess. Perf 12½ (7.4.1942–1944).

438	**99**	50g. deep blue	70	1·50
439		60g. olive	70	1·50
440		80g. reddish purple	70	1·50
441		1z. deep green	70	1·50
		a. Perf 14 (1944)	1·50	20·00
442		1z.20 purple-brown	1·00	2·30
		a. Perf 14 (1944)	3·00	26·00
443		1z.60 violet-indigo	1·00	2·30
		a. Perf 14 (1944)	3·00	33·00
438/443 *Set of* 6			4·25	9·50

1942 (20 Apr). Hitler's 53rd Birthday. As T **99**, but premium inserted in design. Recess. Thick straw-coloured paper. Perf 11.

444		30g.+1z. reddish purple	55	2·50
445		50g.+1z. blue	55	2·50
446		1z.20+1z. brown	55	2·50
444/446 *Set of* 3			1·50	6·75

100 Modern Lublin

101 Copernicus

1942 (15 Aug). 600th Anniversary of Lublin. T **100** and similar design. Photo. Perf 12½.

447	–	12g.+8g. purple	35	1·00
448	**100**	24g.+6g. red-brown	35	1·00
449	–	50g.+50g. dull blue	35	2·00
450	**100**	1z.+1z. green	65	2·50
447/450 *Set of* 4			1·50	5·75

Designs: 12g., 50g. Lublin, after an ancient engraving.

(Des W. Dachauer. Eng F. Lorber. Recess)

1942 (20 Nov). Third Anniversary of German Occupation. T **101** and similar portraits. Perf 13½×14.

451	-	12g.+18g. violet (Veit Stoss (Vit Stvosz))	40	65
452	-	24g.+26g. lake (Hans Dürer)	40	65
453	-	30g.+30g. purple (J. Schuch)	40	65
454	-	50g.+50g. blue (J. Elsner)	40	1·00
455	**101**	1z.+1z. green	40	1·30
451/455 *Set of* 5			1·80	3·75

O102

102 Adolf Hitler

24. MAI 1943

24. MAI 1943

(102a)

(Des W. Kreb. Design photo; value typo)

1943 (16 Feb). OFFICIAL. Perf 14.

O456	**O102**	6g. yellow-brown	55	1·10
O457		8g. grey-blue	35	1·10
O458		10g. light green	35	1·10
O459		12g. violet	35	1·10
O460		16g. brown-orange	35	1·10
O461		20g. brown-olive	35	1·10
O462		24g. brown-lake	35	1·20
O463		30g. reddish purple	35	1·20
O464		40g. blue	35	1·20
O465		60g. olive	35	1·20
O466		80g. dull purple	35	1·20

O467		100g. slate	50	2·20
O456/O467 *Set of 12*			4·00	13·00

(Des W. Dachauer. Eng F. Lorber. Recess)

1943 (20 Apr). Hitler's 54th Birthday. Perf 14.

456	**102**	12g.+1z. violet	50	2·40
457		24g.+1z. carmine	50	2·40
458		84g.+1z. green	50	2·40
456/458 *Set of 3*			1·20	6·50

1943 (24 May). 400th Death Anniversary of Nicolas Copernicus (astronomer). T **101** (colour changed) optd with T **102a**.

459	**101**	1z.+1z. reddish purple	65	2·50

Issued in sheets of ten.

Examples of the 1z. reddish purple without overprint exist; their status is unclear.

103 Cracow Gate, Lublin

103a Lwòw

104 Adolf Hitler

(Des W. Kreb. Frame photo. Centre embossed)

1943 (13 Aug–1 Sept). Third Anniversary of Nazi Party in German-occupied Poland. T **103** and similar designs. Perf 14.

460	**103**	12g.+38g. green	35	1·20
461	-	24g.+76g. red	35	1·20
462	-	30g.+70g. purple	35	1·20
463	-	50g.+1z. blue	35	1·20
464	-	1z.+2z. grey	35	1·20
460/464 *Set of 5*			1·60	5·50

Designs: 24g. Cloth Hall, Cracow; 30g. Administrative Building, Radom; 50g. Bruhl Palace, Warsaw; 1z. Town Hall, Lwòw.

(Des Fahringer (2z., 4z.), F. Prufimeyer (6z.), Gessner (10z.). Eng F. Lorber. Recess)

1943–44. T **103a** and similar horiz designs. Perf 13½×14 or 14×13½ (10z.).

465	-	2z. deep green (10.4.44)	40	65
466	-	4z. slate-violet (10.4.44)	1·10	2·50
467	**103a**	6z. agate (11.2.44)	60	1·60
468	-	10z. grey and chestnut (26.10.43)	65	2·30
465/468 *Set of 4*			2·50	6·25

Designs: 2z. The Barbican, Cracow; 4z. Tyniec Monastery; 10z. Cracow.

(Des W. Kreb. Photo)

1944 (20 Apr). Hitler's 55th Birthday. Perf 14.

469	**104**	12g.+1z. green	30	1·60
470		24g.+1z. red-brown	30	1·60
471		84g.+1z. violet	30	1·60
469/471 *Set of 3*			80	4·25

105 Konrad Celtis

105a Cracow Castle

(Des W. Dachauer. Eng F. Lorber. Recess)

1944 (15 July). Culture Funds. T **105** and similar portraits. Perf 14.

472	**105**	12g.+18g. green	25	2·00
473	-	24g.+26g. red	25	2·00
474	-	30g.+30g. purple	25	2·50
475	-	50g.+50g. blue	25	3·25
476	-	1z.+1z. brown	25	3·25
472/476 *Set of 5*			1·10	11·50

Designs: 24g. Andreas Schlüter; 30g. Hans Boner; 50g. Augustus the Strong; 1z. Georg Gottlieb Pusch.

(Des P. Stubinger. Eng R. Zenziger. Recess)

1944 (26 Oct). Fifth Anniversary of German Occupation. Perf 13½.

477	**105a**	10z.+10z. greenish black and carmine	10·50	65·00
		a. Grey-black and red	10·50	65·00

Issued in sheets of eight.

IV. ISSUES OF POLISH EXILED GOVERNMENT IN LONDON

1941–1944

For correspondence on Polish sea-going vessels and, on certain days, from Polish military camps in Great Britain.

106 Ruins of Ministry of Finance, Warsaw

107 Vickers-Armstrong Wellington and Hawker Hurricanes MK 1 used by Poles in Great Britain

(Eng E. Dawson (5g., 25g., 75g.), P. S. Hall (10g., 80g.), A. B. Hill (25g.), E. Warner (1z.), R. Godbehear (1z.50). Recess Bradbury Wilkinson)

1941 (15 Dec). Types **106/107** and similar designs. Perf 12½×13 (vert) or 11½×12 (horiz).

478	5g. purple	95	1·90
479	10g. myrtle green	1·30	2·50
480	25g. slate-black	1·60	2·50
481	55g. deep blue	2·00	3·75
482	75g. brown-olive	4·50	9·00
483	80g. carmine	4·50	9·00
484	1z. slate-blue	5·75	11·50
485	1z.50 red-brown	5·75	11·50
478/485 *Set of 8*		24·00	46·00

Designs: As T **106**—5g. Ruins of USA Embassy, Warsaw; 25g. Destruction of Mickiewicz Monument, Cracow; 1z.50 Polish submarine *Orzel*. As T **107**—55g. Ruins of Warsaw; 75g. Polish machine gunners; 80g. Polish tank in Great Britain.

108 Vickers-Armstrong Wellington and U-boat

109 Merchant Navy

(Des A. Horowicz. Eng. P. S. Hall (5g., 25g., 55g.), E. Dawson (10g., 75g., 80g.), R. Godbehear (12g.), A. B. Hill (1z.50). Recess Bradbury Wilkinson)

1943 (1 Nov). Types **108/109** and similar designs. Perf 12½×13 (vert) or 11½×12 (horiz).

486	5g. claret	95	1·90
487	10g. bright green	1·30	2·50
488	25g. violet	1·30	2·50
489	55g. ultramarine	1·60	3·25
490	75g. red-brown	2·75	5·75
491	80g. carmine	3·25	6·50
492	1z. blackish olive	4·00	8·25
493	1z.50 black	5·00	10·00
486/493 *Set of 8*		26·00	37·00

Designs: As T **108**—25g. Anti-tank gun in France; 55g. Poles at Narvik; 1z. Saboteurs damaging railway line. As T **109**—75g. The Tobruk road; 80g. General Sikorski visiting Polish troops in Middle East; 1z.50 Underground newspaper office.

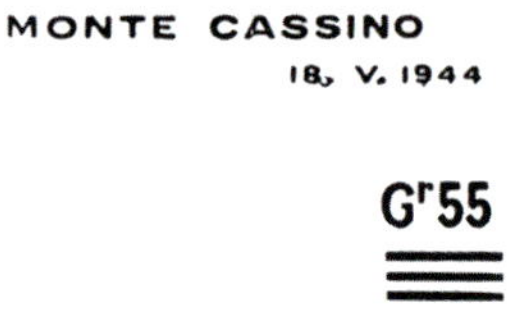

(110)

111 Polish Partisans

1944 (27 June). Capture of Monte Cassino. Nos. 482/485 surch as T **110**, or smaller (No. 497).

494	45g. on 75g. olive-green (B.)	12·50	28·00
495	55g. on 80g. carmine (B.)	12·50	28·00
	a. No stop after '18'	25·00	31·00
496	80g. on 1z. slate-blue (B.)	12·50	28·00
497	1z.20 on 1z.50 red-brown (B.)	12·50	28·00
494/497 *Set of 4*		45·00	£100

(Des A. Horowicz. Eng W. Vacek. Recess De La Rue)

1945 (3 Feb). Relief Fund for Survivors of Warsaw Rising. Perf 11½.

498	**111**	1z.+2z. green	7·50	19·00

V. REPUBLIC

In July 1944 a Provisional Government with Soviet sympathies was formed at Lublin, in the part of Poland reconquered by the Red Army. On 28 June 1945 a Government of National Unity was formed; by 1948 Poland had gradually been transformed into a Communist state.

112 Romuald Traugutt

113 White Eagle

114 Grunwald Memorial, Cracow

(Des J. Ogórkiewicz. Litho J. Pietrzykowski, Lublin)

1944 (7 Sept). National Heroes. T **112** and similar portraits. No gum. Perf 11½.

499	**112**	25g. rose-red (*shades*)	47·00	£130
		a. Imperf (pair)	£250	
		b. Perf 11	90·00	£250
500	-	50g. green (T. Kościuszko)	47·00	£130
		a. Imperf (pair)	£250	
		b. Perf 11	90·00	£250
501	-	1z. blue (H. Dąbrowski)	47·00	£150
		a. Imperf (pair)	£250	
		b. Perf 11	90·00	£325
499/501 *Set of 3*			£140	£375
499b/501b *Set of 3*			£240	£750

(Des J. Grubecki. Photo State Ptg Wks, Moscow)

1944 (13 Sept). Perf 12½.

502	**113**	25g. scarlet	1·30	1·90
503	**114**	50g. slate-green	1·30	1·30

No. 502 was printed in photogravure, but unoverprinted copies also exist from a typographed printing in dull red, which arrived too late for issue in this condition. See Nos. 516*a*, 536*a* and 602.

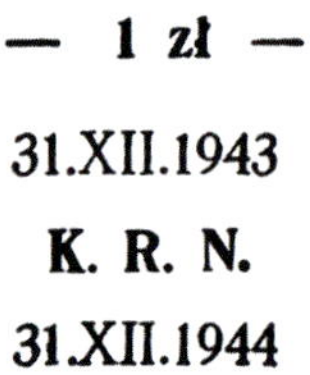

(115)

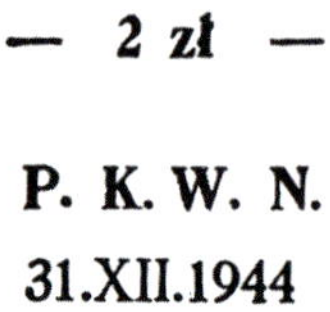

(116)

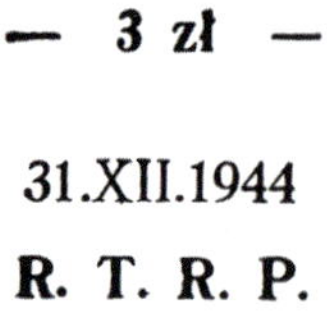

(117)

(118)

K.R.N.=Krajowa Rada Narodowa (National Federal Council).

P.K.W.N.=Polski Komitet Wolnosci Narodowej (Polish National Liberation Committee).

R.T.R.P.=Rzad Tymczasowy Rzeczpospolitej Polskiej (Provisional Government of the Polish Republic).

(Surch typo J. Pietrzykowski, Lublin)

1944–45. No. 502 surch with Types **115/117**.

504	**113**	1z. on 25g. scarlet (31.12.44)	2·20	8·75
505		2z. on 25g. scarlet (15.1.45)	2·20	8·75
506		3z. on 25g. scarlet (15.1.45)	2·20	8·75
504/506 *Set of 3*			6·00	24·00

The 1z. with spacing of 5 mm between the second and third and the third and fourth lines of the surcharge are postal forgeries.

1945 (22 Jan). 82nd Anniversary of 1863 Revolt against Russia. T **112** surch with T **118**.

507	**112**	5z. on 25g. cinnamon	44·00	£150
		a. Opt double	£9500	
		b. Imperf (pair)	£950	

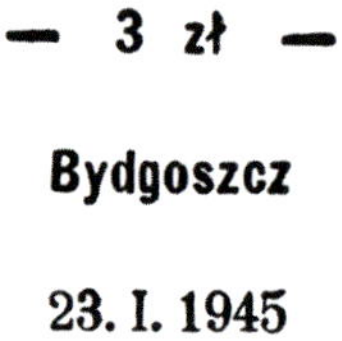

(119)

120 Flag-bearer and War Victim

121 Łódź Factories

1945 (12 Feb). Liberation Issue. No. 502 surch as T **119** (various town names with dates of liberation, as shown below), in blue.

508	3z. on 25g. 'Bydgoszcz 23.1.1945'	5·25	19·00
509	3z. on 25g. 'Częstochowa 17.1.1945'	5·25	19·00
510	3z. on 25g. 'Gniezno 22.1.1945'	5·25	19·00
511	3z. on 25g. 'Kalisz 24.1.1945'	5·25	19·00
512	3z. on 25g. 'Kielce 15.1.1945'	5·25	19·00
513	3z. on 25g. 'Kraków 19.1.1 945'	5·25	19·00
514	3z. on 25g. 'Łódź 19.1.1945'	5·25	19·00
515	3z. on 25g. 'Radom 16.1.1945'	5·25	19·00
516	3z. on 25g. 'Warszawa 17.1.1945'	16·00	38·00
	a. Dull red (typo)	£120	£225
517	3z. on 25g. 'Zakopane 29.1.1945'	7·50	25·00
508/517 *Set of 10*		60·00	£180

(Types **120/121** des J. Ogórkiewicz. Typo Postal Ptg Inst, Łódź)

1945 (9 Mar). Liberation of Warsaw. White or grey paper. Perf 11.

518	**120**	5z. scarlet	1·90	4·50

1945 (15 Mar). Liberation of Łódź. Perf 11.

519	**121**	1z. ultramarine	70	65

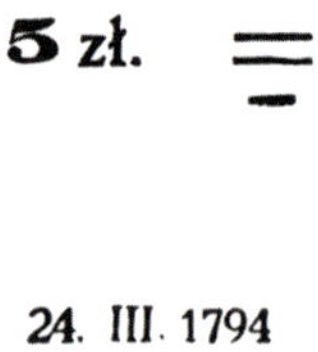

(122)

123 Grunwald Memorial, Cracow

1945 (9 Apr). 151st Anniversary of Kościuszko's Oath of Allegiance. No. 500 surch with T **122**.

520	5z. on 50g. green (R.)	12·50	44·00

USED PRICES. From 1945 most commemorative issues were available cancelled-to-order from the Philatelic Bureau and used prices are for stamps in this condition. Postally used stamps may be worth more.

(Des J. Wilczyk. Photo at Cracow)

1945 (10 Apr). Cracow Monuments. T **123** and similar designs. Perf 11.

521	**123**	50g. chocolate	25	35
		a. Perf 11½	25	35
		b. Designer's name omitted (Perf 11)	95	40
522	-	1z. lake-brown	25	35
		a. Perf 11½	25	35
523	-	2z. blue	65	40
524	-	3z. plum	1·10	65
525	-	5z. blue-green	5·00	15·00
521/525 *Set of* 5			6·50	15·00

Designs: Vert—1z. Kościuszko Memorial; 3z. Copernicus Memorial. Horiz—2z. Cloth Hall; 5z. Wawel Castle.

Nos. 521/525 are also known imperforate (*price* £30 *per set*)

125 *Conrad* (cruiser)

D126 Posthorn and Thunderbolts

(Typo at Łódź)

1945 (24 Apr). 25th Anniversary of Polish Maritime League. T **125** and similar type inscr 'Liga Morska'. Perf 11.

526	**125**	50g.+2z. reddish orange	6·25	24·00
527	-	1z.+3z. royal blue	3·25	12·50
528	-	2z.+4z. scarlet	3·25	12·50
529	-	3z.+5z. deep green	3·25	12·50
526/529 *Set of* 4			14·50	55·00

Designs: Vert—1z. *Dar Pomorza* (full-rigged cadet ship); 2z. Naval ensigns. Horiz—3z. Crane and Old Grain Tower, Gdańsk.

1945 (20 May). POSTAGE DUE. Litho. Size 26×19½ mm. Perf 11.

D530	**D126**	1z. orange-brown	25	30
D531		2z. orange-brown	30	30
D532		3z. orange-brown	50	35
D533		5z. orange-brown	95	40
D530/533 *Set of* 4			1·80	1·20

For stamps in larger size, see Nos. D571/D577 and D646/D652.

126 Town Hall, Poznań

127 Kościuszko Memorial, Łódź

(Des J. Wilczyk. Photo Postal Ptg Inst, Łódź)

1945 (16 June). Postal Employees' Congress. Perf 11.

530	**126**	1z.+5z. green	19·00	50·00

(Des Dobrowald. Litho at Łódź)

1945 (1 July). Perf 11.

531	**127**	3z. purple	3·25	1·90
		a. Perf 9	9·50	10·00

O128

128 Grunwald, 1410

129 Eagle and Manifesto

(Des J. Ogórkiewicz. Photo at Cracow)

1945 (1 July)–**46**. OFFICIAL. With control numbers at bottom right.

(a) Control numbers M-01705 (5z.) or M-01706 (10z.). Perf 11.

O532	**O128**	(5z.) deep violet-blue	30	40
O533		(10z.) red	65	40

(b) Redrawn. Control number M-01709 (May 1946). Perf 11.

O534	**O128**	(5z.) deep violet-blue	65	40
		b. Imperf	65	40
O535		(10z.) red	1·30	40
		b. Imperf	1·30	40

The blue stamps are inscribed 'ZWYKLA' (Ordinary) and the red stamps 'POLECONA' (Registered).

Although the control number is the easiest method of identifying the two issues, it is often blurred with the final figure illegible. The redrawn stamps have fewer lines of shading on the eagle and the diagonal lines in each corner are narrower.

The 10z. stamps can be further distinguished by the horizontal measurement of the design: No. O533 is 17 mm, No. O535 is 16½ mm.

See also Nos. O748 and O805/O806.

(Des M. Wątorski. Photo at Cracow)

1945 (16 July). 535th Anniversary of Battle of Grunwald. Perf 11.

532	**128**	5z. blue	6·25	25·00
		a. Imperf (pair)	£250	

(Des J. Wilczyk. Photo at Cracow)

1945 (22 July). First Anniversary of Liberation. Perf 11.

533	**129**	3z. carmine	9·50	31·00
		a. Imperf (pair)	£1500	

130 Westerplatte

(Des J. Wilczyk. Photo at Cracow)

1945 (1 Sept). Sixth Anniversary of Defence of Westerplatte. Perf 11.

534	**130**	1z.+9z. slate	19·00	55·00
		a. Imperf (pair)	£150	

The premium was for a fund for sanatoria and rest homes.

1 ZŁ

(131)

1·50 zł

(132)

1945 (1–10 Sept). Surch with Types **131**/**132**, in brown.

535	**114**	1z. on 50g. slate-green (10.9)	65	40
		a. Surch inverted	95·00	
536	**113**	1.50z. on 25g. brown-red (1.9)	£650	£650
		a. Dull red (typo)	65	40

133 Crane Tower

135 St John's Cathedral

(Des J. Wilczyk. Photo at Cracow)

1945 (15 Sept). Liberation of Gdańsk. T **133** and similar types inscr 'GDANSK. 30 III 1945'. Perf 11.

537	**133**	1z. blackish olive	25	35
538	-	2z. blue (Stock Exchange)	30	35
539	-	3z. purple (High Gate (*horiz*))	1·30	1·30
		a. Imperf (pair)	1·10	40
537/539 *Set of* 3			1·70	1·80

(Des J. Wilczyk. Photo at Cracow)

1945–46. Warsaw, 1939–1945. T **135** and similar views of Warsaw before and after destruction. Imperf.

540	1.50z. carmine (Royal Castle) (15.10.45)	25	40
541	3z. blue (St John's Cathedral) (25.11.45)	95	40
542	3.50z. green (City Hall) (5.12.45)	1·60	75

543	6z. slate (GPO) (1.1.46)	1·90	40
544	8z. brown (War Ministry) (1.1.46)	6·25	90
545	10z. purple (Church of the Holy Cross) (10.1.46)	1·90	90
540/545 *Set of 6*		11·50	3·50

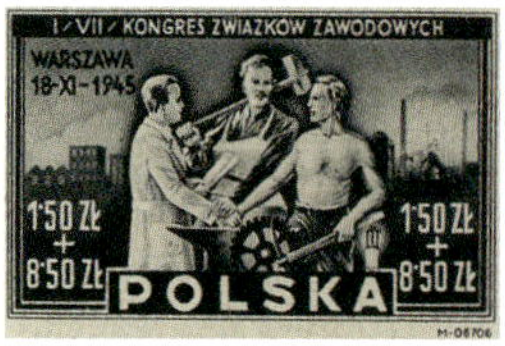

136 United Workers

(Des J. Wilczyk. Photo at Cracow)

1945 (18 Nov). Trades' Union Congress. Perf 11.

546	**136**	1.50z.+8.50z. slate	6·25	16·00

137 Soldiers of 1830 and Jan III Sobieski Statue

(Des J. Wilczyk. Photo at Cracow)

1945 (29 Nov). 115th Anniversary of 1830 Revolt against Russia. Perf 11.

547	**137**	10z. slate	7·50	25·00

WARSZAWA
WOLNA
17 Styczeń
1945—1946

(138)

139 Insurgent

140 Lisunov Li-2 over ruins of Warsaw

1946 (17 Jan). First Anniversary of Liberation of Warsaw. Nos. 540/545 optd with T **138**.

548	1.50z. carmine	3·75	7·50
549	3z. blue	3·75	7·50
	a. Opt inverted	£550	
550	3.50z. green	3·75	7·50
551	6z. slate	3·75	7·50
552	8z. brown	3·75	7·50
	a. Opt inverted	£950	
553	10z. purple	3·75	7·50
548/553 *Set of 6*		20·00	41·00

(Des M. Konarski, after A. Grottger. Photo at Cracow)

1946 (22 Jan). 83rd Anniversary of 1863 Revolt. Perf 11.

554	**139**	6z. blue	12·50	20·00

(Des J. Wilczyk. Photo at Cracow)

1946 (Mar–Nov). AIR. Perf 11.

555	**140**	5z. slate-grey (25.6)	1·00	35
		a. Slate-black	5·00	75
		b. Control Number omitted	13·00	2·50
556		10z. purple (20.5)	1·00	35
557		15z. blue (1.11)	7·50	50
558		20z. claret (5.3)	2·50	40
559		25z. green (10.9)	3·75	75
560		30z. red-orange (15.3)	6·25	75
555/560 *Set of 6*			20·00	2·75

Nos. 557 and 559 are without control 'M-07741' at foot.

141 Fighting in Spain

142 Bydgoszcz

(Des M. Wątorski. Photo at Cracow)

1946 (10 Mar). Polish Legion in the Spanish Civil War. Perf 11.

561	**141**	3z.+5z. scarlet	6·25	19·00

(Des M. Wątorski. Photo at Cracow)

1946 (19 Apr). 600th Anniversary of Bydgoszcz. Perf 11.

562	**142**	3z.+2z. grey-black	6·25	23·00

143 Death over Majdanek Concentration Camp

144 Shield and Soldiers

145 Infantry

(Des J. Wilczyk. Photo at Cracow)

1946 (29 Apr). Majdanek Concentration Camp. Perf 11.

563	**143**	3z.+5z. slate-green	15·00	19·00

(Des M. Wątorski. Photo at Cracow)

1946 (2 May). Silesian Uprisings (1919–1921 and 1939–1945). Perf 11.

564	**144**	3z.+7z. brown	1·90	5·00

(Des S. Jasiński. Photo at Cracow)

1946 (9 May). First Anniversary of Peace. Perf 11.

565	**145**	3z. chocolate	1·30	65

146 Polish Coastline

147 President Bierut, Premier O. Morawski and Marshal Żymierski

(Des P. Marczewski. Photo)

1946 (21 July). Maritime Festival. Perf 11.

566	**146**	3z.+7z. blue	2·50	14·00

(Des T. Gronowski. Photo)

1946 (22 July). Second Anniversary of Polish Committee of National Liberation Manifesto. Perf 11.

567	**147**	3z. violet	7·50	21·00

148 Będzin Castle

149 Crane, Monument and Crane Tower

(Des S. K. Dawski (Nos. 568/569), S. Żechowski (No. 570). Photo)

1946 (Aug–Dec). T **148** and similar designs. Imperf (5z., 10z.) or Perf 11 (6z.).

568	**148**	5z. olive-black (*shades*) (13.8)	40	35
568*a*	**148**	5z. chocolate (*shades*) (14.12)	65	35
569	-	6z. black (1.9)	90	55
570	-	10z. blue (16.12)	1·90	65
568/570 *Set of* 4			3·50	1·70

Designs: Vert—6z. Tombstone of Henry IV. Horiz—10z. Castle at Lanckorona.

1946 (Aug). POSTAGE DUE. Photo. Size 29×21½ mm. Imperf.

D571	**D126**	2z. orange-brown	40	30
D572		3z. orange-brown	40	30
D573		5z. orange-brown	40	30
D574		6z. orange-brown	40	30
D575		10z. orange-brown	40	30
D576		15z. orange-brown	75	40
D577		25z. orange-brown	1·50	55
D571/D577 *Set of* 7			3·75	2·20

See also Nos. D646/D652 for perf stamps.

(Des S. Żechowski. Photo)

1946 (14 Sept). The Fallen in Gdańsk. Perf 11.

571	**149**	3z.+12z. slate	3·75	18·00

150 Schoolchildren at Desk

152 Stojalowski, Bojko, Stapiński and Witos

(Des E. Bartłomiejczyk . Photo Courvoisier)

1946 (10 Oct). Polish Work for Education and Fund for International Bureau of Education. T **150** and similar designs. Granite paper. Perf 11½.

571*a*	**150**	3z.+22z. vermilion	55·00	£120
571*b*	-	6z.+24z. blue	55·00	£120
571*c*	-	11z.+19z. green	55·00	£120
571*a*/571*c* *Set of* 3			£150	£325
MS571*d* 128×80 mm. Nos. 571*a*/571*c* colours slightly changed (*sold at* 25+75z.)			£700	£2250

Designs: 6z. Court of Jagiellonian University. Cracow; 11z. Gregor Piramowicz (1735–1801), founder of the Education Commission.

Nos. 571*a*/571*c* were issued in small sheets of 12.

(Des S. Żechowski. Photo)

1946 (1 Dec). 50th Anniversary of Peasant Movement and Relief Fund. Perf 11.

572	**152**	5z.+10z. blue-green	3·25	14·00
573		5z.+10z. blue	3·25	14·00
574		5z.+10z. brown-olive	3·25	14·00
572/574 *Set of* 3			8·75	38·00

(153)

1947 (4 Feb). Opening of Polish Parliament. No. 567 surch with T **153**.

575	**147**	3z.+7z. violet (R.)	15·00	28·00

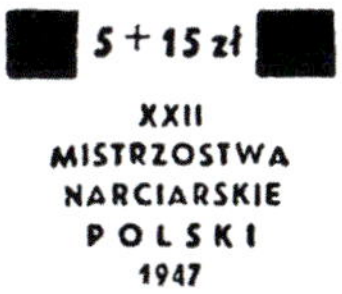

(154)

(155)

1947 (21 Feb). 22nd National Ski Championships, Zakopane. No. 502 surch with T **154**.

576	**113**	5+15z. on 25g. brown-red (B.)	7·50	14·00

1947 (25 Feb). No. 569 surch with T **155**.

577		5z. on 6z. black (R.)	1·30	65
		a. Orange surch	2·30	95

156 Home of Emil Zegadlowicz

157 Frédéric Chopin (musician)

158 Boguslawski, Modrzejewska and Jaracz (actors)

159 Wounded Soldier, Nurse and Child

(Des F. Suknarowski. Photo)

1947 (1 Mar). Emil Zegadlowicz Commemoration. Perf 11.

578	**156**	5z.+15z. grey-green	6·25	15·00

1947 (1 Mar-10 May). Polish Culture (1st issue). As T **157/158** (Polish Celebrities)

(a) Perf 11.

579A	1z. blue (1.3)	65	40
580A	2z. brown (15.3)	65	40
581A	3z. turquoise-green (Type **157**) (31.3)	65	40
582A	5z. greenish black (Type **158**) (30.4)	65	40
583A	15z. red-brown (20.7)	2·50	40
584A	10z. grey (15.3)	3·25	40
585A	15z. slate violet (30.4)	7·50	65
586A	20z. slate-black (10.5)	10·00	90
579A/586A *Set of* 8		23·00	3·50

(b) Imperf.

579B	1z. blue (1.3)	65	65
580B	2z. brown (15.3)	1·30	75
581B	3z. turquoise-green (Type **157**) (31.3)	1·30	65
582B	5z. greenish black (Type **158**) (30.4)	1·30	65
583B	6z. greenish grey (30.4)	5·00	75
584B	10z. grey (15.3)	5·00	65
585B	15z. slate violet (30.4)	7·50	75
586B	20z. slate-black (10.5)	7·50	1·50
579B/586B *Set of* 8		27·00	5·75

Portraits: Horiz—1z. Matejko, Malczewski and Chelmonski (painters); 6z. Swietochowski, Zeromski and Prus (writers); 15z. Wyspianski, Slowacki and Kasprowicz (poets). Vert—2z. Brother Albert of Cracow (founder of Albertine Social Service Order); 10z. Marie Curie (scientist); 20z. A. Mickiewicz (poet).

See also Nos. 587A/595B and **MS**615*a*.

1947 (1 Mar–10 May). Polish Culture (2nd issue). Designs as Types **157/158** (Polish Celebrities).

(a) Perf 11.

587A	1z. blue-skate (18.5)	65	40
588A	2z. orange (18.5)	65	40
589A	3z. grey-olive (Type **157**) (20.7)	3·75	40
590A	5z. sepia (Type **158**) (2.7)	65	40
591A	6z. carmine (20.7)	65	40
592A	10z. pale blue (25.6)	5·00	65
593A	155z. red-brown (20.7)	4·50	65
594A	20z. dull purple (31.10)	4·50	90
587A/594A *Set of* 8		18·00	3·75

(b) Imperf.

587B	1z. blue-skate (18.5)	65	65
588B	2z. orange (18.5)	65	40
589B	3z. grey-olive (Type **157**) (20.7)	3·75	65
590B	5z. sepia (Type **158**) (2.7)	65	40
591B	6z. carmine (20.7)	65	40
592B	10z. pale blue (25.6)	5·00	65
593B	15z. red-brown (20.7)	5·75	1·00
594B	20z. dull purple (31.10)	5·75	1·50
587B/594B *Set of* 8		21·00	5·00

Portraits: Horiz—1z. Matejko, Malczewski and Chelmonski (painters); 6z. Swietochowski, Zeromski and Prus (writers); 15z. Wyspianski, Slowacki and Kasprowicz (poets). Vert—2z. Brother Albert of Cracow (founder of Albertine Social Service Order); 10z. Marie Curie (scientist); 20z. A. Mickiewicz (poet).

(Des M. Konarski. Photo)

1947 (1 June). Red Cross Fund. Cross in red. Perf 11.

595	**159**	5z.+5z. grey and red	7·50	12·50

161 Steelworker

(162)

(Des S. Żechowski and M. Wątorski (15z.). Eng G. Barlangue, Cottet, Dufresne and Mazèlin. Recess Government Printing Works, Paris)

1947 (20 Aug). As T **161** (occupations). Perf 13.

596	**161**	5z. brown-lake	2·50	40
597	-	10z. emerald-green (Harvester)	90	35
598	-	15z. blue (Fisherman)	4·75	50
599	-	20z. black (Miner)	1·90	65
596/599 *Set of* 4			9·00	1·70

1947 (10 Sept). AIR. Nos. 502/503 surch with T **162** or similar surch.

(a) Design photo, surch typo.

600	**114**	40z. on 50g. slate-green (R.)	4·50	2·20
601	**113**	50z. on 25g. scarlet	8·25	6·75
		a. Error. Inscribed 'LOFNICZA' (pos. 23)	45·00	

(b) Design and surch typo.

602	**113**	50z. on 25g. dull red	6·25	4·75
		a. Error. Inscribed 'LOFNICZA' (pos. 23)	45·00	
600/602 *Set of* 3			17·00	12·50

163 Brother Albert of Cracow

164 Sagittarius

(Des S. Żechowski. Photo)

1947 (21 Dec). Winter Relief Fund. Perf 11.

603	**163**	2z.+18z. violet	1·90	14·50

(Des S. Żechowski. Photo)

1948 (9 Feb–25 Apr). AIR. Perf 11.

604	**164**	15z. violet (25.4)	4·75	65
605		25z. blue (25.4)	1·80	35
606		30z. chocolate (25.4)	1·70	60
607		50z. green	2·50	90
608		75z. black (15.3)	2·50	90
609		100z. red-orange	2·50	90
604/609 *Set of* 6			14·00	3·75

165 Chainbreaker

166 Generals H. Dembiński and J. Bem

(T **165** des M. Wątorski; others des S. Żechowski. Photo)

1948 (15 Mar–15 July). Revolution Centenaries. T **165** and portraits as T **166**. Perf 11.

610	**165**	15z. sepia	90	35
611	**166**	30z. sepia (15.7)	2·30	65
612	-	35z. olive-green (15.7)	6·25	90
613	-	60z. scarlet (15.7)	3·25	1·30
610/613 *Set of* 4			11·50	3·00

Portraits: 35z. S. Worcell, P. Ściegienny and E. Dembowski; 60z. Friedrich Engels and Karl Marx.

167 Insurgents

168 Wheel and Streamers

(Des J. Tom. Photo)

1948 (19 Apr). Fifth Anniversary of Warsaw Ghetto Defence. Perf 11.

614	**167**	15z. black	5·75	11·50

(Des T. Gronowski. Design photo, blue portion litho)

1948 (1 May). Warsaw–Prague Cycle Race. Perf 11.

615	**168**	15z. carmine and blue	6·25	3·25

1948 (10 June). Polish Culture (3rd issue). Designs as Types **157/158** (Polish Celebrities). Perf 11½.

MS615*a* 210×128 mm. Designs and colours as Nos. 587A/594A (*sold at* 62+438z.)		£375	£500
	b. Missing control numbers	£1200	

169 Cycle Race

170 *Oliwa* under Construction

(Des N. Jarczewska and K. Witkowski. Photo)

1948 (22 June). Seventh Circuit of Poland Cycle Race. Perf 11.

616	**169**	3z. grey-black	3·50	7·50
617		6z. brown	3·75	9·50
618		15z. green	5·00	11·50
616/618 *Set of* 3			11·00	26·00

(Des T. Gronowski. Photo)

1948 (22 June). Merchant Marine, As T **170**. Perf 11.

619	**170**	6z. bight violet	2·75	6·25
620	-	15z. carmine-lake	4·00	7·50
621	-	35z. slate	5·00	8·25
619/621 *Set of* 3			10·50	20·00

Designs: Horiz—15z. Freighter; 35z. *General M. Zaruski* (cadet ketch).

173 Firework Display

174 Youth

175 Roadway, St Anne's Church and Palace

(Des E. Bartłomiejczyk. Photo)

1948 (15 July). Wroclaw Exhibition. Perf 11.

622	**173**	6z. greenish blue	1·90	90
623		15z. scarlet	2·50	90
624		18z. claret	2·20	90
625		35z. brown	2·20	90
622/625 *Set of* 4			8·00	3·25

(Des T. Tuszewski. Photo)

1948 (8 Aug). International Youth Conference, Warsaw. Perf 11.

626	**174**	15z. blue	1·30	65

(Des Z. Skibiński. Photo)

1948 (1 Sept). Charity. Warsaw Reconstruction Fund. Perf 11.

627	**175**	15z.+5z. green	1·30	65

176 Toruń Ramparts and Mail Coach

177 Streamlined Steam Locomotive PM36-1, Clock and Winged Wheel

(Des A. Suchanek. Photo)

1948 (4 Sept). Philatelic Congress, Toruń. Perf 11.

628	**176**	15z. sepia	2·50	1·30

(Des E. Bartłomiejczyk. Photo)

1948 (6 Oct). European Railway Conference. Perf 11½.

629	**177**	18z. blue	12·50	31·00

178 President Bierut

(Des M. Wątorski. Photo)

1948–49. Perf 11½ (6z.) or 11 (others).

629*a*	**178**	2z. dull orange (15.2.49)	30	20
629*b*		3z. deep blue-green (15.5.49)	30	20
		a. Perf 11½	30	20
630		5z. brown (1.12.48)	35	20
		a. Perf 11½	35	20
631		6z. blue-black (1.12.48)	2·40	40
631*a*		10z. violet (15.5.49)	65	35
		b. Perf 11½	65	35
632		15z. carmine-red (14.10.48)	1·30	35
		a. Perf 11½	1·30	35
633		18z. deep dull green (1.12.48)	3·25	35
		a. Perf 11½	3·25	35
634		30z. blue (1.12.48)	4·00	65
		a. Perf 11½	4·00	65
635		35z. brown-purple (1.12.48)	8·25	1·30
629*a*/635 *Set of 9*			19·00	3·50

179 Workers and Flag

180 Baby

(Des E. John (5z.), T. Gronowski (others). Photo)

1948 (8 Dec). Workers Class Unity Congress. T **179** and similar horiz designs. Perf 11.

636	**179**	5z. carmine-red	3·00	1·30
		a. Perf 11½	3·00	1·30
637	-	15z. blackish purple	1·90	1·30
		a. Perf 11½	1·90	1·30
638	-	25z. brown	3·75	1·30
		a. Perf 11½	3·75	1·30
636/638 *Set of 3*			7·75	3·50

Designs: 15z. Flags and portraits of Engels, Marx, Lenin and Stalin; 25z. Workers marching and portrait of L. Waryński.

1948 (15 Dec). As Nos. 636/638, but colours changed and inscr 'XII 1948' instead of '8 XII 1948'. Perf 11 (25z.) or 11½ (others).

639		5z. plum	2·50	3·25
640		15z. blue	5·00	3·25
641		25z. green	6·75	3·25
639/641 *Set of 3*			13·00	8·75

(Des T. Trepkowski. Photo)

1948 (16 Dec). Anti-tuberculosis Fund. T **180** and similar baby portraits. Perf 11½ (3z.) or 11 (others).

642	**180**	3z.+2z. bronze green	7·50	7·75
643	-	5z.+5z. reddish brown	7·50	7·00
		a. Perf 11½	7·50	7·00
644	-	6z.+4z. plum	6·25	6·25
		a. Perf 11½	6·25	6·25
645	-	15z.+10z. deep rose-red	3·75	5·25
642/645 *Set of 4*			23·00	24·00

Nos. 642/645 were each issued with *se-tenant* stamp-sized labels in ten different designs.

180a President Franklin D. Roosevelt

181 Workers

(Des T. Granowski. Photo Courvoisier)

1948 (30 Dec). AIR. Roosevelt, Pulaski and Kościuszko. T **180a** and similar horiz designs. Perf 11½.

645*a*	**180a**	80z. blackish violet	50·00	50·00
645*b*	-	100z. purple (Pulaski)	50·00	50·00
645*c*	-	120z. blue (Kościuszko)	50·00	50·00
645*a*/645*c* *Set of 3*			£140	£140
MS645*d* 160×95 mm. Nos. 645*a*/645*c* 300+200z. colours changed			£550	£900

Nos. 645*a*/645*c* were issued in small sheets of 16 plus four attached labels.

The sale of this issue was restricted and it is doubtful if many were used, except philatelically.

1949 (15 Feb)–**50**. POSTAGE DUE. Perf 11½ (1z., 2z.) or 11 (others).

D646	**D126**	1z. yellow-brown (1950)	35	30
D647		2z. yellow-brown (1950)	35	30
D648		3z. yellow-brown (1950)	35	30
D649		15z. yellow brown (2.50)	70	40
D650		25z. yellow-brown (1950)	95	75
D651		100z. orange-brown	2·00	1·10
D652		150z. orange-brown	2·75	1·30
D646/652 *Set of 7*			6·75	4·00

(Des E. John. Photo)

1949 (31 May). Trades Union Congress, Warsaw. T **181** and similar types inscr 'II./VIII/. KONGRES ZWIAZKOW ZAWODOWYCH. MAJ. 1949'. Perf 11½.

646	**181**	3z. carmine	2·10	1·30
647	-	5z. blue	2·30	1·30
648	-	15z. green	3·25	3·75
646/648 *Set of 3*			7·00	5·75

Designs: 5z. Factory, tractor and worker; 15z. Three workers.

182 Banks of River Vistula

183 President Bierut

(Des W. Borowski (10z., 15z.), R. Kleczewski (35z.). Eng B. Brandt (10z.), M. R. Polak (15z.), S. Lukaszewski (35z.). Litho)

1949 (22 July). Fifth Anniversary of National Liberation Committee. Types **182/183** and similar vert design. Perf 13.

649	**182**	10z. black	4·00	3·25
650	**183**	15z. deep mauve	4·00	3·25
651	-	35z. grey-blue (Radio station, Raszyn)	4·00	3·25
		a. Perf 11	4·00	3·25
649/651 *Set of 3*			11·00	8·75

184 Mail Coach and Map

185 Worker and Tractor

(Des R. Kleczewski. Eng B. Brandt (6z.), S. Lukaszewski (30z.) and M. R. Polak (80z.). Recess)

1949 (10 Oct). 75th Anniversary of UPU Various forms of transport as T **184** inscr '75 LAT SWIATOWEGO ZWIAZKU POCZTOWEGO'. Perf 13×12½.

652	**184**	6z. slate-purple	2·00	3·25
653	-	30z. deep blue (Liner)	3·50	3·75
654	-	80z. myrtle green (aeroplane)	6·50	6·75
652/654 *Set of* 3			11·00	12·50

(Des L. Dąbrowski and D. Piotrowski. Eng S. Lukaszewski. Recess)

1949 (Nov–Dec). Congress of Peasant Movement. Perf 13×12½.

655	**185**	5z. claret (20.12)	2·30	40
656		10z. red (20.12)	50	30
657		15z. green (26.11)	50	30
658		35z. brown (20.12)	3·50	1·90
655/658 *Set of* 4			6·00	2·50

186 Frédéric Chopin

187 Mickiewicz and Pushkin

188 Postman

(Des M. Wątorski. Eng M. R. Polak (10z.), S. Lukaszewski (15z.) and B. Brandt (35z.). Recess)

1949 (5 Dec). T **186** and similar portraits. Perf 12½×13.

659	-	10z. purple (Adam Mickiewicz)	3·25	3·25
660	**186**	15z. brown-red	5·00	4·50
661	-	35z. blue (Julius Slowacki)	5·50	6·25
659/661 *Set of* 3			12·50	12·50

(Des M. Milberger. Eng B. Brandt. Recess)

1949 (15 Dec). Polish-Russian Friendship Month. Perf 12½×13.

662	**187**	15z. slate-violet	4·75	8·25

(Des R. Kleczewski. Eng B. Brandt. Recess)

1950 (21 Jan). Third Congress of Postal Workers. Perf 12½×13.

663	**188**	15z. bright purple	4·00	5·25

189 Mechanic, Hangar and Aeroplane

D190

190 President Bierut

(Des W. Borowski. Eng B. Brandt. Recess)

1950 (6 Feb). AIR. Perf 12½×13.

664	**189**	500z. brown-lake	11·50	12·50

(Des R. Kleczewski. Eng S. Lukaszewski. Recess)

1950 (Feb–Oct). POSTAGE DUE. Perf 12×12½.

D665	**D190**	5z. brown-red (20.10)	30	30
D666		10z. brown-red (25.2)	30	30
D667		15z. brown-red (5.7)	40	40
D668		20z. brown-red (20.10)	40	40
D669		25z. brown-red (5.7)	50	40
D670		50z. brown-red (24.5)	1·30	45
D671		100z. brown-red (20.10)	1·90	55
D665/D671 *Set of* 7			4·50	2·50

See also Nos. D701/D712, D804/D814 and D2699/D2702.

(Des W. Borowski. Eng M. R. Polak. Recess)

1950 (22 Feb). Perf 12×12½.

665	**190**	15z. red	2·50	40

191 Julian Marchlewski

192 Workers

193 Worker and Flag

(Des from photo by W. Kwinta. Photo)

1950 (23 Mar). 25th Death Anniversary of Julian Marchlewski (patriot). Perf 11½.

666	**191**	15z. blue-black	3·50	1·00
		a. Perf 11	3·50	1·00

(Des M. Bylina. Photo)

1950 (15 Apr). Reconstruction of Warsaw. Perf 12.

667	**192**	5z. deep brown	65	35
		a. Perf 11	65	35
		b. Perf 13×11	65	35
		c. Perf 11½×12	65	35
		d. Perf 13×11½	65	35

See also No. 695.

(Des E. John (10z.), M. Bylina (15z.). Photo)

1950 (26 Apr). 60th Anniversary of May Day Manifesto. T **193** and vert type inscr '1 MAJ 1890 1950'. Perf 11½×12 (horiz) or 12×11½ (vert).

668	**193**	10z. magenta	3·75	75
669	-	15z. olive-green	3·75	1·10

Design: Vert—15z. Three workers and flag.

194 Statue

195 Dove and Globe

195a President Bierut

(Des J. Wilczyk. Photo)

1950 (27 Apr). 23rd International Fair, Posnań. Perf 11½.

670	**194**	15z. red-brown	65	45

(Des T. Trepkowski. Photo)

1950 (15 May). International Peace Conference. Perf 11.

671	**195**	10z. deep green	3·25	40
672		15z. deep sepia	1·00	30
		a. Perf 11½	1·00	30

(Des W. Borowski. Eng S. Lukaszewski. Recess)

1950 (25 June–20 Oct). Perf 12×12½.

673	**195a**	5z. green (25.7)	40	30
674		10z. scarlet (10.8)	40	30
675		15z. blue (20.10)	4·50	65
676		20z. violet	1·30	40
677		25z. red-brown (25.7)	1·30	40
678		30z. claret (10.8)	1·30	65
679		40z. brown	2·50	40
680		50z. brown-olive	5·75	95
673/680 *Set of* 8			16·00	3·75

See also Nos. 687/694.

196 Industrial and Agricultural Worker

197 Hibner, Kniewski, Rutkowski

198 Worker and Dove

(Des W. Zakrzewski. Eng M. R. Polak. Recess)

1950 (20 July). Six Year Reconstruction Plan. Perf 12½×13.

681	**196**	15z. ultramarine (Plate I)	75	40
		a. Grey-blue (Plate II)	2·75	40

For similar stamps see Nos. 696/696*e* and **MS**721*a*.

(Des Cz. Kaczmarczyk. Photo at Cracow)

1950 (18 Aug). 25th Death Anniversary of Hibner, Kniewski and Rutkowski (revolutionaries). Perf 11½.

682	**197**	15z. deep blue-grey	5·50	1·50

(Des T. Gronowski. Eng M. R. Polak. Recess)

1950 (31 Aug). First Polish Peace Congress. Perf 12½×13.

683	**198**	15z. grey-green	1·30	95

Currency Revaluation

100 Old Zlotys = 1 New Groszy

By a decree of 28 October 1950 1 old zloty became worth 1 new groszy and all post offices were empowered to handstamp existing stocks of stamps with the word 'Groszy' or 'gr'. About 50 types of these handstamps are known. These are outside the scope of this catalogue.

The stamps which were authorised for handstamping are Nos. 579/594 perf and imperf, 596/615, 619/645, 646/658, 673/680, D530/D533, D571/D577, D646/D652 and D665/D671. Handstamps on other stamps were not authorised.

199 Dove (after Picasso)

I.

II.

In Type II the '5' slopes more, the 'R' has a long tail and there are six lines of shading below the '4' instead of nine.

(Eng B. Brandt. Recess)

1950 (13 Nov). Second World Peace Congress, Warsaw. Perf 13×12½.

684	**199**	40g. grey-blue	3·75	80
685		45g. claret (Type I)	5·00	95
		a. Type II	85	65

200 General Bem and Battle of Piski

(Des E. Horvath. Eng M. R. Polak and B. Brandt. Recess)

1950 (10 Dec). Death Centenary of General Bem. Perf 12½×13.

686	**200**	45g. blue	5·00	4·25

1950 (16 Dec). Currency revalued. As T **195a**, but values in 'groszy'. Perf 12×12½.

687	**195a**	5g. violet	40	30
688		10g. blue-green	40	30
689		15g. yellow-green	40	30
690		25g. Venetian red	70	35
		a. Perf 11½	25·00	12·50
691		30g. scarlet	70	35
692		40g. red-orange	1·30	35
693		45g. blue	4·00	35
694		75g. brown	2·75	35
687/694 *Set of 8*			9·50	2·40

1950 (16 Dec). Currency revalued. As No. 667, but value in 'groszy'. Perf 11.

695	**192**	15g. green	45	35
		a. Perf 12½×11	45	35
		b. Perf 11½×11	45	35
		c. Perf 13×11½	45	35

1951 (8 Jan–3 June). Currency revalued. As No. 681, but new values. Perf 12½×13.

696	**196**	45g. dull ultramarine (Plate I) (8.1)	65	35
		a. Re-engraved. Plate II	4·75	40
696*b*		75g. blackish brown (15.4)	95	35
		c. Perf 11½	2·50	40
696*d*		1z.15 green (15.4)	2·50	50
696*e*		1z.20 scarlet (3.6)	1·90	40
696/696*e* *Set of 4*			5·50	1·40

In No. 696a there is stronger shading in the face and behind the figures of value and the size is 22.3×28.1 mm instead of 22×27.8 mm.

See also No. **MS**721*a*.

201 Woman with Doves

202 Battle Scene and J. Dąbrowski

(Des B. Brandt. Eng S. Lukaszewski. Recess)

1951 (2 Mar). Women's League Congress. Perf 12½×13.

697	**201**	45g. carmine	90	75

(Des B. Brandt. Eng M. R. Polak and C. Slania. Recess)

1951 (24 Mar). 80th Anniversary of Paris Commune. Perf 12×12½.

698	**202**	45g. green	1·30	40

45 gr

(203)

1951 (20 Apr). Unissued stamp as No. 685, surch with T **203**.

699	**199**	45g. on 15z. claret	1·40	45
		a. Surch double	£900	

204 Worker with Flag

205 Smelting Works

206 Pioneer and Badge

(Des S. Lukaszewski. Photo)

1951 (25 Apr). Labour Day. Perf 13×11.

700	**204**	45g. scarlet	1·30	40
		a. Perf 11×14	1·30	40

1951 (25 Apr)–**52**. POSTAGE DUE. Currency revalued. As Nos. D665/D671.

D701	**D190**	5g. brown-red	30	30
D702		10g. brown-red	30	30
D703		15g. brown-red (9.51)	30	30
D704		20g. brown-red	30	30
D705		25g. brown-red (9.51)	30	30
D706		30g. brown-red	30	30
D707		50g. brown-red (10.51)	30	30
D708		60g. brown-red	30	30
D709		90g. brown-red (9.51)	1·90	1·30
D710		1z. brown-red	40	30

D711		2z. brown-red (10.51)	65	35
D712		5z. slate-purple (1952)	1·60	55
D701/D712 *Set of* 12			6·25	4·50

See also Nos. D804/D814 and D2699/D2702.

(Des B. Brandt. Eng E. Konecki. Recess)

1951 (9 May–15 June). Perf 13×12½.

701	**205**	40g. blue	60	30
		a. Perf 11½	40	30
702		45g. black	65	30
702*a*		60g. brown (15.6)	60	30
		b. Perf 11½	40	30
702*c*		90g. lake (15.6)	3·00	35
701/702*c* *Set of* 4 (*cheapest*)			4·00	1·10

(Des S. Lukaszewski. Photo)

1951 (1 June). International Children's Day. T **206** and similar vert design. Perf 12½×13.

703	**206**	30g. brown-olive	2·30	1·60
704	-	45g. turquoise (Boy, girl and map)	12·00	2·30

BLOCKED VALUES. Starting with Nos. 705/10 most commemorative issues up to 1963 contained one 'blocked value" which was not available at most post offices but could only be obtained in strictly limited quantities at the Philatelic Bureau. Their relative scarcity is reflected in the prices quoted. It is understood that this practice was intended to restrict the export of stamps by private individuals.

207 St Staszic

208 Wróblewski and Olszewski

(Des M. R. Polak (25g.), S. Lukaszewski (40g.), C. Slania (45g.), B. Brandt (60g., 1z.20), R. Kleczewski (1z.15). Photo)

1951 (25 June). First Polish Scientific Congress. T **207** and similar vert designs and T **208**. Perf 14×10½ (45g.) or 12½×13 (others).

705	**207**	25g. carmine	10·00	5·00
706	-	40g. blue (Marie Curie)	85	75
707	**208**	45g. violet	17·00	3·50
708	-	60g. green (M. Nencki)	1·10	65
709	-	1z.15 purple (Copernicus)	1·10	95
710	-	1z.20 grey (Dove and book)	2·50	1·10
705/710 *Set of* 6			29·00	11·00

209 F. Dzerierzński

210 President Bierut, Industry and Agriculture

(Des B. Brandt. Eng S. Lukaszewski. Recess)

1951 (5 July). 25th Death Anniversary of Dzerierzński (Russian politician). Perf 12×12½.

711	**209**	45g. brown	75	45

(Des S. Lukaszewski. Eng M. R. Polak and C. Slania. Recess)

1951 (22 July). Seventh Anniversary of People's Republic. Perf 12½×13.

712	**210**	45g. carmine	2·75	1·00
713		60g. grey-green	31·00	13·00
714		90g. deep blue	8·75	2·10
712/714 *Set of* 3			38·00	14·50

211 Young People and Globe

45 gr

(212)

(Des B. Brandt. Photo)

1951 (5 Aug). Third World Youth Festival, Berlin. Perf 11.

715	**211**	40g. blue	2·50	60
		a. Perf 12½×10½	2·50	60

1951 (1 Sept). Unissued stamp as Nos. 673/680 surch with T **212**.

716	**195a**	45g. on 35z. orange	1·10	45
		a. Figure '4' shorter than '5'	12·50	6·25
		b. Opt inverted		£2250

213 Sports Badge

214 Stalin

(Des E. Konecki. Photo)

1951 (8 Sept). Spartacist Games. Perf 14×11.

717	**213**	45g. green	2·30	95
		a. Perf 12½×13	6·25	3·00

(Des and eng S. Lukaszewski. Recess)

1951 (30 Oct). Polish–Soviet Friendship. Perf 12½×13.

718	**214**	45g. brown-carmine	65	20
719		90g. blackish brown	1·30	55

215 Frederic Chopin and Stanislaw Moniuszko

(Des and eng E. Konecki. Recess)

1951 (15 Nov). Polish Music Festival. Perf 13×12½.

720	**215**	45g. black	65	50
721		90g. red	2·50	1·60

1951 (15 Nov). Warsaw Stamp Day. Sheet 90×120 mm comprising Nos. 696*a*/696*e* printed in red-brown. Perf 12½×13.

MS721*a* Sold at 5z.	34·00	31·00

216 Mining Machinery

217 Building Modern Flats

218 Installing Electric Cable

(Des and eng C. Slania. Recess)

1951 (4 Dec)–**52**. Six Year Plan (Mining). Perf 13×12½.

722	**216**	90g. purple-brown	55	30
723		1z.20 grey-blue	55	30
724		1z.20+15g. red-orange (18.10.52)	65	40
722/724 *Set of* 3			1·60	90

(Des R. Kleczewski. Eng B. Brandt. Recess)

1951 (10 Dec)–**52**. Six Year Plan (Reconstruction). Perf 12½×13.

725	**217**	30g. green	50	30
		a. Perf 12×11½	50	30
726		30g.+15g. brown-red (1.6.52)	75	40
727		1z.15 maroon	50	30
		a. Perf 12×11½	50	30
725/727 *Set of* 3			1·60	90

(Des R. Kleczewski. Eng M. R. Polak. Recess)

1951 (15 Dec)–**52**. Six Year Plan (Electrification). Perf 12½×13.

728	**218**	30g. black	50	30
729		45g. scarlet	75	35
730		45g.+15g. brown (1.6.52)	1·10	40
728/730 *Set of* 3			2·10	95

219 M. Nowotko

220 Women and Banner

221 General Świerczewski

(Des C. Slania, eng E. Konecki (45g.); des and eng B. Brandt (90g.); des M. R. Polak, eng S. Lukaszewski (1z.15). Recess)

1952 (18 Jan). Tenth Anniversary of Polish Workers' Coalition. T **219** and similar vert portrait designs. Perf 12½×13.

731	**219**	45g.+15g. lake	40	30
732	-	90g. chocolate (P. Finder)	75	50
733	-	1z.15 orange-red (M. Fornalska)	40	40
731/733 *Set of* 3			1·40	1·10

(Des and eng S. Lukaszewski. Recess)

1952 (8 Mar). International Women's Day. Perf 12½×12.

734	**220**	45g.+15g. purple-brown	65	40
735		1z.20 scarlet	1·30	95

(Des and eng C. Slania. Recess)

1952 (28 Mar). Fifth Death Anniversary of General Świerczewski. Perf 12½×13.

736	**221**	45g.+15g. purple-brown	90	30
737		90g. indigo	90	1·30

IMPERF STAMPS. From 1952 until 1961 some sets exist imperf from limited printings and issued at special prices by the Philatelic Bureau. We do not list these but they are mentioned in footnotes.

222 Ilyushin Il-12 over Farm

223 President Bierut

(Des C. Slania (55g., 1z.40), B. Brandt (others). Eng B. Brandt (55g.), E. Konecki (90g.), C. Slania (1z.40) and M. R. Polak (5z.). Recess)

1952 (10 Apr). AIR. T **222** and similar horiz designs showing aeroplanes and views. Perf 12×12½.

738	-	55g. grey-blue (Tug and freighters)	80	65
739	**222**	90g. deep green	90	65
740	-	1z.40 maroon (Warsaw)	1·10	75
741	-	5z. black (Steelworks)	1·80	90
738/741 *Set of* 4			4·25	2·75

These exist imperforate.

(Des Rolicz. Eng B. Brandt. Recess)

1952 (18 Apr). President Bierut's 60th Birthday. Perf 13×12½.

742	**223**	45g.+15g. scarlet	90	80
743		90g. grey-green	2·50	2·00
744		1z.20+15g. bright blue	1·10	80
742/744 *Set of* 3			4·00	3·25

224 Cyclists and City Arms

225 Workers and Banner

226 J. I. Kraszewski

(Des P. Świątkowski and K. Maleszewski. Photo)

1952 (25 Apr). Fifth Warsaw–Berlin–Prague Peace Cycle Race. Perf 13×12½.

745	**224**	40g. blue	3·25	2·10

(Des S. Lukaszewski. Eng B. Brandt. Recess)

1952 (1 May). Labour Day. Perf 12½×13.

746	**225**	45g.+15g. scarlet	65	50
747		75g. green	1·80	1·50

1952–53. OFFICIAL. As No. O534 but no control number and litho. Inscr 'ZWYKLA'. Perf 11.

O748	**O128**	(60g.) pale blue	50	40
O749		(1z.55) brown-red (1953)	90	40

See also Nos. O805/O806.

(Des and eng M. R. Polak. Recess)

1952 (5 May). 140th Birth Anniversary of Józef Ignacy Kraszewski (writer). Perf 12½×13.

748	**226**	25g. maroon	1·30	75

227 Maria Konopnicka

228 H. Kollątaj

229 Leonardo da Vinci

(Des and eng E. Konecki. Recess)

1952 (10 May). 110th Birth Anniversary of Maria Konopnicka (poet). Perf 12½×13.

749	**227**	30g.+15g. deep green	1·30	1·90
750		1z.15 brown-red	1·50	1·10

(Des and eng S. Lukaszewski. Recess)

1952 (20 May). 140th Death Anniversary of Hugo Kollątaj (educationist and politician). Perf 12½×13.

751	**228**	45g.+15g. brown	65	60
752		1z. olive-green	1·30	95

(Des M. R. Polak. Eng B. Brandt. Recess)

1952 (1 June). 500th Birth Anniversary of Leonardo da Vinci (artist). Perf 12½×13.

753	**229**	30g.+15g. deep blue	1·90	1·50

230 President Bierut and Children

231 N. V. Gogol

(Des C. Slania. Photo)

1952 (1 June). International Children's Day. Perf 14.

754	**230**	45g.+15g. blue	5·00	2·20

(Des B. Brandt. Eng C. Slania. Recess)

1952 (5 June). Death Centenary of Nikolai Gogol (Russian writer). Perf 12½×13.

755	**231**	25g. deep green	1·90	1·50

232 Cement Works

233 Swimmers

(Des C. Slania. Eng B. Brandt. Recess)

1952 (17 June). Construction of Cement Works, Wierzbica. Perf 12½×13.

756	**232**	3z. black	3·25	65
757		10z. scarlet	6·25	2·50

(Des P. Świątkowski. Photo)

1952 (21 June). Sports Day. T **233** and similar vert designs. Perf 12½×13.

758	**233**	30g.+15g. blue	6·25	2·10
759	-	45g.+15g. violet (Footballers)	1·90	50
760	-	1z.15 green (Runners)	8·75	3·25
761	-	1z.20 rose-red (High jumper)	1·90	1·80
758/761 *Set of 4*			17·00	7·00

234 Yachts

235 Young Workers

(Des B. Brandt (30g.), C. Slania (45g.), R. Kleczewski (90g.). Eng M. R. Polak (30g.), S. Lukaszewski (45g.). E. Konecki (90g.). Recess)

1952 (28 June). Shipbuilders' Day. T **234** and similar designs. Perf 13×12½ (30g.) or 12½×13 (others).

762	**234**	30g.+15g. dull blue-green	6·25	3·00
763	-	45g.+15g. deep violet-blue	2·30	1·80
764	-	90g. maroon	2·20	3·25
762/764 *Set of 3*			9·75	7·25

Designs: Vert—45g. *Dar Pomorza* (full-rigged cadet ship); 90g. *Brygada Makowskiego* (freighter) under construction.

(Des R. Kleczewski (30g.), B. Brandt (45g.) and M. R. Polak (90g.). Eng B. Brandt (45g.), S. Lukaszewski (others). Recess)

1952 (17 July). Youth Festival, Warsaw. T **235** and similar designs with flag inscr '20 22 VII WARSZAWA 1952'. Perf 12×12½ (45g.) or 12½×12 (others).

765	**235**	30g.+15g. deep green	70	50
766	-	45g.+15g. scarlet	75	50
767	-	90g. brown	1·40	1·80
765/767 *Set of 3*			2·50	2·50

Designs: Horiz—45g. Girl and boy students. Vert—90g. Boy bugler.

POLISH PEOPLE'S REPUBLIC

The above title was officially adopted on 22 July 1952.

236 New Constitution

237 L. Waryński

(Des T. Gronowski. Photo)

1952 (22 July). Adoption of New Constitution. Perf 11×11½ (45g.) or 11½×13 (3z.).

768	**236**	45g.+15g. green and purple-brown	5·00	50
769		3z. violet and deep brown	1·30	95

(Des R. Kleczewski. Eng C. Slania. Recess)

1952 (31 July). 70th Anniversary of the Party 'Proletariat'. Perf 13×12½.

770	**237**	30g.+15g. brown-red	1·00	50
771		45g.+15g. purple-brown	2·30	1·20

238 Jaworzno Power Station

239 Frydman

240 Pilot and Glider

(Des C. Slania. Eng E. Konecki. Recess)

1952 (7 Aug). Electricity Power Station, Jaworzno. Perf 13×12½.

772	**238**	45g.+15g. red	1·90	40
773		1z. black	5·00	90
774		1z.50 deep green	1·90	40
		a. Perf 11½×12	10·50	2·75
772/774 *Set of 3*			8·00	1·50

(Des Z. Polasińska. Photo)

1952 (18 Aug). Pieniny Mountain Resorts. T **239** and similar vert designs. Perf 12½×13.

775	**239**	45g.+15g. dull purple	1·70	2·00
776	-	60g. green (Grywald)	1·70	1·40
777	-	1z. rose-red (Niedzica)	5·50	65
		a. Error 'NIEDZIGA'	14·00	3·00
775/777 *Set of 3*			8·00	3·75

(Des E. Konecki, eng B. Brandt (30g.). Des C. Slania, eng M. R. Polak (45g.). Des and eng S. Lukaszewski (90g.). Recess)

1952 (23 Aug). Aviation Day. T **240** and similar horiz designs. Perf 13×12½.

778	**240**	30g.+15g. deep green	2·10	1·50
779	-	45g.+15g. scarlet	4·00	1·50
780	-	90g. deep blue	1·60	75
778/780 *Set of 3*			7·00	3·50

Designs: 45g. Pilot and Yakovlev Yak-18U; 90g. Parachutists descending.

241 Avicenna

242 Victor Hugo

243 Shipbuilding

(Des and eng C. Slania. Recess)

1952 (1 Sept). Birth Millenary of Avicenna (Arab physician). Perf 12½×13.

781	**241**	75g. brown-red	70	45

(Des E. Konecki. Eng C. Slania. Recess)

1952 (1 Sept). 150th Birth Anniversary of Victor Hugo (French author). Perf 12½×13.

782	**242**	90g. chocolate	1·30	45

(Des B. Świderska. Eng E. Konecki. Recess)

1952 (10 Sept). Gdańsk Shipyards. Perf 12½×13.

783	**243**	5g. deep green	45	30
		a. Perf 11½	45	30
784		15g. brown-red	90	30

244 H. Sienkiewicz (author)

245 Assault on Winter Palace, Petrograd

(Des R. Kleczewski. Eng C. Slania. Recess)

1952 (25 Oct). Perf 12½×13.

785	**244**	45g.+15g. chocolate	80	50

(Des and eng B. Brandt. Recess)

1952 (7 Nov). 35th Anniversary of Russian Revolution. Perf 12×12½.

786	**245**	45g.+15g. brown-red	1·70	55
787		60g. blackish brown	1·10	80

These exist imperforate.

246 Lenin

247 Miner

248 H. Wieniawski (violinist)

(Des and eng M. R. Polak. Recess)

1952 (7 Nov). Polish–Soviet Friendship Month. Perf 12½×13.

788	**246**	30g.+15g. dull purple	80	50
789		45g.+15g. brown	1·60	80

(Des E. Konecki. Eng S. Lukaszewski. Recess)

1952 (4 Dec). Miners' Day. Perf 12½×13.

790	**247**	45g.+15g. brown-black	80	35
791		1z.20+15g. brown	1·50	80

(Des K. Sopoćko. Photo)

1952 (5 Dec). Second Wieniawski International Violin Competition. Perf 12½×13.

792	**248**	30g.+15g. deep green	1·60	1·30
793		45g.+15g. violet	2·50	1·20

249 Car Factory, Zeran

250 Dove of Peace

251 Soldier and Flag

(Des and eng C. Slania. Recess)

1952 (12 Dec). Zeran Car Workers' Fund. Perf 13×12½.

794	**249**	45g.+15g. deep grey-green	45	30
795		1z.15 brown	1·30	65

(Des R. Kleczewski. Photo)

1952 (12 Dec). Peace Congress, Vienna. Perf 12½×13.

796	**250**	30g. green	1·30	75
		a. Dot under 'P' of 'POKOJU'	4·50	3·25
797		60g. bright blue	2·30	1·50

(Des E. Szancer. Photo)

1953 (2 Feb). Tenth Anniversary of Battle of Stalingrad. Perf 11.

798	**251**	60g. carmine-red and grey-olive	9·50	4·25
799		80g. carmine-red and slate	2·50	70

252 Lorry Factory

253 Karl Marx

254 Globe and Flag

(Des C. Slania. Eng M. R. Polak. Recess)

1953 (20 Feb). Lublin Lorry Builders' Fund. Perf 13×12½.

800	**252**	30g.+15g. deep blue	1·50	70
801		60g.+20g. dull purple	50	30

1953 (14 Mar). 70th Death Anniversary of Marx. Perf 12½×13.

802	**253**	60g. grey-blue	35·00	26·00
803		80g. sepia	2·50	65

1953 (Apr). POSTAGE DUE. As Nos. D701/D712 but photo and without imprint at foot. Perf 12×12½.

D804	**D190**	5g. red-brown	30	25
		a. Perf 11	30	25
D805		10g. red-brown	30	25
		a. Perf 12½×11	30	25
D806		15g. red-brown	30	25
D807		20g. red-brown	30	25
D808		25g. red-brown	30	25
D809		30g. red-brown	30	25
D810		50g. red-brown	30	25
D811		60g. red-brown	45	30
D812		90g. red-brown	40	25
D813		1z. red-brown	30	25
		a. Perf 10×13	30	25
D814		2z. red-brown	70	55
D804/D814 *Set of* 11			3·50	2·75

1953–54. OFFICIAL. As Nos. O534/O535 but no control number and litho. Inscr 'ZWYKLA' (60g.) or 'POLECONA' (1.55z.). Perf 11 to 14 and compound.

O805	(60g.) indigo (1954)	65	35
O806	(1.55z.) red	90	35

(Des Cz. Kaczmarczyk. Photo)

1953 (28 Apr). Labour Day. Perf 12½×13.

804	**254**	60g. dull vermilion	20·00	7·00
805		80g. carmine-red	95	65

255 Cyclists and Arms of Warsaw

256 Boxer

(Des Cz. Kaczmarczyk. Photo)

1953 (30 Apr). Sixth International Peace Cycle Race. T **255** and similar vert designs. Perf 12½×13.

806	–	80g. deep green	1·50	65
807	**255**	80g. sepia	1·50	65
808	–	80g. brown-red	31·00	19·00
806/808 *Set of* 3			31·00	18·00

Designs: No. 806, Cyclists and Arms of Berlin; No. 808, Cyclists and Arms of Prague.

(Des C. Borowczyk (95g.), L. Jagodziński (others). Photo)

1953 (17 May). European Boxing Championship, Warsaw. T **256** and similar vert design. Perf 12½×13.

809	**256**	40g. red-brown	1·50	65
810		80g. orange	31·00	19·00
811	–	95g. dull purple (Boxers in ring)	1·50	65
809/811 *Set of* 3			31·00	18·00

257 Copernicus (after Matejki)

(Des and eng B. Brandt (20g.). Des J. M. Szancer, eng S. Lukaszewski (80g.). Recess)

1953 (22 May). 480th Birth Anniversary of Copernicus. T **257** and similar vert design inscr '1473–1543'. Perf 12×12½ (20g.) or 12½×12 (80g.).

812	20g. brown	2·75	95
	a. Perf 11×11½	3·50	1·30
813	80g. deep blue (Copernicus and diagram)	31·00	26·00

258 *Dalmor* (trawler)

259 Warsaw Marketplace

260 Students' Badge

(Des and eng B. Brandt (80g.). Des J. Ostrowski. Eng S. Lukaszewski (1z.35). Recess)

1953 (15 July). Merchant Navy Day. T **258** and similar horiz design. Perf 13×12½.

814	**258**	80g. deep dull green	3·25	75
815	-	1z.35 deep blue (*Czech* (freighter))	6·25	5·75

(Des E. John. Photo)

1953 (15 July). Polish National Day. Perf 12½×13.

816	**259**	20g. deep brown-red	40	30
817		2z.35 blue	8·50	6·50

(Des E. John (40g.), J. Ostrowski (1z.35), Fangor-Tchórzewski (1z.50). Photo)

1953 (24 Aug). Third World Students' Congress, Warsaw.

(a) POSTAGE. T **260** *and other designs. Perf 13×12½ (40g.) or 12½×13 (others).*

818	-	40g. deep brown	45	30
819	**260**	1z.35 green	1·30	50
820	-	1z.50 blue	7·50	5·00

(b) AIR. As T **260** *but inscr 'POCZTA LOTNICZA' instead of dates and with aeroplane. Imperf.*

821	**260**	55g. plum	3·75	85
822		75g. deep orange-red	3·50	2·50
818/822 *Set of 5*			15·00	8·25

Designs: Horiz—40g. Students and globe. Vert—1z.50 Woman and dove.

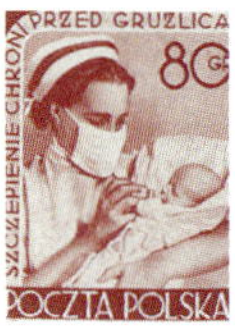

261 Nurse feeding Baby

262 M. Kalinowski

263 Jan Kochanowski (poet)

(Des L. Zaturski. Photo)

1953 (21 Sept). Social Health Service. T **261** and similar vert design. Perf 12½×13.

823	**261**	80g. carmine	15·00	12·00
824	-	1z.75 green (Nurse, mother and baby)	65	50

(Des B. Brandt (45g.), J. Ostrowski (80g.), C. Slania (1z.35). Photo)

1953 (10 Oct). Tenth Anniversary of Polish People's Army. T **262** and similar designs. Perf 13×12½ (80g.) or 12½×13 (others).

825	**262**	45g. red-brown	8·75	7·00
826	-	80g. carmine-red	95	40
827	-	1z.75 bronze-green	95	40
825/827 *Set of 3*			9·50	7·00

Designs: Horiz—80g. Russian and Polish soldiers. Vert—1z.75 R. Paziński.

(Des C. Slania (80g.), M. R. Polak (others). Eng S. Lukaszewski (20g.), C. Slania (80g.), B. Brandt (1z.35). Recess)

1953 (10 Nov). Renaissance Commemoration. T **263** and similar designs. Perf 13×12½ (80g.) or 12½×13 (others).

828	**263**	20g. red-brown	40	30
		a. Perf 11½	40	30
829	-	80g. deep reddish purple	1·00	40
		a. Perf 11½	1·00	40
830	-	1z.35 indigo	5·00	3·50
828/830 *Set of 3*			5·75	3·75

Designs: Horiz—80g. Wawel Castle. Vert—1z.35 Mikolaj Rej (writer).

264 Palace of Science and Culture

265 Dunajec Canyon, Pieniny Mountains

(Des E. John. Eng S. Lukaszewski (80g.), B. Brandt (1z.75), M. R. Polak (2z.). Recess)

1953 (30 Nov). Reconstruction of Warsaw. T **264** and similar horiz designs inscr 'WARSZAWA'. Perf 12×12½.

831	**264**	80g. rose-red	19·00	2·20
832	-	1z.75 deep blue	3·25	50
833	-	2z. dull purple	9·75	7·00
831/833 *Set of 3*			29·00	8·75

Designs: 1z.75 Constitution Square; 2z. Old City Market, Warsaw.

(Des B. Brandt (20g.), M. R. Polak (80g.), S. Lukaszewski (others). Photo)

1953 (16 Dec). Tourist Series. Views as T **265**. Perf 12½×13 (vert) or 13×12½ (horiz).

834	-	20g. brown-lake and blue	40	30
		a. Perf 13	40	30
835	-	80g. deep lilac and blue-green	6·50	4·75
836	**265**	1z.75 slate-green and bistre-brown	1·70	40
837	-	2z. black and vermilion	1·70	40
834/837 *Set of 4*			9·25	5·25

Designs: Horiz—20g. Krynica Spa; 2z. Ciechocinek Spa. Vert—80g. Morskie Oko Lake, Tatra Mountains.

266 Skiing

267 Infants Playing

(Des J. Rajewicz (80g.), H. Przeździecka (95g.), T. Gronowski (2z.85). Litho)

1953 (31 Dec). Winter Sports. T **266** and similar vert designs. Perf 13×12½ (95g.) or 12½×13 (others).

838	-	80g. pale blue (Iceskating)	2·50	65
839	**266**	95g. blue-green	2·10	65
840	-	2z.85 brown-red (Ice hockey)	6·00	2·75
838/840 *Set of 3*			9·50	3·75

(Des H. Tomaszewski (1z.50), J. Ostrowski (others). Photo)

1953 (31 Dec). Children's Education. T **267** and similar horiz designs. Perf 13×12½.

841	**267**	10g. violet	35	30
842	-	80g. lake-brown	1·50	65
843	-	1z.50 slate-green	14·00	6·25
841/843 *Set of 3*			14·50	6·50

Designs: 80g. Girls and school; 1z.50 Two schoolgirls writing.

268 Class EP 02 Electric Locomotive, 1953

(Des Cz. Kaczmarczyk. Eng S. Lukaszewski (60g.), B. Brandt (80g.). Recess)

1954 (26 Jan). Electrification of Railways. T **268** and similar horiz design. Perf 13×12½.

844	-	60g. Prussian blue	14·50	10·00
845	**268**	80g. red-brown	1·30	80

Design: 60g. Class EW54 electric commuter train 1953.

269 Mill Girl

270 Flags and Mayflowers

271 Warsaw–Berlin–Prague

(Des S. Lukaszewski (20g.), H. Przeździecka (others). Photo)

1954 (24 Mar). International Women's Day. T **269** and similar vert designs. Perf 12½×13.

846	**269**	20g. slate-green	4·50	4·25
847	-	40g. deep blue (Postwoman)	90	30
848	-	80g. chocolate (Woman driving tractor)	1·00	35
846/848 *Set of 3*			5·75	4·50

(Des R. Kleczewski. Photo)

1954 (28 Apr). Labour Day. Perf 12½×13.

849	**270**	40g. chocolate	1·20	50
850		60g. blue	2·75	50
851		80g. bright carmine-red	1·10	60
849/851 *Set of 3*			4·50	1·40

(Des H. Przeździecka. Photo)

1954 (29 Apr). Seventh International Peace Cycle Race. T **271** and similar vert design. Perf 12½×12.

852		80g. brown (Type **271**)	1·40	30
853		80g. deep blue (Dove and cycle wheel)	1·60	1·00
		a. Perf 12×11	1·60	1·00

272 Symbols of Labour

272a Postal Coach and Aeroplane

273 Glider and Flags

(Des B. Brandt. Eng J. Miller. Recess)

1954 (30 Apr). Third Trades Union Congress, Warsaw. Perf 12×11½.

854	**272**	25g. indigo	3·50	2·50
855		80g. lake	65	65

(Des R. Kleczewski. Eng B. Brandt. Recess)

1954 (23 May). AIR. Third Polish Philatelic Society Congress. Sheet 57×76 mm. Perf 12½×13.

MS855*a*	**272a**	5z.+(2z.50) greyish green	60·00	44·00

Exists imperforate and blue (*price* £4750 *unused*, £500 *used*).

(Des Cz. Kaczmarczyk. Photo)

1954 (31 May). International Gliding Competition. T **273** and similar horiz designs. Perf 13 (Nos. 857, 859*a*) or 13×12½ (others).

856	–	45g. deep green	1·30	35
857	**273**	60g. deep lilac	3·50	2·75
858		60g. brown	2·30	35
859	–	1z.35 dull blue	4·50	1·60
		a. Light blue	3·50	1·00
856/859*a* *Set of* 4 (*cheapest*)			9·50	4·00

Designs: 45g. Glider with clouds in frame; 1z.35 Glider in large cloud (No. 859 blue clouds, No. 859*a* white clouds).

274 Paczków

275 Fencing

276 Spartacist Games Badge

(Des B. Brandt (1z.50), C. Slania (others). Eng J. Miller (60g.), C. Slania (80g., 1z.50), S. Lukaszewski (1z.15), B. Brandt (1z.55), M. R. Polak (1z.95). Recess)

1954 (13 July). AIR. T **274** and similar vert designs. Perf 12½×13.

860	**274**	60g. myrtle green	50	35
861	-	80g. scarlet	50	35
		a. Perf 12×11½	50	35
862	-	1z.15 black	4·00	3·50
863	-	1z.50 claret	1·30	35
864	-	1z.55 deep blue	1·10	35
		a. Perf 12×11½	1·30	35
		b. 'WARSZAWA' printed double	90·00	3·25
865	-	1z.95 deep brown	2·20	70
860/865 *Set of* 6			8·75	5·00

Designs: Ilyushin Il-12 aeroplane over—80g. Marketplace, Kazimierz Dolny; 1z.15 Wawel Castle, Cracow; 1z.50 Town Hall, Wroclaw; 1z.55 Lazienki Palace, Warsaw; 1z.95 Cracow Tower, Lublin.

(Des H. Przeździecka (1z.), L. Jagodziński (others). Photo)

1954 (17 July). Second Spartacist Games (1st issue). T **275** and similar designs. Perf 13 (60g.) or 13×12½ (others).

866	**275**	25g. dull purple	3·00	90
867	-	60g. greenish blue	2·75	65
868	-	1z. ultramarine	5·25	1·80
866/868 *Set of* 3			10·00	3·00

Designs: Vert—60g. Gymnastics. Horiz—1z. Running.

See also Nos. 869/870.

(Des K. Mann. Photo)

1954 (17 July). Second Spartacist Games (2nd issue). Perf 12×12½.

869	**276**	60g. red-brown	1·50	70
870		1z.55 deep slate-blue	2·75	1·90

O277

277 Battlefield

(Des B. Brandt. Eng W. Falkowski. Recess)

1954 (18 Aug). OFFICIAL. Perf 11×11½.

O871	**O277**	(60g.) deep blue	50	35
O872		(1.55z.) red	90	35
		a. Perf 12×12½	90	35

No. O872 is inscribed 'POLECONA'.

(Des J. Ostrowski. Photo)

1954 (24 Aug). Tenth Anniversary of Liberation and Battle of Studzianki. T **277** and similar horiz design. Perf 12½×13.

871	**277**	60g. green	3·25	50
872	-	1z. ultramarine	9·50	6·25

Design:—1z. Soldier, airman and tank.

278 Steel Works

279 Steam Train and Signal

(Des Cz. Kaczmarczyk. Eng (*b*) S. Lukaszewski (10g., 60g.), J. Miller (20g., 25g.), M. R. Polak (40g., 1z.15), B. Brandt (45g., 2z.10), C. Slania (1z.40, 1z.55). (*a*) Centres litho. (*b*) Centres recess. Frames photo)

1954 (Aug)–**55**. Tenth Anniversary of Second Republic, T **278** and similar horiz designs. Perf 12½×12.

873	-	10g. sepia and red-brown (*b*) (23.12.54)	1·00	35
874	-	20g. deep myrtle-green and rose (*b*) (23.12.54)	80	35
875	**278**	25g. grey-black and yellow-brown (*a*)	9·50	2·50
876		25g. grey-black and yellow-brown (*b*) (1955)	5·00	1·30
877	-	40g. purple-brown and orange-yellow (*b*) (23.12.54)	80	35
878	-	45g. dull purple and dull mauve (*b*) (23.12.54)	1·10	35
879	-	60g. purple-brown and green (*a*)	4·00	90
880	-	60g. purple-brown and green (*b*) (1955)	3·25	65
881	-	1z.15 black and bright blue-green (*b*) (23.12.54)	2·20	40
882	-	1z.40 deep brown and orange (*b*) (23.12.54)	23·00	7·25
883	-	1z.55 deep blue and dull greenish blue (*b*) (23.12.54)	5·00	1·30
884	-	2z.10 deep blue and cobalt (*b*) (23.12.54)	4·75	2·40
873/884 *Set of* 12			55·00	16·00

Designs: 10g. Coal mine; 20g. Soldier and flag, 40g. Worker on holiday; 45g. House builders; 60g. Tractor and binder; 1z.15 Lublin Castle; 1z.40 Customers in bookshop; 1z.55 *Soldek* (freighter) alongside wharf; 2z.10 Battle of Lenino.

(Des T. Gronowski (40g.), E. John, after A. Porebski (60g.). Photo)

1954 (9 Sept). Railway Workers' Day. T **279** and similar vert design. Perf 13 (40g.) or 12½×13 (60g.).

885	**279**	40g. deep blue	9·75	3·25
886	-	60g. black (steam night express)	7·50	1·50

280 Picking Apples

281 Elblag

(Des H. Przeździecka. Photo)

1954 (15 Sept). Polish–Russian Friendship. Perf 12½×13.

887	**280**	40g. slate-violet	3·75	2·30
888		60g. black	70	65

(Des S. Żukowski (45g.), K. Górska (1z.40), E. John (1z.55), Cz. Kaczmarczyk (others). Eng B. Brandt (20g.), M. R. Polak (45g.), J. Miller (60g.), S. Lukaszewski (1z.40), C. Slania (1z.55). Recess)

1954 (16 Oct). 500th Anniversary of Return of Pomerania to Poland. T **281** and similar horiz designs showing mediaeval views. Perf 12×12½.

889	**281**	20g. carmine/*blue*	4·25	1·90
		a. Perf 11×12	27·00	5·75
890	-	45g. brown/*lemon* (Gdańsk)	50	30
891	-	60g. deep blue-green/*pale green* (Toruń)	55	30
892	-	1z.40 deep ultramarine/*pink* (Malbork)	1·00	30
893	-	1z.55 chocolate/*cream* (Olsztyn)	1·30	30
889/893 *Set of* 5			6·75	2·75

282 Chopin and Grand Piano

283 Battle Scene

(Des Cz. Kaczmarczyk. Photo)

1954 (8 Nov). Fifth International Chopin Piano Competition, Warsaw (1st issue). Perf 12½×13.

894	**282**	45g. deep brown	65	25
895		60g. deep myrtle-green	75	30
		a. Perf 11	44·00	5·00
896		1z. blue	4·50	2·50
894/896 *Set of* 3			5·25	2·75

See also Nos. 906/907.

(Des after W. Kossak (40g.), after J. Matejko (60g.). Eng S. Lukaszewski (40g.), C. Slania (60g.). Des and eng B. Brandt (1z.40). Recess)

1954 (30 Nov). 160th Anniversary of Kościuszko's Insurrection. T **283** and similar horiz designs. Perf 14×13.

897	**283**	40g. blackish olive	1·00	30
898	-	60g. deep brown-purple	1·30	40
899	-	1z.40 slate-black	3·25	2·10
897/899 *Set of* 3			5·00	2·50

Designs: 60g. Kościuszko on horseback with insurgents; 1z.40 Street battle.

284 European Bison

285 The Liberator

(Des C. Borowczyk. Eng B. Brandt (45g.), S. Lukaszewski (60g.), M. R. Polak (1z.90), C. Slania (3z.). Background photo; remainder recess)

1954 (22 Dec). Protected Animals. Vert designs as T **284**. Perf 12.

900	**284**	45g. black-brown and deep yellow-green	65	30
901	-	60g. brown and bright green	65	30
902	-	1z.90 black-brown and cobalt	1·70	35
903	-	3z. brown and deep turquoise-green	2·50	1·90
900/903 *Set of* 4			5·00	2·50

Designs: 60g. Elk; 1z.90 Chamois; 3z. Eurasian Beaver.
These exist imperforate.

(Des J. Ostrowski (40g.), T. Trepkowski (60g.). Photo)

1955 (17 Jan). Tenth Anniversary of Liberation of Warsaw. T **285** and similar horiz design. Perf 12½×13.

904	**285**	40g. chocolate	3·25	2·40
905	-	60g. grey-blue (Spirit of Poland)	3·25	40

286 Bust of Chopin (after L. Isler)

287 Mickiewicz Monument

288 Flags and Tower

(Des K. Podlasiecki. Eng C. Slania. Recess)

1955 (22 Feb). Fifth International Chopin Piano Competition, Warsaw (2nd issue). Perf 12½×13.

906	**286**	40g. purple-brown	45	30
907		60g. deep blue	3·75	1·60

(Des R. Kleczewski (15g., 45g., 1z.55), E. John (others). Eng M. R. Polak (5g.), S. Lukaszewski (10g., 45g.), J. Miller (15g., 20g.), C. Slania (40g.), B. Brandt (60g., 1z.55). Recess)

1955 (Mar–May). Warsaw Monuments. T **287** and similar vert designs. Perf 12½×13.

908	-	5g. myrtle green/*olive-yellow*	35	25
		a. Perf 12×11½	35	25
909	-	10g. maroon/*yellow*	35	25
		a. Perf 12×11½	35	25
910	-	15g. brownish black/*pale green*	35	25
		a. Perf 12×11½	35	25
911	-	20g. deep blue/*pink* (31.5)	35	25
		a. Perf 12×11½	35	25
912	-	40g. deep violet/*reddish lilac* (31.5)	35	25
		a. Perf 12×11½	35	25
913	-	45g. purple brown/*pale orange*	1·60	40
914	**287**	60g. blue/*olive-grey* (31.5)	35	25
		a. Perf 12×11½	35	25
915	-	1z.55 deep bluish green/*olive-grey*	5·75	4·00
908/915 *Set of* 8			8·50	5·25

Designs: Vert—5g. Siren; 10g. D Żerzhińsky Statue; 15g. King Sigismund III Statue; 20g. Brotherhood in Arms; 40g. Copernicus Monument; 45g. Marie Curie Statue; 1z.55 Kiliński Statue.

(Des E. Kleczewski (40g.), W. Borowczyk (60g.). Photo)

1955 (21 Apr). Tenth Anniversary of Russo-Polish Treaty of Friendship. T **288** and similar vert design. Perf 11½×11.

916	**288**	40g. rose-red	40	25
		a. Perf 12½×12	40	25
917		40g. chestnut	2·10	1·90
		a. Perf 12½×12	2·10	1·90
918	-	60g. turquoise-blue	40	25
		a. Perf 12½×12	40	25
919	-	60g. deep olive-brown	40	25
		a. Perf 12½×12	40	25
916/919 *Set of* 4			3·00	2·40

Design:—60g. Statue of Friendship.

289

290 Town Hall, Poznań

291 Festival Emblem

(Des Cz. Kaczmarczyk (40g.), S. Jasiński (60g.). Photo)

1955 (25 Apr). Eighth International Peace Cycle Race. T **289** and similar vert design. Perf 12½×13 (40g.) or 13 (60g.).

920	**289**	40g. purple-brown	95	95
921	-	60g. cobalt	40	30

Design: 60g. 'VIII' and doves of peace.

(Des Cz. Kazmarczyk. Photo)

1955 (10 June). 24th International Fair, Poznań. Perf 12½×13.

922	**290**	40g. deep bright blue	80	65
923		60g. red	40	30

See also Nos. **MS**926*a*/**MS**926*b*.

(Des W. Chomicz. Litho)

1955 (16 June). Cracow Festival T **291** and similar design. Perf 12.

924	**291**	20g. ochre, sepia, red-brown and bluish green	1·70	65
925	-	40g. bluish green, black, chestnut and lilac	65	30
926	**291**	60g. yellow-brown, black, rose and blue	70	65
924/926 *Set of 3*			2·75	1·40

Design: Horiz—40g. Centre as T **291**.

1955 (7 July). Sixth Polish Philatelic Exhibition, Poznań. Two sheets 50×70 mm as T **290**. Imperf.

MS926*a*	2z.+(1z.) black and blue-green	6·50	6·50
MS926*b*	3z.+(1z.50) black and carmine	33·00	25·00

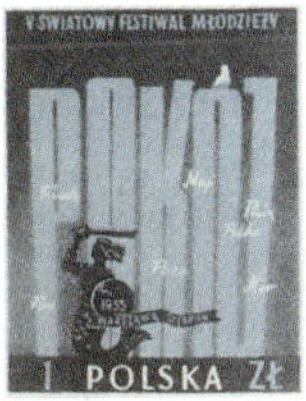

292 Peace

293 Motorcyclists

294 Stalin Palace of Culture and Science, Warsaw

(Des J. Woźnicki (Nos. 928, 931), S. Malecki (others). Litho)

1955 (13 July). Fifth International Youth Festival, Warsaw. T **292** and similar vert designs. Perf 12.

927	-	25g. purple-brown, rose and yellow	30	25
928	-	40g. grey and pale blue	30	25
		a. Perf 11	30	25
929	-	45g. lake, magenta and yellow	85	25
930	**292**	60g. ultramarine and pale blue	65	25
		a. Perf 11	65	25
931	-	60g. black and yellow-orange	65	25
932	**292**	1z. deep slate-purple and pale blue	1·90	1·30
927/932 *Set of 6*			4·25	2·30

Designs: 25g., 45g. Pansies and dove; 40g., 60g. (No. 931), Dove and tower.

These exist imperforate.

See also Nos. **MS**944*a*/**MS**944*b*.

(Des J. Woźnicki. Photo)

1955 (20 July). 13th International Tatra Mountains Motorcycle Race. Perf 12½×13.

933	**293**	40g. deep brown	1·50	65
934		60g. green	40	30

(Des K. Podlasiecki. Photo)

1955 (21 July). Polish National Day. Perf 12½×13.

935	**294**	60g. bright blue	30	25
		a. Pair. Nos. 935/936	65	55
936		60g. bluish grey	30	25
937		75g. turquoise-green	80	80
		a. Pair. Nos. 937/938	1·70	1·80
938		75g. brown	80	80
935/938 *Set of 4*			2·00	1·90

Nos. 935/936 and 937/938 were printed together in sheets containing alternate vertical rows of each colour *se-tenant*.

295 Athletes

296 Szczecin

297 Peasants and Flag

(Des J. Karolkiewicz. Photo)

1955 (27 July). Second International Games. T **295** and similar designs. Perf 13×12½ (60g.) or 12½×13 (others).

939	**295**	20g. sepia	30	25
940	-	40g. brown-purple	40	25
941	-	60g. dull greenish blue	75	30
942	-	1z. red-orange	1·00	35
943	-	1z.35 dull purple	1·40	40
944	-	1z.55 blue-green	3·25	1·90
939/944 *Set of 6*			6·50	3·00

Designs: Vert—40g. Throwing the hammer; 1z. Netball; 1z.35 Sculling; 1z.55 Swimming. Horiz—60g. Stadium.

These exist imperforate.

1955 (3 Aug). International Philatelic Exhibition, Warsaw. Two sheets 61×84 mm. Imperf.

MS944*a*	1z.(+1z.) As No. 929	6·25	3·25
MS944*b*	2z.(+1z.) As No. 932	36·00	29·00

(Des S. Jasiński. Eng B. Brandt (25g.), J. Miller (40g.), M. R. Polak (others). Recess)

1955 (22 Sept). Tenth Anniversary of Return of Western Territories. T **296** and similar vert designs. Perf 12½×13.

945	**296**	25g. deep blue-green	30	25
		a. Perf 12×11½	30	25
946	-	40g. red-brown (Wrocław)	65	30
947	-	60g. deep violet-blue (Zielona Góra)	90	35
948	-	95g. brown-black (Opole)	2·75	1·90
945/948 *Set of 4*			4·25	2·50

(Des M. Bylina. Photo)

1955 (30 Sept). 50th Anniversary of 1905 Revolution. Perf 12½×13.

949	**297**	40g. sepia	1·70	1·30
950		60g. carmine-red	40	30

298 Adam Mickiewicz

299 Statue

(Des H. Przeździecka (20g.), W. Chmielewski (others). Photo)

1955 (10 Oct). Death Centenary of Adam Mickiewicz (poet). T **298** and vert designs as T **299**. Perf 12×12½ (20g.) or 12½×13 (others).

951	**298**	20g. sepia	40	25
952	**299**	40g. sepia and brown-orange	40	25
953	-	60g. sepia and dull green (Sculptured head)	40	30
954	-	95g. black and brown-red (Statue)	3·00	2·00
951/954 *Set of 4*			3·75	2·50

300 Teacher and Pupil

301 Rook and Hands

302 Ice Skates

(Des R. Kleczewski (40g.), H. Przeździecka (60g.). Photo)

1955 (21 Oct). 50th Anniversary of Polish Teachers' Union. T **300** and similar vert design. Perf 12½×13.

955	**300**	40g. brown	3·25	65
956	-	60g. bright blue (Open book and lamp)	6·25	3·50

(Des Cz. Kaczmarczyk. Photo)

1956 (9 Feb). First World Chess Championship for the Deaf and Dumb. T **301** and similar vert design. Perf 12½×13.

957	**301**	40g. brown-red	4·50	3·75
958	-	60g. dull greenish blue	2·20	40

Design:—60g. Knight and hands.

(Des Cz. Kaczmarczyk. Litho)

1956 (7 Mar). 11th World Students' Winter Sports Championship. T **302** and similar vert designs. Perf 12½×13.

959	**302**	20g. black and blue	7·50	5·75
960	-	40g. ultramarine and bright blue-green	1·10	35
		a. Perf 11	1·10	35
961	-	60g. claret and mauve	90	35
		a. Perf 11	90	35
959/961 *Set of 3*			8·50	5·75

Designs: 40g. Ice hockey sticks and puck; 60g. Skis and ski sticks.

303 Officer and *Kilinski* (freighter)

304 Racing Cyclist

(Des S. Lukaszewski. Eng J. Miller (10g.), M. R. Polak (45g.), S. Lukaszewski (60g.), B. Brandt (others). Recess)

1956 (16 Mar). Merchant Navy. T **303** and similar horiz designs. Perf 12×12½.

962	**303**	5g. deep bluish green	40	25
		a. Perf 11×11½	40	25
963	-	10g. crimson	40	25
		a. Perf 11×11½	40	25
964	-	20g. deep blue	45	25
		a. Perf 11×11½	45	25
965	-	45g. red-brown	2·75	2·00
		a. Perf 11×11½	2·75	2·00
966	-	60g. deep violet-blue	55	30
		a. Perf 11×11½	55	30
962/966 *Set of* 5			4·00	2·75
962a/966a *Set of* 5			4·00	2·75

Designs: 10g. Tug and barges; 20g. *Pokój* (freighter) in dock; 45g. Building *Marceli Nowatka* (freighter); 60g. *Fryderyk Chopin* (freighter) and *Rudunia* (trawler).

(Des H. Przeździecka. Photo)

1956 (25 Apr). Ninth International Peace Cycle Race. Perf 13×12½.

967	**304**	40g. deep blue	2·50	1·30
968		60g. deep green	40	30

305 Lodge, Tatra Mountains

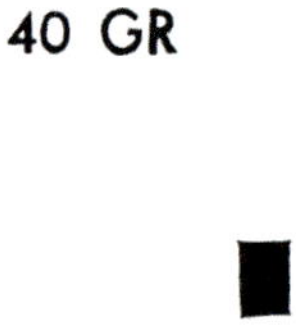

(306)

(Des Cz. Kaczmarczyk, J. Kończak and S. Jasinski. Photo)

1956 (25 May). Tourist Propaganda. T **305** and similar vert designs. Perf 12½×13.

969	**305**	30g. bottle green	50	30
		a. Perf 13	50	30
970	-	40g. chestnut	50	30
971	-	60g. blue	3·50	1·10
972	-	1z.15 deep dull purple	65	40
969/972 *Set of* 4			4·75	1·90

Designs: 40g. Compass, rucksack and map; 60g. Canoe and map; 1z.15 Skis and mountains.

1956 (6 July). No. 829 surch as T **306**.

973	10g. on 80g. deep reddish purple	1·70	60
974	40g. on 80g. deep reddish purple	40	25
	a. Perf 11½	40	25
975	60g. on 80g. deep reddish purple	50	30
	a. Perf 11½	50	30
976	1z.35 on 80g. deep reddish purple	4·50	3·25
973/976 *Set of* 4		6·50	4·00

307 Ghetto Heroes Monument

308 Economic Co-operation

(Des E. John. Eng C. Slania (30g.), M. R. Polak (40g.), E. Konecki (1z.55). Recess)

1956 (10 July). Warsaw Monuments. T **307** and similar vert designs. Perf 12½×13.

977	**307**	30g. black	40	25
		a. Perf 12×11½	40	25
978	-	40g. red-brown/*green*	2·50	1·00
979	-	1z.55 brown-purple/*pink*	40	30
		a. Perf 12×11½	40	30
977/979 *Set of* 3			3·00	1·40

Designs: 40g. Statue of King Jan III Sobieski; 1z.55 Statue of Prince Joseph Poniatowski.

(Des S. Gospodarek (40g.), S. Malecki (60g.). Litho)

1956 (14 Sept). Russo–Polish Friendship Month. T **308** and similar horiz design. Perf 12½×12.

980	-	40g. deep brown and rose-pink	1·50	1·20
		a. Perf 11	1·50	75
981	**308**	60g. red and bistre	40	30

Design: 40g. Polish and Russian dancers.

309 Ludwika Wawrzyńska (teacher)

310 *Lady with a Weasel* (Leonardo da Vinci)

(Des H. Przeździecka. Photo)

1956 (17 Sept). Ludwika Wawrzyńska Commemoration. Perf 13.

982	**309**	40g. chocolate	2·30	1·80
983		60g. deep blue	40	30

(Des Cz. Kaczmarczk. Eng E. Konecki (40g.), S. Lukaszewski (60g.), B. Brandt (1z.55). Recess)

1956 (23 Oct–19 Nov). International Campaign for Museums. T **310** and similar vert designs. Perf 11½×11.

984	-	40g. myrtle-green (19.11)	5·75	2·50
985	-	60g. deep violet (19.11)	1·30	40
986	**310**	1z.55 blackish chocolate (23.10)	3·25	40
984/986 *Set of* 3			9·25	3·00

Designs: 40g. Niobe (bust); 60g. Madonna (Vit Stvosz).

310a Music Quotation and Profiles of Chopin and Liszt

311 *Apis mellifera* (Bee) and Hive

(Des S. Gospodarek. Photo)

1956 (25 Oct). Stamp Day. Sheet 55×75 mm. Imperf.

MS986*a* **310a** 4z.(+2z.) deep bluish green		35·00	28·00

(Des J. Kończak (40g.), S. Gospodarek (60g.). Litho)

1956 (30 Oct). 50th Death Anniversary of Jan Dżierzon (apiarist). T **311** and similar vert design. Perf 12½×13.

987	**311**	40g. brown/*orange-yellow*	2·75	95
988	-	60g. brown/*orange-yellow* (Dr J. Dżierzon)	40	25

312 Fencing

313 15th-century Postman

(Des Cz. Kaczmarczyk. Eng E. Konecki (10g.), S. Lukaszewski (20g.), M. R. Polak (25g.), B. Brandt (40g.), C. Slania (60g.), J. Miller (1z.55). Centres recess (except No. 995, photo); frames litho)

1956 (2 Nov–12 Dec). Olympic Games. T **312** and similar designs inscr 'MELBOURNE 1956'. Perf 11½.

989	**312**	10g. brown and slate	30	25
990	-	20g. blackish lilac and bistre-brown	30	25
		a. 'MELBOURNE 1956' inverted	£32000	
991	-	25g. black and pale blue	1·00	30
992	-	40g. chocolate and blue-green	40	25
993	-	60g. brown-black and carmine	90	30
994	-	1z.55 sepia and bright violet	5·00	1·50
995	-	1z.55 reddish brown and orange (12.12)	1·90	50
989/995 *Set of* 7			8·75	3·00

Designs: 20g. Boxing; 25g. Rowing; 40g. Steeplechase; 60g. Javelin; No. 994, Gymnastics; No. 995, Long jump (Elizabeth Krzesińska's-Duńska gold medal).

(Des S. Bernacińsky. Litho)

1956 (30 Nov). Re-opening of Postal Museum, Wroclaw. Perf 12½×13.

996 **313** 60g. grey-black/*pale blue* .... 6·00 5·00

314 Snow Crystals and Skier of 1907

315 Apple Tree and Globe

(Des J. Konczak. Photo)

1957 (18 Jan). Fifty years of Skiing in Poland. T **314** and similar designs. Perf 13.

997	**314**	40g. blue	35	25
998	-	60g. deep bluish green	35	25
999	-	1z. purple	1·30	1·00
997/999 *Set of 3*			1·80	1·40

Designs: Vert—60g. Snow crystals and skier jumping Horiz—1z. Snow crystals and skier standing.

(Des S. Malecki. Photo)

1957 (26 Feb). United Nations Organisation. T **315** and similar designs. Perf 12½×12 (5g.) or 12×12½ (others).

1000	**315**	5g. crimson and deep turquoise-blue.	65	35
1001	-	15g. blue and pale grey	90	35
1002	-	40g. blue-green and pale grey	1·50	1·30
1000/1002 *Set of 3*			2·75	1·80

MS1002*a* 55×70 mm. 1z.50 blue and bright blue-green. Imperf .... 33·00 26·00

Designs: Vert—15g. UNO emblem; 40g., 1z.50 UNO Headquarters, New York.

Nos. 1000/1002 exist imperforate.

316 Skier

(Des S. Gospodarek. Photo)

1957 (22 Mar). 12th Death Anniversary of Bronislaw Czech and Hanna Marusarzówna (skiers). Perf 12½×13.

1003	**316**	60g. deep brown	2·10	1·00
1004		60g. blue	65	35

317 Winged Letter

318 Foil, Sword and Sabre on Map

(Des S. Jasiński. Photo)

1957 (28 Mar–18 May). AIR. Seventh Polish National Philatelic Exhibition, Warsaw. Perf 11½.

1005 **317** 4z.+2z. blue (28.3) .... 5·00 5·00

MS1005*a* 55×75 mm. 4z.+2z. violet-blue (Type **317**). Imperf (18.5) .... 11·00 9·50

No. 1005 is printed in sheets of 12 stamps with four labels.

(Des J. Kończak (40g.), S. Jasiński (others). Photo)

1957 (20 Apr). World Youth Fencing Championships, Warsaw. T **318** and similar horiz designs. Perf 13×12½.

1006	**318**	40g. purple	80	30
1007	-	60g. deep rose-red	40	25
		a. Pair. Nos. 1007/1008	85	55
1008	-	60g. bright blue	40	25
1006/1008 *Set of 3*			1·40	70

Designs: Nos. 1007/1008 are arranged in *se-tenant* pairs in the sheet, and together show two fencers duelling.

319 Dr S. Petrycy (philosopher)

(Des J. Desselberger. Eng J. Miller (10g.), B. Brandt (20g., 3z.), M. R. Polak (40g.), E. Konecki (60g., 1z.35), S. Lukaszewski (2z.50). Recess and typo)

1957 (27 Apr–30 Sept). Polish Doctors. T **319** and similar designs. Perf 12×11½.

1009	**319**	10g. sepia and ultramarine	30	25
1010	-	20g. lake and emerald	30	25
1011	-	40g. black and rose-red	30	25
1012	-	60g. dull purple and pale blue	2·10	45
1013	-	1z. blue-grey and yellow-orange (30.9)	40	30
1014	-	1z.35 black-brown and blue-green	40	30
1015	-	2z.50 slate-violet and cerise	40	30
1016	-	3z. deep olive-brown and violet	45	30
1009/1016 *Set of 8*			4·25	2·20

Portraits: 20g. Dr W. Oczko; 40g. Dr J. Sniadecki; 60g. Dr T. Chalubinski; 1z. Dr W. Bieganski; 1z.35 Dr J. Dietl; 2z.50 Dr B. Dybowski; 3z. Dr H. Jordan.

320 Cycle Wheel and Flower

321 Fair Emblem

322 Carline Thistle

(Des S. Szymański. Photo)

1957 (4 May). Tenth International Peace Cycle Race. T **320** and similar design. Perf 12½×13.

1017	60g. blue	65	30
1018	1z.50 rose-magenta (Cyclist)	90	40

(Des A. Borys. Litho)

1957 (8 June). 26th International Fair, Poznań. Perf 13 (60g.) or 12½×13 (2z.50).

1019	**321**	60g. light ultramarine	40	30
1020		2z.50 blue-green	90	40

(Des Cz. Borowczyk. Photo)

1957 (12 Aug). Wild Flowers. T **322** and similar floral designs. Perf 12×12½.

1021	60g. yellow, blue-green and pale grey	65	30
1022	60g. deep blue-green and pale blue	65	30
1023	60g. olive-green and grey	65	30
1024	60g. yellow, brown-red and pale bluish green	1·60	50
1025	60g. maroon and blue-green	65	30
1021/1025 *Set of 5*		3·75	1·50

Designs: No. 1021, T **322**; 1022, Sea Holly; 1023, Edelweiss; 1024, Lady's Slipper Orchid; 1025, Turk's Cap Lily.

323 Fireman

324 Town Hall, Leipzig

325 The Letter (after Fragonard)

(Des S. Szymański (40g.), S. Gospodarek (60g.), S. Malecki (2z.50). Photo)

1957 (11 Sept). International Fire Brigades Conference, Warsaw. T **323** and similar vert designs. Perf 12×12½.

1026	**323**	40g. black and red	30	25
1027	-	60g. deep bluish green and orange-red	35	25

1028 - 2z.50 violet and vermilion 70 35
1026/1028 *Set of 3* .... 1·20 75
Designs: 60g. Flames enveloping child; 2z.50 Ear of corn in flames.

(Des H. Macierewicz. Photo)

1957 (25 Sept). Fourth International Trade Unions Congress, Leipzig. Perf 12½×13.
1029 **324** 60g. violet 40 35

(Des H. Przeździecka. Photo)

1957 (9 Oct). Stamp Day. Perf 12×12½.
1030 **325** 2z.50 deep myrtle green .... 1·30 35

326 Red Banner

327 Karol Libelt (founder)

328 H. Wieniawski (violinist)

(Des Cz. Kaczmarczyk. Photo)

1957 (7 Nov). 40th Anniversary of Russian Revolution. T **326** and similar vert design. Perf 12½×13.
1031 **326** 60g. red and deep blue 35 25
a. Red (flag) omitted £250
1032 - 2z.50 chestnut and black 45 30
Design: 2z.50 Lenin Monument, Poronin.

(Des J. Skoracki. Photo)

1957 (15 Nov). Centenary of Poznań Scientific Society. Perf 12½×13.
1033 **327** 60g. crimson 45 35

(Des S. Jasiński. Photo)

1957 (2 Dec). Third Wieniawski International Violin Competition. Perf 12½×13.
1034 **328** 2z.50 blue 65 40

329 Ilyushin Il-14P SP-LAG over Steel Works

330 Multiple Posthorns

There are four different types of W **330**, which also come inverted.

(Des J. Miller. Eng S. Lukaszewski (90g.), E. Konecki (1z.50), J. Miller (3z.40, 3z.90), M. R. Polak (4z.), B. Brandt (15z.). Recess, background photo)

1957 (6 Dec)–**58**. AIR. Pictorial designs as T **329**. W **330** (5z., 10z., 20z., 30z., 50z.) or no wmk (others). Perf 12½.
1035 **329** 90g. black and pink 35 25
1036 - 1z.50 brown and salmon 40 30
1037 - 3z.40 sepia and buff 75 35
1038 - 3z.90 deep brown and olive-yellow .... 1·60 1·00
1039 - 4z. Prussian blue and pale green 90 40
1039*a* - 5z. brown-purple and grey (15.12.58) 90 40
1039*b* - 10z. sepia and pale turquoise (15.12.58) .... 1·60 65
1040 - 15z. deep bluish violet and turquoise-blue .... 3·25 80
1040*a* - 20z. slate-violet and pale yellow (15.12.58) .... 3·25 1·30
1040*b* - 30z. olive-green and buff (15.12.58) .... 4·75 3·50
1040*c* - 50z. deep blue and pale drab (15.12.58) .... 11·00 5·00
1035/1040*c* *Set of 11* .... 26·00 12·50
Designs: Ilyushin Il-14P SP-LAG over—1z.50 Castle Square, Warsaw; 3z.40 Market, Cracow; 3z.90 Szczecin; 4z. Karkonosze Mountains; 5z. Old Market, Gdańsk; 10z. Liw Castle; 15z. Lublin; 20z. Cable railway, Kasprowy Wierch; 30z. Porabka Dam; 50z. *Batory* (liner).
For stamp as No. 1039*b*, but printed in slate-purple only, see No. 1095.

330a J. A. Komensky (Comenius)

(Des S. Jasiński. Photo)

1957 (11 Dec). 300th Anniversary of Publication of Komensky's *Opera Didactica Omnia*. Perf 12.
1041 **330a** 2z.50 bright carmine 65 35

331 A. Strug

332 Joseph Conrad and *Torrens* (full-rigged sailing ship)

(Des S. Szymański. Photo)

1957 (16 Dec). 20th Death Anniversary of Andrzej Strug (writer). Perf 12½×13.
1042 **331** 2z.50 brown 65 35

(Des S. Lukaszewski. Recess)

1957 (30 Dec). Birth Centenary of Joseph Conrad (Korzeniowski) (author). Perf 12×12½.
1043 **332** 60g. chocolate/*turquoise* 40 25
1044 2z.50 deep blue/*pink* .... 1·00 50

333 Postman of 1558

(Des S. Malecki. Litho)

1958 (24 Feb). 400th Anniversary of Polish Postal Service (1st issue). Perf 12½×13.
1045 **333** 2z.50 blackish violet and blue 65 35
a. Error '00LAT' instead of '400 LAT' (pos. 92) .... 12·50 10·00
b. Dot inside 'K' of 'POLSKA' (pos. 62)
See also Nos. 1063/1067.

334 Town Hall, Biecz

335 Zander (*Lucioperca lucioperca*)

I.

II.

Two types of 20g.:

I. Central part of building more lightly shaded; no stops in engraver's name.

II. Building evenly shaded; stops in engraver's name.

III. IV.

Two types of 40g.:

III. Second needle from bottom on right-hand side of roof very long; triangular area at top of door unshaded.

IV. Second needle same size as other needles; triangular area shaded.

(Des S. Gospodarek. Eng B. Szymańska (20g., 40g., 2z.10), E. Tirdiszek (others). Recess)

1958 (29 Mar). Ancient Polish Town Halls. Designs as T **334**. Perf 12×11½ (2z.50), 12½×13 (20g., 40g., 2z.10) or 13×12½ (60g.).

1046	**334**	20g. blue-green (Type I)	35	25
		a. Type II	2·50	40
		ab. Perf 12×11½	35	25
1047	-	40g. brown (Wroclaw) (III)	35	25
		a. Type IV	2·50	40
		ab. Perf 12×11½	35	25
1048	-	60g. deep blue (Tarnow) (*horiz*)	35	25
1049	-	2z.10 lake (Gdańsk)	40	25
1050	-	2z.50 violet (Zamosc)	1·00	40
1046/1050 *Set of* 5			2·20	1·30

(Des S. Malecki. Photo)

1958 (22 Apr). Fish. Designs as T **335**. Perf 12×12½ (vert) or 12½×12 (horiz).

1051	40g. yellow, black and deep turquoise-blue	45	25
1052	60g. ultramarine, indigo and light green	65	30
1053	2z.10 yellow, indigo and blue	1·10	40
1054	2z.50 green, black and reddish violet	2·75	65
1055	6z.40 bistre-brown, vermilion, black and deep turquoise-green	1·40	75
1051/1055 *Set of* 5		5·75	2·10

Designs: Vert—60g. Atlantic Salmon (*Salmo salar*); 2z.10 Northern Pike (*Esox lucius*); 2z.50 Brown Trout (*Salmo trutta m. fario*). Horiz—40g. T **335**; 6z.40 European Grayling (*Thymallus thymallus*).

336 Warsaw University

337 Fair Emblem

338

(Des S. Jasiński. Photo)

1958 (14 May). 140th Anniversary of Warsaw University. Perf 12½×13.

1056	**336**	2z.50 deep violet-blue	65	30

(Des Z. Kaja. Litho)

1958 (9 June). 27th International Fair, Poznań. Perf 12½×13.

1057	**337**	2z.50 red and black	65	30

(Des J. Desselberger. Litho)

1958 (14 June). Seventh International Gliding Championships. T **338** and similar vert design. Perf 12½×13.

1058	**338**	60g. black and slate-blue	30	25
1059	-	2z.50 black and grey	75	35

Design:—2z.50 as T **338** but design in reverse.

339 Armed Postman

340 Polar Bear on Iceberg

(Des Cz. Kaczmarczyk. Eng E. Konecki. Recess)

1958 (1 Sept). 19th Anniversary of Defence of Gdańsk Post Office. Perf 11×11½.

1060	**339**	60g. deep blue	45	30

(Des S. Jasiński. Photo)

1958 (30 Sept). International Geophysical Year. T **340** and similar vert design. Perf 12½×12.

1061	60g. black	40	25
1062	2z.50 blue	1·60	40

Designs: 60g. T **340**; 2z.50 *Sputnik* and track of rocket.

341 Tomb of Prosper Prowano (First Polish Postmaster)

342 Envelope, Quill and Postmark

(Des S. Malecki. Litho)

1958 (8 Oct). 400th Anniversary of Polish Postal Service (2nd issue). T **341** and similar vert designs. Perf 12½×13.

1063	40g. maroon and cobalt	75	30
1064	60g. black and lilac	30	25
1065	95g. violet and yellow-bistre	30	25
1066	2z.10 ultramarine and grey	2·20	75
1067	3z.40 red-brown and turquoise-blue	95	65
1063/1067 *Set of* 5		4·00	2·00

Designs: 40g. T **341**; 60g. Mail coach and Church of Our Lady, Cracow; 95g. Mail coach (rear view); 2z.10 16th-century postman; 3z.40 Kogge.

Nos. 1064/1067 show various forms of modern transport in clear silhouette in the background.

(Des S. Gospodarek. Litho)

1958 (9 Oct). Stamp Day. Perf 12½×13.

1068	**342**	60g. blue-green, red and black	2·20	90

343 Partisans' Cross

344 Mail Coach in the Kielce District (after painting by A. Kedzierski)

(Des Cz. Kacmarczyk. Photo)

1958 (10 Oct). 15th Anniversary of Polish People's Army. Polish decorations as T **343**. Perf 11.

1069	40g. buff, black and green	30	25
1070	60g. brown, yellow, black and blue	40	30
1071	2z.50 yellow, black, red and green	2·00	50
1069/1071 *Set of* 3		2·40	95

Decorations: 40g. T **343**; 60g. Virtuti Military Cross; 2z.50 Grunwald Cross.

(Des H. Przeździecka. Eng S. Lukaszewski. Recess)

1958 (26 Oct). Polish Postal Service 400th Anniversary Exhibition. W **330**. Perf 12½×13.

1072	**344**	2z.50 olive-black/*buff*	2·50	1·90

No. 1072 was printed in sheets of six (*price £19 unused*). These sheets normally measure 139 mm in height but examples also exist 20 mm taller with an extra line of perforations in the top margin. These were attached to the fronts of special brochures (*price £170 unused*).

See also No. **MS**1078*a*.

345 Galleon

346 UNESCO Headquarters, Paris

347 S. Wyspiański (dramatist and painter)

(Des S. Jasiński. Photo)

1958 (29 Oct). 350th Anniversary of Polish Emigration to America. T **345** and similar vert design inscr '1608' etc. Perf 11.

1073	**345**	60g. blackish green	40	30
1074	-	2z.50 carmine-red (Polish emigrants)	2·30	65

(Des Cz. Kaczmarczyk. Photo)

1958 (3 Nov). Inauguration of UNESCO Headquarters Buildings, Paris. Perf 13×12½.

1075	**346**	2z.50 black and green	1·30	65

(Des J. Kończak. Eng B. Brandt (60g.), E. Tirdiszek (2z.50). Recess)

1958 (25 Nov). Famous Poles. T **347** and similar vert design. Perf 12½×13.

1076	60g. violet	40	25
1077	2z.50 deep green	90	40

Portraits: 60g. T **347**; 2z.50 S. Moniuszko (composer).

348 Human Rights

348a Coach and Horses (after A. Kędzierski)

(Des S. Gospodarek. Litho)

1958 (10 Dec). Tenth Anniversary of Declaration of Human Rights. Perf 12½×13.

1078	**348**	2z.50 red-brown and light brown	1·30	40

(Des H. Przeździecka. Eng S. Lukaszewski. Recess on silk)

1958 (12 Dec). 400th Anniversary of Polish Postal Service. Sheet 86×76 mm. Imperf.

MS1078*a*	**348a**	50z. slate-blue	33·00	31·00

349 Party Flag

350 Yacht

(Des A. Balcerzak. Photo)

1958 (16 Dec). 40th Anniversary of Polish Communist Party. Perf 12½×13.

1079	**349**	60g. red and reddish purple	40	25

(Des J. Macierewicz. Photo)

1959 (3 Jan). Sports. T **350** and similar vert designs. Perf 12½×13.

1080	40g. ultramarine and pale blue	65	35
1081	60g. deep purple and salmon	65	35
1082	95g. purple and green	1·30	40
1083	2z. deep blue and pale green	65	35
1080/1083	*Set of* 4	3·00	1·30

Designs: 40g. T **350**; 60g. Archer; 95g. Footballers; 2z. Horseman.

351 The Guiding Hand

352 *Amanita phalloides*

(Des J. Kończak (40g.), S. Biernaciński (60g.), S. Malecki (1z.55). Photo)

1959 (10 Mar). Third Polish United Workers' Party Congress. T **351** and similar designs. W **330**. Perf 13×12½ (60g.) or 12½×13 (others).

1084	40g. black, yellow-brown and red	40	25
1085	60g. black, red, yellow and bluish green	40	25
1086	1z.55 vermilion, grey, purple and black	90	65
1084/1086	*Set of* 3	1·50	1·00

Designs: Horiz—60g. Hammer and ears of corn. Vert—40g. T **351**; 1z.55 Nowa Huta foundry.

(Des C. Borowczyk. Photo)

1959 (8 May). Mushrooms. Triangular designs as T **352**. W **330**. Perf 11½.

1087	20g. yellow, brown and green	3·25	2·30
1088	30g. red, olive, brown and orange-yellow	1·40	50
1089	40g. red, green, yellow and dull mauve	90	35
1090	60g. yellow, brown, green and deep green	90	35
1091	1z. yellow, brown, green and blue	90	35
1092	2z.50 sepia, green and blue	1·50	65
1093	3z.40 red, yellow, green and black	2·20	65
1094	5z.60 chocolate, green and olive-yellow	7·50	2·30
1087/1094	*Set of* 8	17·00	6·75

Mushrooms: 20g. T **352**; 30g. *Suillus luteus* (*Boletus luteus*); 40g. *Boletus edulis*; 60g. *Lactarius deliciosus*; 1z. *Cantharellus cibarius*; 2z.50 *Agaricus campestris* (*Psalliota campestris*); 3z.40 *Amanita muscaria*; 5z.60 *Leccinum scabrum* (*Boletus scaber*).

1959 (23 May). AIR. 65 Years of Philately in Poland and Sixth Polish Philatelic Association Congress, Warsaw. Design as No. 1039*b* but in one colour only. Litho and photo. W **330**. Perf 12½.

1095	10z. slate-purple	6·25	6·00

No. 1095 is printed in sheets of six stamps *se-tenant* with variously inscribed labels in slate-purple and pale green each bearing a premium '+5 zl.' (*price* £75).

353 Storks (after Chelmoński)

354 Miner

355 Sheaf of Wheat (Agriculture)

(Des J. Desselberger. Eng E. Konecki (40g.), B. Szymańska (60g.), S. Lukaszewski (1z.), M. R. Polak (1z.50), J. Miller (6z.40). Recess)

1959 (29 June–22 Sept). Polish Paintings. Various designs as T **353**. W **330**. Perf 13×12 (1z.) or 12 (others).

1096	40g. bronze-green	30	25
1097	60g. deep maroon	55	35
1098	1z. black (22.9)	65	40
1099	1z.50 sepia	1·50	65
1100	6z.40 deep blue	5·00	1·30
1096/1100	*Set of* 5	7·25	2·75

Paintings: Vert—60g. Motherhood (after Wyspiański); 1z. Madame de Romanet (after Rodakowski); 1z.50 Death (after Malczewski). Horiz—40g. T **353**; 6z.40 The Sandmen (after Gierymski).

(Des S. Malecki. Litho)

1959 (1 July). Third International Miners' Congress, Katowice. W **330**. Perf 12½×13.

1101	**354**	2z.50 multicoloured	2·20	40

(Des S. Malecki. Litho)

1959 (21 July). 15th Anniversary of People's Republic. T **355** and similar vert designs inscr 'XV LAT PRL'. W **330**. Perf 12×12½.

1102	40g. blue-green and black	25	25
1103	60g. red and black	30	30
1104	1z.50 pale blue and black	50	35
1102/1104	*Set of* 3	95	80

Designs: 40g. T **355**; 60g. Crane (Building); 1z.50 Corinthian column, and book (Culture and Science).

356 Dr L. Zamenhof

357 Flowering Pink (Map of Austria)

358

(Des B. Brandt (60g.), R. Dudzicki (1z.50). Litho)

1959 (24 July). International Esperanto Congress, Warsaw, and Birth Centenary of Dr Ludwig Zamenhof (inventor of Esperanto). T **356** and similar vert design. W **330**. Perf 12½×13.

1105	60g. black and green/*light olive*	40	30
1106	1z.50 blue-green, red and violet/*grey*	4·00	1·10

Designs: 60g. T **356**; 1z.50 Esperanto Star, and Globe.

(Des E. Konecki. Litho)

1959 (27 July). Seventh World Youth Festival, Vienna. W **330**. Perf 12½×13.

1107	**357**	60g. multicoloured	40	30
1108		2z.50 multicoloured	1·60	80

(Des J. Kończak. Litho)

1959 (24 Aug). 30th Anniversary of Polish Airlines LOT. W **330**. Perf 13×12½.

1109	**358**	60g. light blue, bluish violet and black..	40	30

359 Parliament House, Warsaw

BALPEX I - GDAŃSK 1959

(360)

(Des S. Jasiński. Litho)

1959 (27 Aug). 48th Inter-Parliamentary Union Conference, Warsaw. W **330**.

1110	**359**	60g. green, red and black	40	30
1111		2z.50 dull purple, red and black	1·70	1·10

1959 (30 Aug). Baltic States' International Philatelic Exhibition, Gdańsk. No. 890 optd with T **360**.

1112		45g. brown/*lemon* (B.)	1·50	1·30
		a. Error. Missing accent above 'n' in 'Gdańsk' (pos. 1 and 7)	17·00	15·00

361 Dove and Globe

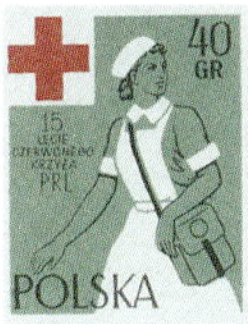

362 Nurse with Bag

363 Emblem of Polish–Chinese Friendship Society

(Des A. Balcerzak and S. Nargiello. Photo)

1959 (1 Sept). Tenth Anniversary of World Peace Movement. W **330**. Perf 13×12½.

1113	**361**	60g. grey and blue	40	30

(Des Cz. Kaczmarczyk. Litho)

1959 (21 Sept). 40th Anniversary of Polish Red Cross. T **362** and similar designs. W **330**. Perf 11 (2z.50) or 12½×13 (others).

1114		40g. red, black and green	30	25
1115		60g. red, brown and yellow-brown	40	30
1116		2z.50 red, black and light Venetian red	3·00	65
1114/1116 *Set of 3*			3·25	1·10

Designs: Vert—40g. T **362**; 60g. Nurse with bottle and bandages. Square 23×23 mm—2z.50 J. H. Dunant.

(Des S. Malecki. Litho)

1959 (28 Sept). Polish–Chinese Friendship. W **330**. Perf 11.

1117	**363**	60g. red, yellow, blue and violet	2·10	1·10
1118		2z.50 red, yellow, blue and blue-green...	50	40

364

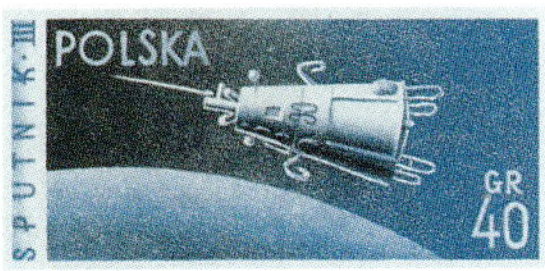

365 *Sputnik 3*

(Des S. Bernaciński. Litho)

1959 (9 Oct). Stamp Day. W **330**. Perf 12½×13.

1119	**364**	60g. red, olive-green and light turquoise	30	25
1120		2z.50 violet-blue, blue-green and red	65	35

(Des Cz. Kaczmarczyk. Photo)

1959 (7 Nov). Cosmic Flights. T **365** and similar horiz designs. W **330**. Perf 12½.

1121		40g. black and turquoise-blue	30	25
1122		60g. black and brown-lake	40	30
1123		2z.50 deep blue and blue-green	2·10	1·00
1121/1123 *Set of 3*			2·50	1·40

Designs: 40g. T **365**; 60g. Rocket *Mieczta* encircling Sun; 2z.50 Moon rocket *Lunik 2*.

Nos. 1121/1123 exist imperforate.

366 Schoolgirl

367 Charles Darwin

(40g. des W. Górka; eng B. Szymańska. Recess, background photo. 60g. des H. Hilscher; eng E. Tirdiszek. Recess and typo, background photo)

1959 (14 Nov). 1000 Schools for Polish Millennium. T **366** and similar vert design inscr 'TYSIAC SZKOL NA TYSIACLECIE'. W **330**. Perf 11½.

1124		40g. sepia and deep green	35	25
1125		60g. red, black and blue	40	30

Designs: 40g. T **366**; 60g. Children going to school.

(Des S. Chludziński. Eng E. Tirdiszek (20g.), E. Konecki (40g.), J. Miller (60g.), B. Brandt (1z.50), B. Kowalska (1z.55), S. Lukaszewski (2z.50). Recess)

1959 (10 Dec). Famous Scientists. Vert portraits as T **367**. W **330**. Perf 11×11½.

1126	**367**	20g. deep blue	20	20
1127	-	40g. deep olive (Mendeleev)	25	20
1128	-	60g. brown-purple (Einstein)	30	25
1129	-	1z.50 chocolate (Pasteur)	45	30
1130	-	1z.55 deep myrtle-green (Newton)	75	40
1131	-	2z.50 violet (Copernicus)	2·20	65
1126/1131 *Set of 6*			3·75	1·80

368 Costumes of Rzeszów

369 Costumes of Rzeszów

(Des Cz. Kaczmarczyk. Eng S. Lukaszewski (20g.), B. Konecki (60g.), J. Miller (1z.), B. Brandt (2z.50), M. R. Polak (5z.60). Recess; background photo)

1959 (18 Dec). Provincial Costumes (1st series). Types **368**/**369** and similar vert designs. W **330**. Perf 12.

1132	**368**	20g. greenish black and grey-green	25	20
		a. Pair. Nos. 1132/1133	55	45
1133	**369**	20g. greenish black and grey-green	25	20
1134	-	60g. agate and salmon-pink	30	25
		a. Pair. Nos. 1134/1135	65	55
1135	-	60g. agate and salmon-pink	30	25
1136	-	1z. brown-red and pale blue	35	30
		a. Pair. Nos. 1136/1137	75	65
1137	-	1z. brown-red and pale blue	35	30
1138	-	2z.50 blue-green and lavender-grey	85	35
		a. Pair. Nos. 1138/1139	1·80	75
1139	-	2z.50 blue-green and lavender-grey	85	35
1140	-	5z.60 Prussian blue and greenish yellow	2·10	55
		a. Pair. Nos. 1140/1141	4·50	1·20
1141	-	5z.60 Prussian blue and greenish yellow	2·10	55
1132/1141 *Set of 10*			7·00	3·00

Designs: Male and female costumes of—Nos. 1134/1135, Kurpie; Nos. 1136/1137, Silesia; Nos. 1138/1139, Górale; Nos. 1140/1141, Szamotuly.

Stamps of the same value were issued together in *se-tenant* pairs within their sheets.

These also exist imperforate.

See also Nos. 1150/1159.

370 Piano

(Des S. Malecki. Litho (60g., 1z.50). Eng B. Kowalska. Recess (2z.50))

1960 (22 Feb). 150th Birth Anniversary of Chopin. Chopin Music Competition, Warsaw. T **370** and similar vert designs inscr '1810–1960'. W **330**. Perf 12 (60g., 1z.50) or 12½×12 (2z.50).

1142	**370**	60g. black and bright violet	65	30
1143	-	1z.50 black, red and light blue	1·30	40
1144	-	2z.50 blackish brown	4·50	2·50
1142/1144 *Set of 3*			5·75	3·00

Designs: 22×35½ mm—1z.50 Portion of Chopin's music. 25×39½ mm—2z.50 Portrait of Chopin.

371 Polish 10k. Stamp of 1860 and Postmark

372 Discus

(Des A. Balcerzak. Litho)

1960 (21 Mar). Stamp Centenary. T **371** and similar vert designs. W **330**. Perf 11½×11.

1145	40g. rose, blue, black and light turquoise-blue	30	25
1146	60g. blue, black and violet	40	30
1147	1z.35 blue, red and grey	1·30	75
1148	1z.55 carmine, black and bluish green	1·90	50
	a. Black missing	£750	£650
1149	2z.50 deep myrtle-green, black and light yellow-olive	2·50	90
1145/1149 *Set of 5*		5·75	2·40

Designs: 40g. T **371**; 1z.35 Emblem inscr '1860 1960'. Reproductions of Polish stamps—60g. No. 356; 1z.55 No. 533; 2z.50 No. 1030; with appropriate postmarks.

A set of five miniature sheets, each containing a value of Nos. 1145/1149 in block of four, was presented to subscribers to the first volume of *Polskie Znaki Pocztowe* (*price* £1000 *mint per set*).

(Des Cz. Karczmarczyk. Eng M. R. Polak (No. 1150), S. Lukaszewski (Nos. 1152, 1156), B. Brandt (No. 1154), E. Konecki (No. 1155), B. Szymańska (No. 1157), E. Tirdiszek (No. 1158), J. Miller (others). Recess; background photo)

1960 (28 May). Provincial Costumes (2nd series). Vert designs as Types **368/369**. W **330**. Perf 12.

1150	40g. carmine and light blue	25	20
	a. Pair. Nos. 1150/1151	55	45
1151	40g. carmine and light blue	25	20
1152	2z. ultramarine and greenish yellow	30	25
	a. Pair. Nos. 1152/1153	65	55
1153	2z. ultramarine and greenish yellow	30	25
1154	3z.10 grey-green and sage green	40	30
	a. Pair. Nos. 1154/1155	85	65
1155	3z.10 grey-green and sage green	40	30
1156	3z.40 brown and pale blue	80	40
	a. Pair. Nos. 1156/1157	1·70	85
1157	3z.40 brown and pale blue	80	40
1158	6z.50 violet and green	1·70	65
	a. Pair. Nos. 1158/1159	3·75	1·40
1159	6z.50 violet and green	1·70	65
1150/1159 *Set of 10*		6·00	3·25

Designs: Male and female costumes of—Nos. 1150/1151, Cracow; Nos. 1152/1153, Lowicz; Nos. 1154/1155, Kujawy; Nos. 1156/1157, Lublin; Nos. 1158/1159, Lubski.

Stamps of the same value were issued together in *se-tenant* pairs within their sheets.

These also exist imperforate.

(Des S. Malecki. Litho centres embossed)

1960 (15 June). Olympic Games, Rome. T **372** and similar horiz designs. Perf 12×13.

1160	60g. greenish blue and black	40	30
	a. Block of 4. Nos. 1160/1163	1·70	
1161	60g. magenta and black	40	30
1162	60g. bright violet and black	40	30
1163	60g. bright blue-green and black	40	30
1164	2z.50 ultramarine and black	1·30	65
	a. Block of 4. Nos. 1164/1167	5·50	
1165	2z.50 orange-brown and black	1·30	65
1166	2z.50 orange-vermilion and black	1·30	65
1167	2z.50 emerald and black	1·30	65
1160/1167 *Set of 8*		6·00	3·50

Designs: Polish successes in previous Olympic Games—No. 1160 T **372**; No. 1161, Running; No. 1162, Cycling; No. 1163, Show jumping; No. 1164, Trumpeters; No. 1165, Boxing; No. 1166, Olympic Flame; No. 1167, Long jump.

Stamps of the same value were issued together in *se-tenant* blocks of four stamps within the sheet, each block illustrating a complete circuit of the stadium track.

These also exist imperforate.

373 King Wladislaw Jagiello's Tomb, Wawel Castle

374 1860 Stamp and Postmark

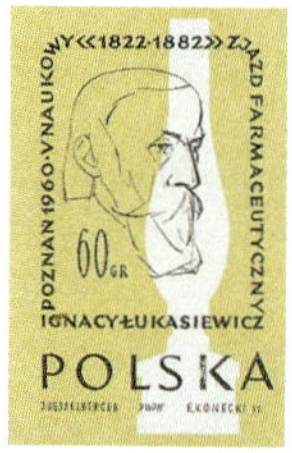

375 I. Lukasiewicz (inventor of paraffin lamp)

(Des Cz. Kaczmarczyk. Eng E. Konecki (60g.), S. Lukaszewski (90g.), J. Miller (2z.50). Recess)

1960 (15 July). 550th Anniversary of Battle of Grunwald. T **373** and other designs inscr 'GRUNWALD 1410–1960'. W **330**. Perf 11×11½.

1168	60g. chocolate	65	40
1169	90g. deep bronze-green	1·30	65
1170	2z.50 black	5·75	2·10
1168/1170 *Set of 3*		7·00	2·75

Designs: Vert—60g. T **373**; 90g. Proposed Grunwald monument. Horiz 78×35½ mm—Battle of Grunwald (after Matejko).

(Des A. Balcerzak. Litho)

1960 (4 Sept). International Philatelic Exhibition, Warsaw. W **330**. Perf 11×11½.

1171	**374**	10z.+10z. red, black and blue	12·00	11·50
		a. Balck omitted	£500	

Printed in sheets of four and sold only at the Exhibition (*prices* £75 *unused*, £70 *used*).

Sheets of four with black omitted are also known (*price* £2750).

(Des J. Desselberger. Eng E. Konecki. Recess; background photo)

1960 (14 Sept). Lukasiewicz Commemoration and Fifth Pharmaceutical Science Congress, Poznań. W **330**. Perf 11×11½.

1172	**375**	60g. black and olive-yellow	45	30

376 The Annunciation

377 Paderewski

(Des R. Kleczewski. Eng E. Konecki (20g., 2z.50), E. Tirdiszek (30g.), B. Brandt (40g.), B. Szymańska (60g.), J. Miller (5z.60), S. Lukaszewski (10z.). Recess)

1960 (20 Sept). Altar Wood Carvings of St Mary's Church, Cracow, by Veit Stoss. T **376** and similar horiz designs. W **330**. Perf 12½×12 or imperf (10z.).

1173	20g. slate-blue	40	25
1174	30g. red-brown	40	25
1175	40g. violet	40	30
1176	60g. deep grey-green	40	35
1177	2z.50 deep claret	1·90	65
1178	5z.60 sepia	11·50	8·25
1173/1178 *Set of 6*		13·50	9·00
MS1178*a* 86×107 mm. 10z. grey-black		14·00	9·75

Designs: 20g. T **376**; 30g. The Nativity; 40g. Homage of the Three Kings; 60g. The Resurrection; 2z.50 The Ascension; 5z.60 The Descent of the Holy Ghost. Vert 72×95 mm—10z. The Assumption of the Virgin.

(Des J. Desselberger. Eng E. Konecki. Recess)

1960 (26 Sept). Birth Centenary of Paderewski. W **330**. Perf 13×12½.

1179	**377**	2z.50 black	65	40

(378)

379 Gniezno

1960 (9 Oct). Stamp Day. T **371** Optd with T **378**.

1180	**371**	40g. rose, blue, black and light turquoise-blue	2·50	1·30

(Des W. Chomicz. Eng S. Lukaszewski (5g., 1z.15, 3z.10), A. Szklarczyk (10g., 50g., 5z.60), B. Kowalska (20g., 60g. (No. 1187)), E. Tirdiszek (40g., 95g., 1z.50, 2z.10), E. Konecki (60g. (No. 1186), 90g., 1z.35, 1z.55, 2z.50), B. Brandt (80g.), J. Miller (1z., 2z.). Recess)

1960 (15 Nov)–**61**. Old Polish Towns. Horiz designs as T **379**. Perf 13×12½ (95g.) or 11½×12 (others).

1181	5g. red-brown	20	20
	a. Perf 13×12½	20	20
1182	10g. blue-green	20	20
	a. Perf 13×12½	20	20
1183	20g. sepia	25	20
	a. Perf 13×12½	25	20
1184	40g. vermilion	25	20
	a. Perf 13×12½	25	20
1185	50g. violet	50	40
1186	60g. brown-lilac	30	25
	a. Perf 13×12½	30	25
1187	60g. dull ultramarine (12.5.61)	45	25
1188	80g. deep violet-blue	35	25
	a. Perf 13×12½	35	30
1189	90g. brown (12.5.61)	1·40	40
1190	95g. blackish olive	40	30
1191	1z. orange-red and pale lilac	35	30
1192	1z.15 bottle green and pale orange (28.12.60)	40	30
1193	1z.35 magenta and pale green (28.12.60)	40	30
1194	1z.50 bistre-brown and pale blue (28.12.60)	40	30
1195	1z.55 brown-lilac and pale yellow (28.12.60)	40	30
1196	2z. deep blue and pale lilac (28.12.60)	50	35
1197	2z.10 agate and pale yellow (28.12.60)	60	35
1198	2z.50 violet and pale green (28.12.60)	50	40
1199	3z.10 bright scarlet and pale grey (28.12.60)	1·90	85
1200	5z.60 slate and light grey-green (28.12.60)	4·75	2·00
1181/1200	*Set of 20*	13·00	7·25

Towns: 5g. T **379**; 10g. Cracow; 20g. Warsaw; 40g. Poznań; 50g. Plock; 60g. (No. 1186) Kalisz; 60g. (No. 1187) Tczew; 80g. Frombork; 90g. Toruń; 95g. Puck; 1z. Slupsk; 1z.15 Gdańsk; 1z.35 Wroclaw; 1z.50 Szczecin; 1z.55 Opole; 2z. Kolobrzeg; 2z.10 Legnica; 2z.50 Katowice; 3z.10 Łódź; 5z.60 Walbrzych.

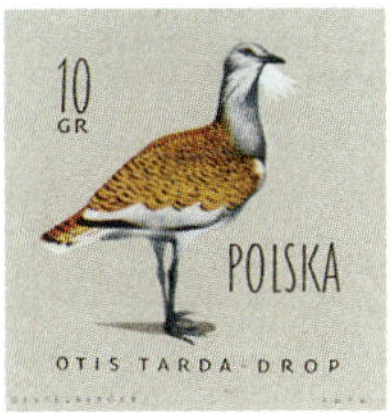

380 Great Bustard (*Otis tarda*)

381 Front page of newspaper *Prolètaryat* (1883)

(Des J. Desselberger. Photo)

1960 (26 Nov). Birds. T **380** and similar square designs. Multicoloured. Perf 11½.

1201	10g. Type **380**	40	25
1202	20g. Common Raven (*Corvus corax*)	40	25
1203	30g. Great Cormorant (*Phalacrocorax carbo*)	40	25
1204	40g. Black Stork (*Ciconia nigra*)	65	30
1205	50g. Eagle Owl (*Bubo bubo*)	65	30
1206	60g. White-tailed Sea Eagle (*Haliaeetus albicilla*)	90	30
1207	75g. Golden Eagle (*Aquila chrysaëtos*)	90	30
1208	90g. Short-toed Eagle (*Circaëtus gallicus*)	1·30	40
1209	2z.50 Rock Thrush (*Montcola saxatilis*)	6·75	3·25
1210	4z. River Kingfisher (*Alcedo atthis*)	5·00	1·50
1211	5z.60 Wallcreeper (*Tichodroma muraria*)	9·50	1·90
1212	6z.50 European Roller (*Coracias garrulus*)	12·50	4·50
1201/1212	*Set of 12*	35·00	12·00

(Des Cz. Kaczmarczyk. Litho; '300' embossed)

1961 (3 Jan). 300th Anniversary of Polish Newspaper Press. T **381** and similar vert designs. W **330**. Perf 12.

1213	-	40g. green, blue and black	65	40
1214	**381**	60g. yellow, brown-red and black	65	40
1215	-	2z.50 blue, violet and black	6·50	5·00
1213/1215		*Set of 3*	7·00	5·25

Designs: As T **381** but showing front page of newspapers—40g. *Merkuriusz* (first issue, 1661); 2z.50 *Rzeczpospolita* (1944).

382 Ice Hockey

383 Congress Emblem

(Des J. Grabiański. Litho)

1961 (1 Feb). First Winter Military Spartakiad. T **382** and similar vert designs. W **330**. Perf 12.

1216	40g. black, olive-yellow and lilac	65	40
1217	60g. black, carmine, violet-blue and cobalt	65	50
1218	1z. olive, black, red, deep blue and light blue	12·50	4·50
1219	1z.50 black, yellow and light turquoise-blue	65	65
1216/1219	*Set of 4*	13·50	5·50

Designs: 40g. T **382**; 60g. Ski jumping; 1z. Rifle shooting; 1z.50 Slalom.

(Des S. Jasiński. Litho)

1961 (11 Feb). Fourth Polish Engineers' Conference. W **330**. Perf 12½×13.

1220	**383**	60g. black and red	35	35

384 Yuri Gagarin

385 Fair Emblem

(Des A. Heidrich. Photo)

1961 (27 Apr). World's First Manned Space Flight. T **384** and similar horiz design inscr '12.1V.1961'. W **330**. Perf 12.

1221	40g. black, red and brown-red	1·00	35
1222	60g. red, black and blue	1·10	65

Designs: 40g. T **384**; 60g. Globe and star.

(Des Z. Kaja. Litho)

1961 (25 May). 30th International Fair, Poznań. W **330**. Perf 12½.

1223	**385**	40g. black, orange-red and blue	30	25
1224		1z.50 black, blue and orange-red	65	35

See also No. **MS**1245*a*.

386 King Mieszko I

(Des A. Heidrich. Eng A. Szklarczyk (No. 1225), S. Lukaszewski (No. 1226), J. Miller (No. 1227), E. Tirdiszek (No. 1228), E. Konecki (No. 1229), B. Kowalska (No. 1230). Recess; background photo)

1961 (15 June). Famous Poles (1st series). T **386** and similar horiz portrait designs. W **330**. Perf 11×12.

1225	60g. black and blue	40	30
1226	60g. black and claret	40	30
1227	60g. black and grey-green	40	30
1228	60g. black and violet	1·30	40
1229	60g. black and light brown	40	30
1230	60g. black and olive-brown	40	30
1225/1230	*Set of 6*	3·00	1·70

Portraits: No. 1225, T **386**; No. 1226, King Casimir the Great; No. 1227, King Casimir Jagiellon; No. 1228, Copernicus; No 1229, A. F. Modrzewski; No. 1230, Kościuszko.

See also Nos. 1301/1306 and 1398/1401.

387 *Leskov* (trawler support ship)

(Des J. Desselberger. Litho)

1961 (24 June). Shipbuilding Industry. T **387** and similar horiz designs. Multicoloured. Perf 11.

1231	60g. Type **387**	40	25
1232	1z.55 *Severodvinsk* (depot ship)	75	35
1233	2z.50 *Rambutan* (coaster)	1·10	50
1234	3z.40 *Krynica* (freighter)	1·60	65
1235	4z. Type B54 (freighter)	2·75	1·30
1236	5z.60 *Baysk* (tanker)	6·25	3·00
1231/1236	*Set of* 6	11·50	5·50

Sizes: As T **387**—60g., 2z.50. 81×21 mm—1z.55, 3z.40, 4z. 108×21 mm—5z.60.

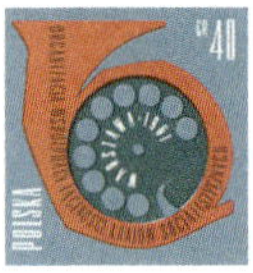

388 Posthorn and Telephone Dial

389 Opole Seal

390 Beribboned Paddle

(Des S. Malecki. Litho)

1961 (26 June). Communications Ministers' Conference, Warsaw. T **388** and similar designs. No wmk or W **330** (No. **MS**1239*a*). Perf 11.

1237	**388**	40g. orange-red, deep green and slate-blue	35	25
1238	-	60g. brown, violet, yellow and light slate-purple	35	25
1239	-	2z.50 ultramarine, light blue and bistre-brown	1·10	40
1237/1239		*Set of* 3	1·60	75
MS1239*a*		108×66 mm. Nos. 1237/1239 (*sold at* 5z.)	12·00	5·75

Designs: Posthorn and 60g. Radar screen; 2z.50 Conference emblem.

(Des Cz. Kaczmarczyk. Eng A. Szklarczyk (1240), E. Konecki (1241, 1243), S. Lukaszewski (1242), B. Kowalska (1243), E. Tirdiszek (1243, 1244), J. Miller (1245). Recess and photo)

1961 (21 July)–**62**. Polish Western Provinces. T **389** and similar designs. W **330**. Perf 11.

1240	40g. deep chocolate and grey-brown	30	20
	a. Pair. Nos. 1240/1241 plus label	65	45
1241	40g. deep chocolate and grey-brown	30	20
1242	60g. deep reddish violet and pink	35	25
	a. Pair. Nos. 1242/1243 plus label	75	55
1243	60g. deep reddish violet and pink	35	25
1243*a*	95g. myrtle green and turquoise-blue (23.2.62)	55	35
	ab. Pair. Nos. 1243*a*/1243*b* plus label	1·20	75
1243*b*	95g. myrtle green and turquoise-blue (23.2.62)	55	35
1244	2z.50 bronze green and yellow-olive	1·10	65
	a. Pair. Nos. 1244/1245 plus label	2·30	1·40
1245	2z.50 bronze green and yellow-olive	1·10	65
1240/1245	*Set of* 8	4·25	2·50

Designs: Vert—No. 1240, T **389**; No. 1242, Henry IV's tomb; No. 1243*a*, Seal of Conrad II; No. 1244, Prince Barnim's seal. Horiz—No. 1241, Opole cement works; No. 1243, Wroclaw apartment house; No. 1243*b*, Factory interior, Zielona Góra; No. 1245, Szczecin harbour.

Stamps of the same value were issued together *se-tenant* with 23 stamp-size inscribed label.

See also Nos. 1308/1313.

1961 (29 July). Intermess II Stamp Exhibition. Sheet 121×51 mm containing pair of No. 1224 but imperf.

MS1245*a*	1z.50×2 (*sold at* 4z.50+2z.50)	9·50	5·25

(Des R. Dudzicki. Litho)

1961 (18 Aug). Sixth European Canoeing Championships. T **390** and similar designs. W **330**. Perf 12½.

1246	40g. red, yellow, green, blue and turquoise	35	25
1247	60g. red, yellow, violet and blue	35	25
1248	2z.50 red, yellow, violet, grey-green and slate	2·50	1·00
1246/1248	*Set of* 3	3·00	1·40

Designs: Vert—2z.50 T **390**. Horiz—40g. Two canoes within letter 'E'; 60g. Two four-seater canoes at finishing post.

These also exist imperforate.

391 Titov and Orbit within Star

392 Monument

(Des S. Bernaciński. Photo)

1961 (24 Aug). Second Russian Manned Space Flight. T **391** and similar horiz design inscr '700,000 KM W KOSMOSIE' etc. Perf 12×13.

1249	40g. black, red and pale pink	80	30
1250	60g. blue and black	90	40

Designs: 40g. T **391**; 60g. Dove and spaceman's orbit around globe.

(Des J. Desselberger. Litho)

1961 (15 Sept). 40th Anniversary of Third Silesian Uprising. T **392** and similar vert design inscr '40 ROCZNICA TRZECIEGO' etc. W **330**. Perf 12.

1251	60g. grey and emerald	30	25
1252	1z.55 grey and light blue	50	30

Designs: 60g. T **392**; 1z.55 Cross of Silesian uprisers.

393 PKO Emblem and Ant

394 Mail Cart (after J. Chelmonski)

(Des S. Malecki. Litho)

1961 (30 Sept). Savings Month. T **393** and similar horiz designs. W **330**. Perf 12.

1253	40g. orange-red, yellow and black	30	25
1254	60g. brown, yellow and black	35	30
1255	60g. blue, violet and pink	35	30
1256	60g. green, orange-red and black	50	30
1257	2z.50 magenta, grey and black	3·75	1·90
1253/1257	*Set of* 5	4·75	2·75

Designs: No. 1253, Savings Bank motif; No. 1254, T **393**; No. 1255, Bee; No. 1256, Squirrel; No. 1257, Savings Bank book.

(Des Cz. Kaczmarczyk. Eng J. Miller. Recess)

1961 (9 Oct). Stamp Day and 40th Anniversary of Postal Museum. W **330**. Perf 12×12½.

1258	**394**	60g. chocolate	50	35
1259		60g. deep green	50	35

395 Congress Emblem

396 Emblem of Kopasyni mining family, 1284

(Des S. Jasiński. Eng B. Kowalska. Recess)

1961 (20 Nov). Fifth World Federation of Trade Unions' Congress, Moscow. W **330**. Perf 12×12½.

1260	**395**	60g. black	40	30

(Des S. Miklaszewski. Litho)

1961 (4 Dec). Millenary of Polish Mining Industry. As T **396**, inscr 'TYSIACLECIE GORNICTWA POLSKIEGO'. W **330**. Perf 11×11½.

1261	40g. brown-purple, orange and light orange	25	20
1262	60g. grey-blue, ultramarine and light blue	30	25
1263	2z.50 green, black and light green	1·30	40
1261/1263	*Set of* 3	1·70	75

Designs: 40g. T **396**; 60g. 14th-century seal of Bytom; 2z.50 Emblem of International Mine Constructors' Congress, Warsaw, 1958.

397 Child and Syringe

(Des S. Gospodarek. Litho)

1961 (11 Dec). 15th Anniversary of UNICEF. T **397** and similar designs inscr '1961 XV ROCZNICA POWSTANIA UNICEF'. W **330**. Perf 12×12½ (60g.) or 12½×12 (others).

1264	40g. black and light blue	30	25
1265	60g. black and yellow-orange	35	30
1266	2z.50 black and turquoise-green	1·00	40
1264/1266	*Set of* 3	1·50	85

Designs: Horiz—60g. Children of three races. Vert—40g. T **397**; 2z.50 Mother and child, and feeding bottle.

398 Cogwheel and Wheat

399 *Calosoma sycophanta*

(Des Cz. Kaczmarczyk. Litho)

1961 (12 Dec). 15th Economic Co-operative Council Meeting, Warsaw. T **398** and similar horiz design. W **330**. Perf 12.

1267	40g. crimson, yellow and black	30	30
1268	60g. red, light blue and ultramarine	40	35

Designs: 40g. T **398**; 60g. Oil pipeline map, Eastern Europe.

(Des J. Desselberger (Nos. 1269/1274), A. Balcerzak (Nos. 1275/1278), A. Heidrich (Nos. 1279/1280). Photo)

1961 (30 Dec). Insects. T **399** and similar multicoloured designs. Perf 13×12 (20g. to 80g.) or 11½ (1z.15 to 5z.60).

1269	20g. Type **399**	35	25
1270	30g. *Carabus violaceus*	35	25
1271	40g. *Rosalia alpina*	35	25
1272	50g. *Cerambyx cerdo*	35	25
1273	60g. *Carabus auronitens*	40	30
1274	80g. *Lucanus cervus*	40	30
1275	1z.15 *Parnassius mnemosyne*	70	30
1276	1z.35 *Acherintia atropos*	70	30
1277	1z.50 *Iphiclides podalirius* (*Papilio podalirius*)	1·40	40
1278	1z.55 *Parnassius apollo*	1·10	40
1279	2z.50 *Formica rufa*	2·75	85
1280	5z.60 *Bombus lucorum*	12·50	5·25
1269/1280	*Set of* 12	19·00	8·25

Sizes: As T **399**—20g. to 80g. 36½×36½ mm—1z.15 to 5z.60.

400 Worker with Flag and Dove

401 Two Skiers Racing

(Des J. Desselberger. Litho)

1962 (5 Jan). 20th Anniversary of Polish Workers' Coalition. T **400** and similar vert designs. Perf 12½×12.

1281	60g. sepia, black and vermilion	40	25
1282	60g. bistre, black and vermilion	40	25
1283	60g. violet, black and vermilion	40	25
1284	60g. slate-green, black and vermilion	40	25
1285	60g. grey-blue, black and vermilion	40	25
1281/1285	*Set of* 5	1·80	1·10

Designs: No. 1281 T **400**; No. 1282, helmsman; No. 1283, Worker with hammer; No. 1284, Soldier with weapon; 1No. 285, Worker with trowel and rifle.

(Des S. Toepfer. Litho. Central figures embossed in colour)

1962 (14 Feb). FIS International Ski Championships, Zakopane. T **401** and similar designs. Perf 12×12½ (1z.50), 12½×12 (40, 60g.) or imperf (10z.).

1286	**401**	40g. slate-blue, grey and red	30	25
1287		40g. grey-blue, bistre-brown and red	1·30	40
1288	–	60g. slate-blue, grey and red	35	30
1289	–	60g. indigo, bistre-brown and red	1·90	90
1290	–	1z.50 slate-blue, grey and red	40	30
1291	-	1z.50 violet, grey and red	3·75	1·90
1286/1291		*Set of* 6	7·25	3·75
MS1291*a*		67×80 mm. 10z.(+5z.) slate-blue, grey and red	7·50	6·25

Designs: Horiz—40g. T **401**; 60g. Skier racing. Vert—1z.50 Ski-jumper; 10z. FIS emblem.

Nos. 1286, 1288 and 1290 also exist in sheets of four, perf 11×11½ or 11½×11 (*price per set of 3 sheets £325 unused*).

402 Majdanek Monument

(Des S. Jasiński. Eng J. Miller (40g.), E. Konecki (60g.), B. Kowalska (1z.50). Recess)

1962 (2 Apr). Concentration Camp Monuments. T **402** and similar designs. W **330**. Perf 11½.

1292	40g. deep blue	30	25
1293	60g. black	40	30
1294	1z.50 violet	70	40
1292/1294	*Set of* 3	1·30	85

Designs: Horiz—60g. T **402**. Vert 20×31 mm—40g. Broken carnations and portion of prison clothing (Oswiecim or Auschwitz Camp); 1z.50 Treblinka Monument.

403 Racing Cyclist

(Des S. Malecki. Litho)

1962 (27 Apr). 15th International Peace Cycle Race. T **403** and similar horiz designs. W **330**. Perf 12.

1295	60g. black and blue	40	30
1296	2z.50 black and yellow	1·00	40
1297	3z.40 black and light reddish violet	2·00	70
1295/1297	*Set of* 3	3·00	1·30

Designs: As T **403**—60g. T **403**; 3z.40 Arms of Berlin, Prague and Warsaw, and cycle wheel. 74½×22 mm—2z.50 Cyclists and 'XV'.

405 Lenin walking

406 General K. Swierczewski-Walter (monument)

407 *Crocus scepusiensis* (Borb)

(Des S. Malecki. Eng E. Tirdiszek (40g.), A. Szklarczyk (60g.), B. Kowalska (2z.50). Recess)

1962 (25 May). 50th Anniversary of Lenin's Sojourn in Poland. T **405** and similar vert designs inscr '1912–1962'. W **330**. Perf 11×11½.

1298	40g. deep bluish green and pale green	65	40
1299	60g. lake and pale pink	40	30
1300	2z.50 sepia and pale yellow	1·30	50
1298/1300 *Set of* 3		2·10	1·10

Designs: 40g. T **405**; 60g. Lenin; 2z.50 Lenin wearing cap, and St Mary's Church, Cracow.

(Des A. Heidrich; eng S. Lukaszewski (No. 1301), J. Miller (No. 1302). Recess; background photo. Des A. Heidrich. Litho (others))

1962 (20 June). Famous Poles (2nd series). Portrait designs as T **386**. W **330**. Perf 11×12 (Nos. 1301/1302) or 12×12½ (others).

1301	60g. black and light grey-green	40	30
1302	60g. black and orange-brown	40	30
1303	60g. black and blue	40	30
1304	60g. black and brown-bistre	40	30
1305	60g. black and reddish purple	40	30
1306	60g. black and deep bluish green	40	30
1301/1306 *Set of* 6		2·20	1·60

Portraits: No. 1301, A. Mickiewicz (poet); No. 1302, J. Slowacki (poet); No. 1303, F. Chopin (composer); No. 1304, R. Traugutt (patriot); No. 1305, J. Dabrowski (revolutionary); No. 1306, Maria Konopnicka (poet).

(Des S. Jasiński. Eng J. Miller. Recess)

1962 (14 July). 15th Anniversary of Death of General K. Swierczewski-Walter (patriot). Perf 11×11½.

1307	**406**	60g. black	40	30

(Des Cz. Kaczmarczyk. Eng E. Tirdszek (No. 1308), A. Szklarczyk (No. 1309), Z. Kowalski (No. 1310), E. Konecki (Nos. 1311, 1312), J. Miller (No. 1313). Recess and photo)

1962 (21 July). Polish Northern Provinces. Designs as T **389**. Perf 11.

1308	60g. deep violet-blue and bluish grey	30	25
	a. Pair. Nos. 1308/1309 plus label	65	55
1309	60g. deep violet-blue and bluish grey	30	25
1310	1z.55 sepia and pale yellow	40	30
	a. Pair. Nos. 1310/1311 plus label	85	65
1311	1z.55 sepia and pale yellow	40	30
1312	2z.50 greenish slate and greenish grey	90	40
	a. Pair. Nos. 1312/1313 plus label	1·90	85
1313	2z.50 greenish slate and greenish grey	90	40
1308/1313 *Set of* 6		3·00	1·70

Designs: Vert—No. 1308, Princess Elizabeth's seal; No. 1310, Gdańsk Governor's seal; No. 1312, Frombork Cathedral. Horiz—No. 1309, Insulator factory, Szczecinek; No. 1311, Gdańsk shipyard; No. 1313, Laboratory of Agricultural College, Kortowo.

Stamps of the same value were issued together *se-tenant* with 23 stamp-size inscribed label.

(Des A. Balcerzak. Photo)

1962 (8 Aug). Polish Protected Plants. T **407** and similar vert designs. Plants in natural colours. Perf 12.

1314	60g. yellow	30	25
1315	60g. cinnamon	1·30	65
1316	60g. pink	30	25
1317	90g. yellow-green	40	30
1318	90g. yellow-olive	40	30
1319	90g. green	40	30
1320	1z.50 grey-blue	65	40
1321	1z.50 light green	65	40
1322	1z.50 bluish green	65	40
1323	2z.50 grey-green	1·50	90
1324	2z.50 turquoise	1·90	90
1325	2z.50 violet-blue	2·10	90
1314/1325 *Set of* 12		9·50	5·25

Plants: No. 1314, T **407**; No. 1315, *Platanthera bifolia* (Rich); No. 1316, *Aconitum callibotryon* (Rchb); No. 1317, *Gentiana clusii* (Perr. et Song); No. 1318, *Dictamnus albus* (L); No. 1319, *Nymphaea alba* (L.); No. 1320, *Daphne mezereum* (L.); No. 1321, *Pulsatilla vulgaris* (Mill.); No. 1322, *Anemone Silvestris* (L.); No. 1323, *Trollius europaeus* (L.); No. 1324, *Galanthus nivalis* (L.); No. 1325, *Adonis vernalis* (L.).

408 The Poisoned Well, after J. Malczewski

409 Pole Vault

(Des J. Desselberger. Eng E. Tirdiszek. Recess)

1962 (25 Aug). FIP Day (1st September, Federation Internationale de Philatélie). W **330**. Perf 11½.

1326	**408**	60g. black/*cream*	90	65

No. 1326 was printed in sheets of 40 stamps *se-tenant* with labels inscribed 'FILA-TELISTYKA ZBLIZA LUDZI WSZYSTKICH KRAJOW' (Philately unites people of all countries).

It also exists in sheets of four stamps and four labels (*price* £55).

(Des R. Dudzicki. Litho)

1962 (12 Sept). Seventh European Athletic Championships, Belgrade. T **409** and similar horiz designs. Multicoloured. Perf 11.

1327	40g. Type **409**	25	20
1328	60g. 400 m relay	25	20
1329	90g. Javelin	30	25
1330	1z. Hurdling	30	25
1331	1z.50 High jump	30	30
1332	1z.55 Discus	30	30
1333	2z.50 100 m final	45	30
1334	3z.40 Hammer throwing	1·70	40
1327/1334 *Set of* 8		3·50	2·00

The above exist imperforate.

410 *Anopheles* sp (mosquito)

(Des S. Malecki. Litho)

1962 (1 Oct). Malaria Eradication. T **410** and similar vert designs. W **330**. Perf 13×12 or imperf (3z.).

1335	60g. olive-brown and deep bluish green	30	25
1336	1z.50 pink, grey, violet and red	35	30
1337	2z.50 orange, yellow-green, ultramarine and greenish grey	1·50	65
1335/1337 *Set of* 3		2·00	1·00
MS1337*a* 60×81 mm. 3z. multicoloured		2·50	1·50

Designs: 60g. T **410**; 1z.50 Malaria parasites in blood; 2z.50 Cinchona plant; 3z. *Anopheles* mosquito.

411 Cosmonauts in Flight

(Des J. Desselberger. Litho)

1962 (6 Oct). First Team Manned Space Flight. T **411** and similar vert design. W **330**. Perf 12½×12 or 11½×11 (10z.).

1338	60g. yellow-green, black and bluish violet	40	30
1339	2z.50 red, black and turquoise-blue	1·00	40
	a. 'PWPW' missing (pos. 11)	25·00	12·50
MS1339*b* 70×94 mm. 10z. red, black and turquoise-blue		5·00	3·50

Designs: 60g. T **411**; 2z.50, 10z. Two stars (representing spaceships) in orbit.

412 A Moment of Determination (after painting by A. Kamiński)

413 Mazovian Princes' Mansion, Warsaw

(Des H. Przeździecka. Eng B. Kowalska. Recess)

1962 (9 Oct). Stamp Day. W **330**. Perf 13×12.

1340	**412**	60g. black	40	30
1341		2z.50 red-brown	1·10	40

(Des Cz. Kaczmarczyk. Litho)

1962 (13 Oct). 25th Anniversary of Polish Democratic Party. W **330**. Perf 13×12.

1342	**413**	60g. black/*red*	40	30

414 *Aurora* (Russian cruiser)

415 J. Korczak (bust after Dunikowski)

(Des S. Malecki. Eng Z. Kowalski. Recess and photo)

1962 (3 Nov). 45th Anniversary of Russian Revolution. W **330**. Perf 11.

1343	**414**	60g. grey-blue and orange-red	40	30

(Des J. Srokowski. Litho)

1962 (12 Nov). 20th Death Anniversary of Janusz Korczak (child educator). T **415** and similar vert designs. Perf 13×12.

1344	40g. sepia, light bistre and red-brown	30	25
1345	60g. multicoloured	40	30
1346	90g. multicoloured	90	40
1347	1z. multicoloured	90	40
1348	2z.50 multicoloured	1·30	90
1349	5z.60 multicoloured	3·75	1·50
1344/1349	*Set of 6*	6·75	3·50

Designs: 40g. T **415**; 60g. to 5z.60 Illustrations from Korczak's children's books.

416 Old Town, Warsaw

417 Master Buncombe

(Des A. Heidrich. Litho)

1962 (26 Nov). Fifth Trade Unions Congress, Warsaw. W **330**. Perf 11.

1350	**416**	3z.40 grey-blue, red, black and cream	1·50	65

Also printed in sheets of four (*price* £12·00).

(Des J. M. Szancer. Litho)

1962 (31 Dec). Maria Konopnicka's Fairy Tale *The Dwarfs and Orphan Mary*. T **417** and similar vert designs. Multicoloured. Perf 12½×12.

1351	40g. Type **417**	1·00	30
1352	60g. Lardie the Fox and Master Buncombe	3·75	1·30
1353	1z.50 Bluey and the frog	1·10	40
1354	1z.55 Peter's kitchen	1·10	65
1355	2z.50 Saraband's concert	1·30	65
1356	3z.40 Orphan Mary and Subearthy	4·50	3·25
1351/1356	*Set of 6*	11·50	6·00

418 R. Traugutt (insurgent leader)

419 Tractor and Wheat

(Des A. Heidrich. Litho)

1963 (31 Jan). Centenary of January (1863) Rising. W **330**. Perf 11½×11.

1357	**418**	60g. black, pale pink and turquoise-blue	40	30

(Des A. Heidrich. Litho)

1963 (25 Feb). Freedom from Hunger. T **419** and similar horiz designs. Multicoloured. W **330**. Perf 12×12½.

1358	40g. Type **419**	30	25
1359	60g. Millet and hoeing	1·00	40
1360	2z.50 Rice and mechanical harvester	2·10	75
1358/1360	*Set of 3*	3·00	1·30

420 Cocker Spaniel

421 Egyptian Galley (15th Century, BC)

(Des J. Grabiański. Litho)

1963 (25 Mar). Dogs. Designs as T **420**. Perf 12½.

1361	20g. orange, red, black and lilac	25	20
1362	30g. black and carmine	30	25
1363	40g. yellow-ochre, black and lilac	30	30
1364	50g. yellow-ochre, black and blue	40	30
1365	60g. black and light blue	65	40
1366	1z. black and yellow-green	90	40
1367	2z.50 brown, yellow and black	1·90	75
1368	3z.40 black and vermilion	4·50	1·90
1369	6z.50 black and greenish yellow	10·00	7·50
1361/1369	*Set of 9*	17·00	11·00

Dogs: Horiz—20g. T **420**; 30g. Sheepdog; 40g. Boxer; 2z.50 Gundog Ogar; 6z.50 Great Dane. Vert—50g. Airedale terrier; 60g. French bulldog; 1z. French poodle; 3z.40 Podhale sheepdog.

(Des S. Malecki. Eng Z. Kowalski (5g., 1z.15), A. Szklarczyk (10g., 60g.), J. Miller (20g.), B. Kowalska (30g., 40g.), E. Tirdiszek (1z.). Recess and photo)

1963 (5 Apr). Sailing Ships (1st series). Horiz designs as T **421**. Perf 11½×12.

1370	5g. red-brown/*light bistre*	20	20
1371	10g. deep bluish green/*light green*	20	20
1372	20g. ultramarine/*light violet*	20	20
1373	30g. black/*yellow-olive*	25	20
1374	40g. blue/*light blue*	30	25
1375	60g. purple/*light grey-brown*	30	30
1376	1z. black/*light blue*	40	35
1377	1z.15 green/*light pink*	75	40
1370/1377	*Set of 8*	2·30	1·90

Ships: 5g. T **421**; 10g. Phoenician merchantman (15th century BC); 20g. Greek trireme (5th century BC); 30g. Roman merchantman (3rd century AD); 40g. *Mora* (Norman ship, 1066); 60g. Hanse kogge (14th century); 1z. Holk (14th century); 1z.15 Carrack (15th century).

See also Nos. 1451/1466.

422 Insurgent

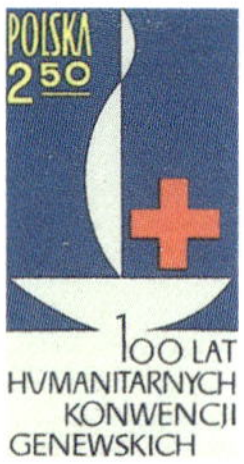

423 Centenary Emblem

(Des S. Jasiński. Eng J. Miller. Recess and photo)

1963 (19 Apr). 20th Anniversary of Warsaw Ghetto Uprising. W **330**. Perf 11½×11.

1378	**422**	2z.50 deep purple-brown and pale blue	65	40

(Des F. Winiarski. Litho)

1963 (8 May). Red Cross Centenary. Perf 12½×12.

1379	**423**	2z.50 red, blue and greenish yellow	1·50	40
		a. *Tête-bêche* (pair)	6·25	3·75

No. 1379 is arranged in sheets with alternate horizontal rows inverted.

424 Lizard

425 Epée, Foil, Sabre and Knight's Helmet

(Des J. Desselberger. Photo)

1963 (10 June). Protected Reptiles and Amphibians. T **424** and similar designs. Reptiles in natural colours; inscriptions and values black; background colours given. Perf 11½.

1380	30g. grey-green	25	20
1381	40g. olive	30	20
1382	50g. light brown	30	20
1383	60g. drab	30	20
1384	90g. myrtle	30	25
1385	1z.15 grey	30	25
1386	1z.35 grey-blue	45	30
1387	1z.50 turquoise-green	55	30
1388	1z.55 pale grey-blue	95	40
1389	2z.50 lavender	95	40
1390	3z. myrtle-green	1·90	65
1391	3z.40 slate-purple	4·50	3·75
1380/1391	*Set of 12*	10·00	6·50

Reptiles: 30g. T **424**; 40g. Copperhead (snake); 50g. Marsh tortoise; 60g. Grass snake; 90g. Blindworm; 1z.15 Tree toad; 1z.35 Mountain newt; 1z.50 Crested newt; 1z.55 Green toad; 2z.50 Bombina toad; 3z. Salamander; 3z.40 Natterjack toad.

(Des K. Tarkowska. Litho)

1963 (29 June). World Fencing Championships. Gdańsk. T **425** and similar designs. Perf 11×11½ (No. **MS**1397*a*), 13×12 (6z.50) or 12×13 (others).

1392	20g. orange-yellow and red-brown	20	20
1393	40g. light blue and blue	25	20
1394	60g. light red and carmine-red	30	25
1395	1z.15 light green and green	40	30
1396	1z.55 reddish violet and violet	90	40
1397	6z.50 yellow, brown-purple and light bistre-brown	2·75	90
1392/1397	*Set of 6*	4·25	2·00
MS1397*a*	110×93 mm. Nos. 1393/1396	70·00	70·00

Designs: Horiz 20g. T **425**. Fencers with background of—40g. Knights jousting; 60g. Dragoons in sword fight; 1z.15 18th-century duellists; 1z.55 Old Gdańsk. Vert–6z.50 Inscription and Arms of Gdańsk.

(Des A. Heidrich. Litho)

1963 (20 July). Famous Poles (3rd series). Portrait designs as T **386**. W **330**. Perf 12×12.

1398	60g. black and brown-red	45	30
1399	60g. black and sepia	45	30
1400	60g. black and light greenish blue	45	30
1401	60g. black and green	45	30
1398/1401	*Set of 4*	1·60	1·10

Portraits: No. 1398, L. Waryński (patriot), No. 1399, L. Krzywicki, (economist); No. 1400, M. Sklodowska-Curie (scientist); No. 1401, K. Świerczewski (patriot).

426 Bykovsky and *Vostok 5*

(Des T. Michaluk. Litho)

1963 (26 Aug). Second Team Manned Space Flights. T **426** and similar horiz designs. Perf 11.

1402	40g. black, green and blue	30	25
1403	60g. black, blue and bluish green	40	30
1404	6z.50 green, blue, black and red	2·10	65
1402/1404	*Set of 3*	2·50	1·10

Designs: 40g. T **426**; 60g. Tereshkova and *Vostok 6*; 6z.50 *Vostok 5* and *Vostok 6* in orbit.

427 Basketball

428 Missile

(Des T. Michaluk. Litho)

1963 (16 Sept). 13th European (Men's) Basketball Championships, Wroclaw. T **427** and similar designs. Perf 11½ or imperf (10z.).

1405	**427**	40g. green, brown black and yellow	20	20
1406	-	50g. green, black and pink	25	20
1407	-	60g. black, light green and red	30	25
1408	-	90g. violet, red-brown, black and light emerald	30	30
1409	-	2z.50 black, orange, red-brown and cobalt	40	35
1410	-	5z.60 black, cream, light green and blue	2·75	40
1405/1410		*Set of 6*	3·75	1·50
MS1410*a*		76×86 mm 10z.(+5z.) multicoloured	3·50	2·00

Designs: 50g. to 2z.50, As T **427** but with ball, players and hands in various positions; 5z.60 Hands placing ball in net; 10z. Town Hall, People's Hall and Arms of Wroclaw.

(Des R. Dudzicki. Litho)

1963 (1 Oct). 20th Anniversary of Polish People's Army. T **428** and similar horiz designs. Multicoloured. Perf 12×12½.

1411	20g. Type **428**	20	20
1412	40g. *Błyskawica* (destroyer)	20	20
1413	60g. Mikoyan Gurevich MiG-21C	25	20
1414	1z.15 Radar scanner	30	25
1415	1z.35 Tank	30	30
1416	1z.55 Missile carrier	40	30
1417	2z.50 Amphibious troop carrier	65	35
1418	3z. Ancient warrior, modern soldier and two swords	1·30	40
1411/1418	*Set of 8*	3·25	2·00

429 A Love Letter (after Czachorski)

23–28. X. 1963
W. F. Bykowski
w Polsce

(430)

(Des Cz. Kaczmarczyk. Eng E. Konecki. Recess)

1963 (9 Oct). Stamp Day. Perf 11½.

1419	**429**	60g. red-brown	45	30

1963 (23 Oct). Visit of Soviet Cosmonauts to Poland. Nos. 1402/1404 optd diagonally as T **430**, or horiz in small capitals at foot (6z.50).

1420	40g. black, green and blue (R.)	65	40
1421	60g. black, blue and bluish green	65	40
1422	6z.50 green, blue, black and red	2·75	1·90
1420/1422	*Set of 3*	3·75	2·40

431 Tsiolkovsky's Rocket and Formula

432 Mazurian Horses

(Des J. Desselberger. Litho)

1963 (25 Nov). The Conquest of Space. T **431** and similar vert designs. Perf 13×12.

1423	30g. deep turquoise-green and black	20	20
1424	40g. yellow-olive and black	25	20
1425	50g. violet-blue and black	30	20
1426	60g. orange brown and black	30	20
1427	1z. blue-green and black	30	25
1428	1z.50 brown-red and black	40	25
1429	1z.55 blue and black	40	25
1430	2z.50 purple and black	65	30
1431	5z.50 yellow-green and black	1·30	35
1432	6z.50 turquoise-blue and black	2·50	40
1423/1432 *Set of* 10		6·00	2·30
MS1432*a* 78×106 mm. Nos. 1431/1432 (two of each)		80·00	80·00

Designs: 30g. T **431**; 40g. *Sputnik 1*; 50g. *Explorer 1*; 60g. Banner carried by *Lunik 2*; 1z. *Lunik 3*; 1z.50 *Vostok 1*; 1z.55 *Friendship 7*; 2z.50 *Vostok 3* and *Vostok 4*; 5z.60 *Mariner 2*; 6z.50 *Mars 1*.

The perforations on No. **MS**1432*a* extend top and bottom.

No. **MS**1432*a* also exists without perforations extending into the margins at the top of the sheet (*price* £150 *unused*., £150 *used*).

(Des L. Maciąg. Photo)

1963 (31 Dec). Polish Horse Breeding. Designs as T **432**. Multicoloured. Perf 11½×11 (20g., 30g., 40g.), 12½×12 (50g., 90g., 4z.) or 13×12 (others).

1433	20g. Arab stallion, Comet	20	20
1434	30g. Wild horses	20	20
1435	40g. Sokólski horse	25	20
1436	50g. Arab mares and foals	30	25
1437	60g. Type **432**	30	25
1438	90g. Steeplechasers	40	30
1439	1z.55 Arab stallion, Witez II	90	35
1440	2z.50 Head of Arab horse (facing right)	1·50	40
1441	4z. Mixed breeds	3·75	90
1442	6z.50 Head of Arab horse (facing left)	5·00	4·00
1433/1442 *Set of* 10		11·50	6·25

Sizes: Triangular 55×27½ mm—20g., 30g., 40g. Horiz 75×26 mm—50g., 90g., 4z. Vert as T **432**, 60g., 1z.55, 2z.50, 6z.50.

433 Ice Hockey

434 Flourishing Tree

(Des F. Winiarski. Litho)

1964 (25 Jan). Winter Olympic Games, Innsbruck. Horiz designs as T **433**. Multicoloured. Perf 12×13 or 11×11½ (No. **MS**1450*a*).

1443	20g. Type **433**	20	20
1444	30g. Slalom	25	20
1445	40g. Downhill skiing	30	25
1446	60g. Speed skating	40	30
1447	1z. Ski jumping	50	35
1448	2z.50 Tobogganing	1·00	40
1449	5z.60 Cross-country skiing	2·10	90
1450	6z.50 Pairs, figure skating	3·25	1·30
1443/1450 *Set of* 8		7·25	3·50
MS1450*a* 110×94 mm. Nos. 1448 and 1450 (two of each)		44·00	41·00

(Des S. Malecki 5g. to 1z.15 eng as Nos. 1370/7; others eng E. Konecki (1z.35, 3z.40), E. Tirdiszek (1z.50), A. Szklarczyk (1z.55), Z. Kowalski (2z., 2z.50), J. Miller (2z.10), B. Kowalska (3z.). Recess)

1964 (19 Mar)–**65**. Sailing Ships (2nd series). Designs as T **421** but without coloured backgrounds. Perf 12½×13 (vert) or 13×12½ (horiz).

1451	5g. reddish brown (25.1.65)	20	20
1452	10g. deep dull green (25.1.65)	20	20
1453	20g. slate-blue (25.1.65)	20	20
	a. Perf 11½×12	20	20
1454	30g. bronze green (25.1.65)	25	20
1455	40g. grey-blue (25.1.65)	30	20
1456	60g. deep claret (25.1.65)	30	20
	a. Perf 11½×12	30	20
1457	1z. chestnut (25.1.65)	30	20
	a. Perf 11½×12	30	20
1458	1z.15 red-brown (25.1.65)	30	20
1459	1z.35 blue	30	25
	a. Perf 12×11½	30	25
1460	1z.50 maroon	30	25
1461	1z.55 black	30	25
	a. Perf 12×11½	30	25
1462	2z. deep reddish violet	40	30
1463	2z.10 blue-green	50	30
	a. Perf 11½×12	50	30
1464	2z.50 magenta	65	35
1465	3z. deep olive	90	35
	a. Perf 11½×12	90	35
1466	3z.40 brown	1·40	40
	a. Perf 12×11½	1·40	40
1451/1466 *Set of* 16		6·00	3·75

Ships: Horiz—5g. to 1z.15 As Nos. 1370/1377; 1z.50 *Ark Royal* (English galleon, 1587); 2z.10 Ship of the line (18th century); 2z.50 Sail frigate (19th century); 3z. *Flying Cloud* (clipper, 19th century). Vert—1z.35 *Santa Maria* (Columbus's ship); 1z.55 *Wodnik* (17th-century Polish warship); 2z. Dutch fleute (17th century); 3z.40 *Dar Pomorza* (cadet ship).

(Des A. Heidrich. Litho)

1984 (15 Apr). 20th Anniversary of People's Republic (1st issue). T **434** and similar horiz design. Perf 12×12½.

1467	60g. red, ochre, blue, black and green (Type **434**)	40	30
1468	60g. black, orange-yellow and red	40	30

Design: No. 1468, Emblem composed of symbols of agriculture and industry.

See also Nos. 1497/1506.

435 European Cat

436 King Casimir the Great (founder)

(Des J. Grabianski. Litho)

1964 (30 Apr). Domestic Cats. T **435** and similar designs. Perf 12½.

1469	30g. black and greenish yellow	30	20
1470	40g. light grey-green, pink, black and orange	30	20
1471	50g. black, turquoise-green and yellow	40	25
1472	60g. multicoloured	40	25
1473	90g. multicoloured	60	30
1474	1z.35 yellow-ochre, yellow-orange, black and emerald	65	35
1475	1z.55 sepia, light blue, black and ultramarine	75	40
1476	2z.50 greenish yellow, black and violet	1·00	65
1477	3z.40 grey-violet, orange, black and rose-carmine	5·00	1·50
1478	6z.50 black, yellow-green, cerise and violet	8·75	3·75
1469/1478 *Set of* 10		16·00	7·00

Cats: Vert (European)—30g. 40g., 2z.50, 6z.50 (Siamese)—50g. (Persian)—3z.40. Horiz (European)—60g., 1z.55 (Persian)—90g. 1z.35.

(Des S. Malecki. Eng E. Tirdiszek (No. 1479), J. Miller (No. 1480), E. Konecki (No. 1481), Z. Kowalski (No. 1482), B. Kowalska (No. 1483). Recess)

1964 (5 May). 600th Anniversary of Jagiellonian University, Cracow. T **436** and similar designs. Perf 11½ (2z.50) or 11×11½ (others).

1479	40g. purple (Type **436**)	30	20
1480	40g. deep green	30	20
1481	60g. Violet	40	25
1482	60g. deep violet-blue	80	30
1483	2z.50 sepia	90	40
1479/1483 *Set of* 5		2·40	1·20

Portraits: No. 1480, Hugo Kollataj (educationist and politician); No. 1481, Jan Dlugosz (geographer and historian); No. 1482, Copernicus (astronomer); No. 1483, (36×37 mm), King Wladyslaw Jagiello and Queen Jadwiga.

437 Northern Lapwing (*Vanellus vanellus*)

(Des J. Desselberger. Photo)

1964 (5 June). Birds. Designs as T **437**. Multicoloured. Perf 11½.

1484	30g. Type **437**	25	20
1485	40g. Bluethroat (*Luscinia svecica*)	30	20
	a. Blue omitted	£200	
1486	50g. Black-tailed Godwit (*Limosa limosa*)	35	25
1487	60g. Osprey (*Pandion haliaëtus*)	40	30
1488	90g. Grey Heron (*Ardea cinerea*)	65	30
1489	1z.35 Little Gull (*Larus minutus*)	90	35
1490	1z.55 Common Shoveler (*Spatula clypeata*)	90	40
1491	5z.60 Black-throated Diver (*Gavia arctica*)	2·10	90
1492	6z.50 Great Crested Grebe (*Podiceps cristatus*)	3·25	1·50
1484/1492	*Set of* 9	8·25	4·00

Nos. 1487/1489 are vert (35×48 mm), the rest as T **437**.

438 Red Flag on Brick Wall

(Des A. Heidrich (No. 1493), R. Dudzicki (others). Litho)

1964 (15 June). Fourth Polish United Workers' Party Congress, Warsaw. T **438** and similar horiz designs. Multicoloured. Perf 11.

1493	60g. Type **438**	40	30
	a. Black omitted	£150	
1494	60g. Beribboned hammer	40	30
1495	60g. Hands reaching for Red Flag	40	30
1496	60g. Hammer and corn emblems	40	30
1493/1496	*Set of* 4	1·40	1·10

439 Factory and Cogwheel **440** Gdańsk Shipyard

(Des T. Michaluk. Photo (Nos. 1497/1500). Des S. Malecki (others). Eng E. Tirdiszek (No. 1501), J. Miller (No. 1502), B. Kowalska (No. 1503), Z. Kowalski (No. 1504). E. Konecki (Nos. 1505/1506). Recess and photo)

1964 (21 July). 20th Anniversary of People's Republic (2nd issue). Various designs. Perf 11.

*(a) As T **439**.*

1497	60g. black and blue (Type **439**)	40	30
1498	60g. black and green	40	30
1499	60g. red and orange	40	30
1500	60g. ultramarine and grey	40	30

Designs: Vert—No. 1498, Tractor and ear of wheat; No. 1499, Mask and symbols of the arts; No. 1500, Atomic symbol and book.

*(b) As T **440**.*

1501	60g. ultramarine and turquoise-green	40	30
1502	60g. reddish violet and magenta	40	30
1503	60g. sepia and slate-violet	40	30
1504	60g. bronze-green and green	40	30
1505	60g. reddish purple and salmon-red	40	30
1506	60g. sepia and olive-yellow	40	30
1497/1506	*Set of* 10	3·50	2·75

Designs: Horiz—No. 1501, T **440**; No. 1502, Lenin Foundry. Nowa Huta; No. 1503, Cement works, Chelm; No. 1504, Turoszów power station; No. 1505, Petro-chemical plant, Plock; No. 1505, Tarnobrzeg sulphur mine.

441 Battle Scene **442** Relay Racing

(Des R. Dudzicki. Litho)

1964 (1 Aug). 20th Anniversary of Warsaw Insurrection. Perf 12½×12.

1507	**441**	60g. multicoloured	40	30

(Des J. Korolkiewicz and J. Jaworowski (No. **MS**1515*b*). Litho)

1964. Olympic Games, Tokyo.

*(a) T **442** and similar designs. Multicoloured. Perf 11×11½ (5z.60, 6z.50) or 11½ (others) (25 August).*

1508	20g. Triple jump	20	20
1509	40g. Rowing	25	20
1510	60g. Weightlifting	30	25
1511	90g. Type **442**	30	30
1512	1z. Boxing	40	30
1513	2z.50 Football	65	40
1514	5z.60 High jump (women)	1·90	65
1515	6z.50 High diving	2·75	90
1508/1515	*Set of* 8	6·00	3·00
MS1515*a*	83×111 mm. Nos. 1514/1515 (two of each) (31.8)	65·00	55·00

Sizes: Diamond—20g. to 60g. Square—90g. to 2z.50. Vert 23×36 mm—5z.60, 6z.50.

(b) Sheet 79×106 mm containing four diamond-shaped stamps. Multicoloured. Imperf (31 August).

MS1515*b*	2z.50 Rifle shooting; 2z.50 Canoeing; 5z. Fencing; 5z. Basketball	4·75	2·50

443 Congress Emblem **444** Hand holding Hammer **445** S. Żeromski

(Des T. Michaluk. Litho)

1964 (7 Sept). 15th International Astronautical Congress, Warsaw. Perf 13×12.

1516	**443**	2z.50 black and bright violet	90	40

(Des F. Winiarski. Litho)

1964 (21 Sept). Third Congress of Fighters for Freedom and Democracy Association, Warsaw. Perf 11×11½.

1517	**444**	60g. red, black and blue-green	40	30

(Des M. Żeromska. Photo)

1964 (21 Sept). Birth Centenary of Stefan Żeromski (writer). Perf 12½×13.

1518	**445**	60g. olive-brown	40	30

446 Globe and Red Flag

447 18th-century Stage Coach (after J. Brodowski)

(Des J. Desselberger. Photo)

1964 (28 Sept). Centenary of First International. Perf 12½.
1519 **446** 60g. black and orange-red 40 30

(Des A. Heidrich. Eng B. Kowalska. Recess)

1964 (9 Oct). Stamp Day. Perf 11½.
1520 **447** 60g. green 40 30
1521 60g. bistre-brown 40 30

448 Eleanor Roosevelt

449 Battle of Studzianki (after S. Żółtowski)

(Des A. Heidrich. Eng E. Konecki. Recess)

1964 (10 Oct). 80th Birth Anniversary of Eleanor Roosevelt. Perf 12½×13.
1522 **448** 2z.50 sepia 65 40

(Des S. Malecki. Eng J. Miller (No. 1523), E. Konecki (No. 1524), E. Tirdiszek (Nos. 1525, 1527), Z. Kowalski (No. 1526). Recess)

1964 (16 Nov). Poland's Struggle (World War II) (1st issue). T **449** and similar designs. Perf 11×11½ (horiz) or 11½×11 (vert).

1523	40g. black	30	25
1524	40g. slate-violet	30	25
1525	60g. deep blue	40	30
1526	60g. deep bluish green	40	30
1527	60g. bronze-green (Type **449**)	40	30
1523/1527	*Set of* 5	1·60	1·30

Designs: Vert—No. 1523, Virtuti Militari Cross; No. 1524, Westerplatte Memorial, Gdańsk; No. 1525, Bydgoszcz Memorial. Horiz—No. 1526. Soldiers crossing the Oder (after S. Zoltowski).

Printed in sheets of 50 stamps and 20 inscribed labels or 56 stamps and 14 labels.

See also Nos. 1610/1612.

449a W. Komarov

450 Cyclamen

(Des A. Heidrich. Litho)

1964 (20 Nov). Russian Three-manned Space Flight. Sheet 114×63 mm depicting crew. Perf 11½.
MS1527*a* 60g. black and red (Type **449a**); 60g. black and green (Feoktistov); 60g. black and blue (Yegorov) .... 2·50 1·30

(Des A. Balcerzak. Photo)

1964 (30 Nov). Garden Flowers. T **450** and similar designs. Multicoloured. Perf 11½ (20g. to 90g.) or 13×12 (others).

1528	20g. Type **450**	20	20
1529	30g. Freesia	20	20
1530	40g. Rose	25	20
1531	50g. Peony	30	20
1532	60g. Lily	35	25
1533	90g. Poppy	35	25
1534	1z.35 Tulip	40	30
1535	1z.50 Narcissus	1·30	65
1536	1z.55 Begonia	40	30
1537	2z.50 Carnation	1·40	40
1538	3z.40 Iris	1·90	65
1539	5z.60 Japanese Camelia	3·25	1·50
1528/1539	*Set of* 12	9·25	4·50

Sizes: As T **450**—20g. to 90g. Vert 26½×37 mm—others.

Nos. 1528/1539 were also available in individual sheets of ten stamps (*price per set of* 12 *sheets* £170).

451 Spacecraft of the Future

452 Siren of Warsaw

(Des T. Michaluk. Litho)

1964 (30 Dec). Space Research. T **451** and similar designs. Multicoloured. Perf 13×12.

1540	20g. Type **451**	20	20
1541	30g. Launching rocket	25	20
1542	40g. Dog Laika and rocket	30	25
1543	60g. *Lunik 3* and Moon	30	30
1544	1z.55 Satellite	40	35
1545	2z.50 *Elektron 2*	75	40
1546	5z.60 *Mars 1*	1·90	75
1547	6z.50+2z. Gagarin seated in capsule	2·50	1·40
1540/1547	*Set of* 8	6·00	3·50

(Des T. Michaluk. Eng E. Konecki. Recess)

1965 (15 Jan). 20th Anniversary of Liberation of Warsaw. Perf 11×11½.
1548 **452** 60g. grey-green 40 30

453 Edaphosaurus

(Des A. Heidrich. Litho)

1965 (5 Mar). Prehistoric Animals (1st series). T **453** and similar designs. Multicoloured. Perf 12½.

1549	20g. Type **453**	25	20
1550	30g. Cryptocleidus (*vert*)	30	20
1551	40g. Brontosaurus	30	25
1552	60g. Mesosaurus (*vert*)	30	25
1553	90g. Stegosaurus	30	30
	a. Error. Missing face value		
1554	1z.15 Brachiosaurus (*vert*)	40	30
	a. Error. Missing face value		
1555	1z.35 Styracosaurus	40	35
1556	3z.40 Corythosaurus (*vert*)	1·50	50
1557	5z.60 Rhamphorhynchus (*vert*)	3·00	90
1558	6z.50 Tyrannosaurus	4·75	1·30
1549/1558	*Set of* 10	10·50	4·00

Nos. 1549/1558 were also available in individual sheetlets of ten stamps (*price per set of* 10 *sheets* £250).

See also Nos. 1639/1647.

454 Petro-chemical Works, Plock, and Polish and Soviet Flags

(Des S. Malecki. Litho)

1965 (21 Apr). 20th Anniversary of Polish–Soviet Friendship Treaty. T **454** and similar design. Perf 13×12 (No. 1559) or 13×12½ (No. 1560).

1559	-	60g. carmine, black, yellow and grey-green	40	30
1560	**454**	60g. black, carmine, red and yellow-olive	40	30

Design: Vert 27×38½ mm—No. 1559, Seal.

455 Polish Eagle and Civic Arms

456 Dove of Peace

(Des T. Michaluk. Eng E. Konecki. Recess)

1965 (8 May). 20th Anniversary of Return of Western and Northern Territories to Poland. Perf 11½.

1561	**455**	60g. carmine-red	40	30

(Des S. Jasiński. Litho)

1965 (8 May). 20th Anniversary of Victory. Perf 12×12½.

1562	**456**	60g. red and black	40	30

457 ITU Emblem

458 Clover-leaf Emblem and *The Friend of the People* (journal)

(Des S. Malecki. Litho)

1965 (17 May). Centenary of International Telecommunications Union. Perf 13×12.

1563	**457**	2z.50 black, reddish violet and new blue	1·00	40

(Des A. Kalczyńska. Litho)

1965 (5 June). 70th Anniversary of Peasant Movement. T **458** and similar design. Perf 11×11½ (40g.) or 11½×11 (60g.).

1564	**458**	40g. green, black, drab and light bluish violet	30	25
1565	-	60g. yellow-orange, ultramarine, black and bluish green	40	30

Design: Horiz—60g. Ears of corn and industrial plant.

459 Dragon Class Yachts

460 Marx and Lenin

(Des J. Jaworowski and R. Dudzicki (15z.). Litho)

1965 (14 June). World Finn Class Sailing Championships, Gdynia. T **459** and similar designs. Multicoloured. Perf 12 or 11 (15z.).

1566	30g. Type **459**	20	20
1567	40g. 5.5 m class	25	20
1568	50g. Finn dinghies (*horiz*)	30	25
1569	60g. V dinghies	30	30
1570	1z.35 Cadet dinghies (*horiz*)	45	35
1571	4z. Star yachts (*horiz*)	1·40	50
1572	5z.60 Flying Dutchman class	2·30	70
1573	6z.50 Amethyst dinghies (*horiz*)	3·75	1·20
1566/1573	*Set of* 8	8·00	3·25
MS1573*a*	79×59 mm. 15z. Finn dinghies	3·75	2·30

Nos. 1566/1573 were also available in individual sheetlets of ten stamps (*price for set of 8 sheets £275*).

(Des J. Desselberger. Eng E. Konecki. Recess and photo)

1965 (14 June). Postal Ministers' Congress, Peking. Perf 11½×11.

1574	**460**	60g. black/*red*	40	30

461 17th-century Arms of Warsaw

462 Nike Memorial and Old Warsaw Seal

(Des Cz. Kaczmarczyk. Eng E. Konecki (5g.), B. Kowalska (10g., 2z.50), E. Tirdiszek (20g., 60g.), J. Miller (40g., 1z.55), Z. Kowalski (1z.50). Recess. Des S. Malecki. Eng E. Konecki (3z.40). Recess and photo)

1965 (21 July). 700th Anniversary of Warsaw. T **461** and similar designs and T **462**. Perf 11½×12 (5g., 10g.) or 12×11½ (others).

1575	5g. carmine	20	20
	a. Perf 12×12½	20	20
1576	10g. myrtle green	20	20
	a. Perf 12×12½	20	20
1577	20g. deep blue	25	20
	a. Perf 12½×12	25	20
1578	40g. red-brown	30	20
	a. Perf 12½×12	30	20
1579	60g. orange-red	30	25
	a. Perf 12½×12	30	25
1580	1z.50 black	35	30
	a. Perf 12½×12	35	30
1581	1z.55 greenish blue	40	30
	a. Perf 12½×12	40	30
1582	2z.50 reddish purple	75	40
	a. Perf 12½×12	75	40
1575/1582	*Set of* 8	2·50	1·80
MS1583	51×62 mm 3z.40 black and bistre	1·90	1·10

Designs: Vert—5g. T **461**; 10g. 13th-century antiquities. Horiz—20g. Tombstone of last Masovian dukes; 40g. Old Town Hall; 60g. Barbican; 1z.50 Arsenal; 1z.55 National Theatre; 2z.50 Staszic Palace; 3z.40 T **462**.

463 IQSY Emblem

464 *Odontoglossum grande*

(Des T. Michaluk. Litho)

1965 (9 Aug). International Quiet Sun Year. T **463** and similar designs. Multicoloured; background colours given. Perf 11½.

1584	**463**	60g. ultramarine	40	25
1585		60g. bluish violet	40	25
1586	-	2z.50 red	65	30
1587	-	2z.50 brown-red	65	30
1588	-	3z.40 orange	1·00	40
1589	-	3z.40 greyish olive	1·00	40
1584/1589		*Set of* 6	3·75	1·70

Designs: 2z.50 Solar scanner; 3z.40 Solar System.

(Des G. Dokalski. Photo)

1965 (6 Sept). Orchids. T **464** and similar vert designs. Multicoloured. Perf 13×12.

1590	20g. Type **464**	20	20
1591	30g. *Cypripedium hibridum*	25	20
1592	40g. *Lycaste skinneri*	30	25
1593	50g. *Cattleya warszewicza*	35	30
1594	60g. *Vanda sanderiana*	40	30
1595	1z.35 *Cypripedium hibridum (different)*	65	40
1596	4z. *Sobralia*	1·90	70
1597	5z.60 *Disa grandiflora*	2·10	75
1598	6z.50 *Cattleya labiata*	3·75	2·10
1590/1598	*Set of 9*	9·00	4·75

Nos. 1590/1598 were also available in individual sheetlets of ten stamps (*price for set of 9 sheets £140*).

465 Weightlifting

466 The Post Coach (after P. Michalowski)

(Des S. Malecki. Photo)

1965 (8 Oct). Olympic Games, Tokyo. Polish Medal Winners. T **465** and similar vert designs. Multicoloured with backgrounds of bronze (7z.10), silver (50g., 90g.) or gold (others), according to medals. Perf 13×12.

1599	30g. Type **465**	20	20
1600	40g. Boxing	25	20
1601	50g. Relay racing	30	25
1602	60g. Fencing	35	30
1603	90g. Hurdling (women's 80 m)	40	35
1604	3z.40 Relay racing (women's)	80	40
1605	6z.50 Triple jump	1·90	95
1606	7z.10 Volleyball (women's)	2·20	1·10
1599/1606	*Set of 8*	5·75	3·50

Nos. 1599/1606 were each issued in sheets of eight, two panes of four being divided by two *se-tenant* labels showing the reverse and obverse of the medals (price for each sheet £70).

Nos. 1599/1606 were also available in individual sheetlets of ten stamps (*price per set of 8 sheets £65*).

(Des A. Balcerzak. Eng B. Kowalska (60g.), E. Tirdiszek (2z.50). Recess)

1965 (9 Oct). Stamp Day. T **466** and similar horiz design. Perf 11×11½.

1607	**466**	60g. brown	40	30
1608	-	2z.50 bronze-green	65	40

Design: 2z.50 Coach about to leave (after P. Michalowski).

Nos. 1607/1608 were each in sheets of 50 with attached *se-tenant* labels inscr 'DZIEN ZNACZKA 1965 R.'.

467 UN Emblem

468 Memorial, Holy Cross Mountains

(Des A. Kalczyńska. Litho)

1966 (24 Oct). 20th Anniversary of UNO. Perf 13×12.

1609	**467**	2z.50 bright blue	65	40

(Des S. Malecki. Eng E. Tirdiszek (No. 1610), B. Kowalska (No. 1611), J. Miller (No. 1612). Recess)

1965 (29 Nov). Poland's Struggle (World War II) (2nd issue). T **468** and similar designs. Perf 11×11½ (No. 1612) or 11½×11 (others).

1610	**468**	60g. deep brown	40	30
1611	-	60g. bronze-green	40	30
1612	-	60g. blackish brown	40	30
1610/1612		*Set of 3*	1·10	80

Designs: Vert—No. 1611, Memorial, Plaszow. Horiz—No. 1612, Memorial, Chelm-on-Ner.

Nos. 1610/1611 were each printed in sheets of 56 stamps and 14 inscribed labels.

No. 1612 in sheets of 50 stamps and 20 labels.

469 Wolf

(Des J. Desselberger. Photo)

1965 (30 Nov). Forest Animals. T **469** and similar designs. Multicoloured. Perf 11½.

1613	20g. Type **469**	25	20
1614	30g. Lynx	30	20
1615	40g. Red Fox	30	25
1616	50g. Eurasian Badger	35	30
1617	60g. Brown Bear	40	30
1618	1z.50 Wild Boar	75	35
1619	2z.50 Red Deer	85	40
1620	5z.60 European Bison	1·90	45
1621	7z.10 Elk	3·75	90
1613/1621	*Set of 9*	8·00	3·00

470 Gig

(Des J. Miller. Litho)

1965 (30 Dec). Horse-drawn Carriages in Lańcut Museum. T **470** and similar horiz designs. Multicoloured. Perf 11.

1622	20g. Type **470**	25	20
1623	40g. Coupé	30	20
1624	50g. Ladies' 'basket' (trap)	30	20
1625	60g. 'Vis-à-vis'	30	25
1626	90g. Cab	35	30
1627	1z.15 Berlinka	40	35
1628	2z.50 Hunting brake	1·00	40
1629	6z.50 Barouche	2·75	90
1630	7z.10 English brake	4·00	2·10
1622/1630	*Set of 9*	8·75	4·50

Nos. 1627/9 are 77×22 mm and No. 1630 is 10×22 mm.

471 Congress Emblem and Industrial Products

(Des A. Heidrich. Litho)

1966 (10 Feb). Fifth Polish Technicians Congress. Katowice. Perf 11.

1631	**471**	60g. multicoloured	40	30

No. 1631 was printed in sheets of 20 stamps and 20 *se-tenant* commemorative labels.

(Des A. Heidrich. Litho)

1966 (10 Feb–21 May). 20th Anniversary of Industrial Nationalisation. Designs similar to T **471**. Multicoloured. Perf 11.

1632	60g. Pithead gear (10.2)	40	30
1633	60g. *Henryk Jedza* (freighter)	40	30
1634	60g. Petrochemical works, Plock	40	30
1635	60g. Combine-harvester	40	30
1636	60g. Class EN 57 electric train	40	30
1637	60g. Exhibition Hall, 35th Poznań Fair	40	30
1638	60g. Crane	40	30
1632/1638	*Set of 7*	2·50	1·90

Nos. 1632 and 1638 are vertical.

Each stamp has *se-tenant* commemorative label.

(Des A. Heidrich. Litho)

1966 (5 Mar). Prehistoric Animals (2nd series). Designs as T **453**. Multicoloured. Perf 12½.

1639	20g. Terror fish (Dinichthys) (fossil)	25	20
1640	30g. Lobefin (Eusthenopteron) (fossil)	30	20
1641	40g. Ichthyostega	35	25
1642	50g. Mastodonsaurus	40	30
1643	60g. Cynognathus	65	35
1644	2z.50 Archaeopteryx (*vert*)	90	35
1645	3z.40 Brontotherium	1·30	40
1646	6z.50 Machairodus	2·75	90
1647	7z.10 Mammuthus	4·50	1·50
1639/1647 *Set of 9*		10·50	4·00

472 H. Sienkiewicz (novelist)

473 Footballers (Montevideo, 1930)

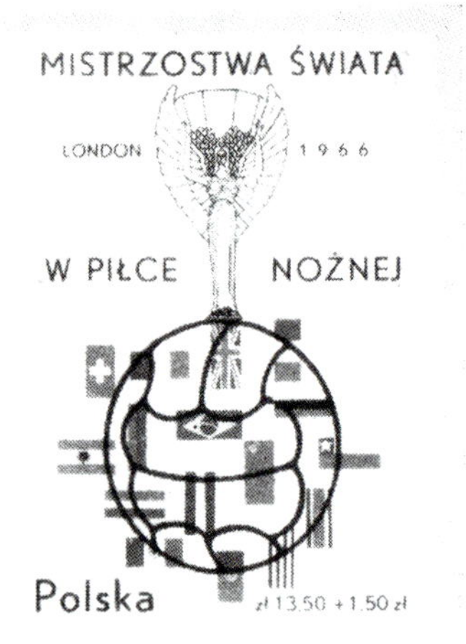

474 Jules Rimet Cup, Flags and Football

(Des T. Michaluk. Eng E. Tirdiszek. Recess)

1966 (30 Mar). 50th Death Anniversary of Henryk Sienkiewicz. Perf 11½×11.

1648	**472**	60g. blackish brown/*light buff*	40	30

(Des J. Jaworowski. Litho)

1966 (6 May). World Cup Football Championship.

*(a) T **473** and similar vert designs showing football scenes representing World Cup finals. Multicoloured. Perf 13×12.*

1649	20g. Type **473**	20	20
1650	40g. Rome, 1934	25	20
1651	60g. Paris, 1938	30	25
1652	90g. Rio de Janeiro, 1950	40	30
1653	1z.50 Bern, 1954	1·60	40
1654	3z.40 Stockholm, 1958	1·60	45
1655	6z.50 Santiago, 1962	2·50	1·30
1656	7z.10 London, 1966 (elimination match, Glasgow, 1965)	3·75	2·50
1649/1656 *Set of 8*		9·50	5·00

(b) Sheet 61×81 mm. Litho. Multicoloured. Imperf.

MS1657 **474**	13z.50+1z.50	6·00	3·00

Nos. 1649/1650 were also available in individual sheetlets of ten stamps (*price per set of 8 sheets £170*).

475 Soldier with Flag and Dove of Peace

476 Women's Relay Racing

477 Long-distance Running

(Des T. Michaluk. Eng E. Konecki. Typo, litho and recess)

1966 (9 May). 21st Anniversary of Victory Day. Perf 11×11½.

1658	**475**	60g. red and black/*silver*	40	30

(Des S. Malecki. Litho)

1966 (18 June). Eighth European Athletic Championships, Budapest. T **476** and similar designs. Multicoloured. Perf 11½×11 (vert) or 11×11½ (horiz).

1659	20g. Runner starting race	20	20
1660	40g. Type **476**	25	20
1661	60g. Javelin	30	25
1662	90g. Women's hurdles	35	30
1663	1z.35 Discus	40	35
1664	3z.40 Finish of race	1·20	40
1665	6z.50 Hammer throwing	1·60	75
1666	7z.10 High jump	1·80	1·10
1659/1666 *Set of 8*		5·50	3·25
MS1667 **477**	110×66 mm. 5z. Imperf.	3·50	1·90

The 20g., 60g., 1z.35 and 6z.50 are vert.

478 White Eagle

479 Flowers and Produce

(Des F. Winiarski. Photo and embossed)

1966 (21 July). Polish Millenary (1st issue). Each printed in red and black on gold. Perf 12½×12.

1668	60g. Type **478**	40	30
	a. Pair. Nos. 1668/1669	85	65
1669	60g. Polish flag	40	30
1670	2z.50 Type **478**	65	40
	a. Pair. Nos. 1670/1671	1·40	85
1671	2z.50 Polish flag	65	40
1668/1671 *Set of 4*		1·90	1·30

Nos. 1668/1669 and 1670/1671 were issued respectively in *se-tenant* pairs within sheets of ten stamps.

See also Nos. 1717/1718.

(Des H. Matuszewska. Photo)

1966 (15 Aug). Harvest Festival. T **479** and similar designs. Multicoloured. Perf 11.

1672	40g. Type **479**	55	30
1673	60g. Woman and loaf	65	40

	a. Silver (value and bottom inscr) omitted	£150	
1674	3z.40 Festival bouquet	1·30	75
1672/1674	*Set of* 3	2·30	1·30

The 60g. is vert as T **479** and the 3z.40 is 49×48 mm.

480 Chrysanthemum

481 Tourist Map

(Des S. Malecki. Photo)

1966 (1 Sept). Flowers. T **480** and similar designs. Multicoloured. Perf 11½.

1675	10g. Type **480**	20	20
1676	20g. Poinsettia	25	20
1677	30g. Centaury	30	25
1678	40g. Rose	35	30
1679	60g. Zinnia	40	35
1680	90g. Nasturtium	50	40
1681	5z.60 Dahlia	1·90	65
1682	6z.50 Sunflower	2·50	90
1683	7z.10 Magnolia	3·75	1·00
1675/1683	*Set of* 9	9·25	3·75

(Des T. Michaluk. Eng J. Miller (10g., 60g. (No. 1688), 1z.35), B. Kowalska (20g., 1z.15), Z Kowalski (40g., 2z.), E. Tirdiszek (60g. (No. 1687)), B. Brandt (1z.55). Recess)

1966 (15 Sept). Tourism. T **481** and similar horiz designs. Perf 13×12½.

1684	10g. rose	20	20
	a. Perf 11½×12	20	20
1685	20g. drab	20	20
	a. Perf 11½×12	20	20
1686	40g. slate-blue	20	20
	a. Pert 11½×12	20	20
1687	60g. brown	25	20
	a. Perf 11½×12	25	20
1688	60g. black	25	20
	a. Perf 11½×12	25	20
1689	1z.15 deep green	30	25
	a. Perf 11½×12	30	25
1690	1z.35 vermilion	35	30
	a. Perf 11½×12	35	30
1691	1z.55 deep reddish violet	40	30
	a. Perf 11½×12	40	30
1692	2z. slate-green	75	40
	a. Perf 11½×12	75	40
1684/1692	*Set of* 9	2·50	2·00
1684a/1692a	*Set of* 9	2·50	2·00

Designs: 10g. T **481**; 20g. Hela Lighthouse; 40g. Yacht; 60g. (No. 1687), Poniatowski Bridge, Warsaw; 60g. (No. 1688), Mining Academy, Kielce; 1z.15 Dunajec Gorge; 1z.35 Old oaks, Rogalin; 1z.55 Silesian Planetarium; 2z. *Batory* (liner).

482 Roman Capital

483 Stableman with Percherons

(Des R. Dudzicki. Eng E. Tirdiszek. Recess and photo)

1966 (7 Oct). Polish Culture Congress. Perf 11½.

1693	**482**	60g. cerise and deep chocolate	40	30

(Des J. Miklaszewski (after paintings by P. Michalowski). Eng E. Konecki (60g.), E. Tirdiszek (2z.50). Recess)

1966 (8 Oct). Stamp Day. T **483** and similar horiz design. Perf 11×12.

1694	60g. sepia	40	30
1695	2z.50 myrtle-green	75	40

Design: 60g. T **483**; 2z.50 Stablemen with horses and dogs.

484 Soldier in Action

485 Woodland Birds

(Des A. Heidrich. Litho)

1966 (20 Oct). 30th Anniversary of Jaroslav Dabrowski Brigade in Spain. Perf 11×11½.

1696	**484**	60g. black, olive-green and red	40	30

(Des T. Michaluk (10g.), J. Desselberger (others). Photo)

1966 (17 Nov). Woodland Birds. T **485** and similar square designs. Multicoloured. Perf 11½.

1697	10g. Type **485**	30	20
1698	20g. Green Woodpecker (*Picus viridis*)	30	20
1699	30g. Jay (*Garrulus glandarius*)	30	20
1700	40g. Golden Oriole (*Oriolus oriolus*)	35	25
1701	60g. Hoopoe (*Upupa epops*)	40	30
1702	2z.50 Common Redstart (*Phoenicurus phoenicurus*)	90	55
1703	4z. Spruce Siskin (*Carduelis spinus*)	2·50	65
1704	6z.50 Chaffinch (*Fringilla coelebs*)	2·75	1·30
1705	7z.10 Great Tit (*Parus major*)	3·25	1·40
1697/1705	*Set of* 9	10·00	4·50

T **485** shows the species depicted on Nos. 1698/1705.

486 Ram (ritual statuette)

487 *Vostok 1*

(Des K. Tarkowska. Eng E. Konecki (No. 1706), Z. Kowalski (No. 1707), B. Kowalska (No. 1708). Recess)

1966 (10 Dec). Polish Archaeological Research. T **486** and similar designs. Perf 11½×11 (No. 1708) or 11×11½ (others).

1706	60g. slate-blue	40	30
1707	60g. myrtle-green	40	30
1708	60g. brown	40	30
1706/1708	*Set of* 3	1·10	80

Designs: Vert—No. 1706, T **486**; No. 1707, Plan of Biskupin settlement. Horiz—No. 1708, Brass implements and ornaments.

(Des T. Michaluk. Litho)

1966 (20 Dec). Space Research. T **487** and similar vert designs showing spacecraft. Multicoloured. Perf 11½×11.

1709	20g. Type **487**	20	20
1710	40g. Gemini	25	20
1711	60g. *Ariel 2*	25	20
1712	1z.35 *Proton 1*	40	25
1713	1z.50 *FR 1*	65	30
1714	3z.40 *Alouette*	90	35
1715	6z.50 *San Marco 1*	2·50	40
1716	7z.10 *Luna 9*	3·00	75
1709/1716	*Set of* 8	7·25	2·40

488 Polish Eagle and Hammer

(Des S. Malecki. Litho)

1966 (20 Dec). Polish Millenary (2nd issue). T **488** and similar horiz design. Perf 11.

1717	40g. purple-brown, lilac and light red	30	25
1718	60g. purple-brown, sage-green and light red	40	30

Designs: 40g. T **488**; 60g. Polish eagle and agricultural and industrial symbols.

489 Dressage

(Des B. Kamiński. Photo)

1967 (25 Feb). 150th Anniversary of Racehorse Breeding in Poland. T **489** and similar horiz designs. Multicoloured. Perf 12½.

1719	10g. Type **489**	25	20
1720	20g. Cross-country racing	30	25
1721	40g. Horse jumping	35	30
1722	60g. Jumping fence in open country	40	35
1723	90g. Horse trotting	65	40
1724	5z.90 Playing polo	1·90	90
1725	6z.60 Stallion, Ofir	3·25	1·40
1726	7z. Stallion, Skowronek	4·75	1·50
1719/1726 *Set of* 8		10·50	4·75

490 Black-wedged Butterflyfish (*Chaetodon melanotus*)

491 Auschwitz Memorial

(Des J. Desselberger. Litho)

1967 (1 Apr). Exotic Fish. T **490** and similar horiz designs. Multicoloured. Perf 11×11½.

1727	5g. Type **490**	20	20
1728	10g. Emperor Angelfish (*Pomacanthus imperator* juv.)	25	20
1729	40g. Racoon Butterflyfish (*Chaetodon fasciatus*)	25	20
1730	60g. Clown Triggerfish (*Balistoides conspicillum*)	30	25
1731	90g. Undulate Triggerfish (*Balistapus undulatus*)	30	25
1732	1z.50 Picasso Triggerfish (*Rhinecanthus aculeatus*)	40	35
1733	4z.50 Black-finned Melon Butterflyfish (*Chaetodon melapterus*)	2·00	40
1734	6z.60 Semicircle Angelfish (*Pomacanthus semicirculatus*)	2·75	1·50
1735	7z. Saddle Butterflyfish (*Chaetodon ephippium*)	3·00	65
1727/1735 *Set of* 9		8·50	3·50

(Des K. Rogaczewska. Eng E. Tirdiszek (Nos. 1736, 1738), B. Kowalska (No. 1737). Recess)

1967 (10 Apr). Polish Martyrdom and Resistance, 1939–1945 (1st series). T **491** and similar designs. Perf 11½×11 (No. 1736) or 11×11½ (others).

1736	**491**	40g. olive-brown	40	30
1737	–	40g. black	40	30
1738	–	40g. deep reddish purple	40	30
1736/1738 *Set of* 3			1·10	80

Designs: Vert—No. 1737, Auschwitz-Monowitz Memorial; No. 1738, Memorial guide's emblem.

See also Nos. 1770/1772, 1798/1799, 1865/1869.

492 Cyclists

(Des T. Michaluk. Litho)

1967 (2 May). 20th International Peace Cycle Race. Perf 11.

1739	**492**	60g. multicoloured	40	30

493 Running

494 Socialist Symbols

(Des F. Winiarski. Litho)

1967 (24 May). Olympic Games (1968). T **493** and similar horiz designs. Multicoloured. Perf 11.

1740	20g. Type **493**	20	20
1741	40g. Horse jumping	25	20
1742	60g. Relay running	25	20
1743	90g. Weightlifting	30	25
1744	1z.35 Hurdling	40	30
1745	3z.40 Gymnastics	1·10	40
1746	6z.60 High jump	1·50	75
1747	7z. Boxing	2·50	1·30
1740/1747 *Set of* 8		5·75	3·25
MS1748 65×86 mm. 10z.+5z. multicoloured. Imperf.		4·00	2·50

Design: Diamond 30×30 mm—10z. Kusociński winning 10,000 m race at Olympic Games, Los Angeles, 1932.

The face value is expressed outside the stamp which has facsimile perforations.

Nos. 1740/1747 are each in sheets of eight (2×4) with intervening *se-tenant* labels showing the Olympic torch and rings.

(Des A. Heidrich. Litho)

1967 (2 June). Polish Trade Unions Congress, Warsaw. Perf 11.

1749	**494**	60g. multicoloured	50	40

No. 1749 was issued with *se-tenant* label showing Congress emblem, both in sheets in 20 and sheets of four.

495 *Arnica montana*

496 Katowice Memorial

(Des A. Heidrich. Litho)

1967 (14 June). Protected Plants. T **495** and similar vert designs. Multicoloured. Perf 11½×11.

1750	40g. Type **495**	25	20
1751	60g. *Aquilegia vulgaris*	30	25
1752	3z.40 *Gentiana punctata*	75	30
1753	4z.50 *Lycopodium clavatum*	90	30
1754	5z. *Iris sibirica*	1·30	40
1755	10z. *Azalea pontica*	2·20	50
1750/1755 *Set of* 6		5·25	1·80

(Des R. Dudzicki. Litho)

1967 (21 July). Inauguration of Katowice Memorial. Perf 11½.

1756	**496**	60g. multicoloured	40	30

497 Marie Curie

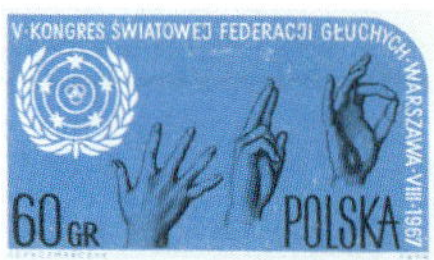

498 Fifth Congress of the Deaf (sign language)

(Des S. Malecki. Eng J. Miller (No. 1757), E. Tirdiszek (No. 1758), B. Kowalska (No. 1759). Recess)

1967 (1 Aug). Birth Centenary of Marie Curie. T **497** and similar vert designs. Perf 11½×11.

1757	**497**	60g. lake	40	30
1758	–	60g. sepia	40	30
1759	–	60g. violet	40	30
1757/1759		*Set of* 3	1·10	80

Designs: No. 1758, Marie Curie's Nobel Prize diploma; No. 1759, Statue of Marie Curie, Warsaw.

(Des Cz. Kaczmarczyk. Litho)

1987 (1 Aug). Fifth World Federation of the Deaf Congress, Warsaw. Perf 11×12.

1760	**498**	60g. black and new blue	40	30

499 Bouquet

500 Wilanów Palace (from painting by W. Kasprzycki)

(Des T. Michaluk. Photo)

1967 (5 Sept). Flowers of the Meadow. T **499** and similar square designs. Multicoloured. Perf 11½.

1761	20g. Type **499**	25	20
1762	40g. Red Poppy	25	20
1763	60g. Field Bindweed	25	25
1764	90g. Wild Pansy	30	25
1765	1z.15 Tansy	40	30
1766	2z.50 Corn Cockle	65	40
1767	3z.40 Field Scabious	1·10	60
1768	4z.50 Scarlet Pimpernel	3·25	65
1769	7z.90 Chicory	3·25	1·30
1761/1769	*Set of* 9	8·75	3·75

(Des K. Rogaczewska. Eng B. Kowalska (No. 1770), J. Miller (No. 1771), E. Tirdiszek (No. 1772). Recess)

1967 (9 Oct). Polish Martyrdom and Resistance, 1939–1945 (2nd series). Designs as T **491**. Perf 11½×11 (No. 1770) or 11×11½ (others).

1770	40g. ultramarine	35	30
1771	40g. bronze green	35	30
1772	40g. black	35	30
1770/1772	*Set of* 3	95	80

Designs: Horiz—No. 1770, Stutthof Memorial. Vert—No. 1771, Walcz Memorial; No. 1772, Łódź-Radogoszcz Memorial.

(Des S. Malecki. Eng J. Miller. Recess and photo)

1967 (9 Oct). Stamp Day. Perf 11½.

1773	**500**	60g. olive-brown and pale blue	40	35

501 *Aurora* (Russian Cruiser)

(Des K. Tarkowska. Litho)

1967 (9 Oct). 50th Anniversary of October Revolution. T **501** and similar horiz designs. All in black, grey and brown-red. Perf 11.

1774	60g. Type **501**	40	35
1775	60g. Lenin	40	35
1776	60g. *Luna 10*	40	35
1774/1776	*Set of* 3	1·10	95

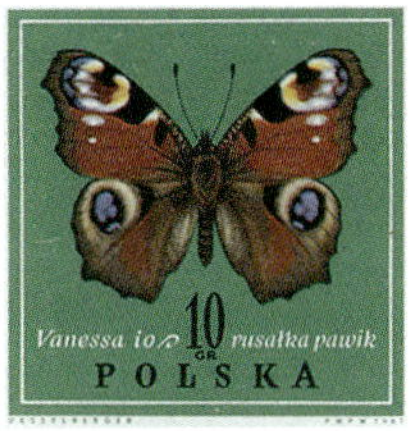

502 *Inachis io* (*Vanessa io*)

503 Kościuszko

(Des J. Desselberger. Litho)

1967 (14 Oct). Butterflies. T **502** and similar square designs. Multicoloured. Perf 11½.

1777	10g. Type **502**	25	20
1778	20g. *Papilio machaon*	30	25
1779	40g. *Aglais urticae* (*Vanessa urticae*)	35	30
1780	60g. *Nymphalis antiopa* (*Vanessa antiopa*)	40	30
1781	2z. *Apatura iris*	55	35
1782	2z.50 *Vanessa atlanta* (*Pyrameis atalanta*)	70	35
1783	3z.40 *Colias hyale*	75	40
1784	4z.50 *Melanargia galathea*	3·75	1·30
1785	7z.90 *Maculinea arion*	4·00	1·50
1777/1785	*Set of* 9	10·00	4·50

(Des R. Dudzicki. Eng E. Konecki. Recess and photo)

1967 (14 Oct). 150th Death Anniversary of Tadeusz Kościuszko (national hero). Perf 12×11.

1786	**503**	60g. chocolate and light yellow-brown	40	30
1787		2z.50 myrtle-green and carmine	50	40

504 *The Lobster* (Jean de Heem)

505 W. S. Reymont

(Des J. S. Miklaszewski. Photo)

1967 (15 Nov). Famous Paintings. T **504** and similar designs. Perf 11×11½ (4z.50, 6z.60) or 11½×11 (others).

1788	20g. multicoloured	30	20
1789	40g. multicoloured	35	30
1790	60g. multicoloured	40	35
1791	2z. multicoloured	75	40
1792	2z.50 multicoloured	90	60
1793	3z.40 multicoloured	1·30	65
1794	4z.50 multicoloured	2·10	1·30
1795	6z.60 multicoloured	3·25	1·50
1788/1795	*Set of* 8	8·50	4·75

Paintings from the National Museums, Warsaw and Cracow: Vert—20g. *Lady with a Weasel* (Leonardo da Vinci); 40g. *The Polish Lady* (Watteau); 60g. *Dog Fighting Heron* (A. Hondius); 2z. *Fowler Tuning Guitar* (J.-B. Greuze); 2z.50 *The Tax Collectors* (M. van Reymerswaele); 3z.40 *Daria Fiodorowna* (F. S. Rokotov). Horiz—4z.50 T **504**; 6z.60 *Parable of the Good Samaritan* (landscape, Rembrandt).

Printed in sheets of five stamps with one stamp-size *se-tenant* label.

(Des R. Dudzicki. Litho)

1967 (12 Dec). Birth Centenary of W. S. Reymont (novelist). Perf 11×11½.

1796	**505**	60g. sepia, red and ochre	40	35

506 J. M. Ossoliński (medallion), Book and Flag

(Des R. Dudzicki. Litho)

1967 (12 Dec). 150th Anniversary of Ossolineum Foundation. Perf 11.

1797	**506**	60g. yellow-brown, red, greenish blue and light blue	40	35

(Des K. Rogaczewska. Eng B. Kowalska (No. 1798), E. Tirdiszek (No. 1799). Recess)

1967 (28 Dec). Polish Martyrdom and Resistance, 1939–1945 (3rd series). Designs as T **491**. Perf 11×11½ (No. 1798) or 11½×11 (No. 1799).

1798	40g. claret	35	30
1799	40g. brown	35	30

Designs: Vert—No. 1798, Żagań Memorial. Horiz—No. 1799, Lambinowice Memorial.

507 Ice Hockey

508 *Puss in Boots*

(Des F. Winiarski. Litho)

1968 (10 Jan). Winter Olympic Games, Grenoble. T **507** and similar horiz designs. Multicoloured. Perf 11×11½.

1800	40g. Type **507**	20	20
1801	60g. Downhill	25	20
1802	90g. Slalom	30	25
1803	1z.35 Speed skating	35	30
1804	1z.55 Ski walking	40	30
1805	2z. Tobogganing	65	40
1806	7z. Rifle shooting on skis	1·30	65
1807	7z.90 Ski jumping	2·50	80
1800/1807	*Set of* 8	5·25	2·75

(Des H. Matuszewska. Litho)

1968 (15 Mar). Fairy Tales. T **508** and similar vert designs. Multicoloured. Perf 12½.

1808	20g. Type **508**	25	20
1809	40g. *The Raven and the Fox*	35	25
1810	60g. *Mr Twardowski*	40	30
1811	2z. *The Fisherman and the Fish*	65	30
1812	2z.50 *Little Red Riding Hood*	75	35
1813	3z.40 *Cinderella*	1·10	40
1814	5z.50 *The Waif*	2·50	90
1815	7z. *Snow White*	3·00	1·30
1808/1815	*Set of* 8	8·00	3·50

509 *Passiflora quadrangularis*

510 Peace (poster by H. Tomaszewski)

(Des T. Michaluk. Litho)

1968 (15 May). Flowers. T **509** and similar square designs. Multicoloured. Perf 11½.

1816	10g. *Clianthus dampieri*	20	20
1817	20g. Type **509**	25	20
1818	30g. *Strelitzia reginae*	30	25
1819	40g. *Coryphanta vivipara*	30	25
	a. Error. 'POISKA'	50·00	
1820	60g. *Odontonia*	35	30
1821	90g. *Protea cynaroides*	40	35
1822	4z.+2z. *Abutilon*	2·00	90
1823	8z.+4z. *Rosa polyantha*	4·50	2·00
1816/1823	*Set of* 8	7·50	4·00

(Des A. Heidrich. Litho)

1968 (29 May). Second International Poster Biennial, Warsaw. T **510** and similar vert design. Multicoloured. Perf 11½×11.

1824	60g. Type **510**	35	30
1825	2z.50 Gounod's Faust (poster by Jan Lenica)	50	40

511 Zephyr Glider SP-1127

512 Child with Stamp

(Des J. Jaworowski. Litho)

1968 (29 May). 11th World Gliding Championships, Leszno. T **511** and similar horiz designs showing gliders. Multicoloured. Perf 12½.

1826	60g. Type **511**	25	20
1827	90g. Stork glider SP-1135	35	30
1828	1z.50 Swallow glider SP-1050	40	35
1829	3z.40 Fly glider	90	40
1830	4z. Seal glider SP-1201	1·90	50
1831	5z.50 Pirate glider SP-250	2·30	65
1826/1831	*Set of* 6	5·50	2·20

(Des T. Michaluk. Litho)

1968 (2 July). 75 Years of Polish Philately. T **512** and similar vert design. Multicoloured. Perf 11½×11.

1832	60g. Type **512**	40	35
	a. Pair. Nos. 1832/1833	85	75
1833	60g. Balloon over Poznań	40	35

Nos. 1832/1833 were printed together *se-tenant* in sheets of 12.

513 Part of Monument

514 Relay Racing

(Des W. Chrucki. Eng B. Brandt. Recess and photo)

1968 (20 July). Silesian Insurrection Monument, Sosnowiec. Perf 11×11½.

1834	**513**	60g. black and bright purple	40	35

(Des T. Michaluk. Litho)

1968 (2 Sept). Olympic Games, Mexico. T **514** and similar horiz designs. Multicoloured. Perf 11×11½ or 11½ (10z.).

1835	30g. Type **514**	20	20
1836	40g. Boxing	25	20
1837	60g. Basketball	30	25
1838	90g. Long jump	35	25
1839	2z.50 Javelin	40	30
1840	3z.40 Gymnastics	55	35
1841	4z. Cycling	65	40
1842	7z.90 Fencing	1·00	55
1843	10z.+5z. Torch Runner and Aztec bas-relief (56×45 mm)	3·25	95
1835/1843	*Set of* 9	6·25	3·00

515 *Knight on a Bay Horse* (P. Michalowski)

516 *September, 1939* (Bylina)

(Des A. Heidrich. Photo)

1968 (10 Oct). Polish Paintings. T **515** and similar multicoloured designs. Perf 11½×11 (vert) or 11×11½ (horiz).

1844	40g. Type **515**	25	20
1845	60g. *Fisherman* (L. Wyczółkowski)	30	25
1846	1z.15 *Jewish Woman with Lemons* (A. Gierymski)	35	30
1847	1z.35 *Eliza Parenska* (S. Wyspiański)	40	35
1848	1z.50 *Manifesto* (W. Weiss)	70	40
1849	4z.50 *Stańczyk* (Jan Matejko)	90	55
1850	5z. *Children's Band* (T. Makowski)	1·50	55
1851	7z. *Feast II* (Z. Waliszewski)	2·50	90
1844/1851	*Set of* 8	6·25	3·25

The 4z.50, 5z. and 7z. are horiz designs.
Printed in sheets of four stamps and two labels.

(Des S. Malecki. Eng E. Konecki (Nos. 1852, 1854, 1860, 1861), E. Tirdiszek (Nos. 1853, 1856, 1859), B. Brandt (No. 1855), B. Kowalska (No. 1857), J. Miller (No. 1858). Recess, typo and photo)

1968 (12 Oct). 25th Anniversary of Polish People's Army. T **516** and similar horiz designs, showing paintings. Perf 11½.

1852	40g. reddish violet and olive/*pale yellow*	30	25
1853	40g. deep ultramarine and reddish violet/*pale lilac*	30	25
1854	40g. olive-green and deep blue/*pale grey*	30	25
1855	40g. black and orange-brown/*pale orange*	30	25
1856	40g. purple and bronze-green/*pale green*	30	25
1857	60g. blackish brown and ultramarine/*pale blue*	40	30
1858	60g. maroon and olive-green/*pale yellow-green*	40	30
1859	60g. blackish olive and carmine-red/*pale pink*	40	30
1860	60g. emerald-green and chocolate/*pale rose*	40	30
1861	60g. indigo and turquoise/*pale greenish blue*	40	30
1852/1861	*Set of* 10	3·25	2·50

Paintings and painters: No. 1852, T **516**; No. 1853, *Partisans* (Maciag); No. 1854 *Lenino* (Bylina); No. 1855, *Monte Cassino* (Boratyński); No. 1856, *Tanks before Warsaw* (Garwatowski); No. 1857, *Neisse River* (Bylina); No. 1858, *On the Oder* (Mackiewicz); No. 1859, *In Berlin* (Bylina); No. 1860, *Błyskawica* (destroyer) (Mokwa); No. 1861, *Pursuit* (Mikoyan Gurevich MiG-17 aircraft) (Kulisiewicz).

517 *Party Members* (F. Kowarski)

(Des F. Winiarski. Litho)

1968 (11 Nov). Fifth Polish United Workers' Party Congress, Warsaw. T **517** and similar multicoloured designs showing paintings. Perf 11×11½ (horiz) or 11½×11 (vert).

1862	60g. Type **517**	40	30
1863	60g. *Strike* (S. Lentz) (*vert*)	40	30
1864	60g. *Manifesto* (W. Weiss) (*vert*)	40	30
1862/1864	*Set of* 3	1·10	80

(Des K. Rogaczewska. Eng E. Tirdiszek (Nos. 1865, 1867), J. Miller (No. 1866), B. Kowalska (No. 1868), B. Brandt (No. 1869). Recess)

1968 (15 Nov). Polish Martyrdom and Resistance, 1939–1945 (4th series). Designs as T **491**. Perf 11½×11 (horiz) or 11×11½ (vert).

1865	40g. slate-grey	30	25
1866	40g. blackish brown	30	25
1867	40g. sepia	30	25
1868	40g. deep ultramarine	30	25
1869	40g. lake-brown	30	25
1865/1869	*Set of* 5	1·40	1·10

Designs: Horiz—No. 1865, Tomb of Unknown Soldier, Warsaw; No. 1866, Partisans' Monument, Kartuzy. Vert—No. 1867, Insurgents' Monument, Poznań; No. 1868, People's Guard Insurgents' Monument, Polichno; No. 1869, Rotunda, Zamość.

518 *Start of Hunt* (W. Kossak)

(Des S. Malecki. Litho)

1968 (20 Nov). Paintings. Hunting Scenes. T **518** and similar horiz designs. Multicoloured. Perf 11.

1870	20g. Type **518**	20	20
1871	40g. *Hunting with Falcon* (J. Kossak)	25	20
1872	60g. *Wolves' Raid* (A. Wierusz-Kowalski)	30	25
1873	1z.50 *Home-coming with a Bear* (J. Falat)	40	30
1874	2z.50 *The Fox-hunt* (T. Sutherland)	50	35
1875	3z.40 *The Boar-hunt* (F. Snyders)	75	40
1876	4z.50 *Hunters' Rest* (W. G. Pierow)	2·40	75
1877	8z.50 *Hunting a Lion in Morocco* (Delacroix)	2·50	1·00
1870/1877	*Set of* 8	6·50	3·00

519 Maltese Terrier **520** House Sign

(Des J. Grabiański. Litho)

1969 (2 Feb). Pedigree Dogs. Multicoloured designs as T **519**. Perf 11½×11 (vert) or 11×11½ (horiz).

1878	20g. Type **519**	30	20
1879	40g. Wire-haired Fox-terrier (*vert*)	40	25
1880	60g. Afghan Hound	50	30
1881	1z.50 Rough-haired Terrier	65	30
1882	2z.50 English Setter	90	35
1883	3z.40 Pekinese	1·30	40
1884	4z.50 Alsatian (*vert*)	2·50	65
1885	8z.50 Pointer (*vert*)	4·50	1·30
1878/1885	*Set of* 8	10·00	3·50

(Des K. Rogaczewska. Litho)

1969 (23 Feb). Ninth Polish Democratic Party Congress. Perf 11½×11.

1886	**520**	60g. carmine-red, black and grey	40	30

521 Dove and Ears of Wheat **522** Running

(Des K. Śliwka. Litho)

1969 (29 Mar). Fifth Congress of United Peasants' Party. Perf 11½.

1887	**521**	60g. multicoloured	40	30

(Des J. Jaworowski. Litho)

1969 (25 Apr). 75th Anniversary of International Olympic Committee and 50th Anniversary of Polish Olympic Committee. T **522** and similar vert designs. Multicoloured. Perf 11½×11.

1888	10g. Type **522**	20	20
1889	20g. Gymnastics	25	20
1890	40g. Weightlifting	30	25
1891	60g. Javelin	35	20
1892	2z.50+50g. Discus	40	25
1893	3z.40+1z. Running	65	35
1894	4z.+1z.50 Wrestling	1·30	40

1895	7z.+2z. Fencing	1·90	65
1888/1895	*Set of* 8	4·75	2·30

523 Pictorial Map of Świętokrzyski National Park

(Des A. Heidrich. Litho)

1969 (20 May). Tourism (1st series). T **523** and similar multicoloured designs. Perf 11.

1896	40g. Type **523**	20	20
1897	60g. Niedzica Castle (*vert*)	25	20
1898	1z.35 Kolobrzeg Lighthouse and yacht	30	25
1899	1z.50 Szczecin Castle and Harbour	35	30
1900	2z.50 Toruń and River Vistula	40	35
1901	3z.40 Klódźko, Silesia (*vert*)	65	40
1902	4z. Sulejów	90	50
1903	4z.50 Kazimierz Dolny marketplace (*vert*)	1·00	55
1896/1903	*Set of* 8	3·75	2·50

Nos. 1896/1903 were each issued with *se-tenant* half stamp-size labels showing either flora or Arms.

See also Nos. 1981/1985.

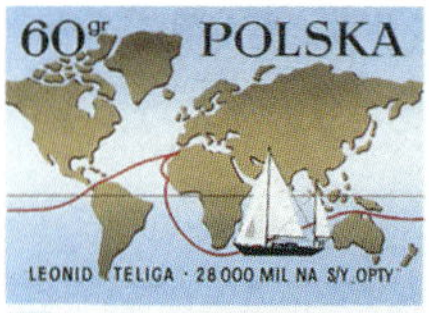

524 Route Map and *Opty*

525 Copernicus (after woodcut by T. Stimer) and Inscription

(Des A. Heidrich. Litho)

1969 (21 June). Leonid Teliga's World Voyage in Yacht *Opty*. Perf 11×11½.

1904	**524**	60g. multicoloured	40	35

(Des H. Chyliński. Eng Z. Kowalski (40g.), E. Konecki (60g.), B. Kowalska (2z.50). Recess and litho)

1969 (26 June). 500th Birth Anniversaryersary of Copernicus (1973) (1st issue). T **525** and similar horiz designs. Perf 11½.

1905	40g. blackish brown, red and yellow	35	30
1906	60g. deep slate-blue, red and light grey-green	40	35
	a. Full point after 'GR'	7·50	4·50
1907	2z.50 olive, red and light brown-purple	90	40
1905/1907	*Set of* 3	1·50	95

Designs: 40g. T **525**; 60g. Copernicus (after J. Falck) and 15th-century globe; 2z.50 Copernicus (after painting by J. Matejko) and diagram of heliocentric system.

See also Nos. 1995/1997, 2069/2072, 2167/**MS**2171, 2213/2214, 2217/2221.

526 Memory Flame and Badge

527 Frontier Guard and Arms

528 Coal Miner

529 Astronauts and Module on Moon

(Des T. Michaluk. Eng E. Tirdiszek. Recess, litho and typo)

1969 (19 July). Fifth National Alert of Polish Boy Scout Association. T **526** and similar vert designs. Perf 11×11½.

1908	60g. black, red and light blue	40	35
1909	60g. red, black and green	40	35
1910	60g. black, green and rose	40	35
1908/1910	*Set of* 3	1·10	95

Designs: No. 1908, T **526**; No. 1909, Defence eagle and badge; No. 1910, Labour map and badge.

(Des I. Michaluk. Litho and embossed (Nos. 1911/1915). Des F. Winiarski. Litho (others))

1969 (21 July). 25th Anniversary of Polish People's Republic. Multicoloured. Perf 11.

*(a) Vert designs as T **527**.*

1911	60g. Type **527**	40	35
	a. Horiz strip of 5. Nos. 1911/1915	2·10	
1912	60g. Lódź petro-chemical plant	40	35
1913	60g. Combine-harvester	40	35
1914	60g. Grand Theatre, Warsaw	40	35
1915	60g. Curie statue and University, Lublin	40	35

*(b) Horiz designs as T **528**.*

1916	60g. Type **528**	40	35
	a. Horiz strip of 4. Nos. 1916/1919	1·70	
1917	60g. Sulphur worker	40	35
1918	60g. Steel worker	40	35
1919	60g. Shipbuilder	40	35
1911/1919	*Set of* 9	3·25	2·75

Nos. 1911/1915 and 1916/1919 respectively were issued in vertical and horizontal *se-tenant* strips within their sheets.

(Des A. Balcerzak. Litho)

1969 (21 Aug). First Man on the Moon. Perf 12×12½.

1920	**529**	2z.50 multicoloured	1·50	90

Issued in sheets of eight stamps and two different stamp-size *se-tenant* labels.

530 *Motherhood* (S. Wyspiański)

531 Nike Statue

(Des R. Dudzicki. Photo)

1969 (4 Sept). Polish Paintings. Multicoloured designs as T **530**. Perf 11½×11 (vert) or 11×11½ (horiz).

1921	20g. Type **530**	20	20
1922	40g. *Hamlet* (J. Malczewski)	25	20
1923	60g. *Indian Summer* (J. Chełmoński)	30	25
1924	2z. *Two Girls* (O. Boznańska) (*vert*)	35	30
1925	2z.50 *The Sun of May* (J. Mehoffer) (*vert*)	40	35
1926	3z.40 *Woman combing her Hair* (W. Ślewiński)	65	50
1927	5z.50 *Still Life* (J. Pankiewicz)	1·50	65
1928	7z. *Abduction of the King's Daughter* (W. Wojtkiewicz)	2·50	90
1921/1928	*Set of* 8	5·50	3·00

Issued in sheets of four stamps and two *se-tenant* labels inscribed with the artist's name.

(Des K. Śliwka. Litho)

1969 (19 Sept). Fourth Congress of Fighters for Freedom and Democracy Association. Perf 11½×11.

1929	**531**	60g. red, black and bistre	40	35

532 Majdanek Memorial

533 Krzczonów (Lublin) Costumes

(Des K. Rogaczewska. Litho)

1969 (20 Sept). Inauguration of Majdanek Memorial. Perf 11.

1930	**532**	40g. black and bright mauve	35	30

(Des S. Malecki. Litho)

1969 (30 Sept). Provincial Costumes. T **533** and similar vert designs. Multicoloured. Perf 11½×11.

1931	40g. Type **533**	20	20
1932	60g. Lowicz (Łódź)	25	20
1933	1z.15 Rozbark (Katowice)	30	25
1934	1z.35 Lower Silesia (Wroclaw)	40	30
1935	1z.50 Opoczno (Łódź)	65	35
1936	4z.50 Sacz (Cracow)	1·00	40
1937	5z. Highlanders (Cracow)	1·30	65
1938	7z. Kurpie (Warsaw)	1·80	75
1931/1938	*Set of* 8	5·25	2·75

534 Pedestrians Keep Left

535 Welding and ILO Emblem

(Des K. Śliwka. Litho)

1969 (4 Oct). Road Safety. T **534** and similar red designs. Multicoloured. Perf 11.

1939	40g. Type **534**	35	25
1940	60g. Drive Carefully (Horses on road)	40	30
1941	2z.50 Do Not Dazzle (cars on road at night)	50	40
1939/1941	*Set of* 3	1·10	85

(Des J. Desselberger. Litho)

1969 (20 Oct). 50th Anniversary of International Labour Organisation. Perf 11×11½.

1942	**535**	2z.50 chalky blue and gold	40	35

536 The Bell-founder

537 'Angel" (19th century)

(Des J. Rapnicki and F. Winiarski. Litho)

1969 (12 Nov). Miniatures from *Behem's Code* of 1505. T **536** and similar vert designs. Multicoloured. Perf 12½.

1943	40g. Type **536**	20	20
1944	60g. The Painter	25	20
1945	1z.35 The Woodcarver	30	25
1946	1z.55 The Shoemaker	40	30
1947	2z.50 The Cooper	50	35
1948	3z.40 The Baker	75	40
1949	4z.50 The Tailor	1·30	65
1950	7z. The Bowyer	2·10	75
1943/1950	*Set of* 8	5·25	2·75

(Des S. Malecki. Litho)

1969 (19 Dec). Polish Folk Sculpture. T **537** and similar vert designs. Multicoloured. Perf 11½×11 (5z.50, 7z.) or 12½ (others).

1951	20g. Type **537**	20	20
1952	40g. Sorrowful Christ (19th century)	25	20
1953	60g. Sorrowful Christ (19th century) (*different*)	30	25
1954	2z. Weeping Woman (19th century)	35	30
1955	2z.50 Adam and Eve (F. Czajkowski)	40	35
1956	3z.40 Girl with Birds (L. Kudla)	65	40
1957	5z.50+1z.50 Choir (A. Zegadlo)	1·80	75
1958	7z.+1z.50 Organ-grinder (Z. Skrętowicz)	2·50	1·00
1951/1958	*Set of* 8	5·75	3·00

Nos. 1957/1958 are larger, 25×35 mm.

538 Leopold Staff

539 Nike Monument

(Des R. Dudzicki. Eng B. Kowalska (40g.), J. Miller (60g., 2z.50, 3z.40), E. Konecki (others). Recess, typo and photo)

1969 (30 Dec). Modern Polish Writers. T **538** and similar horiz portraits. Perf 11×11½.

1959	40g. black, olive-green and pale sage-green	20	20
1960	60g. black, carmine-red and pale pink	25	20
1961	1z.35 black, royal blue and pale blue	30	20
1962	1z.50 black, deep bluish violet and pale lilac.	35	25
1963	1z.55 black, deep emerald and pale turquoise-green	40	30
1964	2z.50 black, ultramarine and pale blue	50	30
1965	3z.40 black, red-brown and pale brown	75	40
1959/1965	*Set of* 7	2·50	1·70

Designs: 40g. T **538**; 60g. Wladyslaw Broniewski; 1z.35 Leon Kruczkowski; 1z.50 Julian Tuwim; 1z.55 Konstanty Ildefons Galczyński; 2z.50 Maria Dąbrownka; 3z.40 Zofia Nalkowska.

(Des F. Barącz. Photo)

1970 (17 Jan). 25th Anniversaryersary of Liberation of Warsaw. Perf 11½.

1966	**539**	60g. multicoloured	40	35

540 Early Printing Works and Colour Dots

541 Mallard

(Des A. Heidrich. Litho)

1970 (20 Jan). Centenary of Printers' Trade Union. Perf 11½×11.

1967	**540**	60g. multicoloured	40	35

(Des J. Desselberger. Litho)

1970 (28 Feb). Game Birds. T **541** and similar square designs. Multicoloured. Perf 11½.

1968	40g. Type **541**	20	20
1969	60g. Common Pheasant	25	20
1970	1z.15 Eurasian Woodcock	35	25
1971	1z.35 Ruff	40	30

1972	1z.50 Wood Pigeon	50	35
1973	3z.40 Black Grouse	65	40
1974	7z. Grey Partridge	4·50	1·30
1975	8z.50 Western Capercaillie	5·00	1·60
1968/1975 *Set of* 8		10·50	4·25

542 Lenin at Desk

(Des K. Tarkowska. Eng J. Miller (40g.), E. Konecki (60g.), B. Brandt (2z.50). Recess and typo)

1970 (22 Apr–10 Oct). Birth Centenary of Lenin. T **542** and similar horiz designs. Perf 11.

1976	40g. deep olive-grey and brown-red	35	30
1977	60g. sepia and magenta	40	35
1978	2z.50 black and vermilion	65	40
1976/1978 *Set of* 3		1·30	95
MS1979 134×81 mm. No. 1977×4 (10.10)		5·00	1·90

Designs: 40g. T **542**; 60g. Lenin addressing meeting; 2z.50 Lenin at Party Conference.

No. **MS**1979 was issued for Cracow Philatelic Exhibition.

543 Polish and Russian Soldiers in Berlin

544 Polish Flower

(Des A. Heidrich. Litho)

1970 (9 May). 25th Anniversaryersary of Liberation. Perf 11×11½.

1980	**543**	60g. multicoloured	40	35

(Des A. Heidrich. Litho)

1970 (9 May). Tourism (2nd series). Multicoloured designs as T **523**. Perf 11.

1981	60g. Town Hall, Wroclaw (*vert*)	40	35
1982	60g. View of Opole	40	35
1983	60g. Legnica Castle	40	35
1984	60g. Bolków Castle	40	35
1985	60g. Town Hall, Brzeg	40	35
1981/1985 *Set of* 5		1·80	1·60

Issued with *se-tenant* labels as described for the first series.

(Des K. Rogaczewska. Eng E. Konecki. Recess, litho and typo)

1970 (9 May). 25th Anniversary of Return of Western Territories. Perf 11½.

1986	**544**	60g. red, silver and deep bluish green	40	35

545 Movement Flag

546 UPU Emblem and New Headquarters

(Des K. Syta. Litho)

1970 (15 May). 75th Anniversary of Peasant Movement. Perf 11½.

1987	**545**	60g. multicoloured	40	35

(Des H. Chyliński. Litho)

1970 (20 May). New UPU Headquarters Building, Bern. Perf 11½.

1988	**546**	2z.50 bright blue and light greenish blue	40	40

547 Footballers

548 Hand with Lamp of Learning

(Des H. Matuszewska. Litho)

1970 (30 May). Gornik Zabrze v Manchester City, Final of European Cup Winners Cup Championship. Perf 11½×11.

1989	**547**	60g. multicoloured	60	50

No. 1989 was issued with *se-tenant* stamp-size label with inscription giving results of previous matches.

(Des H. Chyliński. Litho)

1970 (3 June). 150th Anniversary of Plock Scientific Society. Perf 11½.

1990	**548**	60g. yellow-olive, red and black	40	35

549 Olympic Runners (from Greek amphora)

(Des F. Winiarski (Nos. 1991 and 1993), W. Skoczylas (No. 1992), Z. Kamiński (1994). Photo)

1970 (16 June). Tenth Session of International Olympic Academy. T **549** and similar horiz designs. Perf 11×12.

1991	60g. vermilion, orange-yellow and black	40	35
1992	60g. deep violet-blue, bright blue and black	40	35
1993	60g. multicoloured	40	35
1991/1993 *Set of* 3		1·10	95
MS1994 71×101 mm. 10z.+5z. multicoloured. Imperf.		4·50	2·10

Designs: No. 1991 T **549**; No. 1992, The Archer; No. 1993, Modern runners; No. **MS**1994, Horse of Fame emblem of Polish Olympic Committee.

550 Copernicus (after miniature by Bacciarelli), and Bologna

(Des H. Matuszewska. Eng E. Tirdiszek (40g.), B. Kowalska (60g.), B. Brandt (2z.50). Recess, photo and typo)

1970 (26 June). 500th Birth Anniversary of Copernicus (1973) (2nd issue). Vert designs as T **550**. Perf 11½.

1995	40g. bronze-green, red-orange and reddish lilac	35	30
1996	60g. reddish lilac, bronze-green and orange-yellow	40	35
1997	2z.50 brown, ultramarine and light emerald	1·00	40
1995/1997 *Set of* 3		1·60	95

Designs: 40g. T **550**; 60g. Copernicus (after miniature by Lesseur), and Padua; 2z.50 Copernicus (by Zinck after lost Goluchowska portrait), and Ferrara.

551 *Aleksander Orlowski* (self-portrait)

552 UN Emblem within Eye

(Des T. Michaluk. Litho and photo)

1970 (27 Aug). Polish Miniatures. T **551** and similar vert portraits. Multicoloured. Perf 11½×11.

1998	20g. Type **551**	20	20
1999	40g. *Jan Matejko* (self-portrait)	25	20
2000	60g. *Stefan Batory* (unknown artist)	30	25
2001	2z. *Maria Leszczyńska* (unknown artist)	35	30
2002	2z.50 *Maria Walewska* (Marie-Victorie Jacquetot)	40	35
2003	3z.40 *Tadeusz Kosciuśzko* (J. Rustem)	50	40
2004	5z.50 *Samuel Linde* (G. Landolfi)	1·30	65
2005	7z. *Michal Ogiński* (Nanette Windisch)	2·50	70
1998/2005	*Set of 8*	5·25	2·75

Issued in sheets of four stamps and two inscribed stamp-sized *se-tenant* labels.

(Des F. Bąracz. Photo)

1970 (8 Sept). 25th Anniversary of United Nations. Perf 11½.

2006	**552**	2z.50 multicoloured	50	40

553 Piano Keyboard and Chopin's Signature

554 Population Pictograph

(Des S. Malecki. Eng E. Tirdiszek. Recess and photo)

1970 (8 Sept). Eighth International Chopin Piano Competition. Perf 11.

2007	**553**	2z.50 black and violet	50	40

(Des K. Rogaczewska. Litho)

1970 (15 Sept). National Census. T **554** and similar vert design. Multicoloured. Perf 11½×11.

2008	40g. Type **554**	35	25
2009	60g. Family in house	40	35

555 *Piorun* (destroyer)

(Des K. Rogaczewska. Eng B. Kowalska (40g.), E. Tirdiszek (60g.), B. Brandt (2z.50). Recess and photo)

1970 (25 Sept). Polish Warships of World War II. T **555** and similar horiz designs. Perf 11½×11.

2010	40g. blackish brown	35	30
2011	60g. black	40	35
2012	2z.50 deep brown	1·00	40
2010/2012	*Set of 3*	1·60	95

Designs: 40g. T **555**; 60g. *Orzel* (submarine); 2z.50 HMS *Garland* (destroyer loaned to Polish Navy).

556 *Expressions* (Maria Jarema)

557 *Luna 16* landing on Moon

(Des S. Malecki. Photo)

1970 (9 Oct). Stamp Day. Contemporary Polish Paintings. T **556** and similar multicoloured designs. Perf 11½×12 (vert) or 12×11½ (horiz).

2013	20g. *The Violin-cellist* (J. Nowosielski) (*vert*)	20	20
2014	40g. *View of Łódź* (B. Liberski) (*vert*)	25	20
2015	60g. *Studio Concert* (W. Taranczewski) (*vert*)	30	25
2016	1z.50 *Still Life* (Z. Pronaszko) (*vert*)	35	25
2017	2z. *Hanging-up Washing* (A. Wróblewski) (*vert*)	40	30
2018	3z.40 Type **556**	50	35
2019	4z. *Canal in the Forest* (P. Potworowski)	1·00	40
2020	8z.50 *The Sun* (W. Strzemiński)	2·10	70
2013/2020	*Set of 8*	4·50	2·40

(Des Z. Stasik. Litho)

1970 (20 Nov). Moon Landing of *Luna 16*. Perf 11½×11.

2021	**557**	2z.50 multicoloured	75	40

Issued in sheets of eight stamps and two different stamp-size *se-tenant* labels, showing Space scenes.

558 Stag (detail from Daniel tapestry)

559 Cadet Ship *Dar Pomorza*

(Des H. Matuszewska. Photo)

1970 (23 Dec). Tapestries in Wawel Castle. T **558** and similar vert designs. Multicoloured. Perf 11½.

2022	60g. Type **558**	25	20
2023	1z.15 White Stork (detail)	30	20
2024	1z.35 Panther fighting Dragon	40	25
2025	2z. Man's Head (detail, Deluge tapestry)	50	25
2026	2z.50 Child with Bird (detail, Adam Tilling the Soil tapestry)	65	35
2027	4z. God, Adam and Eve (detail, Happiness in Paradise tapestry)	1·30	40
2028	4z.50 Royal Monogram tapestry	1·60	65
2022/2028	*Set of 7*	4·50	2·10
MS2029		5·00	3·75

The designs on the miniature sheets are larger, 45×55 mm.

(Des S. Malecki. Photo)

1971 (20 Feb). Polish Ships. T **559** and similar horiz designs. Multicoloured. Perf 11.

2030	40g. Type **559**	25	20
2031	60g. Liner *Stefan Batory*	25	20
2032	1z.15 Icebreaker *Perkun*	30	25
2033	1z.35 Lifeboat *R-1*	35	30
2034	1z.50 Bulk carrier *Ziemia Szczecińska*	40	35
2035	2z.50 Tanker *Beskidy*	50	40
2036	5z. Fast freighter *Hel*	1·20	50
2037	8z.50 Ferry *Gryf*	2·30	90
2030/2037	*Set of 8*	5·00	2·75

560 Chęciny Castle

(Des T. Michaluk. Litho)

1971 (5 Mar). Polish Castles. T **560** and similar horiz designs. Multicoloured. Perf 11×12.

2038	20g. Type **560**	25	25
2039	40g. Wiśnicz	25	25
2040	60g. Będzin	30	25
2041	2z. Ogrodzieniec	35	25
2042	2z.50 Niedzica	40	30
2043	3z.40 Kwidzyń	50	35
2044	4z. Pieskowa Skala	80	40
2045	8z.50 Lidzbark Warmiński	1·90	75
2038/2045 *Set of 8*		4·25	2·50

561 Battle of Pouilly, J. Dabrowski and W. Wróblewski

562 Plantation

(Des H. Matuszewska. Litho)

1971 (10 Mar). Centenary of Paris Commune. Perf 12½.

2046	**561**	60g. purple-brown, bright blue and rosine	40	35

(Des Z. Stasik. Photo)

1971 (30 Mar). Forestry Management. T **562** and similar vert designs. Multicoloured. Perf 12½ (60g.) or 11½×11 (others).

2047	40g. Type **562**	35	25
2048	60g. Forest (27×47 mm)	40	35
2049	1z.50 Tree felling	55	40
2047/2049 *Set of 3*		1·20	90

563 Bishop Marianos

564 Revolutionaries

(Des H. Chyliński. Photo)

1971 (20 Apr). Fresco Discoveries made by Polish Expedition at Fares, Nubia. T **563** and similar vert designs. Multicoloured. Perf 11½×11.

2050	40g. Type **563**	25	25
2051	60g. St Anne	25	25
2052	1z.15 Archangel Michael	30	25
2053	1z.35 The Hermit, Anamon	35	30
2054	1z.50 Head of Archangel Michael	40	35
2055	4z.50 Evangelists' Cross	95	40
2056	5z. Christ protecting a nobleman	1·00	50
2057	7z. Archangel Michael (half-length)	1·50	75
2050/2057 *Set of 8*		4·50	2·75

(Des J. W. Brzoza. Photo)

1971 (3 May–17 June). 50th Anniversary of Silesian Insurrection. Perf 11.

2058	**564**	60g. red-brown and gold	50	40
MS2059 108×106 mm. No. 2058×3 (17.6)			5·00	2·20

No. 2058 was issued in sheets of 15 stamps with half stamp-size *se-tenant* labels dated 1971.

No. **MS**2059 also contains three such labels, and was issued in connection with a Philatelic Exhibition at Katowice.

565 Soldiers

566 Fair Emblem

(Des H. Matuszewska from children's drawings. Photo)

1971 (29 May). 25th Anniversary of UNICEF Children's Drawings. T **565** and similar multicoloured designs. Perf 11½×11 (vert) or 11×11½ (horiz).

2060	20g. Peacock (*vert*)	25	25
2061	40g. Type **565**	25	25
2062	60g. Lady Spring (*vert*)	30	25
2063	2z. Cat and Ball	40	30
2064	2z.50 Flowers in Jug (*vert*)	50	35
2065	3z.40 Friendship	65	40
2066	5z.50 Clown (*vert*)	1·20	55
2067	7z. Strange Planet	1·80	75
2060/2067 *Set of 8*		4·75	2·75

(Des H. Chyliński. Photo)

1971 (1 June). 40th International Fair, Poznań. Perf 11½×11.

2068	**566**	60g. multicoloured	40	35

567 Copernicus's House, Toruń

568 Folk Art Pattern

569 *Head of Worker* (X. Dunikowski)

(Des A. Heidrich. Litho)

1971 (1 June). 500th Birth Anniversary of Copernicus (1973) (3rd series). T **567** and similar multicoloured designs. Perf 11.

2069	40g. Type **567**	35	25
2070	60g. Collegium Maius, Jagiellonian University, Cracow (*horiz*)	40	30
2071	2z.50 Olsztyn Castle (*horiz*)	55	35
2072	4z. Frombork Cathedral	1·00	40
2069/2072 *Set of 4*		2·10	1·20

Each value issued with different half stamp-size *se-tenant* label showing Copernicus (40g.) or aspects of his work.

(Des J. Jaworowski. Recess and photo)

1971 (12 July). Folk Art Paper Cut-outs. T **568** and similar vert designs showing different patterns. Perf 12×11½.

2073	**568**	20g. black, emerald and pale blue	35	30
2074	-	40g. indigo, deep olive and pale cream	35	30
2075	-	60g. deep brown, greenish blue and pale grey	35	30
2076	-	1z.15 maroon, yellow-brown and pale buff	35	30
2077	-	1z.35 deep bluish green, vermilion and pale yellow-green	35	30
2073/2077 *Set of 5*			1·60	1·40

(Des J. W. Brzoza. Photo)

1971 (21 July–27 Oct). Modern Polish Sculpture. T **569** and similar vert designs. Multicoloured. Perf 11½×11.

2078	40g. Type **569**	35	30
2079	40g. *Foundryman* (X. Dunikowski)	35	30
2080	60g. *Miners* (M. Więcek)	40	35
2081	60g. *Harvester* (S. Horno-Poplawski)	40	35
2078/2081 *Set of 4*		1·40	1·20
MS2082 158×85 mm. Nos. 2078/2081. Perf 12½×12 (27.10)		6·25	2·40

No. **MS**2082 was issued in connection with a Philatelic Exhibition at Szczecin.

570 Congress Emblem and Computer Tapes

571 Angel (J. Mehoffer)

(Des H. Chyliński. Litho)

1971 (2 Sept). Sixth Polish Technical Congress, Warsaw. Perf 11×11½.

2083	**570**	60g. violet and red	40	35

(Des K. Tarkowska. Photo)

1971 (15 Sept). Stained Glass Windows. T **571** and similar vert designs. Multicoloured. Perf 11½×11.

2084	20g. Type **571**	25	25
2085	40g. Lilies (S. Wyspiański)	25	25
2086	60g. Iris (S. Wyspiański)	30	25
2087	1z.35 Apollo (S. Wyspiański)	35	30
2088	1z.55 Two Wise Men (14th century)	40	35
2089	3z.40 The Flight into Egypt (14th century)	65	40
2090	5z.50 Jacob (14th century)	1·10	50
2091	8z.50+4z. Madonna (15th century)	1·80	1·00
2084/2091	*Set of* 8	4·50	3·00

The 40g., 60g., 1z.35 and 8z.50 are larger, 26×39 mm.

572 *Mrs Fedorowicz* (W. Pruszkowski)

573 PZL P-11C Fighters

(Des K. Śliwka. Litho)

1971 (25 Sept). Contemporary Art from National Museum, Cracow. T **572** and similar multicoloured designs. Perf 11×11½.

2092	40g. Type **572**	25	25
2093	50g. *Woman with Book* (T. Czyżewski)	25	25
2094	60g. *Girl with Chrysanthemums* (O. Boznańska)	30	25
2095	2z.50 *Girl in Red Dress* (J. Pankiewicz) (*horiz*)	40	30
2096	3z.40 *Reclining Nude* (L. Chwistek) (*horiz*)	55	30
2097	4z.50 *Strange Garden* (J. Mehoffer)	80	35
2098	5z. *Wife in White Hat* (Z. Pronaszko)	95	40
2099	7z.+1z. *Seated Nude* (W. Weiss)	1·40	1·00
2092/2099	*Set of* 8	4·50	2·75

Issued in sheets of four stamps and two stamp-size *se-tenant* labels bearing inscription.

(Des J. Brodowski. Photo)

1971 (14 Oct). Polish Aircraft of World War II. T **573** and similar horiz designs. Multicoloured. Perf 11×11½.

2100	90g. Type **573**	40	30
2101	1z.50 PZL 23A Karaś fighters	65	35
2102	3z.40 PZL P-37 Loś bomber	80	40
2100/2102	*Set of* 3	1·70	95

574 Royal Castle, Warsaw (pre-1939)

575 Astronauts in Moon Rover

(Des K. Śliwka. Photo)

1971 (14 Oct). Reconstruction of Royal Castle, Warsaw. Perf 11×11½.

2103	**574**	60g. black, red and gold	40	35

(Des A. Balcerzak. Photo)

1971 (17 Nov). Moon Flight of *Apollo 15*. Perf 11×11½.

2104	**575**	2z.50 multicoloured	1·00	40
MS2105		122×157 mm. No. 2104×6 plus two stamp-size *se-tenant* labels, showing Space scenes	13·00	6·50

576 *Lunokhod 1*

577 Worker at Wheel

578 Shipbuilding

(Des Z. Stasik. Photo)

1971 (17 Nov). Moon Flight of *Lunik 17* and *Lunokhod 1*. Perf 11½×11.

2106	**576**	2z.50 multicoloured	1·00	40
MS2107		158×118 mm. No. 2106×6 plus 2 stamp-size *se-tenant* labels, showing Space scenes	13·00	6·50

(Des S. Malecki (Nos. 2108/2109) or J. W. Brzoza (others). Photo)

1971 (16 Dec)–**72**. Sixth Polish United Workers' Party Congress.

(a) Party Posters. T ***577*** *and similar vert design. Perf 11½×11.*

2108	**577**	60g. red, violet-blue and pale grey	40	35
		a. Strip. Nos. 2108/2109 plus label	85	75
2109	–	60g. red and pale grey (Worker's head)	40	35

(b) Industrial Development. T ***578*** *and similar horiz designs. Each gold, black and red. Perf 11×11½.*

2110	60g. Type **578**	40	35
	a. Block of 6. Nos. 2110/2115	2·50	
2111	60g. Building construction	40	35
2112	60g. Combine-harvester	40	35
2113	60g. Motor car production	40	35
2114	60g. Pithead	40	35
2115	60g. Petro-chemical plant	40	35
2108/2115	*Set of* 6	3·00	2·50
MS2116	102×115 mm. Nos. 2110/2115 (4.72)	3·25	2·00

Nos. 2108/2109 were issued *se-tenant* within the sheet with an intervening stamp-size label inscr 'PZPR'.

Nos. 2110/2115 were issued together *se-tenant* in blocks of six within the sheet, forming an outline map of Poland.

579 *Prunus cerasus*

(Des A. Balcerzak. Litho)

1971 (28 Dec). Flowers of Trees and Shrubs. T **579** and similar horiz designs. Multicoloured. Perf 12½.

2117	10g. Type **579**	25	25
2118	20g. *Malus niedzwetzkyana*	25	25
2119	40g. *Pyrus L.*	25	25
2120	60g. *Prunus persica*	25	25
2121	1z.15 *Magnolia kobus*	30	25
2122	1z.35 *Crataegus oxyacantha*	35	30
2123	2z.50 *Malus M.*	40	35
2124	3z.40 *Aesculus carnea*	65	40
2125	5z. *Robinia pseudoacacia*	1·40	55

2126	8z.50 *Prunus avium*	3·00	1·00
2117/2126	*Set of* 10	6·50	3·50

580 *Worker* (sculpture, J. Januszkiewicz)

(Des J. Brzoza. Recess and photo)

1972 (5 Jan). 30th Anniversaryersary of Polish Workers' Coalition. Perf 11½.

2127	**580**	60g. black and red	40	35

581 Tobogganing

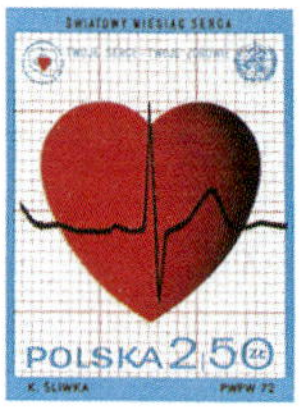

582 Heart and Cardiogram Trace

(Des H. Matuszewska. Photo)

1972 (12 Jan). Winter Olympic Games, Sapporo, Japan. T **581** and similar multicoloured designs. Perf 11.

2128	40g. Type **581**	30	25
2129	60g. Slalom (*vert*)	40	30
2130	1z.65 Biathlon (*vert*)	55	35
2131	2z.50 Ski jumping	80	40
2128/2131	*Set of* 4	1·80	1·20
MS2132	85×68 mm. 10z.+5z. Downhill skiing. Imperf	4·75	2·75

(Des K. Śliwka. Photo)

1972 (28 Mar). World Heart Month. Perf 11½×11.

2133	**582**	2z.50 multicoloured	50	40

583 Running

584 Cyclists

(Des W. Świerzy. Photo)

1972 (25 Apr). Olympic Games, Munich. T **583** and similar vert designs. Multicoloured. Perf 11½×11.

2134	20g. Type **583**	25	25
2135	30g. Archery	25	25
2136	40g. Boxing	25	25
2137	60g. Fencing	30	25
2138	2z.50 Wrestling	35	30
2139	3z.40 Weightlifting	40	35
2140	5z. Cycling	75	40
2141	8z.50 Shooting	1·40	55
2134/2141	*Set of* 8	3·50	2·30
MS2142	70×80 mm. 10z.+5z. As 30g	3·25	1·60

(Des T. Michaluk. Photo)

1972 (2 May). 25th International Peace Cycle Race. Perf 11.

2143	**584**	60g. multicoloured	40	35

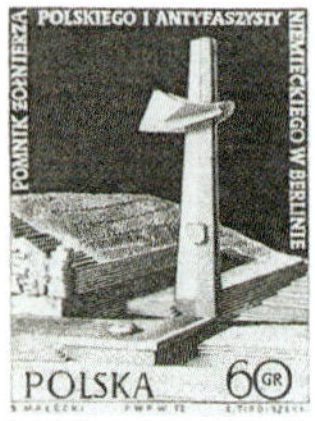

585 Polish War Memorial, Berlin

(Des S. Malecki. Eng E. Tirdiszek. Recess)

1972 (9 May). Victory Day, 1945. Perf 11½×11.

2144	**585**	60g. blackish green	40	35

586 Rodlo Emblem

587 Polish Knight of 972 AD

(Des J. Klopocka. Photo)

1972 (28 May). 50th Anniversary of Polish Posts in Germany. Perf 11½×11.

2145	**586**	60g. scarlet, myrtle-green and pale bistre	40	35

(Des J. Wysocki. Photo)

1972 (12 June). Millenary of Battle of Cedynia. Perf 11½×11.

2146	**587**	60g. multicoloured	40	35

588 Cheetah (*Acinonyx jubatus*)

589 L. Waryński (founder)

(Des J. Grabiański. Litho)

1972 (21 Aug). Zoo Animals. T **588** and similar multicoloured designs on pale buff paper. Perf 12½.

2147	20g. Type **588**	25	25
2148	40g. Giraffe (*Giraffa camelopardalis*) (*vert*)	30	25
2149	60g. Toco Toucan	35	25
2150	1z.35 Chimpanzee (*Pan troglodytes*)	50	30
2151	1z.65 Common Gibbon (*Hylobates lar*)	70	35
2152	3z.40 Crocodile	1·20	40
2153	4z. Red Kangaroo (*Macropus rufus*)	1·90	80
2154	4z.50 Tiger (*Panthera tigris sumatrae*) (*vert*)	5·00	2·40
2155	7z. Mountain Zebra (*Equus zebra*)	6·75	3·00
2147/2155	*Set of* 9	15·00	7·25

(Des K. W. Brzoza. Photo)

1972 (1 Sept). 90th Anniversary of Proletarian Party. Perf 11.

2156	**589**	60g. multicoloured	45	40

No. 2156 was issued together with *se-tenant* stamp-sized labels showing a facsimile of the front page of *Proletaryat*.

590 F. Dzierzyński

591 Global Emblem

(Des Z. Stasik. Photo)

1972 (11 Sept). 95th Birth Anniversary of Feliks Dzierzyński (Russian politician). Perf 11×11½.

2157	**590**	60g. black and red	40	35

(Des M. Wieczorek. Photo)

1972 (15 Sept). 25th International Co-operative Federation Congress. Perf 11½×11.

2158	**591**	60g. multicoloured	40	35

592 Scene from *In Barracks* (ballet)

(Des J. Desselberger. Eng B. Kowalska (10g., 2z.50), B. Brandt (20g., 1z.35, 1z.55), E. Tirdiszek (40g., 60g.) and E. Konecki (1z.15). Recess and photo)

1972 (15 Sept). Death Centenary of Stanislaus Moniuszko (composer). Scenes from Works. T **592** and similar vert designs. Perf 11½.

2159	10g. violet and gold	25	25
2160	20g. black and gold	25	25
2161	40g. myrtle-green and gold	25	25
2162	60g. indigo and gold	30	25
2163	1z.15 deep blue and gold	35	25
2164	1z.35 deep blue and gold	40	30
2165	1z.55 olive-grey and gold	50	35
2166	2z.50 blackish brown and gold	85	40
2159/2166 *Set of 8*		2·75	2·10

Designs: 10g. T **592**; 20g. *The Countess* (opera); 40g. *The Haunted Manor* (opera); 60g. *Halka* (opera); 1z.15 *New Don Quixote* (ballet); 1z.35 *Verbum Nobile* (opera); 1z.55 *Ideal* (operetta); 2z.50 *Pariah* (opera).

593 Copernicus the Astronomer

(Des W. Andrzejewski. Eng B. Kowalska (10z.). Litho or recess and typo (10z.))

1972 (28 Sept). 500th Birth Anniversary of Nicolas Copernicus (1973) (4th issue), and Polska 73 Stamp Exhibition, Poznań. T **593** and similar designs. Perf 11×11½ or 11½ (10z.).

2167	40g. black and bright blue	35	30
2168	60g. black and yellow-orange	40	35
2169	2z.50 black and bright red	75	40
2170	3z.40 black and yellow-green	1·20	60
2167/2170 *Set of 4*		2·40	1·50
MS2171	62×102 mm 10z.+5z. multicoloured	5·00	2·40

Designs: Horiz—40g. T **593**; 60g. Copernicus and Medal of 1530; 2z.50 Copernicus and Polish eagle; 3z.40 Copernicus and page of book. Vert 29×48 mm—10z.+5z. Copernicus charting the planets.

594 *Amazon* (P. Michalowski)

(595)

(Des T. Michaluk. Photo)

1972 (28 Sept). Stamp Day. Polish Paintings. T **594** and similar multicoloured designs. Perf 11.

2172	30g. Type **594**	25	25
2173	40g. *Ostafi Laskiewicz* (J. Metejko)	25	25
2174	60g. *Summer Idyll* (W. Gerson)	25	25
2175	2z. *The Neapolitan Woman* (A. Kotsis)	30	25
2176	2z.50 *Girl Bathing* (P. Szyndler)	35	30
2177	3z.40 *The Princess of Thum* (A. Grottger)	40	35
2178	4z. *Rhapsody* (S. Wyspiański)	2·20	40
2179	8z.50+4z. *Young Woman* (J. Malczewski) (*horiz*)	2·75	65
2172/2179 *Set of 8*		6·00	2·40

1972 (2 Oct–17 Nov). Provisionals. Nos. 1578/1579 surch as T **595**.

2180	50g. on 40g. red-brown (R.) (17.11)	25	25
2181	90g. on 40g. red-brown (R.) (17.11)	30	25
2182	1z. on 40g. red-brown (R.)	30	25
2183	1z.50 on 60g. orange-red	35	25
2184	2z.70 on 40g. red-brown (R.)	40	25
2185	4z. on 60g. orange-red	55	25
2186	4z.50 on 60g. orange-red	65	35
2187	4z.90 on 60g. orange-red	90	40
2180/2187 *Set of 8*		3·25	2·00

On Nos. 2180/2182 and 2184 the old denominations are obliterated by crosses.

596 The Little Soldier (E. Piwowarski)

597 Royal Castle, Warsaw (E. J. Dahlberg, 1656)

(Des T. Michaluk. Litho)

1972 (16 Oct). Children's Health Centre. Perf 11½.

2188	**596**	60g. black and pink	40	35

(Des A. Heidrich. Photo)

1972 (16 Oct). Restoration of Royal Castle, Warsaw. Perf 11×11½.

2189	**597**	60g. black, reddish violet and light blue	40	35

598 Chalet, Chocholowska Valley

599 Trade Union Banners

(Des A. Balcerzak. Photo)

1972 (13 Nov). Tourism. Mountain Chalets. T **598** and similar multicoloured designs. Perf 11.

2190	40g. Type **598**	25	25
2191	60g. Hala Ornak (*horiz*)	25	25
2192	1z.55 Hala Gasienicowa	30	25
2193	1z.65 Valley of Five Lakes (*horiz*)	40	30
2194	2z.50 Morskie Oko	50	35
2190/2194	*Set of* 5	1·50	1·30

(Des K. Śliwka. Photo)

1972 (13 Nov). Seventh Polish Trade Unions Congress. Perf 11½×11.

2195	**599**	60g. multicoloured	40	35

600 Congress Emblem

601 Japanese Azalea

(Des A. Heidrich. Photo)

1972 (15 Dec). Fifth Socialist Youth Union Congress. Perf 11½.

2196	**600**	60g. multicoloured	40	35

(Des A. Balcerzak. Litho)

1972 (15 Dec). Flowering Shrubs. T **601** and similar horiz designs. Multicoloured. Perf 12½.

2197	40g. Type **601**	25	25
2198	50g. Alpine rose	25	25
2199	60g. Pomeranian Honeysuckle	30	25
2200	1z.65 Chinese Quince	35	25
2201	2z.50 Korean Cranberry	40	30
2202	3z.40 Pontic Azalea	85	35
2203	4z. Delavay's White Syringa	2·00	40
2204	8z.50 Common Lilac (Massena)	3·00	1·00
2197/2204	*Set of* 8	6·75	2·75

602 Piast Knight (10th century)

(Des L. Maciąg. Photo)

1972 (28 Dec). Polish Cavalry Through the Ages. T **602** and similar multicoloured designs. Perf 11.

2205	20g. Type **602**	25	25
2206	40g. 13th-century knight	30	25
2207	60g. Knight of Wladyslaw Jagiello's Army (15th century) (*horiz*)	35	25
2208	1z.35 17th-century hussar	40	30
2209	4z. Lancer of National Guard (18th century)	1·20	35
2210	4z.50 Congress Kingdom cavalry officer (1831)	1·30	40
2211	5z. Trooper of Light Cavalry (1939) (*horiz*)	2·10	65
2212	7z. Trooper of People's Army (1945)	2·50	85
2205/2212	*Set of* 8	7·50	3·00

603 Copernicus

604 Couple with Hammer and Sickle

605 *Copernicus as a Young Man* (Bacciarelli)

(Des A. Heidrich. Photo)

1972 (28 Dec). Coil Stamps. 500th Birth Anniversary of Copernicus (1973) (5th issue). Perf 14.

2213	**603**	1z. brown-lake	35	30
2214		1z.50 deep ochre	40	35

(Des T. Konarski and J. Wysocki. Photo)

1972 (30 Dec). 50th Anniversary of USSR. T **604** and similar vert design. Perf 11½×11.

2215	**604**	40g. multicoloured	35	30
2216	–	60g. vermilion, ultramarine and black	40	35

Design: 60g. Red Star and globe.

(Des H. Chyliński. Photo)

1973 (18 Feb). 500th Birth Anniversary of Copernicus (6th issue). T **605** and similar multicoloured portraits. Perf 11×11½ (4z.90) or 11½×11 (others).

2217	1z. Type **605**	25	25
2218	1z.50 *Copernicus* (anon)	30	25
2219	2z.70 *Copernicus* (Zinck Nor)	65	35
2220	4z. Copernicus (from Strasbourg clock)	80	40
2221	4z.90 *Copernicus* (Jan Matejko) (*horiz*)	1·30	65
2217/2221	*Set of* 5	3·00	1·70

606 Coronation Sword

607 Statue of Lenin

(Des S. Malecki. Photo)

1973 (28 Mar). Polish Art. T **606** and similar vert designs. Multicoloured. Perf 11½×11.

2222	50g. Type **606**	25	25
2223	1z. *Krużlowa Madonna* (detail)	30	25
2224	1z. Armour of hussar	30	25
2225	1z.50 Carved head from Wawel Castle	40	30
2226	1z.50 Silver cockerel	40	30
2227	2z.70 Armorial eagle	60	40
2228	4z.90 *Skarbimierz Madonna*	1·10	55
2229	8z.50 *Portrait of Tenczynski* (anon)	2·00	90
2222/2229	*Set of* 8	4·75	3·00

(Des S. Malecki. Litho)

1973 (28 Apr). Unveiling of Lenin's Statue, Nowa Huta. Perf 11×11½.

2230	**607**	1z. multicoloured	40	35

608 Coded Letter

610 Salyut

609 Wolf (*Canis lupus*)

(Des H. Chyliński. Photo)

1973 (5 May). Introduction of Postal Codes. Perf 11×11½.

2231	**608**	1z.50 multicoloured	40	35

(Des I. Konarski and J. Wysocki. Photo)

1973 (21 May). International Hunting Council Congress and 50th Anniversary of Polish Hunting Association. Game Animals. T **609** and similar horiz designs. Multicoloured. Perf 11.

2232	50g. Type **609**	25	25
2233	1z. Mouflon (*Ovis ammon musimon*)	25	25
2234	1z.50 Elk (*Alces alces*)	30	25
2235	2z.70 Western Capercaillie (*Tetrao urogallus*)	35	25
2236	3z. Roe Deer (*Capreolus capreolus*)	50	30
2237	4z.50 Lynx (*Lynx lynx*)	1·10	40
2238	4z.90 Red Deer (*Cervus elaphus*)	3·25	70
2239	5z. Wild Boar (*Sus scrofa*)	4·25	95
2232/2239 *Set of* 8		9·25	3·00

(Des Z. Stasik. Photo)

1973 (20 June). Cosmic Research. T **610** and similar horiz design. Multicoloured. Perf 11×11½.

2240	4z.90 Type **610**	95	40
2241	4z.90 *Copernicus* (US satellite)	95	40

Nos. 2240/2241 were respectively issued in sheets of six stamps plus two *se-tenant* stamp-sized labels depicting (No. 2240) *Soyuz 11* or Soviet astronauts; (No. 2241) Copernicus or constellations.

611 Open Book and Flame

(Des R. Dudzicki. Litho)

1973 (26 June). Second Polish Science Congress, Warsaw. Perf 11½.

2242	**611**	1z.50 multicoloured	40	35

612 Ancient Seal of Poznań

(Des W. Andrzejewski. Eng E. Konecki (10z.). Litho or recess and litho (10z.))

1973 (30 June–19 Aug). Polska 73 Philatelic Exhibition, Poznań. T **612** and similar multicoloured designs. Perf 11×11½ (4z.) or 11½×11 (others).

2243	1z. Type **612**	25	25
2244	1z.50 Tombstone of N. Tomicki	30	25
2245	2z.70 Kalisz paten	40	30
2246	4z. Bronze gates, Gniezno Cathedral (*horiz*)	70	40
2243/2246 *Set of* 4		1·50	1·10
MS2247	91×66 mm. 10z.+5z. deep purple and pale olive. Imperf	3·50	1·80
MS2248	91×66 mm. 10z.+5z. deep purple and pale lilac. Imperf	12·50	8·50

Design: 68×32 mm—10z. Poznań in 1740.

No. **MS**2248 was sold only with entrance tickets to the exhibition.

613 M. Nowotko **614** Cherry Blossom

(Des J. Wysocki. Litho)

1973 (8 Aug). 80th Birth Anniversary of Marceli Nowotko (party leader). Perf 11½×11.

2249	**613**	1z.50 black and vermilion	40	35

(Des H. Matuszewska. Photo)

1973 (20 Aug). Protection of the Environment. T **614** and similar horiz designs. Multicoloured. Perf 11.

2250	50g. Type **614**	25	25
2251	90g. Cattle in meadow	25	25
2252	1z. White stork on nest	30	25
2253	1z.50 Fresh water life	35	30
2254	2z.70 Meadow flora	40	35
2255	4z.90 Ocean fauna	70	40
2256	5z. Forest life	3·50	70
2257	6z.50 Agricultural produce	4·25	1·10
2250/2257 *Set of* 8		9·00	3·25

615 Motorcyclist

(Des W. Andrzejewski. Photo)

1973 (2 Sept). World Speedway Championships, Chorzów. Perf 11½.

2258	**615**	1z.50 multicoloured	40	35

616 *Copernicus* (M. Bacciarelli)

(Des A. Heidrich. Photo)

1973 (27 Sept). Stamp Day. Perf 11×11½.

2259	**616**	4z.+2z. multicoloured	1·20	55

617 Tank

(Des T. Michaluk. Litho)

1973 (4 Oct). 30th Anniversary of Polish People's Army. T **617** and similar horiz designs. Multicoloured. Perf 12½.

2260	1z. Type **617**	35	30
2261	1z. Mikoyan Gurevich MiG-21D aeroplane	35	30
2262	1z.50 Guided missile	40	35
2263	1z.50 *Puck* (missile boat)	40	35
2260/2263 *Set of* 4		1·40	1·20

618 G. Piramowicz and Title Page

(Des S. Malecki. Eng E. Tirdiszek (1z.) and B. Brandt (1z.50). Recess and photo)

1973 (13 Oct). Bicentenary of National Education Commission. T **618** and similar horiz design. Perf 12×11½.

2264	**618**	1z. blackish brown and pale yellow	30	25
2265	-	1z.50 bronze-green and pale grey-green	40	35

Design: 1z.50 J. Śniadecki, H. Kollataj and J. U. Niemcewicz.

619 Pawel Strzelecki (explorer) and Red Kangaroo

620 Polish Flag

(Des T. Michaluk. Photo)

1973 (30 Nov). Polish Scientists. T **619** and similar vert designs. Multicoloured. Perf 11.

2266	1z. Type **619**	30	25
2267	1z. Henryk Arctowski (Polar explorer) and Adélie Penguins	30	25
2268	1z.50 Stefan Rogoziński (explorer) and *Lucy-Margaret* (schooner)	35	25
2269	1z.50 Benedykt Dybowski (zoologist) and Sable, Lake Baikal	35	25
2270	2z. Bronislaw Malinowski (anthropologist) and New Guinea dancers	45	30
2271	2z.70 Stefan Drzewiecki (oceanographer) and submarine	65	35
2272	3z. Edward Strasburger (botanist) and classified plants	90	40
2273	8z. Ignacy Domeyko (geologist) and Chilean desert landscape	2·10	60
2266/2273	*Set of* 8	4·75	2·40

(Des K. Śliwka. Photo)

1973 (15 Dec). 25th Anniversary of Polish United Workers' Party. Perf 11½×11.

2274	**620**	1z.50 red, ultramarine and gold	55	40

621 Jelcz-Berliet Coach

622 Iris

(Des T. Konarski and J. Wysocki. Photo)

1973 (28 Dec). Polish Motor Vehicles. T **621** and similar horiz designs. Multicoloured. Perf 11×11½.

2275	50g. Type **621**	25	25
2276	90g. Jelcz 316 truck	30	25
2277	1z. Polski-Fiat 126p saloon	35	30
2278	1z.50 Polski-Fiat 125p saloon	45	35
2279	4z. Nysa M-521 utility van	80	40
2280	4z.50 Star 660 truck	1·60	55
2275/2280	*Set of* 6	3·50	1·90

(Des J. Brodowski. Eng B. Kowalska (50g., 1z.), E. Konecki (1z.50, 3z.), A. Ostrowska (4z., 4z.50). Recess)

1974 (22 Jan). Flowers. Drawings by S. Wyspiański. T **622** and similar vert designs. Perf 12×11½.

2281	50g. purple	30	25
2282	1z. turquoise-green	35	25
2283	1z.50 vermilion	35	25
2284	3z. violet	55	30
2285	4z. ultramarine	80	35
2286	4z.50 blue-green	95	40
2281/2286	*Set of* 6	3·00	1·60

Flowers: 50g. T **622**; 1z. Dandelion; 1z.50 Rose; 3z. Thistle; 4z. Cornflower; 4z.50 Clover.

623 Cottage, Kurpie

624 19th-century Mail Coach

(Des F. Winiarski. Photo)

1974 (5 Mar). Wooden Architecture. T **623** and similar horiz designs. Multicoloured. Perf 11×11½.

2287	1z. Type **623**	25	25
2288	1z.50 Church, Sękowa	30	25
2289	4z. Town Hall, Sulmierzyce	55	35
2290	4z.50 Church, Lachowice	70	40
2291	4z.90 Windmill, Sobienie-Jeziory	1·10	55
2292	5z. Orthodox Church, Ulucz	1·40	70
2287/2292	*Set of* 6	3·75	2·30

(Des T. Michaluk. Photo)

1974 (30 Mar). Centenary of Universal Postal Union. Perf 11½.

2293	**624**	1z.50 multicoloured	40	35

625 Cracow Motif

626 Association Emblem

(Des H. Matuszewska. Photo)

1974 (7–19 May). SOCPHILEX IV International Stamp Exhibition, Katowice. Regional Floral Embroideries. T **625** and similar vert designs. Multicoloured. Perf 11½×11.

2294	50g. Type **625**	25	25
2295	1z.50 Lowicz motif	40	30
2296	4z. Silesian motif	60	40
2294/2296	*Set of* 3	1·10	85
MS2297	69×171 mm. No. 2296×3. Imperf (*sold at* 17z.) (19.5)	2·50	1·80

The normal, imperforate, version of No. **MS**2297 has bluish violet borders, showing a lace pattern in white. The miniature sheet also exists perforated from a limited printing with white borders and the lace pattern in silver.

(Des K. Śliwka. Litho)

1974 (8 May). Fifth Congress of Fighters for Freedom and Democracy Association, Warsaw. Perf 11½.

2298	**626**	1z.50 red and brownish grey	40	35

627 Soldier and Dove

(Des T. Michaluk. Litho)

1974 (9 May). 29th Anniversary of Victory over Fascism in Second World War. Perf 11½×11.

2299	**627**	1z.50 multicoloured	40	35

628 Comecon Headquarters, Moscow

629 World Cup Emblem

(Des Z. Stasik. Litho)

1974 (15 May). 25th Anniversary of Council for Mutual Economic Aid. Perf 11×11½.

2300	**628**	1z.50 ochre, red and cobalt	40	35

(Des H. Chyliński. Photo)

1974 (6 June). World Cup Football Championship, West Germany. T **629** and similar horiz design. Multicoloured. Perf 11×11½.

2301	4z.90 Type **629**	95	40
2302	4z.90 Players and Olympic Gold Medal of 1972	95	40
MS2303	116×83 mm. Nos. 2301/2302×2	14·50	12·00

See also No. **MS**2315.

630 Model of 16th-century Galleon

631 Title page of *Chess* by Jan Kochanowski, 1564

(Des W. Andrzejewski. Litho)

1974 (29 June). Sailing Ships. T **630** and similar vert designs. Multicoloured. Perf 11½×11.

2304	1z. Type **630**	25	25
2305	1z.50 Trans-Atlantic sloop *Dal* (1934)	30	25
2306	2z.70 Yacht *Opty* (Teliga's circumnavigation, 1969)	40	30
2307	4z. *Dar Pomorza* (full-rigged cadet ship)	70	35
2308	4z.90 Yacht *Polonez* (Baranowski's circumnavigation 1973)	1·40	40
2304/2308	*Set of* 5	2·75	1·40

(Des A. Heidrich. Litho)

1974 (15 July). Tenth International Chess Festival, Lublin. T **631** and similar vert design. Multicoloured. Perf 11½×11.

2309	1z. Type **631**	35	30
2310	1z.50 *Education* (1790s engraving by D. Chodowiecki)	40	35

632 Lazienkowska Road Junction

633 Face on Map of Poland

(Des M. Wieczorek. Litho)

1974 (21 July). Opening of Lazienkowska Road Junction. Perf 11×11½.

2311	**632**	1z.50 multicoloured	40	35

(Des J. W. Brzoza. Photo)

1974 (21 July). 30th Anniversary of Polish People's Republic. T **633** and similar designs. Perf 11½×11.

2312	**633**	1z.50 black, gold and vermilion	40	35
2313	-	1z.50 multicoloured (silver background)	40	35
2314	-	1z.50 multicoloured (scarlet background)	40	35
2312/2314		*Set of* 3	1·10	95

Designs: 31×43 mm—Nos. 2313 and 2314, Polish Eagle.

(Des H. Chyliński. Photo)

1974 (21 July). Poland. Third Place in World Cup Football Championship. Sheet 107×121 mm containing four stamps as No. 2301, but with inscr in silver instead of black, and two labels. Perf 11×11½.

MS2315	4z.90×4 multicoloured	8·00	3·50

634 Strawberries

635 Civic Militia and Security Service Emblem

(Des K. Śliwka. Photo)

1974 (10 Sept). 19th International Horticultural Congress, Warsaw. T **634** and similar vert designs. Multicoloured. Perf 11½.

2316	50g. Type **634**	25	25
2317	90g. Blackcurrants	25	25
2318	1z. Apples	30	25
2319	1z.50 Cucumbers	35	30
2320	2z.70 Tomatoes	40	35
2321	4z.50 Peas	95	40
2322	4z.90 Pansies	2·30	45
2323	5z. Nasturtiums	2·75	65
2316/2323	*Set of* 8	6·75	2·50

(Des W. Surowiecki. Photo)

1974 (3 Oct). 30th Anniversary of Polish Civic Militia and Security Service. Perf 11½×11.

2324	**635**	1z.50 multicoloured	40	35

636 *Child in Polish Costume* (L. Orlowski)

(Des W. Andrzejewski. Photo)

1974 (9 Oct). Stamp Day. Polish Paintings of Children. T **636** and similar vert designs. Multicoloured. Perf 11½×11.

2325		50g. Type **636**	25	25
2326		90g. *Girl with Pigeon* (anon)	25	25
2327		1z. *Portrait of Girl* (S. Wyspiański)	25	25
2328		1z.50 *Orphan from Poronin* (W. Slewiński)	30	25
2329		3z. *Peasant Boy* (K. Sichulski)	40	30
2330		4z.50 *Florence Page* (A. Gierymski)	70	35
2331		4z.90 *Tadeusz and Dog* (P. Michalowski)	95	40
2332		6z.50 *Boy with Doe* (A. Kotsis)	1·50	80
2325/2332 *Set of 8*			4·25	2·50

637 *The Crib*, Cracow

638 Angler and Fish

(Des S. Malecki. Litho)

1974 (2 Dec). Polish Art. T **637** and similar vert designs. Multicoloured. Perf 11½×11.

2333		1z. Type **637**	25	25
2334		1z.50 *The Flight to Egypt* (15th-century polyptych)	30	25
2335		2z. King Sigismund III Vasa (16th-century miniature)	40	30
2336		4z. King Jan Olbracht (16th-century title page)	1·80	40
2333/2336 *Set of 4*			2·50	1·10

(Des T. Michaluk. Eng B. Kowalska (1z.), M. Kopecki (1z.50). Recess)

1974 (30 Dec). Polish Folklore. 16th-century wood carvings (1st series). T **638** and similar horiz design. Perf 12×11.

2337	**638**	1z. black	30	25
2338	-	1z.50 blue-black	35	25

Design: 1z.50 Hunter and wild animals.

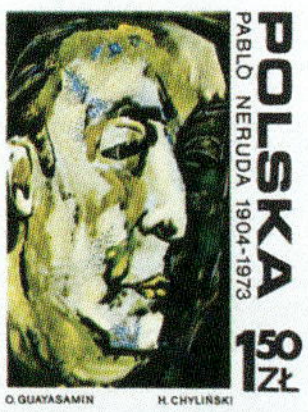

639 *Pablo Neruda* (O. Guayasamin)

(Des H. Chyliński. Litho)

1974 (31 Dec). 70th Birth Anniversary of Pablo Neruda (Chilean poet). Perf 11½×11.

2339	**639**	1z.50 multicoloured	40	35

640 Nike Memorial and National Opera House

641 Male Lesser Kestrel (*Falco naumanni*)

(Des H. Chyliński. Photo)

1975 (17 Jan). 30th Anniversary of Liberation of Warsaw. Perf 11.

2340	**640**	1z.50 multicoloured	40	35

(Des J. Desselberger. Photo)

1975 (23 Jan). Birds of Prey. T **641** and similar vert designs. Multicoloured. Perf 11½×12.

2341		1z. Type **641**	30	25
		a. Pair. Nos. 2341/2342		
2342		1z. Female Lesser Kestrel	30	25
2343		1z.50 Male Western Red-footed Falcon (*Falco vespertinus*)	40	25
		a. Pair. Nos. 2343/2344		
2344		1z.50 Female Western Red-footed Falcon	40	25
2345		2z. Northern Hobby (*Falco subbuteo*)	70	30
2346		3z. Common Kestrel (*Falco tinnunculus*)	1·10	40
2347		4z. Merlin (*Falco columbarius*)	3·25	1·00
2348		8z. Peregrine Falcon (*Falco peregrinus*)	5·00	1·40
2341/2348 *Set of 8*			10·50	3·75

Nos. 2341/2342 and 2343/2344 were issued in *se-tenant* pairs within their sheets.

642 Broken Barbed Wire

643 Hurdling

(Des Z. Stasik. Recess and photo)

1975 (27 Jan). 30th Anniversary of Auschwitz Concentration Camp Liberation. Perf 11½×11.

2349	**642**	1z.50 black and red	40	35

(Des W. Andrzejewski. Litho (Nos. 2350/2353) or recess and photo (No. 2354))

1975 (8 Mar). Sixth European Indoor Athletics Championships, Katowice. T **643** and similar horiz designs. Multicoloured. Perf 11×11½.

2350		1z. Type **643**	30	25
2351		1z.50 Pole vault	40	25
2352		4z. Triple jump	70	30
2353		4z.90 Running	95	40
2350/2353 *Set of 4*			2·10	1·10
MS2354 72×63 mm. 10z.+5z. deep turquoise-green and silver (Montréal Olympics emblem) (26×31 mm). Perf 11½			4·25	1·80

No. **MS**2354 has both the stamp and the outer edges of the sheet perforated.

644 St Anne (Veit Stoss)

645 Globe and Radio Waves

(Des A. Heidrich. Photo)

1975 (15 Apr). Arphila 1975 International Stamp Exhibition, Paris. Perf 11×11½.

2355	**644**	1z.50 multicoloured	40	35

(Des S. Malecki. Litho)

1975 (15 Apr). International Amateur Radio Union Conference, Warsaw. Perf 11½.

2356	**645**	1z.50 multicoloured	40	35

646 Stone Pine and Tatra Mountains

647 Hands holding Tulips and Rifle

(Des A. Balcerzak. Photo)

1975 (30 Apr). Centenary of National Mountain Guides' Association. T **646** and similar multicoloured designs. Perf 11.

2357	1z. Type **646**	25	25
	a. Pair. Nos. 2357/2358	55	55
2358	1z. Gentian and Tatra Mountains	25	25
2359	1z.50 Sudety Mountains (*horiz*)	40	30
	a. Pair. Nos. 2359/2360	85	65
2360	1z.50 Yew-tree branch (*horiz*)	40	30
2361	4z. Beskidy Mountains	60	40
	a. Pair. Nos. 2361/2362	1·30	85
2362	4z. Arnica blossoms	60	40
2357/2362 *Set of 6*		2·30	1·70

Designs of the same value were issued in *se-tenant* pairs forming composite designs.

(Des H. Chyliński. Photo)

1975 (9 May). 30th Anniversary of Victory over Fascism. Perf 11½×11.

2363	**647**	1z.50 multicoloured	40	35

648 Flags of Member Countries

649 Hens

(Des W. Surowiecki. Photo)

1975 (14 May). 20th Anniversary of Warsaw Treaty Organisation. Perf 11½×11.

2364	**648**	1z.50 multicoloured	40	35

(Des A. Balcerzak. Photo)

1975 (23 June). 26th European Zootechnical Federation Congress, Warsaw. T **649** and similar horiz designs. Multicoloured. Perf 11½.

2365	50g. Type **649**	25	25
2366	1z. Geese	25	25
2367	1z.50 Cattle	30	25
2368	2z. Cow	35	30
2369	3z. Wielkopolska horse	40	35
2370	4z. Arab horses	80	40
2371	4z.50 Pigs	3·50	55
2372	5z. Sheep	3·50	1·00
2365/2372 *Set of 8*		8·50	3·00

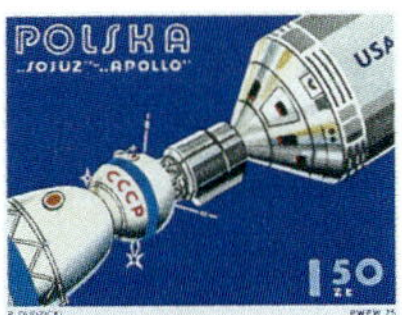

650 Apollo and Soyuz Spacecraft linked

(Des R. Dudzicki. Photo)

1975 (30 June). Apollo-Soyuz Space Link. T **650** and similar horiz designs. Multicoloured. Perf 11×11½.

2373	1z.50 Type **650**	40	30
2374	4z.90 Apollo spacecraft	1·10	40
	a. Pair. Nos. 2374/2375	2·30	85
2375	4z.90 Soyuz spacecraft	1·10	40
2373/2375 *Set of 3*		2·30	1·00
MS2376 119×156 mm. Nos. 2373×2, 2374×2 and 2375×2		10·50	6·00

Nos. 2374/2375 were issued together in *se-tenant* pairs within the sheet.

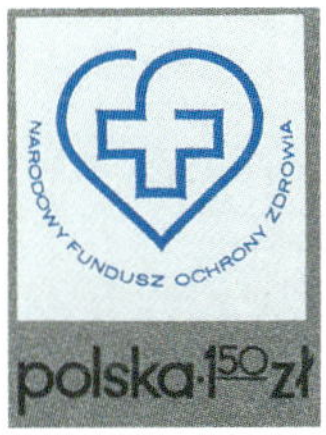

651 Organisation Emblem

652 UN Emblem

(Des K. Tarkowska. Photo)

1975 (12 July). National Health Protection Fund. Perf 11½×11.

2377	**651**	1z.50 blue, black and silver	40	35

(Des A. Heidrich. Litho)

1975 (25 July). 30th Anniversary of United Nations Organisation. Perf 11×11½.

2378	**652**	4z. multicoloured	80	40

653 Polish Flag within 'E' for Europe

654 Bolek and Lolek

(Des H. Chyliński. Litho)

1975 (30 July). European Security and Co-operation Conference, Helsinki. Perf 11×11½.

2379	**653**	4z. multicoloured	75	70

(Des H. Matuszewska. Photo)

1975 (30 Aug). Children's Television Characters. T **654** and similar horiz designs. Multicoloured. Perf 11×11½.

2380	50g. Type **654**	25	25
2381	1z. Jacek and Agatka	30	25
2382	1z.50 Reksio (Dog)	40	30
2383	4z. Telesfor (Dragon)	95	40
2380/2383 *Set of 4*		1·70	1·10

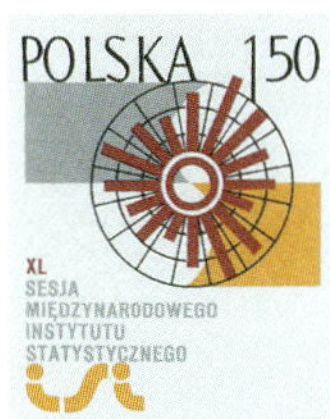

655 Institute Emblem

656 Women's Faces

(Des K. Rogaczewska. Litho)

1975 (1 Sept). 40th Session of International Institute of Statistics. Perf 11½×11.

2384	**655**	1z.50 multicoloured	40	35

(Des S. Malecki. Photo)

1975 (8 Sept). International Women's Year. Perf 11.

2385	**656**	1z.50 multicoloured	40	35

657 Albatros Biplane

658 *Mary and Margaret* (emigrant ship) and Polish Settlers

(Des J. Brodowski. Litho)

1975 (25 Sept). 50th Anniversary of First Polish Airmail Stamps. T **657** and similar horiz design. Multicoloured. Perf 11×11½.

2386		2z.40 Type **657**	40	35
2387		4z.90 Tail of Ilyushin Il-62M aeroplane of LOT	80	40

(Des T. Michaluk. Litho)

1975 (26 Sept). Bicentenary of American Revolution. T **658** and similar horiz designs. Multicoloured. Perf 11×11½.

2388		1z. Type **658**	25	25
2389		1z.50 Polish glassworks, Jamestown	30	25
2390		2z.70 Helena Modrzejewska (actress)	40	30
2391		4z. K. Pulaski (soldier)	70	40
2392		6z.40 T. Kościuszko (soldier)	1·10	70
2388/2392		*Set of* 5	2·50	1·70
MS2393		117×102 mm. 4z.90 Washington; 4z.90 Kościuszko; 4z.90 Pulaski. Perf 12	2·75	1·60

No. **MS**2393 was issued with three *se-tenant* labels.

659 Frédéric Chopin

660 Self-portrait

661 Marketplace, Kazimierz Dolny

(Des S. Malecki. Photo)

1975 (7 Oct). Ninth International Chopin Piano Competition. Perf 11½.

2394	**659**	1z.50 black, lavender and gold	50	45

No. 2394 was issued with *se-tenant* stamp-size label.

(Des H. Matuszewska. Photo)

1975 (9 Oct). Stamp Day and Birth Centenary of Xawery Dunikowski (sculptor). T **660** and similar vert designs. Multicoloured. Perf 11½×11.

2395		50g. Type **660**	25	25
2396		1z. *Breath*	30	25
2397		1z.50 *Maternity*	40	35
2398		8z.+4z. *Silesian Insurrectionists*	2·00	80
2395/2398		*Set of* 4	2·75	1·50

(Des S. Malecki. Photo)

1975 (11 Nov). European Architectural Heritage Year. T **661** and similar design. Perf 14.

2399	**661**	1z. deep olive	35	30
2400	-	1z.50 lake	40	35

Design: Vert—1z.50 Town Hall, Zamość.

662 Łódź (W. Strzemiński)

663 Henry IV's Eagle Gravestone Head (14th century)

(Des Z. Stasik. Litho)

1975 (22 Nov). Łódź 1975 National Stamp Exhibition. Perf 12½.

2401	**662**	4z.50 multicoloured	70	40
MS2402		80×101 mm. No. 2401	2·50	1·60

(Des H. Matuszewska. Eng M. Kopecki (1z.). Des H. Matuszewska and K. Tarkowska. Eng M. Kopecki (1z.50). Des K. Tarkowska. Eng W. Morycińska (4z.))

1975 (29 Nov). Piast Dynasty of Silesia. T **663** and similar horiz designs. Perf 11½×12.

2403		1z. deep dull green	25	25
2404		1z.50 sepia	30	25
2405		4z. deep lilac	70	40
2403/2405		*Set of* 3	1·10	80

Designs: 1z. T **663**; 1z.50 Prince Boleslaw seal (14th century); 4z. Prince Jerzy Wilhelm coin (17th century).

664 Symbolised figure '7'

665 Ski Jumping

(Des W. Surowiecki (1z.), Z. Horodecki (1z.50). Photo)

1975 (8 Dec). Seventh Polish United Workers' Party Congress. T **664** and similar design. Perf 11½×11.

2406	**664**	1z. multicoloured	35	30
2407	-	1z.50 vermilion, ultramarine and silver	40	35

Design: 32×43 mm—1z.50 Party Initials (PZPR).

(Des H. Matuszewska. Photo)

1976 (10 Jan). Winter Olympic Games, Innsbruck. T **665** and similar horiz designs. Multicoloured. Perf 11×11½.

2408		50g. Type **665**	25	25
2409		1z. Ice hockey	25	25
2410		1z.50 Skiing	30	25
2411		2z. Skating	40	25
2412		4z. Tobogganing	60	30
2413		6z.40 Shooting (Biathlon)	1·10	40
2408/2413		*Set of* 6	2·50	1·50

666 R. Trevithick's Steam Railway Locomotive, 1803

(Des S. Malecki. Photo)

1976 (13 Feb). History of the Railway Locomotive. T **666** and similar horiz designs. Multicoloured. Perf 11½.

2414		50g. Type **666**	25	25
2415		1z. Murray and Blenkinsop's steam locomotive and carriage, 1810	25	25
2416		1z.50 George Stephenson's locomotive *Rocket*, 1829	25	25
2417		1z.50 Polish Universal electric locomotive No. ET22-001, 1969	30	25
2418		2z.70 Robert Stephenson's locomotive *North Star*, 1837	35	25
2419		3z. Joseph Harrison's locomotive, 1840	40	30
2420		4z.50 Thomas Rogers, Locomotive 1855, USA.	1·80	35
2421		4z.90 A. Xiezopolski (locomotive engineer) and series Ok22 steam locomotive, 1922	2·20	40
2414/2421		*Set of* 8	5·25	2·10

667 Flags of Member Countries

(Des Z. Stasik. Litho)

1976 (8 Mar). 20th Anniversary of International Nuclear Research Institute. Perf 11½.

2422	**667**	1z.50 multicoloured	40	35

668 Early Telephone, Satellites and Radar **669** Jantar Glider

(Des Z. Stasik. Photo)

1976 (10 Mar). Telephone Centenary. Perf 11.

2423	**668**	1z.50 multicoloured	40	35

(Des J. Brodowski. Recess)

1976 (27 Mar)–**78**. AIR. Contemporary Aviation. T **669** and similar vert designs. Perf 11½.

2424	5z. deep blue-green	75	30
2425	10z. sepia	1·50	35
2425*a*	20z. blackish olive (15.2.77)	3·50	40
2425*b*	50z. brown-lake (2.2.78)	6·25	1·30
2424/2425*b*	*Set of* 4	11·00	2·10

Designs: 5z. T **669**; 10z. Mil MI-6 helicopter; 20z. PZL-106 Kruk spraying crops; 50z. PZL-Mielec TS-11 Iskra jet trainer over Warsaw Castle.

670 Player **671** Polish UN Soldier

(Des T. Michaluk. Photo)

1976 (8 Apr). World Ice Hockey Championships, Katowice. T **670** and similar vert design. Multicoloured. Perf 11½×11.

2426	1z. Type **670**	35	30
2427	1z.50 Player (*different*)	40	35

(Des B. Berg. Photo)

1976 (30 Apr). Polish United Nations Troops in Sinai. Perf 11×11½.

2428	**671**	1z.50 multicoloured	70	60

No. 2428 was issued with a *se-tenant* stamp-size label.

672 *Glory to the Sappers* (S. Kulon) **673** 'Interphil 76'

(Des K. Tarkowska. Photo)

1976 (8 May). War Memorials. T **672** and similar vert design. Multicoloured. Perf 11½.

2429	1z. Type **672**	40	35
2430	1z. 1st Polish Army Monument, Sandau/ Laba (B. Koniuszy)	40	35

(Des T. Michaluk. Litho)

1976 (20 May). Interphil 1976 International Stamp Exhibition, Philadelphia. Perf 11½×11.

2431	**673**	8z.40 multicoloured	1·40	70

674 Wielkopolski and Tawny Owl

(Des J. Brodowski. Photo)

1976 (22 May). National Parks. T **674** and similar horiz designs. Multicoloured. Perf 11½.

2432	90g. Type **674**	25	25
2433	1z. Woliński and White-tailed Sea Eagle	30	25
2434	1z.50 Slowiński and Seagull	40	25
2435	4z.50 Bieszczadzki and Lynx	70	30
2436	5z. Ojcowski and Bat	85	35
2437	6z. Kampinoski and Elk	1·20	40
2432/2437	*Set of* 6	3·25	1·60

675 Peace Dove within Globe **676** Fencing

(Des S. Malecki. Litho)

1976 (29 June). 25th Anniversary of United Nations Postal Administration. Perf 11×11½.

2438	**675**	8z.40 multicoloured	1·50	40

(Des T. Michaluk. Photo (Nos. 2439/2444). Eng M. Kopecki. Recess and photo (No. 2445))

1976 (30 June). Olympic Games, Montréal. T **676** and similar horiz designs. Multicoloured. Perf 11×11½.

2439	50g. Type **676**	25	25
2440	1z. Cycling	25	25
2441	1z.50 Football	30	25
2442	4z.20 Boxing	70	25
2443	6z.90 Weightlifting	1·10	40
2444	8z.40 Athletics	1·50	55
2439/2444	*Set of* 6	3·75	1·80
MS2445	78×94 mm. 10z.+5z. black and bright rose-red (Volleyball) (23×29 mm). Perf 11½	3·75	2·00

No. **MS**2445 has both the stamp and the outer edges of the sheet perforated.

677 National Theatre

678 Aleksander Czekanowski and Baikal landscape

(Des S. Malecki. Litho)

1976 (12 July). Centenary of National Theatre, Poznań. Perf 11×11½.

2446	**677**	1z.50 deep yellow-green and orange	40	30

(Des T. Michaluk. Photo)

1976 (3 Sept). Death Centenary of Aleksander Czekanowski (geologist). Perf 11×11½.

2447	**678**	1z.50 multicoloured	40	30

679 Sphinx

680 Warszawa M-20

(Des H. Matuszewska. Photo)

1976 (30 Sept). Stamp Day. Corinthian Vase Paintings (7th century BC). T **679** and similar multicoloured designs. Perf 11×11½ (vert) or 11×11½ (horiz).

2448	1z. Type **679**	20	25
2449	1z.50 Siren (*horiz*)	25	25
2450	2z. Lion (*horiz*)	40	30
2451	4z.20 Bull (*horiz*)	70	35
2452	4z.50 Goat (*horiz*)	80	40
2453	8z.+4z. Sphinx (*different*)	2·20	80
2448/2453	*Set of* 6	4·00	2·10

(Des W. Surowiecki. Photo)

1976 (6 Nov). 25th Anniversary of Żerań Motor Car Factory, Warsaw, T **680** and similar horiz designs. Multicoloured. Perf 11.

2454	1z. Type **680**	25	25
2455	1z.50 Warszawa 223	30	25
2456	2z. Syrena 104	40	30
2457	4z.90 Polski Fiat 125P	80	55
2454/2457	*Set of* 4	1·60	1·20
MS2458	137×109 mm. Nos. 2454/2457	5·50	2·75

No. **MS**2458 was issued with two *se-tenant* labels.

681 Molten Steel Ladle

682 Congress Emblem

683 Wirzbieto Epitaph (painting on wood, 1425)

(Des M. Zabaglo. Litho)

1976 (26 Nov). Huta Katowice Steel Works. Perf 11.

2459	**681**	1z.50 multicoloured	40	30

(Des S. Malecki. Photo)

1976 (6 Dec). Eighth Polish Trade Unions Congress. Perf 11.

2460	**682**	1z.50 red-orange, bistre and sepia	40	30

(Des S. Malecki. Litho)

1976 (15 Dec). Polish Art. T **683** and similar vert design. Multicoloured. Perf 11×11½.

2461	1z. Type **683**	30	25
2462	6z. Madonna and Child (painted carving, *circa* 1410)	95	40

684 *Zawrat* (tanker) at Oil Terminal, Gdańsk

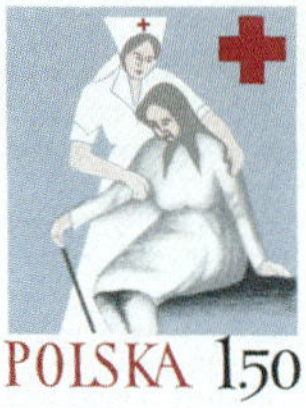

685 Nurse and Patient

(Des S. Malecki. Photo)

1976 (29 Dec). Polish Ports. T **684** and similar horiz designs. Multicoloured. Perf 11.

2463	1z. Type **684**	25	25
2464	1z. *Gryf* (ferry) at Gdańsk	25	25
2465	1z.50 Loading *General Bem* (container ship), Gdynia	30	25
2466	1z.50 *Stefan Batory* (liner) leaving Gdynia	30	25
2467	2z. *Ziemia Szczencinska* (bulk carrier) loading at Szczecin	40	30
2468	4z.20 Loading coal, Świnoujście	80	35
2469	6z.90 Hydrofoil and river boat, Kolobrzeg	1·20	40
2470	8z.40 Bulk carrier, tanker and coastal map	1·40	70
2463/2470	*Set of* 8	4·50	2·50

(Des E. Nożko-Paprocka. Litho)

1977 (24 Jan). Polish Red Cross. Perf 11½×11.

2471	**685**	1z.50 multicoloured	40	30

686 Order of Civil Defence Service

687 Ball in Road

(Des E. Nożko-Paprocka. Litho)

1977 (26 Feb). Polish Civil Defence. Perf 11.

2472	**686**	1z.50 multicoloured	40	30

(Des J. Raczko. Photo)

1977 (12 Mar). Child Road Safety Campaign. Perf 11.

2473	**687**	1z.50 multicoloured	40	30

688 Dewberries (*Rubus caesius*)

689 Computer Tape

(Des A. Balcerzak. Photo)

1977 (17 Mar). Wild Fruits. T **688** and similar vert designs. Multicoloured. Perf 11½×11.

2474	50g. Type **688**	25	25
2475	90g. Cowberries (*Vaccinium vitis-idaea*)	25	25
2476	1z. Wild Strawberries (*Fragaria vesca*)	30	25
2477	1z.50 Bilberries (*Vaccinium myrtillus*)	35	25
2478	2z. Raspberries (*Rubus idaeus*)	40	25
2479	4z.50 Sloes (*Prunus spinosa*)	60	25
2480	6z. Rose hips (*Rosa canina*)	90	30

2481 6z.90 Hazelnuts (*Corylus avellana*) .... 1·80 40
2474/2481 *Set of* 8 .... 4·25 2·00

(Des W. Surowiecki. Litho)

1977 (4 Apr). 30th Anniversary of Russian–Polish Technical Co-operation. Perf 11½×11.
2482 **689** 1z.50 multicoloured 40 30

690 Pendulum Traces and Emblem

691 *Toilet of Venus*

(Des K. Śliwka. Litho)

1977 (22 Apr). Seventh Polish Congress of Technology. Perf 11½×11.
2483 **690** 1z.50 multicoloured 40 30

(Des T. Michaluk. Recess (8z.), litho (others))

1977 (30 Apr). 400th Birth Anniversary of Peter Paul Rubens (artist). T **691** and similar designs. Multicoloured. Perf 11½.
2484 1z. Type **691** 25 25
2485 1z.50 *Bathsheba at the Fountain* (detail) 30 25
2486 5z. *Hélèna Fourment with Fur Coat* 80 30
2487 6z. Self-portrait 90 40
2484/2487 *Set of* 4 .... 2·00 1·10
MS2488 76×62 mm. 8z.+4z. sepia (*The Stoning of St Stephen*) (21×26 mm). Perf 11½ .... 3·25 1·50

No. **MS**2488 has both the stamp and the outer edges of the sheet perforated. It also exists printed in black with the face value obliterated with wavy lines; this was not valid for postage.

692 Dove

693 Cyclist

(Des W. Freudenreich. Litho)

1977 (6 May). World Peace Congress, Warsaw. Perf 11×11½.
2489 **692** 1z.50 bright blue, black and lemon 40 30

(Des T. Michaluk. Photo)

1977 (6 May). 30th International Peace Cycle Race. Perf 11×11½.
2490 **693** 1z.50 multicoloured 40 30

694 Wolf (*Canis lupus*)

695 *The Violinist* (Jacob Toorenvliet)

(Des H. Matuszewska. Photo)

1977 (12 May). Endangered Animals. T **694** and similar vert designs. Multicoloured. Perf 11½×11.
2491 1z. Type **694** 35 25
2492 1z.50 Great Bustard (*Otis tarda*) 55 30
2493 1z.50 Common Kestrel (*Falco tinnunculus*) 55 30
2494 6z. European Otter (*Lutra lutra*) .... 1·20 40
2491/2494 *Set of* 4 .... 2·40 1·10

1977 (16 May). Amphilex 77 International Stamp Exhibition, Amsterdam. Perf 11½×11.
2495 **695** 6z. multicoloured 90 60

Printed in sheets of six.

696 Midsummer's Day Bonfire

(Des K. Tarkowska. Photo)

1977 (13 June). Folk Customs. T **696** and similar designs from 19th-century wood engravings. Multicoloured. Perf 11×11½ (horiz) or 11½×11 (vert).
2496 90g. Type **696** 25 25
2497 1z. Easter cock (*vert*) 30 25
2498 1z.50 'Śmigus' (dousing of women on Easter Monday, Miechów district) (*vert*) 35 25
2499 3z. Harvest Festival, Sandomierz district (*vert*) 40 25
2500 6z. Children with Christmas crib (*vert*) 95 30
2501 8z.40 Mountain wedding dance .... 1·60 40
2496/2501 *Set of* 6 .... 3·50 1·50

697 H. Wieniawski and Music Clef

698 *Parnassius apollo*

(Des Z. Kaja. Litho)

1977 (30 June). Wieniawski International Music Competition, Poznań. Perf 11½×11.
2502 **697** 1z.50 black, gold and red-orange 40 30

(Des J. Wysocki. Photo)

1977 (22 Aug). Butterflies. T **898** and similar horiz designs. Multicoloured. Perf 11.
2503 1z. Type **698** 30 25
2504 1z. *Nymphalis polychloros* 30 25
2505 1z.50 *Nymphalis antiopa* 55 30
2506 1z.50 *Papilio machaon* 70 30
2507 5z. *Fabriciana adippe* .... 1·40 40
2508 6z.90 *Argynnis paphia* .... 3·00 90
2503/2508 *Set of* 8 .... 5·50 2·20

699 Keyboard and Arms of Slupsk

700 Feliks Dzierzyński

(Des S. Malecki. Litho)

1977 (3 Sept). Piano Festival, Slupsk. Perf 11½.
2509 **699** 1z.50 bright mve, black and grey-green. 40 30

(Des W. Surowiecki. Litho)

1977 (10 Sept). Birth Centenary of Feliks E. Dzierzyński (Russian politician). Perf 11½×11.
2510 **700** 1z.50 bistre-brown and deep brown-ochre 40 30

701 *Sputnik* circling Earth

702 Silver Dinar (11th century)

(Des Z. Stasik. Litho)

1977 (1 Oct). 60th Anniversary of Russian Revolution and 20th Anniversary of First Artificial Satellite (1st issue). Perf 11×11½.

2511	**701**	1z.50 ultramarine and cerise	55	40
MS2512		99×125 mm. No. 2511×3 plus three labels. Perf 12	2·00	1·40

No. 2511 was issued *se-tenant* with a label depicting the Winter Palace, Leningrad.

See also No. 2527.

(Des Z. Horodecki. Photo)

1977 (9 Oct). Stamp Day. Polish Coins. T **702** and similar vert designs. Multicoloured. Perf 11½×11.

2513	50g. Type **702**	25	25
2514	1z. Cracow grosz, 14th century	30	25
2515	1z.50 Legnica thaler, 17th century	40	25
2516	4z.20 Gdańsk guilder, 18th century	70	30
2517	4z.50 Silver 5z. coin, 1936	80	35
2518	6z. Millenary 100z. coin, 1966	95	40
2513/2518	*Set of* 6	3·00	1·60

703 Wolin Gate, Kamień Pomorski

704 *Sputnik 1* and Mercury Capsule

(Des J. Brodowski. Photo)

1977 (21 Nov). Architectural Monuments. T **703** and similar designs. Multicoloured. Perf 11½×11 (vert) or 11×11½ (horiz).

2519	1z. Type **703**	30	25
2520	1z. Larch church, Dębno	30	25
2521	1z.50 Monastery, Przasnysz (*horiz*)	40	30
2522	1z.50 Plock cathedral (*horiz*)	40	30
2523	6z. Kórnik Castle (*horiz*)	95	35
2524	6z.90 Palace and garden, Wilanów (*horiz*)	1·10	40
2519/2524	*Set of* 6	3·00	1·70

1977 (12 Dec). Polish Folklore. 16th-century Wood Carvings (2nd series). Horiz designs as T **638**. Recess. Perf 11½×11.

2525	4z. blackish olive	70	35
2526	4z.50 deep brown	80	40

Designs: 4z. Bird snaring; 4z.50 Beekeeper and hives.

1977 (28 Dec). 20th Anniversary of First Artificial Satellite (2nd issue). Photo. Perf 11×11½.

2527	**704**	6z.90 multicoloured	1·10	70
		a. *Tête-bêche* (horiz pair)	2·30	1·50
		b. Sheet of 6. No. 2527, plus 2 labels	8·00	5·50

No. 2527 was issued in sheets of six stamps and two different labels, depicting *Sputnik* 1 or *Explorer 1*. The sheet was arranged in four rows of two, the labels being in the top right and bottom left positions. The latter label and the three stamps of the right-hand vertical row were printed inverted.

705 DN Category Iceboats

(Des M. Raducki. Litho)

1978 (6 Feb). Sixth World Ice Sailing Championships. T **705** and similar horiz design. Perf 11.

2528	**705**	1z.50 black, pale grey-blue and azure	40	30
		a. Vert strip of 2. Nos. 2528/2529 plus label	85	65
2529	-	1z.50 black, pale grey-blue and azure	40	30

Design: No. 2529, Close-up of DN iceboat.

Nos. 2528/2529 were issued together *se-tenant* with an intervening label bearing the Championships emblem, within sheets of 16 stamps and eight labels.

706 Electric Locomotive and Katowice Railway Station

(Des S. Malecki. Photo)

1978 (28 Feb). Railway Engines. T **706** and similar horiz designs. Multicoloured. Perf 11½.

2530	50g. Type **706**	25	25
2531	1z. Steam locomotive No. Py 27 and tender No. 721, Znin-Gasawa railway	30	25
2532	1z. Streamlined steam locomotive No. Pm36-1 (1936) and Cegielski's factory, Poznań	30	25
2533	1z.50 Electric locomotive and Otwock station	40	25
2534	1z.50 Steam locomotive No. 17KDM and Warsaw Stalowa station	40	25
2535	4z.50 Steam locomotive No. Ty51 and Gdynia station	40	30
2536	5z. Steam locomotive No. Tr21 and locomotive factory, Chrzanów	70	35
2537	6z. Cockerill steam locomotive and Vienna station	1·60	40
2530/2537	*Set of* 8	4·00	2·10

707 Czeslaw Tański and Glider

708 Tackle

(Des J. Brodowski. Photo)

1978 (15 Apr). Aviation History and 50th Anniversary of Polish Aero Club. T **707** and similar multicoloured designs. Perf 11×11½ (horiz) or 11½×11 (vert).

2538	50g. Type **707**	25	25
2539	1z. Franciszek Zwirko and Stanislaw Wigura with RWD-6 SP-AHN aircraft (*vert*)	30	25
2540	1z.50 Stanislaw Skarżyński and RWD-5 bis SP-AJU monoplane (*vert*)	40	25
2541	4z.20 Mil Mi-2 helicopter SP-WXA (*vert*)	70	30
2542	6z.90 PZL-104 Wilga 35 monoplane	1·80	35
2543	8z.40 SZD-45 Ogar powered glider	1·50	40
2538/2543	*Set of* 6	4·50	1·60

1978 (12 May). World Cup Football Championship, Argentina. T **708** and similar horiz design. Multicoloured. Perf 11½×11 (1z.50) or 11×11½ (6z.90).

2544	1z.50 Type **708**	40	30
2545	6z.90 Ball on field	95	40

709 Biennial Emblem

710 Kazimierz Stanislaw Gzowski (bridge engineer)

(Des W. Jankowski. Litho)

1978 (1 June). Seventh International Poster Biennial, Warsaw. Perf 11½.

2546 **709** 1z.50 magenta, greenish yellow and bluish violet 40 30

(Des H. Matuszewska. Photo)

1978 (6 June). Capex 78 International Stamp Exhibition, Toronto. Sheet 68×79 mm. Perf 11½×11.

MS2547 8z.40+4z. multicoloured .... 2·50 1·40

711 Polonez Saloon Car

712 Fair Emblem

1978 (10 June). Car Production. Photo. Perf 11.

2548 **711** 1z.50 multicoloured 40 30

(Des W. Freudenreich. Litho)

1978 (10 June). 50th International Fair, Poznań. Perf 11.

2549 **712** 1z.50 multicoloured 40 30

713 Miroslaw Hermaszewski

714 Globe containing Face

1978 (27 June). First Pole in Space. T **713** and similar horiz design. Multicoloured. Perf 11½×11 (1z.50) or 11×11½ (6z.90).

A. With date 27.6.1978.

2550A 1z.50 Type **713** 40 30
2551A 6z.90 Hermaszewski and globe .... 1·10 40

B. Without date.

2550B 1z.50 Type **713** 40 30
2551B 6z.90 Hermaszewski and globe .... 1·60 70

Nos. 2550B/2551B were each printed in sheets of six stamps and two different labels (*price* £24).

A similar set of stamps portraying Major Jankowski, the stand-by cosmonaut, was prepared but not issued.

(Des S. Malecki. Litho)

1978 (12 July). 11th World Youth and Students' Festival. Havana. Perf 11½.

2552 **714** 1z.50 multicoloured 40 30

715 Flowers

716 *Anopheles maculipennis* and Malaria Organisms

(Des S. Malecki. Photo)

1978 (20 July). 30th Anniversary of Polish Youth Union. Sheet 69×79 mm. Perf 11½×11.

MS2553 1z.50 multicoloured 95 70

(Des T. Konarski. Litho)

1978 (19 Aug). Fourth International Congress of Parasitologists, Warsaw and Cracow. T **716** and similar vert design. Multicoloured. Perf 11½×11.

2554 1z.50 Type **716** 40 30
2555 6z. *Gossina palpalis* and sleeping sickness organisms 95 40

717 Pedunculate Oak (*Quercus robur*)

(Des J. Towpik. Photo German Bank Note Ptg Co, Leipzig)

1978 (6 Sept). Environment Protection. Trees. T **717** and similar vert designs. Multicoloured. Perf 14.

2556 50g. Norway Maple (*Acer platanoides*) 25 25
2557 1z. Type **717** 30 25
2558 1z.50 White Poplar (*Populus alba*) 40 25
2559 4z.20 Scots Pine (*Pinus silvestris*) 65 30
2560 4z.50 White Willow (*Salix alba*) 70 35
2561 6z. Birch (*Betula verrucosa*) 95 40
2556/2561 *Set of 6* .... 3·00 1·60

718 *The Battle of Grunwald* (detail, Jan Matejko)

719 Communications

(Des K. Tarkowska. Photo)

1978 (8 Sept). PRAGA 1978 International Stamp Exhibition. Sheet 69×79 mm. Perf 11½×11.

MS2562 6z. multicoloured .... 2·50 1·30

(Des Z. Stasik. Litho)

1978 (20 Sept). 20th Anniversary of Socialist Countries' Communications Organisation. Perf 11.

2563 **719** 1z.50 dull vermilion, greenish blue and royal blue 40 30

720 *Peace* (André le Brun)

721 Polish Unit of UN Middle East Force

(Des J. Brodowski. Litho)

1978 (30 Sept)–**79**. Perf 12½.

2564	**720**	1z. deep reddish violet	30	25
		a. Perf 11	30	25
2565		1z.50 deep turquoise-blue (28.4.79)	35	25
2565*a*		2z. deep brown (30.11.79)	40	30
2565*b*		2z.50 ultramarine (5.11.79)	70	40
2564/2565*b* *Set of 4*			1·60	1·10

(Des T. Michaluk. Photo)

1978 (6 Oct). 35th Anniversary of Polish People's Army. T **721** and similar horiz designs. Multicoloured. Perf 11½.

2566	1z.50 Colour party of Tadeusz Kościuszko 1st Warsaw Infantry Division	40	30
2567	1z.50 Colour party of Mechanised Unit	40	30
2568	1z.50 Type **721**	40	30
2566/2568 *Set of 3*		1·10	80

726 Wild Horses (*Equus przewalskii*)

727 Party Flag

(Des J. Towpik. Photo)

1978 (10 Nov). 50th Anniversary of Warsaw Zoo. T **726** and similar horiz designs. Multicoloured. Perf 11×11½.

2578	50g. Type **726**	25	25
2579	1z. Polar Bears (*Thalarctos maritimus*)	25	25
2580	1z.50 Indian Elephants (*Elaphas maximus*)	30	25
2581	2z. Jaguars (*Panthera onca*)	40	25
2582	4z.20 Grey Seals (*Halichoerus grypus*)	65	30
2583	4z.50 Hartebeests (*Alcelaphus caama*)	70	35
2584	6z. Mandrills (*Mandrillus sphinx*)	1·80	40
2578/2584 *Set of 7*		4·00	1·80

(Des W. Freudenreich. Photo)

1978 (15 Dec). 30th Anniversary of Polish United Workers' Party. Perf 11×11½.

2585	**727**	1z.50 orange-vermilion, gold and black	40	30

722 *Portrait of a Young Man* (Raphael)

723 Janusz Korczak with Children

(Des J. Wysocki. Photo)

1978 (9 Oct). Stamp Day. Perf 11.

2569	**722**	6z. multicoloured	95	70

(Des T. Konarski. Litho)

1978 (11 Oct). Birth Centenary of Janusz Korczak (pioneer of children's education). Perf 11½×11.

2570	**723**	1z.50 multicoloured	55	40

724 Wojciech Boguslawski

725 Polish Combatants' Monument and Eiffel Tower

(Des S. Malecki. Litho)

1978 (1 Nov). Polish Dramatists. T **724** and similar square designs. Multicoloured. Perf 11½.

2571	50g. Type **724**	25	25
2572	1z. Aleksander Fredro	25	25
2573	1z.50 Juliusz Slowacki	30	25
2574	2z. Adam Mickiewicz	40	30
2575	4z.50 Stanislaw Wyspiański	80	35
2576	6z. Gabriela Zapolska	95	40
2571/2576 *Set of 6*		2·75	1·60

(Des A. Heidrich. Photo)

1978 (2 Nov). Monument to Polish Combatants in France, Paris. Perf 11×11½.

2577	**725**	1z.50 multicoloured	55	40

728 Stanislaw Dubois

729 Ilyushin Il-62M and Fokker F.VIIb/3m P-POZM

(Des J. Brodowski. Photo)

1978 (15 Dec). Leaders of Polish Workers' Movement. T **728** and similar vert designs. Perf 11½×11.

2586	1z.50 steel blue and cerise	40	30
2587	1z.50 blackish lilac and cerise	40	30
2588	1z.50 deep brown-olive and cerise	40	30
2589	1z.50 reddish brown and cerise	40	30
2586/2589 *Set of 4*		1·40	1·10

Portraits: No. 2586, T **728**; No. 2587, Aleksander Zawadzki; No. 2588, Julian Leński; No. 2589, Adolf Warski.

(Des J. Bokiewicz. Photo)

1979 (2 Jan). 50th Anniversary of LOT Polish Airlines. Perf 11×11½.

2590	**729**	6z.90 multicoloured	1·10	40

730 Train

(Des K. Tarkowska. Photo)

1979 (13 Jan). International Year of the Child. T **730** and similar horiz designs showing children's paintings. Multicoloured. Perf 11.

2591	50g. Type **730**	25	25
2592	1z. Mother with children	30	25
2593	1z.50 Children playing	40	30
2594	6z. Family group	1·10	40
2591/2594 *Set of 4*		1·80	1·10

731 *Portrait of Artist's Wife with Foxgloves* (Karol Mondrala)

732 A. Frycz Modrzewski (political writer), King Stefan Batory and J. Zamoyski (chancellor)

(Des S. Malecki. Recess)

1979 (5 Mar). Contemporary Graphics. T **731** and similar designs. Perf 11½.

2595	50g. deep lilac	25	25
2596	1z. blackish olive	30	25
2597	1z.50 indigo	40	30
2598	4z.50 purple-brown	80	35
2595/2598	*Set of* 4	1·60	1·00

Designs: Horiz—50g. *Lightning* (Edmund Bartlomiejczyk); 1z. T **731**. Vert—1z.50 *The Musicians* (Tadeusz Kulisiewicz); 4z.50 *Head of a Man* (Wladyslaw Skoczylas).

(Des T. Michaluk. Recess and photo)

1979 (12 Mar). 400th Anniversary of Royal Tribunal in Piotrkow Trybunalski (1978). Perf 11½.

2599	**732**	1z.50 pale grey-brown and blackish brown	40	30

733 Pole Vault

(Des E. Nożko-Paprocka (10z.), M. Raducki (others). Recess and photo (10z.), photo (others))

1979 (26 Mar–19 May). 60th Anniversary of Polish Olympic Committee. T **733** and similar horiz designs. Perf 11½.

2600	1z. brown-lilac, deep brown and bright crimson	30	25
2601	1z.50 brown-lilac, deep brown and bright crimson	40	25
2602	6z. brown-lilac, deep brown and bright crimson	60	30
2603	8z.40 brown-lilac, deep brown and bright crimson	95	40
2600/2603	*Set of* 4	2·00	1·10
MS2604	102×61 mm. 10z.+5z. blackish brown. Imperf (19.5)	2·00	1·60

Designs: 1z. T **733**; 1z.50 High jump; 6z. Skiing; 8z.40 Horse riding; 10z. Olympic rings.

734 European Flounder (*Platichthys flesus*)

(Des J. Brodowski. Photo)

1979 (26 Apr). Centenary of Polish Angling. T **734** and similar horiz designs. Multicoloured. Perf 11½.

2605	50g. Type **734**	25	25
2606	90g. Eurasian Perch (*Perca fluviatilis*)	25	25
2607	1z. European Greyling (*Thymallus thymallus*)	25	25
2608	1z.50 Atlantic Salmon (*Salmo salar*)	30	25
2609	2z. Brown Trout (*Salmo trutta*)	40	25
2610	4z.50 Northern Pike (*Esox lucius*)	60	30
2611	5z. Common Carp (*Cyprinus carpio*)	1·00	35
2612	6z. Wels (*Silurus glanis*)	1·50	40
2605/2612	*Set of* 8	4·00	2·10

735 30 Years of RWPG

736 Soldier, Civilian and Congress Emblem

(Des W. Freudenreich. Litho)

1979 (30 Apr). 30th Anniversary of Council for Mutual Economic Aid. Perf 11×11½.

2613	**735**	1z.50 orange-vermilion, ultramarine and greenish blue	40	30

(Des S. Malecki. Litho)

1979 (7 May). Sixth Congress of Association of Fighters for Liberty and Democracy, Warsaw. Perf 11.

2614	**736**	1z.50 orange-vermilion and black	40	30

737 St George's Church, Sofia

738 Pope and Auschwitz Concentration Camp Memorial

(Des Z. Stasik. Photo)

1979 (15 May). Philaserdica '79 International Stamp Exhibition, Sofia, Bulgaria. Perf 11×11½.

2615	**737**	1z.50 pale orange, reddish brown and carmine-vermilion	40	30

(Des S. Malecki. Photo)

1979 (2 June). Visit of Pope John Paul II. T **738** and similar vert design. Multicoloured. Perf 11½×11 (50z.) or 11 (others).

2616	1z.50 Pope and St Mary's Church, Cracow	70	35
2617	8z.40 Type **738**	1·40	40
MS2618	68×79 mm. 50z. Framed portrait of Pope (26×35 mm)	12·00	8·25

No. **MS**2618 has a gold frame. A version with a silver frame exists from a limited printing (*price* £60).

739 *Ksiaze Ksawery* (river paddle-steamer) and Old Warsaw

740 Statue of Tadeusz Kościuszko (Marian Konieczny)

(Des S. Malecki. Litho)

1979 (15 June). 150th Anniversary of Navigation on River Vistula. T **739** and similar horiz designs. Multicoloured. Perf 11.

2619	1z. Type **739**	30	25
2620	1z.50 *General Świerczewski* (river paddle-steamer) and Gdańsk	40	25
2621	4z.50 *Zubr* (river tug) and Plock	70	30
2622	6z. *Syrena* (passenger launch) and modern Warsaw	75	40
2619/2622	*Set of* 4	1·90	1·10

(Des J. Brodowski. Photo)

1979 (1 July). Monument to Tadeusz Kościuszko in Philadelphia. Perf 11½.

2623	**740**	8z.40 multicoloured	95	55

741 Mining Machinery

742 Heraldic Eagle

(Des Z. Stasik. Photo German Bank Note Ptg Co, Leipzig)

1979 (14 July). Wieliczka Salt Mine. T **741** and similar horiz design. Perf 14.

2624	**741**	1z. orange-brown and black	30	25
2625	-	1z.50 deep turquoise-green and black	40	30

Design: 1z.50 Salt crystals.

(Des J. Brodowski. Photo)

1979 (21 July–2 Sept). 35th Anniversary of Polish People's Republic. T **742** and similar vert design. Perf 11½×11.

2626	-	1z.50 vermilion, black and silver	40	30
2627	**742**	1z.50 vermilion, silver and greenish blue	40	30
MS2628		120×84 mm. Nos. 2626/2627 plus label (2.9.79)	90	80

Design: No. 2626, Girl and stylised flag.

No **MS**2628 was sold at the Katowice '79 Stamp Exhibition for 10z. including admission.

743 Rowland Hill and 1860 Stamp

(Des S. Malecki. Litho)

1979 (16 Aug). Death Centenary of Rowland Hill. Perf 11½×11.

2629	**743**	6z. dull blue, black and orange	1·10	40

744 *The Rape of Europa* (Bernardo Strozzi)

745 Wojciech Jastrzębowski

(Des Z. Stasik. Photo)

1979 (20 Aug). International Stamp Exhibitions. Sheet 86×63 mm. Perf 11×11½.

MS2630 **744**	10z. multicoloured	2·00	1·40

(Des J. Wysocki. Photo)

1979 (27 Aug). Seventh Congress of International Ergonomic Association, Warsaw. Perf 11½×11.

2631	**745**	1z.50 multicoloured	40	30

746 Monument (Wincenty Kućma)

747 Radio Mast and Telecommunications Emblem

(Des A. Heidrich. Photo)

1979 (1 Sept). Unveiling of Monument to Defenders of Polish Post, Gdańsk, and 40th Anniversary of German Occupation. Perf 11×11½.

2632	**746**	1z.50 brownish grey, sepia and orange-vermilion	40	30
MS2633		79×69 mm. **746** 10z.+5z. brownish grey, sepia and orange-vermilion. Imperf	2·50	1·80

(Des W. Freudenreich. Photo)

1979 (24 Sept). 50th Anniversary of International Radio Communication Advisory Committee. Perf 11×11½.

2634	**747**	1z.50 multicoloured	40	30

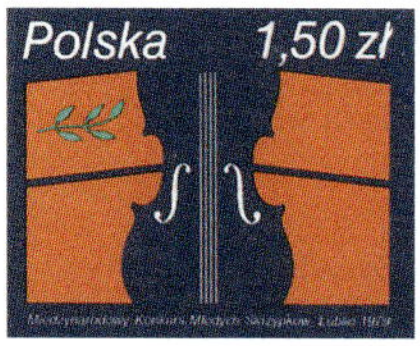

748 Violin

749 Statue of Kazimierz Pulaski, Buffalo (K. Danilewicz)

(Des W. Freudenreich. Photo)

1979 (25 Sept). Wieniawski Young Violinists' Competition, Lublin. Perf 11×11½.

2635	**748**	1z.50 deep ultramarine, red-orange and emerald	40	30

(Des J. Brodowski. Photo)

1979 (1 Oct). Death Bicentenary of Kazimierz Pulaski (American Revolution hero). Perf 11½.

2636	**749**	8z.40 multicoloured	1·50	40

750 Franciszek Jóźwiak (first Commander)

751 Post Office in Rural Area

(Des W. Surowiecki. Photo)

1979 (3 Oct). 35th Anniversary of Civic Militia and Security Force. Perf 11½×11.

2637	**750**	1z.50 blue and gold	40	30

(Des A. Balcerzak. Photo)

1979 (9 Oct). Stamp Day. T **751** and similar horiz designs. Multicoloured. Perf 11½.

2638	1z. Type **751**	30	25
2639	1z.50 Parcel sorting machinery	35	25
2640	4z.50 Loading mail onto train	70	30
2641	6z. Mobile post office	85	40
2638/2641	*Set of 4*	2·00	1·10

752 *The Holy Family* (Ewelina Pękasowa)

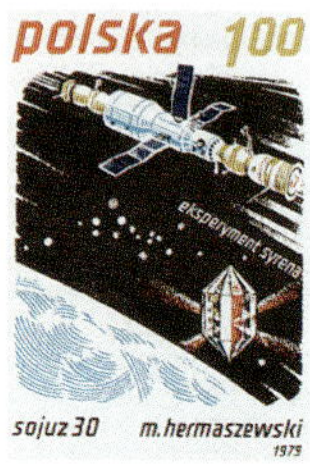

753 *Soyuz 30–Salyut 6* Complex and Crystal

(Des H. Matuszewska. Photo)

1979 (4 Dec). Polish Folk Art. Glass Paintings. T **752** and similar horiz design. Multicoloured. Perf 11½×11 (2z.) or 11×11½ (6z.90).

2642	2z. Type **752**	40	30
2643	6z.90 *The Nativity* (Zdzislaw Walczak)	90	40

(Des Z. Stasik. Photo)

1979 (28 Dec). Space Achievements. T **753** and similar vert designs. Multicoloured. Perf 11½×11.

2644	1z. Type **753** (First Anniversary of first Pole in space)	25	25
2645	1z.50 *Kopernik* and *Copernicus* satellites	30	25
2646	2z. *Lunik 2* and *Ranger 7* spacecraft (20th anniversary of first unmanned Moon landing)	40	25
2647	4z.50 Yuri Gagarin and *Vostok 1*	70	30
2648	6z.90 Neil Armstrong, lunar module and *Apollo 11* (tenth anniversary of first man on Moon)	1·10	40
2644/2648	*Set of 5*	2·50	1·30
MS2649	120×103 mm. Nos. 2644/2648, plus label (*sold at* 20z.90)	3·00	2·30

754 Coach and Four

755 Slogan on Map of Poland

1980 (31 Jan). 150th Anniversary of Sieraków Stud Farm. T **754** and similar vert designs. Multicoloured. Photo. Perf 11½.

2650	1z. Type **754**	25	25
2651	2z. Horse and groom	30	25
2652	2z.50 Sulky racing	40	25
2653	3z. Hunting	50	25
2654	4z. Horse-drawn sledge	65	30
2655	6z. Haywain	85	35
2656	6z.50 Grooms exercising horses	90	35
2657	6z.90 Show jumping	1·00	40
2650/2657	*Set of 8*	4·25	2·20

(Des A. Barecki and Z. Stasik. Photo)

1980 (11 Feb). Eighth Polish United Workers' Party Congress. T **755** and similar vert design. Multicoloured. Perf 11½×11 (No. 2658) or 11½.

2658	2z.50 Type **755**	40	35
2659	2z.50 Poster by Janusz Stann (26×46 mm)	40	35

756 Horse Jumping

1980 (31 Mar). Winter Olympic Games, Lake Placid, and Olympic Games, Moscow. T **756** and similar horiz designs. Multicoloured. Photo. Perf 12×11½.

2660	2z. Type **756**	35	25
2661	2z.50 Archery	40	25
2662	6z.50 Skiing	80	30
2663	8z.40 Volleyball	1·40	40
2660/2663	*Set of 4*	2·75	1·10
MS2664	87×69 mm. 10z.50+5z. Kayak (42×30 mm). Perf 11×11½	3·00	2·75

757 Town Plan and Old Town Hall

(Des Z. Stasik. Litho)

1980 (3 Apr). 400th Anniversary of Zamość. Perf 11½.

2665	**757**	2z.50 buff, reddish brown and deep green	40	25

758 Satellite orbiting Earth

1980 (12 Apr). Intercosmos Space Programme. Sheet 63×79 mm. Photo. Perf 11½×11.

MS2666	6z.90+3z. multicoloured	1·70	1·50

Stamps of a similar design were issued by Bulgaria, Czechoslovakia, East Germany and Russia

759 Seals of Poland and Russia

(Des A. Barecki. Litho)

1980 (21 Apr). 35th Anniversary of Soviet–Polish Friendship Treaty. Perf 11½.

2667	**759**	2z.50 multicoloured	40	35

760 *Lenin in Cracow* (Zbigniew Pronaszko)

761 Workers with Red Flag

(Des J. Brodowski. Photo)

1980 (22 Apr). 110th Birth Anniversary of Lenin. Perf 11.

2668	**760**	2z.50 multicoloured	40	35

(Des K. Tarkowska. Photo)

1980 (1 May). 75th Anniversary of Russian 1905 Revolution. Perf 11½×11.

2669	**761**	2z.50 vermilion, black and lemon	40	35

762 Dove

763 Shield with Crests of Member Nations

(Des H. Matuszewska. Photo)

1980 (9 May). 35th Anniversary of Liberation. Perf 11½.

2670	**762**	2z.50 multicoloured	40	35

(Des Z. Stasik. Litho)

1980 (14 May). 25th Anniversary of Warsaw Pact. Perf 11½×11.

2671	**763**	2z. grey-black and orange-red	40	30

764 Speleological Expedition, Cuba

765 School and Arms

(Photo German Bank Note Ptg Co, Leipzig)

1980 (22 May). Polish Scientific Expeditions. T **764** and similar horiz designs. Multicoloured. Perf 14.

2672	2z. Type **764**	30	25
2673	2z. Antarctic	30	25
2674	2z.50 Archaeology, Syria	40	30
2675	2z.50 Ethnology, Mongolia	40	30
2676	6z.50 Mountaineering, Nepal	95	35
2677	8z.40 Palaeontology, Mongolia	1·90	40
2672/2677	*Set of 6*	3·75	1·70

(Des A. Heidrich. Photo)

1980 (7 June). 800th Anniversary of Malachowianka School, Plock. Perf 11×11½.

2678	**765**	2z. dull yellowish green and black	40	30

766 *Clathrus cancellatus* (*Clathrus ruber*)

767 T. Ziólkowski and *Lwów*

(Des A. Balcerzak. Photo)

1980 (30 June). Fungi. T **766** and similar vert designs. Multicoloured. Perf 11½×11.

2679	2z. Type **766**	30	25
2680	2z. *Xerocomus parasiticus*	30	25
2681	2z.50 *Strobilomyces floccopus*	40	30
2682	2z.50 *Phallus hadriani*	40	30
2683	8z. *Sparassis crispa*	1·20	40
2684	10z.50 *Langermannia gigantea*	1·40	45
2679/2684	*Set of 6*	3·50	1·80

(Des S. Malecki. Litho)

1980 (21 July). Polish Merchant Navy School. Cadet Ships and their Captains. T **767** and similar horiz designs. Perf 11.

2685	2z. black, bright mauve and bright violet	30	25
2686	2z.50 black, greenish blue and new blue	35	25
2687	6z. black, pale green and blue-green	70	25
2688	6z.50 black, olive-yellow and yellow-olive	80	30
2689	6z.90 black, brownish grey and slate-green	95	35
2690	8z.40 black, cobalt and blue-green	1·40	40
2685/2690	*Set of 6*	4·00	1·60

Designs: 2z. T **767**; 2z.50 A. Garnuszewski and *Antoni Garnuszewski*; 6z. A. Ledóchowski and *Zenit*; 6z.50 K. Porebski and *Jan Turlejski*; 6z.90 G. Kański and *Horyzont*; 8z.40 K. Maciejewicz and *Dar Pomorza*.

768 Town Hall

769 *Atropa belladonna*

770 Jan Kochanowski

(Des S. Malecki. Photo)

1980 (26 July). Millenary of Sandomir. Perf 11×11½.

2691	**768**	2z.50 olive-brown and black	55	40

1980 (15 Aug). Medicinal Plants. T **769** and similar vert designs. Multicoloured. Photo. Perf 11½×11.

2692	2z. Type **769**	25	25
2693	2z.50 *Datura innoxia*	30	25
2694	3z.40 *Valeriana officinalis*	40	25
2695	5z. *Mentha piperita*	70	30
2696	6z.50 *Calendula officinalis*	95	35
2697	8z. *Salvia officinalis*	1·60	40
2692/2697	*Set of 6*	3·75	1·60

(Des W. Chomicz. Litho)

1980 (20 Aug). 450th Birth Anniversary of Jan Kochanowski (poet). Perf 11.

2698	**770**	2z.50 multicoloured	55	40

1980 (2 Sept). POSTAGE DUE. As T **D190** but redrawn without imprint at foot. Litho. Perf 12½.

D2699	**D190**	1z. Venetian red	30	25
D2700		2z. drab	40	30
D2701		3z. slate-lilac	55	40
D2702		5z. brown	95	55
D2699/D2702		*Set of 4*	2·00	1·40

771 UN General Assembly

772 Chopin and Trees

(Des J. Bokiewicz. Photo)

1980 (19 Sept). 35th Anniversary of United Nations Organisation. Perf 11×11½.

2703	**771**	8z.40 deep brown, light blue and vermilion	1·50	70

1980 (2 Oct). Tenth International Chopin Piano Competition, Warsaw. Litho. Perf 11½.

2704	**772**	6z.90 multicoloured	95	40

773 Postman emptying Post Box

(Des A. Balcerzak. Photo)

1980 (9 Oct). Stamp Day. T **773** and similar horiz designs. Multicoloured. Perf 11½.

2705	2z. Type **773**	35	25
2706	2z.50 Mail sorting	40	30
2707	6z. Loading mail onto aircraft	95	35
2708	6z.50 Letter boxes	1·40	40
2705/2708	*Set of* 4	2·75	1·20
MS2709	12×94 mm. Nos. 2705/2708	7·00	3·50

774 Child embracing Dove

(Des W. Freudenreich,. Litho)

1980 (21 Nov). United Nations Declaration on Preparation of Societies for Life in Peace. Perf 11×11½.

2710	**774**	8z.40 multicoloured	1·40	40

775 *Battle of Olszynka Grochowska* (Wojciech Kossak)

1980 (29 Nov). 150th Anniversary of Battle of Olszynka Grochowska. Photo. Perf 11.

2711	**775**	2z.50 multicoloured	55	35

776 Fire Engine

777 Honour to Silesian Rebels (statue, Jan Borowczak)

(Des J. Miller. Photo)

1980 (16 Dec). Warsaw Horse-drawn Vehicles. T **776** and similar horiz designs. Multicoloured. Perf 11.

2712	2z. Type **776**	30	25
2713	2z.50 Omnibus	35	25
2714	3z. Brewery dray	40	25
2715	5z. Sledge-cab	70	30
2716	6z. Horse tram	95	40
2717	6z.50 Droshky cab	1·40	50
2712/2717	*Set of* 5	3·75	1·80

(Des A. Heidrich. Recess)

1981 (22 Jan). 60th Anniversary of Silesian Rising. Perf 11½.

2718	**777**	2z.50 deep green	55	40

778 Picasso

779 Jean-François Pilâtre de Rozier and Jules Romain in Hydrogen/Hot Air Balloon, 1785*

(Des W. Freudenreich. Photo)

1981 (10 Mar). Birth Centenary of Pablo Picasso (artist). Perf 11½×11.

2719	**778**	8z.40 multicoloured	1·40	55
MS2720		95×130 mm. No. 2719×2 plus two labels (*sold at* 20z.80)	5·50	2·50

No. 2719 was issued *se-tenant* with a label depicting Picasso's work *Weeping Woman*.

(Des R. Dudzicki. Photo)

1981 (25 Mar). Balloons. T **779** and similar vert designs. Multicoloured. Perf 11½.

2721	2z. Type **779**	30	25
2722	2z. Balloon of J. Blanchard and J. Jeffries, 1785	30	25
2723	2z.50 Eugène Godard's quintuple acrobatic balloon, 1850	35	25
2724	3z. F. Hynek and Z. Burzyński's SP-ADS *Kościuszko*, 1933	35	25
2725	6z. Z. Burzyński and N. Wysocki's *Polonia II*, 1935	95	30
2726	6z.50 Ben Abruzzo, Max Anderson and Larry Newman's *Double Eagle II*, 1978	1·60	40
2721/2726	*Set of* 6	3·50	1·50
MS2727	59×98 mm. 10z.50 Balloon SP-BCU LOPP and Gordon Bennett, statuette. Imperf	1·90	1·60

* No. 2721 is wrongly inscr 'Pilatre de Rozier d'Arlandes 1783'.

780 *Iphigenia* (Anton Maulbertsch)

(Des A. Barecki. Litho)

1981 (11 May). WIPA 1981 International Stamp Exhibition, Vienna. Perf 11½.

2728	**780**	10z.50 multicoloured	2·10	65

781 Wroclaw, 1493

(Des A. Barecki. Photo)

1981 (15 May–28 July). Towns. T **781** and similar designs. Perf 11×11½ (4z., 5z.), 11½×11 (6z., 8z.) or 14 (6z.50).

2729	4z. reddish violet (28.7.81)	80	25
2730	5z. bright blue-green (28.7.81)	1·10	30
2731	6z. red-orange (28.7.81)	1·20	35
2732	6z 50 bistre-brown	1·40	40
2733	8z. blue (28.7.81)	1·80	55
2729/2733	*Set of* 5	5·75	1·70

Designs: Vert—4z. Gdańsk, 1652; 5z. Cracow, 1493. Horiz—6z. Legnica, 1744; 8z. Warsaw, 1618.

Nos. 2734/2743 are vacant.

782 Sikorski

783 Faience Vase

(Des A. Balcerzak. Photo)

1981 (20 May). Birth Centenary of General. Wladyslaw E. Sikorski (statesman). Perf 11½×11.

2744 **782** 6z.50 multicoloured .... 1·30 40

(Des K. Tarkowska (1z., 5z., 8z.40), H. Matuszewska (others). Photo)

1981 (15 June). Pottery. T **783** and similar vert designs. Multicoloured. Perf 11½×11.

2745	1z. Type **783**	30	25
2746	2z. Porcelain cup and saucer in Baranówka design	40	25
2747	2z.50 Porcelain jug, Korzec manufacture	55	25
2748	5z. Faience plate with portrait of King Jan III Sobieski by Thiele	1·00	35
2749	6z.50 Faience Secession vase	1·30	40
2750	8z.40 Porcelain dish, Ćmielów manufacture	1·70	50
2745/2750	*Set of 6*	4·75	1·80

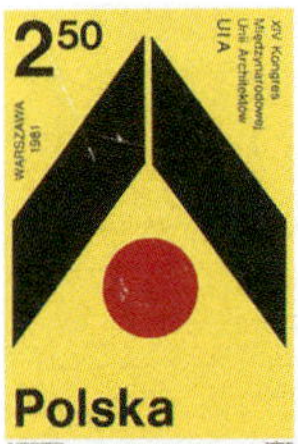

784 Congress Emblem

785 Wild Boar (*Sus scrofa*), Rifle and Oak Leaves

(Des W. Freudenreich. Litho)

1981 (15 June). Architects' Congress. Perf 11½×11.

2751 **784** 2z.50 lemon, black and bright scarlet 55 35

(Des W. Surowiecki. Litho)

1981 (30 June). Game Shooting. T **785** and similar multicoloured designs. Perf 11×11½ (6z.50) or 11½×11 (others).

2752	2z. Type **785**	40	25
2753	2z. Elk (*Alces alces*), rifle and fir twigs	40	25
2754	2z.50 Red Fox (*Vulpes vulpes*), shotgun, cartridges and fir branches	55	30
2755	2z.50 Roe Deer (*Capreolus capreolus*), feeding rack, rifle and fir branches	55	30
2756	6z.50 Mallards, shotgun, basket and reeds	1·40	70
2757	6z.50 Barnacle goose, shotgun and reeds (*horiz*)	1·40	70
2752/2757	*Set of 6*	4·25	2·30

786 European Bison

787 Tennis Player

(Des K. Śliwka. Photo)

1981 (27 Aug). Protection of European Bison (*Bison bonasus*). T **786** and similar vert designs. Multicoloured. Perf 11½×11.

2758	6z.50 Type **786**	1·40	50
	a. Strip of 5. Nos. 2758/2762	7·25	
2759	6z.50 Two Bison (one grazing)	1·40	50
2760	6z.50 Bison with Calf	1·40	50
2761	6z.50 Calf feeding	1·40	50
2762	6z.50 Two Bison (both looking towards right)	1·40	50
2758/2762	*Set of 5*	6·25	2·30

Nos. 2758/2762 were printed together in *se-tenant* strips of five within the sheet each strip forming a composite design.

(Des W. Swierzy. Photo)

1981 (17 Sept). 60th Anniversary of Polish Tennis Federation. Perf 11×11½.

2763 **787** 6z.50 multicoloured .... 1·40 40

788 Boy with Model Aeroplane

(Des J. Brodowski. Photo German Bank Note Ptg Co, Leipzig)

1981 (24 Sept). Model Making. T **788** and similar horiz designs. Multicoloured. Perf 14.

2764	1z. Type **788**	30	25
2765	2z. *Atlas 2* (tug)	40	25
2766	2z.50 Cars	55	25
2767	4z.20 Man with gliders	80	30
2768	6z.50 Racing cars	1·40	40
2769	8z. Man with yachts	1·80	55
2764/2769	*Set of 6*	4·75	1·80

789 Disabled Pictogram

790 17th-century Flintlock Pistol

(Des. R. Dudzicki. Litho)

1981 (25 Sept). International Year of Disabled Persons. Perf 11½×11.

2770 **789** 8z.40 blue-green, light yellowish green and black .... 1·80 55

(Des H. Chyliński. Photo German Bank Note Ptg Co, Leipzig)

1981 (9 Oct). Stamp Day. Antique Weapons. T **790** and similar vert design. Multicoloured. Perf 14.

2771	2z.50 Type **790**	50	35
2772	8z.40 17th-century gala sabre	1·70	50

791 H. Wieniawski and Violin Head

792 Bronislaw Wesolowski

(Des S. Malecki. Photo)

1981 (10 Oct). Wieniawski Young Violinists' Competition. Perf 11½.

2773 **791** 2z.50 multicoloured 55 30

(Des Z. Stasik. Litho)

1981 (15 Oct). Activists of Polish Workers' Movement. T **792** and similar horiz designs. Perf 11½.

2774	50g. green and black	25	25
2775	2z. blue and black	40	25
2776	2z.50 light brown and black	50	25

2777		6z.50 magenta and black	1·20	40
2774/2777		*Set of 4*	2·10	1·00

Designs: 50g. T **792**; 2z. Malgorzata Fornalska; 2z.50 Maria Koszutska; 6z.50 Marcin Kasprzak.

793 FAO Emblem and Globe

794 Helena Modrzejewska (actress)

(Des Z. Stasik. Litho)

1981 (16 Oct). World Food Day. Perf 11½×11.

2778	**793**	6z.90 bistre-brown, dull orange and pale yellow	1·40	40

(Des J. Brodowski. Recess and photo)

1981 (17 Oct). Bicentenary of Cracow Old Theatre. T **794** and similar horiz designs. Perf 12×11½.

2779		2z. maroon, pale grey and bluish violet	40	25
2780		2z.50 deep blue, pale stone and olive-sepia	50	25
2781		6z.50 dull violet, pale grey-blue and brown-olive	1·30	30
2782		8z. bistre-brown, pale sage green and brown-lake	1·60	40
2779/2782		*Set of 4*	3·50	1·10

Designs: 2z. T **794**; 2z.50 Stanislaw Koźmian (politician, writer and theatre director); 6z.50 Konrad Swinarski (stage manager and scenographer); 8z. Old Theatre building.

795 Cracow and Vistula River

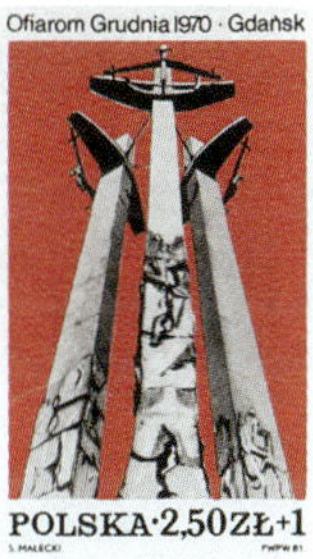

796 Gdańsk Memorial

(Des S. Malecki. Litho)

1981 (20 Nov). Vistula River Project. Sheet 62×51 mm. Perf 11½.

MS2783	10z.50 multicoloured	3·00	2·10

(Des S. Malecki. Litho)

1981 (16 Dec). Memorials to Victims of 1970 Uprising. T **796** and similar vert design. Perf 11½×12 (2z.50) or 11½×11 (6z.50).

2784	**796**	2z.50+1z. olive-grey, black and orange-vermilion	65	30
2785	-	6z.50+1z. olive-grey, black and violet-blue	1·50	50

Design: 26×37 mm—6z.50 Gdynia memorial.

797 *Epyphyllopsis gaertneri*

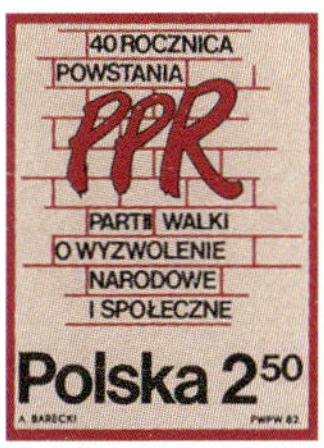

798 Writing on Wall

(Des A. Balcerzak. Photo German Bank Note Ptg Co, Leipzig)

1981 (22 Dec). Succulent Plants. T **797** and similar square designs. Multicoloured. Perf 13.

2786		90g. Type **797**	25	25
2787		1z. *Cereus tonduzii*	30	25
2788		2z. *Cylindropuntia leptocaulis*	40	25
2789		2z.50 *Cylindropuntia fulgida*	50	25
2790		2z.50 *Caralluma lugardi*	50	25
2791		6z.50 *Nopalea chochenillifera*	1·20	40
2792		6z.50 *Lithops helmutii*	1·20	40
2793		10z.50 *Cylindropuntia spinosior*	2·10	60
2786/2793		*Set of 8*	5·75	2·40

UNDERGROUND POST. Between 1982 and 1989, following the imposition of martial law, a large number of unofficial stamps were printed and circulated by the Solidarity Movement, camp internees, and similar organisations. Although most of these were used on clandestine mail some did pass through the normal mail network.

(Des A. Barecki. Photo)

1982 (5 Jan). 40th Anniversary of Polish Workers' Coalition. Perf 11½×11.

2794	**798**	2z.50 salmon-pink, rosine and black	55	35

No. 2794 with overprint '13. XII. 1981r. WOJNA WRON Z NARODEM 13. XII. 1982r.' is a private issue.

799 Faience Plate, Wloclawek

800 Lukasiewicz and Lamp

(Des K. Tarkowska (6z.), H. Matuszewska (others). Photo)

1982 (20 Jan). Polish Ceramics. T **799** and similar vert designs. Multicoloured. Perf 11½×11.

2795		1z. Type **799**	25	25
2796		2z. Porcelain cup and saucer, Korzec	40	25
2797		2z.50 Porcelain tureen and sauce boat, Barnówka	55	25
2798		6z. Porcelain inkpot, Horodnica	1·20	40
2799		8z. Faience Hunter's Tumbler, Lubartów	1·70	50
2800		10z.50 Faience figurine of nobleman, Biala Podlaska	2·30	70
2795/2800		*Set of 6*	5·75	2·10

(Des W. Andrzejewski. Photo)

1982 (22 Mar). Death Centenary of Ignacy Lukasiewicz (inventor of paraffin lamp). T **800** and similar vert designs. Multicoloured. Perf 11½×11.

2801		1z. Type **800**	30	25
2802		2z. Lamp with green shade	45	30
2803		2z.50 Lamp with pink shade	55	35
2804		3z.50 Two lamps	70	40
2805		9z. Lamp with decorated shade	1·90	50
2806		10z. Lamp with globe	2·30	60
2801/2806		*Set of 6*	5·50	2·20

801 Karol Szymanowski

802 RWD-6 SP-AHN, 1932

(Des K. Śliwka. Photo)

1982 (8 Apr). Birth Centenary of Karol Szymanowski (composer). Perf 11½×11.

2807	**801**	2z.50 deep bistre-brown and gold	60	30

(Des J. Brodowski. Photo)

1982 (5 May). 50th Anniversary of First Polish Victory in Tourist Aircraft Challenge Competition. T **802** and similar horiz design. Multicoloured. Perf 11×11½.

2808 27z. Type **802** .... 1·60 40
2809 31z. RWD-9 SP-ORO (winner of 1934 Challenge) .... 2·00 60
MS2810 89×101 mm. Nos. 2808/2809 .... 4·75 3·25

803 Henryk Sienkiewicz (literature, 1905)

804 Football as Globe

(Des W. Freudenreich. Litho)

1982 (10 May). Polish Nobel Prize Winners. T **803** and similar vert designs. Perf 11½×11.

2811 3z. blackish olive and black 35 25
2812 15z. sepia and black 75 35
2813 25z. blue-black 85 40
2814 31z. grey and black .... 2·50 70
2811/2814 *Set of 4* .... 4·00 1·50

Designs: 3z. T **803**; 15z. Wladyslaw Reymont (literature, 1924); 25z. Marie Curie (physics, 1903, and chemistry, 1911); 31z. Czeslaw Milosz (literature, 1980).

(Des J. Konarzewski (25z.), K. Kosmowski (27z.). Photo)

1982 (28 May). World Cup Football Championship, Spain. T **804** and similar horiz design. Multicoloured. Perf 11½×11 (25z.) or 11×11½ (27z.).

2815 25z. Type **804** .... 1·60 50
2816 27z. Bull and football (35×28 mm) .... 1·70 80

805 Maria Kazimiera Sobieska

806 Stanislaw Sierakowski and Boleslaw Domański (former Association presidents)

(Des J. Brodowski. Photo)

1982 (11 June). Philexfrance 82 International Stamp Exhibition, Paris. Sheet 69×86 mm. Perf 11½×11.

MS2817 65z. multicoloured .... 5·75 5·00

(Des S. Malecki. Litho)

1982 (20 July). 60th Anniversary of Association of Poles in Germany. Perf 11½×11.

2818 **806** 4z.50 orange-vermilion and bronze-green 85 40

807 Text around Globe

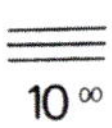

(808)

(Des H. Chyliński. Photo)

1982 (9 Aug). Second United Nations Conference on the Exploration and Peaceful Uses of Outer Space, Vienna. Perf 11½×11.

2819 **807** 31z. multicoloured .... 2·00 70

1982 (20 Aug). No. 2732 surch with T **808**.

2820 **781** 10z. on 6z.50 bistre-brown 75 40

809 Father Augustyn Kordecki (prior)

(Des R. Dudzicki. Photo)

1982 (26 Aug). 600th Anniversary of Black Madonna (icon) of Jasna Góra. T **809** and similar multicoloured designs. Perf 11.

2821 2z.50 Type **809** 45 25
2822 25z. *Siege of Jasna Góra by Swedes, 1655* (detail) (*horiz*) 90 40
a. Missing Ę under first E of OBLĘŻENIE .... 14·50
2823 65z. Black Madonna .... 2·75 65
2821/2823 *Set of 3* .... 3·75 1·20
MS2824 122×108 mm. No. 2823×2 (*sold at* 140z.) .... 15·00 21·00

The premium on No. **MS**2824 was for benefit of the Polish Philatelic Federation.

810 Marchers with Banner

811 Norbert Barlicki

(Des K. Kosmowski. Photo)

1982 (3 Sept). Centenary of Proletarian Party. Perf 11½×11.

2825 **810** 6z. multicoloured 75 40

(Des Z. Stasik. Photo)

1982 (10 Sept). Activists of Polish Workers' Movement. T **811** and similar vert designs. Perf 12×11½.

2826 5z. light new blue, bright blue and black ... 30 25
2827 6z. greenish grey, dull blue-green and black 30 30
2828 15z. salmon-pink, deep carmine and black .. 45 30
2829 20z. mauve, reddish violet and black 75 35
2830 29z. buff, orange-brown and black .... 1·00 40
2826/2830 *Set of 5* .... 2·50 1·40

Designs: 5z. T **811**; 6z. Pawel Finder; 15z. Marian Buczek; 20z. Cezaryna Wojnarowska; 29z. Ignacy Daszyński.

812 Dr Robert Koch

(Des K. Syta. Photo)

1982 (22 Sept). Centenary of Discovery of Tubercle Bacillus. T **812** and similar vert design. Multicoloured. Perf 11½×10.

2831		10z. Type **812**	85	40
2832		25z. Dr Odo Bujwid	2·20	50

813 Head of Woman

813a Head of Ruler

814 Maximilian Kolbe (after M. Koscielniak)

(Des S. Skiba (Nos. 2833/2834), J. Konarzewski (others). Eng W. Zajdel (No. 2840), B. Kowalska (No. 2842), M. Kopecki (No. 2843). Photo German Bank Note Ptg Co, Leipzig (Nos. 2836, 2841, 2843); recess (Nos. 2840, 2842, 2843) or photo (others) Govt Ptg Wks, Warsaw)

1982 (25 Sept)–**89**. Carved Heads from Wawel Castle.

*(a) T **813** and similar vert design. Perf 12×11½.*

2833	**813**	60z. salmon and brown	3·50	1·00
2834	-	100z. ochre and sepia	5·25	1·40

Design: 100z. Man.

*(b) T **813a** and similar vert designs. Perf 14 (Nos. 2836, 2841, 2843) or 11×12 (others).*

2835		3z.50 reddish brown (24.1.85)	35	25
2836		5z. deep bluish green (10.7.84)	35	25
2837		5z. crimson (8.7.85)	35	25
2838		10z. ultramarine (8.7.85)	35	25
2839		15z. lake-brown (22.9.88)	45	25
2840		20z. olive-grey (30.7.86)	70	30
2841		20z. deep dull blue (31.3.89)	35	25
2842		40z. agate (30.7.86)	2·10	40
2843		60z. deep green (15.12.89)	45	30
2843*a*		200z. black (11.11.86)	5·25	1·00
2833/2843*a* *Set of* 12			18·00	5·25

Designs: Nos. 2835, 2841, T **813a**; No. 2836, Warrior; Nos. 2837, 2839, Woman wearing chaplet; No. 2838, Man in cap; No. 2840, Thinker; No. 2842, Man in beret; No. 2843, Young man; No. 2843*a*, Man.

Nos. 2836, 2841 and 2843 were issued in coils, with every fifth stamp numbered on the back.

(Des K. Kosmowski. Photo)

1882 (10 Oct). Sanctification of Maximilian Kolbe (Franciscan concentration camp victim). Perf 11½×11.

2844	**814**	27z. multicoloured	2·40	70

815 Polar Research Station

816 *Log Floats on Vistula River* (drawing by J. Telakowski)

(Des H. Matuszewska. Litho)

1982 (25 Oct). 50th Anniversary of Polish Polar Research. Perf 11½.

2845	**815**	27z. multicoloured	2·50	70

(Des M. Piekarski. Photo)

1982 (2 Nov). Views of Vistula River. T **816** and similar horiz designs. Perf 11½×12.

2846		12z. ultramarine	35	25
2847		17z. cobalt	45	30
2848		25z. deep blue	55	35
2846/2848 *Set of* 3			1·30	80

Designs: 12z. T **806**; 17z. *Kazimierz Dolny* (engraving by Andriollo); 25z. *Danzig* (18th-century engraving).

817 Stanislaw Zaremba

(Des H. Chyliński. Photo)

1982 (23 Nov). Mathematicians. T **817** and similar horiz designs. Perf 11×11½.

2849		5z. reddish purple, ultramarine and black	45	25
2850		6z. orange, violet and black	60	30
2851		12z. cobalt, olive-brown and black	1·20	35
2852		15z. olive-yellow, deep chestnut and black	1·40	40
2849/2852 *Set of* 4			3·25	1·20

Designs: 5z. T **817**; 6z. Waclaw Sierpiński; 12z. Zygmunt Janiszewski; 15z. Stefan Banach.

818 Military Council Medal

1982 (13 Dec). First Anniversary of Military Council. Photo. Perf 12×11½.

2853	**818**	2z.50 black, yellow and rosine	60	30

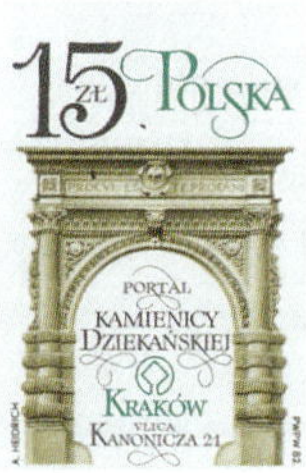

819 Deanery Gate

820 Bernard Wapowski Map, 1526

(Des A. Heidrich. Eng M. Kopecki (65z.). Recess and photo (65z.), litho (others))

1982 (20 Dec). Renovation of Cracow Monuments (1st series). T **819** and similar vert design. Perf 11½×11.

2854		15z. black, yellow-olive and emerald	95	35
2855		25z. black, dull purple and deep magenta	1·60	40
MS2856		75×93 mm. 65z. pale blue-green, dull purple and sepia (22×27 mm). Imperf	3·25	1·90

Designs: 15z. T **819**; 25z. Gateway of Collegium Iuridicum; 65z. Street plan of Old Cracow.

See also Nos. 2904/2905, 2968/2969, 3029/3030, 3116 and 3153.

(Des J. Brodowski. Litho)

1982 (28 Dec). Polish Maps. T **820** and similar square designs. Perf 11½.

2857		5z. multicoloured	35	25
2858		6z. pale cinnamon, black and maroon	35	30
2859		8z. multicoloured	45	30
2860		25z. multicoloured	1·50	50
2857/2860 *Set of* 4			2·40	1·20

Designs: 5z. T **820**; 6z. Map of Warsaw, 1839; 8z. Map of Poland from Eugen Romer's Atlas, 1908; 25z. Plan of Cracow by A. Buchowiecki, 1703, and astrolabe.

821 *The Last of the Resistance* (Artur Grottger)

1983 (22 Jan). 120th Anniversary of January Rising. Photo. Perf 12×11½.

2861	**821**	6z. deep brown	45	30

822 *Grand Theatre, Warsaw, 1838* (Maciej Zaleski)

1983 (24 Feb). 150th Anniversary of Grand Theatre, Warsaw. Photo. Perf 11.

2862	**822**	6z. multicoloured	45	30

823 Wild Flowers

824 Karol Kurpiński (composer)

(Des S. Malecki. Litho)

1983 (24 Mar). Environmental Protection. T **823** and similar square designs. Multicoloured. Perf 11½.

2863	5z. Type **823**	35	25
2864	6z. Mirror carp, European Eel and Mute Swan	45	30
2865	17z. Hoopoe and trees	1·30	50
2866	30z. Redfish, Lumpsucker, Sailfish, Flying-fish and Trunkfish	2·00	85
2867	31z. European Bison and Roe Deer	2·10	90
2868	38z. Fruit	2·50	1·10
2863/2868	*Set of* 6	7·75	3·50

(Des H. Chyliński. Photo)

1983 (25 Mar). Celebrities. T **824** and similar vert designs. Perf 11½×11.

2869	5z. cinnamon and reddish brown	35	25
2870	6z. pale magenta and bluish violet	45	30
2871	17z. pale bluish green and slate-green	90	40
2872	25z. pale yellow-orange and deep orange-brown	1·40	50
2873	27z. new blue and deep ultramarine	1·60	55
2874	31z. reddish lilac and bright violet	2·00	60
2869/2874	*Set of* 6	6·00	2·30

Designs: 5z. T **824**; 6z. Maria Jasnorzewska Pawlikowska (poet); 17z. Stanislaw Szober (linguist); 25z. Tadeusz Banachiewicz (astronomer and mathematician); 27z. Jaroslaw Iwaszkiewicz (writer); 31z. Wladyslaw Tatarkiewicz (philosopher and historian).

825 3000 m Steeplechase

826 Ghetto Heroes Monument (Natan Rappaport)

(Des W. Freudenreich. Photo)

1983 (5 Apr). Sports Achievements. T **825** and similar horiz designs. Perf 11×11½.

2875	5z. pale pink and bright violet	35	25
2876	6z. chestnut, pale pink and black	95	30
2877	15z. stone and deep olive	95	40
2878	27z.+5z. dull violet-blue, deep blue and black	2·10	60
2875/2878	*Set of* 4	3·50	1·40

Designs: 5z. T **825**; 6z. Show jumping; 15z. Football; 27z.+5z. Pole vault.

The 5z., 6z. and 27z. commemorate gold medals won by Polish athletes at the Moscow Olympic Games.

The 15z. commemorates third place in World Cup Football Championship, Spain.

(Des M. Piekarski. Photo)

1983 (19 Apr). 40th Anniversary of Warsaw Ghetto Uprising. Perf 11½×11.

2879	**826**	6z. buff and deep bistre-brown	55	35

No. 2879 was issued with *se-tenant* label showing the Anniversary medal by K. Danielewicz.

827 Customs Officer and Suitcases

828 John Paul II and Jasna Góra Sanctuary

(Des K. Kosmowski. Photo)

1983 (28 Apr). 30th Anniversary of Customs Co-operation Council. Perf 11½×11.

2880	**827**	5z. multicoloured	45	30

(Des R. Dudzicki. Photo)

1983 (16 June). Papal Visit. T **828** and similar horiz design. Multicoloured. Perf 11.

2881	31z. Type **828**	2·20	60
2882	65z. Niepokalanów Church and John Paul holding crucifix	4·25	1·40
MS2883	107×81 mm. No. 2882	4·50	4·00

829 Dragoons

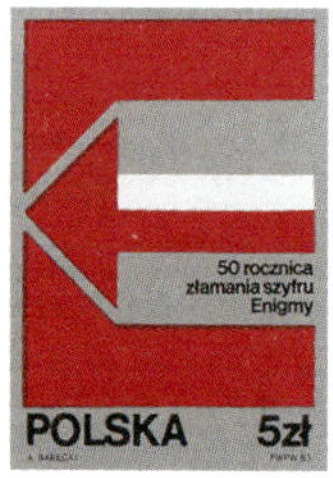

830 Arrow piercing 'E'

(Des R. Dudzicki. Photo)

1983 (5 July). 300th Anniversary of Polish Relief of Vienna (1st issue). Troops of King Jan III Sobieski. T **829** and similar vert designs. Multicoloured. Perf 11½×11.

2884	5z. Type **829**	35	25
2885	5z. Armoured cavalryman	35	25
2886	6z. Infantry non-commissioned officer and musketeer	45	30
2887	15z. Light cavalry lieutenant	1·10	40
2888	27z. Winged hussar and trooper with carbine	1·90	70
2884/2888	*Set of* 5	3·75	1·70

See also Nos. 2893/**MS**2897.

(Des A. Barecki. Litho)

1983 (16 Aug). 50th Anniversary of Deciphering Enigma Machine Codes. Perf 11½×11.

2889	**830**	5z. vermilion, grey and black	45	30

831 Toruń

832 Child's Painting

(Des S. Malecki. Photo)

1983 (25 Aug). 750th Anniversary of Toruń. Perf 11.

2890	**831**	6z. multicoloured	45	30
MS2891		142×116 mm. No. 2890×4	6·50	6·25

The gutter of No. **MS**2891 is inscribed for 14th Polish Philatelic Exhibition, Toruń.

(Des H. Matuszewska. Photo)

1983 (9 Sept). Order of the Smile (politeness publicity campaign). Perf 11½×12.

2892	**832**	6z. multicoloured	45	30

833 King Jan III Sobieski

834 Wanda Wasilewska

(Des S. Malecki. Photo)

1983 (12 Sept). 300th Anniversary of Polish Relief of Vienna (2nd issue). T **833** and similar vert designs. Multicoloured. Perf 11.

2893	5z. Type **833**	35	25
2894	6z. King Jan III Sobieski (*different*)	45	30
2895	6z. *King Jan III Sobieski on Horseback* (Francesco Trevisani)	45	30
2896	25z. *King Jan III Sobieski* (Jerzy Eleuter)	2·20	40
2893/2896	*Set of* 4	3·00	1·10
MS2897	97×75 mm. 65z.+10z. *King Jan III Sobieski at Vienna* (Jan Matejko). Imperf	4·50	3·25

(Des W. Surowiecki (Nos. 2898/2899). Photo)

1983 (12 Oct). 40th Anniversary of Polish People's Army. T **834** and similar designs. Perf 12×11½ (No. 2901) or 11½×12 (others).

2898	5z. multicoloured	35	25
2899	5z. greenish black, blue-green and black	35	25
2900	6z. multicoloured	45	30
2901	6z. multicoloured	45	30
2898/2901	*Set of* 4	1·40	1·00

Designs: Vert—No. 2898, T **934**; No. 2899, General Zygmunt Berling, No. 2900, *The Frontier Post* (S. Poznanski). Horiz—No. 2901, *Taking the Oath* (S. Poznanski).

835 Profiles and WCY Emblem

836 Boxing

(Des N. Chyliński. Photo)

1983 (18 Oct). World Communications Year. Perf 11×11½.

2902	**835**	15z. black, greenish blue and rosine	1·00	40

(Des J. Brodowski. Litho)

1983 (19 Nov). 60th Anniversary of Polish Boxing Federation. Perf 11½×11.

2903	**836**	6z. multicoloured	60	30

(Des A. Heidrich. Litho)

1983 (25 Nov). Renovation of Cracow Monuments (2nd series). Designs as T **819**. Perf 11×11½ (5z.) or 11½×11 (6z.).

2904	5z. brown, purple and black	35	25
2905	6z. black, olive-green and new blue	45	30

Design: Horiz—5z. Cloth Hall. Vert—6z. Town Hall tower.

837 Biskupiec Costume

838 Hand with Sword (poster by Zakrzewski and Krolikowski, 1945)

(Des W. Świerzy. Photo)

1983 (16 Dec). Women's Folk Costumes. T **837** and similar vert designs. Multicoloured. Perf 11½×11.

2906	5z. Type **837**	35	25
2907	5z. Rozbark	35	25
2908	6z. Warmia and Mazuria	45	30
2909	6z. Cieszyń	45	30
2910	25z. Kurpie	1·90	60
2911	38z. Lubsko	3·00	80
2906/2911	*Set of* 6	5·75	2·30

(Des Z. Stasik. Photo)

1983 (31 Dec). 40th Anniversary of National People's Council. Perf 11½×11.

2912	**838**	6z. multicoloured	45	30

839 Badge of General Bem Brigade

840 Dulcimer

(Des W. Surowiecki. Litho)

1983 (31 Dec). 40th Anniversary of People's Army. Perf 11½.

2913	**839**	5z. multicoloured	45	30

(Des Z. Stasik. Photo)

1984 (10 Feb). Musical Instruments (1st series). T **840** and similar vert designs. Multicoloured. Perf 11½×11.

2914	5z. Type **840**	35	25
2915	6z. Kettle drum and tambourine	45	30
2916	10z. Accordion	85	30
2917	15z. Double bass	1·30	40
2918	17z. Bagpipe	1·40	45
2919	29z. Country band (wood carvings by Tadeusz Zak)	2·20	60
2914/2919	*Set of* 6	6·00	2·10

See also Nos. 2994/2999.

841 Wincenty Witos

842 *Clematis lanuginosa*

(Des S. Malecki. Litho)

1984 (2 Mar). 110th Birth Anniversary of Wincenty Witos (leader of Peasants' Movement). Perf 11½×11.

2920	**841**	6z. purple-brown and bright emerald	45	30

(A. Balcerzak. Photo)

1984 (26 Mar). Clematis. T **842** and similar horiz designs. Multicoloured. Perf 11×11½.

2921	5z. Type **842**	35	25
2922	6z. *Clematis tangutica*	45	30
2923	10z. *Clematis texensis*	75	30

2924	17z. *Clematis alpina*	1·40	40
2925	25z. Travellers' joy (*Clematis vitalba*)	2·00	55
2926	27z. *Clematis montana*	2·10	60
2921/2926 *Set of 6*		6·25	2·20

843 *The Ecstasy of St Francis* (El Greco)

844 Handball

(Des J. Konarzewski. Photo)

1984 (21 Apr). España 84 International Stamp Exhibition, Madrid. Perf 11.

2927	**843**	27z. multicoloured	2·30	70

(Des J. Brodowski. Litho)

1984 (25 Apr). Olympic Games, Los Angeles, and Winter Olympics, Sarajevo. T **844** and similar horiz designs. Multicoloured. Perf 11×11½.

2928	5z. Type **844**	35	25
2929	6z. Fencing	45	30
2930	15z. Cycling	1·10	35
2931	16z. Janusz Kusociński winning 10,000 m race, 1932 Olympics, Los Angeles	1·20	40
2932	17z. Stanislawa Walasiewiczówna winning 100 m race, 1932 Olympics, Los Angeles	1·30	45
2933	31z. Women's slalom (Winter Olympics)	2·50	70
2928/2933 *Set of 6*		6·25	2·20
MS2934 129×78 mm. Nos. 2931/2932. Perf 12×13 (*sold at* 43z.)		3·50	2·50

The 10z. premium on No. **MS**2934 was for benefit of the Polish Olympic Committee.

845 Monte Cassino Memorial Cross and Monastery

846 *German Princess* (Lucas Cranach)

(Des S. Malecki. Photo)

1984 (18 May). 40th Anniversary of Battle of Monte Cassino. Perf 11½×11.

2935	**845**	15z. blackish olive and orange-vermilion	1·30	40

(Des R. Dudzicki. Photo)

1984 (15 June). 19th Universal Postal Union Congress, Hamburg. Perf 11½×12.

2936	**846**	27z.+10z. multicoloured	2·50	1·00

No. 2936 was issued with *se-tenant* label bearing text and UPU emblem.

847 *Warsaw from Praga Bank* (detail) (Canaletto)

848 Order of Grunwald Cross

(Des J. Wysocki. Photo)

1984 (20 June). Paintings of Vistula River. T **847** and similar horiz designs. Multicoloured. Perf 11.

2937	5z. Type **847**	35	30
2938	6z. *Trumpet Festivity* (Aleksander Gierymski)	45	35
2939	25z. *The Vistula River near Bielany District* (Józef Rapacki)	1·90	60
2940	27z. *Steamship Harbour in Powiśle District* (Franciszek Kostrzewski)	2·00	65
2937/2940 *Set of 4*		4·25	1·70

(Des J. Desselberger. Photo)

1984 (21 July). 40th Anniversary of Polish People's Republic. T **848** and similar vert designs. Multicoloured. Perf 11½.

2941	5z. Type **848**	35	25
2942	6z. Order of Revival of Poland	45	30
2943	10z. Order of Banner of Labour, First Class	70	30
2944	16z. Order of Builders of People's Poland	1·40	40
2941/2944 *Set of 4*		2·50	1·10
MS2945 156×101 mm. Nos. 2941/2944		9·25	7·00

849 Group of Insurgents

850 Defence of Oksywie Holm and Colonel Stanislaw Dąbek

(Des W. Freudenreich. Photo)

1984 (1 Aug). 40th Anniversary of Warsaw Uprising. T **849** and similar horiz designs. Multicoloured. Perf 11×11½.

2946	4z. Type **849**	35	25
2947	5z. Insurgent on postal duty	35	30
2948	6z. Insurgents fighting	45	30
2949	25z. Tending wounded	2·00	40
2946/2949 *Set of 4*		2·75	1·10

(Des A. Balcerzak. Photo)

1984 (1 Sept). 45th Anniversary of German Invasion. T **850** and similar horiz design. Multicoloured. Perf 12×11½.

2950	5z. Type **850**	35	30
2951	6z. Battle of Bzura River and General Tadeusz Kutrzeba	45	30

See also Nos. 3004/3005, 3062, 3126/3128, 3172/3174 and 3240/3243.

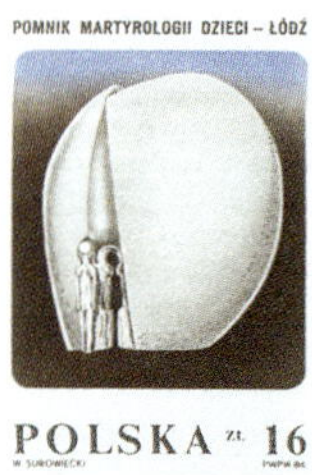

851 Broken Heart (monument, Łódź Concentration Camp)

852 Militiaman and Ruins

(Des W. Surowiecki. Photo)

1984 (17 Sept). Child Martyrs. Perf 11½×11.

2952 **851** 16z. deep bistre-brown, bright blue and blackish brown .... 1·00 40

(Des J. Kroll. Photo)

1984 (29 Sept). 40th Anniversary of Civic Militia and Security Force. T **852** and similar horiz design. Multicoloured. Perf 11×11½.

2953 5z. Type **852** 35 30
2954 6z. Militiaman in control centre 45 30

853 First Balloon Flight, 1784 (after Chrostowski)

854 Weasel (*Mustela nivalis*)

(Des A. Balcerzak. Photo)

1984 (5 Nov). Polish Aviation. T **853** and similar horiz designs. Perf 11×11½.

2955 5z. black, apple-green and mauve 35 25
2956 5z. multicoloured 35 25
2957 6z. multicoloured 45 30
2958 10z. multicoloured 70 30
2959 16z. multicoloured .... 1·10 40
2960 27z. multicoloured .... 2·00 60
2961 31z. multicoloured .... 2·20 70
2955/2961 *Set of 7* .... 6·50 2·50

Designs: No. 2955, T **853**; No. 2956, Michal Scipio del Campo and biplane (first flight over Warsaw, 1911); No. 2957, Balloon *Polonez* (winner, Gordon Bennett Cup, 1983); No. 2958, PWS 101 and Jantar gliders (Lilenthal Medal winners); No. 2959, PZL-104 Wilga SP-APV aerorplane (world precise flight champion, 1983); No. 2960, Jan Nagórski and Farman MF.7 floatplane (Arctic zone flights, 1914); No. 2961, PZL P-37 Loś and PZL P-7 aircraft.

(Des J. Brodowski. Photo)

1984 (4 Dec). Fur-bearing Animals. T **854** and similar multicoloured designs. Perf 11×11½ (horiz) or 11½×11 (vert).

2962 4z. Type **854** 30 25
2963 5z. Stoat (*Mustela erminea*) 35 30
2964 5z. Beech Marten (*Martes foina*) 35 30
2965 10z. Eurasian Beaver (*Castor fiber*) (*vert*) 45 30
2966 10z. Eurasian Otter (*Lutra lutra*) (*vert*) 45 30
2967 65z. Alpine Marmot (*Marmota marmota*) (*vert*) .... 4·00 80
2962/2967 *Set of 6* .... 5·25 2·00

(Des A. Heidrich. Litho)

1984 (10 Dec). Renovation of Cracow Monuments (3rd series). Designs as T **819**. Perf 11½×11 (5z.) or 11×11½ (15z.).

2968 5z. lake-brown, black and deep bluish green 45 30
2969 15z. turquoise-blue, chestnut and black 75 40

Designs: Vert—5z. Wawel cathedral. Horiz—15z. Wawel Castle (royal residence).

855 Protestant Church, Warsaw

856 Steam Fire Hose (late 19th century)

(Des J. Wysocki. Photo)

1984 (28 Dec). Religious Architecture. T **855** and similar multicoloured designs. Perf 11½×12 (vert) or 12×11½ (horiz).

2970 5z. Type **855** 30 25
2971 10z. Saint Andrew's Roman Catholic church, Cracow 45 30
2972 15z. Greek Catholic church, Rychwald 70 30
2973 20z. St Maria Magdalena Orthodox church, Warsaw 95 35
2974 25z. Tykocin synagogue, Kaczorów (*horiz*) .... 1·40 40
2975 31z. Tatar mosque, Kruszyniany (*horiz*) .... 1·70 45
2970/2975 *Set of 6* .... 5·00 1·80

(Des Z. Stasik. Photo)

1985 (25 Feb). Fire Engines. T **856** and similar horiz designs. Multicoloured. Perf 11×11½.

2976 4z. Type **856** 30 25
2977 10z. Polski Fiat, 1930s 45 30
2978 12z. Jelcz 315 fire engine 65 30
2979 15z. Manual fire hose, 1899 .... 75 30
2980 20z. Magirus fire ladder on Jelcz chassis .... 1·00 35
2981 30z. Manual fire hose (early 18th century) .... 2·20 40
2976/2981 *Set of 6* .... 4·75 1·70

857 *Battle of Raclawice* (Jan Styka and Wojciech Kossak)

858 Wincenty Rzymowski

(Des A. Heidrich. Photo)

1985 (4 Apr). Perf 11.

2982 **857** 27z. multicoloured .... 1·50 55

(Des Z. Stasik. Litho)

1985 (11 Apr). 35th Death Anniversary of Wincenty Rzymowski (founder of Polish Democratic Party). Perf 11½×11.

2983 **858** 10z. deep blue-violet and dull vermilion 60 30

859 Badge on Denim

860 Boleslaw III, the Wry-mouthed, and Map

(Des H. Matuszewska and K. Tarkowska. Photo)

1985 (25 Apr). International Youth Year. Perf 11½×11.

2984 **859** 15z. multicoloured .... 1·00 40

(Des. S. Malecki. Litho)

1985 (8 May). 40th Anniversary of Return of Western and Northern Territories to Poland. T **860** and similar square designs. Multicoloured. Perf 11½.

2985 5z. Type **660** 35 25
2986 10z. Wladyslaw Gomulka (vice-president of first post-war government) and map 60 30
2987 20z. Piotr Zaremba (Governor of Szczecin) and map .... 1·30 40
2985/2987 *Set of 3* .... 2·00 85

861 *Victory, Berlin 1945* (Józef Mlynarski)

862 Warsaw Arms and Flags of Member Countries

(Des W. Surowiecki. Photo)

1985 (9 May). 40th Anniversary of Victory over Fascism. Perf 12×11½.

2988	**861**	5z. multicoloured	45	30

(Des S. Tolodziecki. Litho)

1985 (14 May). 30th Anniversary of Warsaw Pact. Perf 11½.

2989	**862**	5z. multicoloured	45	30

863 Wolves in Winter

864 *Iskra* (cadet ship)

(Des J. Brodowski. Photo)

1985 (25 May). Protected Animals. The Wolf (*Canis lupus*). T **863** and similar horiz designs. Multicoloured. Perf 11×11½.

2990	5z. Type **863**	90	35
2991	10z. She-wolf with cubs	1·30	55
2992	10z. Close-up of wolf	1·30	55
2993	20z. Wolves in summer	4·25	1·40
2990/2993	*Set of 4*	7·00	2·50

(Des Z. Stasik. Photo)

1985 (25 June). Musical Instruments (2nd series). Vert designs as T **840**. Multicoloured. Perf 11½×11.

2994	5z. Rattle and tarapata	35	25
2995	10z. Stick rattle and berlo	60	30
2996	12z. Clay whistles	75	30
2997	20z. Stringed instruments	1·30	35
2998	25z. Cow bells	1·60	40
2999	31z. Wind instruments	2·00	55
2994/2999	*Set of 6*	6·00	1·90

(Des M. Piekarski. Eng P. Naszarkowski. Recess and litho)

1985 (29 June). 40th Anniversary of Polish Navy. Perf 11½×11.

3000	**864**	5z. deep violet-blue, greenish yellow and black	45	30

865 Tomasz Nocznicki

866 Hockey Players

(Des J. Konarzewski. Eng W. Zajdel (10z.), M. Kopecki (20z.). Recess)

1985 (26 July). Leaders of Peasants' Movement. T **865** and similar horiz design. Perf 11×11½.

3001	**865**	10z. slate green	45	30
3002	-	20z. chocolate	1·00	70

Design: 20z. Maciej Rataj.

(Des J. Brodowski. Litho)

1985 (22 Aug). 60th Anniversary (1986) of Polish Field Hockey Association. Perf 11½×11.

3003	**866**	5z. multicoloured	45	30

(Des A. Balcerzak. Photo)

1985 (1 Sept). 46th Anniversary of German Invasion. Horiz designs as T **850**. Multicoloured. Perf 12×11½.

3004	5z. Defence of Wizna and Captain Wladyslaw Raginis	35	25
3005	10z. Battle of Mlawa and Colonel Wilhelm Liszka-Lawicz	50	30

867 Type 20k Goods Wagon

868 *Madonna with Child, St John and Angel* (Sandro Botticelli)

(Des H. Chyliński. Litho)

1985 (18 Sept). PAFAWAG Railway Rolling Stock. T **867** and similar horiz designs. Multicoloured. Perf 11½×11.

3006	5z. Type **867**	35	25
3007	10z. Electric locomotive No. ET22-001, 1969	45	30
3008	17z. Type OMMK wagon	90	35
3009	20z. Type 111A passenger carriage	1·00	40
3006/3009	*Set of 4*	2·40	1·20

(Des R. Dudzicki. Photo)

1985 (25 Sept). Italia '85 International Stamp Exhibition, Rome. Sheet 81×108 mm. Perf 11.

MS3010	**868** 65z.+15z. multicoloured	4·75	4·00

A limited quantity of No. **MS**3010 has the additional inscription '35 LAT POLSKIEGO ZWIAZKU FILATELISTÓW' beneath the stamp (*price* £10).

869 Green-winged Teal (*Anas crecca*)

870 UN Emblem and Flags

(Des J. Desselberger. Photo)

1985 (21 Oct). Wild Ducks. T **869** and similar horiz designs. Multicoloured. Perf 11×11½.

3011	5z. Type **869**	35	25
3012	5z. Garganey (*Anas querquedula*)	40	25
3013	10z. Tufted Duck (*Aythya fuligula*)	75	30
3014	15z. Common Goldeneye (*Bucephala clangula*)	1·00	35
3015	25z. Eider (*Somateria mollissima*)	1·50	40
3016	29z. Red-crested Pochard (*Netta rufina*)	1·70	45
3011/3016	*Set of 6*	5·25	1·80

(Des H. Chyliński. Litho)

1985 (24 Oct). 40th Anniversary of United Nations Organisation. Perf 11½×11.

3017	**870**	27z. multicoloured	1·50	55

871 Ballerina

872 *Marysia and Burek in Ceylon*

(Des S. Malecki. Litho)

1985 (4 Dec). Bicentenary of Polish Ballet. T **871** and similar vert design. Perf 11½×11.

3018	**871**	5z. bronze green, yellow-orange and Venetian red	35	25
3019	-	15z. purplish brown, bright reddish violet and reddish orange	75	40

Design: 15z. Male dancer.

(Des K. Śliwka. Photo)

1985 (8 Dec). Birth Centenary of Stanislaw Ignacy Witkiewicz (artist). T **872** and similar multicoloured designs. Perf 11×11½ (No. 3021) or 11½×11 (others).

3020	5z. Type **872**	35	25
3021	10z. *Woman with Fox (horiz)*	75	30
3022	10z. Self-portrait	75	30
3023	20z. *Compositions (1917–1920)*	1·00	35
3024	25z. *Nena Stachurska*	1·50	40
3020/3024	*Set of 5*	4·00	1·40

873 Oliwa Church Organ and Bach

874 Human Profile

(Des R. Dudzicki. Photo)

1986 (30 Dec). 300th Birth Anniversary of Johann Sebastian Bach (composer). Sheet 67×79 mm. Perf 11½×11.

MS3025 **873**	65z. multicoloured	3·50	2·75

No. **MS**3025 also exists with additional inscription '300 rocznica urodzin Jana Sebastian Bacha' from a limited printing (*price* £15).

(Des K. Śliwka. Litho)

1986 (16 Jan). Congress of Intellectuals for Defence of Peaceful Future of the World, Warsaw. Perf 11½×11.

3026	**874**	10z. dull ultramarine, dull violet-blue and deep cobalt	75	35

875 Michal Kamieński and Planetary and Comet's Orbits

876 Sun

(Des Z. Stasik. Litho)

1986 (7 Feb). Appearance of Halley's Comet. T **875** and similar horiz design. Perf 11×11½.

3027	**875**	25z. deep blue and orange-brown	1·40	40
		a. Pair. Nos. 3027/3028	3·00	85
3028	-	25z. indigo, greenish blue and orange-brown	1·40	40

Design: No. 3028, *Vega*, *Planet A*, *Giotto* and *Ice* space probes and comet.

Nos. 3027/3028 were printed together in *se-tenant* pairs within the sheet.

(Des A. Heidrich. Litho)

1986 (20 Mar). Renovation of Cracow Monuments (4th series). Vert designs as T **819**. Perf 11½×11.

3029	5z. bistre-brown, chestnut and black	35	25
3030	10z. yellow-green, yellow-brown and black	45	30

Designs: 5z. Collegium Maius (Jagiellonian University museum); 10z. Kazimierz Town Hall.

(Des H. Chyliński. Photo)

1986 (20 Mar). International Peace Year. Perf 11½×11.

3031	**876**	25z. lemon, greenish blue and blue	1·00	40

877 Grey Partridge (*Perdix perdix*)

878 Kulczyński

(Des H. Chyliński. Photo)

1986 (15 Apr). Game. T **877** and similar multicoloured designs. Perf 11×11½ (horiz) or 11½×11 (vert).

3032	5z. Type **877**	30	25
3033	5z. Common Rabbit (*Oryctolagus cuniculus*)	30	25
3034	10z. Common Pheasants (*Phasianus colchicus*) (*horiz*)	45	30
3035	10z. Fallow Deer (*Dama dama*) (*horiz*)	45	30
3036	20z. Hare (*Lepus europaeus*)	1·00	40
3037	40z. Argali (*Ovis ammon*)	1·90	50
3032/3037	*Set of 6*	4·00	1·80

(Des R. Dudzicki. Eng P. Naszarkowski. Recess and photo)

1986 (3 May). Tenth Death Anniversary (1985) of Stanislaw Kulczyński (politician). Perf 11½×11.

3038	**878**	10z. stone and chocolate	45	30

879 *Warsaw Fire Brigade, 1871* (detail, Józef Brodowski)

(Des Z. Stasik. Eng M. Kopecki. Recess and litho)

1986 (16 May). 150th Anniversary of Warsaw Fire Brigade. Perf 11.

3039	**879**	10z. deep brown and dull brown	45	30

880 Paderewski (composer)

881 Footballers

(Des W. Andrzejewski. Photo)

1986 (22 May). Ameripex '86 International Stamp Exhibition, Chicago. Perf 11½×11.

3040	**880**	65z. deep bright blue, black and brownish grey	3·00	85

(Des R. Dudzicki. Litho)

1986 (26 May). World Cup Football Championship, Mexico. Perf 11½.

3041	**881**	25z. multicoloured	1·00	40

882 *Wilanów*

(Des J. Brodowski. Photo)

1986 (18 June). Passenger Ferries. T **882** and similar horiz designs. Multicoloured. Perf 11.

3042	10z. Type **882**	45	30
3043	10z. *Wawel*	45	30
3044	15z. *Pomerania*	75	35
3045	25z. *Rogalin*	1·00	40
3042/3045 *Set of* 4		2·40	1·20
MS3046 Two sheets, each 116×98 mm. (a) Nos. 3042/3043 (*sold at* 30z.); (b) Nos. 3044/3045 (*sold at* 55z.)		16·00	11·50

Nos. 3042/3045 were each issued with *se-tenant* half stamp-size label depicting features of various harbours.

The premium on Nos. **MS**3046(a) and **MS**3046(b) was for the benefit of the National Association of Philatelists.

883 A. B. Dobrowolski, Map and *Kopenik* (research vessel)

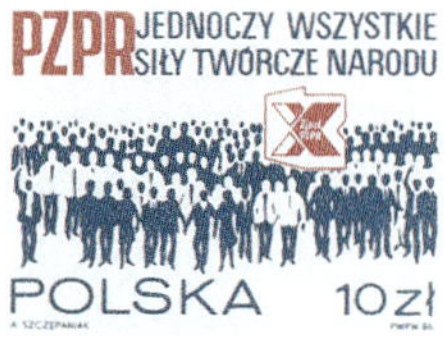

884 Workers and Emblem

(Des S. Malecki. Litho)

1986 (23 June). 25th Anniversary of Antarctic Agreement. T **883** and similar horiz design. Perf 11½×11.

3047	**883**	5z. turquoise-green, olive-black and vermilion	45	30
3048	-	40z. lavender, deep violet and reddish orange	1·90	40

Design: 40z. H. Arctowski, map and *Profesor Siedlecki* (research vessel).

(Des A. Szczepaniak. Photo)

1986 (29 June). Tenth Polish United Workers' Party Congress, Warsaw. Perf 11×11½.

3049	**884**	10z. steel blue and red	45	30

885 *Paulinite Church on Skalka in Cracow* (detail), 1627

886 PZL-106A Kruk SP-AGS (Waclaw Nyez)

(Des A. Heidrich. Photo)

1986 (15 Aug). Treasures of Jasna Góra Monastery. T **885** and similar vert designs. Multicoloured. Perf 11½×11.

3050	5z. Type **885**	30	25
3051	5z. *Tree of Jesse*, 17th century	30	25
3052	20z. Chalice, 18th century	1·40	40
3053	40z. *Virgin Mary* (detail, chasuble column), 15th century	2·20	50
3050/3053 *Set of* 4		3·75	1·30

(Des J. Brodowski. Litho)

1986 (21 Aug). 1985 Polish World Championship Successes. T **886** and similar horiz designs. Multicoloured. Perf 11×11½.

3054	5z. Type **886**	30	25
3055	10z. Windsurfing (Malgorzuta Palasz-Piasecka)	45	30
3056	10z. Glider KUBUZ-3 aerobatics (Jerzy Makula)	45	30
3057	15z. Wrestling (Bogdan Daras)	75	30
3058	20z. Individual road cycling (Lech Piasecki)	1·00	35
3059	30z. Women's modern pentathlon (Barbara Kotowska)	1·50	45
3054/3059 *Set of* 6		4·00	1·80

887 Bird in National Costume carrying Stamp

888 Schweitzer

(Des W. Freudenreich. Photo)

1986 (28 Aug). Stockholmia 86 International Stamp Exhibition. Perf 11×11½.

3060	**887**	65z. multicoloured	3·00	1·00
MS3061 94×80 mm. No. 3060			3·00	2·75

(Des A. Balcerzak. Photo)

1986 (1 Sept). 47th Anniversary of German Invasion. Horiz design as T **850**. Multicoloured. Perf 12×11½.

3062	10z. Battle of Jordanów and Colonel Stanislaw Maczek	45	30

(Des J. Wysocki. Eng T. Lis. Recess and photo)

1986 (26 Sept). 20th Death Anniversary (1985) of Albert Schweitzer (medical missionary). Perf 12×11½.

3063	**888**	5z. agate, cinnamon and ultramarine	35	25

889 Airliner and Postal Messenger

890 Basilisk

(Des S. Malecki. Litho)

1986 (9 Oct). World Post Day. Perf 11×11½.

3064	**889**	40z. sepia, ultramarine and orange-red	1·70	70
MS3065 81×81 mm. No. 3064×2 (*sold at* 120z.)			26·00	18·00

(Des Elzbieta Gaudasińska. Photo)

1986 (28 Oct). Folk Tales. T **890** and similar multicoloured designs. Perf 11×11½ (horiz) or 11½×11 (vert).

3066	5z. Type **890**	35	30
3067	5z. Duke Popiel (*vert*)	35	30
3068	10z. Golden Duck	45	30
3069	10z. Boruta the Devil (*vert*)	45	30
3070	20z. Jánošík the Robber (*vert*)	80	35
3071	50z. Lajkonik (*vert*)	2·50	50
3066/3071 *Set of* 6		4·50	1·80

891 Kotarbiński

892 20th-century Windmill, Zygmuntów

(Des J. Wysocki. Litho)

1986 (19 Nov). Birth Centenary of Tadeusz Kotarbiński (philosopher). Perf 12×11½.

3072	**891**	10z. agate and brown	45	30

(Des M. Piekarski. Photo)

1986 (26 Nov). Wooden Architecture. T **892** and similar horiz designs. Multicoloured. Perf 11½×11 (No. 3073) or 11×11½ (others).

3073	5z. Type **892**	35	25
3074	5z. 17th-century church, Bączal Dolny	35	25
3075	10z. 19th-century Oravian cottage, Zubrzyca Górna	45	30

3076 15z. 18th-century Kashubian arcade cottage, Wdzydze 75 35
3077 25z. 19th-century barn, Grzawa ..... 1·00 40
3078 30z. 19th-century watermill, Siolkowice Stare ..... 1·50 70
3073/3078 *Set of 6* ..... 4·00 2·00

893 Mieszko (Mieczyslaw) I

(Des S. Malecki. Eng P. Naszarkowski (10z.), W. Zajdel (25z.). Recess and photo)

1986 (4 Dec). Polish Rulers (1st series). T **893** and similar vert design showing drawings by Jan Matejko. Perf 11.

3079 **893** 10z. agate and brown-olive ..... 1·00 40
3080 - 25z. brownish black and reddish purple ..... 1·70 1·00

Designs: 25z. Queen Dobrawa (wife of Mieszko I).

See also Nos. 3144/3145, 3193/3194, 3251/3252, 3341/3342, 3351/3352, 3387/3388, 3461/3464, 3511/3512, 3548/3551, 3641/3644, 3705/3708, 3732/3735, 3819/3822 and 3889/3892.

894 Star

(Des W. Freudenreich. Photo)

1986 (12 Dec). New Year. Perf 11×11½.

3081 **894** 25z. multicoloured ..... 1·00 40

895 Trip to Bielany, 1887

896 Joachim Lelewel

(Des W. Surowiecki. Litho)

1986 (19 Dec). Centenary of Warsaw Cyclists' Society. T **895** and similar designs. Perf 13×12½ (3082) or 12½×13 (others).

3082 5z. multicoloured 35 25
3083 5z. bistre-brown, grey-brown and black 30 25
3084 10z. multicoloured 45 30
3085 10z. multicoloured 45 30
3086 30z. multicoloured ..... 1·40 55
3087 50z. multicoloured ..... 1·90 70
3082/3087 *Set of 6* ..... 4·25 2·10

Designs: Horiz—No. 3082, T **895**. Vert—No. 3083, Jan Stanislaw Skrodzki (1895 touring record holder); No. 3084, Dynasy (Society's headquarters, 1892–1937); No. 3085, Mieczyslaw Barański (1896 road cycling champion); No. 3086, Karolina Kocięcka; No. 3087. Henryk Weiss (Race champion).

(Des J. Wysocki. Photo)

1986 (22 Dec). Birth Bicentenary of Joachim Lelewel (historian). Perf 11×12.

3088 **896** 10z.+5z. multicoloured 75 40

The premium was for the benefit of the National Committee for School Aid fund.

897 Krill (*Euphausia superba*) and *Antoni Garnuszewski* (cadet freighter)

898 Portrait of a Woman

(Des S. Malecki. Litho)

1987 (13 Feb). Tenth Anniversary of Henryk Arctowski Antarctic Station, King George Island, South Shetlands. T **897** and similar square designs. Multicoloured. Perf 11½.

3089 5z. Type **897** 35 25
3090 5z. Marbled Rockcod (*Notothenia rossi*), Antarctic Toothfish (*Dissostichus mawsoni*) and *Zulawy* (supply ship) 35 25
3091 10z. Southern Fulmar (*Fulmarus glacialoides*) and *Pogoria* (cadet brigantine) 45 30
3092 10z. Adélie Penguin (*Pigoscelis adeliae*) and *Gedania* (yacht) 45 30
3093 30z. Fur Seal (*Arctocephalus*) and *Dziunia* (research vessel) ..... 1·00 35
3094 40z. Leopard Seal (*Hydrurga leptonyx*) and *Kapitan Ledóchowski* (research vessel) .. 1·60 45
3089/3094 *Set of 6* ..... 3·75 1·70

(Des W. Surowiecki. Photo)

1987 (20 Mar). 50th Death Anniversary (1986) of Leon Wyczólkowski (artist). T **898** and similar multicoloured designs. Perf 11.

3095 5z. *Cineraria Flowers* (*horiz*) 30 25
3096 10z. Type **898** 35 30
3097 10z. *Wooden Church* (*horiz*) 35 30
3098 25z. *Beetroot Lifting* 75 30
3099 30z. *Wading Fishermen* (*horiz*) 85 35
3100 40z. Self-portrait (*horiz*) ..... 1·40 50
3095/3100 *Set of 6* ..... 3·50 1·80

899 Ravage (from *War Cycle*) and Grottger

900 Świerczewski

(Des W. Surowiecki. Photo)

1987 (26 Mar). 150th Birth Anniversary of Artur Grottger (artist). Perf 11.

3101 **899** 15z. brown and stone 45 30

(Des J. Konarzewski. Eng P. Naszarkowski. Recess and photo)

1987 (27 Mar). 90th Birth Anniversary of General Karol Świerczewski. Perf 11½×12.

3102 **900** 15z. olive-green and yellow-olive 45 30

901 Strzelecki

902 Emblem and Banner

(Des M. Piekarski. Photo)

1987 (23 Apr). 190th Birth Anniversary of Pawel Edmund Strzelecki (scientist and explorer of Tasmania). Perf 11½×11.

3103 **901** 65z. blackish olive ..... 1·50 65

(Des A. Szczepaniak. Litho)

1987 (8 May). Second Patriotic Movement for National Revival Congress. Perf 11×11½.

3104	**902**	10z. vermilion, ultramarine and drab	40	25

903 CWS T-1 Motor Car, 1928

(Des J. Brodowski. Photo)

1987 (19 May). Polish Motor Vehicles. T **903** and similar horiz designs. Multicoloured. Perf 12×11½.

3105	10z. Type **903**	30	25
3106	10z. Saurer-Zawrat bus, 1936	30	25
3107	15z. Ursus-A lorry, 1928	45	30
3108	15z. Lux-Sport motor car, 1936	45	30
3109	25z. Podkowa 100 motorcycle, 1939	75	35
3110	45z. Sokól 600 RT motorcycle, 1935	1·60	50
3105/3110	*Set of 6*	3·50	1·80

904 Royal Palace, Warsaw

(Des S. Malecki. Photo)

1987 (5 June). Perf 12×11½.

3111	**904**	50z. multicoloured	1·50	60

A miniature sheet containing No. 3111 and two labels showing Pope John Paul II and President Jaruzelski exists from a limited printing (*price* £85).

905 Pope John Paul II

(Des W. Andrzejewski (50z.), J. Wysocki (others). Photo)

1987 (8 June). Third Papal Visit. T **905** and similar vert designs. Multicoloured. Perf 11.

3112	15z. Type **905**	45	30
	a. Pair. Nos. 3112/3113	1·60	85
3113	45z. Pope and signature	1·00	45
MS3114	77×66 mm. 50z. Profile of Pope (21×27 mm). Perf 12×11½	1·60	1·40

Nos. 3112/13 were printed together in *se-tenant* pairs within the sheet.

906 Polish Settler at Kasubia, Ontario

(Des R. Dudzicki. Photo)

1987 (13 June). Capex '87 International Stamp Exhibition, Toronto. Perf 12×11½.

3115	**906**	50z.+20z. multicoloured	1·70	80

The premium was for the benefit of the Polish Philatelic Union.

(Des A. Heidrich. Litho)

1987 (6 July). Renovation of Cracow Monuments (5th series). Horiz design as T **819**. Perf 11×11½.

3116	10z. magenta, black and yellowish green	35	25

Design: 10z. Barbican.

907 Ludwig Zamenhof (inventor) and Star

908 *Poznań Town Hall* (Stanislaw Wyspiański)

(Des A. Szczepaniak. Litho)

1987 (25 July). Centenary of Esperanto (invented language). Perf 11×11½.

3117	**907**	45z. grey-brown, emerald and black	1·50	45

(Des A. Heidrich. Litho)

1987 (8 Aug). Poznań 87 National Stamp Exhibition. Perf 11½×11.

3118	**908**	15z. black and salmon	45	30

909 Queen Bee

910 1984 Olympic Stamp and Laurel Wreath

(Des K. Śliwka. Photo)

1987 (20 Aug). Apimondia '87 International Beekeeping Congress, Warsaw. T **909** and similar vert designs. Multicoloured. Perf 11½×11.

3119	10z. Type **909**	35	25
3120	10z. Worker bee	35	25
3121	15z. Drone	45	30
3122	15z. Hive in orchard	45	30
3123	40z. Worker bee on clover flower	1·20	40
3124	50z. Forest beekeeper collecting honey	1·60	50
3119/3124	*Set of 6*	4·00	1·80

(Des H. Chyliński. Litho German Bank Note Ptg Co, Leipzig)

1987 (28 Aug). Olymphilex '87 Olympic Stamps Exhibition, Rome. Sheet 83×57 mm. Perf 14.

MS3125	**910**	45z.+10z. multicoloured	1·80	1·70

The premium was for the benefit of the Polish Olympic Committee's fund.

(Des B. Wróblewski and A. Balcerzak. Photo)

1987 (1 Sept). 48th Anniversary of German Invasion. Horiz designs as T **850**. Multicoloured. Perf 12×11½.

3126	10z. Battle of Mokra and Colonel Julian Filipowicz	35	30
3127	10z. Fighting at Oleszyce and Brigadier-General Józef Rudolf Kustroń	35	30
3128	15z. PZL P-7 aircraft over Warsaw and Colonel Stefan Pawlikowski	75	35
3126/3128	*Set of 3*	1·30	85

911 Hevelius and Sextant

(Des J. Brodowski. Litho)

1987 (15 Sept). 300th Death Anniversary of Jan Hevelius (astronomer). T **911** and similar multicoloured design. Perf 11½×11 (15z.) or 11×11½ (40z.).

3129	15z. Type **911**	45	30
3130	40z. Hevelius and map of constellations (*horiz*)	1·20	40

912 High Jump (World Acrobatics Championships, France)

913 *Stacionar 4* Telecommunications Satellite

(Des H. Chyliński. Litho German Bank Note Ptg Co, Leipzig)

1987 (24 Sept). 1986 Polish World Championship Successes. T **912** and similar horiz designs. Multicoloured. Perf 14.

3131	10z. Type **912**	35	25
3132	15z. Two-man canoe (World Canoeing Championships, Canada)	45	30
3133	20z. Marksman (Free pistol event, World Marksmanship Championships, East Germany)	60	30
3134	25z. Wrestlers (World Wrestling Championships, Hungary)	75	35
3131/3134	*Set of 4*	1·90	1·10

(Des Z. Stasik. Photo)

1987 (2 Oct). 30th Anniversary of Launch of *Sputnik 1* (first artificial satellite). Sheet 67×82 mm. Perf 11½×11.

MS3135 **913** 40z. multicoloured .... 1·60 1·40

914 Warsaw Post Office and Ignacy Przebendowski (Postmaster General)

915 *The Little Mermaid*

(Des S. Malecki. Litho)

1987 (9 Oct). World Post Day. Perf 11½×11.

3136	**914**	15z. olive-green and brown-lake	45	30

(Des Emilia Freudenreich. Photo)

1987 (16 Oct). Hafnia 87 International Stamp Exhibition, Copenhagen. Hans Christian Andersen's Fairy Tales. T **915** and similar horiz designs. Multicoloured. Perf 11×11½.

3137	10z. Type **915**	35	25
3138	10z. *The Nightingale*	35	25
3139	20z. *The Wild Swans*	60	30
3140	20z. *The Little Match Girl*	60	30
3141	30z. *The Snow Queen*	85	35
3142	40z. *The Brave Tin Soldier*	1·20	45
3137/3142	*Set of 6*	3·50	1·70

916 Colonel Stanislaw Wieckowski (founder)

917 Santa Claus with Christmas Trees

(Des M. Piekarski. Eng P. Naszarkowski. Recess and photo)

1987 (16 Oct). 50th Anniversary of Democratic Clubs. Perf 12×11½.

3143	**916**	15z. black and blue	45	30

(Des S. Malecki. Eng M. Kopecki (10z.), W. Zajdel (25z.). Recess and photo)

1987 (4 Dec). Polish Rulers (2nd series). Vert designs as T **893** showing drawings by Jan Matejko. Perf 11.

3144	10z. blackish olive and turquoise-blue	1·20	60
3145	15z. deep violet-blue and ultramarine	1·00	40

Designs: 10z. Boleslaw I, the Brave; 15z. Mieszko (Mieczyslaw) II.

No. 3144 was issued with a *se-tenant* inscribed label.

(Des Emilia and W. Freudenreich. Photo)

1987 (14 Dec). New Year. Perf 11×11½.

3146	**917**	15z. multicoloured	45	30

918 *Anax imperator*

919 Composition

(Des B. Wróblewski. Photo)

1988 (23 Feb). Dragonflies. T **918** and similar multicoloured designs. Perf 11×11½ (horiz) or 11½×11 (vert).

3147	10z. Type **918**	35	25
3148	15z. *Libellula quadrimaculata* (*vert*)	45	30
3149	15z. *Agrian splendens* (*Calopteryx splendens*)	45	30
3150	20z. *Cordulegaster annulatus* (*vert*)	60	30
3151	30z. *Sympetrum pedemontanum*	85	35
3152	50z. *Aeshna viridis* (*Aeschna viridis*) (*vert*)	1·60	45
3147/3152	*Set of 6*	3·75	1·80

(Des A. Heidrich. Litho)

1988 (8 Mar). Renovation of Cracow Monuments (6th series). Vert design as T **819**. Perf 11½×11.

3153	15z. greenish yellow, chestnut and black	45	30

Design: 15z. Florianska Gate.

(Des W. Freudenreich. Photo)

1988 (28 Apr). International Year of Graphic Design. Perf 11×11½.

3154	**919**	40z. multicoloured	85	75

920 17th-century Friesian Wall Clock with Bracket Case

921 Atlantic Salmon and Reindeer

(Des S. Zieliński. Photo)

1988 (19 May). Clocks and Watches. T **920** and similar multicoloured designs. Perf 11½×12 (vert) or 12×11½ (horiz).

3155	10z. Type **920**	35	25
3156	10z. 20th-century annual clock (*horiz*)	35	25
3157	15z. 18th-century carriage clock	35	30
3158	15z. 18th-century French rococo bracket clock	35	30
3159	20z. 19th-century pocket watch (*horiz*)	45	30
3160	40z. 17th-century tile-cased clock from Gdańsk by Benjamin Zoll (*horiz*)	1·20	40
3155/3160	*Set of* 6	2·75	1·60

(Des J. Brodowski. Photo)

1988 (1 June). Finlandia 88 International Stamp Exhibition, Helsinki. Perf 12×11½.

3161	**921** 45z.+20z. multicoloured	1·50	65

The premium was for the benefit of the Polish Philatelic Union.

922 Triple Jump

923 Kukuczka

(Des J. Konarzewski. Photo)

1988 (27 June). Olympic Games, Seoul. T **922** and similar horiz designs. Multicoloured. Perf 11×11½.

3162	15z. Type **922**	35	25
3163	20z. Wrestling	45	25
3164	20z. Canoeing	45	25
3165	25z. Judo	50	30
3166	40z. Shooting	85	30
3167	55z. Swimming	1·20	40
3162/3167	*Set of* 6	3·50	1·60

(Des J. Konarzewski. Photo)

1988 (17 Aug). Award of Special Olympic Silver Medal to Jerzy Kukuczka for Mountaineering Achievements. Sheet 84×66 mm. Perf 11×11½.

MS3168	**923** 70z.+10z. multicoloured	1·80	1·70

The premium was for the benefit of the Polish Olympic Committees fund.

924 Wheat as Graph on VDU

925 PZL P-37 Łoś

(Des S. Malecki. Photo)

1988 (22 Aug). 16th European Conference of Food and Agriculture Organ Cracow. T **924** and similar vert design. Perf 11½×11.

3169	15z. Type **924**	45	30
3170	40z. Factory in forest	85	40

(Des A. Szczepaniak. Photo)

1988 (23 Aug). 70th Anniversary of Polish Republic (1st issue). 60th Anniversary of Polish State Aircraft Works. Perf 11×11½.

3171	**925** 45z. multicoloured	90	45

See also Nos. 3175, 3177, 3181/**MS**3189 and 3190/3192.

(Des B. Wróblewski and A. Balcerzak. Photo)

1988 (1 Sept). 49th Anniversary of German Invasion. Horiz designs as T **850**. Multicoloured. Perf 12×11½.

3172	15z. Battle of Modlin and Brigadier-General Wiktor Thommée	65	30
3173	20z. Battle of Warsaw and Brigadier-General Walerian Czuma	75	40
3174	20z. Battle of Tomaszów Lubelski and Brigadier-General Antoni Szylling	75	40
3172/3174	*Set of* 3	1·90	1·00

(Des A. Szczepaniak. Photo)

1988 (5 Sept). 70th Anniversary of Polish Republic (2nd issue). 50th Anniversary of Stalowa Wola Ironworks. Horiz design as T **925**. Multicoloured. Perf 11×11½.

3175	15z. View of plant	45	30

926 Postal Emblem and Tomasz Arciszewski (Postal Minister, 1918–1919)

927 On the Field of Glory Medal

(Des S. Malecki. Litho)

1988 (9 Oct). World Post Day. Perf 11½×11.

3176	**926** 20z. multicoloured	45	30

Issued both in sheets of 30 stamps and in sheets of 15 stamps and 15 labels showing current postal emblem (*price* £1).

Price for No. 3176 is with label.

(Des A. Szczepaniak. Photo)

1988 (12 Oct). 70th Anniversary of Polish Republic (3rd issue). 60th Anniversary of Military Institute for Aviation Medicine. Horiz design as T **925**. Multicoloured. Perf 11×11½.

3177	20z. Hanriot XIV hospital aircraft (38×28 mm)	45	30

(Des R. Dudzicki. Photo)

1988 (12 Oct). Polish People's Army Battle Medals (1st series). T **927** and similar vert design. Multicoloured. Perf 11½×11.

3178	20z. Type **927**	45	30
3179	20z. Battle of Lenino Cross	45	30

See also Nos. 3249/3250.

928 *Stanislaw Malachowski* and *Kazimierz Nestor Sapieha*

929 Ignacy Daszyński (politician)

(Des A. Heidrich. Photo)

1988 (16 Oct). Bicentenary of Four Years Diet (political and social reforms). Paintings of Diet Presidents by Józef Peszko. Perf 11.

3180	**928** 20z. multicoloured	45	30

(Des M. Piekarski. Photo)

1988 (11 Nov). 70th Anniversary of Polish Republic (4th issue). Personalities. T **929** and similar vert designs. Perf 12×11½.

3181	15z. olive-green, rosine and black	35	30
3182	15z. olive-green, rosine and black	35	30
3183	20z. brown, vermilion and black	45	30
3184	20z. brown, vermilion and black	45	30
3185	20z. brown, vermilion and black	45	30
3186	200z. slate-purple, bright scarlet and black	3·00	1·10
3187	200z. slate-purple, bright scarlet and black	3·00	1·10
3188	200z. slate-purple, bright scarlet and black	3·00	1·10
3181/3188	*Set of* 8	10·00	4·25
MS3189	102×60 mm. Nos. 3186/3188	41·00	40·00

Designs: No. 3181, T **929**; No. 3182, Wincenty Witos (politician); No. 3183, Julian Marchlewski (trade unionist and economist); No. 3184, Stanislaw Wojciechowski (politician); No. 3185, Wojciech Korfanty (politician); No. 3186, Ignacy Paderewski (musician and politician); No. 3187, Marshal Józef Pilsudski; No. 3188, Gabriel Narutowicz (President, 1922).

(Des A. Szczepaniak. Photo)

1988 (28 Nov–Dec). 70th Anniversary of Polish Republic (5th issue). Horiz designs as T **925**. Multicoloured. Perf 11×11½.

3190	15z. Coal wharf, Gdynia Port (65th Anniversary) (38×28 mm) (12.12)	35	30
3191	20z. Hipolit Cegielski (founder) and steam locomotive (142nd Anniversary of H. Cegielski Metal Works, Poznań) (38×28 mm)	45	30
3192	40z. Upper Silesia Tower (main entrance) (60th Anniversary of International Poznań Fair) (21.12)	80	45
3190/3192 *Set of* 3		1·40	95

(Des S. Malecki. Eng M. Kopecki (10z.), P. Naszarkowski (15z.). Recess and photo)

1988 (4 Dec). Polish Rulers (3rd series). Vert designs as T **893** showing drawings by Jan Matejko. Perf 11.

3193	10z. deep chocolate and lake-brown	75	40
3194	15z. deep chocolate and brown	1·20	70

Designs: 10z. Queen Rycheza; 15z. Kazimierz (Karol Odnowiciel) I.

930 Snowman

931 Flag

(Des W. Freudenreich. Photo)

1988 (9 Dec). New Year. Perf 11×11½.

3195	**930**	20z. multicoloured	45	30

(Des J. Wysocki. Photo)

1988 (15 Dec). 40th Anniversary of Polish United Workers' Party. Perf 11½×12.

3196	**931**	20z. bright scarlet and black	45	30

932 *Blysk*

933 Ardennes

(Des M. Piekarski. Litho German Bank Note Ptg Co, Leipzig)

1988 (29 Dec). Fire Boats. T **932** and similar horiz designs. Multicoloured. Perf 14.

3197	10z. Type **932**	35	25
3198	15z. *Plomień*	35	30
3199	15z. *Żar*	35	30
3200	20z. *Strażak 11*	50	30
3201	20z. *Strażak 4*	50	30
3202	45z. *Strażak 25*	90	45
3197/3202 *Set of* 6		2·75	1·70

(Des H. Chyliński. Photo)

1989 (6 Mar). Horses. T **933** and similar multicoloured designs. Perf 11.

3203	15z. Lippizaner (*horiz*)	35	25
3204	15z. Type **933**	35	25
3205	20z. English thoroughbred (*horiz*)	45	30
3206	20z. Arab	45	30
3207	30z. Great Poland racehorse (*horiz*)	65	35
3208	70z. Polish horse	1·70	45
3203/3208 *Set of* 6		3·50	1·70

934 Wire-haired Dachshund

935 General Wladyslaw Anders and Plan of Battle

(Des J. Wysocki. Photo)

1989 (3 May). Hunting Dogs. T **934** and similar vert designs. Multicoloured. Perf 11½×11.

3209	15z. Type **934**	30	25
3210	15z. Cocker Spaniel	30	25
3211	20z. Czech Fousek Pointer	35	30
3212	20z. Welsh Terrier	45	30
3213	25z. English Setter	65	30
3214	45z. Pointer	90	40
3209/3214 *Set of* 6		2·75	1·60

(Des H. Chyliński. Photo)

1989 (18 May). 45th Anniversary of Battle of Monte Cassino. Perf 11½×12.

3215	**935**	80z. multicoloured	85	70

See also Nos. 3227, 3247, 3287 and 3327.

A 50z. stamp showing General Broni Grzegorz Korczyński was prepared in 1989 but not issued.

936 Marianne

937 Polonia House

(Des J. Wysocki. Litho)

1989 (3 July). Bicentenary of French Revolution. Perf 11½×11.

3216	**936**	100z. brownish black, bright scarlet and ultramarine	1·00	40
MS3217		93×118 mm. No. 3216×2 plus two labels (*sold at* 270z.)	2·30	2·10

No. 3216 was issued with *se-tenant* label bearing the exhibition emblem.

No. **MS**3217 perforations a right hand margin.

The premium on No. **MS**3217 was for the benefit of the Polish Philatelic Union.

(Des A. Szczepaniak. Photo)

1989 (16 July). Opening of Polonia House (cultural centre), Pultusk. Perf 12×11½.

3218	**937**	100z. multicoloured	1·00	40

938 Monument (Bohdan Chmielewski)

939 Xaweri Dunikowski (artist)

(Des Z. Stasik. Photo)

1989 (21 July). 45th Anniversary of Civic Militia and Security Force. Perf 11×11½.

3219	**938**	35z. slate-blue and yellow-brown	45	30

(Des J. Wysocki. Photo)

1989 (21 July). Recipients of Order of Builders of the Republic of Poland. T **939** and similar vert designs. Multicoloured. Perf 11½×11.

3220 35z. Type **939** 45 30
3221 35z. Stanislaw Mazur (farmer) 45 30
3222 35z. Natalia Gąsiorowska (historian) 45 30
3223 35z. Wincenti Pstrowski (initiator of worker performance contests) 45 30
3220/3223 *Set of* 4 .... 1·60 1·10

940 Astronaut

941 Firemen

(Des Z. Stasik. Photo)

1989 (21 July). 20th Anniversary of First Manned Landing on Moon. Perf 11×11½.

3224 **940** 100z. multicoloured .... 1·00 40
MS3225 85×85 mm. No. 3224 .... 5·50 3·50

No. **MS**3225 also exists imperforate from a limited printing (*price* £41).

(Des W. Surowiecki. Photo)

1989 (25 July). World Firefighting Congress, Warsaw. Perf 11½×11.

3226 **941** 80z. multicoloured 75 40

(Des H. Chyliński. Photo)

1989 (21 Aug). 45th Anniversary of Battle of Falaise. Horiz design as T **935**. Multicoloured. Perf 12×11½.

3227 165z. Plan of battle and General Stanislaw Maczek (*horiz*) .... 1·50 70

No. 3228 is vacant.

942 Daisy

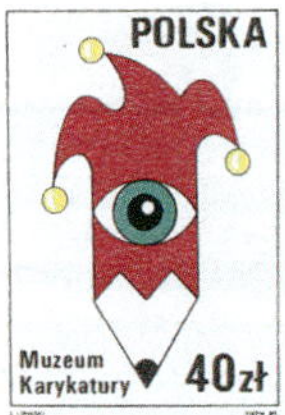

943 Museum Emblem

944 Rafal Czerwiakowski (founder of first university Surgery Department)

(Des S. Malecki. Litho (700z.) or photo (others))

1989 (25 Aug)–**91**. Plants. T **942** and similar vert design. Perf 14 (700z.) or 11×12 (others).

3229 **942** 40z. grey-green 45 25
3230 - 60z. deep violet 60 30
3231 **942** 150z. brown-lake (4.12.89) 75 30
3232 - 500z. deep mauve (19.12.89) .... 1·10 40
3233 - 700z. deep bluish green (26.4.91) 45 30
3234 - 1000z. blue (19.12.89) .... 2·00 70
3229/3234 *Set of* 6 .... 4·75 2·00

Designs: 60z. Juniper; 500z. Wild rose; 700z. Lily of the Valley; 1000z. Blue cornflower.

For similar designs printed by lithography and self-adhesive, see Nos. 3297/3298.

Nos. 3235/3239 are vacant.

(Des L. Wróblewski (No. 3243), B. Wróblewski and A. Balcerzak (others). Photo)

1989 (1 Sept). 50th Anniversary of German Invasion. Horiz designs as T **850**. Perf 12×11½.

3240 25z. slate, orange and black 60 30
3241 25z. multicoloured 60 30
3242 35z. multicoloured 85 40
3243 35z. multicoloured 85 40
3240/3243 *Set of* 4 .... 2·50 1·30

Designs: No. 3240, Defence of Westerplatte and Captain Franciszek Dąbrowski; No. 3241, Defence of Hel and Captain Zbigniew Przybyszewski; No. 3242, Battle of. Kock and Brigadier-General Franciszek Kleeberg; No. 3243, Defence of Lwów and Brigadier-General Wladyslaw Langner.

(Des E. Lipiński. Photo)

1989 (15 Sept). Caricature Museum. Perf 11½×11.

3244 **943** 40z. multicoloured 45 30

(Des J. Konarzewski. Photo)

1989 (18 Sept). Polish Surgeons' Society Centenary Congress, Cracow. T **944** and similar horiz design. Perf 11½×12.

3245 **944** 40z. dull ultramarine and black 45 30
3246 - 60z. blue-green and black 60 40

Design: 60z. Ludwik Rydygier (founder of Polish Surgeons' Society).

(Des H. Chyliński. Photo)

1989 (25 Sept). 45th Anniversary of Landing at Arnhem. Vert design as T **935**. Multicoloured. Perf 11½×12.

3247 210z. General Stanislaw Sosabowski and plan of battle .... 1·70 70

945 Emil Kaliński (Postal Minister, 1933–1939)

946 Stamps

(Des S. Malecki. Photo)

1989 (9 Oct). World Post Day. Perf 12×11½.

3248 **945** 60z. multicoloured 75 60

No. 3248 was issued with a *se-tenant* label depicting Polish Mail emblem.

(Des R. Dudzicki. Photo)

1989 (12 Oct). Polish People's Army Battle Medals (2nd series). Vert designs as T **927**. Multicoloured. Perf 11½×11.

3249 60z. For Participation in the Struggle for the Rule of the People Medal 45 30
3250 60z. Warsaw 1939–1945 Medal 45 30

(Des S. Malecki. Eng P. Naszarkowski (20z.), M. Kopecki (30z.). Recess and photo)

1989 (18 Oct). Polish Rulers (4th series). Vert designs as T **893** showing drawings by Jan Matejko. Perf 11.

3251 20z. slate-black and olive-grey 65 30
3252 30z. sepia and yellow-brown .... 1·10 40

Designs: 20z. Boleslaw II, the Bold; 30z. Wladyslaw I Herman.

(Des W. Andrzejewski. Photo)

1989 (14 Nov). World Stamp Expo '89 International Stamp Exhibition, Washington DC. Perf 11×11½.

3253 **946** 500z. multicoloured .... 2·50 1·40

No. 3253 also exists imperforate (price £5·50).

947 Cross and Twig

948 Ignacy Paderewski and Roman Dmowski (Polish signatories)

(Des W. Andrzejewski. Photo)

1989 (17 Nov). 70th Anniversary of Polish Red Cross. Perf 11½×11.

3254 **947** 200z. rosine, bright green and black .... 1·00 40

(Des J. Wysocki. Photo)

1989 (21 Nov). 70th Anniversary of Treaty of Versailles. Perf 11×11½.

3255 **948** 350z. multicoloured .... 1·50 70

949 Photographer and Medal depicting Maksymilian Strasz

951 Painting by Jan Ciągliński

(Des S. Malecki. Photo)

1989 (27 Nov). 150th Anniversary of Photography. T **949** and similar multicoloured design. Perf 12×11½ (40z.) or 11½×12 (60z.).

3256	40z. Type **949**	45	30
3257	60z. Lens shutter as pupil of eye (*horiz*)	60	35

1989 (30 Nov). No. 2729 surch with T **950**.

3258	500z. on 4z. reddish violet	2·20	1·00

(Des S. Malecki. Photo German Bank Note Ptg Co. Leipzig)

1989 (18 Dec). Flower Paintings. T **951** and similar square designs showing paintings by artists named. Multicoloured. Perf 13.

3259	25z. Type **951**	30	25
3260	30z. Wojciech Weiss	30	25
3261	35z. Antoni Kolasiński	30	25
3262	50z. Stefan Nacht-Samborski	35	30
3263	60z. Józef Pankiewicz	35	30
3264	85z. Henryka Beyer	45	30
3265	110z. Wladyslaw Slewiński	55	35
3266	190z. Czeslaw Wdowiszewski	95	40
3259/3266	*Set of* 8	3·25	2·20

952 Christ

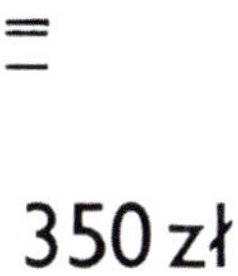

(953)

(Des R. Dudzicki. Photo)

1989 (21 Dec). Icons (1st series). T **952** and similar multicoloured designs. Perf 11.

3267	50z. Type **952**	35	25
3268	60z. Two Saints with books	35	25
3269	90z. Three Saints with books	35	30
3270	150z. Displaying scriptures (*vert*)	45	30
3271	200z. Madonna and child (*vert*)	75	40
3272	350z. Christ with Saints and Angels (*vert*)	1·50	50
3267/3272	*Set of* 6	3·50	1·80

See also Nos. 3345/3350.

REPUBLIC OF POLAND

1990 (31 Jan). No. 2839 surch with T **953**.

3273	350z. on 15z. lake-brown	1·50	70

954 Krystyna Jamroz

955 High Jump

(Des M. Piekarski. Photo)

1990 (9 Feb). Singers. T **954** and similar vert designs. Multicoloured. Perf 12×11½.

3274	100z. Type **954**	35	25
3275	150z. Wanda Wermińska	45	30
3276	350z. Ada Sari	75	30
3277	500z. Jan Kiepura	1·00	40
3274/3277	*Set of* 4	2·30	1·10

(Des J. Brodowski. Photo)

1990 (29 Mar). Sports. T **955** and similar horiz designs. Multicoloured. Perf 11×11½.

3278	100z. Yachting	30	25
3279	200z. Rugby	35	25
3280	400z. Type **955**	35	30
3281	500z. Ice skating	55	30
3282	500z. Diving	55	30
3283	1000z. Gymnastics	75	40
3278/3283	*Set of* 6	2·50	1·60

956 Kozlowski

957 Pope John Paul II

(Des R. Dudzicki. Photo)

1990 (17 Apr). Birth Centenary (1989) of Roman Kozlowski (palaeontologist). Perf 11×11½.

3284	**956** 500z. olive-sepia and rosine	60	30

(Des S. Malecki. Photo)

1990 (18 May). 70th Birthday of Pope John Paul II. Perf 11.

3285	**957** 1000z. multicoloured	75	40

958 1860 10k. Stamp and Anniversary Stamp

959 Ball and Colosseum

(Des S. Malecki. Photo)

1990 (25 May). 130th Anniversary of First Polish Postage Stamp. Sheet 65×68 mm. Perf 12×11½.

MS3286	1000z. red-orange and dull blue	2·20	1·40

(Des H. Chyliński. Photo)

1990 (28 May). 50th Anniversary of Narvik Landings. Vert design as T **935**. Multicoloured. Perf 11½×12.

3287	1500z. General Zygmunt Bohusz-Szyszko and plan of battle	90	40

(Des J. Wysocki. Photo)

1990 (8 June). World Cup Football Championship, Italy. Perf 11½×11.

3288	**959** 1000z. multicoloured	70	30

(960)

961 Memorial

1990 (18 June). No. 3230 surch with T **960** in red.

3289	700z. on 60z. deep violet	55	30

(Des M. Piekarski. Photo)

1990 (28 June). 34th Anniversary of 1956 Poznań Uprising. Perf 12×11½.

3290	**961** 1500z. multicoloured	65	40

962 People and 'ZUS'

963 *Lymnaea stagnalis* (Stagnant Pond Snail)

(Des A. Szczepaniak. Photo)

1990 (5 July). 70th Anniversary of Social Insurance. Perf 11×11½.

3291	**962**	1500z. deep blue, cerise and pale lemon..	65	40

(Des J. Brodowski. Litho)

1990 (16 July). Shells. No value expressed. T **963** and similar horiz design. Perf 11½×12.

3292	-	B (500z.) deep rose-lilac	90	70
		a. Perf 14	70	45
3293	**963**	A (700z.) deep olive	1·00	55
		a. Perf 14	90	55

Design: B, *Viviparus viviparus* (River Snail).

Nos. 3292/3293 were valid for internal postage only.

964 Cross

965 Weather Balloon

(Des W. Freudenreich. Litho)

1990 (20 July). 50th Anniversary of Katyń Massacre. Perf 11½×12.

3294	**964**	1500z. black and vermilion	75	35

(Des J. Konarzewski. Photo)

1990 (27 July). Polish Hydrology and Meteorology Service. T **965** and similar horiz design. Multicoloured. Perf 11×11½.

3295	500z. Type **965**	35	30
3296	700z. Water-height gauge	45	30

(Des S. Malecki. Litho)

1990 (13 Aug). Plants. Vert designs as T **942**. Self-adhesive. Die-cut.

3297	2000z. olive-green	1·20	50
3298	5000z. bluish violet	1·80	90

Designs: 2000z. Water Lily; 5000z. Iris.

Nos. 3299/3304 are vacant.

966 Women's Kayak Pairs

967 Victory Sign

(Des R. Dudzicki. Photo)

1990 (22 Aug). 23rd World Canoeing Championships. T **966** and similar horiz design. Multicoloured. Perf 11×11½.

3305	700z. Type **966**	40	30
3306	1000z. Men's kayak singles	55	40

A miniature sheet containing No. 3306 and an inscribed label was sold only with the Championship programme (*price* £7).

(Des J. Konarzewski. Litho)

1990 (31 Aug). Tenth Anniversary of Solidarity Trade Union. Perf 11½×11.

3307	**967**	1500z. grey, black and vermilion	75	40

968 Jacob's Ladder (*Polemonium coeruleum*)

969 Serving Dish, 1870–1887

(Des A. Balcerzak. Photo)

1990 (24 Sept). Flowers. T **968** and similar vert designs. Multicoloured. Perf 11½×11.

3308	200z. Type **968**	30	25
3309	700z. Floating Heart Water Fringe (*Nymphoides peltata*)	40	30
3310	700z. Dragonhead (*Dracocephalum ruyschiana*)	40	30
3311	1000z. *Helleborus purpurascens*	45	30
3312	1500z. *Daphne cneorum*	90	35
3313	1700z. Campion (*Dianthus superbus*)	1·20	40
3308/3313	*Set of 6*	3·25	1·70

(Des R. Dudzicki. Photo)

1990 (31 Oct). Bicentenary of Ćmielów Porcelain Works. T **969** and similar multicoloured designs. Perf 11×11½ (horiz) or 11½×11 (vert).

3314	700z. Type **969**	30	25
3315	800z. Plate, 1887–1890 (*vert*)	40	30
3316	1000z. Cup and saucer, 1887	50	30
3317	1000z. Figurine of dancer, 1941–1944 (*vert*)	50	30
3318	1500z. Chocolate box, 1930–1990	80	40
3319	2000z. Vase, 1979 (*vert*)	1·10	60
3314/3319	*Set of 6*	3·25	1·90

970 Little Owl (*Athene noctua*)

971 Lech Wałęsa

(Des J. Desselberger. Litho)

1990 (6 Nov). Owls. T **970** and similar vert designs. Multicoloured. Perf 14.

3320	200z. Type **970**	35	25
3321	500z. Tawny Owl (*Strix aluco*) (value at left)	45	30
3322	500z. Tawny Owl (*different*) (value at right)	45	30
3323	1000z. Short-eared Owl (*Asio flammeus*)	75	40
3324	1500z. Long-eared Owl (*Asio otus*)	1·70	70
3325	2000z. Barn Owl (*Tyto alba*)	2·20	1·00
3320/3325	*Set of 6*	5·25	2·75

(Des M. Piekarski. Litho)

1990 (12 Dec). Lech Wałęsa, 1984 Nobel Peace Prize Winner and new President. Perf 11×11½.

3326	**971**	1700z. multicoloured	85	50

(Des H. Chyliński. Photo)

1990 (21 Dec). 50th Anniversary of Battle of Britain. Vert designs as T **935**. Multicoloured. Perf 11½×12.

3327	1500z. Emblem of 303 Squadron, Polish Fighter Wing RAF and Hawker Hurricane Mk 1	1·10	70

972 Collegiate Church, Tum (12th century)

973 *King Zygmunt II August* (anon)

(Des J. Wysocki. Litho)

1990 (28 Dec). Historic Architecture. T **972** and similar vert designs. Multicoloured. Perf 11½×11.

3328	700z. Type **972**	50	30
3329	800z. Reszel castle (14th century)	55	30
3330	1500z. Chelmno Town Hall (16th century)	1·10	40
3331	1700z. Church of the Nuns of the Visitation, Warsaw (18th century)	1·50	60
3328/3331	*Set of 4*	3·25	1·40

No. 3331 was issued with *se-tenant* label bearing Polska '93 International Stamp Exhibition emblem.

(Des A. Szczepaniak. Photo)

1991 (11 Jan). Paintings. T **973** and similar vert designs. Multicoloured. Perf 11.

3332	500z. Type **973**	35	25
3333	700z. Adoration of the Magi (*Pultusk Codex*)	45	30
3334	1000z. St Matthew (*Pultusk Codex*)	50	30
3335	1500z. *Expelling of Merchants from Temple* (Nikolai Haberschrack)	90	35
3336	1700z. The Annunciation (miniature)	1·10	40
3337	2000z. *The Three Marys* (Nikolai Haberschrack)	1·50	70
3332/3337	*Set of 6*	4·25	2·10

974 Silver Fir (*Abies alba*)

975 Radziwill Palace

(Des A. Balcerzak. Photo)

1991 (22 Feb). Cones. T **974** and similar vert design. Multicoloured. Perf 12×11½.

3338	700z. Type **974**	75	30
3339	1500z. Weymouth Pine (*Pinus strobus*)	90	40

See also Nos. 3483/3484 and 3557/3558.

(Des J. Wysocki. Litho)

1991 (15 Mar). Admission of Poland into European Postal and Telecommunications Conference. Perf 11×12.

3340	**975**	1500z. multicoloured	1·60	40

1500 zł

(976)

977 Chmielowski

(Des S. Malecki. Eng W. Zajdel (1000z.), P. Naszarkowski (1500z.). Recess and photo)

1991 (25 Mar). Polish Rulers (5th series). Vert designs as T **893** showing drawings by Jan Matejko, surch as T **976** in red. Perf 11.

3341	1000z. on 40z. brownish black and bronze green	1·10	40
3342	1500z. on 50z. blue-black and crimson	1·60	85

Designs: 1000z. Boleslaw III, the Wry Mouthed; 1500z. Wladyslaw II, the Exile.

Nos. 3341/3342 were not issued unsurcharged.

(Des M. Piekarski. Litho)

1991 (29 Mar). 75th Death Anniversary of Adam Chmielowski (Brother Albert) (founder of Albertine Sisters). Perf 12×11½.

3343	**977**	2000z. multicoloured	90	40

978 Battle (detail of miniature, *Schlackenwerth Codex*, 1350)

979 Title Page of Constitution

(Des F. Lüdtke. Recess and litho State Ptg Wks, Berlin)

1991 (9 Apr). 750th Anniversary of Battle of Legnica. Perf 14.

3344	**978**	1500z. multicoloured	1·50	70

A stamp of a similar design was issued by Germany.

(Des R. Dudzicki. Photo)

1991 (22 Apr). Icons (2nd series). Vert designs as T **952**. Multicoloured. Perf 11.

3345	500z. Madonna of Nazareth	30	25
3346	700z. Christ the Acheirophyte	40	30
3347	1000z. Madonna of Vladimir	45	30
3348	1500z. Madonna of Kazan	90	35
3349	2000z. St John the Baptist	1·50	40
3350	2200z. Christ the Pentocrator	1·70	70
3345/3350	*Set of 6*	4·75	2·10

(Des S. Malecki. Eng W. Zajdel (1000z.), M. Kopecki (1500z.). Recess and photo)

1991 (30 Apr). Polish Rulers (6th series). Vert designs as T **893** showing drawings by Jan Matejko. Perf 11.

3351	1000z. blue-black and brown-red	1·10	40
3352	1500z. brownish black and new blue	1·60	85

Designs: 1000z. Boleslaw IV, the Curly; 1500z. Mieszko (Mieczyslaw) III, the Old.

(Des A. Heidrich. Photo (3000z.) or litho (others))

1991 (2 May). Bicentenary of 3rd May Constitution. T **979** and similar vert designs. Perf 11½×11.

3353	2000z. deep brown, buff and vermilion	1·10	40
3354	2500z. deep brown, stone and vermilion	1·20	70
MS3355	85×85 mm. 3000z. multicoloured	1·80	1·70

Designs: 2000z. T **979**; 2500z. *Administration of Oath by Gustav Taubert* (detail, Johann Friedrich Bolt); 3000z. *Constitution, 3 May 1791* (Jan Matejko).

980 Satellite in Earth Orbit

981 Map and Battle Scene

(Des J. Wysocki. Litho)

1991 (6 May). Europa. Europe in Space. Perf 12×11.

3356	**980**	1000z. multicoloured	3·75	85

(Des J. Brodowski. Photo)

1991 (27 May). 50th Anniversary of Participation of *Piorun* (destroyer) in Operation against *Bismarck* (German battleship). Perf 12×11½.

3357 **981** 2000z. multicoloured .... 1·30 40

982 Arms of Cracow

983 Pope John Paul II

984 Bearded Penguin

(Des S. Malecki. Litho)

1991 (28 May). European Security and Co-operation Conference Cultural Heritage Symposium, Cracow. Perf 12×11½.

3358 **982** 2000z. deep claret and deep ultramarine. 1·50 70

(Des J. Wysocki. Litho)

1991 (1 June). Papal Visit. T **983** and similar vert design. Multicoloured. Perf 11½×11.

3359 1000z. Type **983** 75 30

3360 2000z. Pope in white robes .... 1·30 40

(Des S. Malecki. Litho)

1991 (21 June). 30th Anniversary of Antarctic Treaty. Perf 12×11½.

3361 **984** 2000z. multicoloured .... 1·10 40

985 Making Paper

986 Prisoner

(Des Z. Stasik. Litho)

1991 (8 July). 500th Anniversary of Paper Making in Poland. Perf 11½.

3362 **985** 2500z. turquoise-blue and brown-lake 90 40

(Des W. Freudenreich. Litho)

1991 (28 July). Commemoration of Victims of Stalin's Purges. Perf 11½×12.

3363 **986** 2500z. bright scarlet and black 90 40

987 Pope John Paul II

988 Ball and Basket

(Des J. Wysocki. Photo)

1991 (15 Aug). Sixth World Youth Day, Częstochowa. Perf 11½×11.

MS3364 70×87 mm. **987** 3500z. multicoloured .... 2·30 2·10

(Des J. Konarzewski. Litho)

1991 (19 Aug). Centenary of Basketball. Perf 11×11½.

3365 **988** 2500z. multicoloured .... 1·10 40

989 Self-portrait (Leon Wyczólkowski)

990 Twardowski

(Des R. Dudzicki. Photo)

1991 (7 Sept). Bydgoszcz '91 National Stamp Exhibition. Perf 11½×12.

3366 **989** 3000z. brown-olive and sepia .... 1·20 70

MS3367 155×92 mm. No. 3366×4 .... 5·50 5·50

(Des J. Konarzewski. Photo)

1991 (10 Oct). 125th Birth Anniversary of Kazimierz Twardowski (philosopher). Perf 11×11½.

3368 **990** 2500z. black and brownish grey .... 1·50 70

991 Swallowtail (*Papilio machaon*)

(Des D. Opresco. Hologram and litho (No. 3375) or litho (others))

1991 (16 Nov). Butterflies and Moths. T **991** and similar horiz designs. Multicoloured. Perf 12½.

3369 1000z. Type **991** 35 30

a. Block of 6. Nos. 3369/3367 .... 4·00

3370 1000z. Dark Crimson Underwing (*Mormonia sponsa*) 35 30

3371 1500z. Painted Lady (*Vanessa cardui*) 45 30

3372 1500z. Scarce Swallowtail (*Iphiclides podalirius*) 45 30

3373 2500z. Scarlet Tiger Moth (*Panaxia dominula*). 1·10 40

3374 2500z. Peacock (*Nymphalis io*) .... 1·10 40

3369/3374 *Set of* 6 .... 3·50 1·80

MS3375 127×63 mm. 15000z. Black-veined White (*Aporia crataegi*) (46×33 mm) plus label for Phila Nippon '91 International Stamp Exhibition .... 4·25 4·00

Nos. 3369/3374 were issued together in *se-tenant* blocks of six within the sheet.

No. **MS**3375 is known with the hologram printed at the bottom of the miniature sheet; causing the perforations to cut through the hologram (*price* £450).

Many varieties of No. **MS**3375 are known; including missing or double holograms, shifted image (see above note) and imperforate sheets.

992 *The Shepherd's Bow* (Francesco Solimena)

(Des R. Dudzicki. Photo)

1991 (25 Nov). Christmas. Perf 11.

3376 **992** 1000z. multicoloured 85 40

993 General Stanislaw Kopański and Battle Map

(Des J. Brodowski. Photo)

1991 (10 Dec). 50th Anniversary of Participation of Polish Troops in Battle of Tobruk. Perf 12×11½.

3377	**993**	2000z. multicoloured	1·50	70

994 Brigadier-General Michal Tokarzewski Karaszewicz

995 Lord Baden-Powell (founder)

(Des S. Malecki. Litho)

1991 (20 Dec). World War II Polish Underground Army Commanders. T **994** and similar vert designs. Perf 12×11½.

3378	2000z. blue-black and vermilion	1·00	40
3379	2500z. crimson and violet	1·40	85
3380	3000z. deep violet and bright magenta	1·70	85
3381	5000z. brown and deep olive	2·50	1·40
3382	6500z. deep brown and orange-brown	3·25	1·70
3378/3382	*Set of* 5	8·75	4·75

Designs: 2000z. T **994**, 2500z. General Broni Kazimierz Sosnkowski; 3000z. Lieutenant-General Stefan Rowecki; 5000z. Lieutenant-General Tadeusz Komorowski; 6500z. Brigadier-General Leopold Okulicki.

(Des M. Piekarski. Photo)

1991 (30 Dec). 80th Anniversary of Scout Movement in Poland. T **995** and similar vert designs. Perf 12×11½.

3383	1500z. greenish yellow and emerald	75	30
3384	2000z. new blue and bright lemon	90	35
3385	2500z. bright bluish violet and chrome yellow	1·10	40
3386	3500z. bistre-brown and orange-yellow	1·80	85
3383/3386	*Set of* 4	4·00	1·70

Designs: 1500z. T **995**; 2000z. Andrzej Malkowski (Polish founder); 2500z. *Watch on the Vistula* (Wojciech Kossak); 3500z. Polish scout in Warsaw Uprising, 1944.

(Des S. Malecki. Eng W. Zajdel (1500z.), T. Zlotkowski (2000z.). Recess and photo)

1992 (15 Jan). Polish Rulers (7th series). Vert designs as T **893** showing drawings by Jan Matejko. Perf 11.

3387	1500z. sepia and brown-olive	1·10	40
3388	2000z. blue-black and deep turquoise-blue	1·40	85

Designs: 1500z. Kazimierz II, the Just; 2000z. Leszek I, the White.

996 Sébastien Bourdon

997 Skiing

(Des M. Piekarski. Photo)

1992 (16 Jan). Self-portraits. T **996** and similar vert designs. Multicoloured. Perf 11.

3389	700z. Type **996**	35	25
3390	1000z. Sir Joshua Reynolds	45	30
3391	1500z. Sir Godfrey Kneller	75	30
3392	2000z. Bartolomé Estéban Murillo	90	35
3393	2200z. Peter Paul Rubens	1·10	40
3394	3000z. Diego de Silva y Velázquez	1·50	70
3389/3394	*Set of* 6	4·50	2·10

(Des J. Konarzewski. Litho)

1992 (8 Feb). Winter Olympic Games, Albertville. T **997** and similar horiz design. Multicoloured. Perf 11×11½.

3395	1500z. Type **997**	75	30
3396	2500z. Ice hockey	1·10	40

998 Manteuffel

999 Nicolas Copernicus (astronomer)

(Des M. Jędrysik. Photo)

1992 (5 Mar). 90th Birth Anniversary of Tadeusz Manteuffel (historian). Perf 11½×11.

3397	**998**	2500z. light brown	1·10	40

(Des J. Wysocki. Photo)

1992 (3 May). Famous Poles. T **999** and similar horiz designs. Multicoloured. Perf 11×11½.

3398	1500z. Type **999**	60	30
3399	2000z. Frédéric Chopin (composer)	90	40
3400	2500z. Henryk Sienkiewicz (writer)	1·10	70
3401	3500z. Marie Curie (physicist)	1·50	85
3398/3401	*Set of* 4	3·75	2·00
MS3402	80×81 mm. 5000z. Kazimierz Funk (biochemist)	2·30	2·10

No. **MS**3402 commemorates Expo '92 World's Fair, Seville.

1000 Columbus and Left-hand Detail of Map

1001 River Czarna Wiselka

(Des J. Wysocki. Litho)

1992 (5 May). Europa. 500th Anniversary of Discovery of America by Christopher Columbus. T **1000** and similar horiz design. Multicoloured. Perf 11×11½.

3403	1500z. Type **1000**	45	30
	a. Horiz pair. Nos. 3403/3404	1·90	1·10
3404	3000z. *Santa Maria* and right-hand detail of Juan de la Costa map, 1500	1·30	70

Nos. 3403/3404 were issued together in horizontal *se-tenant* pairs within the sheet, each pair forming a composite design.

(Des J. Brodowski. Photo)

1992 (12 June). Environmental Protection. River Cascades. T **1001** and similar vert designs. Multicoloured. Perf 11½×12.

3405	2000z. Type **1001**	60	25
3406	2500z. River Świder	1·10	45
3407	3000z. River Tanew	1·40	50
3408	3500z. Mickiewicz waterfall	2·00	85
3405/3408	*Set of* 4	4·50	1·80

1002 Prince Józef Poniatowski

1003 Family and Heart

(Des M. Jędrysik. Litho (No. 3411) or photo (others))

1992 (18 June). Bicentenary of Order of Military Virtue. T **1002** and similar vert designs. Multicoloured. Perf 11.

3409 1500z. Type **1002** .... 1·20 30
3410 3000z. Marshal Józef Pilsudski .... 1·10 40
MS3411 108×93 mm. 20000z. Virgin Mary of Częstochowa (icon) (36×57 mm). Imperf. .... 7·50 6·50

(Des J. Wysocki. Litho)

1992 (26 June). Children's Drawings. T **1003** and similar vert design. Multicoloured. Perf 11½×11.

3412 1500z. Type **1003** 45 30
a. Pair. Nos 3412/3413 .... 1·70 1·00
3413 3000z. Butterfly, sun, bird and dog .... 1·10 65

Nos. 3412/3413 were issued together in *se-tenant* pairs within the sheet.

1004 Fencing

1005 Runners

(Des J. Konarzewski. Litho)

1992 (25 July). Olympic Games, Barcelona. T **1004** and similar horiz designs. Multicoloured. Perf 11×11½.

3414 1500z. Type **1004** 35 25
3415 2000z. Boxing 45 30
3416 2500z. Running 90 40
3417 3000z. Cycling .... 1·20 70
3414/3417 *Set of 4* .... 2·50 1·50

(Des H. Chyliński. Photo)

1992 (29 July). Olymphilex '92 Olympic Stamps Exhibition, Barcelona. Sheet 86×81 mm. Perf 11×11½.

MS3418 **1005** 20000z. multicoloured .... 7·00 6·50

No. **MS**3418 also exists imperforate from a limited issue (*price* £17).

1006 Statue of Korczak

1007 Flag and 'V'

(Des J. Brodowski. Photo)

1992 (5 Aug). 50th Death Anniversary of Janusz Korczak (educationist). Perf 11×11½.

3419 **1006** 1500z. black, lake-brown and chrome yellow 75 40

(Des F. Winiarski. Photo)

1992 (14 Aug). Fifth Polish Veterans World Meeting. Perf 11½×11.

3420 **1007** 3000z. multicoloured .... 1·20 70

1008 Wysziński

1009 National Colours encircling World Map

(Des M. Jędrysik. Litho)

1992 (15 Aug). 11th Death Anniversary of Stefan Wysziński (Primate of Poland) (No. 3421) and First Anniversary of Sixth World Youth Day (No. 3422). T **1008** and similar vert design. Multicoloured. Perf 11½×11.

3421 1500z. Type **1008** 90 40
a. Pair. Nos. 3421/3422 plus 2 labels .... 2·20 1·40
3422 3000z. Pope John Paul II embracing youth .... 1·20 85

Nos. 3421/3422 were issued together in blocks of two stamps and two labels showing the arms of either Wyszyński or the Pope.

(Des A. Szczepaniak. Photo)

1992 (19 Aug). World Meeting of Expatriate Poles, Cracow. Perf 12×11½.

3423 **1009** 3000z. multicoloured .... 1·50 85

1010 Polish Museum, Adampol

1011 18th-century Post Office Sign, Slonim

(Des H. Chyliński. Photo)

1992 (15 Sept). 150th Anniversary of Polish Settlement at Adampol, Turkey. Perf 11×11½.

3424 **1010** 3500z. multicoloured .... 1·50 85

(Des Z. Stasik. Photo)

1992 (9 Oct). World Post Day. Perf 11½×11.

3425 **1011** 3500z. multicoloured .... 1·50 85

1012 *Dedication* (self-portrait)

1013 *Seated Girl* (Henryk Wiciński)

(Des J. Konarzewski. Litho)

1992 (26 Oct). Birth Centenary of Bruno Schulz (writer and artist). Perf 11×11½.

3426 **1012** 3000z. multicoloured .... 1·30 70

(Des H. Chyliński. Litho)

1992 (29 Oct). Polish Sculptures. T **1013** and similar square designs. Multicoloured. Perf 11½.

3427 2000z. Type **1013** 75 40
3428 2500z. *Portrait of Tytus Czyżewski* (Zbigniew Pronaszko) 90 40
3429 3000z. *Polish Nike* (Edward Wittig) .... 1·10 70
3430 3500z. *The Nude* (August Zamoyski) .... 1·20 70
3427/3430 *Set of 4* .... 3·50 2·00
MS3431 107×90 mm. Nos. 3427/3430 .... 3·75 3·50

No. **MS**3431 commemorates Polska '93 International Stamp Exhibition.

1014 *10th Theatrical Summer in Zamość* (Jan Mlodożeniec)

1015 Girl skipping with Snake

(Des K. Kupczyk. Litho)

1992 (30 Oct). Poster Art (1st series). T **1014** and similar multicoloured designs. Perf 13½.

3432	1500z. Type **1014**	60	30
3433	2000z. *Red Art* (Franciszek Starowieyski) (*horiz*)	90	40
3434	2500z. *Circus* (Waldemar Świerzy)	1·20	70
3435	3500z. *Mannequins* (Henryk Tomaszewski)	1·50	85
3432/3435	*Set of* 4	3·75	2·00

See also Nos. 3502/3503, 3523/3524, 3585/3586 and 3712/3715.

(Des E. Lutczyn. Photo)

1992 (16 Nov). Polska '93 International Stamp Exhibition, Poznań (1st issue). T **1015** and similar vert designs. Multicoloured. Perf 11.

3436	1500z. Type **1015**	45	30
3437	2000z. Boy on rocking horse with upside-down runners	75	40
3438	2500z. Boy firing bird from bow	1·10	50
3439	3500z. Girl placing ladder against clockwork giraffe	1·50	70
3436/3439	*Set of* 4	3·50	1·70

See also Nos. 3452, 3453/**MS**3457, 3466/3469 and **MS**3476.

1016 Medal and Soldiers

1017 Church and Star

(Des J. Wysocki. Litho)

1992 (20 Nov). 50th Anniversary of Formation of Polish Underground Army. T **1016** and similar multicoloured designs. Perf 13½.

3440	1500z. Type **1016**	45	30
	a. Pair. Nos. 3440/3441	2·10	1·40
3441	3500z. Soldiers	1·50	1·00
MS3442	75×95 mm. 20000z.+500z. 'WP AK' (26×32 mm) (7 contract numbers)	7·00	6·50

Nos. 3440/3441 were issued together in *se-tenant* pairs within the sheet.

No. **MS**3442 was also issued with five control numbers (*price* £375).

(Des J. Brodowski. Photo)

1992 (25 Nov). Christmas. Perf 11½×12.

3443	**1017**	1000z. multicoloured	75	25

1018 Wheat

1019 Arms of Sovereign Military Order

(Des M. Jędrysik. Photo)

1992 (5 Dec). International Nutrition Conference, Rome. T **1018** and similar vert design. Multicoloured. Perf 11½×11.

3444	1500z. Type **1018**	45	30
3445	3500z. Glass, bread, vegetables and jug on table	1·20	70

(Des A. Heidrich. Litho)

1992 (10 Dec). Postal Agreement with Sovereign Military Order of Malta. Perf 11½×11.

3446	**1019**	3000z. multicoloured	1·20	70

1020 Arms, 1295

(Des H. Chyliński. Photo)

1992 (14 Dec). History of the White Eagle (Poland's Arms). T **1020** and similar vert designs. Each black, orange-vermilion and orange-yellow. Perf 11½.

3447	2000z. Type **1020**	75	30
3448	2500z. 15th-century Arms	90	35
3449	3000z. 18th-century Arms	1·10	40
3450	3500z. Arms, 1919	1·20	70
3451	5000z. Arms, 1990	1·80	85
3447/3451	*Set of* 5	5·25	2·30

1021 Exhibition Emblem and Stylised Stamp

(Des J. Wysocki. Litho)

1993 (6 Jan). Centenary of Polish Philately and Polska '93 International Stamp Exhibition, Poznań (2nd issue). Perf 11½.

3452	**1021**	1500z. multicoloured	75	40

1022 Amber

1023 Downhill Skier

(Des A. Jeziorkowski. Litho)

1993 (29 Jan). Polska '93 International Stamp Exhibition, Poznań (3rd issue). Amber. T **1022** and similar multicoloured designs. Perf 13½.

3453	1500z. Type **1022**	45	30
3454	2000z. Pinkish amber	75	40
3455	2500z. Amber in stone	1·20	70
3456	3000z. Amber containing wasp	1·80	1·00
3453/3456	*Set of* 4	3·75	2·20
MS3457	82×88 mm. 20000z. Detail of map with necklace representing amber route (44×29 mm) (6 control numbers)	5·75	5·25

No. **MS**3457 was also issued wiht five small control numbers (*price* £400) or five large control numbers (style as on No. **MS**3457) (*price* £800).

(Des H. Chyliński. Litho)

1993 (5 Feb). Winter University Games, Zakopane. Perf 11½×11.

3458	**1023**	3000z. multicoloured	1·10	70

1024 Flower-filled Heart

1025 Arsenal

(Des S. Malecki. Litho)

1993 (14 Feb). St Valentine's Day. T **1024** and similar vert design. Multicoloured. Perf 11½×11.

3459 1500z. Type **1024** 45 30
3460 3000z. Heart in envelope .... 1·10 70

(Des S. Malecki. Eng W. Zajdel (1500z., 3000z.), T. Zlotkowski (2000z.), M. Kopecki (2500z.). Recess and photo)

1993 (25 Mar). Polish Rulers (8th series). Vert designs as T **893** showing drawings by Jan Matejko. Perf 11.

3461 1500z. blackish brown and yellow-olive 75 40
3462 2000z. blue-black and deep magenta .... 1·30 70
3463 2500z. black and slate-green .... 1·50 85
3464 3000z. deep brown and orange-brown .... 2·75 1·30
3461/3464 *Set of 4* .... 5·75 3·00

Designs: 1500z. Wladyslaw Laskonogi; 2000z. Henryk I; 2500z. Konrad I of Masovia; 3000z. Boleslaw V, the Chaste.

No. 3464 was issued with a *se-tenant* label commemorating Polska '93 International Stamp Exhibition.

(Des A. Szczepaniak. Photo)

1993 (26 Mar). 50th Anniversary of Action by Szare Szeregi (formation of Polish Scouts in the resistance forces) on Warsaw Arsenal. Perf 12×11½.

3465 **1025** 1500z. multicoloured 75 40

1026 Jousters with Lances

1027 Szczecin

(Des F. Winiarski. Photo)

1993 (29 Mar). Polska '93 International Stamp Exhibition, Poznań (4th issue). Jousting at Golub Dobrzyń. T **1026** and similar horiz designs each showing a modern and a medieval jouster. Multicoloured. Perf 11×11½.

3466 1500z. Type **1026** 45 30
3467 2000z. Jousters 75 40
3468 2500z. Jousters with swords .... 1·10 70
3469 3500z. Officials .... 1·50 85
3466/3469 *Set of 4* .... 3·50 2·00

(Des M. Jędrysik. Litho)

1993 (3 Apr). 750th Anniversary of Granting of Town Charter to Szczecin. Perf 11½×11.

3470 **1027** 1500z. multicoloured 90 40

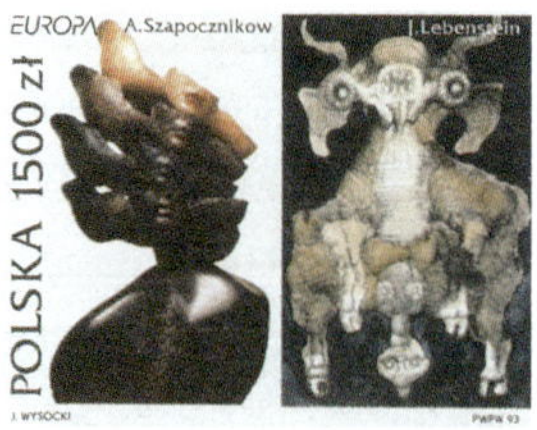

1028 Jew and Ruins

1029 Works by A. Szapocznikow and J. Lebenstein

(Des Ruth Avrahami. Litho)

1993 (18 Apr). 50th Anniversary of Warsaw Ghetto Uprising. Perf 14.

3471 **1028** 4000z. black, lemon and azure .... 1·50 85

No. 3471 was issued in sheets with a row of half stamp-size inscribed labels.

A stamp of a similar design was issued by Israel.

(Des J. Wysocki. Litho)

1993 (30 Apr). Europa. Contemporary Art. T **1029** and similar horiz design. Multicoloured. Perf 11×11½.

3472 1500z. Type **1029** 75 40
a. Pair. Nos. 3472/3473 .... 2·40 1·40
3473 4000z. *CXCIX* (S. Gierawski) and *Red Head* (B. Linke) .... 1·50 85

Nos. 3472/3473 were issued together in *se-tenant* pairs within the sheet.

1030 *King Alexander Jagiellończyk in the Sejm* (Jan Laski, 1505)

(Des A. Jeziorkowski. Photo)

1993 (2 May). 500th Anniversary of Parliament. Perf 11.

3474 **1030** 2000z. multicoloured 75 40

1031 Nullo

(Des R. Dudzicki. Photo)

1993 (5 May). 130th Death Anniversary of Francesco Nullo (Italian volunteer in January 1863 Rising). Perf 11×11½.

3475 **1031** 2500z. multicoloured .... 1·10 70

1032 Lech's Encounter with the White Eagle after Battle of Gniezno

1033 Cap

(Des A. Jeziorkowski. Eng C. Slania. Recess)

1993 (7 May). Polska '93 International Stamp Exhibition, Poznań (5th issue). Sheet 103×86 mm. Perf 13½.

MS3476 50000z. deep brown .... 13·50 12·50

No. **MS**3476 also exists imperforate from a limited issue (*price* £26).

(Des J. Wysocki. Litho)

1993 (21 May). Third World Congress of Cadets of the Second Republic. Perf 11×11½.

3477 **1033** 2000z. multicoloured 90 40

1034 Copernicus and Solar System

1035 Fiki Miki and Lion

(Des J. Konarzewski. Litho)

1993 (24 May). 450th Death Anniversary of Nicolas Copernicus (astronomer). Perf 11×11½.
3478 **1034** 2000z. multicoloured .... 1·10 70

(Des H. Chyliński. Litho)

1993 (1 June). 40th Death Anniversary of Kornel Makuszyński (writer of children's books). T **1035** and similar horiz designs. Multicoloured. Perf 11×11½.
3479 1500z. Type **1035** 45 30
3480 2000z. Billy goat 75 40
3481 3000z. Fiki Miki .... 1·50 70
3482 5000z. Billy goat riding ostrich .... 2·30 1·00
3479/3482 *Set of 4* .... 4·50 2·20

(Des A. Balcerzak. Photo)

1993 (30 June). Cones. Vert designs as T **974**. Multicoloured. Perf 12×11½.
3483 10000z. Arolla Pine (*Pinus cembra*) .... 3·25 2·10
3484 20000z. Scots Pine (*Pinus sylvestris*) .... 6·25 3·50

1036 Eurasian Tree Sparrow (*Passer montanus*)

1037 Soldiers Marching

(Des K. Rogaczewska. Litho)

1993 (15 July). Birds. T **1036** and similar vert designs. Multicoloured. Perf 11½×11.
3485 1500z. Type **1036** 55 30
3486 2000z. Pied Wagtail (*Motacilla alba*) 90 40
3487 3000z. Syrian Woodpecker (*Dendrocopos syriacus*) .... 1·40 60
3488 4000z. Eurasian Goldfinch (*Carduelis carduelis*) 1·80 80
3489 5000z. Common Starling (*Sturnus vulgaris*) .... 2·00 1·40
3490 6000z. Northern Bullfinch (*Pyrrhula pyrrhula*) .. 3·00 1·60
3485/3490 *Set of 6* .... 8·75 4·50

(Des M. Jędrysik. Photo)

1993 (20 July). Bicentenary of Dąbrowski's Mazurka (National Anthem) (1st issue). Perf 11×11½.
3491 **1037** 1500z. multicoloured 75 40
See also Nos. 3526, 3575, 3639 and 3700/**MS**3701.

1038 Madonna and Child (St Mary's Basilica, Leśna Podlaska)

1039 Handley Page HP.61 Halifax A9

(Des J. Wysocki. Litho)

1993 (15 Aug). Sanctuaries to St Mary. T **1038** and similar vert design. Multicoloured. Perf 11×11½ (with one elliptical hole on each vert side).
3492 1500z. Type **1038** 90 30
3493 2000z. 'Madonna and Child" (St. Mary's Church, Swieta Lipka) .... 1·40 50
Each issued in sheets of nine stamps.

(Des M. Jędrysik. Litho)

1993 (15 Sept). The Polish Rangers (Second World War air troop). Perf 11×11½ (with one elliptical hole on each horiz side).
3494 **1039** 1500z. multicoloured 75 40

1040 Trumpet Player

1041 Postman

(Des J. Konarzewski. Litho)

1993 (27 Sept). Jazz Jamboree '93 International Jazz Festival, Warsaw. Perf 11½ (with one elliptical hole on each horiz side).
3495 **1040** 2000z. multicoloured 90 40

(Des S. Malecki. Eng T. Zlotkowski. Recess and photo)

1993 (9 Oct). World Post Day. Perf 11½×11.
3496 **1041** 2500z. agate, lavender-grey and blue....... 1·10 70

1042 St Jadwiga (miniature, *Schlackenwerther Codex*)

1043 Pope John Paul II

(Des A. Heidrich. Litho State Ptg Wks, Berlin)

1993 (14 Oct). 750th Death Anniversary of St Jadwiga of Silesia. Perf 14.
3497 **1042** 2500z. multicoloured .... 1·50 70
A stamp of a similar design was issued by Germany.

(Des J. Wysocki. Litho)

1993 (16 Oct). 15th Anniversary of Election of Pope John Paul II. Sheet 70×92 mm. Perf 11½×11 (with one elliptical hole on each vert side).
MS3498 **1043** 20000z. multicoloured........ 7·50 7·00

1044 Eagle and Crown

1045 St Nicholas

(Des J. Wysocki. Litho)

1993 (11 Nov). 75th Anniversary of Republic. T **1044** and similar vert design. Multicoloured. Perf 11½×11 (with one elliptical hole on each vert side).
3499 4000z. Type **1044** .... 1·80 1·00
MS3500 66×89 mm. 20000z. Silhouette and shadow of flying eagle (31×38 mm)........ 8·50 8·25
On No. **MS**3500 the perforations on each vertical side, as well as containing an elliptical hole, are interrupted along that part of the design showing the eagle.

(Des A. Gosik. Litho)

1993 (25 Nov). Christmas. Perf 12×11½ (with one elliptical hole on each vert side).
3501 **1045** 1500z. multicoloured 90 40

(Des Krystyna Hoffman-Pagowska. Litho)

1993 (10 Dec). Poster Art (2nd series). Vert designs as T **1014**. Multicoloured. Perf 11×11½ (with one elliptical hole on each vert side).
3502 2000z. *Come and see Polish mountains* (M. Urbaniec) .... 1·10 70
3503 5000z. Production of Alban Berg's *Wozzeck* (J. Lenica) .... 1·80 1·00

1046 Daisy shedding Petals

(Des A. Gosik. Litho)

1994 (14 Jan). Greetings Stamp. Perf 11½×11 (with one elliptical hole on each vert side).

3504 **1046** 1500z. multicoloured .... 1·00 40

1047 Cross-country Skiing

1048 Bem and Cannon

(Des M. Urbaniec. Photo)

1994 (12 Feb). Winter Olympic Games, Lillehammer, Norway. T **1047** and similar vert designs. Multicoloured. Perf 11½×11.

3505 2500z. Type **1047** .... 1·40 70
3506 5000z. Ski jumping .... 2·40 1·00
MS3507 81×80 mm. 10000z. Downhill skiing .... 3·75 3·50

The miniature sheet also commemorates the centenary of the International Olympic Committee.

(Des J. Wysocki. Litho)

1994 (14 Mar). Birth Bicentenary of General Józef Bem. Perf 11½ (with one elliptical hole on each horiz side).

3508 **1048** 5000z. multicoloured .... 2·10 1·00

1049 Jan Zamojski (founder)

1050 Cracow Battalion Flag and Scythes

(Des Y. Erol. Litho)

1994 (15 Mar). 400th Anniversary of Zamojski Academy, Zamość. Perf 11½×11 (with one elliptical hole on each vert side).

3509 **1049** 5000z. violet-grey, black and light brown 2·10 1·00

(Des M. Jędrysik. Litho)

1994 (24 Mar). Bicentenary of Tadeusz Kościuszko's Insurrection. Perf 11½×11 (with one elliptical hole on each vert side).

3510 **1050** 2000z. multicoloured 90 40

(Des S. Malecki. Eng T. Zlotkowski (2500z.), W. Zajdel (5000z.). Recess and photo)

1994 (15 Apr). Polish Rulers (9th series). Vert designs as T **893** showing drawings by Jan Matejko. Perf 11.

3511 2500z. black and new blue .... 1·50 70
3512 5000z. blue-black, dull violet and reddish violet .... 3·00 1·40

Designs: 2500z. Leszek II, the Black; 5000z. Przemysl II.

1051 Oil Lamp, Open Book and Spectacles

1052 Madonna and Child

(Des T. Boguslawski. Litho)

1994 (30 Apr). Europa. Inventions and Discoveries. T **1051** and similar vert design. Multicoloured. Perf 11½×11 (with one elliptical hole on each vert side).

3513 2500z. Type **1051** (invention of modern oil lamp by Ignacy Lukasiewicz) .... 1·10 70
3514 6000z. Illuminated filament forming man in the moon (astronomy) .... 2·40 1·40

(Des Z. Stasik. Litho)

1994 (16 May). St Mary's Sanctuary, Kalwaria Zebrzydowska. Perf 11½×11 (with one elliptical hole on each vert side).

3515 **1052** 4000z. multicoloured .... 1·50 85

1053 Abbey Ruins and Poppies

1054 Mazurka

(Des A. Heidrich. Litho)

1994 (18 May). 50th Anniversary of Battle of Monte Cassino. Perf 11×11½ (with one elliptical hole on each horiz side).

3516 **1053** 6000z. multicoloured .... 1·80 1·00

(Des A. Heidrich. Litho)

1994 (25 May). Traditional Dances. T **1054** and similar vert designs showing paintings by Zofia Stryjeńska. Multicoloured. Perf 11½ (with one elliptical hole on each vert side).

3517 3000z. Type **1054** 60 30
3518 4000z. Coralski .... 1·20 45
3519 9000z. Krakowiak .... 2·75 1·10
3517/3519 *Set of 3* .... 4·00 1·70

1055 Cogwheels

1056 Optic Fibre Cable

(Des H. Chyliński. Litho)

1994 (7 June). 75th Anniversary of International Labour Organisation. Perf 11½ (with one elliptical hole on each horiz side).

3520 **1055** 6000z. greenish blue, bright new blue and black .... 1·50 85

(Des J. Górski. Litho)

1994 (10 June). 75th Anniversary of Polish Electricians Association. Perf 11×11½ (with one elliptical hole on each horiz side).

3521 **1056** 4000z. multicoloured .... 1·20 70

1057 Map of Americas on Football

1058 Znaniecki

(Des M. Nadolski. Litho)

1994 (17 June). World Cup Football Championship, USA. Perf 11½×11 (with one elliptical hole on each horiz side).

3522 **1057** 6000z. multicoloured .... 1·80 1·00

1994 (4 July). Poster Art (3rd series). Multicoloured designs as T **1014**. Litho. Perf 11×11½ (4000z.) or 11½×11 (6000z.) (each with one elliptical hole on one side).

3523 4000z. *Monsieur Fabre* (Wiktor Górka) .... 1·10 70
3524 6000z. *8th OISTAT Congress* (Hubert Hilscher) (*horiz*) .... 1·80 1·00

(Des A. Gosik. Litho)

1994 (15 July). 36th Death Anniversary of Professor Florian Znaniecki. Perf 11½ (with one elliptical hole on each vert side).

3525 **1058** 9000z. deep olive, bistre and yellow .... 3·00 1·70

(Des M. Jędrysik. Litho)

1994 (20 July). Bicentenary of Dąbrowski's Mazurka (2nd issue). Horiz designs as T **1037**. Multicoloured. Perf 11×11½.

3526 2500z. Troops preparing to charge .... 1·10 70

1059 Polish Eagle and Ribbon

1060 Stamp protruding from Pocket

(Des Y. Erol. Litho)

1994 (1 Aug). 50th Anniversary of Warsaw Uprising. Perf 11½×11 (with one elliptical hole on each vert side).

3527 **1059** 2500z. multicoloured .... 1·10 70

(Des T. Boguslawski. Litho)

1994 (16 Aug). Philakorea 1994 International Stamp Exhibition, Seoul. Perf 11½×11 (with one elliptical hole on each vert side).

3528 **1060** 4000z. multicoloured .... 1·20 85

1061 Basilica of St Brigida, Gdańsk

1062 Nike (goddess of Victory)

(Des J. Wysocki. Litho)

1994 (28 Aug). Sanctuaries. Perf 11½×11 (with one elliptical hole on each vert side).

3529 **1061** 4000z. multicoloured .... 1·20 85

(Des M. Buszewicz. Litho)

1994 (5 Sept). Centenary of International Olympic Committee. Perf 11×11½ (with one elliptical hole on each horiz side).

3530 **1062** 4000z. multicoloured .... 1·20 85

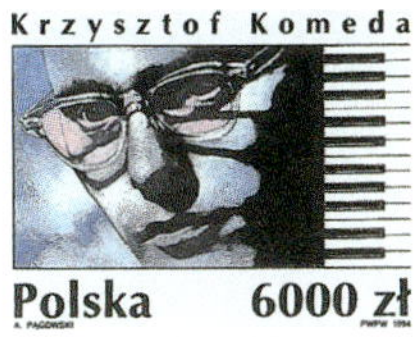

1063 Komeda and Piano Keys

1064 Long-finned Bristle-mouthed Catfish (*Ancistrus dolichopterus*)

(Des A. Pagowski. Litho)

1994 (22 Sept). 25th Death Anniversary of Krzysztof Komeda (jazz musician). Perf 11½ (with one elliptical hole on each horiz side).

3531 **1063** 6000z. multicoloured .... 1·50 85

(Des J. Brodowski. Litho)

1994 (28 Sept). Fish. T **1064** and similar vert designs. Multicoloured. Perf 11½×11 (with one elliptical hole on each vert side).

3532 4000z. Type **1064** .... 1·40 85
a. Horiz strip of 4. Nos. 3532/3535 .... 5·75
3533 4000z. Freshwater Angelfish (*Pterophyllum scalare*) .... 1·40 85
3534 4000z. Red Swordtail (*Xiphophorus helleri*), Neon Tetra (*Paracheirodon innesi*) and Berlin Platy .... 1·40 85
3535 4000z. Neon Tetra and Guppies (*Poecilia reticulata*) .... 1·40 85
3532/3535 *Set of 4* .... 5·00 3·00

Nos. 3532/3535 were issued together in horizontal *se-tenant* strips of four stamps within the sheet, each strip forming a composite design.

1065 Arms of Polish Post, 1858

1066 Kolbe

(Des B. Orliński. Litho)

1994 (9 Oct). World Post Day. Perf 11½×11 (with one elliptical hole on each vert side).

3536 **1065** 4000z. multicoloured .... 1·50 70

(Des M. Jędrysik. Photo)

1994 (24 Oct). Maksymilian Maria Kolbe (concentration camp victim) Year. Perf 11×11½.

3537 **1066** 2500z. multicoloured .... 1·30 95

1067 Pigeon

1068 Musicians playing Carols

(Des Krystyna Rogaczewska. Litho)

1994 (28 Oct). Pigeons. T **1067** and similar horiz designs. Multicoloured. Perf 11×11½ (with one elliptical hole on each horiz side).

3538 4000z. Type **1067** 90 40
a. Block of 4. Nos. 3538/3541 .... 4·50
3539 4000z. Friar Pigeon 90 40
3540 6000z. Silver Magpie Pigeon .... 1·20 85
3541 6000z. Danzig Pigeon (black) .... 1·20 85
3538/3541 *Set of 4* .... 3·75 2·30
MS3542 79×94 mm. 10000z. Short-tail Pigeon .... 3·50 2·75

Nos. 3538/3541 were issued together in *se-tenant* blocks of four within the sheet.

(Des Jadwiga and Z. Okrassa. Litho)

1994 (25 Nov). Christmas. Perf 11×11½ (with one elliptical hole on each horiz side).
3543 **1068** 2500z. multicoloured .... 1·20 40

1069 Landscape and EU Flag

1070 I Love You on Pierced Heart

(Des W. Freudenreich. Litho)

1994 (15 Dec). Application by Poland for Membership of European Union. Perf 11×11½ (with one elliptical hole on each horiz side).
3544 **1069** 6000z. multicoloured .... 2·75 2·00

Currency Reform

10000 Old Zlotys = 1 New Zloty

(Des A. Pagowski. Litho)

1995 (31 Jan). Greetings Stamp. Perf 11½×11 (with one elliptical hole on each vert side).
3545 **1070** 35g. bright crimson and ultramarine.... 1·20 40

1071 Rain, Sun and Water

1072 Flag and Sea

(Des H. Chyliński. Litho)

1995 (31 Jan). 75th Anniversary of Hydrological-Meteorological Service. Perf 11×11½ (with one elliptical hole on each horiz side).
3546 **1071** 60g. multicoloured .... 1·50 70

(Des T. Boguslawski. Litho)

1995 (10 Feb). 75th Anniversary of Poland's Marriage to the Sea (symbolic ceremony commemorating renewal of access to sea). Perf 11×11½ (with one elliptical hole on each horiz side).
3547 **1072** 45g. multicoloured 90 40

(Des S. Malecki. Eng W. Zajdel (35g., 80g.), M. Kopecki (45g., 60g.). Recess and photo)

1995 (28 Feb). Polish Rulers (10th series). Vert designs as T **893** showing drawings by Jan Matejko. Perf 11.
3548 35g. blackish brown, brown and pale yellow-brown 45 30
3549 45g. blackish olive, deep dull green and sage green 75 40
3550 60g. sepia and ochre .... 1·50 70
3551 80g. blue-black and blue .... 1·80 85
3548/3551 *Set of 4* .... 4·00 2·00

Designs: 35g. Waclaw II; 45g. Wladyslaw I; 60g. Kazimierz III, the Great; 80g. Ludwik Węgierski.

1073 St John

1074 Eggs

(Des Z. Okrassa. Litho)

1995 (8 Mar). 500th Birth Anniversary of St John of God (founder of Order of Hospitallers). Perf 12×11½ (with one elliptical hole on each vert side).
3552 **1073** 60g. multicoloured .... 1·10 70

(Des M. Wasilewski. Litho)

1995 (16 Mar). Easter. T **1074** and similar horiz designs, showing decorated Easter eggs. Multicoloured (background colours given). Perf 11½ (with one elliptical hole on each horiz side).
3553 - 35g. red 60 30
3554 - 35g. deep lavender 60 30
3555 - 45g. bright greenish blue .... 1·00 40
3556 **1074** 45g. blue-green .... 1·00 40
3553/3556 *Set of 4* .... 3·00 1·30

(Des A. Balcerzak. Photo)

1995 (27 Mar). Cones. Vert designs as T **974**. Multicoloured. Perf 12×11½.
3557 45g. European Larch (*Larix decidua*) 75 40
3558 80g. Mountain Pine (*Pinus mugo*) .... 1·20 70

1075 Polish Officer's Button and Leaf

1076 Rose and Barbed Wire

(Des. M. Buszewicz. Litho)

1995 (13 Apr). Katyń Commemoration Year. Perf 11×11½ (with one elliptical hole on each horiz side).
3559 **1075** 80g. multicoloured .... 1·50 85

(Des T. Boguslawski. Litho)

1995 (28 Apr). Europa. Peace and Freedom. T **1076** and similar horiz design. Multicoloured. Perf 11×11½ (with one elliptical hole on each horiz side).
3560 35g. Type **1076** (liberation of concentration camps) 75 40
3561 80g. Flowers in helmet .... 1·50 1·00

1077 Storks

1078 Pope and Wadowice Church Font

(Des J. Wysocki. Litho)

1995 (6 May). 50th Anniversary of Return of Western Territories. Perf 11½ (with one elliptical hole on each horiz side).
3562 **1077** 45g. multicoloured 90 40

(Des A. Gosik. Litho)

1995 (18 May). 75th Birthday of Pope John Paul II. Perf 11½ (with one elliptical hole on each vert side).
3563 **1078** 80g. multicoloured .... 1·50 85

1079 Puppets under Spotlight (Miròmagia)

1080 Cockerill Steam Locomotive and Train, Warsaw–Vienna, 1845

(Des H. Chyliński. Litho)

1995 (25 May). 50th Anniversary of Groteska Fairy Tale Theatre. T **1079** and similar multicoloured designs. Perf 11×11½ (horiz) or 11½×11 (vert) (each with one elliptical hole on two opposite sides).
3564 35g. Type **1079** 60 40
a. Pair. Nos. 3564/3565 .... 1·30 85
3565 35g. Puppets in scene from play 60 40

3566	45g. Puppet leaning on barrel (*Thomas Fingerchen*) (*vert*)	90	55
	a. Pair. Nos. 3566/3567	1·90	1·20
3567	45g. Clown (*Bumstara Circus*)	90	55
3564/3567 *Set of 4*		2·75	1·70

Stamps of the same value were issued together in *se-tenant* pairs within their sheets.

(Des M. Jędrysik. Litho)

1995 (9 June). 150th Anniversary of Polish Railways. T **1080** and similar horiz designs. Multicoloured. Perf 11½ (with one elliptical hole on each horiz side).

3568	35g. Type **1080**	60	40
	a. Pair. Nos. 3568/3569	1·80	1·20
3569	60g. Lux-Torpedo diesel railcar, 1927	1·10	70
3570	80g. Electric freight train, 1936	1·40	85
	a. Pair. Nos. 3570/3571	3·50	2·10
3571	1z. EuroCity Sobieski express, Warsaw–Vienna line, 1992	1·80	1·10
3568/3571 *Set of 4*		4·50	2·75

Nos. 3568/3569 and 3570/3571 respectively were issued together in *se-tenant* pairs within their sheets.

1081 Symbols of Nations

1082 Bank

(Des J. Konarzewski. Litho)

1995 (26 June). 50th Anniversary of United Nations Organisation. Perf 11½ (with one elliptical hole on each horiz side).

3572	**1081**	80g. multicoloured	1·50	85

(Des M. Piekarski. Litho)

1995 (30 June). 125th Anniversary of Warsaw Commercial Bank. Perf 11½ (with one elliptical hole on each horiz side).

3573	**1082**	45g. multicoloured	1·20	40

1083 Loaf and Four-leaved Clover

1084 Rowan Berries (*Sorbus aucuparia*)

(Des J. Konarzewski. Litho)

1995 (13 July). Centenary of Peasant Movement. Perf 11×11½ (with one elliptical hole on each horiz side).

3574	**1083**	45g. multicoloured	90	40

(Des M. Jędrysik. Photo)

1995 (20 July). Bicentenary of Dąbrowski's Mazurka (3rd issue). Horiz designs as T **1037**. Multicoloured. Perf 11×11½.

3575	35g. Mounted troops	90	40

(Des A. Balcerzak. Photo)

1995 (31 July). Fruits of Trees. No value expressed. T **1084** and similar vert design. Multicoloured. Perf 12×11½.

3576	B (35g.) Acorns and Sessile Oak leaves (*Quercus petraea*)	1·20	40
	a. Phosphorescent paper	1·50	40
3577	A (45g.) Type **1084**	1·40	40
	a. Phosphorescent paper	1·60	40

1085 Madonna and Child

1086 Marshal Józef Piłsudski

(Des Z. Stasik. Litho)

1995 (2 Aug). Basilica of the Holy Trinity, Leżajsk. Perf 11½×11 (with one elliptical hole on each vert side).

3578	**1085**	45g. multicoloured	90	40

(Des A. Heidrich. Litho)

1995 (14 Aug). 75th Anniversary of Defence of Warsaw and of Riga Peace Conference. Perf 11×11½ (with one elliptical hole on each horiz side).

3579	**1086**	45g. multicoloured	90	40

1087 Dressage

(Des A. Jeziorkowski. Litho)

1995 (23 Aug). World Carriage Driving Championships, Poznań. T **1087** and similar horiz design. Multicoloured. Perf 11½ (with one elliptical hole on each horiz side).

3580	60g. Type **1087**	1·10	70
	a. Pair. Nos. 3580/3581	2·75	1·80
3581	80g. Cross-country event	1·50	1·00

Nos. 3580/3581 were issued together in *se-tenant* pairs within the sheet.

1088 Warsaw Technical University

(Des J. Wysocki. Litho)

1995 (30 Aug). Warsaw '95 National Stamp Exhibition. T **1088** and similar multicoloured design. Perf 11½×11 (with one elliptical hole on two opposite sides).

3582	35g. Type **1088**	75	40
MS3583	94×71 mm. 1z. Castle Place, Warsaw (*horiz*). Perf 11×11½	2·30	1·70

1089 Russian Space Station and US Spacecraft

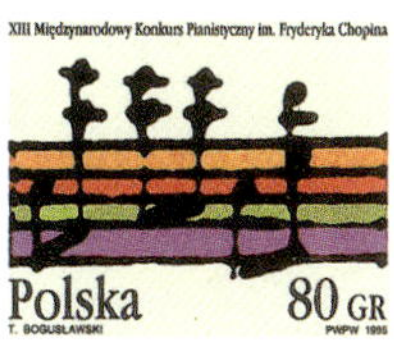

1090 Bar from *Polonaise* (Frédéric Chopin)

(Des Z. Stasik. Litho)

1995 (10 Sept). 11th World Cosmonauts Congress, Warsaw. Perf 11½×11 (with one elliptical hole on each vert side).

3584	**1089**	80g. multicoloured	1·50	85

(Des Krystyna Hoffman-Pagowska. Litho)

1995 (27 Sept). Poster Art (4th series). Vert designs as T **1014**. Multicoloured. Perf 11×11½ (with one elliptical hole on each vert side).

3585	35g. *The Crazy Locomotive* (Jan Sawka)	90	40
3586	45g. *The Wedding* (Eugeniusz Get Stankiewicz)	1·20	55

(Des T. Boguslawski. Litho)

1995 (1 Oct). 13th International Chopin Piano Competition. Perf 11×11½ (with one elliptical hole on each horiz side).
3587 **1090** 80g. multicoloured .... 1·70 85

1091 Postman

1092 Acrobatic Pyramid

(Des M. Jędrysik. Litho)

1995 (9 Oct). World Post Day. T **1091** and similar vert design. Multicoloured. Perf 11½ (with one elliptical hole on each vert side).
3588 45g. Type **1091** 75 40
3589 80g. Feather fixed to envelope by seal .... 1·40 85

(Des J. Brodowski. Litho)

1995 (26 Oct). World Acrobatic Sports Championships, Wroclaw. Perf 11½×11 (with one elliptical hole on each vert side).
3590 **1092** 45g. multicoloured 90 40

1093 Groszkowski and Formula

1094 Crib

(Des A. Pagowski. Litho)

1995 (10 Nov). 11th Death Anniversary of Professor Janusz Groszkowski (radio-electronic scientist). Perf 11½ (with one elliptical hole on each horiz side).
3591 **1093** 45g. multicoloured 90 40

(Des H. Chyliński. Litho)

1995 (27 Nov). Christmas. T **1094** and similar vert design. Multicoloured. Perf 12×11½ (with one elliptical hole on each vert side).
3592 35g. Type **1094** 75 40
a. Horiz pair. Nos. 3592/3593 .... 2·00 1·00
3593 45g. Wise men, Christmas tree and star of Bethlehem .... 1·10 55

Nos. 3592/3593 were issued together in horizontal *se-tenant* pairs within the sheet, each pair forming a composite design.

1095 Blue Tit (*Parus caeruleus*)

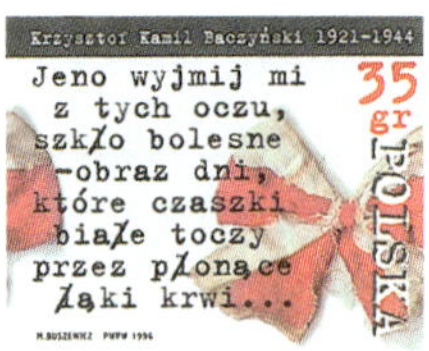

1096 Extract from Poem and Bow

(Des J. Desselberger. Litho)

1995 (15 Dec). Song Birds. T **1095** and similar square designs. Multicoloured. Perf 11½ (with one elliptical hole on each vert side).
3594 35g. Type **1095** 60 40
a. Block of 4. Nos. 3594/3597 .... 4·00
3595 45g. Long-tailed Tit (*Aegithalos caudatus*) 75 40
3596 60g. Great Grey Shrike (*Lanius excubitor*) .... 1·10 70
3597 80g. Hawfinch (*Coccothraustes coccothraustes*) .... 1·40 85
3594/3597 *Set of 4* .... 3·50 2·10

Nos. 3594/3597 were issued together in *se-tenant* blocks of four stamps within the sheet.

(Des M. Buszewicz. Litho)

1995 (22 Jan). 75th Birth Anniversary of Krzysztof Karnil Baczyński (poet). Perf 11×11½ (with one elliptical hole on each horiz side).
3598 **1096** 35g. multicoloured 75 40
a. *Tête-bêche* (pair) .... 2·30 1·40

1097 Cherries and I love you

1098 Romanesque-style Inowlódź Church

(Des T. Boguslawski. Litho)

1996 (31 Jan). Greetings Stamp. Perf 11½×11 (with one elliptical hole on each vert side).
3599 **1097** 40g. multicoloured 75 40

(Des A. Gosik. Litho)

1996 (27 Feb). Architectural Styles. T **1098** and similar vert designs. Multicoloured. Perf 11½ (with one elliptical hole on each vert side).
3600 40g. Type **1098** 75 55
3601 55g. Gothic-style St Mary the Virgin's Church, Cracow .... 1·10 70
3602 70g. Renaissance-style St Sigismund's Chapel, Wawel Castle .... 1·40 85
3603 1z. Baroque-style Church of the Order of the Holy Sacrament, Warsaw .... 2·00 1·30
3600/3603 *Set of 4* .... 4·75 3·00

1099 *Oceania* (experimental sailing ship)

1100 16th-century Warsaw

(Des M. Piekarski. Litho)

1996 (11 Mar). Sailing Ships. T **1099** and similar horiz designs. Multicoloured. Perf 11×11½ (with one elliptical hole on each horiz side).
3604 40g. Type **1099** 75 55
a. Strip of 4. Nos. 3604/3607 .... 5·00
3605 55g. *Zawisza Czarny* (cadet schooner) .... 1·10 70
3606 70g. *General Zaruski* (cadet ketch) .... 1·40 1·00
3607 75g. *Fryderyk Chopin* (cadet brig) .... 1·50 1·10
3604/3607 *Set of 4* .... 4·25 3·00

Nos. 3604/3607 were issued together in *se-tenant* strips of four stamps within the sheet.

(Des A. Heidrich. Litho)

1996 (18 Mar). 400th Anniversary of Warsaw. Perf 11½.
3608 **1100** 55g. multicoloured .... 1·10 70

1101 Bull (Taurus)

1102 Hanka Ordonówna (singer)

(Des M. Jędrysik. Photo)

1996 (21 Mar–31 July). Signs of the Zodiac. T **1101** and similar vert designs. Multicoloured. Perf 12×11½.
3609 5g. Workman in water (Aquarius) (19.7) 25 20
a. Phosphorescent paper 30 20
3610 10g. Fish-person holding fish (Pisces) (31.7) 25 20

	a. Phosphorescent paper	30	20
3611	20g. Type **1101** (21.4)	30	20
	a. Phosphorescent paper	35	25
3612	25g. Twins looking through keyhole (Gemini) (10.5)	35	25
	a. Phosphorescent paper	55	30
3613	30g. Crab smoking pipe (Cancer) (20.5)	45	25
	a. Phosphorescent paper	60	30
3614	40g. Maid and cogwheels (Virgo) (31.5)	45	30
	a. Phosphorescent paper	80	35
3615	50g. Lion in military uniform (Leo) (31.5)	60	30
	a. Phosphorescent paper	1·40	40
3616	55g. Couple with head and shoulders as scales (Libra) (10.6)	65	40
3617	70g. Ram with ram-head (Aries)	75	40
	a. Phosphorescent paper	1·20	55
3618	1z. Woman with scorpion's tail hat (Scorpio) (20.6)	1·20	70
	a. Phosphorescent paper	1·90	1·00
3619	2z. Archer on motorcycle (Sagittarius) (28.6)	2·40	1·50
	a. Phosphorescent paper	3·00	2·00
3620	5z. Office worker shielding face with paper mask (Capricorn) (10.7)	6·00	3·75
	a. Phosphorescent paper	6·75	4·25
3609/3620	*Set of* 12	12·00	7·50

(Des A. Gosik. Litho)

1996 (30 Apr). Europa. Famous Women. T **1102** and similar vert design. Multicoloured. Perf 11½×11 (with one elliptical hole on each vert side).

3621	40g. Type **1102**	1·10	70
3622	1z. Pola Negri (actress)	2·00	1·40

1103 Flag of Osiek and Old Photographs forming '1921"

1104 On Bergamuty Islands

(Des J. Wysocki. Litho)

1996 (2 May). 75th Anniversary of Silesian Uprising. Perf 11×11½ (with one elliptical hole on each horiz side).

3623	**1103**	55g. bright scarlet, bronze green and black	1·10	70

(Des M. Jędrysik. Litho)

1996 (31 May). 50th Anniversary of United Nations Children's Fund. Scenes from fairy tales by Jan Brzechwa. T **1104** and similar vert designs. Multicoloured. Perf 11½×11 (with one elliptical hole on each vert side).

3624	40g. Type **1104**	60	40
3625	40g. Waiters carrying trays of apples (nursery rhyme)	60	40
3626	55g. Vegetable characters (At the Market Stall)	90	55
3627	55g. Chef holding duck (Wacky Duck)	90	55
3628	70g. Woman and birdchild (The Fibber)	1·20	70
3629	70g. Red fox (The Impishness of Witalis Fox)	1·20	70
3624/3629	*Set of* 6	4·75	3·00

1105 *City Walls and Building*

1106 Discus on Ribbon

(Des A. Balcerzak. Litho)

1996 (21 June). Paintings by Stanislaw Noakowski. T **1105** and similar vert designs. Multicoloured. Perf 11½×11 (with one elliptical hole on each vert side).

3630	40g. Type **1105**	75	40
3631	55g. *Renaissance Bedroom*	90	55
3632	70g. *Rural Gothic Church*	1·20	85
3633	1z. *Renaissance Library*	1·80	1·10
3630/3633	*Set of* 4	4·25	2·50

(Des T. Boguslawski. Litho)

1996 (5 July). Olympic Games, Atlanta, and Centenary of Modern Olympic Games. T **1106** and similar multicoloured designs. Perf 11½×11 (vert) or 11×11½ (horiz) (with one elliptical hole on two opposite sides).

3634	40g. Type **1106** (gold medal, Halina Konopacka, 1928)	75	40
3635	55g. Tennis ball (*horiz*)	1·10	55
3636	70g. Polish Olympic Committee emblem (*horiz*)	1·50	85
3637	1z. Bicycle wheel	2·00	1·10
3634/3637	*Set of* 4	4·75	2·50

1107 Tweezers holding Stamp showing Emblem

1108 St Mary of Przeczycka

(Des T. Boguslawski. Litho)

1996 (5 July). Olymphilex '96 International Sports Stamp Exhibition, Atlanta. Perf 11×11½ (with one elliptical hole on each horiz side).

3638	**1107**	1z. multicoloured	1·80	1·00

(Des M. Jędrysik. Photo)

1996 (20 July). Bicentenary of Dąbrowski's Mazurka (4th issue). Horiz design as T **1037**. Multicoloured. Perf 11×11½.

3639	40g. Charge of Polish cavalry at Somosierra	90	40

(Des Z. Stasik. Litho)

1996 (2 Aug). St Mary's Church, Przeczycka. Perf 11½.

3640	**1108**	40g. multicoloured	90	40

(Des S. Malecki. Eng W. Zajdel (40g.), M. Kopecki (55g.) P. Krajewski (others). Recess and photo)

1996 (29 Aug). Polish Rulers (11th series). Vert designs as T **893**. Perf 11.

3641	40g. agate and bistre	75	40
3642	55g. deep reddish lilac and deep mauve	1·10	55
3643	70g. violet-grey and brownish grey	1·50	70
3644	1z. blackish green, grey-green and olive-yellow	2·40	1·00
3641/3644	*Set of* 4	5·25	2·40

Designs: 40g. Queen Jadwiga (wife of Wladyslaw II); 55g. Wladyslaw II Jagiello; 70g. Wladyslaw III Warneńczyk; 1z. Kazimierz IV Jagiellończyk.

1109 Mount Giewont and Edelweiss

1110 Seifert

(Des J. Brodowski. Litho)

1996 (5 Sept). The Tatra Mountains. T **1109** and similar horiz designs. Multicoloured. Perf 11½ (with one elliptical hole on each horiz side).

3645	40g. Type **1109**	60	40
3646	40g. Mount Krzesanica and Spring Gentian	60	40

3647	55g. Mount Kościelec and Leopard's Bane	90	55
3648	55g. Mount Świnica and Clusius Gentian	90	55
3649	70g. Mount Rysy and Ragwort	1·50	70
3650	70g. Mięguszowieckie peaks and Pine Trees	1·50	70
3645/3650	*Set of 6*	5·50	3·00

(Des W. Swierzy. Litho)

1996 (25 Sept). 50th Birth Anniversary of Zbigniew Seifert (jazz musician). Perf 11½ (with one elliptical hole on each vert side).

3651	**1110**	70g. multicoloured	1·50	85

1111 *Changing of Horses at Post Station* (detail, Mieczyslaw Watorski)

1112 Father Christmas on Horse-drawn Sleigh

(Des S. Malecki. Photo)

1996 (9 Oct). World Post Day. 75th Anniversary of Post and Telecommunications Museum, Wroclaw. T **1111** and similar horiz design showing paintings. Multicoloured. Perf 12×11½.

3652	40g. Type **1111**	90	40
MS3653	102×81 mm. 1z.+20g. *Mail Coach at Jagniątków with View over Karkonosze* (Professor Täger) (42×30 mm). Perf 11×11½	2·75	2·50

(Des J. Brodowski. Litho)

1996 (27 Nov). Christmas. T **1112** and similar horiz designs. Multicoloured. Perf 11½×12 (with one elliptical hole on each horiz side).

3654	40g. Type **1112**	60	35
3655	55g. Carol singers with star lantern	90	40

1113 Head of Male

1114 Wislawa Szymborska

(Des J. Wysocki. Litho)

1996 (4 Dec). The European Bison (*Bison bonasus*). T **1113** and similar vert designs. Multicoloured. Perf 11½ (with one elliptical hole on each vert side).

3656	55g. Type **1113**	90	55
	a. Strip of 4. Nos. 3656/3659	3·75	
3657	55g. Head of female	90	55
3658	55g. Pair of bison	90	55
3659	55g. Male	90	55
3656/3659	*Set of 4*	3·25	2·00

Nos. 3656/3659 were issued together in *se-tenant* strips of four stamps within the sheet.

(Des J. Wysocki. Litho)

1996 (10 Dec). Award of Nobel Prize for Literature to Wislawa Szymborska (poet). Perf 11½ (with one elliptical hole on each vert side).

3660	**1114**	1z. multicoloured	1·80	1·00

1115 I Love You on King of Hearts Playing Card

1116 Blessing the Palms

(Des J. Konarzewski. Litho)

1997 (14 Jan). Greetings Stamps. T **1115** and similar horiz design. Multicoloured. Phosphorescent paper. Perf 11×11½ (with one elliptical hole on each horiz side).

3661	B (40g.) Type **1115**	80	35
	a. Vert pair. Nos. 3661/3662	2·10	80
3662	A (55g.) Queen of hearts playing card	1·20	40

Nos. 3661/3662 were issued together in vertical *se-tenant* pairs. each pair forming a composite design.

No. 3661 was sold as the rate for postcards.

No. 3662 for letters up to 20 grams.

(Des Maria Dziekańska. Litho)

1997 (14 Mar). Easter. Traditional Customs. T **1116** and similar horiz designs. Multicoloured. Phosphorescent paper. Perf 11×11½ (with one elliptical hole on each horiz side).

3663	50g. Type **1116**	60	40
3664	60g. Woman and child painting easter eggs	75	40
3665	80g. Priest blessing the food	1·10	70
3666	1z.10 Man throwing water over woman's skirts on Easter Monday	1·50	85
3663/3666	*Set of 4*	3·50	2·10

1117 Long Market and Town Hall (after Mateusz Deisch)

1118 St Adalbert and Monks addressing Pagans

(Des T. Boguslawski. Photo and recess)

1997 (18 Apr). Millenary of Gdańsk. T **1117** and similar design. Each brown, pale cinnamon and carmine-red. Perf 11½×11.

3667	50g. Type **1117**	75	40
MS3668	94×71 mm. 1z.10 St Mary's Church and Hall of the Main Town (after Mateusz Merian) (*horiz*). Perf 11×11½	2·75	2·50

No. **MS**3668 also exists imperforate (*price* £24).

(Des A. Heidrich (50g., 60g.), V. Suchanek (1z.10). Eng C. Slania. Recess)

1997 (19–23 Apr). Death Millenary of St Adalbert (Bishop of Prague). T **1118** and similar designs. Perf 11×11½ (50g.) or 11½×11 (others).

3669	**1118**	50g. sepia	60	35
3670	-	60g. blackish green	75	40
3671	-	1z.10 deep lilac (23.4)	1·50	85
3669/3671		*Set of 3*	2·50	1·40

Designs: Vert—60g. St Adalbert and Anniversary emblem; 1z.10 St Adalbert.

Stamps of a similar design were also issued by Czech Republic, Germany, Hungary and Vatican City.

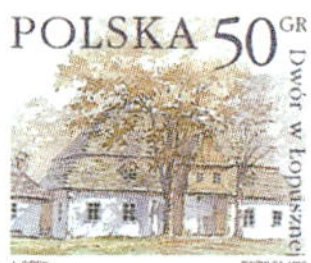

1119 Mansion House, Lopuszna

1120 The Crock of Gold

(Des A. Gosik. Photo)

1997 (30 Apr)–**01**. Polish Manor Houses. T **1119** and similar horiz designs. Multicoloured. Phosphorescent paper. Perf 11½×12.

3672	10g. Lipkowie, Warsaw (20.6.01)	25	20
3672*a*	50g. Type **1119**	75	35
3673	55g. Henryk Sienkewicz Museum, Oblęgorek (3.3.98)	65	40
3674	60g. Zyrzyn	75	40
3675	65g. Stanislaw Wyspiański Museum, Bronowice, near Cracow (3.3.98)	80	55
3675*a*	70g. Medlnica (15.6.99)	90	55
3675*b*	80g. Grabonóg Gostyń (14.4.2000)	1·00	60
3676	90g. Oborg, near Warsaw (3.3.98)	1·20	70
3676*a*	1z. Krzeslawice (15.6.99)	1·30	75
3677	1z.10 Ozarów (23.5.97)	1·40	85
3678	1z.20 Józef Krasnewski Museum, Biala Podlaska (3.3.98)	1·80	1·00
3678*a*	1z.40 Winna Góra (15.6.99)	1·80	1·00
3678*b*	1z.50 Sulejowku, Warsaw (20.6.01)	2·30	1·10

3678*c*	1z.55 Żelazowa Wola (14.4.00)	2·00	1·00
3678*d*	1z.60 Potok Zloty (15.6.99)	2·10	1·10
3678*e*	1z.65 Sucha, Wegrów (14.4.00)	2·20	1·20
3679	1z.70 Tulowice (23.5.97)	2·30	1·40
3679*a*	1z.85 Kąśna Dolna (15.6.99)	2·50	1·20
3679*b*	1z.90 Petrykozach, Mszczonowa (28.2.01)	2·50	1·40
3680	2z.20 Kuznocin (23.5.97)	2·75	1·80
3681	2z.65 Liwia, Wegrów (14.4.00)	3·25	1·80
3682	3z. Janowcu, Pulaw (28.2.01)	3·75	2·10
3683	10z. Koszuty (23.5.97)	12·00	8·50
3672/3683	*Set of 23*	45·00	27·00

No. 3684 is vacant.

(Des M. Wasilewski. Litho)

1997 (5 May). Europa. Tales and Legends. T **1120** and similar horiz design. Phosphorescent paper. Perf 11½×12 (with one elliptical hole on each horiz side).

3685	50g. Type **1120**	90	55
3686	1z.10 Wars, Sawa and mermaid-siren	2·40	1·30

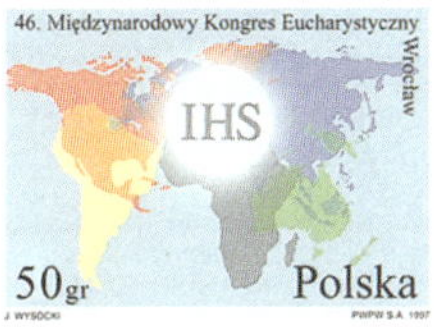

1121 World Map and Emblem

(Des J. Wysocki. Litho)

1997 (6 May). 46th International Eucharistic Congress, Wroclaw. Phosphorescent paper. Perf 11½ (with one elliptical hole on each horiz side).

3687	**1121**	50g. multicoloured	75	40

1122 Golden Gate Bridge

(Des M. Buszewicz. Photo)

1997 (20 May). Pacific 97 International Stamp Exhibition, San Francisco. Phosphorescent paper. Perf 11½×11 (with one elliptical hole on each horiz side).

3688	**1122**	1z.30 multicoloured	1·80	1·00

1123 Pope John Paul II

1124 European Long-eared Bat (*Plecotus auritus*)

(Des J. Wysocki. Litho)

1997 (28 May). Fifth Papal Visit. Sheet 76×90 mm. Phosphorescent paper. Perf 11×11½ (with one elliptical hole on each vert side).

MS3689	1z.10 multicoloured	3·00	2·75

(Des J. Brodowski. Litho)

1997 (30 May). Bats. T **1124** and similar horiz designs. Multicoloured. Phosphorescent paper. Perf 11×11½ (with one elliptical hole on each horiz side).

3690	50g. Type **1124**	60	40
3691	60g. Common Noctule (*Nyctalus noctula*)	75	55
3692	80g. Brown Bat (*Myotis myotis*)	90	70
3693	1z.30 Red Bat (*Vespertilio murinus*)	2·00	1·00
3690/3693	*Set of 4*	3·75	2·40

1125 *Founding of the Main School* (Jan Matejko)

1126 Map highlighting Settled Area

(Des J. Wysocki. Photo)

1997 (6 June). 600th Anniversary of Faculty of Theology, Jagiellonian University, Cracow. Phosphorescent paper. Perf 11.

3694	**1125**	80g. multicoloured	90	55

(Des A. Radziejowski. Litho)

1997 (6 June). Centenary of Polish Migration to Argentina. Phosphorescent paper. Perf 11½ (with one elliptical hole on each vert side).

3695	**1126**	1z.40 multicoloured	1·80	1·10

1127 *Return from War to the Village*

(Des A. Balcerzak. Photo)

1997 (4 July). Paintings by Juliúsz Kossak. T **1127** and similar horiz designs. Multicoloured. Phosphorescent paper. Perf 11.

3696	50g. Type **1127**	75	40
3697	60g. *Cracowian Wedding*	90	55
3698	80g. *In the Stable*	1·20	70
3699	1z.10 *Stablehand with Pair of Horses*	1·70	1·00
3696/3699	*Set of 4*	4·00	2·40

(Des M. Jędrysik. Photo)

1997 (18 July). Bicentenary of Dąbrowski's Mazurka (5th issue). Horiz designs as T **1037**. Phosphorescent paper. Perf 11×11½.

3700	50g. Dąbrowski and Wybicki's arrival in Poznál, 1806	75	40
MS3701	85×77 mm. 1z.10 Manuscript of lyrics and Józef Wybicki (composer)	2·30	2·10

1128 Strzelecki and Route Map around Australia

1129 Flooded Houses

(Des A. Jeziorkowski. Litho)

1997 (20 July). Birth Bicentenary of Pawel Strzelecki (explorer). Phosphorescent paper. Perf 11½ (with one elliptical hole on each horiz side).

3702	**1128**	1z.50 multicoloured	2·30	1·40

(Des M. Jędrysik. Photo)

1997 (18 Aug). Flood Relief Fund. Phosphorescent paper. Perf 11½×12.
3703 **1129** 60g.+30g. multicoloured .... 1·50 1·00

1130 Holy Mother of Consolation (icon)

1131 Kosz

1132 Globe and Posthorn

(Des Z. Stasik. Litho)

1997 (28 Aug). Church of the Holy Mother of Consolation and St Michael the Archangel, Górká Duchowa. Phosphorescent paper. Perf 11½×11 (with one elliptical hole on each vert side).
3704 **1130** 50g. multicoloured 90 40

(Des S. Malecki. Eng P. Krajewski (60g.), W. Zajdel (others). Recess and photo)

1997 (22 Sept). Polish Rulers (12th series). Vert designs as T **893**. Perf 11.
3705 50g. agate, red-brown and olive-bistre 90 40
3706 60g. deep dull purple and grey-blue .... 1·10 55
3707 80g. slate-green, deep dull green and grey-olive .... 1·50 85
3708 1z.10 blackish purple and reddish lilac .... 2·00 1·10
3705/3708 *Set of* 4 .... 5·00 2·50

Designs: 50g. Jan I Olbracht; 60g. Aleksander Jagiellończyk; 80g. Zygmunt I, the Old; 1z.10 Zygmunt II August.

(Des J. Stanny. Litho)

1997 (3 Oct). 24th Death Anniversary of Mieczyslaw Kosz (jazz musician). Phosphorescent paper. Perf 12×11½ (with one elliptical hole on each vert side).
3709 **1131** 80g. multicoloured .... 1·10 70

(Des W. Walkuski. Litho)

1997 (9 Oct). World Post Day. Phosphorescent paper. Perf 11½×12 (with one elliptical hole on each horiz side).
3710 **1132** 50g. multicoloured 90 40

1133 St Basil's Cathedral, Moscow

1134 Nativity

(Des J. Konarzewski. Litho)

1997 (13 Oct). Moskva 97 International Stamp Exhibition, Moscow. Phosphorescent paper. Perf 11×11½ (with one elliptical hole on each horiz side).
3711 **1133** 80g. multicoloured .... 1·30 1·00

(Des A. Pagowski. Litho)

1997 (14 Nov). Poster Art (5th series). Designs as T **1014**. Phosphorescent paper. Perf 11½×11 (No. 3712) or 11×11½ (others) (each with one elliptical hole on two opposite sides).
3712 50g. multicoloured 60 40
3713 50g. black 60 40
3714 60g. multicoloured 75 40
3715 60g. multicoloured 75 40
3712/3715 *Set of* 4 .... 2·40 1·40

Posters: Horiz—No. 3712, Advertisement for Radion washing powder (Tadeusz Gronowski). Vert—No. 3713, Production of Stanislaw Witkiewicz's play *Shoemakers* (Roman Cieślewicz); No. 3714, Production of Aleksander Fredro's play *A Husband and a Wife* (Andrzej Pagowski); No. 3715, Production of ballet *Goya* (Wiktor Sadowski).

(Des Krystyna Pagowska. Litho)

1997 (27 Nov). Christmas. T **1134** and similar multicoloured designs. Phosphorescent paper. Perf 11½×11 (50g., 1z.10) or 11×11½ (60g., 80g.) (each with one elliptical hole on two opposite sides).
3716 50g. Type **1134** 60 40
3717 60g. Christmas Eve feast (*horiz*) 75 45
3718 80g. Family going to church for Midnight Mass (*horiz*) .... 1·10 70
3719 1z.10 Waits (carol singers representing animals) .... 1·50 1·00
3716/3719 *Set of* 4 .... 3·50 2·30

1135 Common Shelducks (*Tadorna tadorna*)

1136 Ski Jumping

(Des J. Desselberger. Litho)

1997 (4 Dec). Precocial Chicks. T **1135** and similar square designs. Multicoloured. Phosphorescent paper. Perf 11½ (with one elliptical hole on each vert side).
3720 50g. Type **1135** 75 60
a. Block of 4. Nos. 3720/3723 .... 3·25
3721 50g. Goosanders (*Mergus merganser*) 75 60
3722 50g. Common Snipes (*Gallinago gallinago*) . 75 60
3723 50g. Moorhens (*Gallinula chloropus*) 75 60
3720/3723 *Set of* 4 .... 2·75 2·20

Nos. 3720/3723 were issued together in *se-tenant* blocks of four stamps within the sheet.

(Des W. Walkuski. Litho)

1998 (5 Jan). Winter Olympic Games, Nagano, Japan. Phosphorescent paper. Perf 11½ (with one elliptical hole on each vert side).
3724 **1136** 1z.40 multicoloured .... 1·80 1·10

1137 Dog wearing Cat T-shirt inscr I Love You

(Des Malgorzata Osa. Litho)

1998 (14 Jan). Greetings Stamps. No value expressed. T **1137** and similar vert design. Multicoloured. Phosphorescent paper. Perf 11½ (with one elliptical hole on each vert side).
3725 B (55g.) Type **1137** .... 1·20 40
3726 A (65g.) Cat wearing dog T-shirt .... 1·30 55

No. 3725 was sold as the rate for postcards.
No. 3726 was sold as the rate for letters up to 20 grams.

(Des A. Gosik. Photo)

1998 (15 Jan). Polish Manor Houses. No value expressed. Horiz designs as T **1119**. Multicoloured. Phosphorescent paper. Perf 11½.
3727 B (55g.) Gluchy .... 1·20 40
3728 A (65g.) Jan Kochanowski Museum, Czarnolas .... 1·30 55

No. 3727 was sold as the rate for postcards.
No. 3728 was sold as the rate for letters up to 20 grams.

1138 Paschal Lamb

(Des A. Pagowski. Litho)

1998 (12 Mar). Easter. T **1138** and similar vert design. Multicoloured. Phosphorescent paper. Perf 11½ (with one elliptical hole on each vert side).

3729	55g. Type **1138**	60	40
3730	65g. The Resurrected Christ	90	55

1139 Polish National Guard and Civilians at Lviv Barricades

1140 Grey Seal (*Halichoerus grypus*)

(Des M. Jędrysik. Eng W. Zajdel. Recess)

1998 (20 Mar). 150th Anniversary of 1848 Revolutions. Phosphorescent paper. Perf 11×11½.

3731	**1139**	55g. blackish brown	75	40

(Des S. Malecki. Eng W. Zajdel (55g.), M. Kopecki (80g.), P. Krajewski (others). Recess and photo)

1998 (31 Mar). Polish Rulers (13th series). Vert designs as T **893**. Perf 11.

3732	55g. reddish brown and yellow-brown	75	40
3733	65g. slate-purple, deep purple and magenta	1·10	55
3734	80g. bottle green and dull yellowish green	1·40	70
3735	90g. blackish lilac, deep purple and magenta	1·50	75
3732/3735	*Set of* 4	4·25	2·20

Designs: 55g. Henryk Walezy; 65g. Queen Anne Jagiellońka (wife of Stefan I); 80g. Stefan I Batory; 90g. Zygmunt III Wasa.

(Des J. Brodowski. Litho)

1998 (28 Apr). Protection of Baltic Sea. Marine Life. T **1140** and similar vert designs. Multicoloured. Phosphorescent paper. Perf 11½×11 (with one elliptical hole on each vert side).

3736	65g. Type **1140**	75	70
	a. Horiz strip of 6. Nos. 3736/3741	4·75	
3737	65g. *Pomatoschistus microps* (fish), jellyfish and shells	75	70
3738	65g. Twaite Shad (*Alosa fallax*) and Pipefish (*Syngnathus typhle*)	75	70
3739	65g. Common Sturgeon (*Acipenser sturio*)	75	70
3740	65g. Atlantic Salmon (*Salmo salar*)	75	70
3741	65g. Common Porpoise (*Phocoena phocoena*)	75	70
3736/3741	*Set of* 6	4·00	3·75
MS3742	76×70 mm. 1z.20 Grey Seal	2·00	1·80

Nos. 3736/3741 were issued together in horizontal *se-tenant* strips of six stamps within the sheet, each strip forming a composite design.

1141 Exhibition Emblem and 1948 Israeli 500m. Stamp

1142 Festival Emblem

(Des M. Buszewicz. Litho)

1998 (30 Apr). Israel '98 International Stamp Exhibition, Tel Aviv. Phosphorescent paper. Perf 11½ (with one elliptical hole on each horiz side).

3743	**1141**	90g. multicoloured	1·40	1·30

(Des W. Freudenreich. Litho)

1998 (5 May). Europa. National Festivals. T **1142** and similar horiz design. Phosphorescent paper. Perf 11½ (with one elliptical hole on each horiz side).

3744	55g. multicoloured	75	70
	a. Pair. Nos. 3744/3745	2·75	2·50
3745	1z.20 black, bright scarlet and ultramarine	1·80	1·70

Designs: 55g. T **1142** (Warsaw Autumn International Festival of Music); 1z.20 State flag and opening bars of *Welcome the May Dawn* (3rd of May Constitution Day).

Nos. 3744/3745 were issued together in *se-tenant* pairs within the sheet.

D1143

1144 Longing Holy Mother

1998 (18 June). POSTAGE DUE. T **D1143** and similar horiz designs. Litho. Perf 14.

D3746	5g. deep violet-blue, bright reddish violet and lemon	30	25
D3747	10g. deep violet-blue, turquoise-blue and lemon	35	30
D3748	20g. indigo, bright green and lemon	45	40
D3749	50g. blue-black and lemon	75	55
D3750	80g. deep violet-blue, orange and lemon	1·30	1·00
D3751	1z. deep violet-blue, bright crimson and lemon	1·70	1·30
D3746/D3751	*Set of* 6	4·25	3·50

(Des J. Konarzewski. Litho)

1998 (28 June). Coronation of Longing Holy Mother (icon in Powsin church). Phosphorescent paper. Perf 11½ (with one elliptical hole on each vert side).

3752	**1144**	55g. multicoloured	90	70

1145 *Triple Self-portrait*

1146 Anniversary Inscription

(Des W. Freudenreich. Litho)

1998 (10 July). 30th Death Anniversary of Nikifor (Epifan Drowniak) (artist) T **1145** and similar vert designs. Multicoloured. Phosphorescent paper. Perf 11½ (with one elliptical hole on each vert side).

3753	55g. Type **1145**	80	75
3754	65g. *Cracow Office*	95	90
3755	1z.20 *Orthodox Church*	1·80	1·70
3756	2z.35 *Ugrybów Station*	3·50	3·25
3753/3756	*Set of* 4	6·25	6·00

(Des W. Freudenreich. Litho)

1998 (13 July). 80th Anniversary of Main Board of Statistics. Phosphorescent paper. Perf 11×11½ (with one elliptical hole on each horiz side).

3757	**1146**	55g. multicoloured	95	75

1147 Madonna and Child

1148 Jesus (stained glass window)

(Des Z. Stasik. Litho)

1998 (14 Aug). Basilica of the Visitation of St Mary the Virgin, Sejny. Phosphorescent paper. Perf 11½×11 (with one elliptical hole on each vert side).

3758	**1147**	55g. multicoloured	95	75

(Des J. Konarzewski. Litho)

1998 (28 Aug). Bicentenary of Diocese of Warsaw. Phosphorescent paper. Perf 11½ (with one elliptical hole on each horiz side).

3759	**1148**	65g. multicoloured	95	75

1149 Szczecin

1150 Pierre and Marie Curie (physicists)

(Des A. Heidrich. Eng C. Slania. Recess and photo)

1998 (18 Sept). 17th Congress of Polish Union of Stamp Collectors. Sheet 114×77 mm containing T **1149** and similar horiz design. Each indigo and cream. Phosphorescent paper. Perf 11×11½.

MS3760	65g.×2 Composite design showing 17th-century engraving of Szczecin from *Descriptio Urbis Stettinensis* by Paul Feideborn	2·10	2·00

No. **MS**3760 also exists imperforate (*price* £31).

(Des T. Boguslawski. Litho)

1998 (18 Sept). Centenary of Discovery of Polonium and Radium. Phosphorescent paper. Perf 11×11½ (with one elliptical hole on each horiz side).

3761	**1150**	1z.20 multicoloured	1·60	1·50

1151 Mazowsze Dancers

1152 Mniszchów Palace

(Des M. Buszewicz. Litho)

1998 (22 Sept). 50th Anniversary of Mazowsze Song and Dance Group. T **1151** and similar vert design. Multicoloured. Phosphorescent paper. Perf 11½×11 (with one elliptical hole on each vert side).

3762	65g. Type **1151**	80	75
	a. Horiz pair. Nos. 3762/3763	1·70	1·60
3763	65g. Dancers (*different*)	80	75

Nos. 3762/3763 were issued together in horizontal *se-tenant* pairs throughout the sheet, each pair forming a composite design.

(Des A. Heidrich. Eng G. Broux. Recess and photo)

1998 (28 Sept). Belgium Embassy, Warsaw. Phosphorescent paper. Perf 11½.

3764	**1152**	1z.20 multicoloured	1·60	1·50

A stamp of a similar design was issued by Belgium.

1153 *King Sigismund* (Studio of Rubens)

1154 Coloured Envelopes

(Des A. Heidrich. Eng C. Slania. Recess)

1998 (3 Oct). 400th Anniversary of Battle of Stångebro. Phosphorescent paper. Perf 11½×11.

3765	**1153**	1z.20 purple-brown	1·80	1·50

A stamp of a similar design was issued by Sweden.

(Des M. Wasilewski. Litho)

1998 (9 Oct). World Post Day. Phosphorescent paper. Perf 11½×11 (with one elliptical hole on each vert side).

3766	**1154**	65g. multicoloured	95	75

1155 Pope John Paul II and People of Different Races

1156 State Flags and 1919 Seal

(Des W. Walkuski. Litho)

1998 (16 Oct). 20th Anniversary of Selection of Karol Wojtyła to Papacy. Phosphorescent paper. Perf 11½ (with one elliptical hole on each vert side).

3767	**1155**	65g. multicoloured	1·20	75

(Des A. Heidrich. Litho)

1998 (11 Nov). 80th Anniversary of Independence. Phosphorescent paper. Perf 11½ (with one elliptical hole on each horiz side).

3768	**1156**	65g. black, vermilion and gold	1·20	75

1157 Nativity

1158 Anniversary Emblem

(Des J. Wysocki. Photo)

1998 (27 Nov). Christmas. *Grudziądz* Polyptych. T **1157** and similar vert design. Multicoloured. Phosphorescent paper. Perf 11½×11.

3769	55g. Type **1157**	80	70
3770	65g. Adoration of the Wise Men	95	75

(Des W. Freudenreich. Litho)

1998 (10 Dec). 50th Anniversary of Universal Declaration of Human Rights. Phosphorescent paper. Perf 11×11½ (with one elliptical hole on each horiz side).

3771	**1158**	1z.20 new blue and deep ultramarine	1·60	1·50

1159 Maryla Wereszczakówna and Moonlit Night

1160 *Piorun* (destroyer), 1942–1946

(Des J. Wysocki. Litho)

1998 (24 Dec). Birth Bicentenary of Adam Mickiewicz (poet). T **1159** and similar multicoloured designs. Phosphorescent paper. Perf 11½ (with one elliptical hole on each horiz side).

3772	55g. Type **1159**	65	60
3773	65g. Cranes flying over tomb of Maria Potocka	80	75
3774	90g. Burning candles and cross	1·10	1·10
3775	1z.20 House, field of flowers and Uhlan's shako	1·40	1·40
3772/3775	*Set of 4*	3·50	3·50
MS3776	61×76 mm. 2z.45 Mickiewicz (bust by Jean David d'Angers) (30×38 mm). Perf 11½×11 (with one elliptical hole on each vert side)	4·00	3·75

(Des T. Boguslawski. Litho)

1999 (4 Jan). 80th Anniversary (1998) of Polish Navy T **1160** and similar horiz design. Multicoloured. Phosphorescent paper. Perf 11×11½ (with one elliptical hole on each horiz side).

3777	55g. Type **1160**	65	60
	a. Pair. Nos. 3777/3778	1·40	1·30
3778	55g. *Piorun* (missile corvette), 1994	65	60

Nos. 3777/3778 were issued together in *se-tenant* pairs within the sheet.

1161 Dominoes

(Des J. Konarzewski. Litho)

1999 (5 Feb). Greetings stamps. Value expressed by letter. T **1161** and similar square design. Multicoloured. Phosphorescent paper. Perf 11½ (with one elliptical hole on each vert side).

3779	B (60g.) Type **1161**	1·20	60
3780	A (65g.) Dominoes (*different*)	1·30	75

No. 3779 was sold as the rate for postcards.

No. 3780 was sold as the rate for letters up to 20 grams.

1162 Ernest Malinowski and Railway Bridge over Verrugas Canyon

(Des J. Konarzewski. Litho)

1999 (12 Feb). Polish Engineers. T **1162** and similar horiz design. Multicoloured. Phosphorescent paper. Perf 11½ (with one elliptical hole on each horiz side).

3781	1z. Type **1162** (death centenary)	1·10	1·10
3782	1z.60 Rudolf Modrzejewski and Benjamin Franklin Bridge over Delaware River, Philadelphia	1·90	1·80

1163 Prayer in Ogrójec

1164 Chinese Ideograms

(Des J. Wysocki. Photo)

1999 (5 Mar). Easter. T **1163** and similar vert designs. Multicoloured. Phosphorescent paper. Perf 11½×11.

3783	60g. Type **1163**	65	60
3784	65g. Carrying the Cross	70	65
3785	1z. Pietà	1·10	1·10
3786	1z.40 Resurrection	1·60	1·50
3783/3786	*Set of 4*	3·75	3·50

Nos. 3783/3784 and 3786 show details of the *Grudziądz* polyptych.

(Des Malgorzata Osa. Litho)

1999 (31 Mar). China '99 International Stamp Exhibition, Peking. Sheet 80×96 mm. Phosphorescent paper. Perf 11½×11 (with one elliptical hole on each vert side).

MS3787	1z.70 multicoloured	3·00	2·75

1165 Victorious St Mary of Kozielsk (sculpture)

(Des J. Wysocki. Litho)

1999 (2 Apr). Images of Virgin Mary made by Polish Prisoners of War. T **1165** and similar vert design. Multicoloured. Phosphorescent paper. Perf 11½ (with one elliptical hole on each vert side).

3788	60g. Type **1165**	65	60
3789	70g. St Mary of Katyń (bas-relief, Stanislaw Balos)	80	75

1166 Jan Skrzetuski passing Zbara Fortress (*With Fire and Sword*)

(Des A. Gosik. Photo)

1999 (6 Apr). Heroes of The Trilogy (novels) by Henryk Sienkiewicz. T **1166** and similar horiz designs. Multicoloured. Phosphorescent paper. Perf 11½ (with one elliptical hole on each horiz side).

3790	70g. Type **1166**	80	75
	a. Block of 6. Nos. 3790/3795	5·00	
3791	70g. Onufry Zagloba and 17th-century map of Poland (at three parts)	80	75
3792	70g. Longinus Podbipięta defending Zbara and three Tartars (*With Fire and Sword*)	80	75
3793	70g. Bohun with Helena Kuncewiczówna on way to Czarci Jar (*With Fire and Sword*)	80	75
3794	70g. Andrzej Kmicic and cannon at Jasna Góra Monastery (*The Deluge*)	80	75
3795	70g. Michel Jerzy Wolodyjowski and Basia Jeziorkowska fencing (*Pan Michael*)	80	75
3790/3795	*Set of 6*	4·25	4·00

Nos. 3790/3795 were issued together in *se-tenant* blocks of six stamps within sheets of 12.

1167 Polish Flag and NATO Emblem

1168 Anniversary Emblem and Headquarters, Strasbourg

(Des J. Kornarzewski. Litho)

1999 (22 Apr). Accession of Poland into and 50th Anniversary of North Atlantic Treaty Organisation. Phosphorescent paper. Perf 11½ (with one elliptical hole on each horiz side).

3796 **1167** 70g. multicoloured 95 80

(Des M. Jędrysik. Litho)

1999 (5 May). 50th Anniversary of Council of Europe. Phosphorescent paper. Perf 11½×11 (with one elliptical hole on each vert side).

3797 **1168** 1z. multicoloured .... 1·60 1·50

1169 Three-toed Woodpecker

1170 Mountain Biking

(Des J. Desselberger. Litho)

1999 (5 May). Europa. Parks and Gardens. Bialowieski National Park. Phosphorescent paper. Perf 11½ (with one elliptical hole on each vert side).

3798 **1169** 1z.40 multicoloured .... 2·40 2·00

(Des J. Kornarzewski. Litho)

1999 (1 June). Youth Sports. T **1170** and similar horiz designs. Multicoloured. Phosphorescent paper. Perf 11½ (with one elliptical hole on each horiz side).

3799 60g. Type **1170** 70 65
3800 70g. Snowboarding 80 75
3801 1z. Skateboarding .... 1·30 1·20
3802 1z.40 Rollerblading .... 1·80 1·70
3799/3802 *Set of* 4 .... 4·25 3·75

1171 St Mary's Church, Cracow, Pope John Paul II and Crowd

(Des J. Wysocki. Litho)

1999 (5 June). Sixth Papal Visit to Poland. T **1171** and similar horiz designs. Multicoloured. Phosphorescent paper. Perf 12×11½ (with one elliptical hole on each vert side).

3803 60g. Type **1171** 60 55
a. Strip of 4. Nos. 3803/3806........
3804 70g. Pope and crowd with crosses........ 80 65
3805 1z. Pope and cheering teenagers........ 1·30 1·10
3806 1z.40 Eiffel Tower (Paris), *Christ the Redeemer* (statue, Rio de Janeiro), Pope and church at Fátima, Portugal........ 1·80 1·50
3803/3806 *Set of* 4 .... 4·00 3·50

1172 Ignacy Paderewski and Roman Dmowski (signatories)

1173 St Mary Carefully Listening (icon)

(Des M. Jędrysic. Litho)

1999 (28 June). 80th Anniversary of Treaty of Versailles. Phosphorescent paper. Perf 11×11½ (with one elliptical hole on each horiz side).

3807 **1172** 1z.40 multicoloured .... 1·80 1·70

(Des Z. Stasik. Photo)

1999 (9 July). St Mary's Sanctuaries. T **1173** and similar vert design. Multicoloured. Phosphorescent paper. Perf 11½×11 (with one elliptical hole on each vert side).

3808 60g. Type **1173** (church of St Mary Queen of Poland, Rokitno)........ 70 65
3809 70g. Mary (statue, Ms. Jazlowiecka), Convent of Order of the Immaculate Conception, Szymanów 80 75

1174 Great Diving Beetle (*Dytiscus marginalis*)

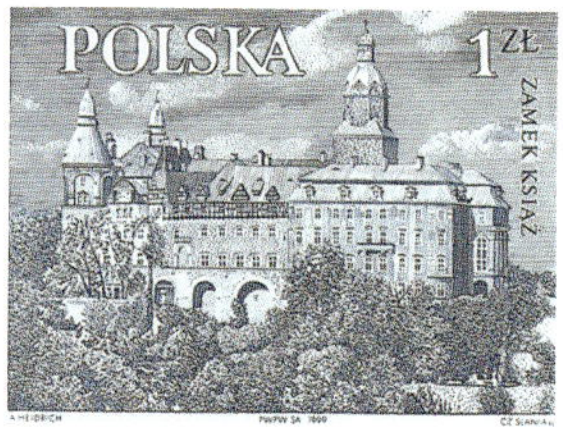

1175 Ksiaz Castle

(Des J. Brodowski. Litho)

1999 (16 July). Water Insects. T **1174** and similar horiz designs. Multicoloured. Phosphorescent paper. Perf 11½×12 (with one elliptical hole on each horiz side).

3810 60g. Type **1174** 80 65
3811 60g. *Corixa punctata* 80 65
3812 70g. *Limnophilus* .... 1·00 75
3813 70g. *Perla marginata* .... 1·00 75
3814 1z.40 Emperor Dragonfly (*Anax imperator*)........ 1·90 1·70
3815 1z.40 *Ephemera vulgata* .... 1·90 1·70
3810/3815 *Set of* 6 .... 6·75 5·50

(Des A. Heidrich. Eng C. Slania. Recess and photo)

1999 (14 Aug). Walbrzych '99 18th National Stamp Exhibition. Sheet 74×105 mm. Phosphorescent paper. Perf 11.

MS3816 1z. deep violet-blue........ 2·20 2·20

No. **MS**3816 also exists imperforate (*price* £24).

1176 Red Deer (*Cervus elaphus*)

1177 Emblem

(Des O. Koszel (No. 3817), J. Brodowski (No. 3818). Litho)

1999 (22 Sept). Eastern Carpathian Mountains International Biosphere Reserve (covering Polish, Ukrainian and Slovakian National Parks). T **1176** and similar horiz design. Multicoloured. Phosphorescent paper. Perf 11×11½ (with one elliptical hole on each horiz side).

3817 1z.40 Type **1176** .... 1·60 1·50
a. Pair. Nos. 3817/3818 .... 3·50 3·25
3818 1z.40 Wild Cat (*Felis silvestris*)........ 1·60 1·50

Stamps of a similar design were issued by Ukraine.

(Des S. Malecki. Eng W. Zajdel. 60g., 70g.) or P. Krajewski (others). Recess and photo)

1999 (25 Sept). Polish Rulers (14th series). Vert designs as T **893**. Phosphorescent paper. Perf 11.

3819 60g. olive-black, grey-olive and brown-olive ... 80 65
3820 70g. reddish brown and orange-brown ... 95 75
3821 1z. blue-black and dull ultramarine ... 1·30 1·10
3822 1z.40 deep dull purple and purple ... 1·90 1·60
3819/3822 *Set of 4* ... 4·50 3·75

Designs: 60g. Wladyslaw IV Waza; 70g. Jan II Kazimierz; 1z. Michal Korybut Wiśniowiecki; 1z.40 Jan III Sobieski.

(Des Agnieszka Sobczyńska. Litho)

1999 (9 Oct). 125th Anniversary of Universal Postal Union. World Post Day. Phosphorescent paper. Perf 11½ (with one elliptical hole on each horiz side).

3823 **1177** 1z.40 multicoloured ... 1·80 1·70

1178 Chopin and Academy of Fine Arts, Warsaw

(Des A. Heidrich. Eng C. Slania. Recess)

1999 (17 Oct). 150th Death Anniversary of Frédéric Chopin (composer). Phosphorescent paper. Perf 11×11½.

3824 **1178** 1z.40 blackish green ... 1·80 1·70

A stamp of a similar design was issued by France.

1179 Popieluszko

(Des M. Jędrysik. Litho)

1999 (19 Oct). 15th Death Anniversary of Father Jerzy Popieluszko. Phosphorescent paper. Perf 11½×11 (with one elliptical hole on each vert side).

3825 **1179** 70g. multicoloured ... 95 75

1180 Barbed Wire

1181 Angel (Silent Night)

(Des T. Boguslawski. Litho)

1999 (21 Oct). Homage to 20th-century Heroes of Poland. Sheet 93×70 mm. Phosphorescent paper. Perf 11½×11 (with one elliptical hole on each vert side).

MS3826 1z. multicoloured ... 1·90 1·80

(Des Agnieszka Sobczyńska. Litho)

1999 (26 Nov). Christmas. T **1181** and similar horiz designs inscr in Polish with the opening lines of carols. Multicoloured. Phosphorescent paper. Perf 11½ (with one elliptical hole on each horiz side).

3827 60g. Type **1181** ... 80 65
3828 70g. Angel (Sleep, Jesus Baby) ... 95 75
3829 1z. Angel (Let's Go Everybody to the Stable) ... 1·30 1·10
3830 1z.40 Angel (The God is Born) ... 1·90 1·60
3827/3830 *Set of 4* ... 4·50 3·75

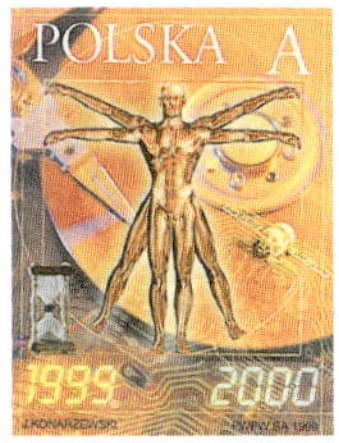

1182 Polish Museum, Rapperswil Castle, Switzerland

1183 Vitruvian Man (da Vinci)

(Des J. Wysocki. Litho)

1999 (6 Dec). Polish Overseas Cultural Buildings. T **1182** and similar vert designs. Multicoloured. Phosphorescent paper. Perf 11½ (with one elliptical hole on each vert side).

3831 1z. Type **1182** ... 1·30 1·10
3832 1z.40 Marian Priests' Museum, Fawley Court, England ... 1·90 1·60
3833 1z.60 Polish Library, Paris, France ... 2·10 1·70
3834 1z.80 Polish Institute and General Sikorski Museum, London, England ... 2·40 2·00
3831/3834 *Set of 4* ... 7·00 5·75

(Des J. Konarzewski. Litho)

2000 (2 Jan). New Year 2000. Phosphorescent paper. Perf 11½ (with one elliptical hole on each vert side).

3835 **1183** A (70g.) multicoloured ... 1·30 75

1184 Bronislaw Malinowski (sociologist)

1185 Otto III granting Crown to Boleslaw I

(Des W. Walkuski. Litho)

2000 (22 Feb). Polish Personalities. T **1184** and similar square design. Multicoloured. Phosphorescent paper. Perf 11½ (with one elliptical hole on each vert side).

3836 1z.55 Type **1184** ... 2·10 1·70
3837 1z.95 Józef Zwierzycki (geologist) ... 2·75 2·10

(Des M. Jędrysik. Photo)

2000 (12 Mar). 1000th Anniversary of the Gniezno Summit and the Catholic Church in Poland. T **1185** and similar multicoloured designs. Phosphorescent paper. Perf 11½×11.

3838 70g. Type **1185** ... 95 65
3839 80g. Archbishop of Gnesna, and Bishops of Cracovina, Wratislavia and Colberga ... 1·10 80
MS3840 77×65 mm. 1z.55 Provincial representatives presenting gifts to Otto III as Roman Emperor (*horiz*). Perf 11×11½ ... 2·40 1·90

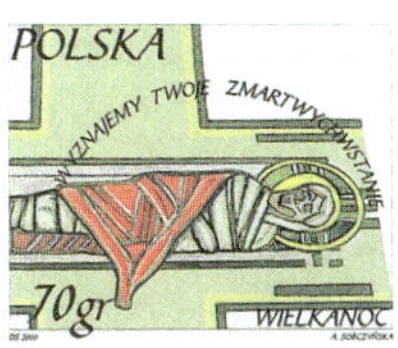

1186 Jesus in Tomb

(Des Agnieszka Sobczyńska. Litho)

2000 (24 Mar). Easter. T **1186** and similar horiz design. Multicoloured. Phosphorescent paper. Perf 11×11½ (with one elliptical hole on each horiz side).

3841 70g. Type **1186** ... 80 65
3842 80g. Resurrected Christ ... 95 80

1187 Saurolophus

(Des J. Brodowski. Litho)

2000 (24 Mar). Prehistoric Animals. T **1187** and similar horiz designs. Multicoloured. Phosphorescent paper. Perf 12×11½ (with one elliptical hole on each vert side).

3843		70g. Type **1187**	80	70
3844		70g. Gallimimus	80	70
3845		80g. Saichania	95	85
3846		80g. Protoceratops	95	85
3847		1z.55 Prenocephale	2·20	1·70
3848		1z.55 Velociraptor	2·20	1·70
3843/3848		*Set of* 6	7·00	5·75
MS3848*a*		150×145 mm. Nos. 3843/3848	12·00	8·75

1191 Dying Rose

(Des W. Walkuski. Litho)

2000 (28 Apr). Stop Drug Addiction Campaign. Phosphorescent paper. Perf 11×11½ (with one elliptical hole on each vert side).

3854	**1191**	70g. multicoloured	1·10	65

1188 Wajda

1189 Pope John Paul kneeling, St Peter's Basilica, Rome

(Des M. Buszewicz. Litho)

2000 (26 Mar). Presentation of American Film Academy Award to Andrzej Wajda (film director). Phosphorescent paper. Perf 11½ (with one elliptical hole on each horiz side).

3849	**1188**	1z.10 black	1·60	1·20
		a. *Tête-bêche* (pair)	3·50	2·50

No. 3849 was issued in *tête-bêche* pairs throughout the sheet.

(Des J. Wysocki. Litho)

2000 (7 Apr). Holy Year 2000. Opening of Holy Door, St Peter's Basilica, Rome. Phosphorescent paper. Perf 11½×11 (with one elliptical hole on each vert side).

3850	**1189**	80g. multicoloured	95	80

1192 Building Europe

1193 Pope John Paul II

(Des J.-P. Cousin. Litho)

2000 (9 May). Europa. Phosphorescent paper. Perf 11½ (with one elliptical hole on each vert side).

3855	**1192**	1z.55 multicoloured	3·25	3·00

(Des and eng C. Slania. Recess and litho (No. 3857) or recess (others))

2000 (9 May). 80th Birthday of Pope John Paul II. T **1193** and similar vert designs. Phosphorescent paper. Perf 13.

3856		80g. deep reddish violet	1·10	90
3857		1z.10 multicoloured	1·40	1·20
3858		1z.55 deep bluish green	2·10	1·70
3856/3858		*Set of* 3	4·25	3·50

Designs: No. 3856, T **1193**; No. 3857, Holy Mother, Częstochowa; No. 3858, Pastoral Staff.

Stamps of a similar design were issued by Vatican City.

1190 Artist and Model, Poster for *Wesele* (play), and Building

(Des M. Jędrysik (Nos. 3851/3852), A. Heidrich (No. 3853). Eng C. Slania (No. 3853). Litho (Nos. 3851/3852) or recess (No. 3853))

2000 (26 Apr). Crakow, European City of Culture. T **1190** and similar horiz designs. Phosphorescent paper. Perf 11½×11 (with one elliptical hole on each horiz side).

3851	**1190**	70g. multicoloured	80	75
3852	-	1z.55 multicoloured	2·40	2·30
MS3853		110×77 mm. 1z.75 blue (39×30 mm). Perf 11×11½	3·25	3·25

Designs: As T **1190**—No. 3852, Jagiellonian University, Pope John Paul II, Queen Jadwiga and Krzysztof Penderecki (composer). 38×30 mm—No. **MS**3853, View of Crackow (wood carving), 1489.

No. **MS**3853 also exists imperforate (*price* £32).

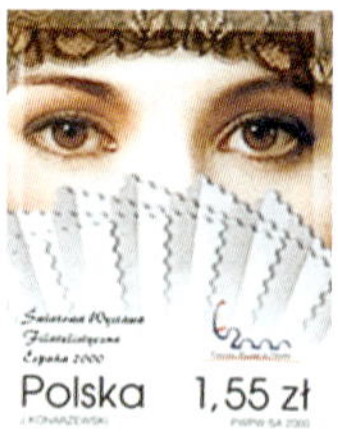

1194 Woman's Face and Fan

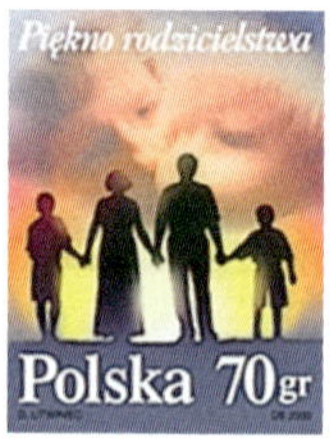

1195 Family

(Des J. Konarzewski. Litho)

2000 (26 May). Espana 2000 International Stamp Exhibition, Madrid. Phosphorescent paper. Perf 11½×11 (with one elliptical hole on each vert side).

3859	**1194**	1z.55 multicoloured	2·10	1·70

(Des D. Litwiniec. Litho)

2000 (31 May). Parenthood. Phosphorescent paper. Perf 11½×11 (with one elliptical hole on each vert side).

3860	**1195**	70g. multicoloured	80	65

1196 Cathedral Façade

(Des A. Gosik. Litho)

2000 (15 June). Millenary of Wroclaw. Sheet 70×90 mm. Phosphorescent paper. Perf 11×11½ (with one elliptical hole on each vert side).

MS3861	**1196** 1z.55 multicoloured	2·40	2·20

(Des M. Jędrysik. Litho)

2000 (23 June). Personalities. T **1197** and similar horiz design. Multicoloured. Phosphorescent paper. Perf 11×11½ (with one elliptical hole on each horiz side).

3862	70g. Type **1197** (founder of Scientific Assistance Association)	80	65
3863	80g. Josemaría Escrivá de Balaguer (founder of Priests' Association of St Cross, 1943)	95	80

1198 Gerwazy and the Count

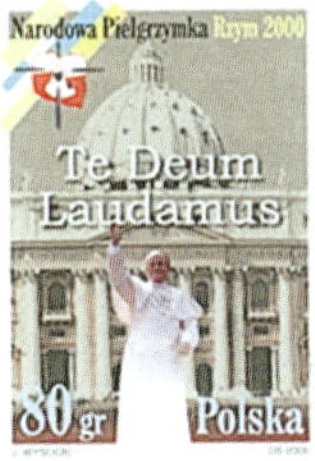

1199 Pope John Paul II and St Peter's Basilica, Rome

(Des A. Heidrich. Eng I. Zlotkowski (Nos. 3864/3865), P. Krajewski (Nos. 3866/3867), W. Zajalel (Nos. 3868/3869). Recess)

2000 (30 June). *Pan Tadeusz* (poem by Adam Mickiewicz). T **1198** and similar vert designs showing illustrations by Michal Elwiro Andriolli from the 1882 edition. Phosphorescent paper. Perf 11.

3864	70g. bistre-brown	80	65
3865	70g. bistre-brown	80	65
3866	80g. slate-green	95	80
3867	80g. slate-green	95	80
3868	1z.10 deep dull purple	1·40	1·20
3869	1z.10 deep dull purple	1·40	1·20
3864/3869	*Set of 6*	5·75	4·75

Designs: No. 3864, T **1198**; No. 3865, Telimenta reclining and the Judge; No. 3866, Father Robak, Judge and Gerwazy; No. 3867, Gathering in forest; No. 3868, Jankiel playing musical instrument; No. 3869, Zosia and Tadeusz.

(Des J. Wysocki. Litho)

2000 (1 July). National Pilgrimage to Rome. T **1199** and similar vert design. Multicoloured. Phosphorescent paper. Perf 11½ (with one elliptical hole on each vert side).

3870	80g. Type **1199**	95	80
3871	1z.55 Cross and Colosseum	2·10	1·70

1200 Self-portrait

1201 Mary and Jesus (painting), Rózanystok

(Des A. Balcerzak. Photo)

2000 (2 July). Birth Bicentenary of Piotr Michalowski (artist). T **1200** and similar multicoloured designs. Phosphorescent paper. Perf 11½×11 (70g., 80g.) or 11½ (others) (with one elliptical hole on each horiz side).

3872	70g. Type **1200**	80	65
3873	80g. *Portrait of a Boy in a Hat*	95	80
3874	1z.10 *Stable boy Bridling Percherons* (*horiz*)	1·40	1·20
3875	1z.55 *Horses with Cart* (*horiz*)	2·10	1·70
3872/3875	*Set of 4*	4·75	4·00

(Des Z. Stasik (No. 3876) and M. Jędrysik (No. 3877). Litho)

2000 (14 Aug). St Mary's Sanctuaries. T **1201** and similar vert design. Multicoloured. Phosphorescent paper. Perf 11½×11 (with one elliptical hole on each vert side).

3876	70g. Type **1201**	80	65
3877	1z.55 Mary with crown supported by Angles, Licheń	2·10	1·70

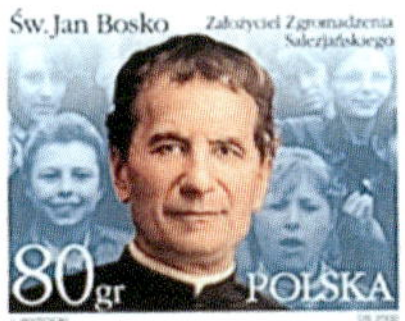

1202 John Bosco (founder of movement)

1203 Victory Sign

(Des J. Wysocki. Litho)

2000 (25 Aug). Salesian Society (religious educational institution) in Poland. Phosphorescent paper. Perf 11×11½ (with one elliptical hole on each horiz side).

3878	**1202**	80g. multicoloured	95	80

(Des T. Boguslaski. Litho)

2000 (31 Aug). 20th Anniversary of Solidarity Trade Union. Sheet 60×78 mm. Phosphorescent paper. Perf 11½ (with one elliptical hole on each vert side).

MS3879	1z.65 multicoloured	3·25	2·75

1204 Running

1205 Postman (Tomasz Wistuba)

(Des J. Wysocki. Litho)

2000 (1 Sept). Olympic Games, Sydney. T **1204** and similar horiz designs. Multicoloured. Phosphorescent paper. Perf 11½ (with one elliptical hole on each horiz side).

3880	70g. Type **1204**	80	65
3881	80g. Diving, windsurfing, sailing and kayaking	95	80
3882	1z.10 Weightlifting, high jump and fencing	1·40	1·20
3883	1z.55 Athletics, basketball and judo	2·10	1·60
3880/3883	*Set of 4*	4·75	3·75

(Des J. Konarzewski. Litho)

2000 (9 Oct). World Post Day. Winning Entries in Children's Painting Competition. T **1205** and similar multicoloured designs. Phosphorescent paper. Perf 11½×11 (70g.) or 11×11½ (others) (with one elliptical hole on two opposite sides).

3884	70g. Type **1205**	80	65
3885	80g. Customers and flying stork in Post Office (Katarzyna Chrzanowska) (*horiz*)	95	80
3886	1z.10 Post Office on stamp (Joanna Zbik) (*horiz*)	1·40	1·20
3887	1z.55 Woman at Post Office counter (Katarzyna Lonak) (*horiz*)	2·10	1·60
3884/3887	*Set of 4*	4·75	3·75

1206 Man with Postage Stamp Wings

(Des R. Konrad. Litho)

2000 (12 Oct). 50th Anniversary of Polish Philatelic Union. Sheet 75×60 mm. Phosphorescent paper. Perf 11×11½ (with one elliptical hole on each horiz side).

MS3888	1z.55 multicoloured	2·40	2·20

(Des S. Malecki. Eng T. Zlotkowski (70g.), P. Krajewski (1z.55), W. Zajdei (others). Recess and photo)

2000 (23 Oct). Polish Rulers (15th series). Vert designs as T **893**. Perf 11.

3889	70g. slate-black, brown-olive and light yellow-olive	1·10	65
3890	80g. black and dull purple	1·30	80
3891	1z.10 blue-black, deep blue and cobalt	1·80	1·20
3892	1z.55 black and purple-brown	2·20	1·60
3889/3892	*Set of 4*	5·75	3·75

Designs: 70g. August II; 80g. Stanislaw Leszczyński; 1z.10 August III; 1z.55 Stanislaw August Poniatowski.

1207 Priest and Cross

(Des J. Wysocki. Litho)

2000 (15 Nov). 60th Anniversary of Katyń Massacre. T **1207** and similar vert design. Multicoloured. Phosphorescent paper. Perf 11½ (with one elliptical hole on each vert side).

3893	70g. Type **1207**	1·00	65
3894	80g. Pope John Paul II kneeling at monument, Muranów	1·30	75

1208 Nativity

1209 Building Façade

(Des M. Jędrysik. Litho)

2000 (27 Nov). Christmas. T **1208** and similar vert designs. Multicoloured. Phosphorescent paper. Perf 11½ (with one elliptical hole on each vert side).

3895	70g. Type **1208**	80	65
3896	80g. Wedding at Cana	95	80
3897	1z.10 The Last Supper	1·40	1·20
3898	1z.55 The Ascension	2·10	1·60
3895/3898	*Set of 4*	4·75	3·75

(Des A. Gosik. Litho)

2000 (4 Dec). Centenary of Warsaw Art Gallery. Phosphorescent paper. Perf 11½×11 (with one elliptical hole on each vert side).

3899	**1209**	70g. multicoloured	80	65

1210 Privately Issued Stamp

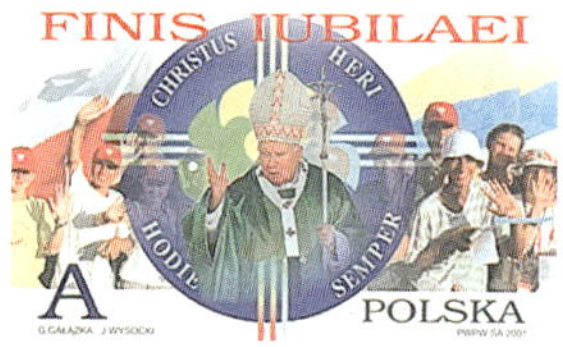

1211 Pope John Paul II, Emblem and Crowd

(Des M. Buszewicz. Litho)

2000 (13 Dec). Underground Post during Martial Law, 1982–1989. Phosphorescent paper. Perf 11½×11 (with one elliptical hole on each vert side).

3900	**1210**	80g. multicoloured	1·30	90
		a. *Tête-bêche* (pair)	2·75	1·90

No. 3900 was issued with a *se-tenant* label forming a composite design of the stamp.

(Des J. Wysocki. Litho)

2001 (6 Jan). End of Holy Year 2000. Value expressed by letter. Phosphorescent paper. Perf 12×11½ (with one elliptical hole on each vert side).

3901	**1211**	A (1z.) multicoloured	1·70	1·10

1212 Mountains reflected in Ski Goggles

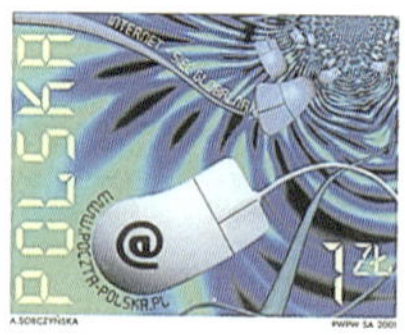

1213 Computer Mouse

(Des J. Konarzewski. Litho)

2001 (7 Feb). 20th University Games, Zakopane. Phosphorescent paper. Perf 11×11½ (with one elliptical hole on each horiz side).

3902	**1212**	1z. multicoloured	1·30	1·10

(Des Agnieszka Sobczyńska. Litho)

2001 (22 Feb). The Internet. Phosphorescent paper. Perf 11×11½ (with one elliptical hole on each horiz side).

3903	**1213**	1z. multicoloured	1·60	1·10

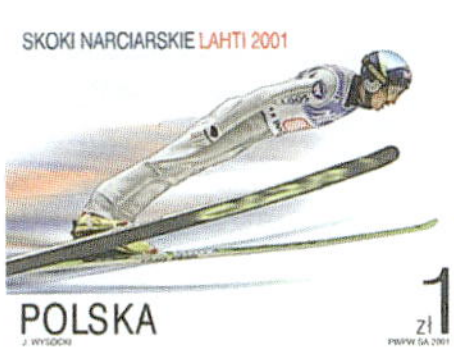

1214 Adam Malysz (ski jumper)

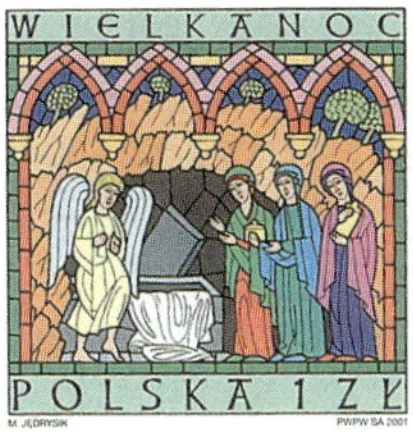

1215 Tomb of the Resurrected Christ

(Des J. Wysocki. Litho)

2001 (23 Feb). World Classic Seniors Championships, Lahti. T **1214** and similar horiz designs. Multicoloured. Phosphorescent paper. Perf 11½ (with one elliptical hole on each horiz side).

3904	1z. Type **1214**	1·30	1·10
3905	1z. As Type **1214** but additionally inscribed 'Adam Malysz'	1·30	1·10
3906	1z. As No. 3905 but additionally inscribed Mistrzem Świata	1·60	1·10
3904/3906	*Set of 3*	3·75	3·00

(Des M. Jędrysik. Litho)

2001 (16 Mar). Easter. T **1215** and similar square design. Multicoloured. Phosphorescent paper. Perf 11½ (with one elliptical hole on each vert side).

3907	1z. Type **1215**	1·30	1·10
3908	1z.90 Resurrected Christ and Apostles	2·40	2·00

1216 Emblem and Basketball Players

(Des D. Litwiniec. Litho)

2001 (28 Apr). 12th Salesian Youth World Championships, Warsaw. Phosphorescent paper. Perf 12×11½ (with one elliptical hole on each vert side).

3909	**1216**	1z. multicoloured	1·30	1·10

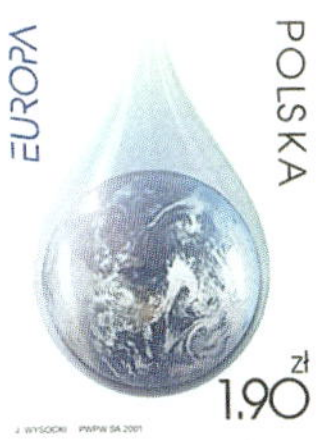

1217 Water Droplet

1218 Man and Mermaid on Beach (Holiday Greetings)

(Des J. Wysocki. Litho)

2001 (5 May). Europa. Water Resources. Phosphorescent paper. Perf 11½×11 (with one elliptical hole on each vert side).

3910	**1217**	1z.90 multicoloured	2·40	2·30

(Des W. Terechowicz. Litho)

2001 (10 May). Greetings Stamps. T **1218** and similar vert design. Multicoloured. Phosphorescent paper. Perf 11½×12 (with one elliptical hole on each vert side).

3911	1z. Type **1218**	1·30	1·10
3912	1z. Man presenting bouquet to woman (Best Wishes)	1·30	1·10

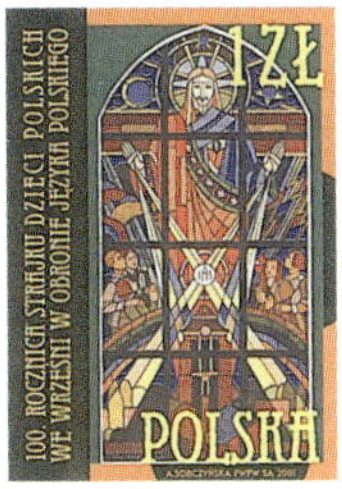

1219 Christ blessing Children of Września (Marian Turwid) (stained glass window), Parish Church, Września

1220 Polish Scientific Institute and Wanda Stachiewicz Library, Montréal, Canada

(Des Agnieszka Sobczyńska. Litho)

2001 (20 May). Centenary of Support of Września Schoolchildren for the Polish Language. Phosphorescent paper. Perf 11½ (with one elliptical hole on each vert side).

3913	**1219**	1z. multicoloured	1·30	1·10

(Des M. Buszewicz. Litho)

2001 (29 June). Polish Institutions Abroad. T **1220** and similar horiz designs. Multicoloured. Phosphorescent paper. Perf 11½ (with one elliptical hole on each horiz side).

3914	1z. Type **1220**	1·60	1·20
	a. *Tête-bêche* (pair)	3·50	2·50
3915	1z.90 Bust of Jósef Pilsudski, Jósef Pilsudski Institute, New York	3·00	2·30
	a. *Tête-bêche* (pair)	6·25	4·75
3916	2z.10 Polonia Museum, Archives and Library, Orchard Lake, Michigan	3·00	2·50
	a. *Tête-bêche* (pair)	6·25	5·25
3917	2z.20 Polish Museum, Chicago	3·25	2·75
	a. *Tête-bêche* (pair)	6·75	5·75
3914/3917	*Set of 4*	9·75	8·00

Nos. 3914/3917 were each issued in sheets of 20 the lower four rows printed *tête-bêche* with the top row upright thus giving eight *tête-bêche* pairs.

1221 Snowdrop (*Galanthus nivalis*) and European Lynx (*Lynx lynx*)

1222 Cardinal Wyszyński and Text

(Des A. Balcerzak. Litho)

2001 (10 July). Convention on International Trade of Wild Animals and Plants Threatened with Extinction (CITES). T **1221** and similar horiz designs. Multicoloured. Phosphorescent paper. Perf 11½ (with one elliptical hole on each horiz side).

3918	1z. Type **1221**	1·40	1·20
3919	1z. Apollo Butterfly (*Parnassius apollo*) and Orchid (*Orchis sambucina*)	1·40	1·20
3920	1z. Eagle Owl (*Bubo bubo*) and *Adonis vernalis* (plant)	1·40	1·20
3921	1z.90 Lady's Slipper Orchid (*Cypripedium calceolus*) and Brown Bear (*Ursus arctos*)	2·75	2·30
3922	1z.90 Peregrine Falcon (*Falco peregrinus*) and *Orchis pallens*	2·75	2·30
3923	1z.90 Wide Leaf Orchid (*Orchis latifolia*) and European Otter (*Lutra lutra*)	2·75	2·30
3918/3923	*Set of 6*	11·00	9·50
MS3924	90×70 mm. 2z. World map and emblem (35×28 mm)	3·25	3·00

(Des J. Konarzewski. Litho)

2001 (3 Aug). Birth Centenary of Cardinal Stefan Wyszyński. (Primate of Poland 1948–1981). Phosphorescent paper. Perf 11½ (with one elliptical hole on each horiz side).

3925	**1222**	1z. multicoloured	1·90	1·20

1223 Kolbe and Handwriting

1224 St Mary of the Beautiful Love (icon)

(Des M. Jędrysik. Litho)

2001 (14 Aug). 60th Death Anniversary of Maksymilian Maria Kolbe (founder of Knighthood of the Immaculate, and concentration camp victim). Phosphorescent paper. Perf 11½ (with one elliptical hole on each horiz side).

3926 **1223** 1z. multicoloured .... 1·90 90

(Des M. Jędrysik (No. 3928) and Z. Stasik (others). Litho)

2001 (14 Aug). St Mary's Sanctuaries. T **1224** and similar vert designs. Multicoloured. Phosphorescent paper. Perf 11½×11 (with one elliptical hole on each vert side).

3927 1z. Type **1224** (Cathedral of St Martin and St Nicolas, Bydgoszcz) .... 1·40 1·20
3928 1z. St Mary of Ludźmierz, Basilica of the Assumption of St Mary, Ludźmierz .... 1·40 1·20
3929 1z.90 St Mary the Winner, Church of St Mary in Piasek, Wroclaw .... 2·75 2·30
3927/3929 *Set of* 3 .... 5·00 4·25

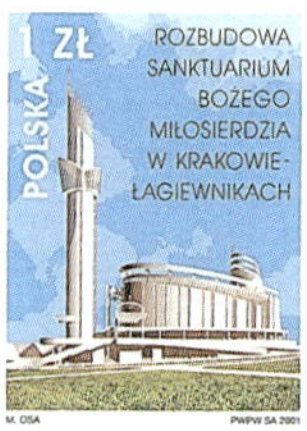

1225 Model of Sanctuary

1226 Ligia, Vinius and Petrinius

(Des M. Osa. Litho)

2001 (31 Aug). Completion of Section of God's Mercy Sanctuary at Cracow-Lagiewniki. Phosphorescent paper. Perf 11½×11 (with one elliptical hole on each vert side).

3930 **1225** 1z. multicoloured .... 1·50 1·30

(Des J. Wysocki. Litho)

2001 (1 Sept). *Quo Vadis* (film directed by Jerzy Kawalerowicz). T **1226** and similar horiz designs depicting scenes from the film. Multicoloured. Phosphorescent paper. Perf 11½ (with one elliptical hole on each horiz side).

3931 1z. Type **1226** .... 1·60 1·30
a. Sheetlet of 6. Nos. 3931/3936 .... 9·75
3932 1z. Nero singing at feast .... 1·60 1·30
3933 1z. St Peter in the catacombs and the baptism of Chilon Chilonides .... 1·60 1·30
3934 1z. Chilon Chilonides and crowd fleeing .... 1·60 1·30
3935 1z. Liga tied to the back of a Bull and in the arms of Ursus .... 1·60 1·30
3936 1z. St Peter blessing Vincius and Liga .... 1·60 1·30
3931/3936 *Set of* 6 .... 8·75 7·00

Nos. 3931/3936 were issued together in *se-tenant* sheetlets of six stamps.

1227 Copper Furnace

(Des and eng M. Jędrysik. Litho (No. 3940) or recess and litho (others))

2001 (1 Sept). Euro Cuprum 2001 European Stamp Exhibition, Lubin. T **1227** and similar horiz designs. Multicoloured. Phosphorescent paper. Perf 11½ (with one elliptical hole on each horiz side).

3937 1z. Type **1227** .... 1·50 1·40
3938 1z.90 Engraver at work and men dressing copper sheets .... 2·75 2·20
3939 2z. Inking plates and engraving press .... 3·00 2·50
3937/3939 *Set of* 3 .... 6·50 5·50
MS3940 88×76 mm. 3z. 18th-century engraving of Lubin and burin (50×39 mm) .... 4·75 4·25

No. **MS**3940 also exists imperforate (*price* £15).

1228 *Battle of Chocim* (detail, Stanislaw Batowski-Kaczor) and Breastplate of Stanislaw Skórkowski's Armour

(Des A. Gosik. Litho)

2001 (10 Sept). One Century Passes it Over to Another Century Exhibition, Polish Military Museum, Warsaw. Phosphorescent paper. Perf 11½ (with one elliptical hole on each horiz side).

3941 **1228** 1z. multicoloured .... 1·60 1·30

1229 Steam and Electric Locomotives

(Des A. Gosik. Litho)

2001 (24 Sept). 75th Anniversary of Polish State Railways. Phosphorescent paper. Perf 12×11½ (with one elliptical hole on each vert side).

3942 **1229** 1z. multicoloured .... 1·60 1·30

1230 Street Scene (Marcin Kuroń)

(Des J. Konarzewski. Litho)

2001 (28 Sept). Winners of Poland in 21st Century (children's painting competition). T **1230** and similar square designs. Multicoloured. Phosphorescent paper. Perf 11½ (with one elliptical hole on each vert side).

3943 1z. Type **1230** .... 1·50 1·30
3944 1z.90 Rockets behind girl and boy (Agata Grzyb) .... 2·75 2·10
3945 2z. Futuristic car and house on wheels (Joanna Sadrakula) .... 3·00 2·30
3943/3945 *Set of* 3 .... 6·50 5·25

1231 Football and Players

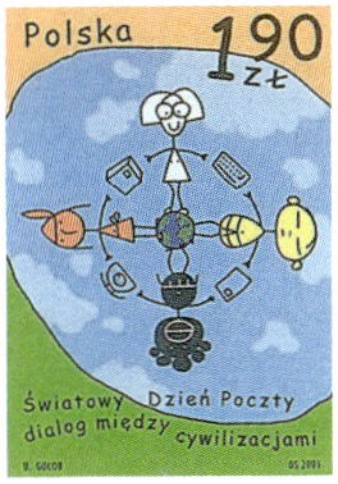

1232 Children encircling Globe

(Des J. Konarzewski. Litho)

2001 (6 Oct). Qualification of Poland for World Cup Football Championship, Japan and South Korea. Phosphorescent paper. Perf 11½×12 (with one elliptical hole on each horiz side).

3946	**1231**	1z. multicoloured	1·60	1·30

(Des Urska Golob. Litho)

2001 (9 Oct). World Post Day. United Nations Year of Dialogue among Civilisations. Phosphorescent paper. Perf 11½ (with one elliptical hole on each vert side).

3947	**1232**	1z.90 multicoloured	3·25	2·30
		a. *Tête-bêche* (pair)	6·75	4·75

1233 *100 Years Ago* (detail, Wlodzimierz Kugler)

1234 Violin Peg Box and Scroll

(Des Agnieszka Sobczyńska. Photo)

2001 (9 Oct). 80th Anniversary of Post and Telecommunication Museum, Wroclaw. Sheet 87×70 mm. Phosphorescent paper. Perf 11×11½.

MS3948	**1233**	3z.+75g. multicoloured	6·50	6·00

(Des M. Buszewicz. Litho)

2001 (13 Oct). 12th Henryk Wieniawski International Violin Competition, Poznań. Phosphorescent paper. Perf 11½ (with one elliptical hole on each horiz side).

3949	**1234**	1z. multicoloured	1·60	1·30

1235 Pope John Paul II

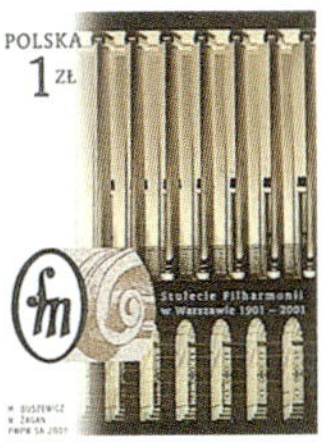

1236 Building Façade

(Des J. Wysocki. Litho)

2001 (14 Oct). Papal Day. Phosphorescent paper. Perf 11½ (with one elliptical hole on each vert side).

3950	**1235**	1z. multicoloured	1·60	1·30

(Des M. Buszewicz and W. Żagan. Litho)

2001 (5 Nov). Centenary of National Philharmonic Orchestra. Phosphorescent paper. Perf 11½ (with one elliptical hole on each vert side).

3951	**1236**	1z. multicoloured	1·60	1·30
		a. *Tête-bêche* (pair)	3·50	2·75

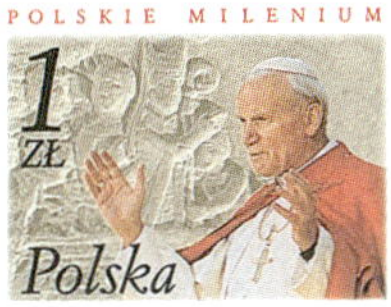

1237 Pope John Paul II

1238 Lower Silesian Crib

(Des T. Boguslawski. Litho)

2001 (11 Nov). New Millennium. T **1237** and similar horiz designs. Multicoloured. Phosphorescent paper. Perf 11½ (with one elliptical hole on each horiz side).

3952	1z. Type **1237**	1·50	1·30
	a. Sheetlet of 16. Nos. 3952/3967	25·00	
3953	1z. President Lech Wałęsa and cover of 1791 constitution	1·50	1·30
3954	1z. Covers of *Glos Wolny Wolność Ubespieczaiacy, Kultura, Zniewolony umysl* and *O skutecznym rad sposobie* (magazines)	1·50	1·30
3955	1z. Wojciech Boguslawski (actor and dramatist) and Jerzy Grotowski (director)	1·50	1·30
3956	1z. General Józef Piłsudski (soldier and President 1918–1922) and posters (1989)	1·50	1·30
3957	1z. NATO emblem and General Kazimierz Pulaski (soldier)	1·50	1·30
3958	1z. Nicolaus Copernicus and Aleksander Wolszczan (astronomers)	1·50	1·30
3959	1z. Jan of Glogów (wood engraving) (mathematician and astronomer) and Tadeusz Kotarbiński (physicist)	1·50	1·30
3960	1z. *Do Broni* (poster, 1920) and *Bitwa pod Grunwaldem* (detail) (painting, Jan Matejko)	1·50	1·30
3961	1z. Leaders of November Uprising, 1830	1·50	1·30
3962	1z. Head of John the Apostle (detail) (wooden altarpiece, Wit Stwosz) and sculpture by Magdalena Abakanowicz	1·50	1·30
3963	1z. Frédérik Chopin, Krzysztof Penderecki (composers) and score of *Mazurka No. 10* by Karol Szymanowski	1·50	1·30
3964	1z. Royal Castle, Warsaw and view of Cracow (wood engraving)	1·50	1·30
3965	1z. Jan III Sobieski (painting) and emblem of European Union	1·50	1·30
3966	1z. Wislawa Szymborska (Nobel Prizewinner for Literature) and Mikolaj Rej (poet)	1·50	1·30
3967	1z. Janusz Kusociński and Robert Korzeniowski (athletes)	1·50	1·30
3952/3967	*Set of* 16	22·00	19·00

Nos. 3952/3967 were issued together in *se-tenant* sheetlets containing two blocks of eight stamps separated by a central gutter.

(Des J. Wysocki. Litho)

2001 (27 Nov). Christmas. T **1238** and similar square design. Multicoloured. Phosphorescent paper. Perf 11½ (with one elliptical hole on each vert side).

3968	1z. Type **1238**	1·40	1·30
3969	1z.90 Lower Silesian Crib (*different*)	2·75	2·10

1239 Radio Station Building and Virgin Mary (statue)

1240 Pear and Apple

(Des J. Brodowski. Litho)

2001 (7 Dec). Tenth Anniversary of Radio Maryja (religious broadcasting station). T **1239** and similar horiz designs. Multicoloured. Phosphorescent paper. Perf 11×11½ (with one elliptical hole on each horiz side).

3970	1z. Type **1239**	1·60	1·30
MS3971	176×78 mm. 1z. Virgin Mary (statue) and crowd; 1z. Type **1239**; 1z. Crowd and crowned Virgin Mary (statue)	4·75	4·50

(Des M. Jędrysik. Litho)

2002 (4 Feb). Valentine's Day. Phosphorescent paper. Perf 11½ (with one elliptical hole on each horiz side).

3972 **1240** 1z.10 multicoloured .... 1·60 1·30

1241 Downhill, Biathlon, Ice Skating and Ski Jumping

(Des J. Konarzewski. Litho)

2002 (8 Feb). Winter Olympic Games, Salt Lake City, USA. Phosphorescent paper. Perf 11½×11 (with one elliptical hole on each horiz side).

3973 **1241** 1z.10 multicoloured .... 2·40 1·70

No. 3973 was issued with a *se-tenant* stamp-size label in sheets of 18 stamps and 18 labels.

1242 Jan Czerski

1243 Gniezno

(Des M. Jędrysik. Litho)

2002 (22 Feb). Explorers. T **1242** and similar horiz designs. Multicoloured. Phosphorescent paper. Perf 11½ (with one elliptical hole on each horiz side).

3974 2z. Type **1242** .... 3·00 2·30
3975 2z. Bronislaw Pilsudski .... 3·00 2·30

2002 (1 Mar)–**08**. Polish Cities. T **1243** and similar multicoloured designs. Phosphorescent paper. Perf 11½.

3976 5g. Sandomierz (*horiz*) (1.1.04) 35 20
3977 20g. Sieradz (29.7.05) 45 30
3978 30g. Katowice (*horiz*) (5.10.05) 55 40
3978*a* 1z.20 Toruń (31.1.03) .... 1·80 1·20
3978*b* 1z.25 Gdańsk (9.1.04) .... 1·90 1·30
3978*c* 1z.30 Poznań (*horiz*) (3.1.05) .... 2·00 1·40
3978*d* 1z.35 Gorzów Wielkopolski (19.1.07) .... 2·20 1·60
3978*e* 1z.45 Racibórz (1.7.08) .... 3·25 2·30
3978*f* 1z.80 Kalisz (1.7.02) .... 2·75 2·00
3978*g* 1z.90 Lódz (*horiz*) (14.5.04) .... 3·00 2·10
3978*h* 2z. Type **1243** 30 25
3978*i* 2z.10 Kraków 35 30
3978*j* 2z.20 Sopot (29.7.05) .... 3·75 2·75
3978*k* 2z.40 Częstochowa (*horiz*) (24.4.06) .... 4·00 3·00
3978*l* 2z.60 Plock (*horiz*) (1.7.02) .... 4·25 3·00
3978*m* 2z.80 Szczecin (*horiz*) (30.5.05) .... 4·50 3·25
3978*n* 3z.20 Warsaw 40 35
3978*o* 3z.40 Kazimierz Dolny (10.4.03) .... 1·80 90
3978*p* 3z.45 Lublin (*horiz*) (23.2.04) .... 1·60 95
3978*q* 3z.50 Przemyśl (bright green and deep green) (30.4.05) .... 5·25 4·00
3978*r* 3z.55 Chorzów (15.6.07) .... 5·50 4·25
3978*s* 3z.65 Jelenia Góra (1.8.08) .... 5·75 4·75
3975*a*/3978*bd* *Set of* 22 .... 65·00 48·00

No. 3978g was issued with a *se-tenant* Priority label.

1244 Flowers

1245 Labrador Retriever and Puppies

(Des A. Gosik. Litho)

2002 (8 Mar). Easter. T **1244** and similar vert design. Multicoloured. Phosphorescent paper. Perf 11½×12 (with one elliptical hole on each horiz side).

3979 1z.10 Type **1244** .... 1·60 90
3980 2z. Chicks .... 2·75 1·50

(Des J. Wysocki. Litho)

2002 (25 Mar). Domestic and Wild Animals. T **1245** and similar horiz designs. Multicoloured. Phosphorescent paper. Perf 12×11½ (with one elliptical hole on each vert side).

3981 1z.10 Type **1245** .... 1·60 90
a. Horiz strip of 4. Nos. 3981/3984 .... 6·75
3982 1z.10 Cat and kittens .... 1·60 90
3983 1z.10 Wolf and cubs .... 1·60 90
3984 1z.10 Lynx and kittens .... 1·60 90
3981/3984 *Set of* 4 .... 5·75 3·25

Nos. 3981/3984 were issued together in horizontal *se-tenant* strips of four stamps within the sheet.

1246 Soldiers marching

1247 Trees (Amanda Żejmis)

(Des M. Osa. Litho)

2002 (26 Mar). 60th Anniversary of Evacuation of General Wladislaw Ander's Army from USSR. Phosphorescent paper. Perf 11½ (with one elliptical hole on each vert side).

3985 **1246** 1z.10 multicoloured .... 1·60 90

(Des M. Buszewicz. Litho)

2002 (17 Apr). Paintings. T **1247** and similar multicoloured designs. Phosphorescent paper. Perf 11½×11 (Nos. 3986/3987) or 11×11½ (others) (with one elliptical hole on each vert (Nos. 3986/3987) or horiz (others) side).

3986 1z.10 Type **1247** .... 1·60 90
3987 1z.10 Vase and ornaments (Henryk Paraszczuk) .... 1·60 90
3988 2z. Landscape (Lucjan Matula) (*horiz*) .... 3·25 1·50
3989 3z.20 Basket of flowers (Józefa Laciak) (*horiz*) .... 4·75 2·75
3986/3989 *Set of* 4 .... 10·00 5·50

1248 Stylised Figures

1249 Radio Microphone

(Des J. Wysocki. Litho)

2002 (30 Apr). National Census. Phosphorescent paper. Perf 11×11½ (with one elliptical hole on each horiz side).

3990 **1248** 1z.10 multicoloured .... 1·60 90

(Des J. Wysocki. Litho)

2002 (2 May). 50th Anniversary of Radio Free Europe. Phosphorescent paper. Perf 12×11½ (with one elliptical hole on each vert side).

3991 **1249** 2z. multicoloured .... 3·00 1·50

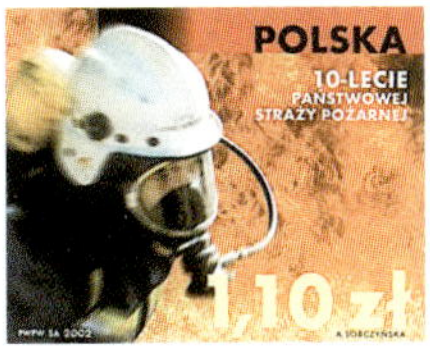

1250 Fireman

1251 Circus Artist

(Des Agnieszka Sobczyńska. Litho)

2002 (4 May). Tenth Anniversary of State Fire Brigade. Phosphorescent paper. Perf 11×11½ (with one elliptical hole on each horiz side).

3992 **1250** 1z.10 multicoloured ..... 1·60 90

(Des A. Pagowski. Litho)

2002 (5 May). Europa. Circus. Phosphorescent paper. Perf 11×11½ (with one elliptical hole on each vert side).

3993 **1251** 2z. multicoloured ..... 3·25 2·30

1252 *Madonna with the Child, St John the Baptist and the Angel* (Sandro Botticelli)

1253 Maria Konopnicka

(Des M. Buszewicz. Litho)

2002 (18 May). 140th Anniversary of the National Gallery, Warsaw. Phosphorescent paper. Perf 11½ (with one elliptical hole on each vert side).

3994 **1252** 1z.10 multicoloured ..... 1·70 90

(Des A. Heidrich. Eng C. Slania. Recess and photo)

2002 (23 May). 160th Birth Anniversary of Maria Konopnicka (poet and writer). Phosphorescent paper. Perf 11½×11.

3995 **1253** 1z.10 brown, ochre and turquoise-green ..... 1·60 90

1254 Scooter

1255 Football and Globe

(Des P. Pyzik. Litho)

2002 (31 May). Children's Games. T **1254** and similar vert designs. Multicoloured Phosphorescent paper. Perf 11½ (with one elliptical hole on each vert side).

3996 1z.10 Type **1254** ..... 1·60 90

a. Horiz strip of 3. Nos. 3996/3998 ..... 5·00

3997 1z.10 Flying kite ..... 1·60 90

3998 1z.10 Badminton ..... 1·60 90

3996/3998 *Set of 3* ..... 4·25 3·25

Nos. 3996/3998 were issued together in horizontal *se-tenant* strips of three stamps within sheets of six, the bottom row inverted, giving three vertical *tête-bêche* pairs (*price per sheet* £13).

(Des J. Konerzewski. Litho)

2002 (1 June). World Cup Football Championship, Japan and South Korea. T **1255** and similar vert design. Multicoloured. Phosphorescent paper. Perf 11½×11 (with one elliptical hole on each vert side).

3999 1z.10 Type **1255** ..... 1·60 90

a. Horiz pair, Nos. 3999/4000 ..... 4·75 2·50

4000 2z. Player chasing ball ..... 3·00 1·50

Nos. 3999/4000 were issued together in horizontal *se-tenant* pairs in sheetlets of four (*price per sheetlet* £12·50).

Nos. 4001/4014 are vacant.

1256 Domeyko and Santiago University, Chile

1257 Hibiscus and Tulips

(Des M. Jędrysik. Litho)

2002 (3 July). Birth Bicentenary of Ignacego Domeyki (scientist). Fluorescent paper. Perf 11½ (with one elliptical hole on each horiz side).

4015 **1256** 2z.60 multicoloured ..... 4·00 2·30

A stamp of a similar design was issued by Chile.

(Des J. Wysocki. Litho)

2002 (12 July). Philakorea 2002 International Philatelic Exhibition, Seoul and Amphile 2002 International Philatelic Exhibition, Amsterdam. Fluorescent paper. Perf 11½ (with one elliptical hole on each horiz side).

4016 **1257** 2z. multicoloured ..... 3·00 1·50

1258 Pope John Paul II and Basilica of Virgin Mary of the Angel, Kalwaria Zebrzydowska

1259 Holy Lady of Assistance

(Des J. Wysocki. Litho)

2002 (5 Aug). Seventh Papal Visit To Poland (1st issue). T **1258** and similar horiz design. Multicoloured. Phosphorescent paper. Perf 11½ (with one elliptical hole on each horiz side).

4017 1z.10 Type **1258** ..... 1·60 90

4018 1z.80 Pope John Paul II and Sanctuary of God's Mercy, Sisters of Virgin Mary's Convent, Łagiewniki ..... 3·25 1·50

See also No. **MS**4022.

(Des Z. Stasik. Litho)

2002 (14 Aug). St Mary's Sanctuaries. T **1259** and similar vert designs. Multicoloured. Phosphorescent paper. Perf 11½×11 (with one elliptical hole on each vert side).

4019 1z.10 Type **1259** (Church of the Holy Lady of Assistance, Jaworzno) ..... 1·60 90

4020 1z.10 Holy Virgin of Opole (Cathedral of Holy Cross, Opole) ..... 1·60 90

4021 2z. Holy Virgin of Trąbki (Church of the Assumption of the Holy Lady, Trąbki Wielkie) ..... 3·25 1·50

4019/4021 *Set of 3* ..... 5·75 3·00

1260 Pope John Paul II and Wawel Castle, Cracow

1262 Cześnik Raptusiewicz and Dyndalski

1261 Spa Building, Ciechocinku

(Des M. Jędrysik. Eng C. Slania. Recess)

2002 (16 Aug). Seventh Papal Visit To Poland (2nd issue). Sheet 73×57 mm. Phosphorescent paper. Perf 11×11½.
MS4022 **1260** 3z.20 black .... 6·50 5·00

(Des A. Heidrich. Eng C. Slania. Recess)

2002 (1 Sept). 18th Polish Philatelic Association Convention, Ciechocinku. Sheet 74×105 mm. Phosphorescent paper. Perf 11.
MS4023 **1261** 3z.20 chocolate .... 4·75 4·50
No. **MS**4023 also exists imperforate (*price* £14·50).

(Des M. Buszewicz. Litho)

2002 (12 Sept). *Zemsta* (Revenge) (film directed by Andrzej Wajda). Sheet 177×137 mm containing T **1262** and similar horiz designs showing scenes from the film. Multicoloured. Phosphorescent paper. Perf 11½ (with one elliptical hole on each horiz side).
MS4024 1z.10 Type **1262**; 1z.10 Klara and Waclaw; 1z.10 Papkin; 1z.10 Regent Milczek and Papkin; 1z.10 Regent Milczek and Cześnik Raptusiewicz; 1z.10 Podstolina and Klara .... 13·00 9·00

1263 Schwarzkopf Okl-359

(Des J. Brodowski. Litho)

2002 (21 Sept). Steam Locomotives. T **1263** and similar horiz designs showing locomotives from Wolsztyn Railway Museum. Multicoloured. Phosphorescent paper. Perf 12×11½ (with one elliptical hole on each vert side).
4025 1z.10 Type **1263** .... 1·60 90
a. Horiz strip of 4. Nos. 4025/4028 .... 10·00
4026 1z.10 Fablok 0149-7 .... 1·60 90
4027 2z. Krolewiec Tki3-87 .... 3·25 1·50
4028 2z. Express locomotive Pm 36-2 .... 3·25 1·50
4025/4028 *Set of* 4 .... 8·75 4·25
Nos. 4025/4028 were issued both separately in sheets of 20 stamps or together in horizontal *se-tenant* strips of four stamps within sheets of 12.
Stamps from the *se-tenant* sheetlets have elliptical holes towards the top of the vertical perforations whereas stamps from the individual sheets have the elliptical hole at the foot.

1264 Hands holding Pens

1265 Emblem

(Des M. Buszewicz. Litho)

2002 (9 Oct). World Post Day. Phosphorescent paper. Perf 11×11½ (with one elliptical hole on each horiz side.
4029 **1264** 2z. multicoloured .... 3·00 1·50

(Des A. Pągowski. Litho)

2002 (25 Oct). Anti-Cancer Campaign. Phosphorescent paper. Perf 11½ (with one elliptical hole on each horiz side).
4030 **1265** 1z.10 multicoloured .... 1·90 90

1266 Emblem

1267 St Stanislaw

(Des J. Wysocki. Litho)

2002 (25 Oct). 50th Anniversary of Polish Television. Sheet 185×115 mm containing T **1266** and similar horiz designs showing emblems of television programmes. Multicoloured. Phosphorescent paper. Perf 11×11½ (with one elliptical hole on each horiz side).
MS4031 1z.10 Type **1266** (TV News); 1z.10 TV Theatre; 1z.10 *Pegaz* (cultural programme); 1z.10 *Teleranek* (children's programme) .... 8·00 4·50

(Des W. Terechowicz. Litho)

2002 (8 Nov). Saints. Sheet 136×165 mm containing T **1267** and similar vert designs. Multicoloured. Fluorescent paper. Perf 11½×11 (with one elliptical hole on each vert side).
MS4032 1z.10 Type **1267**; 1z.10 St Kazimierz; 1z.10 St Faustyna Kowalska; 1z.10 St Benedict; 1z.10 St Cyril and St Methody; 1z.10 St Catherine of Siena .... 9·50 6·00

1268 Christmas Tree Baubles

1269 'POLSKA' superimposed on 'EUROPA'

(Des M. Kamler. Litho)

2002 (27 Nov). Christmas. T **1268** and similar horiz design. Multicoloured. Fluorescent paper. Perf 11×11½ (with one elliptical hole on each horiz side).
4033 1z.10 Type **1268** .... 1·60 90
4034 2z. Small purple and large yellow baubles .... 2·75 1·50

(Des M. Buszewicz. Photo)

2003 (18 Feb). Poland's Accession to European Union (1st issue). Negotiations. Perf 11×11½.
4035 **1269** 1z.20 multicoloured .... 1·90 1·80
See also No. 4067, 4069 and 4120.

1270 Pope John Paul II on Balcony of St Peter's Basilica, 1978

1271 Pope John Paul II

(Des O. Mauro and G. Fabrizio. Litho)

2003 (20 Mar). 25th Anniversary of the Pontificate of Pope John Paul II (1st issue). T **1270** and similar horiz designs. Multicoloured. Perf 14×13½.
4036 1z.20 Type **1270** .... 1·60 90
a. Sheet. Nos. 4036/4060 .... 41·00
4037 1z.20 Celebrating mass, Victory Square, Warsaw, 1979 .... 1·60 90
4038 1z.20 Addressing young people, Parc des Princes Stadium, Paris, 1980 .... 1·60 90
4039 1z.20 Assassination attempt, St Peter Square, 1981 .... 1·60 90
4040 1z.20 Giving homily surrounded by flowers, Portugal, 1982 .... 1·60 90
4041 1z.20 Kneeling in front of Holy Doors, start of Holy Year of Redemption, 1983 .... 1·60 90
4042 1z.20 Meeting Sandro Pertini, President of Italy, 1984 .... 1·60 90
4043 1z.20 International Youth Day, Rome, 1985 .... 1·60 90
4044 1z.20 First visit of Pope to Synagogue, 1986 .... 1·60 90

4045 1z.20 Inaugurating Year of Mary, 1987 ... 1·60 90
4046 1z.20 Visiting European Parliament, Strasbourg, 1988 ... 1·60 90
4047 1z.20 Meeting Mikhail Gorbachev, President Soviet Union, 1989 ... 1·60 90
4048 1z.20 Visiting lepers in Guinea-Bissau, 1990 ... 1·60 90
4049 1z.20 Addressing Bishop's Synod, 1991 ... 1·60 90
4050 1z.20 Pronouncing the Catechism, 1992 ... 1·60 90
4051 1z.20 Enthroned, Assissi, 1993 ... 1·60 90
4052 1z.20 Celebrating Mass in the Sistine Chapel, 1994 ... 1·60 90
4053 1z.20 Addressing the United Nations, 1995 ... 1·60 90
4054 1z.20 Walking through the Brandenburg Gate with Chancellor Helmut Kohl, 1996 ... 1·60 90
4055 1z.20 Celebrating Mass in Sarajevo, 1997 ... 1·60 90
4056 1z.20 With Fidel Castro, Cuba, 1998 ... 1·60 90
4057 1z.20 Opening door, Christmas, 1999 ... 1·60 90
4058 1z.20 With young people, World Youth Day, Rome, 2000 ... 1·60 90
4059 1z.20 Closing door of St Peter's Basilica, 2001 ... 1·60 90
4060 1z.20 Visiting the Italian Parliament, 2002 ... 1·60 90
4036/4060 *Set of 25* ... 36·00 20·00

Nos. 4036/4060 were issued in *se-tenant* sheets of 25 stamps.
Stamps of a similar design were issued by Vatican City.

(Des O. Mauro and G. Fabrizio. Silk screen printed)

2003 (20 Mar). 25th Anniversary of the Pontificate of Pope John Paul II (2nd issue). Die-cut perf 12½×13.

4061 **1271** 10z. silver ... 16·00 15·00

No. 4061 was silk screen printed on silver foil with self-adhesive pad covered by a peel-off protector on the back.
A stamp of a similar design were issued by Vatican City.

1272 Andrzej Modrzewski

1273 Christ Anxious

(Des M. Jędrysik. Eng W. Zajdel. Recess)

2003 (28 Mar). 500th Birth Anniversary of Andrzej Frycz Modrzewski (writer). Perf 11½×11.

4062 **1272** 1z.20 grey-black ... 1·80 90

(Des M. Osa. Photo)

2003 (28 Mar). Easter. Folk Sculpture. T **1273** and similar vert design. Multicoloured. Perf 11½×11.

4063 1z.20 Type **1273** ... 1·60 90
4064 2z.10 Christ Vanquisher ... 3·00 1·70

1274 Poznań Ancient and Modern

(Des A. Jeziorkowski. Eng P. Krajewski (No. 4066). Photo (No. 4065) or Recess (No. 4066))

2003 (15 Apr). 750th Anniversary of Poznań. T **1274** and similar horiz design. Perf 11½.

4065 1z.20 multicoloured ... 1·80 90
MS4066 95×72 mm 3z.40 cinnamon and brownish black (40×31 mm). Perf 11×11½ ... 4·75 3·50

Designs: 1z.20 T **1274**; 3z.40 Ancient view of city and city Arms.

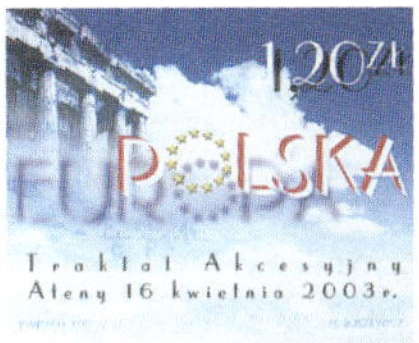

1275 Portico and Clouds

1276 Poster for Vanitas Exhibition (Wieslaw Walkuski)

(Des M. Buszewicz. Photo)

2003 (16 Apr). Poland's Accession to European Union (2nd issue). Perf 11×11½.

4067 **1275** 1z.20 multicoloured ... 1·90 1·40

2003 (5 May). Europa. Poster Art. Photo. Perf 11.

4068 **1276** 2z.10 multicoloured ... 3·25 2·30

1277 'POLSKA' superimposed on 'EUROPA'

1278 Island Palace (south view)

(Des M. Buszewicz. Photo)

2003 (26 May). Poland's Accession to European Union (3rd issue). Referendum. Perf 11×11½.

4069 **1277** 1z.20 multicoloured ... 1·90 1·40

(Des S. Wieczorek. Photo)

2003 (30 May). Royal Baths, Lazienki Park, Warsaw. T **1278** and similar horiz designs. Multicoloured. Perf 11×11½.

4070 1z.20 Type **1278** ... 1·80 90
4071 1z.80 Island Palace (north view) ... 2·50 1·40
4072 2z.10 Myślewicki Palace ... 3·00 1·50
4073 2z.60 Amphitheatre ... 3·75 2·30
4070/4073 *Set of 4* ... 10·00 5·50

1279 Pyramids and Camel (Anna Golębiewska)

2003 (20 June). Children's Paintings. Stamp Design Competition Winners. T **1279** and similar multicoloured designs on theme My Dream Vacation. Photo. Perf 11.

4074 1z.20 Type **1279** ... 1·80 90
4075 1z.80 Girl windsurfing (Marlena Krejpcio) (*vert*) ... 2·50 1·40
4076 2z.10 Windsurfer and fish (Michal Korzeń) ... 3·00 1·50
4077 2z.60 Girl and hens (Ewa Zajdler) ... 3·75 2·30
4074/4077 *Set of 4* ... 10·00 5·50

1280 *Krak* (anonymous)

1281 Katowice Cathedral

(Des J. Stanny. Photo)

2003 (30 June). Fairy Tales. T **1280** and similar vert designs. Multicoloured. Perf 11.

4078	1z.20 Type **1280**	1·80	90
4079	1z.80 *Stupid Mateo* (Josef Kraszewski)	2·50	1·40
4080	2z.10 *Frog Princess* (Antoni Gliński)	3·00	1·50
4081	2z.60 *Crock of Gold* (Jósef Kraszewski)	3·75	2·30
4078/4081	*Set of* 4	10·00	5·50

(Des Magdalena Jonczyk. Eng W. Zajdel. Recess and photo)

2003 (18 Aug). Katowice 2003 National Stamp Exhibition. Sheet 94×71 mm. Perf 11½×11.

MS4082 **1281**	3z.40 brownish black, orange-brown and yellow-ochre	5·50	3·75

No. **MS**4082 also exists imperforate (*price* £16).

1282 Self-portrait

1283 Posthorn

(Des J. Wysocki. Photo)

2003 (30 Sept). Birth Centenary of Julian Falat (artist). T **1282** and similar multicoloured designs. Perf 11½×11 (vert) or 11×11½ (horiz).

4083	1z.20 Type **1282**	1·80	90
4084	1z.80 *Spear Men*	2·50	1·40
4085	2z.10 *Winter Landscape with River and Bird* (*horiz*)	3·00	1·50
4086	2z.60 *Aboard Ship, Merchants of Ceylon* (*horiz*)	3·75	2·30
4083/4086	*Set of* 4	10·00	5·50

(Des A. Gósik. Photo)

2003 (9 Oct). World Post Day. Perf 11½×11.

4087 **1283**	2z.10 multicoloured	3·00	1·50

1284 Holy Virgin of Częstochowa

1285 Motorcycle (1903)

(Des Z. Stasik. Litho)

2003 (14 Oct). St Mary's Sanctuaries. T **1284** and similar vert designs. Multicoloured. Phosphorescent paper. Perf 11½×11.

4088	1z.20 Type **1284** (Church of the Holy Redeemer, Warsaw)	1·60	90
4089	1z.80 Holy Mother Benevolent (Basilica of Assumption of Holy Virgin, Krzeszowice)	2·40	1·40
4090	2z.10 Holy Virgin (Church of the Holy Virgin, Zieleniec)	3·25	1·50
4088/4090	*Set of* 3	6·50	3·50

(Des J. Konarzewski. Photo)

2003 (20 Oct). Centenary of Motorcycle Racing in Poland. T **1285** and similar horiz designs. Multicoloured. Perf 11×11½.

4091	1z.20 Type **1285**	1·60	90
	a. Strip of 3. Nos. 4091/4093	5·00	
4092	1z.20 Rudge (*circa* 1930)	1·60	90
4093	1z.20 NSU (*circa* 1940)	1·60	90
4091/4093	*Set of* 3	4·25	2·40

Nos. 4091/4093 were issued in horizontal *se-tenant* strips of three within sheets of 12 stamps.

1286 Dancers wearing Traditional Costume

1287 Perching Adult holding Fish

(Des J. Konarzewski. Photo)

2003 (29 Oct). 50th Anniversary of Folk Dance Troup Ślask. T **1286** and similar vert design. Multicoloured. Perf 11½×11.

4094	1z.20 Type **1286**	1·60	90
	a. Pair. Nos. 4094/4095	3·50	1·90
4095	1z.20 Dancers (*different*)	1·60	90

Nos. 4094/4095 were issued in horizontal *se-tenant* pairs within sheets of four stamps, each pair forming a composite design (*price for sheet* £9).

(Des J. Brodowski. Photo)

2003 (31 Oct). Endangered Species. Osprey (*Pandion haliaetus*). T **1287** and similar vert designs. Multicoloured. Perf 11½×11.

4096	1z.20 Type **1287**	1·60	90
	a. Strip of 4. Nos. 4096/4099	6·75	
	b. Sheet of 8. Nos. 4096/4099, each×2	17·00	
4097	1z.20 Adult and chicks on nest	1·60	90
4098	1z.20 Adult catching fish (one wing visible)	1·60	90
4099	1z.20 Adult carrying fish (both wings visible)	1·60	90
4096/4099	*Set of* 4	5·75	3·25

Nos. 4096/4099 were issued in horizontal *se-tenant* strips of four within sheets of eight stamps, each strip forming a composite design.

1288 Two White Storks

1289 The Nativity

(Des J. Wysocki. Photo)

2003 (31 Oct). www.poland.gov.pl (Poland on the internet). Perf 11×11½.

4100 **1288**	2z.10 multicoloured	3·00	1·50

(Des A. Gósik. Photo)

2003 (27 Nov). Christmas. T **1289** and similar multicoloured designs. Perf 11½ (with one elliptical hole on each horiz (Nos. 4101/4102) or vert (Nos. 4103/4104) side).

4101	1z.20 Type **1289**	1·80	90
4102	1z.80 Three Kings	2·50	1·40
4103	2z.10 Angel appearing to Mary (*vert*)	3·00	1·50
4104	2z.60 Holy Family (*vert*)	3·75	2·30
4101/4104	*Set of* 4	10·00	5·50

1290 Wislawa Szymborska

1291 Heart

(Des M. Jędrysik. Litho)

2003 (12 Dec). Polish Influence Abroad (1st series). T **1290** and similar designs showing designs from other countries' stamps. Perf 11½ (with one elliptical hole on each vert (Nos. 4106, 4108) or horiz (Nos. 4105, 4108) side).

4105 1z.20 brown-purple, slate-green and black.... 1·80 90
4106 1z.80 ultramarine, bright blue and black (*horiz*) .... 2·50 1·40
4107 2z.10 deep purple, pale azure and black......... 3·00 1·50
4108 2z.60 slate and black (*horiz*) .... 3·75 2·30
4105/4108 *Set of 4*........ 10·00 5·50

Designs: 1z.20 Wislawa Szymborska (writer) (as Sweden No. 2120); 1z.80 Marie Sklodowska-Curie (physicist) (as France No. 1765); 2z.10 Czeslaw Milosz (writer) (as Sweden No. 1299); 2z.60 Holy Virgin of Częstochowa (as Vatican City No. 481).

See also Nos. 4112/4113

(Des Y. Paszkiewicz. Photo)

2004 (5 Jan). Orchestra of Holy Day Assistance (fund raising charity). Perf 11×11½.

4109 **1291** 1z.25 multicoloured .... 1·60 90

1292 Airliner

(Des J. Brodowski. Photo)

2004 (21 Jan). 75th Anniversary of LOT (Polish airlines). Perf 11×11½.

4110 **1292** 1z.25 multicoloured .... 1·90 90

1293 Boy and Girl with Heart-shaped Balloon

(Des E. Luczyn. Photo)

2003 (2 Feb). St Valentine. Perf 11×11½.

4111 **1293** 1z.25 multicoloured .... 1·60 90

1294 Helena Paderewska

1295 Chocolate Rabbit

(Des M. Jędrysik. Litho)

2004 (27 Feb). Polish Influence Abroad (2nd series). T **1294** and similar horiz design. Multicoloured. Perf 11.

4112 2z.10 Type **1294** co-founder of USA Polish White Cross (humanitarian organisation)........ 3·00 1·50
4113 2z.10 Lucjan Bojnowski (New Britain, USA church pioneer)........ 3·00 1·50

(Des T. Boguslawski. Photo)

2004 (12 Mar). Easter. T **1295** and similar horiz design. Multicoloured. Perf 11×11½.

4114 1z.25 Type **1295** .... 1·60 90
4115 2z.10 Ceramic lamb .... 3·00 1·50

1296 Beaver and Frog

1297 Map of Europe and New Members' Flags

(Des J. Brodowski. Litho)

2004 (31 Mar). Fauna. T **1296** and similar horiz designs. Multicoloured. Perf 11½ (with one elliptical hole on each horiz side).

4116 1z.25 Type **1296** .... 1·60 90
a. Strip of 4. Nos. 4116/4119........ 6·75
4117 1z.25 Kingfisher, Crayfish, Roach and Water Beetle........ 1·60 90
4118 1z.25 Grayling, Leech and Water Snail........ 1·60 90
4119 1z.25 Pike, Grebe and Roach........ 1·60 90
4116/4119 *Set of 4*........ 5·75 3·25

Nos. 4116/4119 were issued in horizontal *se-tenant* strips of four within sheets of 20 stamps, each strip forming a composite design.

The strips were laid *tête-bêche* giving three strips upright and two upside down.

(Des J. Golik. Litho)

2004 (1 May). Poland's Accession to European Union (4th issue). Perf 11½ (with one elliptical hole on each vert side).

4120 **1297** 2z.10 multicoloured .... 4·00 2·30

No. 4120 was issued with a *se-tenant* stamp-size label showing arms.

1298 Rucksack as Landscape

1299 Figure (sculpture, St Mariacki Square, Krakow)

(Des J. Konarzewski. Litho)

2004 (5 May). Europa. Holidays. Perf 11½ (with one elliptical hole on each vert side).

4121 **1298** 2z.10 multicoloured .... 3·00 1·50

(Des M. Kopecki. Recess and photo)

2004 (7 May). Tenth Government Postage Stamp Printers' Conference, Krakow. Perf 11×12.

4122 **1299** 3z.45 multicoloured .... 4·75 2·50

No. 4122 was issued with a ½ stamp-size label attached at foot.

1300 Pope John Paul II

1301 Crimson Rosella (*Platycercus elegans*)

(Des M. Olivieri and F. Guarniera. Litho Cartor)

2004 (2 June). Pope John Paul II visits to Poland, 1979–2002. Two sheets, each 115×185 mm containing T **1300** and similar vert designs. Multicoloured. Two phosphor bands. Perf 13½×13.

MS4123 (a) 1z.25×4, Type **1300** (1979); At prayer (1983); Holding reliquary (1987); Resting head against staff (1991). (b) 1z.25×4, Holding staff (1991); With raised hand (1997); Seated facing right (1999); Seated facing left (2002) .... 16·00 13·50

The stamps of **MS**4123(a)/**MS**4123(b) were arranged in strips of three, each stamp with a *se-tenant* label at left and right.

The labels were inscribed with the either the Papal Arms or the Polish Arms and the year of the visit.

Stamps of the same design were issued by Vatican City.

(Des A. Balcerzak. Litho)

2004 (30 June). Birds. T **1301** and similar vert designs. Multicoloured. Perf 11½ (with one elliptical hole on each vert side).

4124	1z.25 Type **1301**	1·60	90
	a. Block of 4. Nos. 4124/4127	6·75	
4125	1z.25 Cockatiel (*Nymphicus hollandicus*)	1·60	90
4126	1z.25 Budgerigar (*Melopsittacus undulates*)	1·60	90
4127	1z.25 Spotted-side Finch (*Poephila guttata*), Gouldian Finch (*Chloebia gouldiae*) and Java Sparrow (*Padda oryzivora*)	1·60	90
4124/4127	*Set of 4*	5·75	3·25

Nos. 4124/4127 were issued in *se-tenant* blocks of four within sheets of eight stamps.

1302 *Self-portrait wearing White*

1303 Sun Wu-Kung (monkey king)

(Des J. Wysoki. Photo)

2004 (15 July). 150th Birth Anniversary of Jacek Malczewski (artist). T **1302** and similar multicoloured designs. Perf 11½×11 (vert) or 11×11½ (horiz).

4128	1z.25 Type **1302**	1·60	90
4129	1z.90 *Ellenai*	2·50	1·40
4130	2z.10 *Tobias with Harpy* (*horiz*)	3·00	1·50
4131	2z.60 *The Unknown Note* (*horiz*)	3·50	2·00
4128/4131	*Set of 4*	9·50	5·25

(Des E. Libera. Litho)

2004 (30 July). Singapore International Stamp Exhibition. Sheet 90×70 mm. Perf 11½ (with one elliptical hole on each horiz side).

MS4132 **1303** 3z.45 multicoloured .... 4·75 3·00

No. **MS**4132 also exists imperforate (*price* £19).

1304 Boxer

1305 Witold Gombrowicz

(Des J. Wysocki. Litho)

2004 (2 Aug). Olympic Games, Athens. Sheet 198×117 mm containing T **1304** and similar horiz designs. Multicoloured. Perf 11½ (with one elliptical hole on each horiz side).

MS4133 1z.25×4, Type **1304**; Hurdler; Show jumper; Wrestler .... 7·25 4·50

The stamps and margin of No. **MS**4133 form a composite design.

(Des B. Paczowski. Litho)

2004 (4 Aug). Birth Centenary of Witold Gombrowicz (writer). Perf 11½. (with one elliptical hole on each vert side).

4134	**1305**	1z.25 ultramarine	1·60	90
		a. *Tête-bêche* (pair)	3·50	1·90

1306 Holy Mother of Miedzna

1307 Czeslaw Niemen

(Des J. Pietras (Nos. 4135, 4137, 4143 and 4149), E. Libera (Nos. 4136, 4139, 4142 and 4146), M. Osa (Nos. 4138 and 4141), M. Jędrysik (Nos. 4140, 4145, 4147/4148 and 4150) or W. Terechowicz (Nos. 4144 and 4151). Litho)

2004 (14 Aug). St Mary's Sanctuaries. T **1306** and similar vert designs. Multicoloured. Perf 11½×11 (with one elliptical hole on each vert side).

4135	1z.25 Type **1306** (Church of the Annunciation of Our Lady of Miedzna)	1·90	90
4136	1z.25 Holy Mary and Family (John the Baptist Basilica, Studiazianna)	1·90	90
4137	1z.25 Holy Virgin of Sianow (Church of the Nativity of Our Lady of Sianów)	1·90	90
4138	1z.25 Holy Mary of Rywald (St Sebastian and Nativity of Our Lady, Rywald)	1·90	90
4139	1z.25 Holy Mary of Piekary (Name of Our Lady and St Bartholome Basilica,Piekary Slaskie)	1·90	90
4140	1z.25 Holy Mary of Ruda (Assumption of Our Lady Church, Ruda)	1·90	90
4141	1z.25 Holy Mary of Lomża (Archangel St Michael Cathedral, Lomża)	1·90	90
4142	1z.25 Holy Mary of Perpetual Assistance (Barefoot Carmelite Convent, Niedzwiady)	1·90	90
4143	1z.25 Holy Mary of Rychwald (St Nicholas and Our Lady of Scapular, Rychwald)	1·90	90
4144	1z.25 Crying Holy Mary (St John the Baptist and Evangelist, Lublin)	1·90	90
4145	1z.25 Holy Mary of Dzików (Assumption of Our Lady Convent, Tarnobrzeg)	1·90	90
4146	1z.25 Holy Mary of Rzeszów (Assumption of Our Lady Church, Rzeszów)	1·90	90
4147	1z.25 Gracious Holy Mary (St Stanislaw, St Peter and St Paul, Lubaczów)	1·90	90
4148	1z.25 Holy Mother of Fátima (Immaculate Heart of Our Lady of Fátima, Szczecin)	1·90	90
4149	1z.25 Pietà of Skrzatusz (Assumption of Our lady Church, Skrzatusz)	1·90	90
4150	1z.25 Pietà of Obory (Visitation of Our Lady Church, Obory)	1·90	90
4151	1z.25 Holy Mary of Jasnagora (Queen of Poland Sanctuary, Jasnagora)	1·90	90
4135/4151	*Set of 17*	29·00	14·00

(Des J. Konarzewski. Litho)

2004 (30 Aug). Czeslaw Wydrzycki (Niemen) (musician) Commemoration. Perf 11½ (with one elliptical hole on each horiz side).

4152	**1307**	1z.25 black	2·40	90

1308 Raft on River Dunajec

1309 Motorcyclists

(Des J. Brodowski. Litho)

2004 (3 Sept). Raft Men working on River Dunajec (bordering Slovakia and Poland). Perf 11½ (with one elliptical hole on each horiz side).

4153	**1308**	2z.10 multicoloured	3·25	1·50

A stamp of the same design was issued by Slovakia.

(Des J. Konarzewski. Litho)

2004 (11 Sept). Motor Sports. T **1309** and similar horiz designs. Multicoloured. Perf 11×11½ (with one elliptical hole on each horiz side).

4154	1z.25 Type **1309**	1·80	90
	a. Strip of 4. Nos. 4154/4157	7·50	
4155	1z.25 Race car	1·80	90
4156	1z.25 Kart racing	1·80	90

4157 1z.25 Motorcyclist (2004 International Six Day's Enduro) .... 1·80 90
4154/4157 *Set of 4* .... 6·50 3·25

Nos. 4154/4157 were issued in *se-tenant* strips of four stamps within the sheet, each strip forming a composite design.

1310 Binary Codes forming Postman

1311 Holy Mary Church, Kraków

(Des M. Jędrysik. Litho)

2004 (9 Oct). World Post Day. Perf 11½ (with one elliptical hole on each horiz side).

4158 **1310** 2z.10 multicoloured .... 3·00 1·50

(Des A. Gósik. Litho)

2004 (20 Oct). World Heritage Sites. T **1311** and similar multicoloured designs. Perf 11½ (with one elliptical hole on each vert (Nos 4159/4161) or horiz side (Nos. 4162/4163)).

4159 1z.25 Type **1311** .... 1·90 90
4160 1z.25 Tower, St John the Baptist and Evangelist Cathedral, Toruń .... 1·90 90
4161 1z.25 Town Hall, Zamość .... 1·90 90
4162 1z.25 Riverside, Warsaw (*horiz*) .... 1·90 90
4163 1z.25 Castle, Malbork (*horiz*) .... 1·90 90
4159/4163 *Set of 5* .... 8·50 4·00

1312 People entering Church

1313 Protoplanet circling Sun

(Des J. Brodowski. Photo)

2004 (5 Nov). Christmas. T **1312** and similar multicoloured design. Perf 11½.

4164 1z.25 Type **1312** .... 1·80 90
4165 2z.10 Decorated window (*horiz*) .... 3·00 1·50

(Des J. Pietras. Litho)

2004 (3 Dec). History of Earth. T **1313** and similar horiz designs. Multicoloured. Perf 11½ (with one elliptical hole on each horiz side).

4166 1z.25 Type **1313** .... 1·80 90
a. Block of 4. Nos. 4166/4169 .... 7·50
4167 1z.25 Asteroids bombarding earth .... 1·80 90
4168 1z.25 Dinosaurs .... 1·80 90
4169 1z.25 International space station in orbit .... 1·80 90
4166/4169 *Set of 4* .... 6·50 3·25

Nos. 4166/4169 were issued in *se-tenant* blocks of four within sheets of eight stamps.

1314 '13'

1315 Konstanty Galczyński

(Des I. Tratkowski and J. Owsiak. Photo). Photo)

2005 (6 Jan). Orchestra of Holy Day Assistance (fund raising charity). Perf 11×11½.

4170 **1314** 1z.30 multicoloured .... 1·80 1·10

(Des A. Gósik. Photo)

2005 (14 Jan). Birth Centenary of Konstanty Ildefons Galczyński (writer). Perf 11½×11.

4171 **1315** 1z.30 multicoloured .... 1·80 1·10
a. *Tête-bêche* (pair) .... 3·75 2·30

1316 Mikolaj Rej

1317 Masked Swordsman and Carved Heart on Tree

(Des M. Buszewicz. Photo)

2005 (26 Jan). 500th Birth Anniversary of Mikolaj Rej (writer). Perf 11½.

4172 **1316** 1z.30 black and scarlet-vermilion .... 2·40 1·10

(Des A. Niemierko. Photo)

2005 (1 Feb). Greetings Stamp. Valentine's Day. Perf 11½.

4173 **1317** 1z.30 multicoloured .... 1·80 1·10

No. 4173 was also available in sheets of 20 stamps and 20 labels which could be personalised by the addition of a photograph, text or image.

1318 Rabbit

1319 *The Little Mermaid*

(Des Agnieszka Sobczyńska. Photo)

2005 (1 Mar). Easter. T **1318** and similar vert design. Multicoloured. Perf 12.

4174 1z.30 Type **1318** .... 1·80 1·10
4175 2z.20 Chick .... 3·00 1·70

(Des Agnieszka Sobczyńska. Litho)

2005 (15 Mar). Birth Bicentenary of Hans Christian Andersen (writer). T **1319** and similar vert design. Multicoloured. Perf 11½ (with one elliptical hole on each vert side).

4176 1z.30 Type **1319** .... 2·40 1·10
4177 1z.30 *The Snow Queen* .... 2·40 1·10

1320 Pope John Paul II

(Des A. Pagowski. Litho)

2005 (8 Apr). Pope John Paul II Commemoration (1st issue). Perf 11½×12 (with one elliptical hole on each vert side).

4178 **1320** 1z.30 multicoloured .... 2·40 1·10

See also No. **MS**4184

1321 Sky Diving

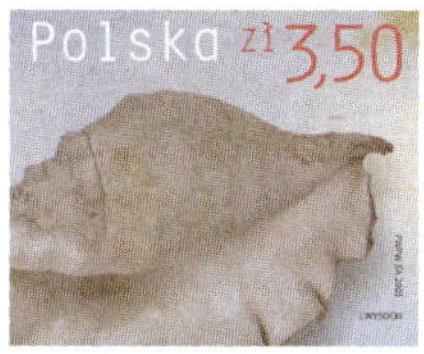

1322 Shell

(Des Magdalena Błażków. Litho)

2005 (15 Apr). Extreme Sports. T **1321** and similar vert designs. Multicoloured. Perf 11½ (with one elliptical hole on each horiz side).

4179 1z.30 Type **1321** .... 1·80 1·10
a. Block of 4. Nos. 4179/4182 .... 7·50
4180 1z.30 Bungee jumping .... 1·80 1·10
4181 1z.30 Rock climbing .... 1·80 1·10
4182 1z.30 White-water rafting .... 1·80 1·10
4179/4182 *Set of 4* .... 6·50 4·00

Nos. 4179/4182 were issued in *se-tenant* blocks of four stamps within the sheet.

(Des J. Wysocki. Litho)

2005 (21 Apr). Pacific Explorer International Stamp Exhibition, Sydney. Sheet 90×70 mm. Perf 11½ (with one elliptical hole on each horiz side).

MS4183 **1322** 3z.50 multicoloured .... 4·50 3·00

No. **MS**4183 was also available imperforate (*price* £22).

1323 Pope John Paul II **1324** Bread

(Des W. Terechowicz. Litho)

2005 (22 Apr). Pope John Paul II Commemoration (2nd issue). Sheet 70×83 mm. Perf 11½ (with one elliptical hole on each vert side).

MS4184 **1323** 3z.50 multicoloured .... 5·50 4·00

(Des M. Błażków and C. Hladki. Litho and embossed)

2005 (5 May). Europa. Gastronomy. Perf 11½ (with one elliptical hole on each horiz side).

4185 **1324** 2z.20 multicoloured .... 4·00 2·50

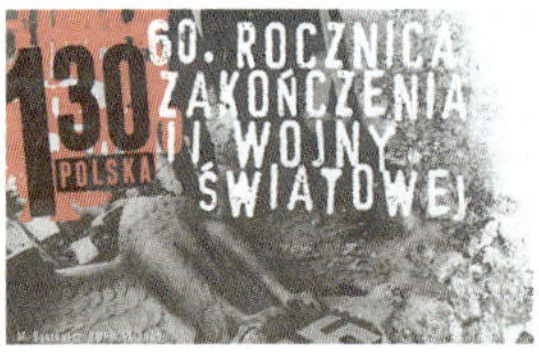

1325 Rubble

(Des M. Buszewicz. Litho)

2005 (6 May). 60th Anniversary of End of World War II. Perf 12×11½ (with one elliptical hole on each vert side).

4186 **1325** 1z.30 black and vermilion .... 1·80 1·10

1326 *The Hour of the Crimson Rose* (M. Krüger) **1327** *Stanislaw Kostka Potocki* (Jacques-Louis David)

(Des Agnieszka Sobczyńska. Litho)

2005 (1 June). Stories. Sheet 124×124 mm containing T **1326** and similar square designs. Multicoloured. Perf 12×11½ (with one elliptical hole on each vert side).

MS4187 1z.30 Type **1326**; 2z. *The Little Prince* (Antoine de Saint-Exupéry); 2z.20 *2000 Leagues under the Sea* (Jules Verne); 2z.80 *In the Desert and the Forest* (H. Sienkiewicz) .... 11·00 8·50

(Des J. Wysocki. Litho)

2005 (21 June). Bicentenary of National Museum, Wilanów. Sheet 95×130 mm containing T **1327** and similar vert designs. Multicoloured. Perf 12.

MS4188 1z.30 Type **1327**; 2z.17th-century Nautilus wine cup; 2z.20 Flower girl (18th-century porcelain); 2z.80 19th-century clock .... 11·00 8·50

1328 Embroidered Rose (Podhale) **1329** Hurdling

(Des E. Skrzypek and M. Malczyńska. Litho)

2005 (15 July). Embroidery. T **1328** and similar vert designs showing embroidered roses. Perf 11½ (with one elliptical hole on each vert side).

4189 1z.30 Type **1328** .... 1·80 1·10
4190 2z. Rose (Lowicz) .... 2·75 1·50
4191 2z.20 Rose (Lowicz) (*different*) .... 3·00 1·70
4192 2z.80 Rose (Lowicz) (*different*) .... 3·75 2·30
4189/4192 *Set of 4* .... 10·00 6·00

(Des Maria Dziekańska. Litho)

2005 (8 Aug). International Athletics Championship, Helsinki. Sheet 200×115 mm containing T **1329** and similar horiz designs. Multicoloured. Perf 11½ (with one elliptical hole on each horiz side).

MS4193 1z.30 Type **1329**; 1z.30 Shot put; 2z. Triple jump; 2z. Pole vault .... 12·00 8·25

1330 Józef Piłsudski (Commander in Chief) **1331** Lech Wałęsa (founder)

(Des Maria Dziekańska. Litho)

2005 (12 Aug). 85th Anniversary of Battle of Warsaw (Miracle on the Vistula). Sheet 70×90 mm. Perf 11½.

MS4194 **1330** 3z.50 multicoloured .... 5·50 4·00

(Des Maria Dziekańska. Litho)

2005 (17 Aug). 25th Anniversary of Solidarity (trade union). Perf 11½ (with one elliptical hole on each vert side).

4195 **1331** 2z.20 scarlet vermilion, dark grey and black .... 3·50 1·80

1332 '80' **1333** Music Score and Frédéric Chopin

(Des Maria Dziekańska. Litho)

2005 (1 Sept). 80th Anniversary of Radio. Perf 11½ (with elliptical hole on each vert side).

4196 **1332** 1z.30 rosine and black .... 1·80 1·10

(Des Maria Dziekańska. Litho)

2005 (16 Sept). Frederick Chopin International Piano Competition. Perf 11½ (with one elliptical hole on each horiz side).
4197 **1333** 2z.20 green, scarlet vermilion and black 3·00 1·80
Issued in sheets of four stamps (*price* £18).

1334 Lemur (*Opole*)

1335 Post Office Building, Cracow

(Des M. Błażków. Litho)

2005 (30 Sept). Zoological Gardens. T **1334** and similar vert designs. Each black. Perf 11½ (with one elliptical hole on each vert side).
4198 1z.30 Type **1334** 1·80 1·10
4199 2z. Siberian Tiger (*Panthera tigris altaica*) (Wroclaw) 2·75 1·50
4200 2z.20 White Rhinoceros (*Ceratotherium simum*) (Poznań) 3·00 1·70
4201 2z.80 Anteater (Warsaw) 3·75 2·30
4198/4201 *Set of* 4 10·00 6·00

(Des M. Błażków. Litho)

2005 (7 Oct). World Post Day. Architecture. Perf 11½ (with one elliptical hole on each horiz side).
4202 **1335** 1z.30 multicoloured 1·80 1·10

1336 Gingerbread Men

1337 St Maciej's Church and St Stefan's Statue, Budapest

(Des A. Wasik and M. Błażków. Litho)

2005 (14 Oct). 60th Anniversary of United Nations. Perf 11½ (with one elliptical hole on each horiz side).
4203 **1336** 2z.20 multicoloured 3·00 1·80

(Des M. Błażków. Litho)

2005 (24 Oct). European Capitals. T **1337** and similar horiz designs. Multicoloured. Perf 11½ (with one elliptical hole on each horiz side).
4204 1z.30 Type **1337** 1·80 1·70
4205 1z.30 Vilnius Cathedral 1·80 1·70
4206 2z.20 Arc de Triomphe, Paris 3·50 2·75
4207 2z.20 Monument to the Discoverers Belém, Lisbon 3·50 2·75
4208 2z.80 Government building, Dublin 3·75 3·50
4204/4208 *Set of* 5 13·00 11·00

1338 *Ploughing in the Ukraine* (L. J. Wyczólkowski)

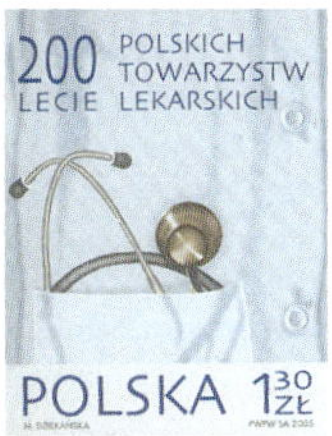

1339 Stethoscope in Pocket

(Des A. Pagowski. Photo)

2005 (3 Nov). Art. Polish Impressionists. Sheet 94×130 mm containing T **1338** and similar horiz designs. Multicoloured. Perf 11½.
MS4209 1z.30×2, Type **1338**; *Still Life* (J. Panekiewicz); 2z.×2, *Flower Sellers* (O. Boznanska); *The Garden* (W. Podkowinski) 11·00 9·50
No. **MS**4209 was issued *se-tenant* with two stamp-size labels.

(Des M. Dziekańska. Litho)

2005 (24 Nov). Bicentenary of Doctors' Association. Perf 11½ (with one elliptical hole on each vert side).
4210 **1339** 1z.30 multicoloured 2·40 1·70

1340 Trees and Angel

1341 Athletes

(Des M. Dziekańska. Photo)

2005 (28 Nov). Christmas. T **1340** and similar vert design. Multicoloured. Perf 12×11½.
4211 1z.30 Type **1340** 1·80 1·70
4212 2z.20 Angel facing left 3·00 2·75

(Des J. Brodowski. Photo)

2006 (7 Feb). Winter Olympic Games, Turin. Perf 12×11½ (with one elliptical hole on each horiz side).
4213 **1341** 2z.40 multicoloured 4·00 3·00
No. 4213 was issued with a *se-tenant* stamp-sized label.

1342 Heart carved in Apple

1343 Wolfgang Mozart

(Des A. Gósik. Photo)

2006 (10 Feb). St Valentines Day. Perf 11½.
4214 **1342** 1z.30 multicoloured 1·90 1·80
No. 4214 was issued with a *se-tenant* label that could be personalised (*price* £5·50 *unused*, £5·25 *used*).

(Des M. Jędrysik. Photo)

2006 (15 Feb). 250th Birth Anniversary of Wolfgang Amadeus Mozart (composer and musician). Perf 12×11½ (with one elliptical hole on each horiz side).
4215 **1343** 2z.40 multicoloured 3·25 3·00

1344 Students

1345 Zygmunt Gloger (first president)

(Des J. Pietras. Photo)

2006 (17 Feb). 25th Anniversary of Independent Students' Union. Perf 12×11½ (with one elliptical hole on each horiz side).
4216 **1344** 1z.30 black and scarlet vermilion 2·40 1·70

(Des J. Konarzewski. Photo)

2006 (20 Feb). Centenary of Polish Touring Society. Perf 12×11½ (with one elliptical hole on each horiz side).
4217 **1345** 1z.30 multicoloured 2·40 1·70

1346 *Pedicularis sudetica*

1347 *Dream II*

(Des A. Balcerzak. Litho)

2006 (14 Mar). Endangered Species. Flowers. T **1346** and similar horiz design. Multicoloured. Perf 12×11½ (with one elliptical hole on each horiz side).

4218	1z.30 Type **1346**	1·80	1·70
4219	2z.40 *Trapa natans*	3·25	3·00

(Des J. Pietras. Photo)

2006 (27 Mar). Contemporary Sculpture. Igor Mitoraj. T **1347** and similar horiz design. Multicoloured. Perf 12×11½ (with one elliptical hole on each horiz side).

4220	1z.30 Type **1347**	2·40	1·20
4221	1z.30 *Lips of Eros*	2·40	1·20

Nos. 4220/4221 were issued both in large sheets and together, each×2, in small sheets of four stamps with enlarged margins (*price for sheet* £14·50 *unused*, £15 *used*).

1348 Floral Procession, Palm Sunday

1349 Tree, Man and Stars

(Des Agnieszka Sancewicz. Litho)

2006 (3 Apr). Easter. T **1348** and similar horiz design. Multicoloured. Perf 12×11½ (with one elliptical hole on each horiz side).

4222	1z.30 Type **1348**	1·40	1·30
4223	2z.40 Śmigus-dyngus (dousing with water), Easter Monday	2·75	2·50

(Des Anna Niemierko. Litho)

2006 (5 May). Europa. Integration. Perf 11½×12 (with one elliptical hole on each vert side).

4224 **1349**	2z.40 multicoloured	4·00	2·75

1350 2006 WASHINGTON

1351 Pope Benedict XVI

(Des Anna Niemierko. Photo)

2006 (19 May). Washington 2006 International Stamp Exhibition. Sheet 115×77 mm. Perf 12.

MS4225 **1350**	2z.40 blue and vermilion	3·50	3·25

No. **MS**4225 was issued *se-tenant* with a stamp-size label.

(Des J. Wysocki. Litho)

2006 (25 May). Visit of Pope Benedict XVI. Perf 11½×12 (with one elliptical hole on each vert side).

4226 **1351**	1z.30 multicoloured	2·20	1·30

1352 Stilo

1353 Spinning Top

(Des Z. Okrassa. Litho)

2006 (29 May). Lighthouses (1st series). T **1352** and similar vert designs. Multicoloured.

4227	2z.40 Type **1352**	3·50	2·00
	a. Sheetlet of 4. Nos. 4227/4230	14·50	
4228	2z.40 Krynica Morska	3·50	2·00
4229	2z.40 Gąski	3·50	2·00
4230	2z.40 Niechorze	3·50	2·00
4227/4230	*Set of 4*	12·50	7·25

See also No. **MS**4275.

(Des Agnieszka Sancewicz. Litho)

2006 (1 June). Toys. T **1353** and similar triangular design. Multicoloured. Perf 11×11½ (with one elliptical hole on each vert side).

4231	1z.30 Type **1353**	2·20	1·30
4232	1z.30 Windmill	2·20	1·30

1354 Baroque Tankard

1355 Workers Procession, Poznań

(Des Wang Huming. Photo)

2006 (20 June). Gold and Silver Ware. T **1354** and similar vert design. Multicoloured. Perf 12×11½.

4233	1z.30 Type **1354**	2·20	1·30
	a. Pair. Nos. 4233/4234	4·75	2·75
4234	1z.30 Empire Lasting Forever Gold Cup	2·20	1·30

Stamps of the same design were issued by People's Republic of China. Nos. 4233/4234 were issued in *se-tenant* pairs within the sheet.

(Des M. Jędrysik. Eng T. Zlotkowski (No. **MS**4235(a)) or W. Zajdel (No. **MS**4235(b)). Recess and photo)

2006 (25–28 June). 50th Anniversary of Workers' Revolt, Poznań (No. **MS**4235(a)) and 30th Anniversary of Workers' Revolt, Radom (No. **MS**4235(b)). Two sheets, each 90×70 mm containing T **1355** and similar horiz design. Perf 12×11½.

MS4235	(a) 3z.50 grey-blue and slate-black. (28.6) (b) 3z.50 deep greenish grey and slate-black	11·00	8·25

Designs: (a) T **1355**. (b) Workers on lorry, Radom.

1356 Jerzy Giedroyc

1357 Edward Szczeklik

(Des J. Konarzewski. Eng M. Kopecki. Recess)

2006 (27 July). Birth Centenary of Jerzy Giedroyc (journalist). Perf 11½×11.

4236 **1356**	1z.30 slate black	2·75	1·30

(Des J. Skakun. Litho)

2006 (8 Sept). Centenary of Internal Medicine Society. T **1357** and similar horiz designs. Multicoloured. Perf 12×11½ (with one elliptical hole on each horiz side).

4237	1z.30 Type **1357**	2·50	1·30
4238	1z.30 Witold Eugeniusz Orlowskil	2·50	1·30

4239 3z. Antoni Wladyslaw Gluzinski .... 4·00 2·75
4237/4239 *Set of* 3 .... 8·00 4·75

1358 Lublin Town Hall

1359 Scream 'E'

(Des Joanna Górska. Eng P. Krajewski. Recess and photo)

2006 (20 Sept). 19th Convention of Polish Philatelic Association. Sheet 90×70 mm. Perf 11½.
MS4240 **1358** 3z.50 multicoloured .... 3·50 3·25
No. **MS**4240 also exists imperforate (*price* £11).

(Des J. Pietras ('A', 'f', 'O', 'Ś'), M. Jędrysik ('B', 'Ć', 'I', 'J', 'U'), W. Terechowicz ('C'), M. Osa ('D', 'E', 'H', 'L'), K. Castellini ('G', 'K', 'Ł'), E. Libera ('M', 'N', 't', 'Z'), A. Niemierko ('P', 'S'), J. Wysocki ('R', 'Y') or K. Syta ('W'). Litho)

2006 (29 Sept). Alphabet. Two sheets, each 130×175 mm containing T **1359** and similar multicoloured designs showing illustrations for letters of the Polish alphabet. Perf 11½ (with one elliptical hole on each vert side).
MS4241 (a) 10g. Type **1359**; 10g. 'I'; 30g. 'A' (44×22 mm); 30g. 'D'; 30g. 'K'; 1z. 'f'; 1z. 'L'; 1z.30 'B'; 1z.30 'C'; 1z.30 'Ć'; 1z.30 'G'; 1z.30 'H'; 1z.30 'J'. (b) 10g. 'N'; 10g. 'Y'; 30g. 'M'; 30g. 'O'; 30g. 'Z' (44×22 mm); 1z. 'P'; 1z. 't'; 1z.30 'Ł'; 1z.30 'R'; 1z.30 'S'; 1z.30 'Ś'; 1z.30 'U'; 1z.30 'W' .... 29·00 26·00

1360 Globe and Flags

1361 Brandenburg Gate, Berlin

(Des J. Ochendzan. Litho)

2006 (9 Oct). World Post Day. Perf 11½.
4242 **1360** 2z.40 multicoloured .... 2·50 2·30

(Des M. Błażków. Litho)

2006 (24 Oct). European Capital Cities. T **1361** and similar horiz designs. Multicoloured. Perf 11½ (with one elliptical hole on each horiz side).
4243 2z.40 Type **1361** .... 3·50 2·30
4244 2z.40 Coliseum, Rome .... 3·50 2·30
4245 2z.40 Royal Theatre, Stockholm .... 3·50 2·30
4246 2z.40 St Alexander Nevski Cathedral, Tallin .... 3·50 2·30
4247 2z.40 St Paul's Cathedral, Valletta .... 3·50 2·30
4243/4247 *Set of* 5 .... 16·00 10·50

1362 Ogar Polski (hound)

1363 The Nativity

(Des M. Błażków. Litho)

2006 (6 Nov). International Dog Show, Poznań. T **1362** and similar horiz designs. Multicoloured. Perf 11½ (with one elliptical hole on each horiz side).
4248 1z.30 Type **1362** .... 2·20 1·30
a. Horiz strip of 5. Nos. 4248/4252 .... 11·50
4249 1z.30 Gonczy Polski (hound) .... 2·20 1·30
4250 1z.30 Polski Owczarek (lowland sheepdog) ... 2·20 1·30
4251 1z.30 Chart Polski (sight hound) .... 2·20 1·30
4252 1z.30 Polski Owczarek Podralański (Tatra mountain dog) .... 2·20 1·30
4248/4252 *Set of* 5 .... 10·00 5·75
Nos. 4248/4252 were issued in horizontal *se-tenant* strips of five stamps within the sheet.

(Des Marzanna Dąbrowska. Photo)

2006 (30 Nov). Christmas. T **1363** and similar horiz design. Multicoloured. Perf 11½.
4253 1z.30 Type **1363** .... 2·20 1·30
a. Pair. Nos. 4253/4254 .... 5·75 4·00
4254 2z.40 Christmas .... 3·25 2·50

1364 Coal bleeding

1365 Heart as Planet

(Des J. Konarzewski. Litho)

2006 (16 Dec). 25th Anniversary of End of Miners' Strike for Solidarity. Perf 11½ (with one elliptical hole on each horiz side).
4255 **1364** 1z.30 multicoloured .... 2·20 1·30

(Des Z. Wlodarczyk, P. Salkowski and J. Owsiak. Photo)

2007 (4 Jan). Orchestra of Holy Day Assistance (fund raising charity). Perf 11½.
4256 **1365** 1z.35 multicoloured .... 2·20 1·30

1366 Ice Dancers

1367 Hearts as Butterflies

(Des J. Górska. Litho)

2007 (22 Jan). European Figure Skating Championships, Warsaw. Perf 11½ (with one elliptical hole on each horiz side).
4257 **1366** 2z.40 multicoloured .... 3·50 2·50

(Des J. Skakun. Litho)

2007 (8 Feb). St Valentine's Day. Perf 11½ (with one elliptical hole on each vert side).
4258 **1367** 1z.35 multicoloured .... 1·80 1·30
No. 4258 was issued with a *se-tenant* label that could be personalised (*price* £5·50 *unused*, £4·25 *used*).

1368 Straw Lamb

1369 Flags

(Des Marzanna Dąbrowska. Photo)

2007 (8 Mar). Easter. T **1368** and similar horiz design. Multicoloured. Perf 11½.
4259 1z.35 Type **1368** .... 2·20 1·30
4260 2z.40 Easter egg chicken .... 3·25 2·50

(Des M. Błażków. Litho)

2007 (20 Mar). 50th Anniversary of Treaty of Europe. Perf 11½ (with one elliptical hole on each vert side).
4261 **1369** 3z.55 multicoloured .... 4·50 4·25

1370 Cake

1371 Recycle Emblem

(Des Joanna Górska. Photo)

2007 (30 Mar). Greetings Stamps. T **1370** and similar horiz designs. Multicoloured. Perf 11½ (with one elliptical perf on each horiz side).
4262 1z.35 Type **1370** .... 2·20 1·30
4263 1z.35 Grapes, wine and bread .... 2·20 1·30
4264 1z.35 Wedding rings .... 2·20 1·30
4262/4264 *Set of* 3 .... 6·00 3·50

(Des A. Niemierko. Litho)

2007 (22 Apr). Earth Day. Perf 11½ (with one elliptical hole on each horiz side).
4265 **1371** 1z.35 multicoloured .... 2·75 1·30

1372 Postal Wagon Type 5G *circa* 1956

1373 Scout

(Des J. Skakun. Photo)

2007 (28 Apr). Railways. T **1372** and similar horiz designs. Multicoloured. Perf 11½ (with one elliptical perf on each horiz side).
4266 1z.35 Type **1372** .... 1·80 1·30
a. Horiz strip of 4. Nos. 4266/4269 .... 9·25
4267 1z.35 Carriage Type Cd21b *circa* 1924 .... 1·80 1·30
4268 2z.40 Carriage Type C3Pr07 *circa* 1909 .... 2·75 2·30
4269 2z.40 Carriage Type Ci29 *circa* 1929 .... 2·75 2·30
4266/4269 *Set of* 4 .... 8·25 6·50

Nos. 4266/4269 were issued in horizontal *se-tenant* strips of four stamps within the sheet.

(Des A. Pękalski. Litho)

2007 (5 May). Europa. Centenary of Scouting. Perf 11½ (with one elliptical hole on each horiz side).
4270 **1373** 3z. multicoloured .... 4·50 4·25

1374 *Little Helen with Vase of Flowers*

1375 Karol Szymanowski

2007 (18 May). Death Centenary of Stanisław Wyspiański (artist and writer). Perf 12×11½ (with one elliptical hole on each horiz side).
4271 **1374** 1z.35 multicoloured .... 1·80 1·70

(Des A. Pagowski and M. Błażków)

2007 (26 May). 125th Birth and 70th Death Anniversary of Karol Szymanowski (composer and writer). Perf 12×11½.
4272 **1375** 1z.35 multicoloured .... 1·80 1·70

1376 Centre of Cracow, Locating Document and City Arms

(Des K. Sowinski. Recess and photo)

2007 (29 May). 750th Anniversary of Cracow. Perf 12.
4273 **1376** 2z.40 multicoloured .... 3·25 3·00

1377 St Catherine of Alexandria Church, St Petersburg

(Des J. Górska. Eng W. Zajdel. Recess and photo)

2007 (29 May). Saint Petersburg 2007 International Philatelic Exhibition. Sheet 90×70 mm. Perf 12.
MS4274 **1377** 3z. multicoloured .... 5·50 4·25

1378 Gdańsk

1379 Virgin Mary and Child

(Des Z. Okrassa. Litho)

2007 (15 June). Lighthouses (2nd series). Sheet 90×125 mm containing T **1378** and similar vert designs. Multicoloured. Perf 12.
MS4275 1z.35 Type **1378**; 2z.40 Rozewie; 3z. Kolobrzeg; 3z.55 Hel .... 16·00 14·00

(Des P. Orzechowska. Litho)

2007 (2 July). 300th Anniversary of Leśniów Monastery. Perf 12 (with one elliptical perf on each vert side).
4276 **1379** 1z.35 multicoloured .... 2·75 1·70

1380 Bay

1381 *Saguinus imperator* (Emperor Tamarin)

(Des Witold Hyszko. Photo)

2007 (31 Aug). Arab Horses. T **1380** and similar vert designs showing horses. Multicoloured. Perf 11½ (with one elliptical perf on each vert side).
4277 1z.35 Type **1380** .... 1·80 1·70
a. Horiz strip of 4. Nos. 4277/4280 .... 17·00
4278 3z. Grey with pink snip .... 4·25 3·75

4279 3z.55 Bright bay with long forelock .... 4·75 4·50
4280 3z.55 Dappled grey .... 4·75 4·50
4277/4280 *Set of 4* .... 14·00 13·00

Nos. 4277/4280 were issued in horizontal *se-tenant* strips of four stamps within the sheet.

(Des M. Błażków. Photo)

2007 (11 Sept). Polish Zoos. T **1381** and similar vert designs showing animals. Multicoloured. Perf 11½ (with one elliptical perf on each vert side).

4281 1z.35 Type **1381** .... 1·80 1·70
4282 3z. *Ciconia nigra* (Black Stork) .... 3·25 3·00
4283 3z. *Loxodonta africana* (African Elephant) .. 4·25 3·75
4284 3z.55 *Uncia uncia* (Snow Leopard) .... 4·75 4·50
4281/4284 *Set of 4* .... 12·50 10·50

1382 Visual Interpretation of Electronic Sound as City Skyline

1383 Performers

(Des M. Dąbrowska. Litho)

2007 (21 Sept). Warsaw Autumn 2007. 50th Anniversary of Festival of Contemporary Music. Perf 12 (with one elliptical perf on each horiz side).

4285 **1382** 3z. multicoloured .... 4·50 3·75

(Des M. Dziekańska. Litho)

2007 (5 Oct). Centenary of Theatre of Silesia, Katowice. Perf 12 (with one elliptical perf on each horiz side).

4286 **1383** 1z.35 multicoloured .... 2·75 1·80

1384 Postmarks

1385 Dragon's Bridge, Ljubljana, Slovenia

(Des M. Dąbrowska. Litho)

2007 (9 Oct). World Post Day. Perf 12 (with one elliptical perf on each horiz side).

4287 **1384** 1z.35 multicoloured .... 2·75 1·80

(Des M. Błażków. Litho)

2007 (24 Oct). Capital Cities of European Union States. T **1385** and similar horiz designs. Multicoloured. Perf 12 (with one elliptical perf on each horiz side).

4288 1z.35 Type **1385** .... 2·50 1·80
4289 1z.35 Roland Monument, Riga, Latvia .... 2·50 1·80
4290 3z. Philharmonic Hall, Luxembourg .... 4·25 3·75
4291 3z. Plaza de Cibeles, Madrid, Spain .... 4·25 3·75
4292 3z.55 Tower Bridge, London, UK .... 5·25 4·50
4288/4292 *Set of 5* .... 17·00 14·00

1386 Pope John Paul II

1387 *Jubilee Self-Portrait*

(Des D. Belloti. Litho)

2007 (30 Oct). 25th Anniversary of Pope John Paul II Foundation. Perf 12 (with one elliptical perf on each horiz side).

4293 **1386** 1z.35 multicoloured .... 3·00 1·80

(Des J. Pietras)

2007 (5 Nov). Jerzy Duda-Gracz (artist) Commemoration. Perf 12 (with one elliptical perf on each horiz side).

4294 **1387** 1z.35 multicoloured .... 2·75 1·80

1388 Teddy and Tree

1389 Script, *Otago* and Joseph Conrad

(Des M. Dąbrowska. Photo)

2007 (27 Nov). Christmas. T **1388** and similar vert design. Multicoloured. Perf 12.

4295 1z.35 Type **1388** .... 2·00 1·80
4296 3z. *Adoration of the Magi* (Mikolaj Haberschrack) .... 4·25 3·75

(Des Maciej Jędrysik. Eng J. M. Kopecki. Recess)

2007 (3 Dec). 150th Birth Anniversary of Józef Teodor Konrad Korzeniowski (Joseph Conrad) (writer and sailor). Perf 11½.

4297 **1389** 3z. black .... 4·25 3·75

1390 Envelope and Quill

1391 Heart as Open Door

(Des Janusz Wysocki. Photo)

2008 (15 Jan). PostEurop (Association of European Public Postal Operators) Plenary Assembly, Krakow. Sheet 70×90 mm. Perf 12 (with one elliptical hole on each vert side).

MS4298 **1390** 3z. multicoloured .... 5·50 4·25

(Des Marzanna Dąbrowska. Litho)

2008 (7 Feb). St Valentine's Day. Perf 12 (with one elliptical hole on each horiz side).

4299 **1391** 1z.35 multicoloured .... 2·75 1·80

1392 Self-portrait, 1858

1393 Easter Eggs

(Des J. Konarzewski. Litho)

2008 (29 Feb). History of Polish Photography. 190th Birth Anniversary of Karol Beyer. T **1392** and similar vert designs. Multicoloured. Perf 12 (with one elliptical hole on each vert side).

4300 1z.35 Type **1392** .... 2·00 1·80
a. Strip of 4. Nos. 4300/4303 .... 8·25
4301 1z.35 Street scene, Wilanów, 1866 .... 2·00 1·80
4302 1z.35 Street scene, Warsaw, 1858 .... 2·00 1·80

4303 1z.35 Russian army tents, 1861 .... 2·00 1·80
4300/4303 *Set of 4* .... 7·25 6·50

Nos. 4300/4303 were issued in horizontal *se-tenant* strips of four stamps within the sheet.

(Des Marzanna Dąbrowska. Litho)

2008 (29 Feb). Easter. T **1393** and similar vert design. Multicoloured. Perf 12.

4304 1z.35 Type **1393** .... 2·00 1·80
4305 2z.40 Eggs (*different*) .... 3·50 3·25

Although not *se-tenant*, Nos. 4304/4305, together, form a composite design.

1394 Emblem

1395 TS-11 ISKRA

(Des Jerzy Skakun. Litho)

2008 (22 Mar). 80th Anniversary of Straż Graniczna (border guard). Perf 12×11½ (with one elliptical hole on each vert side).

4306 **1394** 2z.10 scarlet and black .... 3·50 2·75

(Des Jerzy Skakun. Litho)

2008 (31 Mar). Polish Air Force. T **1395** and similar vert design. Multicoloured. Perf 11½×12 (with one elliptical hole on each vert side).

4307 3z. Type **1395** .... 4·25 3·75
a. Pair. Nos. 4307/4308 .... 9·25 8·50
4308 3z.55 F-16 JASTRZĄB.......... 4·75 4·50

Nos. 4307/4308 were issued in *se-tenant* pairs within sheets of eight stamps.

1396 Sand Storm

1397 Envelope as Plate

(Des Marzanna Dąbrowska. Litho)

2008 (25 Apr). Weather Phenomena. T **1396** and similar horiz designs. Multicoloured. Perf 12×11½ (with one elliptical hole on each horiz side).

4309 1z.35 Type **1396** .... 2·00 1·80
a. Strip of 4. Nos. 4309/4312.......... 11·50
4310 1z.35 Lightning .... 2·00 1·80
4311 2z.40 Rainbow .... 3·50 3·25
4312 2z.40 Tornado .... 3·50 3·25
4309/4312 *Set of 4* .... 10·00 9·00

Nos. 4309/4312 were issued in *se-tenant* strips of four stamps within the sheet.

(Des Joanna Górska. Litho)

2008 (5 May). Europa. The Letter. Perf 12×11½ (with one elliptical hole on each horiz side).

4313 **1397** 3z. black and silver.......... 4·50 4·25
MS4313*a* 90×70 mm. As No. **MS**4313. Imperf.......... 5·50 5·25

1398 Emblem

1399 Magnifier and Emblem

(Des Anna Niemierko. Litho)

2008 (30 May). Euro 2008 European Football Championships, Austria and Switzerland. Perf 11½.

4314 **1398** 1z.35 multicoloured .... 2·00 1·80

(Des Anna Niemierko. Litho)

2008 (30 May). EUROSAI Congress, Kraków. Perf 11½×12 (with one elliptical hole on each vert side).

4315 **1399** 3z.55 multicoloured .... 4·75 4·50

1400 Toy Train

1401 Child and Rug

(Des Marzanna Dąbrowska. Litho)

2008 (1 June). National Children's Day. Toys. T **1400** and similar triangular design. Multicoloured. Perf 11×11½ (with one elliptical hole on each vert side).

4316 1z.35 Type **1400** .... 2·00 1·80
4317 3z. Xylophone.......... 4·25 3·75

(Des Maciej Jędrysik. Litho)

2008 (10 June). Child Refugees to Esfahan, Iran during World War II. Perf 11½ (with one elliptical hole on each vert side).

4318 **1401** 2z.40 multicoloured .... 3·50 3·25

1402 Envelope enclosing Romanian Athenaeum Building

1403 Madonna and Child

(Des Kuba Sowiński. Eng Przemyslaw Krajewski. Recess and photo)

2008 (20 June). EFIRO 2008 International Stamp Exhibition, Bucharest. Sheet 90×70 mm. Perf 11½.

MS4319 **1402** 3z. multicoloured.......... 4·50 4·25

No. **MS**4319 also exists imperforate (*price* £19).

(Des Maciej Jędrysik. Litho)

2008 (21 June). St Mary's Sanctuaries. St Mary of the Snow. Perf 11½.

4320 **1403** 1z.35 multicoloured .... 2·75 1·80

1404 Swimming

1405 Siekierkowski Bridge, Warsaw

(Des Janusz Wysocki. Litho)

2008 (8 Aug). Olympic Games, Beijing. T **1404** and similar horiz designs. Multicoloured. Perf 11½ (with one elliptical hole on each horiz side).

4321 10g. Type **1404** 45 35
a. Strip of 4. Nos. 4321/4324.......... 5·50
4322 10g. Volleyball 45 35
4323 1z.45 Pole vault .... 2·20 2·00
4324 1z.45 Fencing .... 2·20 2·00
4321/4324 *Set of 4* .... 4·75 4·25
MS4325 202×116 mm. Nos. 4321/4324.......... 7·00 6·25

Nos. 4321/4324 were issued in horizontal *se-tenant* strips of four stamps.

(Des Andrzej Gósik. Litho)

2008 (29 Aug). Bridges. T **1405** and similar horiz designs. Multicoloured. Perf 11½ (with one elliptical hole on each horiz side).

4326	1z.45 Type **1405**	2·20	2·00
	a. Strip of 4. Nos. 4326/4329	13·50	
4327	1z.45 Poniatowski Bridge, Warsaw	2·20	2·00
4328	3z. Bridge, Maurzyce	4·25	3·75
4329	3z. Ernest Malinowski Bridge, Toruń	4·25	3·75
4326/4329 *Set of 4*		11·50	10·50

Nos. 4326/4329 were issued in horizontal *se-tenant* strips of four stamps within the sheet.

1406 Prosper Prowana

1407 Wladyslaw Raczkiewicz

(Des Maciej Jędrysik. Eng Przemyslaw Krajewski (Prosper Prowana), Maciej Kopecki (Zygmunt August) or Wanda Zajdel (Sebastian Montelupi). Recess and photo)

2008 (15 Sept). 450th Anniversary of Polish Postal Service (1st issue). Sheet 120×80 mm containing T **1406** and similar multicoloured designs. Perf 11½.

MS4330 1z.45×3, Type **1406**; King Zygmunt August (51×31 mm); Sebastian Montelupi — 7·25 — 6·25

The stamps and margins of No. **MS**4330 form a composite design.

See also No. **MS**4352.

(Des Agnieszka Sobczyńska. Litho)

2008 (24 Sept). Presidents of Government in Exile. Sheet 129×125 mm containing T **1407** and similar horiz designs. Multicoloured. Perf 11½ (with one elliptical hole on each horiz side).

MS4331 1z.45×6, Type **1407**; Edward Raczyński; August Zaleski; Kazimierz Sabbat; Stanisław Ostrowski; Ryszard Kaczorowski — 13·00 — 12·00

The central stamps of No. **MS**4331 form a composite design.

1408 Sports Men and Women

1409 Native American, Settler and Map

(Des Marzanna Dąbrowska. Photo)

2008 (30 Sept). Centenary of Lódź Sports Club. Perf 11½.

4332	**1408**	1z.45 vermilion and silver	2·75	2·00

(Des Agnieszka Sobczyńska. Litho)

2008 (30 Sept). 400th Anniversary of Polish Settlers in America. Perf 11½ (with one elliptical hole on each horiz side).

4333	**1409**	3z. multicoloured	4·25	4·00

1410 Pigeon Post

1411 Mieczysław Karłowicz

(Des Maciej Jędrysik. Litho)

2008 (9 Oct). World Post Day. Perf 11½ (with one elliptical hole on each horiz side).

4334	**1410**	2z.10 multicoloured	3·50	3·00

(Des Jerzy Skakun. Litho)

2008 (18 Oct). Composers. T **1411** and similar vert designs. Multicoloured. Perf 11½ (with one elliptical hole on each vert side).

4335	1z.45 Type **1411**	2·20	2·00
4336	1z.45 Wojciech Kilar	2·20	2·00
4337	1z.45 Henryk Mikolaj Górecki	2·20	2·00
4338	1z.45 Witold Lutosławski	2·20	2·00
4335/4338 *Set of 4*		8·00	7·25

1412 Rijksmuseum, Amsterdam

1413 J. Przybora and J. Wasowski

(Des Magdalena Błażków. Litho)

2008 (24 Oct). Capital Cities of European Union States. T **1412** and similar horiz designs. Multicoloured. Perf 11½ (with one elliptical perf on each horiz side).

4339	1z.45 Type **1412**	2·20	2·00
4340	1z.45 Royal Library, Copenhagen	2·50	2·00
4341	3z. Charles Bridge, Prague	4·25	4·00
4342	3z. Acropolis, Athens	5·50	4·00
4343	3z.65 Parliament, Vienna	5·50	4·75
4339/4343 *Set of 5*		18·00	15·00

(Des Agnieszka Sobczyńska)

2008 (30 Oct). 50th Anniversary of *Kabaret Starszych Panów* (comedy series). Perf 11½ (with one elliptical hole on each vert side).

4344	**1413**	1z.45 multicoloured	2·75	2·00

1414 Maria Konopnicka

1415 National Arms

(Des Joanna Górska)

2008 (7 Nov). Centenary of *Rota* (the Oath (poem)) by Maria Konopnicka. Perf 11½ (with one elliptical hole on each vert side).

4345	**1414**	3z.65 multicoloured	5·50	5·00

No. 4345 was printed in sheets of ten stamps and ten inscribed labels.

(Des Jerzy Pietras. Eng Maciej Kopecki. Recess)

2008 (11 Nov). Centenary of Independence Day. Perf 11½.

4346	**1415**	1z.45 deep carmine	2·75	2·00

1416 Stars

1417 Pope John Paul II

(Des Jerzy Pietras)

2008 (27 Nov). Christmas. T **1416** and similar vert design. Multicoloured. Perf 11½.

4347	1z.45 Type **1416**	2·20	2·00
4348	3z. Stars (*different*)	4·25	4·00

(Des Marzanna Dąbrowska)

2008 (27 Nov). 30th Anniversary of Election of Karol Wojtyła as Pope John Paul II. Perf 11½.
4349 **1417** 2z.40 multicoloured .... 5·25 3·25

1418 Zbigniew Herbert

1419 Emblem

(Des Anna Niemierko)

2008 (1 Dec). Tenth Death Anniversary of Zbigniew Herbert (writer). Perf 11½ (with one elliptical hole on each vert side).
4350 **1418** 2z.10 multicoloured .... 3·00 2·75

(Des Anna Niemierko)

2008 (1 Dec). United Nations Conference on Climate Change, Poznań. Perf 11½.
4351 **1419** 2z.40 multicoloured .... 4·00 3·25

1420 Postal Messenger

2008 (14 Dec). 450th Anniversary of Polish Postal Service (2nd issue). Sheet 106×75 mm. Self-adhesive. Imperf.
MS4352 **1420** 20z. multicoloured........ 29·00 26·00
No. **MS**4352 was screen printed on silk.

1421 Louis Braille

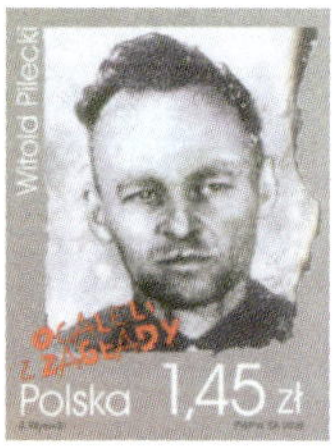

1422 Witold Pilecki (historian)

(Des Anna Niemierko. Litho)

2009 (4 Jan). Birth Bicentenary of Louis Braille (inventor of Braille writing for the blind). Perf 12×11½ (with one elliptical hole on each horiz side).
4353 **1421** 1z.45 multicoloured .... 3·50 2·00
No. 4353 was printed with a *se-tenant* stamp-size label with embossed Braille letters attached at right.

(Des Magdalena Błażków. Litho)

2009 (6 Feb–3 Apr). Camp Survivors. T **1422** and similar vert designs. Multicoloured. Perf 11½ (with one elliptical hole on each vert side).
4354 1z.45 Type **1422** .... 2·20 2·00
a. Horiz strip of 4. Nos. 4354/4357 .... 38·00
b. Strip of 4. Nos. 4354, 4355a and 4356/4357 .... 13·50
4355 2z.10 Wladyslaw Wolski .... 27·00 23·00
a. Inscr 'Jozef Wladyslaw Wolski' (3.4.09)... 3·00 2·75
4356 2z.40 Ignacy Ludwik Jeż........ 3·50 3·25
4357 3z. Stanislawa Maria Sawicka........ 4·25 4·00
4354/4357 *Set of 4*........ 11·50 11·00
Nos. 4354/4357 were printed, *se-tenant*, in horizontal strips of four stamps within sheets of 16.

1423 Heart in Four-leafed Clover

1424 *Zwiastowanie*

(Des Magdalena Błażków. Litho)

2009 (6 Feb). St Valentine's Day. Perf 12×11½ (with one elliptical hole on each horiz side).
4358 **1423** 1z.45 multicoloured .... 3·00 2·00

(Des Malgorzata Osa. Litho)

2009 (6 Mar). Contemporary Polish Sculpture. Tenth Death Anniversary of Wladyslaw Hasior. T **1424** and similar vert designs. Multicoloured. Perf 12 (with one elliptical hole on each vert side).
4359 1z.45 Type **1424** .... 2·20 2·00
4360 1z.45 *Mucha* .... 2·20 2·00
4361 2z.10 *Sztandar Zielonej Poetki* .... 3·00 2·75
4362 2z.40 *Sztandar Rozbieranie do snu* .... 3·50 3·25
4359/4362 *Set of 4*........ 9·75 9·00
MS4363 90×125 mm. Nos. 4359/4362........ 12·50 11·50

1425 *Chrystus Zmartwychwstaly*

1426 Fish

(Des Magdalena Błażków. Litho)

2009 (1 Apr). Easter. Paintings by Szymon Czechowicz. T **1425** and similar multicoloured design. Perf 12.
4364 1z.55 Type **1425** .... 2·30 2·10
4365 3z. *Zlozenie do grobu* (*vert*)........ 4·50 4·25

(Des Ewo Monńko. Litho)

2009 (16 Apr). China 2009 International Stamp Exhibition, Luoyang. Sheet 90×70 mm. Perf 11½ (with one elliptical hole on each vert side).
MS4366 **1426** 3z. multicoloured........ 5·50 5·00

1427 *Berek Joselewicz* (Juliusz Kossak)

1428 Cheetahs

(Des Marzanna Dąbrowska. Litho)

2009 (22 Apr). Polish Year in Israel. Sheet 90×70 mm. Perf 11½ (with one elliptical hole on each horiz side).
MS4367 **1427** 3z. multicoloured........ 5·50 5·00

(Des Tomasz Gudzowaty)

2009 (30 Apr). African Animals. Sheet 124×90 mm containing T **1428** and similar horiz designs. Each black. Perf 11½ (with one elliptical hole on each horiz side).
MS4368 1z.55 Type **1428**; 1z.95 Zebras; 2z.40 Gnu and crocodile; 3z. Elephants........ 14·50 13·00

1429 Numbers as Starburst

1430 Grażyna Bacewicz

(Des Agata Tobolczyk)

2009 (5 May). Europa. Astronomy. Perf 11½ (with one elliptical hole on each horiz side).

4369 **1429** 3z. deep turquoise-blue and new blue .... 5·50 5·00
a. *Tête-bêche* (pair) .... 11·50 10·50

No. 4369 was printed, *tête-beche*, in horizontal pairs within small sheets, each pair forming a composite design.

(Des Agata Tobolczyk)

2009 (28 May). Birth Centenary of Grażyna Bacewicz (composer and violinist). Perf 11½ (with one elliptical hole on each vert side).

4370 **1430** 1z.55 multicoloured .... 2·30 2·10
a. *Tête-bêche* (pair) .... 4·75 4·50

1431 Tytus de Zoo

1432 Lech Wałęsa (leader Trade Union Solidarność)

(Des Ewo Mońko)

2009 (29 May). 50th (2007) Anniversary of *Tytus, Romek and A'Tomek* (comic created by Henryk Jerzy Chmielewski (Papcio Chmiel)). T **1431** and similar vert designs. Multicoloured. Perf 11½ (with one elliptical hole on each vert side).

4371 1z.55 Type **1431** .... 2·30 2·10
a. Horiz strip of 3. Nos. 4371/4374 .... 7·25
4372 1z.55 Romek .... 2·30 2·10
4373 1z.55 A'Tomek .... 2·30 2·10
4371/4373 *Set of 3* .... 6·25 5·75

Nos. 4371/4373 were printed, *se-tenant*, in horizontal strips of three stamps within the sheet.

(Des Agnieszka Sobczyńska)

2009 (30 May). 20th Anniversary of Opposition Electoral Success. Sheet 90×70 mm. Perf 11½ (with one elliptical hole on each vert side).

MS4374 **1432** 3z.75 multicoloured .... 7·25 5·75

1433 Saint Bruno

1434 *Dar Mlodziezy* (frigate of Naval Academy of Gdynia, built,1982)

(Des Bożydar Grozdew)

2009 (19 June). Death Millennary of Saint Bruno of Querfurt (missionary and martyr). Perf 11½ (with one elliptical hole on each vert side).

4375 **1433** 3z. multicoloured .... 4·50 4·25

(Des Kazimierz Bulik. Eng Tomasz Notkowski. Recess and photo)

2009 (30 June). Tall Ships' Races. Gdynia 2009. Sheet 90×70 mm. Perf 11½ (with one elliptical hole on each vert side).

MS4376 **1434** 3z.75 multicoloured .... 7·25 5·75

1435 *Phocoena phocoena* (Porpoise)

1436 Building on Fire

(Des Agata Tobolczyk)

2009 (31 July). Mammals of the Baltic Sea. T **1435** and similar vert designs. Multicoloured. Perf 11½ (with one elliptical hole on each vert side).

4377 1z.55 Type **1435** .... 2·20 1·70
a. Horiz strip of 4. Nos. 4377/4380 .... 11·50
4378 1z.55 *Halichoreus grypus* (Grey Seal) .... 2·20 1·70
4379 1z.95 *Phoca vitulina* (Harbour seal) .... 3·25 2·10
4380 1z.95 *Phoca hispida* (Ringed Seal) .... 3·25 2·10
4377/4380 *Set of 4* .... 9·75 6·75

Nos. 4377/4380 were printed, *se-tenant*, in horizontal strips within the sheet, each strip forming a composite design.

(Des Paweł Myszka. Eng Przemysław Krajewski. Recess and photo)

2009 (1 Aug). 65th Anniversary of Warsaw Uprising against German Occupation. Sheet 90×70 mm. Perf 11½ (with one elliptical hole on each vert side).

MS4381 **1436** 3z.75 black and rosine .... 7·25 5·75

1437 *Cerasus avium* (*Prunus avium*) (Cherry)

1438 Jan Czochralski (specialist in metallurgy and inventor of Czochralski process)

(Des Marzanna Dąbrowska)

2009 (10 Aug). Fruit and Flowers. T **1437** and similar horiz design. Multicoloured. Perf 11½.

4382 1z.95 Type **1437** .... 2·75 2·10
4383 3z.75 *Calendula officinalis* (Pot Marigold) .... 5·50 4·25

(Des Ewa Szydłowska)

2009 (28 Aug). Poles in Exile. T **1438** and similar vert designs. Multicoloured. Perf 11½ (with one elliptical hole on each vert side).

4384 1z.55 Type **1438** .... 2·20 1·70
4385 1z.55 Antoni Norbert Patek (watchmaker) .... 2·20 1·70
4386 1z.95 Ludwik Hirszfeld (microbiologist and serologist) .... 3·25 2·10
4387 1z.95 Marian Rejewski, Henryk Zygalski and Jerzy Różycki (mathematicians and cryptologists who created replica of Enigma, German encrypting machine) .... 3·25 2·10
4384/4387 *Set of 4* .... 9·75 6·75

1439 Juliusz Słowacki

1440 Attack on Węgierska Górka (village in Zywiec County which held out for three days)

(Des Marzanna Dąbrowska)

2009 (31 Aug). Birth Bicentenary of Juliusz Słowacki (poet, playwright and philosopher). Perf 11½.

4388 **1439** 1z.55 multicoloured .... 3·50 1·70

(Des Jacek Dąbrowski)

2009 (1 Sept). Defensive War 1939. T **1440** and similar horiz design. Each black and scarlet-vermilion. Perf 11½.

4389 1z.55 Type **1440** .... 2·75 1·70
4390 2z.40 Wieluń (first town to come under attack) .... 3·50 2·75

1441 Ball and Hoop

1442 Tadeusz Mazowiecki (first premier)

(Des Kazimierz Bulik)

2009 (7 Sept). EuroBasket 2009. European Men's Basketball Championship, Poland. Perf 11½ (with one elliptical hole on each vert side).

4391 **1441** 3z. multicoloured .... 4·50 3·25

(Des Agnieszka Sobczyńska)

2009 (11 Sept). 20th Anniversary of First Non-Communist Government following Elections in June, 1989. Perf 11½ (with one elliptical hole on each horiz side).

4392 **1442** 1z.55 multicoloured .... 3·50 1·70

1443 Player in Motion

1444 Envelope as Kite

(Des L. Walendziuk)

2009 (25 Sept). Women's European Volleyball Championship 2009, Poland. Perf 11½ (with one elliptical hole on each horiz side).

4393 **1443** 3z. multicoloured .... 5·50 3·25

(Des Magdalena Błażków. Litho)

2009 (6 Oct). Capital Cities of European Union States. Horiz designs as T **1412**. Multicoloured. Perf 11½ (with one elliptical perf on each horiz side).

4394 1z.55 Castle, Bratislava .... 2·75 1·70
4395 1z.55 Famagusta Gate, Nicosia .... 2·75 1·70
4396 3z. Town Hall, Brussels .... 4·75 3·25
4397 3z. Courtyard, Warsaw .... 4·75 3·25
4398 3z.75 National Museum, Helsinki .... 5·75 4·25
4394/4398 *Set of 5* .... 19·00 12·50

(Des B. Grozdew. Eng P. Krajewski. Recess and litho)

2009 (9 Oct). World Post Day. Perf 11½.

4399 **1444** 3z. multicoloured .... 5·50 3·25

1445 Jerzy Popiełuszko

1446 Volunteer

(Des M. Dąbrowska)

2009 (19 Oct). 25th Death Anniversary of Jerzy Popiełuszko (priest and solidarity martyr). Perf 11½ (with one elliptical perf on each horiz side).

4400 **1445** 1z.55 multicoloured .... 3·50 1·70

(Des E. Szydlowska)

2009 (24 Oct). Centenary of Voluntary Tatra Mountains Rescue Service. Perf 11½ (with one elliptical perf on each vert side).

4401 **1446** 1z.55 multicoloured .... 3·50 1·70

1447 Paweł Jasienica

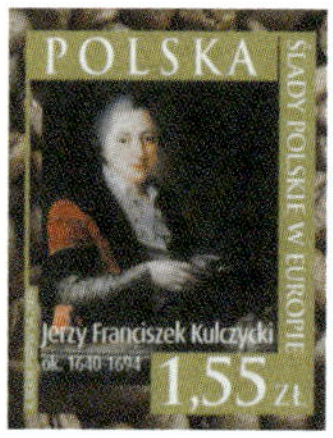

1448 Jerzy Franciszek Kulczycki

(Des E. Mońko)

2009 (10 Nov). Birth Centenary of Leon Lech Beynar (Paweł Jasienica) (writer and historian). Perf 11½.

4402 **1447** 1z.55 multicoloured .... 3·50 1·70

(Des K. Bulik)

2009 (16 Nov). Polish Influence in Europe. Jerzy Franciszek Kulczycki (hero of Battle of Vienna and opened first coffee house in Vienna) Commemoration. Perf 11½ (with one elliptical perf on each vert side).

4403 **1448** 1z.55 multicoloured .... 3·75 2·00

No. 4403 was printed in sheets of eight stamps and eight labels, the whole forming a composite design.

1449 Bookplate *Exlibris Willibald Pirkheimer* (Albrecht Dürer)

1450 Choir

(Des K. Bulik)

2009 (20 Nov). Lost Treasures. Art. T **1449** and similar vert designs. Multicoloured. Perf 11½.

4404 1z.55 Type **1449** .... 2·20 1·70
a. Strip of 3. Nos. 4404/4406 .... 6·75
4405 1z.55 *Christ falls beneath the Cross* (Peter Paul Rubens) .... 2·20 1·70
4406 1z.55 *Joseph recounts his Dream* (Rembrandt) .... 2·20 1·70
4404/4406 *Set of 3* .... 6·00 4·50

Nos. 4404/4406 were printed, *se-tenant*, in horizontal strips of three stamps within the sheet.

(Des E. Szydlowska)

2009 (27 Dec). Christmas. T **1450** and similar vert design. Multicoloured. Perf 11½.

4407	1z.55 Type **1450**	2·75	1·70
4408	2z.40 Holy Family	4·50	2·50

1451 Letter from Kalwaria to Warsaw, franked with 1860 10k. Stamp (As T **1**)

1452 Skiers

(Des Maciej Jędrysik)

2010 (15 Jan). 150th Anniversary of Polish Stamps. Sheet 90×70 mm. Perf 11½ (with one elliptical hole on each vert side).

MS4409	**1451** 4z.15 multicoloured	5·50	4·75

(Des Jacek Brodowski)

2010 (27 Jan). Winter Olympic Games, Vancouver. Perf 11½ (with one elliptical hole on each horiz side).

4410	**1452**	3z. multicoloured	5·50	3·25

1453 British Shorthair

1454 Frédéric Chopin

(Des Andrzej Gósik)

2010 (17 Feb). Cats. Sheet 122×125 mm containing T **1453** and similar vert designs. Multicoloured. Perf 11½ (with one elliptical hole on each vert side).

MS4411	1z.55 Type **1453**; 1z.55 Siamese; 1z.95 Somali; 1z.95 Maine Coon; 3z. Persian; 3z. Tortoiseshell and white exotic	22·00	17·00

(Des Marzanna Dąbrowska)

2010 (22 Feb). Birth Bicentenary of Frédéric Chopin (composer). Sheet 90×70 mm. Perf 11½ (with one elliptical hole on each horiz side).

MS4412	**1454** 4z.15 multicoloured	5·50	5·00
MS4412*a*	4z.15 As Type **1454**. Imperf	36·00	33·00

1456 Warsaw, 1920

1455 Lamb

(Des Jerzy Pietras)

2010 (5 Mar). Easter. T **1455** and similar vert design. Multicoloured. Perf 11½.

4413	1z.55 Type **1455**	2·75	2·10
4414	2z.40 Basket of eggs	4·50	2·75

(Des Jacek Konarzewski)

2010 (31 Mar). History of Polish Photography. Jan Bulhak Commemoration. T **1456** and similar vert designs showing photographs. Multicoloured. Perf 11½ (with one elliptical hole on each vert side).

4415	1z.95 Type **1456**	2·75	2·50
	a. Strip of 4. Nos. 4415/4418	11·50	
4416	1z.95 Doorway, Krakow, 1921	2·75	2·50
4417	1z.95 Old Town Hall, Warsaw, 1920	2·75	2·50
4418	1z.95 Kasimir side altar, Vilnius Cathedral, 1912	2·75	2·50
4415/4418	*Set of* 4	10·00	9·00

Nos. 4415/4418 were printed, *se-tenant*, in strips of four stamps within the sheet.

1457 Anniversary Emblem

(Des Jerzy Pietras)

2010 (6 Apr). 20th Anniversary of Special Services. Perf 11½ (with one elliptical hole on each vert side).

4419	**1457**	1z.55 scarlet-vermilion, indigo and silver	3·50	2·10

1458 Cross of Polish Badges

1459 Tower of Belém, Lisbon

(Des Marzanna Dąbrowska)

2010 (7 Apr). 60th Anniversary of Katyń Massacre. Sheet 70×90 mm. Perf 11½ (with one elliptical hole on each horiz side).

MS4420	**1458** 3z. multicoloured	5·50	4·50

(Des Jacek Konarzewski)

2010 (30 Apr). Portugal 2010 International Stamp Exhibition, Lisbon. Sheet 90×70 mm. Perf 11½ (with one elliptical hole on each vert side).

MS4421	**1459** 3z. multicoloured	5·50	4·50

1460 Boy reading

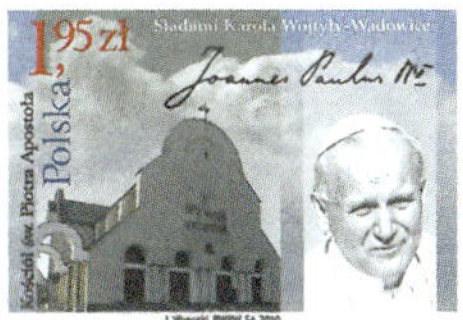

1461 Pope John Paul II and Church of Peter the Apostle, Wadowice

(Des Maciej Jędrysik)

2010 (5 May). Europa. Children's Books. Perf 11½ (with one elliptical hole on each vert side).

4422	**1460**	3z. multicoloured	5·50	4·25

(Des Janusz Wysocki)

2010 (18 May). Pope John Paul II (Karol Józef Wojtyła) Commemoration. Perf 11½ (with one elliptical hole on each horiz side).

4423	**1461**	1z.95 multicoloured	6·00	3·25

No. 4423 was printed, *se-tenant*, with a stamp-size label showing Church of the Presentation of the Virgin, Wadowice (site of baptism of Karol Wojtyła) and Karol Wojtyła as a cardinal.

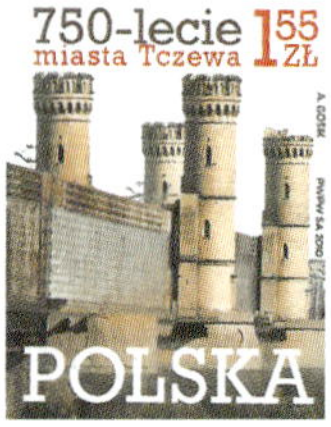

1462 Bridge over the Vistula

1463 Jerzy Popiełuszko

(Des Andrzej Gósik)

2010 (27 May). 750th Anniversary of Tczew. Perf 11½.
4424 **1462** 1z.55 multicoloured .... 3·50 2·10

(Des Jacek Konarzewski)

2010 (6 June). Beatification of Jerzy Popiełuszko (priest and solidarity martyr). Perf 11½ (with one elliptical hole on each horiz side).
4425 **1463** 1z.95 multicoloured .... 4·00 3·00

1464 Convent and Statue of Christ

1465 Battle Scene (Jan Matejko)

1466 Scouts signalling Semaphore Message, 'STO LAT' (100 YEARS)

(Des Jacek Brodowski)

2010 (24 June). 750th Anniversary of Dominican Ursuline Sisters Convent, Sieradtz. Perf 11½.
4426 **1464** 1z.55 multicoloured .... 3·00 2·30

(Des Marzanna Dąbrowska)

2010 (15 July). 600th Anniversary of Battle of Grunvald (First Battle of Tannenberg), during the Polish–Lithuanian–Teutonic War. Sheet 116×82 mm. Perf 11½.
MS4427 **1465** 8z.30 multicoloured........ 18·00 15·00

(Des Małgorzata Osa)

2010 (17 July). Centenary of Polish Scouts' Association. Perf 11½.
4428 **1466** 1z.95 multicoloured .... 4·00 3·00

1467 Forget-me-Not

1468 Lech Wałęsa

(Des Marzanna Dąbrowska)

2010 (10 Aug). Flowers. Perf 11½.
4429 **1467** 4z.15 multicoloured .... 6·75 6·00

(Des Agnieszka Sobczyńska)

2010 (31 Aug). 30th Anniversary of NSZZ 'Solidarność' (Solidarity). Perf 11½ (with one elliptical hole on each horiz side).
4430 **1468** 3z.75 black, silver and red .... 6·25 5·50

1469 Sphalerite

1469a Tower of Postmen

(Des Anna Niemierko)

2010 (3 Sept). Minerals. T **1469** and similar horiz designs. Multicoloured. Perf 11½ (with one elliptical hole on each horiz side).
4431 1z.55 Type **1469** .... 2·50 2·30
a. Strip of 4. Nos. 4431/4434........ 16·00
4432 1z.95 Gypsum .... 3·25 3·00
4433 2z.40 Agate .... 4·00 3·50
4434 3z. Chrysoprase .... 5·00 4·50
4431/4434 *Set of 4* .... 13·50 12·00

Nos. 4431/4434 were printed, *se-tenant*, in strips of four stamps within the sheet.

(Des Maciej Jędrysik)

2010 (9 Oct). World Post Day. Perf 11½.
4435 **1469a** 1z.95 multicoloured .... 5·00 3·00
a. *Tête-bêche* (pair) .... 10·50 6·25

1470 Sofia

1471 'A' and Floral Motif

(Des Magdalena Błażków. Litho)

2010 (24 Oct). Capital Cities of European Union States. T **1470** and similar horiz design. Multicoloured. Perf 11½ (with one elliptical hole on each horiz side).
4436 1z.95 Type **1470** .... 3·50 3·00
4437 3z. Bucharest .... 5·50 4·50

2010 (29 Oct). Personal Stamp. Perf 11½ (with one elliptical hole on each vert side).
4438 **1471** A (1z.55) multicoloured .... 16·00 14·00

No. 4438 was printed, *se-tenant*, with a stamp-sized label which could be personalised by the addition of a photograph or logo.

1472 Players

1473 Ignacy Paderewski

(Des Janusz Wysocki)

2010 (9 Oct). Centenary of Widzew Łódź Football Club. Perf 11½.
4439 **1472** 1z.55 multicoloured .... 4·00 2·30

(Des Marzanna Dąbrowska)

2010 (22 Nov). 150th Birth Anniversary of Ignacy Jan Paderewski (composer and Prime Minister (1919)). Perf 11½ (with one elliptical hole on each vert side).
4440 **1473** 3z. multicoloured .... 6·00 4·75

1474 Shooting Star, Trail and Christmas Tree

1475 'Kocham Cię"

2010 (27 Nov). Christmas. T **1474** and similar horiz design. Multicoloured. Perf 11½.
4441 1z.55 Type **1474** .... 2·50 2·30
4442 2z.40 Shooting star, trail and night sky .... 4·00 3·50

(Des Jan Konarzewski)

2010 (30 Dec). Greetings Stamp. Perf 11½.
4443 **1475** A (1z.55) multicoloured .... 4·00 2·30

1476 Jan Heweliusz

1477 Players

(Des Maciej Jędrysik. Litho)

2011 (28 Jan). 400th Birth Anniversary of Johannes Hevelius (Jan Heweliusz) (brewer and astronomer). Perf 11½ (with one elliptical hole on each horiz side).
4444 **1476** 3z. multicoloured .... 6·00 5·50
No. 4444 was issued in sheets of six stamps and six *se-tenant* labels.

(Des Jacek Brodowski. Litho)

2011 (4 Feb). Men's World Indoor Hockey Championship, Poznań. Perf 11½ (with one elliptical hole on each horiz side).
4445 **1477** 2z.40 multicoloured .... 4·00 3·50

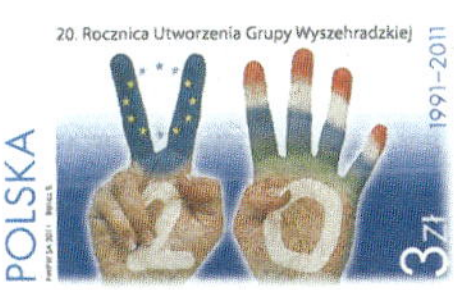

1478 '20', EU Stars and Group Colours on Hands

1478a Students Demonstrating

(Des Barnabas Baticz. Litho)

2011 (11 Feb). 20th Anniversary of Viségrad Group (cultural, education, science and exchange of information). Perf 12.
4446 **1478** 3z. multicoloured .... 7·00 4·50
Stamps of a similar design were also issued by Czech Republic, Hungary and Slovakia.

(Des Agnieszka Sobczyńska. Litho)

2011 (17 Feb). 30th Anniversary of Łódź Independent Students' Association. Perf 11½ (with one elliptical hole on each horiz side).
4446*a* **1478a** 1z. 95 multicoloured .... 4·00 3·00

1479 Child's Face and Tree

1480 Stefan Kisielewski

(Des Jacek Konarzewski. Photo)

2011 (28 Feb). Cystic Fibrosis Awareness Week. Perf 11½×11.
4447 **1479** 1z.55 multicoloured .... 4·00 2·50

(Des Ewa Libera. Litho)

2011 (7 Mar). Birth Centenary of Stefan Kisielewski (writer, composer, music critic and co-founder and member of the Union of Real Politics). Perf 11½ (with one elliptical hole on each horiz side).
4448 **1480** 1z.95 multicoloured .... 6·75 2·75
a. *Tête-bêche* (pair) .... 14·00 5·75
No. 4448 was issued in sheets of 12 stamps.
The elliptical hole can be on either the left or the right-hand of the horizontal.

1481 Chick and Flowers

1482 Cardinal Kozłowiecki

(Des Jan Konarzewski. Photo)

2011 (25 Mar). Easter. T **1481** and similar vert design. Multicoloured. Perf 11½.
4449 1z.55 Type **1481** .... 3·00 2·50
4450 2z.40 Rabbit and flowers .... 5·00 3·50

(Des Maciej Jędrysik)

2011 (31 Mar). Birth Centenary of Cardinal Adam Kozłowiecki. Perf 11×11½.
4451 **1482** 1z.95 multicoloured .... 5·00 3·00

1483 Boy (Burma)

1484 Pope John Paul II

(Des Marzanna Dąbrowska)

2011 (18 Apr). Smile of the World (photographs by Elżbeita Dzikowska). Sheet 120×127 mm containing T **1483** and similar vert designs. Multicoloured. Perf 11½ (with one elliptical hole on each vert side).
MS4452 1z.95 Type **1483**; 1z.95 African girl with plaited hair (Ethiopia); 2z.40 Girl with flowers in hair (Burma); 2z.40 Arab man with camel (Palestinian man); 3z. Indian girl (Nepal); 3z. Woman wearing hat (Peru) .... 26·00 23·00

(Des Marzanna Dąbrowska. Litho)

2011 (28 Apr). Beatification of Pope John Paul II. Sheet 75×100 mm. Perf 11½×11 (with one elliptical hole on each horiz side).
MS4453 **1484** 8z.30 multicoloured .... 20·00 16·00
Stamps of a similar design were issued by Vatican City.

1485 Bison amongst Trees

1486 Guccio

(Des Anna Niemierko)

2011 (5 May). Europa. Forests. Perf 12×11½ (with one elliptical hole on each horiz side).

4454	**1485**	3z. multicoloured	7·00	4·75

(Des Bohdan Butenko)

2011 (27 May). Cartoon Characters created by Bohdan Butenko. T **1486** and similar vert designs. Multicoloured. Perf 11½×12 (with one elliptical hole on each vert side).

4455	1z.55 40 Type **1486**	3·00	2·75
	a. Strip of 4. Nos. 4455/4458	14·50	
4456	1z.55 Cezar	3·00	2·75
4457	2z.40 Kwapiszon	4·00	3·50
4458	2z.40 Gapiszon	4·00	3·50
4455/4458 *Set of 4*		12·50	11·00

Nos. 4455/4458 were printed, *se-tenant*, in horizontal strips of four stamps within the sheet.

1487 Arrows as Figures and Flag

(Des Anna Niemierko)

2011 (30 June). Polish Presidency of EU Council. Perf 12×11½ (with one elliptical hole on each horiz side).

4459	**1487**	3z. multicoloured	6·00	5·50

No. 4459 was printed, *se-tenant*, with a stamp-size label showing stylised figure and stars.

1488 Czesława Miłosz

1489 Maximilian (Maksymilian) Maria Kolbe

(Des Marzanna Dąbrowska. Eng Przemysław Krajewski. Recess and photo)

2011 (30 June). Birth Centenary of Czesława Miłosz (poet and writer). Sheet 70×90 mm.

MS4460 **1488**	4z.15 black and bright rose-carmine	8·00	7·25

(Des Maciej Jędrysik)

2011 (12 Aug). 60th Death Anniversary of Saint Maximilian (Maksymilian) Maria Kolbe (Franciscan friar, who volunteered to die in place of a stranger in Auschwitz concentration camp). Perf 11½×12 (with one elliptical hole on each vert side).

4461	**1489**	1z.95 multicoloured	4·00	3·00

1490 Michał Sędziwój (alchemist, philosopher, and medical doctor)

(Des Janusz Wysocki)

2011 (29 Aug). Personalities. T **1490** and similar horiz designs. Multicoloured. Perf 12×11½ (with one elliptical hole on each horiz side).

4462	1z.55 Type **1490**	2·75	2·50
4463	1z.95 Jan Szczepanik (inventor)	3·25	3·00
4464	3z. Jan Józef Baranowski (astronomer)	6·00	4·75
4465	3z. Rudolf Stefan Weigl (biologist and inventor of first vacine against epidemic typhus)	6·00	4·75
4462/4465 *Set of 4*		16·00	13·50

1491 Jan Dzierżon

1492 Saint Mary's Church, Niegowić (Karol Józef Wojtyła's first parish)

(Des Jacek Konarzewski)

2011 (2 Sept). Birth Bicentenary of Johan (Jan) Dzierżon (pioneering apiarist discover of parthenogenesis in bees and designer of first successful movable-frame beehive). Perf 11½×12 (with one elliptical hole on each vert side).

4466	**1491**	1z.55 multicoloured	3·50	2·50

(Des Janusz Wysocki)

2011 (22 Sept). Pope John Paul II (Karol Józef Wojtyła) Commemoration. Perf 12×11½ (with one elliptical hole on each horiz side).

4467	**1492**	1z.95 multicoloured	5·25	4·50

No. 4467 was printed, *se-tenant*, with a stamp-size label showing Karol Wojtyła as parish priest with children.

1493 Town Hall and Church, St Barbar, Polkowice

1494 *Double Portrait of Eliza Pareńska* (Stanislaw Wyspiański)

(Des Małgorzata Osa)

2011 (30 Sept). Polski Związek Felinologiczny (PZF) (cat lovers and breeders association) Congress, Polkowice. Sheet 70×90 mm. Perf 11½×12 (with one elliptical hole on each vert side).

MS4468 **1493**	4z.15 multicoloured	8·00	7·25

(Des Jacek Konarzewski. Photo)

2011 (21 Oct). Lost Works of Art. T **1494** and similar horiz designs. Multicoloured. Perf 11½.

4469	1z.95 Type **1494**	3·50	3·00
	a. Strip of 3. Nos. 4469/4471	14·00	
4470	2z.40 Scene from the legend of Theophilus of Adana (late 15th-century wooden carving) (Wit Stwosz)	4·50	4·00
4471	3z. *Woman standing* (Jean-Antoine Watteau)	5·50	4·75
4469/4471 *Set of 3*		12·00	10·50

Nos. 4469/4471 were printed, *se-tenant*, in horizontal strips of three stamps within sheets of six.

1495 Satellite

1496 Nobel Medal

(Des Jacek Brodowski)

2011 (4 Nov). First Polish Scientific Satellite. Sheet 90×70 mm. Perf 12×11½ (with one elliptical hole on each horiz side).
MS4472 **1495** 4z.15 multicoloured .... 8·00 7·25

(Des Marzanna Dąbrowska. Eng Piotr Naszarkowski. Recess and litho)

2011 (17 Nov). Centenary of Marie Skłodowska Curie's Nobel Prize for Chemistry. Sheet 84×125 mm containing T **1496** and similar multicoloured design. Perf 13.
MS4473 3z. Type **1496**; 7z.80 Marie Curie (40×55 mm)... 24·00 20·00

A stamp of a similar design was issued by Sweden.

1497 Santa Claus

(Des Marek Kwiatkowski)

2011 (25 Nov). Christmas. T **1497** and similar horiz design. Multicoloured. Perf 11½.

(a) Ordinary gum. Perf 11½×12.
4474 1z.55 Type **1497** .... 2·75 2·50

(b) Self-adhesive. Die-cut perf 12.
4475 2z.40 Holy Family .... 4·50 4·00

1498 School Building

1499 Cloth as Map of Kazakhstan

(Des Maciej Jędrysik)

2011 (2 Dec). 30th Anniversary of Strike at Higher Military Fire Service School in Warsaw. Sheet 70×90 mm. Perf 11½×12 (with one elliptical hole on each vert side).
MS4476 **1498** 4z.15 multicoloured .... 7·50 6·75

(Des Aleksandra Ubukata)

2011 (8 Dec). 20th Anniversary of Independence of Kazakhstan. Perf 11½.
4477 **1499** 2z.40 multicoloured .... 4·50 4·00

1500 *Rubus idaeus* (Raspberry)

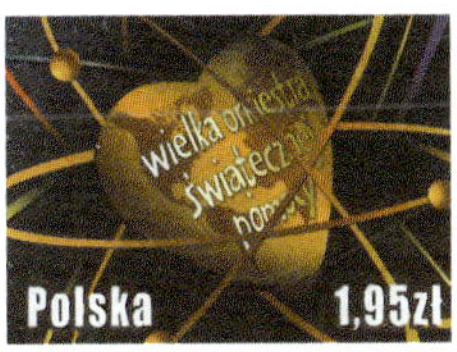

1501 Heart as Globe

(Des Marzanna Dąbrowska)

2011 (16 Dec). Flowers and Fruit. Perf 11½×12.
4478 **1500** 1z.55 multicoloured .... 2·75 2·50

(Des Jerzy Owsiak, Magdalena Jabłońska, Katarzyna Sasin and Krystiana Konieczna)

2012 (8 Jan). 20th Finale of Orchestra of Holy Day Assistance (fund raising charity). Sheet 70×90 mm. Perf 11½ (with one elliptical hole on each horiz side).
MS4479 **1501** 1z.95 multicoloured .... 6·00 3·50

1502 Arms

1503 Zygmunt Krasiński

(Des Marzanna Dąbrowska)

2012 (14 Feb). 70th Anniversary of National Army. Perf 12×11½.
4480 **1502** 1z.55 multicoloured .... 3·50 2·50

(Des Agata Tobolczyk)

2012 (19 Feb). Birth Bicentenary of Count Napoléon Stanisław Adam Ludwig Zygmunt Krasiński (writer). Sheet 90×70 mm. Perf 11½×12 (with one elliptical hole on each vert side).
MS4481 **1503** 4z.15 multicoloured .... 8·00 7·00

1504 Lamb and Flowers

1505 Leopold Kronenberg

(Des Agata Tobolczyk)

2012 (9 Mar). Easter. T **1504** and similar vert designs. Multicoloured. Perf 12×11½.
4482 1z.55 Type **1504** .... 3·00 2·50
4483 1z.95 Egg and flowers .... 4·00 3·00
4484 3z. Rabbit and flowers .... 6·00 4·75
4482/4484 *Set of 3* .... 11·50 9·25

(Des Bożydar Grozdew)

2012 (20 Mar). Birth Bicentenary of Baron Leopold Julian Kronenberg (banker). Perf 11½.
4485 **1505** 2z.40 black and gold .... 4·50 4·00

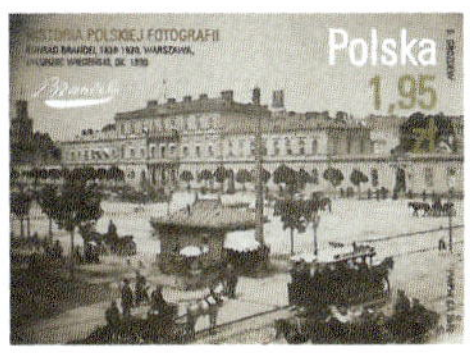

1506 Vienna Station, Warsaw, 1890

(Des Bozydar Grozdew)

2012 (28 Mar). History of Polish Photography. Konrad Brandel Commemoration. T **1506** and similar horiz designs showing photographs. Multicoloured. Perf 12×11½ (with one elliptical hole on each horiz side).
4486 1z.95 Type **1506** .... 3·50 3·00
a. Strip of 4. Nos. 4486/4489 .... 17·00
4487 1z.95 Krakowskie Przedmieście, 1880 .... 3·50 3·00
4488 2z.40 Three Crosses Square, 1875 .... 4·50 4·00
4489 2z.40 Pancera Viaduct, 1890 .... 4·50 4·00
4486/4489 *Set of 4* .... 14·50 12·50

Nos. 4486/4489 were printed, *se-tenant*, in strips of four stamps within the sheet.

1507 Municipal Offices

1508 Ushebti (Funerary figurine), 4th century BC

(Des Bożydar Grozdew)

2012 (30 Mar). 300th Anniversary of Suwałki City. Perf 11½.

4490	**1507**	1z.95 multicoloured	4·00	3·00

(Des Marzanna Dąbrowska)

2012 (30 Apr). 150th Anniversary of First Polish Discoveries in Egypt. Sheet 95×130 mm containing T **1508** and similar vert designs. Multicoloured. Perf 11½.

MS4491 1z.55 Type **1508**; 1z.95 Blue Ushebti (Funerary figurine) 6th/7th century BC; 2z.40 Amulet figurine depicting Nefertum; 3z. Michał Tyszkiewicz (Egyptologist) ..... 16·00 14·50

1509 *Maskerada* (Tadeusz Makowski)

(Des Piotr Stefankiewicz)

2012 (17 May). 150th Anniversary of National Museum, Warsaw. Sheet 110×78 mm. Perf 11½.

MS4492 **1509** 4z.15 multicoloured ..... 8·00 7·00

1510 Signposts showing Attractions

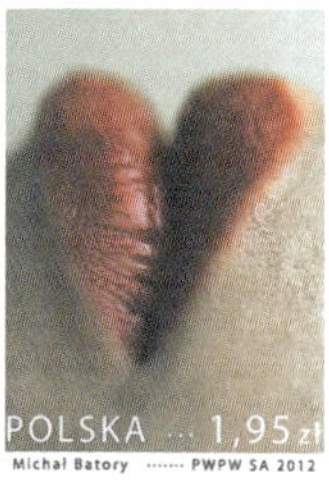

1511 Lips (poster for ARTISAN DE L' AFICHE, Musée des Arts Décoratifs at the Louvre, Paris)

(Des Bożydar Grozdew)

2012 (22 May). Europa. Visit Poland. Perf 11½ (with one elliptical hole on vert side).

4493	**1510**	3z. multicoloured	6·00	4·75

2012 (25 May). Art Work (photography) by Michał Batory. T **1511** and similar design. Perf 11½ (with one elliptical hole on each vert side (No. 4494) or horiz side (No. 4495)).

4494	1z.95 Type **1511** (multicoloured)	3·50	3·00
4495	3z. Fingers (sepia) (*horiz*)	5·50	4·75

1512 Zajączek Parauszek

(Des Piotr Stefankiewicz)

2012 (27 May). Cartoon Characters created by Wojciech Próchniewicz, Anthony Bankowski and Luc Toutounghi. Sheet 90×70 mm. Perf 11½ (with one elliptical hole on each horiz side).

MS4496 **1512** 4z.15 multicoloured ..... 8·00 7·00

1513 Municipal Stadium, Poznań

(Des Bożydar Grozdew)

2012 (8–15 June). Euro 2012, European Football Championships. T **1513** and similar multicoloured designs. Perf 11½ (No. 4501) or 11½ (others) (with one elliptical hole on each horiz side).

4497	1z.55 Type **1513**	3·75	3·00
4498	1z.95 National Stadium, Warsaw	3·50	3·00
4499	2z.40 PGE Area, Gdańsk	5·25	4·00
4500	3z. Municipal Stadium, Wrocław	7·25	5·50
4501	3z. Football (39×39 mm (circular)) (15.6)	6·75	5·50
4497/4501	*Set of* 5	24·00	19·00
MS4502	125×90 mm. Nos. 4497/5400	24·00	18·00

No. 4501 is perforated in a circle around the design, enclosed in an outer perforated square.

1514 Parkland

(Des Marzanna Dąbrowska)

2012 (12 July). World Heritage Site. Muskauer Park. Perf 11½ (with one elliptical hole on each horiz side).

4503	**1514**	3z. multicoloured	7·25	5·50

A stamp of a similar design was issued by Germany.

1515 Sculls

1516 Józef Kraszewski

(Des Agata Tobolczyk)

2012 (27 July). Olympic Games, London. Sheet 199×116 mm containing T **1515** and similar horiz designs. Multicoloured. Perf 12×11½ (with one elliptical hole on each horiz side).

MS4504 1z.55 Type **1515**; 1z.95 Handball; 2z.40 Weightlifting; 3z. Shot put ..... 24·00 20·00

(Des Kazimierz Bulik)

2012 (28 July). Birth Bicentenary of Józef Ignacy Kraszewski (writer, historian and journalist). Perf 12×11½.

4505	**1516**	4z.15 multicoloured	8·00	7·25

No. 4505 was printed *se-tenant* with a stamp-size label at right.

1517 *Russula virescens*

1518 Exhibition Name and National Flags of Poland and Germany

(Des Marzanna Dąbrowska)

2012 (3 Aug). Fungi. Sheet 125×152 mm containing T **1517** and similar horiz designs. Multicoloured. Perf 12×11½ (with one elliptical hole on each horiz side).

MS4506 1z.55 Type **1517**; 1z.95 *Morchella esculenta*; 3z. *Macrolepiota procea*; 4z.15 *Amillaria ostoyae*........... 24·00 20·00

No. **MS**4506 also contains four stamp-size labels showing poisonous fungi.

(Des Bożydar Grozdew)

2012 (6 Sept). Kargowa 2012 Bilateral Polish and German Philatelic Exhibiton. Perf 11½×12 (with one elliptical hole on each vert side).

4507 **1518** 2z.40 multicoloured .... 4·50 4·00

1519 Piotr Skarga

1520 *Bullfinches and Dandelion Seed Heads*

(Des Kazimierz Bulik. Photo)

2012 (27 Sept). 400th Death Anniversary of Piotr Skarga (Jesuit, preacher, hagiographer, polemicist and leading figure of the Counter-reformation in the Polish-Lithuanian Commonwealth). Perf 11½.

4508 **1519** 1z.55 multicoloured .... 4·50 2·75

(Des Agata Tobolczyk. Photo)

2012 (10 Oct). Tenth Death Anniversary of Piotr Kwit (artist). Perf 11½.

4509 **1520** 1z.55 multicoloured .... 3·00 2·75

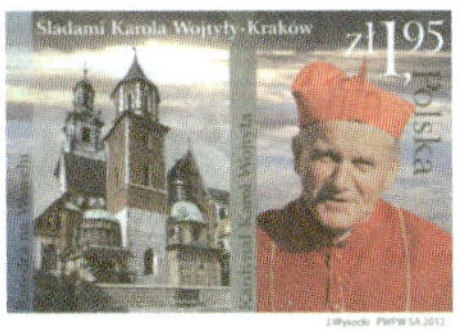

1521 Wawel Cathedral and Karol Wojtyła

1522 Jadwiga Smosarska (actor)

(Des Janusz Wysocki. Litho)

2012 (13 Oct). Pope John Paul II (Karol Józef Wojtyła) Commemoration. In Cracow. Perf 12×11½ (with one elliptical hole on each horiz side).

4510 **1521** 1z.95 multicoloured .... 6·00 3·00

No. 4510 was printed, *se-tenant*, with a stamp size label showing Karol Wojtyła being created a Cardinal on 26 June 1967 by Pope Paul VI.

(Des Marzanna Dąbrowska. Litho)

2012 (31 Oct). Personalities of Theatre and Cinema. T **1522** and similar vert designs. Multicoloured. Perf 11½×12 (with one elliptical hole on each vert side).

4511 1z.55 Type **1522** .... 3·00 2·75
4512 1z.95 Aleksander Zabczyński (actor)................ 5·00 3·50
4513 3z. Eugeniusz Bodo (film director) .... 6·00 4·50
4511/4513 *Set of* 3.................................... 12·50 9·75

MS4514 121×82 mm. 1z.55 Type **1522**; 1z.95 Aleksander Zabczyński (actor); 3z. Eugeniusz Bodo (film director).. 16·00 14·50

See also Nos. 4572/**MS**4575, 4648/**MS**4651 and 4702/**MS**4705.

1523 Turczynek Villa, Milanówek

1524 Angels and Star

(Des Marzanna Dąbrowska. Litho)

2012 (31 Oct). Garden Cities in Poland. Sheet 90×70 mm. Perf 12×11½ (with one elliptical hole on each horiz side).

MS4515 **1523** 4z.15 multicoloured.................................. 8·00 6·75

(Des Agnieszka Sobczyńska. Photo)

2012 (30 Nov). Christmas. T **1524** and similar multicoloured design. Perf 11½.

4516 A (1z.55) Type **1524** .... 3·00 2·30
4517 2z.40 Angels with Christmas gifts (*horiz*)........ 5·00 3·75

1525 Jerzy Turowicz

1526 Emblem

(Des M. Ufnalewski. Litho)

2012 (10 Dec). Birth Centenary of Jerzy Turowicz (Catholic journalist and editor). Perf 12×11½ (with one elliptical hole on each horiz side).

4518 **1525** 1z.55 black and yellow .... 4·00 2·75

(Des Jerzy Owsiak, Magdalena Jabłońska and Katarzyna Sasin. Litho)

2013 (13 Jan). 21st Finale of Orchestra of Holy Day Assistance (fund raising charity). Self-adhesive. Die-cut wavy edge.

4519 **1526** A (1z.60) multicoloured........................ 4·00 2·50

No. 4519 was die-cut around in a circle enclosed in an outer square and printed in sheets of six stamps.

1527 'E'

1528 'P'

(Des Marzanna Dąbrowska. Photo)

2013 (8 Mar). Economic and Priority Stamps. Vert designs as T **1527** (E stamps) or T **1528** (P stamps). Multicoloured (blue). Perf 12×11½.

4520 a (1z.60) Type **1527** .... 3·00 2·30
4521 a (2z.35) Type **1528** .... 4·50 3·25
4522 b (3z.75) As Type **1527** .... 7·00 5·25
4523 b (5z.10) As Type **1528** .... 9·50 7·25
4520/4523 *Set of* 4.................................... 22·00 16·00

Nos. 4520/4523 each have a different geometric centre design.

Nos. 4520/4523 are for use on mail up to 350 grams.

There are two delivery speeds, economic (E) and priority (P).

Those stamps inscribed 'a' are for domestic mail and those inscribed 'b' are for international mail.

(Des Marzanna Dąbrowska. Photo)

2013 (29 Mar). Economic and Priority Stamps. Vert designs as T **1527** (E stamps) or **1528** (P stamps). Multicoloured (green). Perf 12×11½.

4524	a (3z.70) As Type **1527**	6·75	4·75
4525	a (4z.50) As Type **1528**	8·00	5·50
4526	b (4z.75) As Type **1527**	8·50	5·75
4527	b (7z.10) As Type **1528**	13·00	9·00
4524/4527 *Set of 4*		33·00	23·00

Nos. 4524/4527 each have a different geometric centre design.

Nos. 4524/4527 are for use on mail up to 1000 grams.

There are two delivery speeds, economic (E) and priority (P).

Those stamps inscribed 'a' are for domestic mail and those inscribed 'b' are for international mail.

See also Nos. 4535/4538.

1529 *Alcedo atthis*

(Des Marzanna Dąbrowska. Litho)

2013 (12 Apr). Polish Birds. Kingfisher. Sheet 90×70 mm. Perf 11½ (with one elliptical hole on each vert side).

MS4528 **1529** 4z.55 multicoloured .... 9·00 7·50

1530 Wieczław Chrzanowski

1531 Star

(Des Marzanna Dąbrowska. Litho)

2013 (16 Apr). 90th Birth Anniversary (2012) of Wieczław Chrzanowski (politician). Perf 11½ (with one elliptical hole on each horiz side).

4529 **1530** 3z.80 multicoloured .... 6·25 5·50

(Des Marzanna Dąbrowska. Photo)

2013 (19 Apr). 70th Anniversary of Warsaw Uprising (1st issue). Perf 11.

4530 **1531** 3z.80 multicoloured .... 6·25 5·50

See also No. **MS**4606.

1532 Flag

(Des Jacek Konarzewski. Litho)

2013 (2 May). Flag Day of the Republic of Poland. Perf 11½ (with one elliptical hole on each vert side).

4531 **1532** 1z.60 multicoloured .... 3·25 2·50

1533 Peugeot Post Van

1534 Goofy, Minnie and Mickey

(Des Jacek Konarzewski. Litho)

2013 (6 May). Europa. Postal Transport. Perf 11½ (with one elliptical hole on each vert side).

4532 **1533** 4z.60 multicoloured .... 9·00 8·00

(Des Agnieszka Sancewicz)

2013 (1 June). Walt Disney Characters. Sheet 90×70 mm. Perf 11½ (with one elliptical hole on each horiz side).

MS4533 **1534** 4z.60 multicoloured .... 8·00 7·00

No. **MS**4533 is also known imperforate (*price £9 unused, £8 used*).

1535 Darlowo

(Des Jerzy Pietras. Litho)

2013 (14 June). Lighthouses. Sheet 90×125 mm containing T **1535** and similar vert designs. Multicoloured. Perf 11½×11.

MS4534 1z.60 Type **1535**; 2z.35 Jaroslawiec; 3z.75 Ustka; 3z.80 Czolpino .... 19·00 17·00

(Des Marzanna Dąbrowska. Photo)

2013 (20 June). Economic and Priority Stamps. Vert designs as T **1527** (E stamps) or T **1528** (P stamps). Multicoloured (red). Perf 12×11½.

4535	a (6z.30) As Type **1527**	11·00	7·75
4536	b (7z.30) As Type **1527**	13·00	9·00
4537	a (8z.80) As Type **1528**	16·00	11·00
4538	b (10z.90) As Type **1528**	20·00	13·50
4535/4538 *Set of 4*		55·00	37·00

Nos. 4535/4538 each have a different geometric centre design.

Nos. 4535/4538 are for use on mail up to 2000 grams.

There are two delivery speeds, economic (E) and priority (P).

Those stamps inscribed 'a' are for domestic mail and those inscribed 'b' are for international mail.

1536 Boleslaw III Krzywousty (Boleslaw III Wrymouth), Prince of Poland

(Des U. Cancewicz. Eng M. Kopecki. Recess and photo)

2013 (28 June). 900th Anniversary of Chronicles of Gallus Anonymus. Sheet 90×70 mm. Perf 11½.

MS4539 **1536** 8z.50 black and vermilion .... 14·00 12·50

1537 Kashubian Strawberry

1538 Cyclist

(Des Marek Kwiatkowski. Photo)

2013 (18 July). Polish Regional Products. Kashubian Strawberry. Perf 11½.
4540 **1537** 4z.60 multicoloured .... 8·00 6·75

(Des Janusz Wysocki. Litho)

2013 (30 July). Polish Cycle Race. Tour de Pologne. T **1538** and similar circular design. Multicoloured. Multicoloured. Perf 11½.
4541 1z.60 Type **1538** .... 2·40 2·20
a. Pair. Nos. 4541/4542 .... 10·50 9·25
4542 4z.60 Two cyclists .... 7·50 6·75

Nos. 4541/4542 were printed, *se-tenant*, in horizontal pairs within sheets of four stamps.

Each stamp was perforated in a circle contained in an outer perforated square. Each square has one elliptical hole on each vert side.

1539 *BRITE-PL Heweliusz* Satellite

1540 Guitar

(Des Jan Konarzewski. Litho)

2013 (31 July). Poland's Second Scientific Satellite. *BRITE-PL Heweliusz* (named after Polish astronomer Hevelius). Sheet 90×70 mm. Perf 11½ (with one elliptical hole on each horiz side).
MS4543 **1539** 4z.55 multicoloured .... 8·00 7·25

(Des Jerzy Owsiak, Magdalena Jabłońska, Katarzyna Sasin and G. Andrzejewski. Litho)

2013 (1 Aug). Woodstock Free Music Festival, Kostrzyn nad Odrą, Poland (Festiwal Przystanek Woodstock). Self-adhesive. Die-cut perf 11½.
4544 **1540** 2z.35 multicoloured .... 5·00 3·50

No. 4544 was printed on transparent plastic film.

1541 *Fryderyk Chopin* (Polish brig-rigged sailing ship)

(Des Jerzy Pietras. Eng P. Krajewski. Recess and photo)

2013 (3 Aug). Tall Ships' Races, Szczecin 2013. Sheet 90×70 mm. Perf 11.
MS4545 **1541** 8z.50 new blue and black .... 14·00 12·50

1542 Two General Dynamics (now Lockheed Martin) F-16 Fighting Falcons

(Des Jan Konarzewski. Litho)

2013 (14 Aug). Contemporary Polish Army Weapons. T **1542** and similar horiz designs. Multicoloured. Perf 11½ (with one elliptical hole on each vert side).
4546 1z.60 Type **1542** .... 2·50 2·30
a. Vert strip of 3. Nos. 4546/4548 .... 7·75
4547 1z.60 KTO Rosomak (Kolowy Transporter Opancerzony) wheeled armoured vehicle .... 2·50 2·30
4548 1z.60 ORP *Kontradmiral Xawery Czernicki* (multitask logistical support ship) .... 2·50 2·30
4546/4548 *Set of 3* .... 6·75 6·25

Nos. 4546/4548 were printed, *se-tenant*, in vertical strips of three, within sheets of six stamps.

1543 'E' and *Polymmatus senuargus*

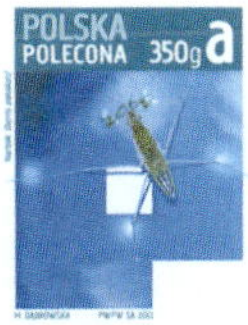

1544 'P' and *Gerris paludum*

(Des Marzanna Dąbrowska. Photo)

2013 (16 Aug). Economic and Priority Stamps. Registered Mail. Insects. Vert designs as T **1543** (E stamps) or T **1544** (P stamps). Multicoloured (blue). Perf 12×11½.
4549 a (4z.20) Type **1543** .... 6·00 5·00
4550 b (5z.50) As Type **1543** but with *Rosalia alpina* .... 10·00 7·50
4551 a (7z.50) Type **1544** .... 12·00 8·75
4552 b (8z.30) As Type **1544** but with *Sympetrum faveclum* .... 16·00 12·00
4549/4552 *Set of 4* .... 40·00 29·00

Nos. 4549/4552 each have a different insect incorporated in the design.

Nos. 4549/4552 are for use on mail up to 350 grams.

There are two delivery speeds, economic (E) and priority (P).

Those stamps inscribed 'a' are for domestic mail and those inscribed 'b' are for international mail.

See also Nos. 4559/4562 and 4564/4567.

1545 Costumes from Bistrița-Năsăud, Romania and Kraków, Poland

(Des Marzanna Dąbrowska. Litho)

2013 (11 Sept). 20th Anniversary of Poland–Romania Friendship Treaty. Traditional Folk Costumes. Sheet 70×90 mm. Perf 11½ (with one elliptical hole on each vert side).
MS4553 **1545** 4z.60 multicoloured .... 8·00 7·25

A stamp of a similar design was issued by Romania.

1546 Halite

1547 Lech Wałęsa

(Des Marek Kwiatkowski. Litho and varnish)

2013 (20 Sept). Polish Minerals. T **1546** and similar horiz designs. Multicoloured. Perf 11½ (with one elliptical hole on each vert side).
4554 1z.60 Type **1546** .... 2·50 2·30
a. Strip of 4. Nos. 4554/4557 .... 13·50
4555 1z.60 Malachite and azurite .... 2·50 2·30

4556 2z.35 Marcasite ... 4·00 3·50
4557 2z.35 Gypsum ... 4·00 3·50
4554/4557 *Set of 4* ... 11·50 10·50

Nos. 4554/4557 were printed, *se-tenant*, in vertical strips of four stamps within sheets of 12.

(Des Jacek Konarzewski. Litho)

2013 (29 Sept). 70th Birth Anniversary of Lech Wałęsa. Perf 11½ (with one elliptical hole on each vert side).
4558 **1547** 3z.80 multicoloured ... 6·50 5·75

(Des Marzanna Dąbrowska. Photo)

2013 (30 Sept). Economic and Priority Stamps. Registered Mail. Insects. Vert designs as T **1543** (E stamps) or T **1544** (P stamps). Multicoloured (green). Perf 12×11½.
4559 a (5z.90) As Type **1543** but with Ladybird ... 10·00 7·75
4560 a (8z.30) As Type **1544** but with Grasshopper ... 12·00 9·00
4561 b (7z.20) As Type **1543** but with Peacock Butterfly ... 12·00 9·25
4562 b (11z.) As Type **1544** but with Ant ... 16·00 12·00
4559/4562 *Set of 4* ... 45·00 34·00

Nos. 4559/4562 each have a different insect incorporated in the design.
Nos. 4559/4562 are for use on mail up to 1000 grams.
There are two delivery speeds, economic (E) and priority (P).
Those stamps inscribed 'a' are for domestic mail and those inscribed 'b' are for international mail.

1548 St Mark's Church, Zagreb, Croatia

(Des Magdalena Błażków. Litho)

2013 (11 Oct). Capital Cities of European Union States. Perf 11½ (with one elliptical hole on each horiz side).
4563 **1548** 4z.60 multicoloured ... 8·00 7·25

(Des Marzanna Dąbrowska. Photo)

2013 (18 Oct). Economic and Priority Stamps. Registered Mail. Insects. Vert designs as T **1543** (E stamps) or T **1544** (P stamps). Multicoloured (red). Perf 12×11½.
4564 a (8z.50) As Type **1543** but with Tiger Moth Butterfly ... 14·00 11·00
4565 b (9z.50) As Type **1543** but with Stag Beetle ... 16·00 12·50
4566 a (11z.) As Type **1544** but with Honey Bee ... 18·00 14·00
4567 b (13z.11) As Type **1544** but with Old World Swallowtail Caterpillar ... 22·00 17·00
4564/4567 *Set of 4* ... 65·00 49·00

Nos. 4564/4567 each have a different insect incorporated in the design.
Nos. 4564/4567 are for use on mail up to 2000 grams.
There are two delivery speeds, economic (E) and priority (P).
Those stamps inscribed 'a' are for domestic mail and those inscribed 'b' are for international mail.

1549 Tree Rings marking Polish Postage from 16th–21st Century

(Des A. Sancewicz)

2013 (18 Oct). World Post Day. 455th Anniversary of Polish Post. Perf 11½.
4568 **1549** 4z.60 multicoloured ... 8·00 7·25

1550 Ludwik Solski as the Guardian in *Treasure* by Leopold Staff

(Des A. Ubukata. Photo)

2013 (21 Oct). Lost Works of Art. Paintings of Ludwik Solski (actor) by Stanislaw Wyspiański (playwright, artist and poet) in 1904. T **1550** and similar horiz designs. Multicoloured. Perf 11½.
4569 1z.60 Type **1550** ... 2·50 2·30
a. Strip of 3. Nos. 4569/4571 ... 13·50
4570 2z.35 As Andrew Aguecheek in William Shakespeare's *Twelfth Night* ... 4·00 3·50
4571 3z.80 As Veteran Defender (the old Wiarus) in *Varsovian Anthem* (Warszawianka), by Stanislaw Wyspianski ... 6·50 5·75
4569/4571 *Set of 3* ... 11·50 10·50

Nos. 4569/4571 were printed, *se-tenant*, in horizontal strips of three stamps within sheets of six.

(Des Marzanna Dąbrowska. Litho)

2013 (31 Oct). Personalities of Theatre and Cinema. Vert designs as T **1522**. Multicoloured. Perf 11½×12 (with one elliptical hole on each vert side).
4572 1z.60 Helena Grossówna (actress and dancer) ... 3·00 2·30
4573 2z.35 Adolf Dymsza (comedy actor) ... 5·00 3·50
4574 3z.80 Mieczysława Ćwiklińska (actress and singer) ... 8·00 5·75
4572/4574 *Set of 3* ... 14·50 10·50
MS4575 121×82 mm. Nos. 4572/4574 ... 20·00 15·00

1551 Krzysztof Penderecki

1552 *Argiope bruennichi*

(Des Anna Niemierko)

2013 (23 Nov). 80th Birth Anniversary of Krzysztof Penderecki (composer and conductor). Perf 11½.
4576 **1551** 3z.80 multicoloured ... 6·50 5·75

(Des Jacek Konarzewski. Litho and varnish)

2013 (29 Nov). Spiders protected in Poland. T **1552** and similar horiz designs. Multicoloured. Perf 12×11½ (with one elliptical hole on each horiz side).
4577 1z.60 Type **1552** ... 3·00 2·75
4578 2z.35 *Atypus muralis* ... 4·00 3·50
4579 3z.80 *Eresus kollari* ... 7·00 6·25
4580 4z.55 *Philaeus chrysops* ... 8·00 7·25
4577/4580 *Set of 4* ... 20·00 18·00

1553 Ski Jump

1554 Oskar Kolberg

(Des Agata Tobolczyk)

2014 (7 Feb). Winter Olympic Games, Sochi. Sheet 126×90 mm containing T **1553** and similar horiz design. Multicoloured. Perf 12×11½ (with one elliptical hole on each horiz side).
MS4581 1z.75 Type **1553**×2; 5z. Nordic skiing×2 ... 32·00 27·00

The stamps and margins of No. **MS**4581 form a composite background design.

(Des Karol Tabaka)

2014 (22 Feb). Birth Bicentenary of Oskar Kolberg (ethnographer, folklorist and composer). Perf 11½×11.

4582 **1554** 4z.20 multicoloured .... 8·00 6·50

1555 Athletes

1556 Easter Egg

(Des Agata Tobolczyk)

2014 (7 Mar). IAAF World Indoor Championships. Perf 11½ (with one elliptical hole on each horiz side).

4583 **1555** 5z. multicoloured .... 8·50 7·75

(Des Agnieszka Sancewicz)

2014 (26 Mar). Easter. T **1556** and similar vert design. Multicoloured. Perf 12×11½.

4584 1z.75 Type **1556** .... 3·50 2·75

4585 5z. Purple egg.................................... 10·50 8·00

See also Nos. 4662/4663 and 4724/4726.

1557 Towers of Wawel Cathedral

1558 Pope John Paul II

(Des Marzanna Dąbrowska. Recess and photo)

2014 (28 Mar). 650th Anniversary of Wawel Cathedral. Sheet 77×77 mm containing T **1557** and similar vert design. Black and carmine-vermilion. Perf 11.

MS4586 4z.20 Type **1557**; 8z.30 Bell and nave................ 22·00 20·00

(Des Marzanna and Jacek Dąbrowscy. Recess and litho (No. **MS**4589) or litho (others))

2014 (2 Apr). Canonisation of Pope John Paul II. Perf 11½ (with one elliptical hole on each vert side).

4587 **1588** 2z.35 multicoloured .... 4·00 3·50

MS4588 75×100 mm. 5z. As T **1558** multicoloured (40×50 mm).. 9·00 7·75

MS4589 75×100 mm. 8z.50 As T **1558** gold (40×50 mm).. 15·00 13·50

Design: 2z.35 Type **1558**; 5z. As Type **1558**; 8z.50 As Type **1558**.

1559 Pope John Paul II

1560 Kamil Stoch

(Des Marzanna and Jacek Dąbrowscy)

2014 (2 Apr). Canonisation of Pope John Paul II and Pope John XXIII. Sheet 120×75 mm containing T **1559** and similar vert design. Multicoloured. Perf 11½×11 (with one elliptical hole on each vert side).

MS4590 5z.×2, Type **1559**; Pope John XXIII..................... 20·00 17·00

(Des Marzanna Dąbrowska)

2014 (11 Apr). Polish Olympic Gold Medalists. Sheet 82×121mm containing T **1560** and similar horiz designs. Multicoloured. Perf 12×11½ (with one elliptical hole on each horiz side).

MS4591 4z.20×3, Type **1560** (double Olympic champion in the normal hill and large hill); Justyna Kowalczyk (Cross-country 10 k. classical Olympic champion); Zbigniew Bródka (Olympic 1500 m. individual speed skating champion)......................... 22·00 20·00

1561 Jan Karski

1562 Paper Plane and EU Stars

(Des Agata Tobolczyk)

2014 (24 Apr). Birth Centenary of Jana Karskiego (World War II resistance movement fighter and professor at Georgetown University). Perf 11½.

4592 **1561** 4z.20 multicoloured .... 8·00 6·50

(Des Magdalena Błażków)

2014 (1 May). Tenth Anniversary of Accession of Poland to European Union. Perf 11×11½ (with one elliptical hole on each horiz side).

4593 **1562** 5z.20 multicoloured .... 8·75 8·00

1563 Traditional Bagpipes in Shape of Goat

1564 Family in the Frame

(Des Małgorzata Myszka. Litho)

2014 (5 May). Europa. Musical Instruments. Perf 11½ (with one elliptical hole on each vert side).

4594 **1563** 5z.20 multicoloured .... 10·00 8·00

(Des Karol Tabaka)

2014 (15 May). International Year of the Family. Perf 11½.

4595 **1564** 2z.35 multicoloured .... 5·00 3·50

1565 Poppy

1566 Crowds and 'Wolności'

(Des Agnieszka Sancewicz)

2014 (18 May). 70th Anniversary of Battle of Monte Cassino. Perf 11½ (with one elliptical hole on each vert side).

4596 **1565** 1z.75 multicoloured .... 4·00 2·75

(Des Agnieszka Sancewićz)

2014 (28 May). Freedom Festival. 25th Anniversary of Anti-Communism Revolutions. Perf 11½×11.

4597 **1566** 2z.35 black, scarlet-vermilion and silver 4·00 3·50

1567 Tinkerbell and the Fairy Pirates

1568 Kazimierz Górski

(Des Jacek Konarzewski)

2014 (1 June). Walt Disney Characters. Sheet 90×70 mm. Perf 11½ (with one elliptical hole on each vert side).

MS4598 **1567** 5z.20 multicoloured.................................. 10·00 8·50

(Des Agata Tobolczyk)

2014 (27 June). Polish Football Coaches. Sheet 115×90mm containing T **1568** and similar horiz designs. Multicoloured. Perf 11½.

MS4599 2z.35×4, Type **1568**; Hubert Wagner; Feliks Stamm; Henryk Łasak.. 16·00 14·50

1569 Zinc Works, Szopienice

(Des Agata Tobolczyk)

2014 (11 July). History of Polish Photography. Henryk Poddębski Commemoration. T **1569** and similar horiz designs showing photographs. Multicoloured. Perf 12×11½ (with one elliptical hole on each horiz side).

4600 1z.75 Type **1569** .... 3·00 2·75
a. Strip of 4. Nos. 4600/4603........................ 22·00
4601 2z.35 Machinery, Coal Mine, Kleofas .... 4·00 3·50
4602 3z.75 Royal foundry.. 6·50 5·75
4603 4z.20 Coal Port, Gdynia .... 7·25 6·50
4600/4603 *Set of 4*... 19·00 17·00

Nos. 4600/4603 were printed, *se-tenant*, in strips of four stamps within the sheet.

1570 Apple

1571 Bee-eater

(Des Agnieszka Sancewicz)

2014 (18 July). Polish Regional Products. Jablko Łąckłe Apple. Perf 11½.

4604 **1570** 5z. multicoloured .... 8·00 7·25

(Des Marzanna Dąbrowska)

2014 (31 July). Polish Birds. Common Bee-eater (*Merops apiaster*). Sheet 90×70 mm. Perf 11½ (with one elliptical hole on each vert side).

MS4605 **1571** 5z.50 multicoloured.................................. 9·00 8·00

1572 Soldier

1573 Józef Piłsudski (statesman and Marshal of Poland)

(Des Agnieszka Sancewicz)

2014 (1 Aug). 70th Anniversary of Warsaw Uprising (2nd issue). Sheet 90×70 mm. Perf 11½ (one elliptical hole on each vert side).

MS4606 **1572** 5z.20 multicoloured.................................. 8·50 7·50

(Des Karol Tabaka. Eng Przemyslaw Krajewski. Recess and litho)

2014 (6 Aug). Polish Legions. Sheet 90×70 mm. Perf 11.

MS4607 **1573** 8z.50 multicoloured.................................. 14·50 13·00

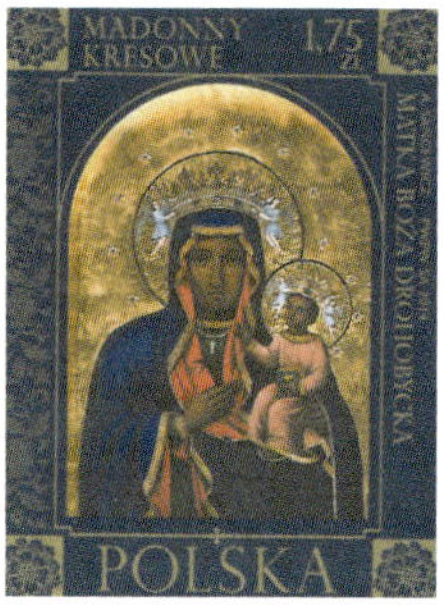

1574 Madonna, Drohobycka

1575 *Cantharellus cibarius*

(Des Agnieszka Sancewicz)

2014 (14 Aug). Madonnas of the Eastern Borderlands. T **1574** and similar vert design. Multicoloured. Perf 11.

4608 1z.95 Type **1574** .... 3·00 2·75
4609 4z.20 Madonna, Kochawińska .... 7·25 6·25

(Des Marzanna Dąbrowska)

2014 (29 Aug). Fungi. Sheet 125×152 mm containing T **1575** and similar horiz designs. Multicoloured. Perf 12×11½ (with one elliptical hole on each horiz side).

MS4610 1z.75 Type **1575**; 2z.35 *Agaricus campestris*; 3z.75 *Russula vesca*; 4z.20 *Boletus edulis*.................... 21·00 19·00

No. **MS**4610 also contains four stamp-size labels showing poisonous fungi.

1576 Player

1577 Stethoscope as Smiling Face

(Des Karol Tabaka)

2014 (30 Aug). FIVB Volleyball Men's World Championship, Poland. Sheet 121×125 mm containing T **1576** and similar vert designs. Multicoloured. Perf 11½ (with one elliptical hole on each vert side).

MS4611 1z.75 Type **1576**; 1z.75 Player 'spiking', blue vest; 2z.35 Player 'blocking', green T-shirt; 5z. Player serving, red T-shirt; 5z.10 Player 'digging', white vest; 5z.50 Player 'spiking', yellow vest........... 40·00 34·00

(Des Agata Tobolczyk)

2014 (5 Sept). Smiles Heal. Dr Clown. Perf 11½.
4612 **1577** 1z.75 multicoloured .... 4·00 2·75

1578 Legends of the Giants (Natalia Rak)

1579 Trees, Buildings, Dam and Raptor

(Des Robert Duczkowski)

2014 (26 Sept). Street Art. Sheet 90×82 mm. Perf 12×11½ (with one elliptical hole on each horiz side).
MS4613 **1578** 4z.20 multicoloured........ 10·00 8·00

(Des Agata Tobolczyk)

2014 (29 Sept). Alternative Energy Sources. T **1579** and similar vert designs. Multicoloured. Perf 11½.
4614 1z.75 Type **1579** .... 3·00 2·75
a. Block of 4. Nos. 4614/4617 .... 22·00
4615 2z.35 Thermal energy production and pylon 4·00 3·50
4616 3z.75 Trees, wind turbine and kite .... 6·50 5·75
4617 4z.20 High-rise buildings and solar array .... 7·25 6·50
4614/4617 *Set of* 4 .... 19·00 17·00

Nos. 4614/4617 were printed, *se-tenant*, in a block of four stamps.
Nos. 4614 and 4617 laid *tête-bêche* to Nos. 4615/4616, within the sheet, the block forming a composite design.

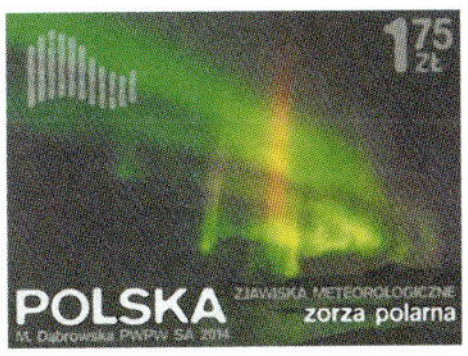

1580 *Aurora Borealis*

1581 Jan Nowaka-Jezlorańskiego

(Des Marzanna Dąbrowska)

2014 (30 Sept). Meteorological Phenomena. T **1580** and similar horiz designs. Multicoloured. Perf 11½ (with one elliptical hole on each horiz side).
4618 1z.75 Type **1580** .... 3·00 2·75
a. Strip of 4. Nos. 4618/4621 .... 24·00
4619 2z.35 Solar halo .... 4·00 3·50
4620 4z.20 Smoke .... 7·25 6·50
4621 5z.50 Hoarfrost .... 9·00 8·00
4618/4621 *Set of* 4 .... 21·00 19·00

Nos. 4618/4621 were printed, *se-tenant*, in strips of four stamps within the sheet.

(Des Karol Tabaka)

2014 (2 Oct). Birth Centenary of Jan Nowaka-Jezlorańskiego. Perf 11½.
4622 **1581** 4z.20 multicoloured .... 8·00 6·50

1582 *Acanthurus sohal*

1583 Stefan Żeromski

(Des Jacek Konarzewski)

2014 (10 Oct). Warszawa 2014 National Philatelic Exhibition. Marine Life. T **1582** and similar vert designs. Multicoloured. Perf 11½.
4623 35g. Type **1582** 60 55
a. Sheet. Nos. 4623/4630, plus 4 labels .... 65·00
4624 45g. *Chaetodon capistratus* 80 70
4625 55g. *Rhinomuraena quaesita* .... 1·00 90
4626 65g. *Hippocampus* sp. .... 1·20 1·10
4627 1z.10 *Balistoides conspicillum* .... 2·00 1·80
4628 1z.20 *Pomacanthus xanthometopon* .... 2·20 2·00
4629 1z.30 *Chelmon rostratus* .... 2·40 2·20
4630 1z.40 *Amphiprion ocellaris* .... 2·50 2·30
4623/4630 *Set of* 8 .... 11·50 10·50

Nos. 4623/4630 were printed in sheets of eight stamps and four stamp-size labels.

(Des Maciej Jędrysik)

2014 (14 Oct). 150th Birth Anniversary of Stefan Żeromski (writer). Perf 11½ (with one elliptical hole on each vert side).
4631 **1583** 4z.20 multicoloured .... 7·00 6·25

1584 Stéphane Antigi

(Des Jacek Konarzewski)

2014 (18 Oct). Poland, Winner of the FIVB Volleyball Men's World Championships. T **1584** and similar horiz designs. Multicoloured. Perf 11½ (with one elliptical hole on each horiz side).
4632 1z. Type **1584** .... 1·60 1·40
a. Sheet. Nos. 4632/4647 plus 4 labels .... 25·00
4633 1z. Piotr Nowakowski ....
4634 1z. Michał Winiarski .... 1·60 1·40
4635 1z. Dawid Konarski .... 1·60 1·40
4636 1z. Rafal Buszek .... 1·60 1·40
4637 1z. Paweł Zagumny .... 1·60 1·40
4638 1z. Karol Kłos .... 1·60 1·40
4639 1z. Andrzej Wrona .... 1·60 1·40
4640 1z. Mariusz Wlazły .... 1·60 1·40
4641 1z. Fabian Drzyzga .... 1·60 1·40
4642 1z. Michał Kubiak .... 1·60 1·40
4643 1z. Krzysztof Ignaczak .... 1·60 1·40
4644 1z. Paweł Zatorski .... 1·60 1·40
4645 1z. Marcin Możdżonek .... 1·60 1·40
4646 1z. Mateusz Mika .... 1·60 1·40
4647 1z. Philippe Blain .... 1·60 1·40
4632/4647 *Set of* 16 .... 22·00 19·00

Nos. 4632/4647 were printed, *se-tenant*, in sheets of 16 stamps and four stamp-size labels.

(Des Marzanna Dąbrowska)

2014 (31 Oct). Personalities of Theatre and Cinema. Vert designs as T **1522**. Multicoloured. Perf 11½×12 (with one elliptical hole on each vert side).
4648 1z.75 Tola Mankiewiczówna (singer and actress) .... 3·00 2·75
4649 2z.35 Antoni Fertner (actor) .... 4·00 3·50
4650 4z.20 Loda Halama (dancer and actress) .... 7·25 6·50
4648/4650 *Set of* 3 .... 13·00 11·50
MS4651 121×82 mm. Nos. 4648/4650 .... 18·00 14·50

1585 Holy Family

1586 Ophelia drowning (scene from *Hamlet*)

(Des Agnieszka Sancewicz)

2014 (14 Nov). Christmas. T **1585** and similar vert design. Multicoloured. Perf 11½.

4652 2z.35 Type **1585** .... 4·00 3·50
4653 5z.20 Adoration of the Magi .... 8·50 7·75

(Des Aleksandra Pietrzak)

2014 (21 Nov). 450th Birth Anniversary of William Shakespeare. Perf 11½×12.

4654 **1586** 4z.20 multicoloured .... 7·00 6·25

1587 Ambassadors to Courts

1588 Circle of Figures

(Des Maciej Jędrysik)

2014 (28 Nov). 600th Anniversary of Poland–Turkey Diplomatic Relations. Sheet 90×70 mm. Perf 11½ (with one elliptical hole on each horiz side).

MS4655 **1587** 5z. multicoloured .... 10·00 8·25

(Des Agnieszka Sancewicz)

2014 (19 Dec). World Youth Day. T **1588** and similar design. Perf 11½ (with one elliptical hole on each horiz side (1z.75) or each vert side (5z.)).

4656 1z.75 gold and bronze .... 5·00 2·75
4657 5z. gold and silver (45×23 mm) .... 10·00 7·50

Designs: 1z.75 T **1588**; 5z. Kracow skyline.

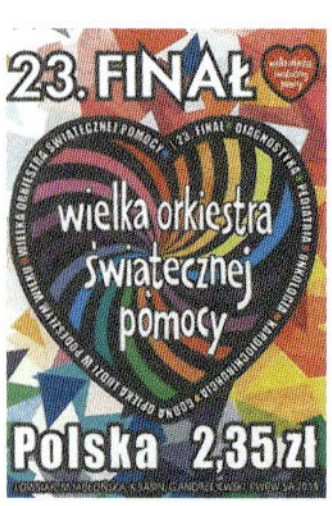

1589 Emblem

1590 Heart

(Des Jerzy Owsiak, Gawel Andrzejewski, Magdalena Jabłońska and Katarzyna Sasin)

2015 (7 Jan). 23rd Finale of Orchestra of Holy Day Assistance (fund raising charity). Perf 11½ (with one elliptical hole on each vert side).

4658 **1589** 2z.35 multicoloured .... 4·00 3·50

(Des Marzanna Dąbrowska. Litho, screen printing)

2015 (6 Feb). I Love You. Perf 11½ (with one elliptical hole on each vert side of outer square).

4659 **1590** 2z.35 multicoloured .... 4·00 3·50

No. 4659 was perforated around the heart-shape enclosed in an outer perforated square. The screen printing gives a glitter effect.

Stamps of a similar design were issued by Vatican City.

1591 Kazimierza Przerwy-Tetmajera

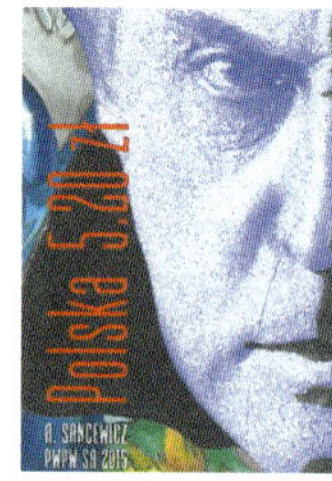

1592 Witkacy

(Des Aleksandra Pietrzak)

2015 (12 Feb). 150th Birth Anniversary of Kazimierza Przerwy-Tetmajera (writer). Perf 11½ (with one elliptical hole on each horiz side).

4660 **1591** 1z.75 multicoloured .... 3·00 2·75

(Des Agnieszka Sancewicz)

2015 (24 Feb). Witkacy, Visionary Creator. 130th Birth Anniversary of Stanisław Ignacy Witkiewicz (Witkacy) (artist, philosopher and writer). Sheet 70×90 mm. Perf 11½.

MS4661 **1592** 5z.20 multicoloured .... 8·50 7·50

(Des Agnieszka Sancewicz)

2015 (6 Mar). Easter. Vert designs as T **1556**. Multicoloured. Perf 12×11½.

4662 2z.35 Purple egg with floral decoration .... 4·00 3·50
4663 5z.20 Burgundy egg with fan-shaped decoration .... 8·00 7·25

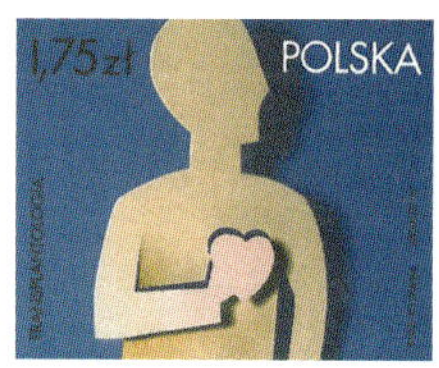

1594 Figure holding Heart

1595 'IDA'

(Des Maciej Jędrysik)

2015 (20 Mar). Organ Transplantation. Perf 11½.

4664 **1594** 1z.75 multicoloured .... 3·00 2·75

(Des Maciej Jędrysik)

2015 (31 Mar). *Ida* (film, directed by Pawel Pawlikowski, 2013). Perf 11½ (with one elliptical hole on each horiz side).

4665 **1595** 1z.75 multicoloured .... 4·00 3·50

1596 Tadeusz Kantor

1597 Symbol of Massacre

(Des Alexander Pietrzak)

2015 (3 Apr). Birth Centenary of Tadeusz Kantor (artist, set designer and theatre director). Perf 11½.

4666 **1596** 1z.75 multicoloured .... 3·00 2·75

(Des Marzanna Dąbrowska)

2015 (7 Apr). 75th Anniversary of Katyń Massacre. Perf 11½ (with one elliptical hole on each vert side).

4667 **1597** 1z.75 multicoloured .... 3·00 2·75

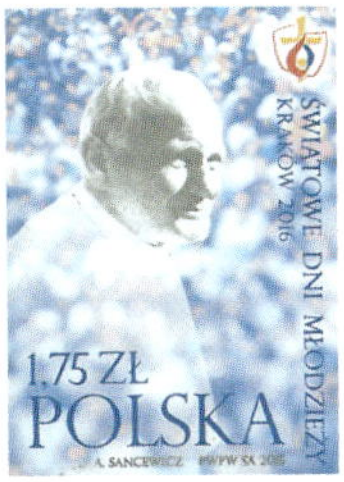

1598 Pope John Paul II

(Des Agnieszka Sancewicz)

1915 (27 Apr). World Youth Day. T **1598** and similar vert design. Multicoloured. Perf 11½.

4668		1z.75 Type **1598**	3·00	2·50
4669		5z. 'In You There Is Hope' (30×39 mm)	9·00	7·25

1599 Homemade Doll

(Des Maciej Jedrysik. Litho)

1915 (5 May). Europa. Old Toys. Perf 11½ (with one elliptical hole on each horiz side).

4670	**1599**	5z. multicoloured	8·00	7·25

1600 Flowers growing from Soldier's Helmet

(Des Alexander Pietrzak)

1915 (8 May). 70th Anniversary of End of World War II. Sheet 90×70 mm. Perf 11½.

MS4671	**1600**	2z.35 multicoloured	5·00	3·50

1601 Apple (Litho)

(Litho)

1915 (28 May). World EXPO 1915, Milan, Italy. Sheet 100×100 mm. Perf 11½.

MS4672	**1601**	5z.20 multicoloured	9·00	7·25

(Des Marzanna Dąbrowska. Litho)

1915 (29 May). Birth Centenary of Jan Twardowski (poet). Perf 11½ (with one elliptical hole on each vert side).

4673		1z.75 Jan Twardowski	4·00	2·20

T **1602** is unavailable.

1603 Anna (from *Frozen*)

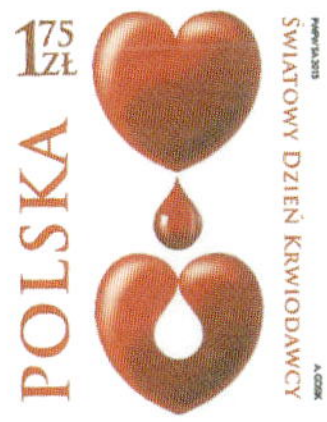

1604 Heart dripping Blood

(Des Agnieszka Sancewicz)

1915 (1 June). Walt Disney Characters. Sheet 121×75 mm containing T **1603** and similar vert design. Multicoloured. Perf 11½ (with one elliptical hole on each horiz side).

MS4674		2z.35×2, Type **1603**; Elsa	9·00	7·25

(Des Andrzej Gosik)

2015 (14 June). World Blood Donor Day. Perf 11½.

4675		1z.75 multicoloured	3·00	2·25

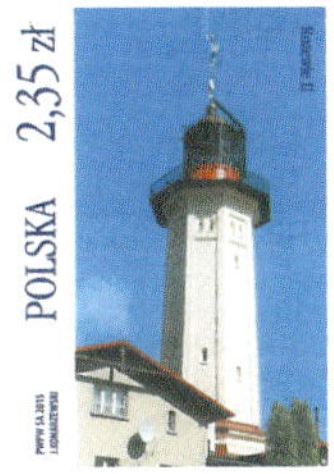

1605 Rozewie II

(Des Jacek Konarzewski)

2015 (19 June). Lighthouses. T **1535** and similar vert designs. Multicoloured. Perf 11½.

4676	2z.35 Type **1605**	3·25	3·00
	a. Sheet. Nos. 4676/4680 plus label	17·00	
4677	2z.35 Kikut	3·25	3·00
4678	2z.35 Świnoujście	3·25	3·00
4679	2z.35 Jastarnia	3·25	3·00
4680	2z.35 Gdańsk Port Pólnocny	3·25	3·00
4676/4680	*Set of 5*	14·50	13·50

Nos. 4676/4680 were printed, *se-tenant*, in sheets of five stamps and one stamp-size label.

1606 Jan Potocki

(Des Maciej Jędrysik)

2015 (25 June). Death Bicentenary of Jan Potocki (traveller and writer). Perf 11½ (with one elliptical hole on each vert side).

4681	**1606**	5z. multicoloured	8·00	6·00

1607 Sunflower

1608 Coloured Rocks

(Des Marzanna Dąbrowska)

2015 (26 June). Flowers and Fruit. Perf 11½.

4682	**1607**	1z. multicoloured	1·40	1·25

(Des Jacek Konarzewski. Litho)

2015 (1 July). Polish Presidency of Council of the Baltic Sea States. Fluorescent paper. Perf 11½ (with one elliptical hole on each vert side).

4683	**1608**	5z. multicoloured	6·75	6·00

1609 Cheese Wheel

(Des Agnieszka Sancewicz. Litho)

2015 (17 July). Polish Regional Products. Koryciński Cheese. Fluorescent paper. Perf 11½ (with one elliptical hole on each horiz side).

4684	**1609**	5z. multicoloured	6·75	6·00

1610 Lower Part of Organ

(Des Marzanna Dąbrowska. Litho)

2015 (30 July). Historic Organs of Poland. Baroque Pipe Organ, Cistercian Abbey, Jędrzejów. Sheet 75×100 mm containing T **1610** and similar horiz design. Multicoloured. Fluorescent paper. Perf 11½ (with one elliptical hole on each horiz side).

MS4685 4z.20 Type **1610**; 8z.30 Upper part of organ	20·00	17·00

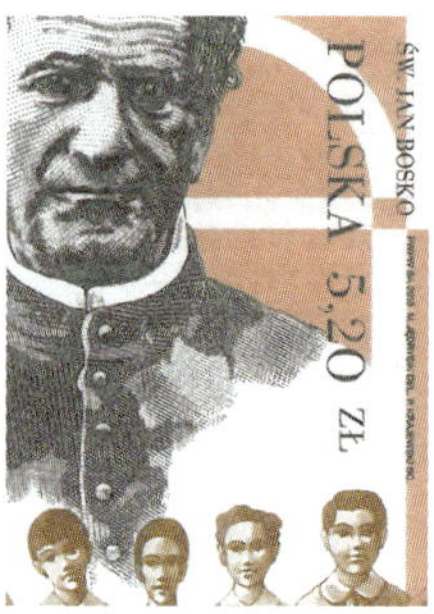

1611 St John Bosco

1612 PZL-130 Orlik Turboprop aircraft

(Des Maciej Jędrysik. Eng Przemyslaw Krajewski. Recess and photo)

2015 (16 Aug). Birth Bicentenary of St John Bosco (founder of the Salesians). Sheet 75×100 mm. Fluorescent paper. Perf 11½.

MS4686 **1611** 5z.20 multicoloured	9·00	7·75

(Des Andrzej Gosik. Litho)

2015 (22 Aug). Radom Airshow, 2015. T **1612** and similar horiz design. Multicoloured. Fluorescent paper. Perf 11½ (with one elliptical hole on each horiz side).

4687	2z.35 Type **1612**	3·25	3·00
	a. Pair. Nos. 4687/4688	6·75	6·25
4688	2z.35 PZL SW-4 Puszczyk Helicopter	3·25	3·00

Nos. 4687/4688 were printed, *se-tenant*, in horizontal and vertical pairs within sheets of eight stamps.

1613 Optimist Dinghies

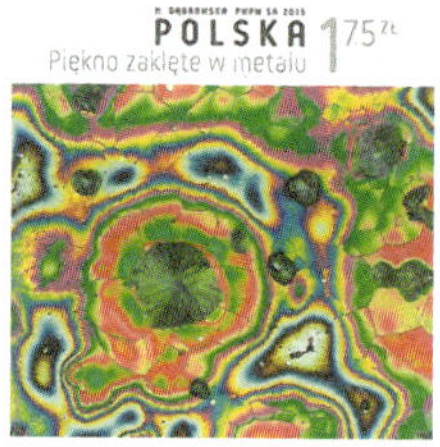

1614 Microstructure of Ductile Iron

(Des Jacek Konarzewski. Litho)

2015 (26 Aug). Optimist World Championship 2015, Dziwnów, Poland. Fluorescent paper. Perf 11½ (with one elliptical hole on each horiz side).

4689	**1613**	1z.75 multicoloured	4·00	2·25

(Des Marzanna Dąbrowska. Litho and varnish)

2015 (11 Sept). Beauty Enchanted in Metal. Microstructures of Metal Castings. Sheet 117×117 mm containing T **1614** and similar square designs. Multicoloured. Fluorescent paper. Perf 11½ (with one elliptical hole on each vert side).

MS4690 1z.75 Type **1614**; 1z.75 Microstructure of aluminium bronze; 2z.35 Microstructure of sheet iron; 2z.35 Microstructure of austempered ductile iron	12·00	11·00

Stamps of a similar design were issued by France.

1615 Water Lily

1616 Early Post Office and Cap

(Des Marzanna Dąbrowska. Gravure)

2015 (15 Sept). Flowers and Fruit. T **1615** and similar horiz design. Multicoloured. Fluorescent paper. Perf 11½.

4691	10g. Type **1615**	45	40
4692	5z. Rose	6·75	6·00

(Des Maciej Jędrysik. Litho)

2015 (23 Sept). Centenary of Warsaw City Post Office. Fluorescent paper. Perf 11½ (with one elliptical hole on each vert side).

4693	**1616**	2z.35 multicoloured	4·00	3·00

1617 'If you want what's best for me, buy me a crocodile, my love' (*Zemsta* Aleksander Fredo

1618 Emblem

(Des Jacek Konarzewski. Litho)

2015 (23 Sept). Quotations. T **1617** and similar horiz design. Multicoloured. Fluorescent paper. Perf 11½ (with one elliptical hole on each vert side).

4694	2z.35 Type **1617**	3·25	3·00
4695	2z.35 'Hounds went into the forest' (*Popioly* (Stefan Żeromski))	3·25	3·00

(Des Maciej Jędrysik. Litho)

2015 (1 Oct). 17th International Frédéric Chopin Piano Competition. Fluorescent paper. Perf 11½ (with one elliptical hole on each vert side).

4696	**1618**	1z.75 multicoloured	4·00	2·75

1619 Symbol of Reconciliation

1620 *Bubo bubo* (Eurasian Eagle Owl)

(Des Maciej Jędrysik. Gravure)

2015 (23 Oct). 50th Anniversary of Letter of Reconciliation from the Polish Bishops to the German Bishops. Fluorescent paper. Perf 11½×11.

4697	**1619**	1z.75 multicoloured	4·00	2·75

(Des Marzanna Dąbrowska. Litho and embossed)

2015 (23 Oct). Polish Birds. Owls. T **1620** and similar horiz designs. Multicoloured. Fluorescent paper. Perf 11½ (with one elliptical hole on each horiz side).

4698	2z.35 Type **1620**	5·00	3·00
	a. Sheet. Nos. 4698/4701 plus 4 labels	21·00	
4699	2z.35 *Aegolius funereus* (Boreal Owl)	5·00	3·00
4700	2z.35 *Tyto alba* (Barn Owl)	5·00	3·00
4701	2z.35 *Strix nebulosa* (Great Grey Owl)	5·00	3·00
4698/4701 *Set of* 4		18·00	11·00

Nos. 4698/4701 were printed, *se-tenant*, in vertical strips of four stamps, each with a stamp-size label attached at right, within sheets of four stamps and four labels

(Des Marzanna Dąbrowska)

2015 (31 Oct). Personalities of Theatre and Cinema. As T **1522**. Vert designs as T **1522**. Multicoloured. Fluorescent paper. Perf 11½×12 (with one star-shaped hole on each vert side).

4702	1z.75 Jerzy Pichelski (actor)	3·00	2·25
4703	2z.35 Hanka Bielicka (singer and actress)	4·00	3·25
4704	4z.20 Aleksander Zelwerowicz (actor)	7·00	5·50
4702/4704 *Set of* 3		12·50	9·75
MS4705 121×82 mm. Nos 4702/4704		16·00	13·50

1621 The Nativity

(Des Maciej Jędrysik. Gravure)

2015 (16 Nov). Christmas. T **1621** and similar vert designs. Multicoloured. Fluorescent paper. Perf 11½.

4706	1z.75 Type **1621**	2·25	2·25
4707	2z.35 The Annuciation	3·50	3·00
4708	5z.20 Adoration of the Magi	9·00	6·50
4706/4708 *Set of* 3		13·50	10·50

1622 *Wojciecha Bogusławskiego* (Józef Rejchan)

(Des Jacek Konarzewski. Gravure)

2015 (19 Nov). 250th Anniversary of National Theatre, Warsaw. Fluorescent paper. Perf 11½×11.

4709	**1622**	1z.35 multicoloured	3·00	2·25

1623 Children

1624 Władysława Bartoszewskiego

(Des Aleksander Pietrzak. Gravure)

2015 (20 Nov). National Day of Children's Rights. Fluorescent paper. Perf 11½×11.

4710	**1623**	1z.75 multicoloured	3·00	2·25

(Des Agnieszka Sancewicz. Gravure)

2015 (25 Nov). Władysława Bartoszewskiego (writer and politician) Commemoration. Fluorescent paper. Perf 11½ (with one elliptical hole on each horiz side).

4711	**1624**	1z.75 multicoloured	3·00	2·25

1625 Jana Długosza

1626 Michał Tomaszk and Zbigniew Strzałkowski

(Des Jacek Konarzewski. Gravure)

2015 (30 Nov). 600th Birth Anniversary of Jana Długosza (priest, soldier and diplomat). Fluorescent paper. Perf 11½.

4712	**1625**	1z.75 multicoloured	3·00	2·25

(Des Aleksander Pietrzak. Litho)

2015 (5 Dec). Beatification of Michał Tomaszk (1960–1991) and Zbigniew Strzałkowski (1958–1991), killed working as Missionaries in Peru. Fluorescent paper. Perf 11½ (with one elliptical hole on each horiz side).

4713 **1626** 1z.75 multicoloured .... 3·00 2·25

1627 Lilac

(Des Marzanna Dąbrowska. Gravure)

2015 (7 Dec). Flowers and Fruit. Fluorescent paper. Perf 11½×12.

4714 **1627** 5g. multicoloured 30 25

1628 St Paraskevia Church, Kwiaton, Poland and St George's Church, Drohobych, Ukraine

(Des Andrzej Gosik. Eng Przemysław Krajewski. Recess and photo)

2015 (18 Dec). World Heritage Sites. Wooden Tserkvas of the Carpathian Region in Poland and Ukraine. Fluorescent paper. Perf 11.

4715 **1628** 5z. multicoloured .... 8·00 6·25

A stamp in a similar design was issued by Ukraine.

1629 Air Balloon (detail)

(Des Jerzy Owsiak, Gawel Andrzejewski and Katarzyna Sasin. Litho and varnish)

2016 (5 Jan). 24th Finale of Orchestra of Holy Day Assistance (fund raising charity). Fluorescent paper. Perf 11½ (with one elliptical hole on each vert side).

4716 **1629** 2z.35 multicoloured .... 4·00 3·25

No. 4716 was perforated in a heart-shape enclosed in an outer perforated square, with varnish applied to the inscription.

1630 Ball enclosing Player

(Des Agata Tobolczyk. Litho)

2016 (15 Jan). Poland Winner of EHF European Men's Handball Championship. T **1630** and similar square design. Multicoloured. Fluorescent paper. Perf 11½ (with one elliptical hole on each horiz side).

4717 2z.35 Type **1630** .... 3·50 3·00

a. Pair. Nos. 4717/4718 .... 11·00 9·50

4718 5z. Hand grasping ball .... 7·00 6·25

Nos. 4717/4718 were perforated in a ball-shape enclosed in an outer perforated square.

Nos. 4717/4718 were printed, *se-tenant*, in vertical and horizontal pairs within sheets of six stamps.

1631 Wrocław Market Square from St Elisabeth Church Tower

1632 Cornflower

(Des Aleksander Pietrzak. Litho)

2016 (15 Jan). Wrocław. European Capital of Culture 2016. Sheet 90×70 mm. Fluorescent paper. Perf 11½ (with one elliptical hole on each horiz side).

MS4719 **1631** 5z. multicoloured .... 7·50 6·75

(Des Marzanna Dąbrowska. Gravure)

2016 (20 Jan). Flowers and Fruit. Fluorescent paper. Perf 11½×12.

4720 **1632** 50g. multicoloured 80 70

1633 Early Coin (detail)

1634 Tree

(Des Agata Tobolczyk. Gravure)

2016 (21 Jan). Release of 250th Anniversary of Warsaw Mint Commemorative Coins. Fluorescent paper. Perf 11½.

4721 **1633** 2z.35 multicoloured .... 4·00 3·00

(Des Agata Tobolczyk. Gravure)

2016 (22 Jan). 50th Anniversary of First Successful Kidney Transplant in Poland. Fluorescent paper. Perf 11½.

4722 **1634** 1z.75 multicoloured .... 3·00 2·25

1635 Soldier

(Des Marzanna Dąbrowska. Gravure)

2016 (28 Feb). Cursed Soldiers (anti-Communist resistance fighters) National Remembrance Day. Fluorescent paper. Perf 11½.

4723 **1635** A (2z.) multicoloured .... 4·00 2·25

(Des Agnieszka Sancewicz)

2016 (3 Mar). Easter. As T **1556**. Multicoloured. Perf 12×11½.

4724 2z. Black egg, bands of crosses at top and bottom .... 2·75 2·50
4725 2z.50 Black egg with flowers, streamers and hearts .... 3·50 3·25
4726 6z. Purple egg with hearts and flowers .... 8·50 7·75
4724/4726 *Set of 3* .... 13·50 12·00

1636 Photographer

1637 *Christianisation of Poland AD 966* (Jan Matejko)

(Des Agata Tobolczyk)

2016 (28 Mar). History of Polish Photography. Jan Kosidowski (Nos. 4727, 4729) or Wiesław Prażuch (others) Commemoration. T **1636** and similar horiz designs showing photographs. Multicoloured. Fluorescent paper. Perf 12×11½ (with one elliptical hole on each horiz side).

4727 2z. Type **1636** .... 2·75 2·50
a. Strip of 4. Nos. 4727/4730 .... 13·00
4728 2z. Construction of a thermal power plant 2·75 2·25
4729 2z.50 'Warszawa al jerozolimskie przy kruczej' .... 3·50 3·25
4730 2z.50 May Day, Warsaw .... 3·50 3·25
4727/4730 *Set of 4* .... 11·50 10·50

Nos. 4727/4730 were printed, *se-tenant*, in vertical strips of four stamps within the sheet.

(Des Charles Tabaka. Eng Przemysław Krajewski. Recess and gravure)

2016 (30 Mar). 1050th Anniversary of Christianisation of Poland. Sheet 70×90 mm. Fluorescent paper. Perf 11½.

MS4731 **1637** 6z. multicoloured .... 8·50 7·75

1638 Compassion of Christ

1639 Team Members

(Des Maciej Jędrysik. Gravure)

2016 (2 Apr). Extraordinary Holy Year of Mercy. Jubilee of Mercy. Fluorescent paper. Perf 11½.

4732 **1638** 2z.50 multicoloured .... 3·50 3·25

(Des Agnieszka Sancewicz. Litho)

2016 (20 Apr). Centenary of Legia Warsaw Football Club. Sheet 90×70 mm. Fluorescent paper. Perf 11½.

MS4733 **1639** 6z. black and gold .... 9·00 8·25

1640 Poppy

1641 Roller painting Contaminated Landscape Green

(Des Marzanna Dąbrowska. Gravure)

2016 (22 Apr). Flowers and Fruit. Fluorescent paper. Perf 11½.

4734 **1640** 10z. multicoloured .... 14·00 13·00

(Des Doxia Sergidou. Litho)

2016 (8 May). Europa. Think Green. Perf 11½ (with one elliptical hole on each horiz side).

4735 **1641** 5z. multicoloured .... 7·00 6·50

Post Europ decided that member countries should issue a joint stamp, Think Green, to that end a design-a-stamp competition was held which was won by Doxia Sergidou of Cyprus.

1642 Young People and Pope Francis

1643 Early Interior

(Des Agnieszka Sancewicz. Eng J. Kopecka, P. Krajewski and K. Michalczuk (No. **MS**4737). Recess and photo (No. **MS**4737) or photo (other))

2016 (10 May). World Youth Day. T **1642** and similar horiz design. Multicoloured. Perf 11½.

4736 2z.50 Type **1642** .... 3·50 3·25
MS4737 104×77 mm. 6z. Pope Francis (54×40 mm)........ 9·00 8·25

A stamp in a similar design was issued by The Vatican City.

(Des Karol Tabaka. Litho)

2016 (13 May). Bicentenary of University of Warsaw. Sheet 70×90 mm. Perf 11½ (with one elliptical hole on each vert side).

MS4738 **1643** 5z. slate-grey and silver .... 7·50 7·00

1644 Reksio collecting Eggs

1645 Stamps as Neon Display

(Des Aleksandra Pietrzak)

2016 (20 May). Reksio (cartoon character created by Lechosław Marszałek). T **1644** and similar horiz design. Multicoloured. Perf 11½.

4739 2z.50 Type **1644** .... 5·00 2·75
a. Pair. Nos. 4739/4740 .... 11·50 6·75
4740 2z.50 Reksio painting hen shed .... 6·00 3·75

Nos. 4739/4740 were printed, *se-tenant*, in horizontal pairs within the sheet.

(Des Agata Tobolczyk. Litho and varnish)

2016 (28 May). International Philatelic Exhibition New York 2016. Sheet 70×100 mm. Perf 11½ (with one elliptical hole on each horiz side).

MS4741 **1645** 6z. multicoloured .... 9·00 8·25

1646 Family

(Des Aleksandra Pietrzak. Litho)

2016 (1 June). Family Values. Perf 12×11½ (with one elliptical hole on each horiz side).

4742 **1646** 3z.70 multicoloured .... 5·25 4·75

1647 'AA'

1648 Father Stanislaw Papczyński

(Des Maciej Jędrysik. Litho)

2016 (2 June). 25th Anniversary of Polish–German Youth Co-operation. Perf 11½ (with one elliptical hole on each horiz side).

4743 **1647** 2z.50 multicoloured .... 4·00 3·25

A stamp in a similar design was issued by Germany.

(Des Marzanna Dąbrowska. Gravure)

2016 (5 June). Canonisation of Father Stanislaw Papczyński. Perf 11½×12 (with one elliptical hole on each vert side).

4744 **1648** 3z.70 multicoloured .... 5·25 4·75

1649 Cumulonimbus capillatus

1650 Jan Jessenius

(Des Marzanna Dąbrowska. Litho)

2016 (15 June). Clouds. T **1649** and similar horiz designs. Multicoloured. Perf 11½×12 (with one elliptical hole on each vert side).

4745 2z. Type **1649** .... 3·00 2·50
a. Strip of 4. Nos. 4745/4748 .... 14·50
4746 2z. Cirrus uninus .... 3·00 2·50
4747 2z.50 Cumulonimbus mammatus .... 4·00 3·25
4748 2z.50 Cumulonimbus capillatus (*different*) .... 4·00 3·25
4745/4748 *Set of 4* .... 12·50 10·50

Nos. 4745/4748 were printed, *se-tenant*, in strips of four stamps within the sheet.

(Des Vladislav Rostoka and Agnieszka Sancewicz. Eng František Horniak. Recess and gravure)

2016 (22 June). 450th Birth Anniversary of Jan Jessenius (physician, politician and philosopher). Perf 11½.

4749 **1650** 6z. multicoloured .... 8·50 7·75

Stamps in a similar design were issued by Czech Republic, Hungary and Slovakia.

1651 Emblem and Castle Square, Warsaw

1652 Crocus

(Des Agata Tobolczyk. Litho)

2016 (24 June). NATO Summit Warsaw, 2016. Perf 11½ (with one elliptical hole on each horiz side (others).

4750 **1651** 5z. multicoloured .... 7·00 6·50

(Des Marzanna Dąbrowska. Gravure)

2016 (6 July). Flowers and Fruit. Fluorescent paper. Perf 11½.

4751 **1652** 20g. multicoloured 90 65

1653 Windsurfer

1654 Suitcase

(Des Agata Tobolczyk. Gravure)

2016 (8 July). Polish Athletes at RIO 2016 Olympic Games, Brazil. Sheet 200×75 mm containing T **1653** and similar horiz designs. Multicoloured. Perf 11½.

MS4752 2z.×4, Type **1653**; Cyclist; Discus thrower; Tennis player .... 15·00 14·00

(Des Agata Tobolczyk. Litho)

2016 (14 July). Postcrossing (people from many countries sending each other traditional postcards). Perf 11½ (with one elliptical hole on each horiz side).

4753 **1654** 5z. multicoloured .... 7·00 6·50

1655 Lily

1656 Honey

(Des Marzanna Dąbrowska. Gravure)

2016 (15 July). Flowers and Fruit. Fluorescent paper. Perf 11½.

4754 **1655** 6z. multicoloured .... 8·50 7·75

(Des Agnieszka Sancewicz. Litho)

2016 (18 July). Polish Regional Products. Honey. Fluorescent paper. Perf 11½ (with one elliptical hole on each horiz side).

4755 **1656** 5z. multicoloured .... 6·75 6·25

1657 General Anders

1658 Iris

(Des Maciej Jędrysik. Litho)

2016 (21 July). General Władysław Anders' Army. Trail of Hope (leading Polish prisonners of USSR to freedom). Perf 11½ (with one elliptical hole on each horiz side).

4756 **1657** 2z.50 multicoloured .... 3·50 3·25

(Des Marzanna Dąbrowska. Gravure)

2016 (30 Aug). Flowers and Fruit. Fluorescent paper. Perf 11½.

4757 **1658** 2z. multicoloured .... 2·75 2·50

1659 Madonna of Fraga

(Des Agnieszka Sancewicz)

2016 (30 Aug). Madonnas of the Eastern Borderlands. T **1659** and similar vert designs. Multicoloured. Perf 11.

4758 2z.50 Type **1659** .... 3·50 3·25
4759 3z.70 Our Lady of Żółkiewska .... 5·00 4·75
4760 6z. Madonna of Biały Kamień .... 8·75 8·25
4761 6z. Arms of Madonna of the Kingdom of Poland .... 8·75 8·25
4758/4761 *Set of 4* .... 23·00 22·00

1660 *Rhodeus sericeus*

(Des Agata Tobolczyk. Litho)

2016 (31 Aug). Endangerd Species. Fish. T **1660** and similar horiz designs. Multicoloured. Perf 11½ (with one elliptical hole on each horiz side).

4762 2z. Type **1660** .... 2·75 2·50
4763 2z.50 *Carassius carassius* .... 3·50 3·25
4764 3z.70 *Rhynchocypris percnurus* .... 5·00 4·75
4765 6z. *Acipenser oxyrinchus* .... 8·50 7·75
4762/4765 *Set of 4* .... 18·00 16·00

1661 Eagle

1662 Town Hall, Iława

(Des Ewa Szydłowska. Gravure)

2016 (1 Sept). 75th Anniversary of First Drop of Cichociemni Paratroopers (Silent Unseen). Perf 11½.

4766 **1661** 3z.70 multicoloured .... 5·00 4·75

(Des Karol Tabaka. Litho)

2016 (8 Sept). XXI General Assembly of PZF Delegates, Iława. Perf 11½ (with one elliptical hole on each horiz side).

4767 **1662** 2z.50 multicoloured .... 4·00 3·75

1663 Władysław Bukowski

1664 The Witcher

(Des Karol Tabaka. Litho)

2016 (11 Sept). Beatification of Władysław Bukowski. Perf 11½ (with one elliptical hole on each vert side.

4768 **1663** 6z. multicoloured .... 8·50 7·75

(Des CD Projekt SA. Gravure)

2016 (16 Sept). The Witcher (Geralt of Rivia) (character created by Andrzej Sapkowsk). Sheet 70×90 mm. Perf 11½.

MS4769 **1664** 6z. multicoloured .... 9·00 8·25

1665 Bible

1666 Our Lady of Perpetual Help

(Des Karol Tabaka. Gravure)

2016 (3 Oct). Bicentenary of Bible Society in Poland. Perf 11½.

4770 **1665** 2z.50 multicoloured .... 3·50 3·25

(Des Ewa Szydłowska. Gravure)

2016 (5 Oct). Our Lady of Perpetual Help. Icon of Love. Perf 11½.

4771 **1666** 3z.70 multicoloured .... 5·25 4·75

1667 Cherries

1668 *Herdsman with Whip* (Józef Chełmoński)

(Des Marzanna Dąbrowska. Gravure)

2016 (20 Oct). Flowers and Fruit. Fluorescent paper. Perf 11½.
4772 **1667** 15g. multicoloured 60 55

(Des Agata Tobolczyk. Gravure)

2016 (24 Oct). Lost Works of Art. T **1668** and similar vert designs. Multicoloured. Perf 11½.

4773 2z. Type **1668** .... 2·75 2·50
a. Strip of 3. Nos. 4773/4775........ 8·50
4774 2z. Self-portrait (Aleksander Gierymski) ..... 2·75 2·50
4775 2z. *Portrait of Olga's Wife* (Leon Chwistek).. 2·75 2·50
4773/4775 *Set of 3*........ 7·50 6·75

Nos. 4773/4775 were printed, *se-tenant*, in vertical strips of three stamps within sheets of six.

1669 Aleksander Gieysztor and Royal Castle, Warsaw

(Des Aleksandra Pietrzak. Gravure)

2016 (29 Oct). Polish Achievements in Science. T **1669** and similar square designs. Multicoloured. Perf 11½.

4776 2z.50 Type **1669** .... 3·50 3·25
a. Sheet. Nos. 4776/4781 .... 22·00
4777 2z.50 Witold Kula and scale........ 3·50 3·25
4778 2z.50 Gerard Labuda and chapel of Mieszko I 3·50 3·25
4779 2z.50 Edmund Faustyn Biernacki and blood drop test tube........ 3·50 3·25
4780 2z.50 Hilary Koprowski and Polio virus .... 3·50 3·25
4781 2z.50 Wladyslaw Kunicki-Goldfinger and bacteria .... 3·50 3·25
4776/4781 *Set of 6*........ 19·00 18·00

Nos. 4776/4781 were printed, *se-tenant*, in sheets of six stamps with enlarged margins.

(Des Marzanna Dąbrowska. Litho)

2016 (31 Oct). Personalities of Theatre and Cinema. Vert designs as T **1522**. Multicoloured. Fluorescent paper. Perf 11½×12 (with one star-shaped hole on each vert side).

4782 2z. Franciszek Brodniewicz (actor) .... 3·00 2·75
4783 2z.50 Maria-Elisabeth Barszczewska Wyrzykowska (Elżbieta Barszczewska) (actress)........ 3·50 3·25
4784 6z. Tadeusz Fijewski (actor)........ 8·50 7·75
4782/4784 *Set of 3*........ 16·00 14·50
MS4785 121×82 mm. Nos. 4782/4784........ 13·50 12·50

1670 The Annunciation

(Des Aleksandra Pietrzak. Gravure)

2016 (16 Nov). Christmas. T **1670** and similar vert designs showing images from the altar of Assumption of the Blessed Virgin Mary church in Książnice Wielkie. Multicoloured. Fluorescent paper. Perf 12×11½.

4786 2z. Type **1670** .... 2·75 2·50
4787 6z. Holy Family .... 8·50 7·75
MS4788 98×60 mm. As Nos. 4786/4787........ 11·50 10·50

1671 Our Lady of Fátima

(Des Marzanna Dąbrowska. Gravure)

2016 (25 Nov). 25th Anniversary of Radio Maryja. Multicoloured. Perf 11×11½.
4789 **1671** A (2z.) Our Lady of Fátima........ 2·75 2·50

1672 Anita Włodarczyk (athletics and hammer throw)

(Des Agnieszka Sancewicz. Gravure)

2016 (28 Nov). Polish Gold Medalists at Rio 2016. Olympic Games, Brazil. T **1672** and similar vert design. Multicoloured. Perf 11.

4790 2z.50 Type **1672** .... 3·50 3·25
4791 2z.50 Natalia Madaj and Magdalena Fularczyk-Kozłowska (rowing) .... 3·50 3·25

1673 Rafał Wilk on a Hand-held Bike

(Des Karol Tabaka. Gravure and iridescent ink)

2016 (3 Dec). Polish Success at Rio 2016. Paralympic Games, Brazil. Perf 11.
4792 **1673** B (2z.50) multicoloured........ 3·50 3·25

1674 Player and Emblem

1675 Syrena Sport Prototype FSO

(Des Karol Tabaka. Gravure)

2016 (9 Dec). Vive Sport Club Kielce. Perf 11.
4793 **1674** 3z.70 multicoloured .... 5·00 4·75

(Des Marzanna Dąbrowska. Litho)

2016 (30 Dec). Polish Design. Sheet 90×70 mm. Perf 11×11½.
MS4794 **1675** 6z. multicoloured........ 9·00 8·25

1676 Erwin Axer

1677 *Adoration of the Magi* (Santi di Tito)

(Des Jaroslaw Ochendzan. Litho)

2017 (2 Jan). Birth Centenary of Erwin Axer (theatre director, writer and university professor). Perf 11½ (with one elliptical hole on each vert side).
4795 **1676** 2z.50 multicoloured .... 5·00 3·25

(Des Andrzej Gosik. Gravure)

2017 (6 Jan). Epiphany. Perf 11½×11.
4796 **1677** B (2z.50) multicoloured .... 4·00 3·25

1678 Waves

(Des Agnieszka Sancewicz. Litho and screen printing)

2017 (30 Jan). Year of the Vistula River. Perf 11½ (with one elliptical hole on each vert side).
4797 **1678** 6z. multicoloured .... 8·50 7·75

1679 Mariusz Zaruski

1680 Tadeusz Kościuszko

(Des Karol Tabaka. Litho)

2017 (31 Jan). 150th Birth Anniversary of Mariusz Zaruski (sailing and maritime education pioneer, Brigadier General and mountaineer). Perf 11½ (with one elliptical hole on each vert side).
4798 **1679** B (2z.50) multicoloured .... 4·00 3·25

(Des Jaroslaw Ochendzan. Litho)

2017 (4 Feb). Death Bicentenary of Andrzej Tadeusz Bonawentura Kościuszko (military engineer and leader). Perf 11½ (with one elliptical hole on each horiz side).
4799 **1680** 3z.20 multicoloured .... 4·50 4·00

1681 Clasped Hands

1682 Love for truth and the desire to reveal it are the reason that Wittenberg is going to carry out the debate over the following theses (Martin Luther)

(Des Karol Tabaka. Gravure)

2017 (11 Feb). World Day of the Sick. Perf 11×11½.
4800 **1681** 5z. multicoloured .... 7·00 6·50

(Des Andrzej Gosik. Gravure)

2017 (28 Feb). 500th Anniversary of the Reformation. Perf 11½×11.
4801 **1682** 3z.20 multicoloured .... 4·50 4·00

1683 Franciszek Majewski's Neck Badge

1684 Our Lady of Fátima

(Des Marzanna Dąbrowska. Gravure and embossed)

2016 (28 Feb). Cursed Soldiers (anti-Communist resistance fighters) Gorgets (neck badges). Sheet 117×117 mm containing T **1683** and similar square design. Multicoloured. Fluorescent paper. Perf 11½ (with one elliptical hole on each vert side).
MS4802 6z.×2, Type **1683**; Mieczysław Dziemieszkiewicz's badge........ 18·00 16·00

(Des Atelier Design&etc. Litho)

2017 (12 Mar). Centenary of the Fátima Apparitions. Sheet 125×95 mm. Perf 11½ (with one cross-shaped hole on each horiz side).
MS4803 **1684** 6z.80 multicoloured........ 10·00 9·25

Stamps of a similar design were issued by Luxembourg, Portugal and Slovakia

(Des Andrzej Gosik. Gravure)

2017 (15 Mar). 700th Anniversary of City of Lublin. Horiz design showing Lublin past and present. Multcoloured. Perf 11½.
4804 2z.60 Panorama of Lublin view of the city in 1618........ 3·50 3·25

T **1685** is unavailable.

1686 White Egg **1687** Lech and Maria Kaczyński

(Des Agnieszka Sancewicz)

2017 (5 Mar). Easter. Multicoloured. Fluorescent paper. Perf 12×11½.

4805 **1686** A (2z.60) White egg, red, green and yellow flower shape .... 3·50 3·25

4806 - 6z. Black egg, star-shaped central design with yellow and red star bursts .... 8·50 7·75

(Des Andrzej Gosik. Litho and embossed)

2017 (10 Apr). We Remember 10.04.2010. Death of Lech Kaczyński, his wife Maria and other Delegates in Air Disaster. Sheet 98×154 mm. Perf 11½ (with one elliptical hole on each horiz side).

MS4807 **1687** 5z. multicoloured .... 7·50 7·00

1688 Pieskowa Skała Castle **1689** Władysław Reymont

(Des Karol Tabaka. Litho)

2017 (5 May). Europa. Castles. Perf 11½ (with one elliptical hole on each horiz side).

4808 **1688** 5z. multicoloured .... 7·00 6·50

(Des Ewa Szydłowska. Gravure)

2017 (7 May). 150th Birth Anniversary of Władysław Reymont (writer and winner of 1924 Nobel Prize for Literature). Perf 11½.

4809 **1689** 2z.60 multicoloured .... 4·00 3·25

1690 Jackson Storm **1691** General Jozef Haller von Hallenburg

(Des Agnieszka Sancewicz. Litho and varnish)

2017 (30 May). Walt Disney Characters. *Cars*. Sheet 115×75 mm containing T **1690** and similar horiz design. Perf 11½ (with one elliptical hole on each horiz side).

MS4810 3z.20 Type **1690**; 5z. Lightning McQueen .... 12·00 11·00

(Des Ewa Szydłowska. Litho)

2017 (31 May). Centenary of Creation of Blue Army (Polish legion fighting in France wearing French issued blue uniforms). Perf 11½ (with one elliptical hole on each vert side).

4811 **1691** 2z.60 multicoloured .... 4·00 3·25

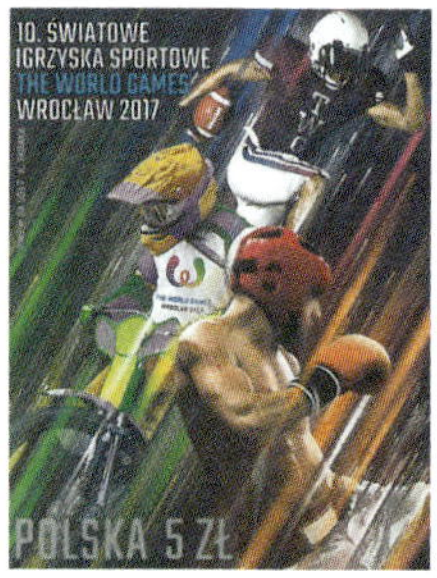

1692 Franciszek Stefczyk (founder) **1693** Athletes

(Des Karol Tabaka. Gravure)

2017 (8 June). Polish Credit Unions. Perf 11½.

4812 **1692** 2z.60 multicoloured .... 4·00 3·25

(Des Karol Tabaka. Litho)

2017 (9 June). World Games, Wroclaw 2017. Perf 11½ (with one elliptical hole on each vert side).

4813 **1693** 5z. multicoloured .... 7·00 6·50

1694 Emblem **1695** Adam Chmielowski

(Des Andrzej Gosik. Litho)

2017 (16 June). Astana EXPO 2017 International Exhibition. Perf 11½ (with one elliptical hole on each vert side).

4814 **1694** 2z.60 multicoloured .... 4·00 3·75

(Des Andrzej and Teresa Sowińscy. Litho and varnish)

2017 (17 June). Death Centenary (2016) of Adam Hilary Bernard Chmielowski (Adam Chmielowski) (painter, Franciscan friar and founder of Congregation of the Brothers Albertines). Perf 11½ (with one elliptical hole on each vert side).

4815 **1695** 2z.60 multicoloured .... 3·50 3·25

No. 4815 was perforated in a heart shape contained in an outer perforated square.

1696 Emblem

(Des Karol Tabaka. Litho)

2017 (20 June). Fighting Solidarity. Perf 11½ (with one elliptical hole on each horiz side).

4816 **1696** 2z.60 multicoloured .... 3·50 3·25

1697 Mountain Peaks

(Des Agnieszka Sancewicz. Gravure)

2017 (30 June). Crown of Polish Mountains (list of 28 peaks, one for each of the mountain ranges of Poland). Sheet 90×70 mm. Perf 11½.

MS4817	**1697** 6z. multicoloured	9·00	8·25

No. 4818 is vacant.

1698 Algeria

(Des Karol Tabaka)

2017 (31 July). Bicentenary of Janów Podlaski Stud. T **1698** and similar horiz designs. Multicoloured. Perf 11½ (with one elliptical hole on each vert side).

4819	2z.60 Type **1698**	3·50	3·25
	a. Sheet. Nos. 4819/4827	32·00	
4820	2z.60 Pilarka	3·50	3·25
4821	2z.60 Bandos	3·50	3·25
4822	2z.60 Etruria	3·50	3·25
	a. Strip of 3. Nos. 4822/4824	10·00	
4823	2z.60 Pinga	3·50	3·25
4824	2z.60 Pianissima	3·50	3·25
4825	2z.60 Pogrom	3·50	3·25
	a. Strip of 3. Nos. 4825/4827	10·00	
4826	2z.60 Ecaho	3·50	3·25
4827	2z.60 Bandola	3·50	3·25
4819/4827 *Set of* 9		28·00	26·00

Nos. 4819/4821, 4822/4824 and 4825/4827 were printed, *se-tenant*, in vertical strips of three stamps, within sheets of nine.

1699 *Kapitan Borchardt*

1700 Player

(Des Jarosław Ochendzan. Gravure)

2017 (5 Aug). Tall Ships Race 2017, Szczecin. Sheet 90×70 mm. Perf 11½.

MS4828	**1699** 6z. multicoloured	9·00	8·25

(Des Jarosław Ochendzan)

2017 (5 Aug). European Men's Volleyball Championship Gdańsk, Poland 2017. T **1700** and similar square designs. Multicoloured. Perf 11½ (with one elliptical hole in each vert side).

4829	2z.60 Type **1700**	3·50	3·25
	a. Strip. Nos. 4829/4832	14·50	
4830	2z.60 Two-handed hit	3·50	3·25
4831	2z.60 Jumping	3·50	3·25
4832	2z.60 Two players	3·50	3·25
4829/4832 *Set of* 4		12·50	11·50

Nos. 4829/4832 were perforated in a circle around the design, enclosed in an outer perforated square and were printed, *se-tenant*, in horizontal strips of four stamps.

1701 Our Lady of Licheń

1702 Our Lady of Częstochowa

(Des Karol Tabaka. Gravure)

2017 (12 Aug). 50th Anniversary of Coronation of the Image of our Lady of Licheń. Perf 11½.

4833	**1701**	2z.60 multicoloured	3·50	3·25

(Des Marzanna Dąbrowska. Gravure)

2017 (26 Aug). 300th Anniversary of Coronation of the Image of our Our Lady of Częstochowa. Perf 11½.

4834	**1702**	2z.60 multcoloured	3·50	3·25

1703 *Centaurea cyanus*

1704 *St Francis* (El Greco)

(Des Agnieszka Sancewicz)

2017 (31 Aug). Polish Herbarium. T **1703** and similar square designs. Multicoloured. Perf 11½ (with one elliptical hole on each vert side).

4835	2z.60 Type **1703**	3·50	3·25
	a. Sheet. Nos. 4835/4838	14·50	
4836	2z.60 *Matricaria chamomilla*	3·50	3·25
4837	2z.60 *Achillea millefolium*	3·50	3·25
4838	2z.60 *Thymus serphyllum*	3·50	3·25
4835/4838 *Set of* 4		12·50	11·50

Nos. 4835/4838 were printed, *se-tenant*, in sheets of four stamps.

(Des Ewa Szydlowska)

2017 (2 Sept). Art. European Art in Polish Collections. Perf 11½×11 (with one elliptical hole on each vert side).

4839	**1704**	2z.60 multicoloured	3·50	3·25

1705 Baroque Organ, Central Basilica of the Assumption, Peplin.

1706 Rope

(Des Marzanna Dąbrowska)

2017 (16 Sept). Historic Organs of Poland. Sheet 75×100 mm. Perf 11½×11 (with one elliptical hole on each vert side).
MS4840 **1705** 11z. multicoloured .... 18·00 16·00

(Des Agnieszka Sancewicz)

2017 (20 Sept). 80th Anniversary of the Execution of Ethnic Poles by the Russian Soviet Security Service (NKVD). Perf 12×11½.
4841 **1706** A (2z.60) multicoloured .... 3·50 3·25

1707 Holy Mary of Piekary (painting)

(Des Adam Kultys)

2017 (13 Oct). Holy Mary of Piekary. Perf 11½×12.
4842 **1707** 5z. multicoloured .... 7·00 6·50

1708 Our Lady of the Immaculate Conception

(Des Zenon Święch)

2017 (14 Oct). Centenary of the Militia of the Immaculata (evangelical movement) (founded by Maximilian Kolbe). Perf 11½.
4843 **1708** 5z. multicoloured .... 7·50 7·00

No. 4843 was printed, *se-tenant*, with a stamp-size label showing Maximilian Kolbe

1709 Feliks Selmanowicz

1710 A Horse's Health (Ariadna Kruszy)

(Des Zenon Święch)

2017 (18 Oct). Feliks Selmanowicz, 1904–1946 (Polish decorated soldier, executed after fighting for the anti-communist guerillas). Perf 11½ (with one elliptical hole on each vert side).
4844 **1709** 3z.20 multicoloured .... 4·50 4·00

(Des Roch Stefaniak)

2017 (25 Oct). World through the Eyes of Young People. Winning Designs in Drawing Competition. T **1710** and similar horiz designs. Multicoloured. Perf 11½×11 (with one elliptical hole on each vert side).
4845 2z.60 Type **1710** .... 3·50 3·25
a. Sheet. Nos. 4845/4847 .... 11·00
4846 2z.60 The Personification of Health (Kamila Rylska) .... 3·50 3·25
4847 2z.60 Time for Health (Sandra Marwitz) .... 3·50 3·25
4845/4847 *Set of 3* .... 9·50 8·75

Nos. 4845/4847 were printed, *se-tenant*, in strips of three stamps, with the name of the design and the designer inscribed in the right margin.

1711 Cover of *Kurjer Bloku* (international avant-garde art magazine) (cover designed by Mieczysław Szczuka)

1712 Mieczysław Cybulski

(Des Agata Tobolczyk)

2017 (27 Oct). Centenary of Polish Avant-Garde. Sheet 75×260 mm containing T **1711** and similar vert designs. Perf 11×11½ (with one elliptical hole on each vert side).
MS4848 2z.60 myrtle-green and vermilion; 2z.60 black and vermilion; 3z.20 black and pale blue-green; 3z.70 bright royal blue and olive-yellow.................. 17·00 16·00

Designs: 2z.60, T **1711**; 2z.60, *Sixth! Sixth!* (play by Tadeusz Peiper) (cover design by Władysław Strzemiński); 3z. 20, *Modernist Quarterly* (Polish avant-garde magazine) (cover designed by Henryk Stażewski); 3z.70, *The Source* (bi-weekly art magazine) (cover designed by Władysław Skotarek)

(Des Marzanna Dąbrowska)

2017 (30 Oct). Personalities of Theatre and Cinema. T **1712** and similar vert designs. Multicoloured. Perf 11½ (with a star-shaped hole in each horiz corner).
4849 2z.60 Type **1712** .... 3·50 3·25
4850 3z.20 Ina Benita.. 4·50 4·00
4851 3z.70 Kazimierz Junosza-Stępowski .... 5·00 4·75
4849/4851 *Set of 3*.. 14·00 13·00
MS4852 121×83 mm. 9z.50 As Nos. 4849/4851................ 11·50 11·00

1713 Wojtek carrying Ammunition

1714 St Martin's Croissant from Poznań

(Des Roch Stefaniak)

2017 (31 Oct). Corporal Wojtek (Bear bought by soldiers and enlisted in order to provide him with food and transport. Served with 22nd Artillery Supply Company in Italy). Perf 11½×11.
4853 **1713** A (2z.60) multicoloured .... 3·50 3·25

(Des Agnieszka Sancewicz. Litho and embossed)

2017 (3 Nov). Polish Regional Products. Perf 11½ (with one elliptical hole on each horiz side).
4854 **1714** 5z. multicoloured .... 6·75 6·25

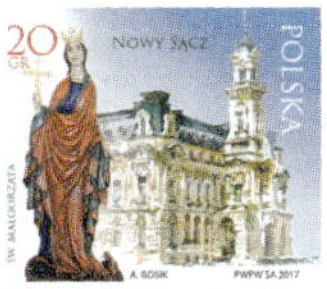

1715 Marie Curie **1716** Symbols of Nowy Sącz

(Des Agata Tobolczyk)

2017 (7 Nov). 150th Birth Anniversary of Maria Skłodowska-Curie. Perf 11½ (with one elliptical hole on each vert side).

4855 **1715** 6z. multicoloured .... 8·00 7·50

(Des Andrzej Gosik)

2017 (16 Nov). Polish Cities. Nowy Sącz. Perf 12×11½ .

4856 **1716** 20g. multicoloured 60 55

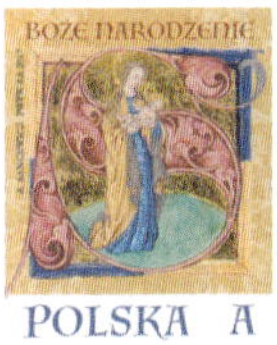

1717 Mary and Jesus **1718** Snowflake

(Des Agnieszka Sancewicz)

2017 (16 Nov). Christmas. T **1717** and similar vert designs. Multicoloured. Perf 12×11½.

4857	A (2z.60) Type **1717**	3·50	3·25
4858	B (3z.20) Adoration of the Magi	4·50	4·00
4859	6z. The Annunciation	8·00	7·50
4857/4859	*Set of 3*	14·50	13·50

2017 (18 Nov). Success of Polish Ski Jumpers. Perf 11½ (with one elliptical hole on each vert side).

4860 **1718** 2z.60 multicoloured .... 3·50 3·25

1719 Jarek Śmietana

(Des Agata Tobolczyk)

2017 (27 Nov). Polish Jazz Musicians. Jarek Śmietana, 1951–2013. Perf 11½ (with one elliptical hole on each horiz side).

4861 **1719** 2z.60 multicoloured .... 3·50 3·25

1720 *Bubo scandius* (Snowy Owl) **1721** Ex Libris, Maciej Drzewicki (Bishop of Włocławek)

(Des Marzanna Dąbrowska. Litho and embossed)

2017 (30 Nov). Polish Birds. Owls. Sheet 126×153 mm containing T **1720** and similar horiz designs. Multicoloured. Perf 11½ (with one elliptical hole on each horiz side).

MS4862 5z.×4, Type **1720**; *Athene noctua* (Little Owl); *Surnia ulula* (Northern Hawk-Owl); *Asio otus* (Long-eared Owl) .... 29·00 27·00

(Des Maciej Jędrysik)

2017 (3 Dec). Polish Bookplates. Sheet 90×70 mm. Perf 11×11½ (with) one elliptical hole on each horiz side).

MS4863 **1721** 6z. multicoloured .... 8·50 7·75

1722 Józef Piłsudski in Uniform **1723** General Anders and Soldiers

(Des Agata Tobolczyk. Litho and gold foil)

2017 (5 Dec). 150th Birth Anniversary of Józef Klemens Piłsudski (statesman and First Marshal of Poland). Perf 12×11.

4864 **1722** 10z. multicoloured .... 14·00 13·00

(Des Andrzej Gosik. Litho)

2017 (6 Dec). General Władysław Anders' Army. Trail of Hope (leading Polish prisoners of USSR to freedom). Perf 11½ (with one elliptical hole on each horiz side).

4865 **1723** 5z. multicoloured .... 12·00 11·00

A stamp of a similar design was issued by Kazakhstan.

1724 Faces of the Miners **1725** United Nations Building

(Des Maciej Jędrysik)

2017 (16 Dec). Nine of Wujek (striking miners killed by militia at Wujek coal mine, Katowice, 16 December 1981). Perf 12×11½.

4866 **1724** 2z.60 multicoloured .... 3·50 3·25

(Des Andrzej Gosik. Litho)

2017 (29 Dec). Poland in the United Nations Security Council, 2018–2019. Perf 11×11½.

4867 **1725** 3z.70 multicoloured .... 5·25 4·75

1726

1727 NEVER AGAIN!

(Des Agata Tobolczyk. Litho and gold foil)

2017 (29 Dec). Centenary of the Supreme Court. Perf 11½×11.
4868 **1726** 3z.70 multicoloured .... 5·25 4·75

(Des Marzanna Dąbrowska. Litho)

2018 (27 Jan). Never Again! (Auschwitz Birkenau Concentration and Extermination Camp, 1940–1945). Fluorescent paper. Perf 11×11½ (with one elliptical hole on each horiz side).
4869 **1727** 2z.60 black, carmine and grey .... 3·50 3·25

1728 Emblem

1729 Mother of God, Teacher of Youth (Maria Wollenberg-Kluza, from Władysława Papis' vision of apparition)

(Des Michał Korolec)

2018 (12 Feb). Winter Olympic Games, Pyeongchang, Korea. Fluorescent paper. Perf 11½×11 (with one elliptical hole on each horiz side).
4870 **1728** 5z.20 multicoloured .... 7·25 6·75

(Des Bożydar Grozdew. Litho)

2018 (24 Feb). Mother of God. Teacher of Youth. Fluorescent paper. Perf 11½ (with one elliptical hole on each vert side).
4871 **1729** 2z.60 multicoloured .... 3·50 3·25

1730 Skier

(Des Karol Tabaka. Gravure)

2018 (8 Feb). Winter Paralympic Games, Pyeongchang, Korea. Fluorescent paper. Perf 11.
4872 **1730** 5z.20 multicoloured .... 7·25 6·75

1731 Neck Badge of Captain Witold Pilecki (code name 'Witold')

(Des Marzanna Dąbrowska. Litho and embossed)

2018 (1 Mar). Cursed Soldiers (anti-Communist resistance fighters) Gorgets (neck badges). Sheet 117×117 mm containing T **1731** and similar vert design. Multicoloured. Fluorescent paper. Perf 11½ (with one elliptical hole on each vert side).
MS4873 6z.×2, Type **1731**; Neck badge of Danuta Sieikówna (code name 'Inka') (nurse)........ 18·00 16·00

(Des Agnieszka Sancewicz. Gravure)

2018 (6 Mar). Easter. As T **1686**. Perf 12×11.
4874 B (3z.20) Red egg, with white and yellow flower decoration .... 4·50 4·00

T **1732** is unavailable.

1733 Daffodil

(Des Marzanna Dąbrowska. Litho)

2018 (9 Mar). Flowers and Fruit. Fluorescent paper. Perf 11½×12.
4875 **1733** 25g. multicoloured 50 45

(Des Jacek Konarzewski. Gravure)

2018 (24 Mar). Tenth Death Anniversary of Irene Stanisława Sendler (humanitarian, social worker, and nurse who served in the Polish Underground Resistance during World War II in German-occupied Warsaw), 1910–2008. Horiz design. Multicoloured. Fluorescent paper. Perf 11×11½.
4876 2z.60 Irene Sendler .... 3·50 3·25

T **1734** is unavailable.

(Des Maciej Jędrysik. Gravure)

2018 (31 Mar). Bar Confederation, 1768–1772 (association of Polish nobles formed at Bar Fortress, Podolia to defend the independence of the Polish–Lithuanian Commonwealth magnates against Russian influence, King Stanislaus II Augustus and reformers). Vert design. Multicoloured. Fluorescent paper. Perf 12×11½.
4877 1z. Soldier wearing confederation uniform 1·40 1·25

T **1735** is unavailable.

(Des Ewa Bilan-Stoch. Gravure)

2018 (14 Apr). Kamil Stoch (ski jump multiple champion, oldest individual Olympic gold medalist and World Cup title holder). Horiz design. Multicoloured. Fluorescent paper. Perf 11½×12.
4878 3z.70 Kamil Stoch .... 5·25 4·75

T **1736** is unavailable.

(Des Jarosław Ochendzan. Litho)

2018 (24 Apr). History of Polish Photography. Ignacy Krieger (photographer) Commemoration. Four vert designs showing photographs. Multicoloured. Fluorescent paper. Perf 11½ (with one elliptical hole on each vert side).
4879 2z.60 Ignacy Krieger smoking pipe (blue background) .... 3·50 3·25
a. Strip of 4. Nos. 4879/4882 .... 17·00
4880 2z.60 Two chimney sweeps (blue background) .... 3·50 3·25
4881 3z.20 Man, seated .... 4·50 4·00
4882 3z.20 Boy selling bagels from a tray (violet background) .... 4·50 4·00
4879/4882 *Set of 4* .... 14·50 13·00

Nos. 4879/4822 were printed, *se-tenant,* alternating in a checkerboard fashion within sheets of 12 stamps, giving three horizontal strips of four stamps.

T **1737** is unavailable.

(Des Bożydar Grozdew. Gravure)

2018 (2 May). My Homeland. Vert design. Multicoloured. Fluorescent paper. Perf 12×11½.

4883 A (2z.60) Red and white rosette (National Colours) .... 4·50 4·00

T **1738** is unavailable.

(Des Roch Stefaniak. Litho)

2018 (2 May). Europa. Bridges. Vert design. Multicoloured. Fluorescent paper. Perf 11½×11 (with one elliptical hole on each vert side).

4884 5z. Tczew Bridge .... 7·00 6·50

T **1739** is unavailable.

(Des Marzanna Dąbrowska. Gravure)

2018 (11 May). Flowers and Fruit. Horiz design. Multicoloured. Fluorescent paper. Perf 11½×12.

4885 A (6z.80) Lily of the Valley .... 9·50 8·75

T **1740** is unavailable.

1741 Mother of Zagłębie (detail)

(Des Agnieszka Sancewicz. Gravure)

2018 (19 May). Mother of Zagłębie. Multicoloured. Fluorescent paper. Perf 11½×12.

4886 **1741** B (3z.20) multicoloured .... 4·50 4·25

(Des Joanna Fleszar. Litho)

2018 (30 May). Polish Animated Cartoons. *Proszę słonia*. Sheet 121×75 mm containing two horiz designs. Multicoloured. Fluorescent paper. Perf 11½ (with one elliptical hole on each horiz side).

MS4887 2z.60 Boy riding Elephant; 3z.20 Boy riding on Elephant's head with two boys sitting on sofa behind him .... 9·00 8·25

T **1742** is unavailable.

(Des Marzanna Dąbrowska. Litho)

2018 (3 June). Historic Organs. Sheet 75×100 mm. Vert design. Multicoloured. Fluorescent paper. Perf 11×11½ (with one elliptical hole on each horiz side).

MS4888 6z.80 Mannerist-Baroque organ, Franciscan Church of St Trinity, Gdańsk .... 10·00 9·25

T **1743** is unavailable.

(Des Bożydar Grozdew. Gravure)

2018 (14 June). Robert Lewandowski (captain of National Football Team). Vert design. Multicoloured. Fluorescent paper. Perf 12×11½.

4889 6z. Robert Lewandowski .... 8·50 8·00

T **1744** is unavailable.

(Des Marzanna Dąbrowska. Gravure)

2018 (16 June). 50th Death Anniversary of St Padre Pio (Francesco Forgione, Pio of Pietrelcina). Vert design. Multicoloured. Fluorescent paper. Perf 11½×11.

4890 2z.60 St Padre Pio .... 4·00 3·75

T **1745** is unavailable.

(Des Andrzej Gosik. Gravure)

2018 (22 June). Jubilee of the Bishopric in Poznań (968–2018). Vert design. Multicoloured. Fluorescent paper. Perf 11.

4891 A (2z.60) Bishop Jordan and outline of Poznań Cathedral .... 4·00 3·75

T **1746** is unavailable.

(Des Andrzej Gosik. Gravure)

2018 (22 June). Polish Cities. Horiz design as T **1716**. Multicoloured. Fluorescent paper. Perf 11½×12.

4892 10z. St Florian with Żywiec Castle in the background .... 14·00 13·00

T **1747** is unavailable.

(Gravure)

2018 (24 June). Blessed Dorota of Montau (Mąty). Vert design. Multicoloured. Fluorescent paper. Perf 11½×11.

4893 2z.60 *Blessed Dorothea, Montoviensis, Reclusa 1347–1394* (Krzysztof Izdebski-Cruz), St Mary's Basilica in Gdańsk .... 4·00 3·75

T **1748** is unavailable.

(Des Agnieszka Sobczyńska. Litho)

2018 (27 June). 550th Anniversary of the Parliamentary Movement in Poland. Square design. Multicoloured. Fluorescent paper. Perf 11 (with one elliptical hole on each horiz side).

4894 3z.20 Polish Seym under King Sigismund III Vasa (meeting of the combined chambers in the Senator's Hall in the presence of the monarch) (Giacomo Lauro) .... 4·50 4·00

T **1749** is unavailable.

1750 Wieliczka Salt Mine

(Des Marzanna Dąbrowska. Litho)

2018 (23 July). Tourism. Poland, See More. T **1750** and similar horiz design. Multicoloured. Fluorescent paper. Perf 11½×11 (with one elliptical hole on each horiz side).

4895 2z.60 Type **1750** .... 3·75 3·50

a. Pair. Nos. 4895/4896 .... 12·00 11·00

4896 5z.20 Baltic Sea coast .... 7·50 7·00

Nos. 4895/4896 were printed, *se-tenant*, in horizontal and vertical pairs within sheets of eight stamps.

1751 Madonna

1752 General Władysław Sikorski

(Des Agnieszka Sancewicz. Gravure)

2018 (27 July). 300th Anniversary of the Canonical Coronation of Our Lady of Takai (icon). Fluorescent paper. Perf 11.

4897 **1751** 3z.20 multicoloured .... 4·50 4·00

No. 4897 was printed, *se-tenant*, with a stamp-size label at right in sheets of two stamps and two labels.

A stamp of a similar design was issued by Lithuania.

(Des Ryszard Kufel. Litho)

2018 (28 July). General Władysław Sikorski (military and political leader). Fluorescent paper. Perf 11½ (with one elliptical hole on each vert side).

4898 **1752** 2z.60 multicoloured .... 4·25 3·75

1753 Lisiecka Sausage

1754 Our Lady of Swiętolipskiej

(Des Agnieszka Sancewicz. Litho and embossed)

2018 (30 July). Polish Regional Products. Fluorescent paper. Perf 11½ (with one elliptical hole on each horiz side).

4899 **1753** 6z. multicoloured .... 9·50 8·50

(Des Bożydar Grozdew. Gravure)

2018 (11 Aug). 50th Anniversary of the Canonical Coronation of Our Lady of Swiętolipskiej (icon). Fluorescent paper. Perf 11½×11.

4900 **1754** 2z.60 multicoloured .... 4·25 3·75

1758 Lilac Avenue

(Des Jacek Konarzewski. Litho)

2018 (10 Sept). Bicentenary of University of Warsaw Botanical Gardens. Fluorescent paper. Perf 11½×11 (with one elliptical hole on each vert side).

4908 **1758** 3z.20 multicoloured .... 5·00 4·50

1755 St Stanisław Kostka (1550–1568)

1756 Our Lady of Lusk

(Des Bożydar Grozdew. Gravure)

2018 (19 Aug). Patrons of Poland. Fluorescent paper. Perf 11×11½.

4901 **1755** 2z.60 multicoloured .... 4·25 3·75

(Des Agnieszka Sancewicz. Gravure)

2018 (23 Aug). Madonnas of the Eastern Borderlands. T **1756** and similar vert design. Multicoloured. Fluorescent paper. Perf 11.

4902 2z.60 Type **1756** .... 4·25 3·75
4903 2z.60 Our Lady, Queen of the Polish Crown from Kałusz .... 4·25 3·75
4904 2z.60 Our Lady, Queen of the Polish Crown from Porchowa, Buczacz .... 4·25 3·75
4905 2z.60 Our Lady of Zbaraska .... 4·25 3·75
4902/4905 *Set of* 4 .... 15·00 13·50

1759 Polish Flag against World Map

1760 Wacław Sieroszewski

(Des Roch Stefaniak. Litho)

2018 (20 Sept). World Congress of Polish Diaspora and Poles from Abroad. Fluorescent paper. Perf 11×11½ (with one elliptical hole on each horiz side).

4909 **1759** 2z.60 multicoloured .... 4·25 3·75

(Des Ryszard Kufel. Gravure)

2018 (24 Sept). Poles in Siberia. Wacław Sieroszewski (writer, independence activist, senator of the Republic of Poland, exile and researcher of distant cultures). Fluorescent paper. Perf 11×11½.

4910 **1760** 5z.20 multicoloured .... 8·25 7·25

1757 TkT48 Steam Locomotive

(Des Jacek Konarzewski. Litho)

2018 (31 Aug). Centenary of Kędzierzyn-Koźle Steam Locomotive Factory. T **1757** and similar horiz design. Multicoloured. Fluorescent paper. Perf 11½ (with one elliptical hole on each vert side).

4906 2z.60 Type **1757** .... 4·25 3·75
a. Pair. Nos. 4906/4907 .... 9·50 8·50
4907 3z.20 Ty42 Steam Locomotive .... 5·00 4·50

Nos. 4906/4907 were printed, *se-tenant*, in horizontal and vertical pairs within sheets of 12 stamps.

1761 Necessary Changes (Oliwia Gola)

(Des Roch Stefaniak. Litho)

2018 (26 Sept). The World through the Eyes of Young People. Fight Climate Change Campaign. Sheet 98×153 mm containing T **1761** and similar horiz designs. Multicoloured. Fluorescent paper. Perf 11½×11 (with one elliptical hole on each horiz side).

MS4911 2z.60×3, Type **1761**; To Rescue our Planet (Benjamin Tchaikovsky); Fighting the Smog (Natalia Gąski) .... 13·00 11·50

1762 *Oryctes nasicornis*

(Des Andrzej Gosik. Litho)

2018 (28 Sept). Beetles. T **1762** and similar diamond-shaped design. Multicoloured. Fluorescent paper. Perf 11 (with one elliptical hole on each vert side).

4912 3z.20 Type **1762** .... 5·00 4·50
4913 3z.20 *Cucujus cinnaberinus* .... 5·00 4·50

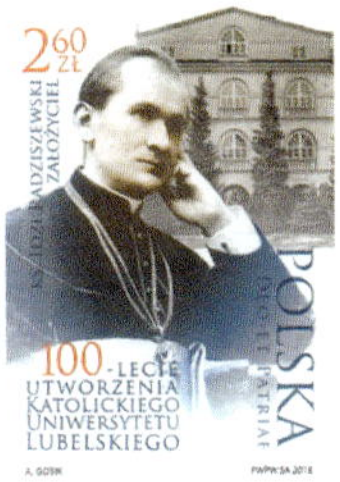

1763 Idzi Radziszewski (founder)

1764 Via Carpatia and Łańcut Castle

(Des Andrzej Gosik. Gravure)

2018 (1 Oct). Centenary of Catholic University of Lublin. Fluorescent paper. Perf 11½×11.

4914 **1763** 2z.60 multicoloured .... 4·25 3·75

(Des Jacek Konarzewski. Gravure)

2018 (3 Oct). Via Carpatia (road from the Black Sea through the Carpathians to the Baltic Sea, connecting Lithuania, Poland, Slovakia, Hungary, Romania, Bulgaria, Greece, Ukraine and Turkey) (Łańcut Declaration on transport co-operation). Fluorescent paper. Perf 12×11½.

4915 **1764** 20g. multicoloured 30 25

1765 Poznań Town Hall

1766 Pope John Paul II

(Des Jacek Konarzewski. Litho)

2018 (3 Oct). Poznań 2018, Polish Philatelic Exhibition. Fluorescent paper. Perf 11½ (with one elliptical hole on each vert side).

4916 **1765** 2z.60 multcioloured .... 4·25 3·75

It is reported that No. 4916 was also available imperforate.

(Des Marzanna Dąbrowska. Litho)

2018 (16 Oct). 40th Anniversary of the Election of Cardinal Karol Wojtyła as Pope. Fluorescent paper. Perf 11½×11 (with one elliptical hole on each vert side).

4917 **1766** 3z.20 multicoloured .... 5·00 4·50

(Des Agnieszka Sancewicz. Eng Przemysław Krajewski and Krystian Michalczuk. Recess and embossed)

2018 (18 Oct). 460 Years of the Polish Post. Sheet 121×75 mm. Sepia and gold. Fluorescent paper. Perf 11½×11 (with one elliptical hole on each vert side).

MS4918 *Swift and Stella* (Margaret Isabel Dicksee) .... 17·00 14·50

T **1767** is unavailable.

1768 Cardinal Hlond

1769 Brühl Palace in Warsaw

(Des Jarosław Ochendzan. Gravure)

2018 (22 Oct). 70th Death Anniversary of Cardinal August Hlond (arrested by Gestapo and critic of Soviet communism), 1881–1948. Fluorescent paper. Perf 12×11½.

4919 **1768** 5z. multicoloured .... 8·00 7·00

(Des Jarosław Ochendzan. Gravure)

2018 (31 Oct). Centenary of Polish Foreign Service. Fluorescent paper. Perf 11×11½.

4920 **1769** 2z.60 multicoloured .... 4·25 3·75

1770 *View of Zamość* (Marcin Zaleski)

1771 Stefan Jaracz

(Des Bożydar Grozdew. Gravure)

2018 (31 Oct). Lost Works of Art. T **1770** and similar horiz designs. Black, gold and magenta. Fluorescent paper. Perf 11×11½.

4921 2z.60 Type **1770** .... 4·25 3·75
a. Vert strip of 3. Nos. 4921/4923 .... 13·50
4922 2z.60 *Przystań na Solcu* (Aleksander Gierymski) .... 4·25 3·75
4923 2z.60 *View of Krakow* (Juliana Fałat) .... 4·25 3·75
4921/4923 *Set of 3* .... 11·50 10·00

Nos. 4921/4923 were printed, *se-tenant*, in vertical strips of three stamps within sheets of six.

(Des Marzanna Dąbrowska. Litho)

2018 (31 Oct). Personalities of Theatre and Cinema. T **1771** and similar vert designs. Multicoloured. Fluorescent paper. Perf 11½ (with a star-shaped hole on each vert side).

4924 2z.60 Type **1771** .... 4·25 3·75
4925 2z.60 Adam Brodzisz .... 4·25 3·75
4926 3z.20 Maria Bogda .... 5·00 4·50
4924/4926 *Set of 3* .... 12·00 11·00
MS4926*a* 121×83 mm. 8z.40 As Nos. 4924/4926 .... 14·00 12·50

1772 Polish and Israeli Flags in the Shape of a Butterfly

1773 Poppies in a Grenade

(Des Ronen Goldberg. Litho Cartor)

2018 (5 Nov). Poland–Israel Common Heritage. Fluorescent paper. Perf 13.
4927 **1772** 6z.50 multicoloured .... 4·25 3·75

(Des Jan Konarzewski. Litho)

2018 (11 Nov). Centenary of End of World War I (1st issue). Fluorescent paper. Perf 11 (with one elliptical hole on each vert side).
4928 **1773** 2z.60 multicoloured .... 4·25 3·75

1774 Silesian Insurgents

(Des Andrzej Gosik. Litho)

2018 (11 Nov). Centenary of End of World War I (2nd issue). The First Days of Independence. Sheet 150×110 mm containing T **1774** and similar multicoloured designs. Fluorescent paper. Self-adhesive. Die-cut perf 11½.
MS4929 2z.60×5, Type **1774**; Edward Śmigły-Rydz (*vert*); Franciszek Ksawery Latinik (*vert*); Three soldiers (*vert*); Group of soldiers................................ 22·00 19·00

The stamps of No. **MS**4929 were additional die-cut 3 mm outside the perforation to facilitate removal of the stamps.

1775 Historic Armed Forces

1776 Armed Forces

(Des Maciej Jędrysik. Gravure)

2018 (11 Nov). Centenary of End of World War I (3rd issue). Army of the Republic of Poland Reborn. Sheet 162×131 mm containing T **1775** and similar horiz designs forming the overall designs T **1776**. Multicoloured. Fluorescent paper. Perf 11.
MS4930 2z.60×5, Type **1775**; Armed forces; Armed forces; Armed forces; Armed forces (108×27 mm).... 22·00 19·00

1777 Ignacy Jan Paderewski

1778 Triggo Electric Vehicle, 2010 (Rafał Budweil)

(Des Marzanna Dąbrowska. Litho)

2018 (11 Nov). Centenary of Poland regaining Independence. Sheet 120×168 mm containing T **1777** and similar vert design. Multicoloured. Fluorescent paper. Perf 11½ (with one elliptical hole on each vert side).
MS4931 2z.60×8, Type **1777**; Józef Piłsudski; Roman Dmowski; Order of Polonia Restituta; Our Lady of the Hetman of the Polish Soldier (icon); Wincenty Witos; Ignacy Daszyński; Wojciech Korfanty............. 35·00 32·00

(Des Roch Stefaniak. Litho)

2018 (26 Nov). Centenary of the Polish Patent Office. Sheet 150×109 mm containing T **1778** and similar horiz designs. Multicoloured. Fluorescent paper. Perf 11½×11 (with one elliptical hole on each horiz side).
MS4932 3z.20×4, Type **1778**; Aeroscope, 1908 (Kazimierz Proszynski); Bulletproof vest (Kazimierz Żegleń, 1897 and Jan Szczepanik, 1901); Human brain atlas, 1997 (Wieslaw L Nowinski)...................... 21·00 19·00

1779 Jędrzej Śniadecki and University Of Vilinius

1780 Bridge on Central Trans-Andean Railway

(Des Jan Konarzewski. Gravure)

2018 (30 Nov). 250th Birth Anniversary of Jędrzej Śniadecki (writer, scientist and philosopher). Fluorescent paper. Perf 11×11½.
4933 **1779** 2z.60 multicoloured .... 4·25 3·75

(Des Karol Tabaka. Litho)

2018 (10 Dec). Birth Bicentenary of Ernest Malinowski (civil engineer, constructed Ferrovias Central in Peru). Fluorescent paper. Perf 11½ (with one elliptical hole on each horiz side).
4934 **1780** 5z.20 multicoloured .... 8·25 7·25

1781 *Girl sitting* (Henryk Jędrysik)

1782 Insurgents' Flag and Cap

(Des Marzanna Dąbrowska. Litho)

2018 (21 Dec). Polish Industrial Design. T **1781** and similar square design. Multicoloured. Fluorescent paper. Perf 11 (with one elliptical hole on each vert side).

4935 2z.60 Type **1781** .... 4·25 3·75
a. Pair. Nos. 4935/4936 .... 8·75 7·75
4936 2z.60 RM58 chair (Roman Modzelewski) .... 4·25 3·75

Nos. 4935/4936 were printed, *se-tenant*, in horizontal and vertical pairs within sheets of four stamps.

(Des Jan Konarzewski. Litho)

2018 (27 Dec). Centenary of the Wielkopolskie Uprising (the Great Poland Uprising). Fluorescent paper. Perf 11½.

4937 **1782** 2z.60 multicoloured .... 4·25 3·75

1783 Piotr Nowakowski

(Des Jarosław Ochendzan. Litho)

2018 (28 Dec). Gold Medalists of the FIVB Men's Volleyball World Championship, Italy and Bulgaria, 2018. Sheet 183×210 mm containing T **1783** and similar vert designs. Multicoloured. Fluorescent paper. Perf 11½ (with one elliptical hole on each vert side).

MS4938 1z.×16, Type **1783**; Dawid Konarski; Bartosz Kurek; Artur Szalpuk; Damian Schulz; Damian Wojtaszek; Fabian Drzyzga; Grzegorz Łomacz; Michał Kubiak; Aleksandra Śliwka; Jakub Kochanowski; Paweł Zatorski; Bartosza Kwolek; Mateusz Bienek; Vital Heynena (coach); Trophy and medal.......... 27·00 23·00

No. **MS**4938 also contains four central stamp-size labels, showing crowd and competition emblem.

1784 Chimpanzee (*Pan troglodytes*)

(Des Andrzej Gosik. Litho)

2018 (28 Dec). Animals and their Young. T **1784** and similar vert design. Multicoloured. Fluorescent paper. Perf 11½ (with one elliptical hole on each vert side).

4939 1z.30 Type **1784** .... 2·10 1·75
4940 1z.30 Indian Rhinoceros (*Rhinoceros unicornis*).......... 2·10 1·75
4941 3z. Two-toed Sloth (*Choloepus didactylus*). 4·75 4·25
4942 3z. Rothschild's Giraffe (*Giraffa camelopardis*) .... 4·75 4·25
4939/4942 *Set of 4* .... 12·50 11·00

1785 Self-portrait

1786 Red Cross

(Des Jarosław Ochendzan. Gravure)

2019 (15 Jan). 150th Birth Anniversary of Stanisław Mateusz Ignacy Wyspiański (artist, writer and designer), 1869–1907. Perf 11½×11.

4943 **1785** 3z.20 multicoloured .... 5·00 4·50

(Des Jan Konarzewski. Litho)

2019 (17 Jan). Centenary of Polish Red Cross. Perf 11½×11 (with one elliptical hole on each vert side).

4944 **1786** 3z.20 scarlet and black .... 5·00 4·50

1787 Ignacy Jan Paderewski (composer and prime minister)

(Des Agnieszka Próchniak. Eng Przemysław Krajewski. Recess and litho)

2019 (25 Jan). Centenary of the Polish Security Printing Works. Sheet 150×75 mm. Perf 11×11½.

MS4945 **1787** 14z.50 multicoloured.......... 24·00 21·00

1788 Anniversary Emblem

1789 Achille Ratti (Pope Pius XI) (assigned 1918) and Stanislaw Gall (assigned 1919)

(Des Jan Konarzewski. Litho)

2019 (31 Jan). 90th Anniversary of Polish Airlines (LOT). Perf 11½ (with one elliptical hole on each horiz side).

4946 **1788** 5z.20 multicoloured .... 8·25 7·25

(Des Roch Stefaniak. Gravure)

2019 (5 Feb). Centenary of the Field Ordinance (military ordinariate of the Catholic Church). Perf 11×11½.
4947 **1789** 2z.60 multicoloured .... 4·25 3·75

1790 Archive

1791 Anniversary Emblem

(Des Ryszard Kufel. Gravure)

2019 (7 Feb). Centenary of the State Archives. Perf 11½×11.
4948 **1790** 3z.20 multicoloured .... 5·00 4·50

(Des Karol Tyczyński. Gravure)

2019 (7 Feb). Centenary of PKO Bank Polski. Perf 11½×11.
4949 **1791** 3z.20 multicoloured .... 5·00 4·50

1792 Building Façade

(Des Jaroslaw Ochendzan. Litho and die-stamped)

2019 (7 Feb). Centenary of the Supreme Audit Office. Perf 11½ (with one elliptical hole on each horiz side).
4950 **1792** 5z. multicoloured .... 8·00 7·00

1793 Badge

(Des Roch Stefaniak. Gravure)

2019 (8 Feb). Centenary of the Polish Prison Service. Perf 11×11½.
4951 **1793** 2z.60 multicoloured .... 4·25 3·75

(Des Jan Konarzewski. Litho)

2019 (8 Feb). Centenary of Legislative Sejm (lower house of the Polish Parliament). Perf 11½×11 (with one elliptical hole on each vert side).
4952 5z. *Wojciech Trąmpczyński* (first Marshal of the Legislative Sejm) by Antoni Cygan. 8·00 7·00

T **1794** is unavailable.

1795 Branicki Palace

1796 Marian Bernaciak (Orlik) welcomed by People of Ryki, July 26, 1944

(Des Andrzej Gosik. Gravure)

2019 (19 Feb). Polish Cities. Białystok. Perf 11½.
4953 **1795** 5z. multicoloured .... 8·00 7·00

(Des Marzanna Dąbrowska. Gravure)

2019 (1 Mar). National Day of Remembrance of Cursed Soldiers (anti-Communist resistance fighters). Perf 11½.
4954 **1796** 2z.60 multicoloured .... 4·25 3·75

1797 Athletes

1798 Decorated Egg from Lowicz

(Des Dorota Sancewicz. Litho)

2019 (7 Mar). Special Olympics World Games, Abu Dhabi 2019. Perf 11½ (with one elliptical hole on each horiz side).
4955 **1797** 2z.60 multicoloured .... 4·25 3·75

(Des Agnieszka Sancewicz. Gravure)

2019 (18 Mar). Easter. T **1798** and similar vert design. Perf 11½.
4956 A (2z.60) Type **1798** .... 4·25 3·75
4957 6z. Kashubian Easter egg........ 9·50 8·50

1799 The Ulma Family Who were all Executed for Hiding Jewish Families

1800 *Dar Młodzieży* (watercolour by Andrzej Filipowicz)

(Litho)

2019 (24 Mar). Poles who Rescued Jewish Families. Perf 11×11½ (with one elliptical hole on each vert side).
4957*a* **1799** 3z.30 multicoloured .... 5·25 4·50

(Des Jaroslaw Ochebdzan. Litho)

2019 (28 Mar). Independence Cruise (round-the-world cruise marking the centenary of Polish independence). Perf 11 (with one elliptical hole on each vert side).
4958 **1800** 3z.30 multicoloured .... 5·25 4·50

1801 Marshal Józef Piłsudski, Pope Benedict XV, Belvedere Palace and Dome of St. Peter's Basilica

1802 Captain Charles de Gaulle

(Des Stefano. Litho)

2019 (29 Mar). Centenary of of the Restoration of Diplomatic Relations between Poland and the Holy See. Perf 11×11½ (with one elliptical hole on each vert side).

4959 **1801** 5z. multicoloured .... 8·00 7·00

Stamps of a similar design were issued by Vatican City.

(Des Maciej Jedrysik. Litho)

2019 (2 Apr). Centenary of the Renewal of Polish–French Diplomatic Relations. Sheet 121×75 mm containing T **1802** and similar vert design. Multicoloured. Perf 11½ (with one elliptical hole on each vert side).

MS4960 5z.×2, Type **1802**; Lieutenant General Józef Haller........ 17·00 14·50

Stamps of a similar design were issued by France.

1803 Athletes

1804 *Fringilla coelebs* (Chaffinch)

(Des Agnieszka Sancewicz. Gravure)

2019 (17 Apr). 150th Anniversary of the Sokół Gymnastic Society. Perf 11½×11.

4961 **1803** 3z.30 black and gold .... 5·25 4·50

(Des Andrzej Gosik. Litho)

2019 (24 Apr). Europa. Birds. Perf 11 (with one elliptical hole on each vert side).

4962 **1804** 5z. multicoloured .... 8·00 7·00

1805 St Wojciech

1806 Symbols of Greece and Poland

(Des Bożydar Grozdew. Gravure)

2019 (27 Apr). Patrons of Poland. Perf 11×11½.

4963 **1805** 3z.30 multicoloured .... 5·25 4·50

(Des Eleni Apostolou. Litho)

2019 (30 Apr). Centenary of Polish–Greek Diplomatic Relations. Perf 11×11½ (with one elliptical hole on each horiz side).

4964 **1806** 3z.30 ultramarine, scarlet and grey .... 5·25 4·50

Stamps of a similar design were issued by Greece.

1807 Fields and Forest, Central Poland

1808 Anniversary Emblem

(Des Bożydar Grozdew. Litho)

2019 (30 Apr). Polish Landscapes. T **1807** and similar horiz designs. Multicoloured. Perf 11×11½ (with one elliptical hole on each horiz side).

4965 3z.30 Type **1807** .... 5·25 4·50
a. Sheet. Nos. 4965/4968 .... 22·00
4966 3z.30 Island, Warta River Delta .... 5·25 4·50
4967 3z.30 Valley path, meadow and forest, Tatra Mountains .... 5·25 4·50
4968 3z.30 Snow-covered forest, Bieszczady........ 5·25 4·50
4965/4968 *Set of 3* .... 19·00 16·00

(Des Małgorzata Osa. Litho)

2019 (1 May). 15th Anniversary of Poland's Accession to the European Union. Perf 11×11½ (with one elliptical hole on each vert side).

4969 **1808** 3z.30 multicoloured .... 5·25 4·50

1809 Stanisław Moniuszko

1810 Race

(Des Jaroslaw Ochendzan. Gravure)

2019 (5 May). Birth Bicentenary of Stanisław Moniuszko (composer), 1819–1872. Perf 11½×11.

4970 **1809** 3z.30 multicoloured .... 5·25 4·50

(Des Agnieszka Sancewicz. Litho)

2019 (5 May). 80th Anniversary of Toru Służewiec Racetrack. Perf 11×11½ (with one elliptical hole on each horiz side).

4971 **1810** 3z.30 multicoloured .... 5·25 4·50

1811 Portrait of Heliodor Święcicki (first rector) by Józef Bronisław Czarnecki

(Des Bożydar Grozdew. Gravure)

2019 (7 May). Centenary of University of Poznań. Sheet 70×90 mm. Perf 11½×11.

MS4972 **1811** 8z.40 multicoloured........ 14·00 12·50

1812 Symbols of the Olympics

(Des Jerzy Pietras. Litho)

2019 (16 May). Centenary of the Polish Olympic Committee. Perf 11×11½ (with one elliptical hole on each horiz side).

4973 **1812** 4z.10 multicoloured .... 6·50 5·75

1813 Castle

(Des Maciej Jędrysik. Litho)

2019 (29 May). 400th Anniversary of the Royal Castle, Warsaw. Perf 11½ (with one elliptical hole on each vert side).

4974 **1813** 3z.30 multicoloured .... 5·25 4·50

1816 Marshal's Cane given for the Bicentenary of the Constitution

1817 *108 Polish Martyrs of World War II* by Stanisław Baj

(Des Andrzej Gosik. Litho)

2019 (4 June). 30th Anniversary of the Revival of the Senate and Free Elections. Perf 11½ (with one elliptical hole on each horiz side).

4977 **1816** 5z. multicoloured .... 8·00 7·00

(Des Jerzy Pietras. Gravure)

2019 (15 June). Blessed 108 Polish Martyrs. Perf 11.

4978 **1817** 3z.30 multicoloured .... 5·25 4·50

1814 Gymnasium, Baku designed by Konstanty Borysoglebski

1815 Pope John Paul II

(Des Maciej Jędrysik. Litho)

2019 (31 May). Polish Architects in Azerbaijan. Sheet 193×148 mm containing T **1814** and similar vert designs. Multicoloured. Perf 11×11½ (with one elliptical hole on each vert side).

MS4975 3z.30×8, Type **1814**; Baku City Council building, designed by Józef Gosławski; Tagijewo Women's School, Baku, designed by Józef Gosławski; Melikowa's house, Baku, designed by Józef Gosławski; Hajj Soltan-Ali Mosque, Baku, designed by Józef Płoszko; Murtuza Muchtarow's house, Baku, designed by Józef Płoszko; Villa Aga-Bały Kulijewa, Baku, designed by Eugeniusz Skibiński; Rothschild building, Baku, designed by Kazimierz Skórewicz .... 42·00 38·00

(Des Jerzy Pietras. Litho)

2019 (2 June). 40th Anniversary of the First Pilgrimage of Pope John Paul II to Poland. Sheet 70×90 mm. Perf 11½ (with one elliptical hole on each vert side).

MS4976 **1815** 8z.40 multicoloured .... 14·00 12·50

1818 Emblem of Culture Week painted by Michael Kliś

1819 Organ from Cathedral Basilica of St. John the Baptist and Evangelist, Toruń

(Gravure)

2019 (19 June). Beskid Culture Week. Perf 11½.

4979 **1818** 4z.10 multicoloured .... 6·50 5·75

(Des Marzanna Dąbrowska. Litho)

2019 (21 June). Historic Organs. Sheet 75×100 mm. Perf 11×11½ (with one elliptical hole on each horiz side).

MS4980 **1819** 6z.60 multicoloured .... 11·00 9·50

The stamp and margin of **MS**4980 form a composite design.

1820 Anna Walentynowicz

1821 General Sikorski

(Des Maciej Jędrysik. Gravure)

2019 (24 June). 90th Birth Anniversary of Anna Walentynowicz (Co-founder of Solidarity), 1929–2010. Perf 11½.
4981 **1820** 8z.70 multicoloured .... 14·00 12·00

(Des Agnieszka Sancewicz. Litho)

2019 (25 June). Polish Varieties of Clematis. Sheet 90×149 mm containing T **1821** and similar vert designs. Multicoloured. Perf 11½.
MS4982 3z.30×4, Type **1821**; Cardinal Wyszyński; Solidarity; Maria Skłodowska-Curie.......................... 22·00 18·00
The stamps of **MS**4982 form a composite background design.

1822 *The Apparition*, Barbara Samulowska and Justyna Szafryńska

1823 Family Arms

(Des Jerzy Pietras. Gravure)

2019 (27 June). Apparitions of Our Lady in Gietrzwałd, 1877. Perf 11½×11.
4983 **1822** 3z.30 multicoloured .... 5·25 4·50

(Des Jerzy Pietras. Gravure)

2019 (28 June). The Tęczyński Family. Perf 11½×11.
4984 **1823** 3z.30 multicoloured .... 5·25 4·50

1824 Garlic

1825 *Unia Lubelska* by Jan Matejko

(Des Agnieszka Sancewicz. Litho and embossed)

2019 (28 June). Polish Regional Products. Perf 11½.
4985 **1824** 6z. multicoloured .... 9·50 8·50

(Des Jaroslaw Ochendzan. Gravure)

2019 (1 July). 450th Anniversary of the Union of Lublin. Sheet 70×90 mm. Perf 11½×11.
MS4986 **1825** 8z.40 multicoloured.................................. 14·00 12·50

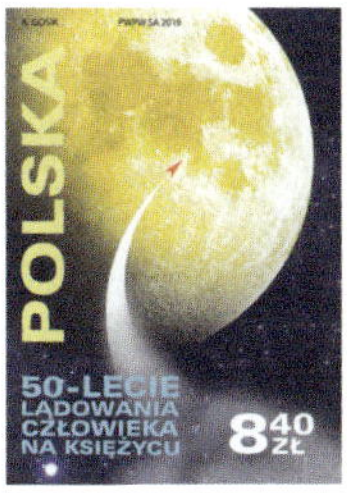

1826 The Moon

1827 Józef Kozubkiewicz and Traffic Policeman

(Des Andrzej Gosik. Litho)

2019 (20 July). 50th Anniversary of the First Moon Walk. Sheet 90×70 mm. Perf 11½.
MS4987 **1826** 8z.40 multicoloured.................................. 14·00 12·50

(Des Rocj Stefaniak. Gravure)

2019 (24 July). Centenary of the State Police. Perf 11½×11.
4988 **1827** 3z.30 multicoloured .... 5·25 4·50

1828 Henryk Sławik

1829 Football and Field

(Des Łukasz Kobiela. Gravure)

2019 (26 July). Henryk Sławik, Righteous Among the Nations (politician who saved Jewish refugees, executed by the SS), 1894–1944. Perf 11½.
4989 **1828** 4z. multicoloured .... 6·50 5·50

(Des Mateusz Sadowski. Litho)

2019 (30 July). Centenary of the Polish Football Association. Perf 11½ (with one elliptical hole on each vert side).
4990 **1829** 4z. multicoloured .... 6·50 5·50

1830 Brigadier General Zbigniew Scibor-Rylsk and Memorial Wall

1831 Runners

(Des Bożydar Grozdew. Litho)

2019 (1 Aug). World War II. 75th Anniversary of the Warsaw Uprising. Sheet 70×90 mm. Perf 11½ (with one elliptical hole on each vert side).
MS4991 **1830** 7z.30 black and gold................................. 12·00 10·50

(Des Jerzy Pietras. Gravure)

2019 (20 Aug). NSZZ SOLIDARNOŚĆ National Road Run, Kołobrzeg. Perf 11½.
4992 **1831** 30g. multicoloured 50 40

1832 Stefan Frelichowski

1833 Kazimierz Deyna

(Des Andrzej Filipowicz. Gravure)

2019 (8 Aug). Blessed Stefan Wincenty Frelichowski (died in Dachau), 1913–1945. Perf 11½.

4993 **1832** 6z.30 multicoloured .... 10·00 8·75

(Des Jarosław Ochendzan. Gravure)

2019 (12 Aug). 30th Death Anniversary of Kazimierz Deyna (footballer), 1947–1989. Perf 11½.

4994 **1833** 5z.90 multicoloured .... 9·50 8·25

1834 Alfons Zgrzebniok

1835 Steam Roller and Surveyors

(Des Adam Kultys. Litho)

2019 (16 Aug). Centenary of the First Silesian Uprising. Perf 11½ (with one elliptical hole on each vert side).

4995 **1834** 3z.30 sepia and scarlet .... 5·25 4·50

(Des Maciej Jędrysik. Gravure)

2019 (28 Aug). Bicentenary of the Central Road Administration. Perf 11×11½.

4996 **1835** 3z.30 black and greenish yellow .... 5·25 4·50

1836 Jerzy Milian

1837 Armed Employees of the Polish Post in Uniform

(Des Bożydar Grozdew. Litho)

2019 (30 Aug). Polish Jazz Musicians. Jerzy Milian, 1935–2018. Perf 11½×11 (with one elliptical hole on each vert side).

4997 **1836** 3z.30 multicoloured .... 5·25 4·50

(Des Maciej Jędrysik. Litho)

2019 (1 Sept). 80th Anniversary of the Defense of the Polish Post in Gdańsk against German Aggression. Perf 11½ (with one elliptical hole on each vert side).

4998 **1837** 3z.30 multicoloured .... 5·25 4·50

1838 'KPN'

(Des Maciej Jędrysik. Gravure)

2019 (1 Sept). 40th Anniversary of the Establishment of the Confederation of Independent Poland (KPN). Perf 11×11½.

4999 **1838** 3z.30 multicoloured .... 5·25 4·50

1839 Battleship

(Des Anna Niemierko. Gravure)

2019 (1 Aug). 80th Anniversary of the Start of World War II. Perf 11.

5000 **1839** 3z.30 multicoloured .... 5·25 4·50

1840 Equipment and Operators

1841 Emblem

(Des Jarosław Ochendzan. Gravure)

2019 (12 Sept). Centenary of Military Communications School, Zegrze. Perf 11½.

5001 **1840** 3z.30 multicoloured .... 5·25 4·50

(Des Roch Stefaniak. Litho)

2019 (20 Sept). Centenary of Independent Financial Institutions in Poland and 250th Anniversary of Budget History. Sheet 154×98 mm containing T **1841** and similar vert designs. Perf 11×11½.

MS5002 3z.30×3, greenish grey; brown-olive; light brown .... 17·00 14·50

Designs: Type **1841**; Arms of the Polish-Lithuanian Commonwealth during the reign of Stanisław August Poniatowski; Emblem of the National Tax Administration

1842 Fighting Poland Emblem

(Des Jerzy Pietras. Gravure)

2019 (27 Sept). 80th Anniversary of the Polish Underground State. Perf 11×11½.

5003	**1842**	3z.30 multicoloured	5·25	4·50

1843 Rumiany Sad (Paulina Malarz)

1844 Origami Stork

(Des Roch Stefaniak. Litho)

2019 (27 Sept). World through the Eyes of Young People. Let's Bring Back Traditional Orchards. Sheet 97×154 mm containing T **1843** and similar horiz designs. Multicoloured. Perf 11×11½ (with one elliptical hole on each horiz side).

MS5004	3z.30×3, Type **1843**; Beauty of the Orchard (Karolina Rupik); Bees' Paradise (Patryk Zielański)	17·00	14·50

(Des Roch Stefaniak. Litho)

2019 (30 Sept). Fukudenkai. House of Hope (Japanese charity working in Poland). Perf 11½×11 (with one elliptical hole on each vert side).

5005	**1844**	3z.30 multicoloured	5·25	4·50

1845 Mahatma Gandhi

1846 Sculpture at Piaśnica Memorial

(Des Maciej Jędrysik. Gravure)

2019 (30 Sept). 150th Birth Anniversary of Mohandas (Mahatma) Gandhi, 1869-1948. Perf 11½×11.

5006	**1845**	3z.30 multicoloured	5·25	4·50

(Gravure)

2019 (5 Oct). Massacre at Piaśnica Wielka of Gdańsk Pomeranians, Jews, Czechoslovakians and Mental Patients . Perf 11½×11.

5007	**1846**	2z.60 multicoloured	4·25	3·75

1847 Renaissance Organ, St Andrew the Apostle Church, Olkusz

(Des Marzanna Dąbrowska. Litho)

2019 (5 Oct). Historic Organs. Sheet 74×100 mm. Perf 11½×11 (with one elliptical hole on each horiz side).

MS5008	**1847**	6z.60 multicoloured	11·00	9·50

1848 Group in Traditional Costume

1849 Michaô Znicz, 1888–1943

(Des Joanna Fleszar. Litho)

2019 (19 Oct). 300th Anniversary of the Poznań Bambers (descendants of settlers from Bamberg who came at the invitation of the city authorities). Perf 11½×11 (with one elliptical hole on each horiz side).

5009	**1848**	3z.30 multicoloured	5·25	4·50

(Des Marzanna Dąbrowska. Litho)

2019 (25 Oct). Personalities of Theatre and Cinema. T **1849** and similar vert designs. Multicoloured. Perf 11½×11 (with one star-shaped hole on each vert side).

5010	3z.30 Type **1849**	5·25	4·50
5011	3z.30 Jadwiga Andrzejewska, 1915–1977	5·25	4·50
5012	3z.30 Józefa Węgrzyn, 1884–1952	5·25	4·50
5010/5012	*Set of* 3	14·00	12·00
MS5013	121×82 mm. 3z.30×3, As Nos. 5010/5012	17·00	14·00

1850 Radio Operator

1851 *The Sermon of St John the Baptist* (Pieter Brueghel the Younger)

(Des Marzanna Dąbrowska. Gravure)

2019 (26 Oct). World War II. 75th Anniversary of the Liberation of Breda. Perf 11½×11.

5014	**1850**	3z.30 black, blue and scarlet	5·25	4·50

(Des Maciej Jędrysik. Litho)

2019 (28 Oct). European Art in Polish Collections. Perf 11½×11 (with one elliptical hole on each horiz side).

5015 **1851** 6z. multicoloured .... 9·50 8·50

No. 5015 was printed in sheets of five stamps and one stamp-sized label.

1852 *Anthracoceros albirostris* (Oriental Pied Hornbill)

1853 Lieutenant General Józef Haller

(Des Sonny Lee (Hornbill) or Andrzej Gosik (Peregrine). Litho)

2019 (30 Oct). Birds of Singapore and Poland. Sheet 90×69 mm containing T **1852** and similar vert design. Multicoloured. Perf 11½×11 (with one elliptical hole on each vert side).

MS5016 3z.30×2, Type **1852**; *Falco peregrinus* (Peregrine Falcon).......... 11·00 9·50

Stamps of a similar design were issued by Singapore.

(Des Andrzej Gosik. Litho)

2019 (11 Nov). First Days of Independence 1919. Sheet 150×110 mm containing T **1853** and similar multicoloured designs. Self-adhesive. Rouletted.

MS5017 3z.30×6, Type **1853**; Polish cavalry parade in Sejny (*horiz*); Vilnius is seized (*horiz*); Lieutenant General Józef Dowbor-Muśnicki; Government of Jędrzej Moraczewski (*horiz*); Regaining independence, Białystok (*horiz*);.......... 32·00 29·00

1854 Woman

1855 *Wilson and Paderewski* (Ignacy Jan Paderewski and Woodrow Wilson) (fragment of Postcard by Artur Szyk)

(Des Agnieszka Sancewicz. Litho)

2019 (28 Nov). Centenary of Women's Suffrage in Poland. Perf 11½×11 (with one elliptical hole on each vert side).

5018 **1854** 3z.30 multicoloured .... 5·25 4·50

(Des Roch Stefaniak. Litho)

2019 (20 Dec). Centenary of USA–Poland Diplomatic Relations. Perf 11½×11 (with one elliptical hole on each vert side).

5019 **1855** 3z.30 multicoloured .... 5·25 4·50

1856 Monument of Gratitude to Greater Poland Insurgents and the Town Hall, Leszno

1857 Rat

(Des Andrzej Gosik. Gravure)

2020 (17 Jan). Polish Cities. Perf 11½.

5020 **1856** 3z.30 multicoloured .... 5·25 4·50

(Des Andrzej Gosik. Litho)

2020 (27 Jan). Chinese New Year. Year of the Rat. Perf 11½ (with one elliptical hole one each horiz side (outer square)).

5021 **1857** 3z.30 multicoloured .... 5·25 4·50

1858 Anniversary Memorial

1859 10k. Russian Province Stamp (As T **1**)

(Des Roch Stefaniak. Gravure)

2020 (27 Jan). 75th Anniversary of the Liberation of Auschwitz Concentration Camp. Perf 11½.

5022 **1858** 3z.30 multicoloured .... 5·25 4·50

(Des Bożydar Grozdew. 11½)

2020 (31 Jan). 160th Anniversary of the First Polish Postage Stamp. Perf 11½×11 (with one elliptical hole on each vert side).

5023 **1859** 3z.30 multicoloured .... 5·25 4·50

1860 *Poland's Wedding to the Sea* (Wojciech Kossak)

1861 Mugs and Heart

(Des Jarosław Ochendzan. Litho)

2020 (10 Feb). Centenary of Poland Regaining Access to the Baltic Sea. The Marriage to the Sea. Perf 11×11½ (with one elliptical hole on each horiz side).

5024 **1860** 3z.30 multicoloured .... 5·25 4·50

(Des Marzanna Dąbrowska. Litho)

2020 (14 Feb). Greetings Stamp. I Love You. Perf 11×11½ (with one elliptical hole on each horiz side).

5025 **1861** 3z.30 new blue, scarlet and black.......... 5·25 4·50

1862 Fatala Khan Khojski and Stanisław Patek (foreign ministers of Azerbaijan and Poland in 1920)

1863 Neck Badge of Władysław 'Sem' Gurgacz, 1914–1949

(Des Maciej Jędrysik. Litho)

2020 (20 Feb). Centenary of Azerbaijan–Poland Diplomatic Relations. Perf 11½ (with one elliptical hole on each horiz side).

5026 **1862** 3z.30 multicoloured .... 5·25 4·50

(Des Marzanna Dąbrowska. Litho)

2020 (1 Mar). Cursed Soldiers (anti-Communist resistance fighters) Gorgets (neck badges). Sheet 117×117 mm containing T **1863** and similar square design. Multicoloured. Perf 11 (with one elliptical hole on each vert side).

MS5027 6z.×2, Type **1863**; Neck badge of Henryk 'Zbych' Jastrzębski, 1917–1948.......... 20·00 18·00

No. **MS**5027 also includes two stamp-size labels showing the soldiers.

1864 Demonstration in Poznań, June 1956

1865 Edward Raczyński

(Des Maciej Jędrysik. Litho)

2020 (8 Mar). The Road to Freedom. Sheet 170×120 mm containing T **1864** and similar horiz designs. Multicoloured. Perf 11½ (with one elliptical hole one each horiz side).

MS5028 3z.30×9, Type **1864**; June 1956 in Poznań;, Celebration of the Millennium of the Baptism of Poland in 1966; Student demonstrations in 1968; December revolt in 1970; Workers' strikes in 1976; First pilgrimage of Pope John Paul II to Poland in 1979; Strike at the Gdańsk Shipyard in 1980; Pacification of the Wujek mine in 1981; Street demonstrations in 1982 .... 50·00 42·00

(Des Jarosław Ochendzan. Gravure)

2020 (25 Mar). Poles who Rescued Jewish Families. Perf 11½×11.

5029 **1865** 3z.30 multicoloured .... 5·25 4·50

1866 Anniversary Memorial

1867 President Lech Kaczyński (killed in the crash), Flag and Arms of Poland and Georgia

(Des Marzanna Dąbrowska. Litho)

2020 (4 Apr). 80th Anniversary of the Katyn Massacre. Perf 11½ (with one elliptical hole on each vert side).

5030 **1866** 3z.30 scarlet and black .... 5·25 4·50

(Des Roch Stefaniak. Litho)

2020 (10 Apr). We Remember. Tenth Anniversary of the Smolensk Air Disaster. Perf 11½ (with one elliptical hole on each horiz side).

5031 **1867** 3z.30 multicoloured .... 5·25 4·50

A stamp of a similar design was issued by Georgia.

1868 Team Members, 1920

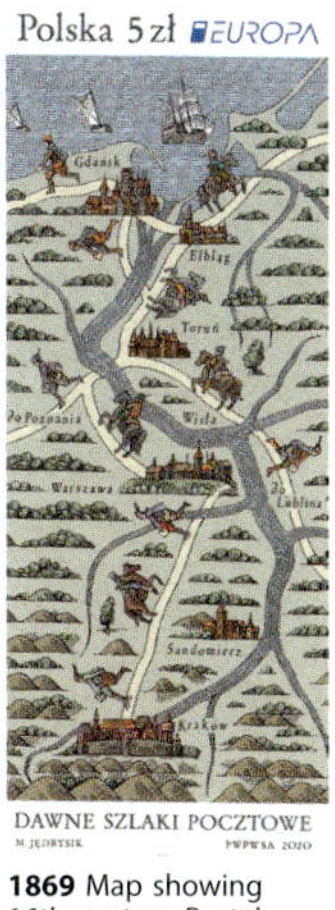

1869 Map showing 16th-century Postal Routes

(Des Agnieszka Sancewicz. Litho)

2020 (20 Apr). Centenary of of the Ruch Chorzów Sports Club. Perf 11 (with one elliptical hole on each horiz side).

5032 **1868** 3z.30 multicoloured .... 5·25 4·50

No. 5032 was printed in sheets of five stamps and a stamp-size label.

(Des Maciej Jędrysik. Litho)

2020 (29 Apr). Europa. Old Postal Routes. Perf 11×11½ (with one elliptical hole on each horiz side).

5033 **1869** 5z. multicoloured .... 8·00 7·00

No. 5033 was printed in sheets of six stamps.

1870 Chamomile Flower

(Des Marzanna Dąbrowska. Gravure)

2020 (7 May). Flowers and Fruit. Perf 11½.

5034 **1870** 8z.40 multicoloured .... 13·50 12·00

1871 Pope John Paul II

(Des Maciej Jedrysik. Litho)

2020 (13 May). Birth Centenary of Pope John Paul II. Perf 11½ (with one elliptical hole on each horiz side).

5035 **1871** 5z. multicoloured .... 8·00 7·00

1872 Andrzej Bobola

1873 Leopold Tyrmand

(Des Bożydar Grozdew. Gravure)

2020 (16 May). Patrons of Poland. Saint Andrzej Bobola, 1591–1657. Perf 11½.

5036 **1872** 3z.30 multicoloured .... 5·25 4·50

(Des Bożydar Grozdew. Litho)

2020 (16 May). Birth Centenary of Leopold Tyrmand (writer), 1920–1985. Perf 11½ (with one elliptical hole on each vert side).

5037 **1873** 3z.30 multicoloured .... 5·25 4·50

1874 'Safe Passage - Barrier to Risk'

1875 Emblem

(Des Jan Konarzewski. Litho)

2020 (30 May). Rail Crossing Safety Awareness . Perf 11½.

5038 **1874** 30g. multicoloured 50 40

(Des Jarosław Ochendzan. Litho)

2020 (30 May). Centenary of Jagielonia Białystok Sports Club. Perf 11½ (with one elliptical hole on each horiz side).

5039 **1875** 3z.30 multicoloured .... 5·25 4·50

1876 Quill

1877 *Lemur catta* (Ring-tailed Lemur)

(Des Piotr Waliszewski. Litho)

2020 (15 June). Centenary of Rzeczpospolita Daily Newspaper. Perf 11½ (with one elliptical hole on each horiz side).

5040 **1876** 3z.30 multicoloured .... 5·25 4·50

(Des Andrzej Gosik. Litho)

2020 (15 June). Animals and Their Young. T **1877** and similar vert designs. Multicoloured. Perf 11½ (with one elliptical hole on each vert side1877).

5041 3z.30 Type **1877** .... 5·25 4·50
5042 3z.30 *Osphranter* (Macropus) *rufus* (Red Kangaroo) .... 5·25 4·50
5043 3z.30 *Acinonyx jubatus* (Cheetah) .... 5·25 4·50
5044 3z.30 *Camelus bactrianus* (Bactrian Camel) .... 5·25 4·50
5041/5044 *Set of* 4 .... 19·00 16·00

1878 Luk Muzakowa Geopark

1879 Jan Kowalewski

(Des Marzanna Dąbrowska. Litho)

2020 (29 June). Tourism. Poland, See More. T **1878** and similar horiz design. Multicoloured. Perf 11½ (with one elliptical hole on each vert side).

5045 3z.30 Type **1878** .... 5·25 4·50
a. Pair. Nos. 5045/5046 .... 11·00 9·25
5046 3z.30 Biebrza National Park .... 5·25 4·50

Nos. 6045/5046 were printed, *se-tenant*, in horizontal and vertical pairs within sheets of eight stamps.

(Des Jarosław Ochendzan. Litho)

2020 (30 June). Jan Kowalewski (cryptologist and intelligence officer), 1892–1965. Perf 11½.

5047 **1879** 1z.80 multicoloured .... 3·00 2·50

1880 Abai Qunanbaiuly

(Des Maciej Jedrysik. Litho)

2020 (30 June). 175th Anniversary of the Birth of Abai Qunanbaiuly (Kazakh poet), 1845–1904. Perf 11½ (with one elliptical hole on each vert side).

5048 **1880** 3z.30 multicoloured .... 5·25 4·50

1881 *Sigismund Augustus and Barbora in Radziwill Manor in Vilnius* (Jan Mateika)

(Des Bozhydar Grozdew. Gravure)

2020 (1 Aug). 500th Birth Anniversary of Sigismund Augustus, the Grand Duke of Lithuania and King of Poland, 1520–1572. Perf 11.

5049 **1881** 3z.30 multicoloured .... 5·25 4·50

1882 Woman Soldier

1883 Andrzej Mielecki (doctor and activist)

(Des Roch Stefaniak. Litho)

2020 (15 Aug). Centenary of the Battle of Warsaw. T **1882** and similar horiz designs. Multicoloured. Perf 11½ (with one elliptical hole on each horiz side).

5050 3z.30 Type **1882** .... 5·25 4·50
5051 3z.30 Soldiers and flag .... 5·25 4·50
5052 3z.30 Cavalry .... 5·25 4·50
5053 3z.30 Virgin Mary purportedly on the battlefield .... 5·25 4·50
5050/5053 *Set of* 4 .... 19·00 16·00
MS5054 120×80 mm 6z.60 Priest and soldiers .... 11·00 9·50

(Des Adam Kultys. Litho)

2020 (20 Aug). Centenary of the Silesian Uprising. Perf 11½ (with one elliptical hole on each vert side).

5055 **1883** 3z.30 multicoloured .... 5·25 4·50

1884 Father Bocheński

1885 Emblem

(Des Jacek Konaezewski. Litho)

2020 (30 Aug). Father Józef Maria Bocheński (1902–1995)'s Year. Perf 11½ (with one elliptical hole on each horiz side).
5056 **1884** 3z.30 multicoloured .... 5·25 4·50

(Des Jacek Konarzewski. Gravure)

2020 (31 Aug). 40th Anniversary of the Solidarity Trade Union Movement. Perf 11½.
5057 **1885** 4z.70 multicoloured .... 7·50 6·50

1886 *Battle of Cecora* (Witold Piwnicki)

(Des Jarosław Ochendzan. Gravure)

2020 (18 Sept). 400th Anniversary of the Battle of Cecora. Perf 11.
MS5058 **1886** 8z.70 multicoloured........................ 14·50 12·50

1887 Blessed Eusebius **1888** Building

(Des Jarosław Ochendzan. Gravure)

-**2020** (21 Sept). Blessed Eusebius of Esztergom, 1200–1270, Founder of the Order of St Paul. Perf 11½.
5059 **1887** 3z.30 multicoloured .... 5·25 4·50

(Des Agnieszka Sancewicz. Gravure)

2020 (25 Sept). 900th Anniversary of the Collegiate Chapter in Glogów. Perf 11½.
5060 **1888** 1z. multicoloured .... 1·60 1·40

1889 Figures of all Ages and Abilities protected by Umbrella

(Des Roch Stefaniak. Litho)

2020 (28 Sept). World through the Eyes of Young People. Sheet 98×154 mm containing T **1889** and similar horiz designs. Multicoloured. Perf 11½ (with one elliptical hole on each horiz side).
MS5061 3z.30×3, Type **1889**; Children of all abilities enjoying woodland walk (A. Pietroń); People of all abilities and ages joined together (K. Peterko)........ 17·00 14·50

1890 *Hypericum perforatum* **1891** Interior

(Des Agnieszka Sancewicz. Litho)

2020 (30 Sept). Polish Herbarium. Sheet 117×117 mm containing T **1890** and similar square designs. Multicoloured. Perf 11½ (with one elliptical hole on each vert side).
MS5062 3z.30×4, Type **1890**; *Urtica dioica*; *Equisetum arvense*; *Valeriana officinalis*........................ 22·00 19·00

(Des Poczta Polska SA. Gravure)

2020 (7 Oct). Stargard Collegiate Church. The Jewel of Western Pomerania. Perf 11½.
5063 **1891** 4z. multicoloured .... 6·50 5·50

1892 *Danaus plexippus* **1893** Queen of Peace

(Des Andrzej Gosik. Gravure)

2020 (8 Oct). Butterflies. T **1892** and similar horiz designs. Multicoloured. Perf 11½ (with one elliptical hole on each vert side).

5064		3z.30 Type **1892**	5·25	4·50
		a. Block of 4. Nos. 5064/5067	22·00	
5065		3z.30 *Agrias narcissus*	5·25	4·50
5066		3z.30 *Morpho helene*	5·25	4·50
5067		3z.30 *Morpho portis*	5·25	4·50
5064/5067		*Set of 4*	19·00	16·00

Nos. 5064/5067 were printed, *se-tenant*, in blocks of four stamps within the sheet.

(Des Marzanna Dabrowska. Litho)

2020 (13 Oct). The 12 Stars in the Crown of the Queen of Peace. Perf 11½ (with one elliptical hole on each vert side).
5068 **1893** 3z.30 multicoloured .... 5·25 4·50

1894 Pope John Paul II **1895** Monument

(Des Agnieszka Sobczynska. Litho)

2020 (16 Oct). Birth Centenary of Pope John Paul II, 1920–2005. Perf 11½ (with one elliptical hole on each horiz side).
5069 **1894** 5z. multicoloured .... 8·00 7·00

(Des Pczta Polska SA. Litho)

2020 (23 Oct). 150th Anniversary of the Polish Museum in Rapperswil, Switzerland. Perf 11½ (with one elliptical hole on each vert side).
5070 **1895** 4z. multicoloured .... 6·50 5·50

Stamps of a similar design were issued by Vatican City.

1896 Symbols of UN

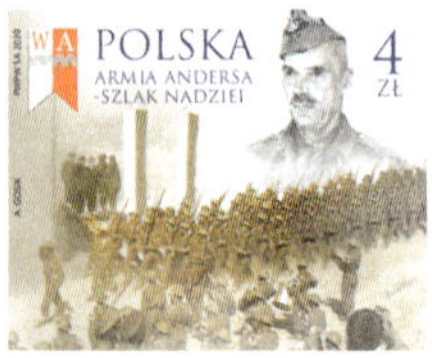

1897 Soldiers

(Des Jan Konarzewski. Gravure)

2020 (24 Oct). 75th Anniversary of the United Nations Organisation. Perf 11½.
5071 **1896** 3z.30 multicoloured .... 5·25 4·50

(Des Andrzej Gosik. Litho)

2020 (28 Oct). General Władysław Anders' Army. Trail of Hope (leading Polish prisoners of USSR to freedom). Perf 11½ (with one elliptical hole on each horiz side).
5072 **1897** 4z. multicoloured .... 6·50 5·50

1898 Spitfire

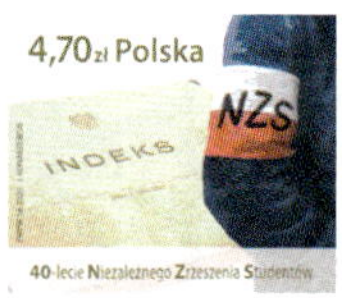

1899 Arm Band

(Des Jaroslaw Ochendzan. Litho)

2020 (28 Oct). 80th Anniversary of the Battle of Britain. Sheet 90×70 mm. Perf 11½ (with one elliptical hole on each horiz side).
MS5073 **1898** 8z.70 multicoloured........ 14·50 12·50

(Des Jacek Konarzewski. Gravure)

2020 (30 Oct). 40th Anniversary of the Independent Students Association. Perf 11½.
5074 **1899** 4z.70 multicoloured .... 7·50 6·50

1900 Train

1901 Maciej Rataj, 1884–1940

(Des Adam Kultys. Gravure)

2020 (6 Nov). 75th Anniversary of the Upper Silesian Deportations to USSR Labour Camps. Perf 11½.
5075 **1900** 3z.30 multicoloured .... 5·25 4·50

(Des Jaroslaw Ochendzan. Litho)

2020 (11 Oct). Marshals of the Second Polish Parliament. Sheet 120×170 mm containing T **1901** and similar vert designs. Multicoloured. Perf 11½ (with one elliptical hole on each vert side).
MS5076 3z.30×6, Type **1901**; Ignacy Dasznsk, 1866–1936; Kazimierz Switalski, 1886–1962; Stanislaw Car, 1882–1938; Walery Slawek, 1879–1939; Waclaw Makowski, 1888–1932........ 32·00 29·00
No. **MS**5076 also contains three stamp-size labels.

1902 The Nativity

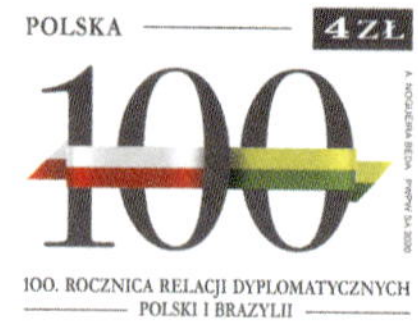

1903 '100'

(Des Agniezska Sancewicz. Gravure)

2020 (16 Nov). Christmas. Perf 11½.
5077 **1902** 8z. multicoloured .... 13·00 11·00

(Des Alessandro Nogueira Beda. Litho)

2020 (19 Nov). Centenary of Poland–Brazil Diplomatic Relations. Perf 11½ (with one elliptical hole on each horiz side).
5078 **1903** 4z. multicoloured .... 6·50 5·50

1904 Coelophysis

(Des Alessandro Nogueira Beda. Litho)

2020 (25 Nov). Dinosaurs. T **1904** and similar horiz designs. Multicoloured. Perf 11½ (with one elliptical hole on each vert side).

5079	3z.30 Type **1904**	5·25	4·50
	a. Strip. Nos. 5079/5081	17·00	
5080	3z.30 Dilophosaurus	5·25	4·50
5081	3z.30 Scelidosaurus	5·25	4·50
5079/5081	*Set of 3*	14·00	12·00

Nos. 5079/5081 were printed, *se-tenant*, in vertical strips of three stamps within sheets of six.

1905 Bydgoszcz

1906 White Stork (*Ciconia ciconia*)

(Des Waldemar Kawiński. Litho)

2020 (30 Nov). Polish Cities. Perf 11½.
5082 **1905** 95g. multicoloured .... 1·50 1·40

(Des Marzanna Dabrowska. Litho)

2020 (30 Nov). Polish Birds. Sheet 125×152 mm containing T **1906** and similar horiz designs. Multicoloured. Perf 11½ (with one elliptical hole on each vert side).
MS5083 3z.30×4, Type **1906**; Black Stork (*Ciconia nigra*); Great Egret (*Ardea alba*); Grey Heron (*Ardea cinerea*)........ 22·00 19·00
The stamps of No. **MS**5083 were each printed with a *se-tenant* stamp-size label at right, each stamp and label combination forming a composite design.

1907 Emblem

1908 Ludwig van Beethoven,

(Des Marzanna Dabrowska. Gravure)

2020 (4 Dec). Pocztowy Dar (Postal Gift) Foundation. Perf 11½.
5084 **1907** 4z.10 red and gold .... 6·50 5·75

(Des Bozydar Grozdew. Litho)

2020 (15 Dec). 250th Anniversary of the Birth of Ludwig van Beethoven, 1770–1827. Perf 11½ (with one elliptical hole on each horiz side).

5085	**1908**	3z.30 black and gold	5·25	4·50

1909 Ceramic Stove with Bird

1910 K. K. Baczynski

(Des Andrzej Gosik. Litho)

2020 (21 Dec). Polish Ceramic Stoves. T **1909** and similar vert designs. Multicoloured. Perf 11½ (with one elliptical hole on each horiz side).

5086	3z.30 Type **1909**	5·25	4·50
	a. Strip. Nos. 5086/5089	22·00	
5087	3z.30 Corner stove with pediment	5·25	4·50
5088	3z.30 Rectangular tiled stove	5·25	4·50
5089	3z.30 Semi-circular stove with legs and decorative top	5·25	4·50
5086/5089 *Set of 4*		19·00	16·00

Nos. 5086/5089 were printed, *se-tenant*, in horizontal strips of four stamps in sheets of eight.

(Des Jaroslaw Ochendzan. Litho)

2021 (21 Jan). Birth Centenary of Krystof Kamil Baczynski (resistance leader during WWII), 1921–1944. Perf 11½ (with one elliptical perf on each vert side).

5090	**1910**	4z.10 multicoloured	6·50	5·75

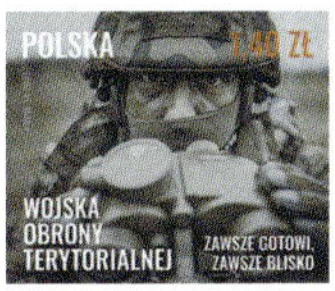

1911 Soldier

1912 Anniversary Emblem

(Des Poczta Polska S.A.. Gravure)

2021 (14 Feb). Territorial Defence Forces. Perf 11½.

5091	**1911**	1z.40 multicoloured	2·25	2·00

(Des Agnieszka Sobczyńska. Litho)

2021 (15 Feb). 30th Anniversary of the Visegrad Group. Perf 11½ (with one elliptical perf on each horiz side).

5092	**1912**	8z. multicoloured	13·00	11·00

Stamps of a similar design were issued by Czech Republic, Hungary and Slovakia

1913 Dyed Egg

1914 Sister Faustina and Pope John Paul II

(Des Agnieszka Sobczyńska. Gravure)

2021 (19 Feb). Easter. Perf 11½.

5093	**1913**	8z. multicoloured	13·00	11·00

(Des Poczta Polska S.A.. Gravure)

2021 (22 Feb). 90th Anniversary of the Revelations to Sister Faustina, 1920–2005. Sheet 158×104 mm. Perf 11.

MS5094 **1914**	11z.50 multicoloured	19·00	17·00

1915 Bull

1916 Kazimierz Górski

(Des Andrzej Gosik. Litho)

2021 (26 Feb). Chinese New Year. Year of the Bull. Perf 11½.

5095	**1915**	3z.30 multicoloured	5·25	4·50

No. 5095 was perforated in a circle contained in an outer perforated square.

(Des Jaroslaw Ochendzan. Gravure)

2021 (26 Feb). Birth Centenary of Kazimierz Górski (footballer and coach), 1921–2006. Perf 11½.

5096	**1916**	4z. multicoloured	6·50	5·50

1917 Lukasz Cieplinksi, 1913–1951

1918 Map

(Des Marzanna Dąbrowska. Gravure)

2021 (1 Mar). National Day of Remembrance of Cursed Soldiers. Perf 11½.

5097	**1917**	3z.30 black and magenta	5·25	4·50

(Des Jan Konarzewski. Litho)

2021 (18 Mar). Centenary of the Treaty of Riga. Perf 11½ (with one elliptical perf on each vert side).

5098	**1918**	3z.30 multicoloured	5·25	4·50

1919 Monument

1920 Michał Jankowski

(Des Jan Konarzewski. Gravure)

2021 (24 Mar). Poles Who Rescued Jews During The Holocaust. Perf 11½.

5099	**1919**	3z.30 multicoloured	5·25	4·50

(Des Jan Konarzewski. Gravure)

2021 (25 Mar). Michał Jankowski (scientist), 1842–1912. Perf 11½.

5100	**1920**	1z. multicoloured	1·60	1·40

1921 Jerzy Iwanow-Szajnowicz

(Des Agnieszka Sancewicz. Gravure)

2021 (26 Mar). Jerzy Iwanow-Szajnowicz (resistance leader), 1911–1943. Perf 11½.

5101	**1921**	8z. multicoloured	13·00	11·00

1922 Pendolino

(Des Jacek Konarzewski. Litho)

2021 (31 Mar). European Year of Rail. Modern Railway Rolling Stock. T **1922** and similar horiz designs. Multicoloured. Perf 11½ (with one elliptical perf on each vert side).

5102	3z.30 Type **1922**	5·25	4·50
	a. Sheet. Nos. 5102/5107	32·00	
5103	3z.30 Dart	5·25	4·50
5104	3z.30 Impuls	5·25	4·50
5105	3z.30 Pt31 64	5·25	4·50
5106	3z.30 Flirt	5·25	4·50
5107	3z.30 Elf II	5·25	4·50
5102/5107 *Set of 6*		28·00	24·00

Nos. 5102/5107 were printed, *se-tenant*, in sheets of six stamps.

1923 Bull and Bear **1924** Lynx

(Des Jacek Konarzewskii. Litho)

2021 (16 Apr). 30th Anniversary of the Warsaw Stock Exchange. Perf 11½ (with one elliptical perf on each vert side).

5108	**1923**	3z.30 multicoloured	5·25	4·50

(Des Bozydar Grozdew. Litho)

2021 (21 Apr). Europa. Endangered National Wildlife. Perf 11½ (with one elliptical perf on each horiz side).

5109	**1924**	3z.30 multicoloured	5·25	4·50

1925 Celebration **1926** *Andrena nigroaenea*

(Des Jan Konarzewski. Litho)

2021 (21 Apr). 230th Anniversary of the May 3rd Constitution. Perf 11½ (with one elliptical perf on each horiz side).

5110	**1925**	3z.30 multicoloured	5·25	4·50

(Des Andrzej Gosik. Litho)

2021 (30 Apr). Beneficial Insects. T **1926** and similar square designs. Multicoloured. Perf 11½ (with one elliptical perf on each horiz side).

5111	3z.30 Type **1926**	5·25	4·50
5112	3z.30 *Dasypoda hirtipes*	5·25	4·50
5113	3z.30 *Halictus quadricinctus*	5·25	4·50
5114	3z.30 *Apis mellifera*	5·25	4·50
5115	3z.30 *Sphecodes albilabris*	5·25	4·50
5116	3z.30 *Bombus pascuorum*	5·25	4·50
5111/5116 *Set of 6*		28·00	24·00

1927 St Joseph **1928** Wojciecch Korfanty

(Des Jaroslaw Ochendzan. Gravure)

2021 (1 May). Year of St Joseph. Perf 11½.

5117	**1927**	3z.30 multicoloured	5·25	4·50

(Des Adam Kultys. Litho)

2021 (2 May). Centenary of the Silesian Uprising. Perf 11½ (with one elliptical perf on each vert side).

5118	**1928**	3z.30 multicoloured	5·25	4·50

1929 Kornel Morawieck **1930** Stanisław Szczepanowsk (bishop and martyr)

(Des Poczta Polska S.A.. Gravure)

2021 (3 May). 80th Birth Anniversary of Kornel Morawieck (politician), 1941–2019. Perf 11½.

5119	**1929**	3z.30 multicoloured	5·25	4·50

(Des Bożydar Grozdew. Gravure)

2021 (8 May). Patrons of Poland. Perf 11½.

5120	**1930**	3z.30 multicoloured	5·25	4·50

1931 Bread **1932** Athletes

(Des Jan Konarzewski. Gravure)

2021 (12 May). 40th Anniversary of the Solidarity Union of Farmers. Perf 11½.

5121	**1931**	5z. multicoloured	10	10

(Des Poczta Polska S.A.. Litho)

2021 (28 May). European Team Athletics Championships, Silesia Region. Perf 11½.

5122	**1932**	4z. multicoloured	6·50	5·50

No. 5122 was perforated in a circle contained in an outer perforated square.

1933 Minsk Mazowiecki

(Des Andrzej Gosik. Gravure)

2021 (29 May). Polish Cities. Perf 11½.

5123	**1933**	4z. multicoloured	6·50	5·50

1934 Madonna from Bilszwici, Ukraine

1935 Emblem

(Des Agnieszka Sancewicz. Gravure)

2021 (31 May). Madonnas of the Eastern Borderlands. T **1934** and similar vert designs. Multicoloured. Perf 11½.

5124	4z. Type **1934**	6·50	5·50
5125	4z. Madonna from Marjampole, Lithuania	6·50	5·50
5126	4z. Madonna from Lviv, Ukraine	6·50	5·50
5127	4z. Madonna from Ternopil, Ukraine	6·50	5·50
5124/5127 *Set of 4*		23·00	20·00

(Des Marzanna Dąbrowska. Litho)

2021 (12 June). Centenary of Post and Telecommunication Museum, Wrocław. Perf 11½ (with one elliptical perf on each horiz side).

5128	**1935**	3z.30 multicoloured	5·25	4·50

1936 Henryk Arctowski

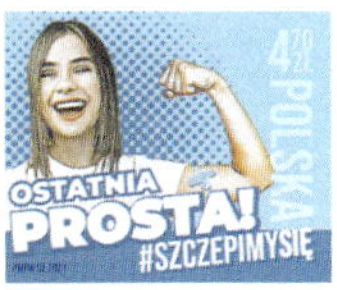

1937 Girl

(Des Paweł Myszka. Litho)

2021 (15 July). 150th Birth Anniversary of Henryk Arctowski (Antarctic explorer). Perf 11½ (with one elliptical perf on each vert side).

5129	**1936**	3z.30 multicoloured	5·25	4·50

(Des Poczta Polska S.A.. Gravure)

2021 (15 July). Combat Corona Campaign. We Vaccinate. Perf 11½.

5130	**1937**	4z.70 multicoloured	7·50	6·50

1938 Table Tennis Player

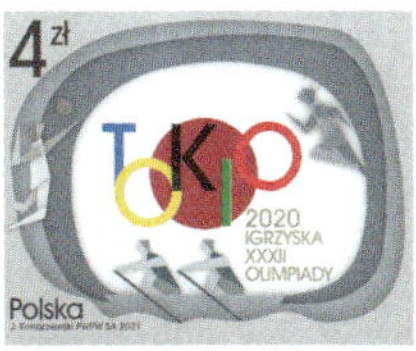

1939 Emblem

(Des Jan Konarzewski. Litho)

2021 (15 July). Paralympic Games, Tokyo. Perf 11½ (with one elliptical perf on each horiz side).

5131	**1938**	4z. multicoloured	6·50	5·50

(Des Paweł Myszka. Litho)

2021 (15 July). Olympic Games, Tokyo. Perf 11½ (with one elliptical perf on each horiz side).

5132	**1939**	4z. multicoloured	6·50	5·50

1940 *Polonia*

(Des Marzanna Dąbrowska. Litho)

2021 (23 July). Polish Transatlantic Ships. T **1940** and similar horiz designs. Multicoloured. Perf 11½ (with one elliptical perf on each vert side).

5133	3z.30 Type **1940**	5·25	4·50
	a. Strip. Nos. 5133/5135	17·00	
5134	3z.30 *Kościuszko*	5·25	4·50
5135	3z.30 *Pulaski*	5·25	4·50
5133/5135 *Set of 3*		14·00	12·00

Nos. 5133/5135 were printed, *se-tenant*, in vertical strips of three stamps within sheets of six stamps.

1941 Hiker

1942 Jan Michon, Alfons Flisykowski and Konrad Guderski

(Des Marzanna Dąbrowska. Gravure)

2021 (25 July). Year of St James the Apostle. Perf 11½.

5136	**1941**	4z.10 multicoloured	6·50	5·75

(Des Robert Kotowicz. Litho)

2021 (1 Sept). Defense of the Polish Post in Gdańsk against German Aggression. Perf 11½ (with one elliptical perf on each horiz side).

5137	**1942**	3z.30 multicoloured	5·25	4·50

1943 *Bitwa pod Chocimiem* (Jozef Brandt), 1867

(Des Jaroslaw Ochendzan. Litho)

2021 (2 Sept). 400th Anniversary of the Battle of Khotyn. Sheet 100×75 mm. Perf 11½ (with one elliptical perf on each vert side).

MS5138	**1943**	8z. multicoloured	13·50	11·50

1944 Krzysztof Krawczyk

1945 Cardinal Stefan Wyszyński

(Des Marzanna Dąbrowska. Litho)

2021 (3 Sept). Krzysztof Krawczyk (singer and musician), 1946–2021. Perf 11½ (with one star-shaped perf on each vert side).

5139 **1944** 4z. multicoloured .... 6·50 5·50

(Des Marzanna Dąbrowska. Litho)

2021 (12 Sept). Beatification of Cardinal Stefan Wyszyński. Perf 11½ (with one elliptical perf on each horiz side).

5140 **1945** 4z. multicoloured .... 6·50 5·50

1950 Statue

1951 Expo

(Litho)

2021 (30 Sept). Congress of the PZF. Perf 11½ (with one elliptical perf on each vert side).

5145 **1950** 3z.30 multicoloured .... 5·25 4·50

(Des Jan Konarzewski. Litho)

2021 (1 Oct). Expo 2020, Dubai, United Arab Emirates 2021. Sheet 70×90 mm. Perf 11½ (with one elliptical perf on each vert side).

MS5146 **1951** 8z. multicoloured.. 13·50 11·50

1946 Player

1947 Mother Elżbieta Róża Czacka

(Des Jan Konarzewski. Litho)

2021 (12 Sept). 2021 European Amputee Football Championship, Kraków. Perf 11½ (with one elliptical perf on each vert side).

5141 **1946** 4z. multicoloured .... 6·50 5·50

(Des Bożydar Grozdew. Litho)

2021 (12 Sept). Beatification of Mother Elżbieta Róża Czacka. Perf 11½ (with one elliptical perf on each horiz side).

5142 **1947** 4z. black .... 6·50 5·50

1952 Anniversary Emblem

1953 Emblem

(Des Jacek Konarzewski. Gravure)

2021 (6 Oct). 30th Anniversary of Caritas Poland. Perf 11½.

5147 **1952** 10z. carmine .... 16·00 14·00

(Des Jan Konarzewski. Gravure)

2021 (16 Oct). 25th Anniversary of Poland in the OECD. Perf 11½.

5148 **1953** 3z.30 multicoloured .... 5·25 4·50

1948 Stanislaw Lem

1949 C. K. Norwid

(Des Bożydar Grozdew. Litho)

2021 (12 Sept). Birth Centenary of Stanislaw Lem (writer), 1921–2006. Perf 11½ (with one elliptical perf on each vert side).

5143 **1948** 4z. blue-grey and black.. 6·50 5·50

(Des Jaroslaw Ochendzan. Gravure)

2021 (24 Sept). Birth Bicentenary of Cyprian Kamil Norwid (writer and artist), 1821–1883. Perf 11½ (with one elliptical perf on each vert side).

5144 **1949** 3z.30 multicoloured .... 5·25 4·50

1954 Czesław Słania

(Des Marzanna Dąbrowska. Eng Przemysław Krajewski and P. Sihlberg. Recess and litho)

2021 (22 Oct). Birth Centenary of Czesław Słania, 1921–2005. Perf 11½ (with one elliptical perf on each horiz side).

MS5149 **1954** 15z.30 multicoloured.. 25·00 22·00

Stamps of a similar design were issued by Sweden.

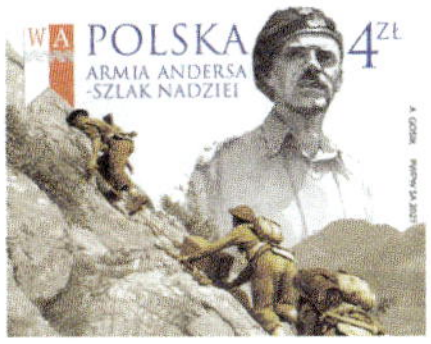

1955 Aleksander Ładoś **1956** General Anders

(Des Agnieszka Sancewicz. Litho)

2021 (23 Oct). Aleksander Ładoś and the Ładoś Group. Perf 11½ (with one elliptical perf on each vert side).

5150 **1955** 4z. multicoloured .... 6·50 5·50

(Des Andrzej Gosik. Litho)

2021 (17 Nov). General Władysław Anders' Army. Trail of Hope (leading Polish prisoners of USSR to freedom). Perf 11½ (with one elliptical perf on each horiz side).

5151 **1956** 4z. multicoloured .... 6·50 5·50

1957 Early Team **1958** Father Jan Franciszek Macha

(Des Agnieszka Sancewicz. Litho)

2021 (19 Nov). 110th Anniversary of Polonia Warszawa Football Club. Perf 11½ (with one elliptical perf on each horiz side).

5152 **1957** 3z.30 multicoloured .... 5·25 4·50

(Des Ewa Burdzicka. Litho)

2021 (20 Nov). Beatification of Father Jan Franciszek Macha. Perf 11½ (with one elliptical perf on each vert side).

5153 **1958** 4z. multicoloured .... 6·50 5·50

1959 Bochnia Salt Mine, Poland **1960** Pope John Paul II and Virgin Mary

(Des Alenka Lalić and Marzanna Dąbrowska. Litho)

2021 (2 Dec). Natural Wealth. Salt. T **1959** and similar horiz design. Perf 11½ (with one elliptical perf on each horiz side).

5154 4z. Type **1959** .... 6·50 5·50
a. Pair. Nos. 5154/5155 .... 13·50 11·50
5155 4z. Ston Saltworks, Croatia .... 6·50 5·50

Nos. 5154/5155 were printed, *se-tenant*, in horizontal pairs within the sheet.

Stamps of a similar design were issued by Croatia.

(Des Poczta Polska S.A.. Litho)

2021 (4 Dec). 30th Anniversary of Radio Maryja. Perf 11½ (with one elliptical perf on each vert side).

5156 **1960** 4z.10 multicoloured .... 6·50 5·75

1961 Virgin and Child **1962** Marek Edelman

(Des Bożydar Grozdew. Litho)

2021 (8 Dec). Mother of God of the Elections. Perf 11½ (with one elliptical perf on each vert side).

5157 **1961** 4z.10 multicoloured .... 6·50 5·75

(Des Jaroslaw Ochendzan. Gravure)

2022 (2 Jan). Marek Edelman (Leader of Warsaw Ghetto Uprising), 1919—2009. Perf 11½.

5158 **1962** 4z.50 multicoloured .... 7·25 6·25

1963 Emblem **1964** Uniform Badges

(Des Jan Konarzewski. Litho)

2022 (24 Jan). Winter Olympics and Paralympics, Beijing 2022. T **1963** and similar multicoloured design. Perf 11½ (with one elliptical perf on each vert side) (No. 5159) or 11½ (with one elliptical perf on each horiz side) (No. 5160).

5159 4z. Type **1963** .... 6·50 5·50
5160 4z. Iweta Faron and Witold Skupien (paralympic cross country skiers) (*horiz*) .... 6·50 5·50

(Des Poczta Polska S.A.. Gravure)

2022 (27 Jan). Polish Uniform. Perf 11½.

5161 **1964** (3z.60) multicoloured .... 5·75 5·00

1965 Baku City Hall

(Des Poczta Polska S.A. Gravure)

2022 (31 Jan). Poles Abroad, Józef Gosławski (architect in Baku). Perf 11½.

5162 **1965** 4z. multicoloured .... 6·50 5·50

1966 Tiger

(Des Andrzej Gosik. Litho)

2022 (1 Feb). Chinese New Year. Year of the Tiger. Perf 11½ (inner circle) and 11½ (with one elliptical perf on each horiz side) (outer square).
5163 **1966** 4z. multicoloured .... 6·50 5·50
No. 5163 was perforated in a circle around the design enclosed in an outer perforated square.

1967 Iwona Krugłowska (soldier and post office worker)

1968 Anniversary Emblem

(Des Jaroslaw Ochendzan. Litho)

2022 (14 Feb). 80th Anniversary of Formation of Armia Krajowa (home army (underground military organization in Central Europe during World War II)). Perf 11½ (with one elliptical perf on each horiz side).
5164 **1967** 3z.60 multicoloured .... 5·75 5·00

(Des Jacek Konarzeski. Gravure)

2022 (17 Feb). Centenary of Polish Civil Service. Perf 11½.
5165 **1968** 3z.60 scarlet, ultramarine and black........ 5·75 5·00

1969 Embassy

1970 Józef Franczak

(Des Poczta Polska S.A.. Litho)

2022 (28 Feb). Polish Diplomatic Posts Overseas. Ankara, Turkey. Perf 11½ (with one elliptical perf on each horiz side).
5166 **1969** 4z. multicoloured .... 6·50 5·50

(Des Adam Kultys . Gravure)

2022 (1 Mar). National Day of Remembrance of Cursed Soldiers. Perf 11½.
5167 **1970** 4z.50 black and scarlet.................................. 7·25 6·25

1971 Louis Pasteur

1972 Ignacy Łukasiewicz

(Des Jan Konarzewski. Gravure)

2022 (7 Mar). Birth Bicentenary of Louis Pasteur (chemist and microbiologist), 1822–1895. Perf 11½.
5168 **1971** 30g. ultramarine, scarlet and gold......... 50 40

(Des Mirosław Szponar. Litho)

2022 (8 Mar). Birth Bicentenary of Ignacy Łukasiewicz (petroleum industry pioneer), 1822–1882. Sheet 121×82 mm. Perf 11½ (with one elliptical perf on each vert side).
MS5169 **1972** 11z.50 multicoloured.................................. 19·00 17·00
No. **MS**5169 also contains two stamp-sized labels.

1973 *Glory to the Resurrected Jesus* (Guido Reni) (detail)

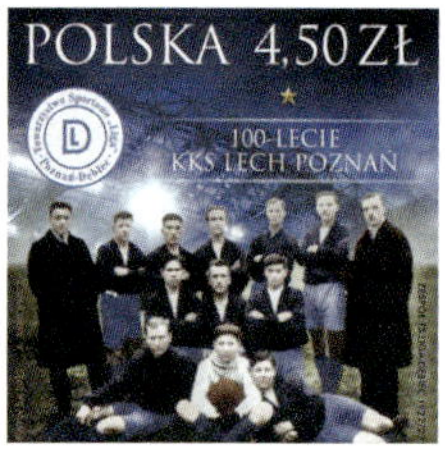

1974 Early Team

(Des Poczta Polska S.A.. Gravure)

2022 (17 Mar). Easter. Perf 11½.
5170 **1973** (4z.50) multicoloured .... 7·25 6·25

(Des Agnieszka Sancewicz. Gravure)

2022 (19 Mar). Centenary of KKS Lech Poznań Football Club. Perf 11½ (with one elliptical perf on each vert side).
5171 **1974** 4z.50 multicoloured .... 7·25 6·25

1975 Family of Bronisława and Adam Kowalski

1976 Flags of Ukraine and Poland as Clasped Hands

(Des Jan Konarzewski. Gravure)

2022 (24 Mar). Poles Who Rescued Jews During The Holocaust. Perf 11½.
5172 **1975** 3z.60 multicoloured .... 5·75 5·00

(Des Pawel Myszka. Gravure)

2022 (25 Mar). We are with You!. Perf 11½.
5173 **1976** (4z.50) multicoloured .... 7·25 6·25

1977 Jozef Mackiewicz

1978 Wawel

(Des Jacek Konarzewski. Gravure)

2022 (1 Apr). 120th Birth Anniversary of Jozef Mackiewicz (writer), 1902–1965. Perf 11½.

5174 **1977** 30g. Black 50 40

(Des Maciej Jedrysik. Litho)

2022 (21 Apr). Europa. Stories and Myths. Perf 11½ (with one elliptical perf on each horiz side).

5175 **1978** 4z.50 multicoloured .... 7·25 6·25

1979 Bernese Mountain Dog

1980 Nuthatch (*Sita europea*)

(Des Andrzej Gosik. Litho)

2022 (25 Apr). Dogs. Sheet 121×125 mm containing T **1979** and similar vert designs. Multicoloured. (11½ with one elliptical perf on each vert side).

MS5176 3z.60×6, Type **1979**; Golden Retriever; Scottish Setter (Gordon); French Bulldog; West Highland White Terrier; Miniature Long-haired Dachshund. Perf or imperf........ 35·00 30·00

(Des Pawel Myszka. Litho)

2022 (27 Apr). Birds of Polish Parks. T **1980** and similar horiz designs. Multicoloured. Perf 11½ (with one elliptical perf on each horiz side).

5177 3z.60 Type **1980** .... 5·75 5·00
a. Block. Nos. 5177/5180........ 24·00
5178 3z.60 Great Tit (*Parus major*)........ 5·75 5·00
5179 3z.60 House sparrow (*Passer domesticus*)........ 5·75 5·00
5180 3z.60 Blue Tit (*Cyanistes caeruleus*)........ 5·75 5·00
5177/5180 *Set of 4*........ 21·00 18·00

Nos. 5177/5180 were printed, *se-tenant*, in blocks of four stamps within sheets of eight stamps.

1981 Drohiczyn

1982 Gianna Beretta Molla

(Des Jaroslaw Ochendzan. Litho)

2022 (28 Apr). Tourism. The Beauty of Poland. Sheet 150×154 mm containing T **1981** and similar horiz designs. Multicoloured. Perf 11½ (with one elliptical perf on each vert side).

MS5181 3z.60×6, Type **1981**; Białowieża National Park; Catholic Church of St. Trinity in Tykocin; Muslim Mosque in Kruszyniany; Orthodox Monastery of the Annunciation of the Most Holy Theotokos in Supraśl Branicki Palace in Bialystok........ 35·00 30·00

(Des Agnieszka Sancewicz. Gravure)

2022 (30 Apr). Birth Centenary of Saint Gianna Beretta Molla (patron saint of mothers and physicians), 1922–1962. Perf 11½.

5182 **1982** 3z.60 mmulticoloured........ 5·75 5·00

1983 Black Madonna of Jasnogórska

1984 Zbigniew Wodecki

(Des Bozydar Grozdew. Litho)

2022 (3 May). Patrons of Poland. Perf 11½ (with one elliptical perf on each horiz side).

5183 **1983** 8z. multicoloured........ 13·00 11·00

(Des Agnieszka Sancewicz. Litho)

2022 (6 May). Zbigniew Wodecki (musician and actor), 1950–2017. Perf 11½ (with one star-shaped perf on each vert side).

5184 **1984** 4z.50 multicoloured........ 7·25 6·25

1985 Books and 'Big Ben'

1986 Aleksander Czekanowski

(Des Jan Konarzewski. Litho)

2022 (8 May). 80th Anniversary of the POSK Polish Library in London. Perf 11½ (with one elliptical perf on each horiz side).

5185 **1985** 4z.50 multicoloured........ 7·25 6·25

(Des Jaroslaw Ochendzan. Gravure)

2022 (23 May). Poles in Siberia. Perf 11½.

5186 **1986** 3z.60 black and gold........ 5·75 5·00

1987 Kajko and Kokosz

1988 Karol De Forbin-Jansen (1785–1844)

(Des Joanna Fleszar-Hapert and Radoslaw Gieremek. Litho)

2022 (31 May). 50th Anniversary of the *Kajko and Kokosz* (comic by Janusz Christa). Sheet 90×70 mm . Perf 11½ (with one elliptical perf on each vert side).

MS5187 **1987** 8z multicoloured........ 13·50 11·50

(Des Agnieszka Sancewicz. Gravure)

2022 (3 June). Jubilees of the Pontifical Mission Societies. Sheet 158×104 mm containing T **1988** and similar vert designs. Multicoloured. Perf 11½.

MS5188 4z.50×3, Type **1988**; Joanna Bigand (1859–1934); Paulina Jaricot (1799–1862)........ 23·00 20·00

1989 Jan Olszewski

1990 Arms and Cathedral

(Des Poczta Polska S.A.. Gravure)

2022 (4 June). Jan Olszewski (politician and prime minister), 1930–2019. Perf 11½.

5189 **1989** 4z.50 multicoloured .... 7·25 6·25

(Des Jaroslaw Ochendzan. Gravure)

2022 (6 June). 30th Anniversary of the Establishment of the Elbląg Diocese. Perf 11½.

5190 **1990** (3z.60) multicoloured .... 7·25 6·25

1991 Badge and Arms

1992 Statue and church, Lubliniec

(Des Roch Stefaniak. Gravure)

2022 (9 June). Centenary of the Silesian Voivodeship Police. Perf 11½.

5191 **1991** (3z.60) multicoloured .... 7·25 6·25

(Des Andrzej Gosik. Gravure)

2022 (17 June). Polish Cities. Perf 11½.

5192 **1992** (3z.60) multicoloured .... 7·25 6·25

1993 Welcoming General Stanisław Szeptycki, Market Square, Katowice

1994 Hubal

(Des Adam Kultys. Litho)

2022 (20 June). Centenary of the Return of Upper Silesia to Poland. Perf 11½ (with one elliptical perf on each vert side).

5193 **1993** 3z.60 multicoloured .... 7·25 6·25

(Des Miroslaw Szponar. Litho)

2022 (22 June). 125th Birth Anniversary of Henryk Dobrzański (Hubal) (soldier and resistance fighter), 1897–1940. Perf 11½ (with one elliptical perf on each vert side).

5194 **1994** 3z.60 multicoloured .... 7·25 6·25

1995 Knight

1996 Town Hall and Market Square, Zamość

(Des Jaroslaw Ochendzan. Litho)

2022 (24 June). 1050th Anniversary of the Battle of Cedynia. Perf 11½ (with one elliptical perf on each vert side).

5195 **1995** 3z.60 multicoloured .... 7·25 6·25

(Des Roch Stefaniak. Litho)

2022 (28 June). Tourism. Poland, View More. Multicoloured. Perf 11½ (with one elliptical perf on each horiz side).

5196 3z.60 Type **1996** .... 7·25 6·25

a. Pair. Nos. 5196/5197 .... 15·00 13·00

5197 3z.60 Czocha Castle .... 7·25 6·25

Nos. 5196/5197 were printed, *se-tenant*, in vertical and horizontal pairs within sheets of eight stamps.

1997 Anniversary Emblem

1998 Miron Bialoszewski

(Des Bozydar Grozdew. Gravure)

2022 (30 June). 75th Anniversary of *Kultura* Emigrant Cultural Magazine. Perf 11½.

5198 **1997** 3z.60 black .... 7·25 6·25

(Des Pawel Myszka. Gravure)

2022 (30 June). Birth Centenary of Miron Bialoszewski (writer), 1922–1983. Perf 11½.

5199 **1998** 3z.60 multicoloured .... 7·25 6·25

1999 Castle in Pińczów

(Des Jaroslaw Ochendzan. Litho)

2022 (30 June). Lost Architectural Treasures. T **1999** and similar horiz design showing engravings of buildings that have been lost. Multicoloured. Perf 11½ (with one elliptical perf on each horiz side).

5200 3z.60 Type **1999** .... 7·25 6·25

a. Pair. Nos. 5200/5201 .... 15·00 13·00

5201 3z.60 Saxon Palace .... 7·25 6·25

Nos. 5200/5201 were printed, *se-tenant*, in horizontal and vertical pairs within sheets of eight stamps.

MACHINE LABELS

1996 (1 Nov). Design showing asterisks surrounding face value. Face values from 40g. to 29z.

ML1 No fixed steps available ....

1998. Multicoloured designs showing a postal horn emblem. Date shown as day/month/year, re-issued later in the year reversed. Face values from 55g. to 35z.70.

ML2 No fixed steps available ....

GERMAN OCCUPATION OF POLAND 1915–1918

A German offensive in Galicia on 1 May 1915 broke through the Russian lines and all Poland was in German hands by the end of August. In 1916 Poland was named the General-Government, Warsaw and on 5 November 1916, Germany and Austria proclaimed a Polish Kingdom; Piłsudski sat on the Council of State of this until he resigned in protest against German control. On 15 October 1917, the Germans set up a Regency Council, which exercised control under German supervision, and took charge of affairs on 12 October 1918 when the Central Powers were on the verge of collapse.

100 Pfennig = 1 Mark

(1)

(2)

Contemporary stamps of Germany overprinted.

1915 (12 May). With T **1**.

1	**17**	3pf. brown	1·30	65
2		5pf. green	1·30	65
3		10pf. carmine	1·30	1·00
4		20pf. ultramarine	8·50	1·00
5		40pf. black and carmine	7·75	4·50
1/5 *Set of 5*			18·00	7·00

Nos. 1/5 were for use in the Łódź region.

1916 (1 Aug)–**17**. With T **2**.

6	**24**	2½pf. grey	1·20	2·50
7	**17**	3pf. brown	1·20	3·75
8		5pf. green	1·30	4·50
9	**24**	7½pf. orange	1·40	2·75
10	**17**	10pf. carmine	5·25	2·75
11	**24**	15pf. yellow-brown	4·50	4·00
12		15pf. slate-violet (1917)	1·30	2·75
13	**17**	20pf. deep blue	8·50	3·25
		a. Violet-blue	90·00	£150
		b. Ultramarine	5·25	7·75
14		30pf. black and orange/*buff*	10·50	18·00
15		40pf. black and carmine	4·00	2·75
16		60pf. magenta	4·00	3·75
6/16 *Set of 11 (cheapest)*			36·00	46·00

The area north-east of Warsaw was part of the Eastern Military Command Area, which also included the Baltic Provinces of Russia.

German stamps overprinted 'Postgebiet Ob. Ost' were used in this area; these are listed in Stanley Gibbons *Germany* catalogue.

During the period of German occupation several municipal councils organised local postal delivery services. Most used handstamps to indicate payment but the following towns issued stamps, some of which were quickly suppressed by the military authorities: Sosnowiec, Warsaw, Zawiercie. Bialystok (in the Eastern Command Area).

Przedborz and Zarki in the Austrian occupied area also issued stamps.

Polish Military Post

I. POLISH CORPS IN RUSSIA, 1918

In 1917 Poles serving in the Russian Army were transferred into Polish units so that an autonomous Polish Army could be organised. The Polish First Corps was formed on 21 August 1917. By January 1918 the Corps was based at Bobruisk, virtually surrounded by German troops.

An agreement with the Germans in February 1918 established an area of Polish Occupation and the forwarding of Polish mail to Warsaw by the German field post. Post offices operated from 1 April to 29 June 1918, after which the Corps was disbanded.

100 Kopeks = 1 Rouble

(M1)

(M2)

1918 (1 Mar). 1912–1918 stamps of Russia optd with T **M1**, by Mr Podzuinski, Bobruisk. No wmk.

(a). Perf 14½.

M1	**22**	3k. carmine-red	£150	£150
M2	**23**	4k. red	£150	£150
M3	**22**	5k. brown-lilac	34·00	27·00
M4	**23**	10k. deep blue	34·00	27·00
M5	**22**	10k. on 7k. deep blue (No. 170)	£950	£1100
M6	**10**	15k. blue and purple-brown	6·75	11·00
M7	**14**	20k. scarlet and blue	13·50	12·00
M8	**10**	25k. violet and deep green	£160	£140
M9		35k. deep green and brown-purple	6·75	11·00
M10	**14**	50k. green and dull purple	27·00	20·00

(b). Imperf.

M11	**10**	70k. vermilion and brown	£500	£400

1918 (1 Mar). Stamps of Russia surch as T **M2**, by the Corps Printing Works. No wmk.

(a). Perf 14×14½.

M12A	**22**	10k. on 3k. carmine-red	6·75	6·75
M13A		35k. on 1k. orange	£100	£100
		ba. Surch inverted	£325	
M14A		50k. on 2k. light green	6·75	6·75
		a. Surch inverted		
M15A		1r. on 3k. carmine-red	£140	£120

(b). Imperf.

M12B	**22**	10k. on 3k. carmine-red	4·00	4·00
		a. Surch overprint		
M13B		35k. on 1k. orange	2·75	2·75
		a. Surch double		
		b. Surch inverted		
M14B		50k. on 2k. light green	4·00	4·00
M15B		1k. on 3k. carmine-red	6·75	6·75
		a. Surch double		
		b. Surch inverted		

II. POLISH ARMY IN RUSSIA, 1942

After the German invasion of Russia in 1941, Polish prisoners of war taken by the Russians in 1939 were released and formed into an army which, after training in the Soviet Union, went to fight in Italy.

M3 We Shall Return

(Eng Polkowski. Typo)

1942 (18 Aug). Issued at Jangi-Jul, near Tashkent. Thick carton paper. Imperf×perf 11½.

M16	**M3**	50k. brown (*shades*)	£300	£800
		a. *Tête-bêche* (pair)	£800	£1600

Stamps with no full point after 'KOP' are forgeries.

Polish Occupation

CENTRAL LITHUANIA

A force of Poles under General Zeligawski seized Vilna and district from the Lithuanians on 9 October 1920.

100 fenigi = 1 mark.

IMPERF STAMPS. With the exception of Nos. 4/13 all the following exist imperf and perf and the prices are the same.

1

(**2** Arms of Poland and Lithuania)

(Des F. Zaniewski. Litho J. Zawadski)

1920 (20 Oct). White or greyish paper. Perf 11½ or imperf.

1	**1**	25f. dull red	60	95
2		1m. blue	60	95
3		2m. grey-violet	60	95

See also Nos. 20/22.

1920 (23 Nov). Nos. 50, etc, of Lithuania. Surch as T **2**, in black (Blk.) or blue (sideways on Nos. 8/10).

4	**5**	2m. on 15s. mauve	70·00	£100
5		4m. on 10s. orange-red	70·00	£100
6		4m. on 20s. Prussian blue (Blk.)	70·00	£100
7		4m. on 30s. bistre	70·00	£100
8	**6**	6m. on 50s. yellow-green	70·00	£100
		a. Error. 4m. on 50s.	£350	
		b. Error. 10m. on 50s.	£350	
9		6m. on 60s. red and violet	70·00	£100
		a. Error. 4m. on 60s.	£350	
		b. Error. 10m. on 60s.	£350	
10		6m. on 75s. red and bistre	70·00	£100
		a. Error. 4m. on 75s.	£350	
		b. Error. 10m. on 75s.	£350	
11	**7**	10m. on 1a. red and grey	£140	£225
12		10m. on 3a. red and brown	£2000	£3500
13		10m. on 5a. red and blue-green	£2000	£3500

3 Girl

4 Warrior

5 Ostrabrama Gate, Vilnius

6 St Stanislaus Cathedral and Tower, Vilnius

7 Rector's Insignia

8 General Zeligowski

(Res F. Ruszczyc. Litho Laskow, Vilna)

1920 (Dec). White or greyish paper. Perf 11½ or imperf.

14	**3**	25f. grey	35	85
15	**4**	1m. orange	35	85
16	**5**	2m. dull claret	70	1·40
17	**6**	4m. olive and yellow	1·00	2·00
18	**7**	6m. grey and carmine	3·50	5·50
19	**8**	10m. yellow and black-brown	4·75	8·00
14/19 *Set of 6*			9·50	16·00

1921 (6 Feb). Colours changed. White paper (2m.) also on greyish. Perf 11½ or imperf.

20	**1**	25f. deep green	60	95
21		1m. sepia	60	95
22		2m. yellow	60	95
20/22 *Set of 3*				

D9 Government Offices

D10 Castle Hill, Vilnius

(Des F. Ruszczyc. Litho Chominski)

1921 (Feb–July). POSTAGE DUE. Types **D9**/**D10** and similar designs. Perf 11½ or imperf.

D23	**D9**	50f. claret	70	2·00
D24	**D10**	1m. bright green	70	2·00
D25	-	2m. purple	70	2·00
D26	-	3m. purple	1·40	2·75
D27	-	5m. purple	1·40	4·00
D28	-	20m. vermilion (7.21)	2·40	5·50
D23/28 *Set of 6*			6·50	16·00

Designs: Horiz—2m. Castle on Troki Island. Vert—3m. Ostrabrama Gate, Vilnius; 5m. St Stanislaus Cathedral; 20m. (larger) St Nicholas Cathedral.

NA

ŚLĄSK
2 M.

(9)

+1

(10)

+1 M

(11)

1921 (Feb-Apr). Fund for Polish participation in Plebiscite for Upper Silesia. Surch with T **9**, in red or green (G,), by J. Zawadski.

23	**1**	25f.+2m. dull red (G.)	2·00	5·50
24		25f.+2m. deep green	2·00	5·50
25		1m.+2m. blue	2·00	5·50
26		1m.+2m. sepia	2·00	5·50
27		2m.+2m. grey-violet	2·00	5·50
28		2m.+2m. yellow	2·00	5·50
23/28 *Set of 6*			11·00	30·00

1921 (15 Mar). Red Cross Fund. Surch with T **10** or T **11**, in red. Perf 11½ or imperf.

29	**5**	2m.+1.(m.) pale claret	1·70	3·50
30	**6**	4m.+1.m. olive and yellow	1·70	3·50

(12)

1921 (21 Apr). White Cross Fund. Types **5**, **6** and **8** with white cross added as in T **12**. White or greyish paper. Perf 11½ or imperf.

31	**5**	2m.+1m. bright claret	1·00	2·00
32	**6**	4m.+1m. olive and buff	1·00	2·00
33	**8**	10m.+2m. yellow and black-brown	1·00	2·00
31/33 *Set of 3*			2·75	5·50

13 Church of St Anne in Vilnius

14 St Stanislaus Cathedral

(Litho State Ptg Wks, Warsaw)

1921 (Apr–July). T **13/14** and similar types. Perf 13½, 14 or imperf.

34	**13**	1m. yellow and slate (7.21)	1·00	2·00
35	**14**	2m. green and carmine (7.21)	1·00	2·00
36	-	3m. myrtle-green	1·00	2·00
37	-	4m. chocolate and brown (7.21)	1·00	2·00
38	-	5m. red-brown	1·00	2·00
39	-	6m. buff and myrtle (7.21)	1·00	2·00
40	-	10m. buff and purple (7.21)	1·40	4·00
41	-	20m. buff and sepia (7.21)	1·40	4·00
34/41 *Set of* 8			8·00	18·00

Design: Vert—3m. Coat of Arms in oval; 5m. Arms in shield. Horiz—4m. Queen Jadwiga and King Wladislaw Jagiello; 6m. Poczobut Observatory, Vilnius University; 10m. Union of Lithuania and Poland, 1569; 20m. Kosciuszko and Mickiewicz.

21 Entry into Vilnius

22 General Żeligowski

(Litho Chominski)

1921 (Nov). First Anniversary of Entry of General Żeligowski into Vilnius. Perf 11½ or imperf.

42	**21**	100m. blue and bistre (17.11)	3·75	8·75
43	**22**	150m. olive-green and brown	5·00	11·50

23 Agriculture

24 Arms

25 National Assembly, Vilnius

26 Industry

(Litho Chominski)

1922 (Feb). Opening of National Parliament. Perf 11½ or imperf.

44	**23**	10m. chestnut	5·50	11·00
45	**24**	25m. carmine and buff	5·50	13·50
46	**25**	50m. deep blue	8·00	20·00
47	**26**	75m. lilac	8·00	38·00
44/47 *Set of* 4			24·00	75·00

After a plebiscite Central Lithuania was incorporated in Poland on 8 April 1922. The Russians returned it to Lithuania on 10 October 1939 after dividing Poland with the Germans but in August 1940 it was incorporated in the Soviet Union as part of the Lithuanian SSR.

Polish Post Offices Abroad

CONSTANTINOPLE

100 Fenigów = 1 Marka

The following were used for franking correspondence handed in to the Polish Consulate at Constantinople.

LEVANT

(1)

(2)

1919 (May). Stamps of Poland optd as T **1** (larger on mark values), in carmine. Perf 11½.

1A	**15**	3f. brown	£160	£190
2A		5f. yellow-green	£160	£190
3A		10f. purple	£160	£190
4A		15f. lake	£160	£190
5A	**16**	20f. blue	£160	£190
6A		25f. olive	£160	£190
7A		50f. green	£160	£190
8A	**17**	1m. violet	£190	£225
9A		1m.50 green	£190	£225
10A		2m. brown	£190	£225
11A	**18**	2m.50 red-brown	£190	£225
12A	**19**	5m. violet	£190	£225
1A/12A *Set of* 12			£1900	£2250

1919 (1 Oct). Shiny ink.

1B	**15**	3f. brown	1·40
2B		5f. yellow green	1·40
3B		10f. purple	1·40
4B		15f. lake	1·40
5B	**16**	20f. blue	1·40
6B		25f. olive	1·40
7B		50f. green	1·40
8B	**17**	1m. violet	1·90
9B		1m.50 green	1·90
10B		2m. brown	1·90
11B	**18**	2m.50 red-brown	1·90
12B	**19**	5m. violet	2·30
1B/12B *Set of* 12			18·00

1921 (25 May). Stamps of Poland surch as T **2** (larger on T **19**), in red-brown.

13	**25**	1m. carmine	2·00
14		2m. green	3·50
15		3m. pale blue	3·00
16		4m. rose	4·00
17	**19**	6m. rose-carmine	5·00
18		10m. vermilion	9·00
19		20m. green	15·00
13/19 *Set of* 7			37·00

Nos. 13/19 were not issued.

This office was closed down in 1923 under the terms of the Treaty of Lausanne.

ODESSA

100 Fenigów = 1 Marka

The following stamps were issued at the Polish Consulate during the occupation of Odessa by General Denikin as the normal postal connections with Poland were interrupted.

(Optd typo by E. I. Fesenko, Odessa)

1919 (Nov). Arms (Types **15** and **16**) and Agriculture (T **17**) issue for Northern Poland optd 'ODESA'. Perf 11½.

1	**15**	10f. purple	£500	£500
		a. Opt inverted	£3000	
		b. Red opt	£5000	£5000
2		15f. scarlet	£52000	
3	**16**	20f. blue	£500	£500
		a. Opt inverted	£2000	
4		25f. olive	£3250	£3250
		a. Opt inverted	£4000	
5		50f. green	£500	£500
		a. Opt inverted	£2250	
		b. Red opt	£5000	£5000
6	**17**	1m. violet	£475	£475
		a. Opt inverted	£2500	

The sheets of 100 were overprinted twice in settings of 50. Some smaller blocks were also overprinted.

Only six examples of the 15f. were overprinted, of which four still exist; one is in the Polish Postal Museum and two are in a pair. 50 examples each of the red overprints were made.

This postal agency was closed on 31 January 1920.

Allenstein

100 Pfennig = 1 Mark

On 11 July 1920 a plebiscite was held under the Treaty of Versailles in this district of East Prussia. There was a vote of 98% in favour of remaining in Germany. The district was occupied by Soviet troops in 1945 and has since been administered by Poland under the name of Olsztyn.

PLÉBISCITE

OLSZTYN
ALLENSTEIN

(1)

(2)

1920 (3 Apr–3 Aug). Types of Germany (wmk Lozenges) optd with T **1** at State Printing Office, Berlin. Mark values (*a*) Engraved, (*b*) Surface-printed.

1	**17**	5pf. green	65	2·00
2		10pf. carmine	65	2·00
3	**24**	15pf. slate-violet	65	2·00
4		15pf. dull purple-brown (3.8)	9·00	20·00
5	**17**	20pf. violet-blue	65	2·50
6		30pf. black and orange/*buff*	65	2·50
7		40pf. black and carmine	65	2·00
8		50pf. black and purple/*buff*	65	2·00
9		75pf. black and dark green-black	65	2·00
10	**18**	1m. red (*a*)	2·50	10·00
		a. Opt double	£450	£1800
11		1m.25 yellow-green (*b*)	2·50	8·75
		a. Opt double		
12		1m.50 brown (*b*)	1·60	7·00
13	**20**	2m.50 lilac-rose (*b*)	70·00	£250
		a. Claret	4·00	18·00
		b. Purple	4·00	26·00
14	**21**	3m. violet-black (*a*)	4·00	10·50
		a. Opt double	£450	£1800
1/14 *Set of* 14 (*cheapest*)			26·00	80·00

1920 (May–June). Stamps as last, but optd with T **2**.

15	**17**	5pf. green	65	1·60
16		10pf. carmine	65	1·60
17	**24**	15pf. slate-violet	65	1·60
18		15pf. dull purple brown (25.6)	33·00	65·00
19	**17**	20pf. violet-blue	1·00	2·50
20		30pf. black and orange/*buff*	65	1·60
21		40pf. black and carmine	65	1·60
22		50pf. black and purple/*buff*	65	1·60
23		75pf. black and dark green-black	1·00	2·50
24	**18**	1m. red (*a*)	2·30	6·50
		a. Opt inverted	£750	£1300
25		1m.25 yellow-green (*b*)	2·30	6·50
26		1m.50 brown (*b*)	1·60	6·50
27	**20**	2m.50 claret (*b*)	4·00	10·50
		a. Purple (*b*)	5·25	21·00
28	**21**	3m. violet-black (*a*)	2·75	5·25
		a. Opt inverted	£600	£1500
		b. Opt double	£325	£950
15/28 *Set of* 14			47·00	£100

The 40pf. carmine, No. 144a, was also overprinted and placed on sale after the plebiscite but was only used on internal parcels and also exists cancelled by favour.

The international use of these stamps was discontinued on 20 August but they could be used internally until the end of October.

Danzig

1920. 100 Pfennig = 1 Mark
1923. 100 Pfennig = 1 Danzig Gulden

FREE CITY

By the Treaty of Versailles, 28 June 1919, Danzig, with surrounding territory, was created a Free City as from 10 January 1920. Unoverprinted stamps of Germany were in use from 10 January to 13 June 1920.

> **USED PRICES**. Used prices for Nos. 1/177 are for cancelled-to-order examples.

Stamps of Germany overprinted

17

18

20

21

22

24

30 LVG Schneider Biplane

Danzig (1)

10 (2)

(Optd by State Ptg Wks, Berlin)

1920 (14 June–21 Dec). Stamps of Germany, 1905–1920, optd with T **1**.

1	**17**	5pf. green	50	80
		a. Pair, one with opt omitted	£130	
		b. Optd double		
2	**30**	10pf. carmine	50	50
3	**24**	15pf. dull purple-brown	50	50
4	**17**	20pf. violet-blue	50	1·70
5		30pf. black and orange/*buff*	50	50
		a. Pair, one with opt omitted		
6		40pf. carmine (No. 144a) (13.9)	50	50
7		50pf. black and purple/*buff*	65	50
		a. Pair, one with opt omitted		
8	**18**	1m. carmine (No. 113)	65	90
		a. Pair, one with opt omitted	£130	
9		1m.25 blackish green-blue	65	90
10		1m.50 brown (20.7)	1·30	2·50
11	**20**	2m. blue (No. 94B)	4·50	10·50
		a. Optd double	£600	
12		2m.50 claret	4·50	7·25
		a. Pair, one with opt omitted		

13	**21**	3m. violet-black (No. 95B) (20.7)	13·00	18·00
		a. Pair, one with opt omitted		
14	**17**	4m. carmine and black (21.12)	6·25	9·00
15	**22**	5m. carmine and black (No. 96A)	£4000	
15*a*		5m. carmine and black (No. 96B)	4·00	5·75
		ab. Frame inverted	£23000	
		ac. Optd double	£1400	
1/15*a* (ex. 15) *Set of 15*			35·00	55·00

Nos. 89 and 140/141 of Germany also exist with this overprint, but were not sold to the public.

(Surch by J. Sauer, Danzig)

1920 (10 Aug–20 Nov). Nos. 4 and 5 with additional surch as T **2**.

16		5 on 30pf. (V.) (1.11)	40	40
17		10 on 20pf. (R.) (17.8)	40	40
		a. Surch double	£170	
18		25 on 30pf. (G.) (10.8)	40	40
		a. Surch inverted	£130	£400
19		60 on 30pf. (Br.) (20.11)	1·00	1·70
		a. Surch double	£130	£450
20		80 on 30pf. (V.) (20.11)	1·00	1·70
16/20 *Set of 5*			3·00	4·25

(3)

(3a)

(Optd by J. Sauer, Danzig)

1920 (20–30 Aug). Stamps of Germany optd.

*(a) With T **3** or larger (1m.).*

21	**24**	2pf. grey (B.) (30.8)	£160	£300
22		2½pf. grey (B.) (30.8)	£225	£450
23	**17**	3pf. brown (B.) (30.8)	16·00	26·00
		a. Opt double	£160	
24		5pf. green (B.)	80	1·20
		a. Opt double	£160	
25	**24**	7½pf. orange (B.) (30.8)	60·00	85·00
26	**17**	10pf. carmine (B.) (30.8)	5·25	10·50
		a. Opt double		
27	**24**	15pf. slate-violet (B.)	1·00	1·20
		a. Opt double	£160	
28	**17**	20pf. dark violet blue (B.)	1·00	1·20
29		25pf. black and red/*yellow* (R.)	1·00	1·20
30		30pf. black and orange/*buff* (R.) (30.8)	80·00	£140
31		40pf. black and carmine (R.) (30.8)	3·25	4·00
		a. Opt double		
		b. Opt inverted	£325	
32		50pf. black and purple/*buff* (R.) (30.8)	£250	£450
32*a*		60pf. magenta (B.) (30.8)	£1800	£3250
33		75pf. black and blue-green (30.8) (R.)	1·00	1·20
34		80pf. black and carmine/*rose* (R.) (30.8)	3·75	6·50
34*a*	**18**	1m. carmine (R.) (30.8)	£1800	£3250
		ab. Opt double		

*(b) With T **3a**.*

34*b*	**20**	2m. blue (94B) (R.) (30.8)	£1800	£3250
		a. Opt double	£1800	£3250

(4)

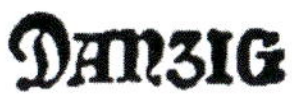
(5)

(8)

(9)

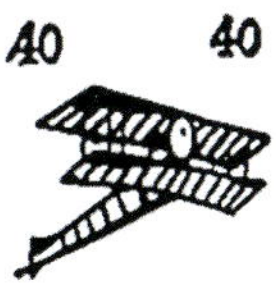
(10)

(12)

(Surch by J. Sauer, Danzig)

1920. No. 5 of Danzig and Types **17** and **24** of Germany, but with burelé background added, surch as Types **4** to **9**.

A. Burelé background with points upward toward the right.

35A	**17**	1m. on 30pf. black and orange/*buff*	1·30	2·30
36A		1¼m. on 3pf. brown (R.)	1·60	2·30
37A	**24**	2m. on 35pf. red-brown (B.)	2·30	2·30
38A		3m. on 7½pf. orange (G.)	1·60	2·30
39A		5m. on 2pf. grey (R.)	1·60	3·25
40A		10m. on 7½pf. orange	4·00	11·50

B. Burelé background with points downward toward the left.

36B	**17**	1¼m. on 3pf. brown (R.)	50·00	65·00
37B	**24**	2m. on 35pf. red-brown (B.)	£650	£425
38B		3m. on 7½pf. orange (G.)	39·00	26·00
39B		5m. on 2pf. grey (R.)	39·00	46·00
40B		10m. on 7½pf. orange	8·50	20·00

A. Burelé background with points upward toward the right.

40A*a*	**17**	1m. on 30pf.	£130	48·00
40A*b*		1¼m. on 3pf. (R.)	7·50	9·50
40A*c*	**24**	2m. on 35pf. (B.)	19·00	55·00
40A*d*		3m. on 7½pf. (G.)	3·25	3·75
40A*e*		5m. on 2pf. (R.)	1·90	3·75
40A*f*		10m. on 7½pf.	1·90	3·25

B. Burelé background with points downward toward the left.

40B*a*	**17**	1m. on 30pf.	1·90	3·75
40B*b*		1¼m. on 3pf. (R.)	10·00	16·00
40B*c*	**24**	2m. on 35pf. (B.)	44·00	75·00
40B*d*		3m. on 7½pf. (G.)	65·00	£130
40B*e*		5m. on 2pf. (R.)	12·50	12·50
40B*f*		10m. on 7½pf.	20·00	44·00

The bar in T **9** is of network pattern, not solid as shown in our illustration. All values exist without burelé background, and all except Nos. 39A and 37B/40B with background double.

1920 (29 Sept). AIR. No. 6 of Danzig surch as Types **10** and **12**.

41	**17**	40 on 40pf. carmine (B.)	2·00	4·50
		a. Surch double	£250	£400
42		60 on 40pf. carmine (R.)	2·00	4·50
		a. Surch double	£200	£400
43		1m. on 40pf. carmine (B.)	2·00	4·50
		a. Surch double	£200	£400

On the 60pf. the aeroplane is reversed.

13 Hanse Kogge

14

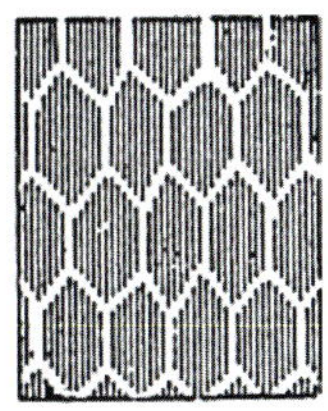
14a Large Honeycomb

(Typo J. Sauer, Danzig)

1921 (31 Jan–11 Mar). Constitution of 1920. W **14a**.

(a) Zigzag roulette (31 January).

44	**13**	5pf. purple and brown	40	40
		a. Centre inverted	£140	
45		10pf. slate-violet and orange	40	40
		a. Centre inverted	£140	
46		25pf. carmine and green	80	1·00
		a. Centre inverted	£140	
47		40pf. carmine	5·75	5·25
48		80pf. ultramarine	65	80
49	**14**	1m. slate and red	2·50	3·25
		a. Centre inverted	£160	
50		2m. deep green and blue	7·75	7·75
		a. Centre inverted	£160	
51		3m. emerald and black	3·25	4·50
		a. Centre inverted	£160	
52		5m. red and slate	3·25	4·50
		a. Centre inverted	£160	
53		10m. chestnut and deep green	4·00	7·25
		a. Centre inverted	£160	

(b) Perf 14 (11 March).

54	**13**	25pf. carmine and green	80	1·30
		a. Centre inverted	65·00	

55		40pf. carmine	80	1·30
56		80pf. ultramarine	9·00	16·00

Nos. 44 and 45 but with centres in red are believed to be proofs.
All values exist imperforate (*Price for set of* 10 £550 *un*).

15 Sabaltnig P111 over Danzig

16

(17)

(Des M. Buchholz. Typo J. Sauer, Danzig)

1921 (3 May)–**22**. AIR. Perf 14 (T **15**) or zigzag roulette (T **16**). W **14a**.

57	**15**	40pf. emerald	40	65
		b. Wmk sideways	90·00	£130
58		60pf. dull purple	40	65
		b. Wmk sideways	£160	£200
59		1m. carmine	40	65
60		2m. bistre-brown	40	65
		b. Wmk sideways	£130	£275
61	**16**	5m. blue-violet	2·00	3·25
		b. Wmk sideways	£2250	£4000
		ba. Imperf pair	£4750	£8500
62		10m. olive-green (15.5.22)	3·25	7·25
		b. Wmk sideways	39·00	£200

Nos. 57/62 are also known imperforate (*Price per set of* 6 £325)
See also Nos. 112/119.

1921 (6 May). No. 33 surch with T **17**, in blue-black.

63	60 on 75pf. black and blue-green	1·60	1·30
	a. Surch double	£160	£170
	b. Surch double, one inverted	£130	£120

18

19

(O20)

(Des Professor Petersen. Typo J. Sauer)

1921 (3 June)–**22**. W **14a**. Perf 14.

64	**18**	5pf. orange	25	25
65		10pf. grey-brown	25	25
66		15pf. green	25	25
67		20pf. slate	25	25
68		25pf. deep green	25	25
69		30pf. red and blue	25	25
		a. Centre inverted	£130	£225
70		40pf. red and green	25	25
		a. Centre inverted	£130	£225
71		50pf. red and deep green	25	25
72		60pf. carmine	65	65
73		75pf. purple (1.2.22)	40	40
74		80pf. red and slate-black	50	65
75		80pf. bright green (1.2.22)	40	40
76		1m. red and orange	80	65
		a. Centre inverted	£130	£225
77		1.20m. blue	2·00	2·00
78		1.25m. red and purple (1.2.22)	40	40
79		1.50m. slate (29.7.22)	25	65
80		2m. red and grey	4·50	8·50
81		2m. carmine (1.2.22)	40	40
82		2.40m. carmine and sepia (1.2.22)	2·00	3·25
83		3m. red and purple (*wmk sideways*)	13·00	16·00
		a. Wmk upright	£130	£250
84		3m. carmine (29.7.22)	25	65
85		4m. indigo (1.2.22)	2·00	3·25
86		5m. deep green (9.11.22)	25	50
		a. Wmk sideways	49·00	90·00
87		6m. carmine (30.10.22)	25	50
88		8m. pale blue (29.7.22)	80	2·50
89		10m. orange (9.11.22)	25	50
90		20m. yellow-brown (30.10.22)	25	50

See also Nos. 106/111.

(Des M. Buchholz. Typo J. Sauer)

1921 (1 Aug)–**22**. W **14a**. Zigzag roulette.

91	**19**	5m. green, black and red	2·00	4·50
		a. Wmk sideways	2·00	5·25
91*b*		9m. orange and red (1.2.22)	4·50	13·00
		ba. Wmk sideways	4·50	12·50
92		10m. blue, black and red (1922)	2·00	4·50
		a. Wmk sideways	2·00	5·25
93		20m. black and red	2·00	4·50
		a. Wmk sideways	2·00	5·25

Nos. 76 to 93 have a background of faint grey network. Some stamps in this and the following issues are known without network.

1921 (25 Aug)–**22**. OFFICIAL. Optd with T **O20**. W **14a**.

O94	**18**	5pf. orange	40	40
		a. Opt double	£160	
O95		10pf. grey-brown	40	40
		a. Opt double	50·00	
		b. Opt inverted	90·00	
O96		15pf. green	40	40
O97		20pf. slate	40	40
		a. Opt inverted		
O98		25pf. deep green	40	40
		a. Opt double	50·00	
		b. Wmk sideways	£450	£650
O99		30pf. red and blue	90	90
		a. Opt double	50·00	
O100		40pf. red and green	40	40
		a. Opt double	50·00	
O101		50pf. red and deep green	40	40
O102		60pf. carmine	40	40
O103		75pf. purple (15.2.22)	25	65
		a. Opt double	85·00	
O104		80pf. red and slate-black	1·30	2·00
O105		80pf. bright green (15.2.22)	25	4·25
		a. Wmk sideways	13·00	50·00
O106		1m. red and orange	40	40
O107		1.20m. blue	2·00	2·00
O108		1.25m. red and purple (15.2.22)	25	65
O109		1.50m. slate (29.7.22)	50	80
O110		2m. red and grey	26·00	21·00
		a. Opt inverted	£170	
O111		2m. carmine (15.2.22)	25	65
O112		2.40m. carmine and sepia (15.2.22)	2·00	4·25
O113		3m. red and purple (*wmk sideways*)	16·00	18·00
O114		3m. carmine (29.7.22)	50	80
O115		4m. indigo (15.2.22)	2·00	1·60
		a. Opt inverted		
O116		5m. deep green (21.11.22)	50	80
		a. Wmk sideways	13·00	20·00
O117		6m. carmine (30.10.22)	50	80
O118		10m. orange (21.11.22)	50	80
O119		20m. yellow-brown (16.12.22)	50	80

D20

20

21

1921 (1 Oct)–**22**. POSTAGE DUE. Typo. W **14a** (sideways). Perf 14.

(a) Value in 'pfennig' (figures only).

D94	**D20**	10pf. purple	50	80
D95		20pf. purple	50	80
		a. Wmk upright	£200	
D96		40pf. purple	50	80
D97		60pf. purple	50	80
D98		75pf. purple (10.6.22)	50	80
		a. Wmk upright	£130	
D99		80pf. purple	50	80
		a. Wmk upright	£130	
D100		120pf. purple	50	80
D101		200pf. purple (10.6.22)	1·30	1·70
D102		240pf. purple	50	1·70
		a. Wmk upright	£200	
D103		300pf. purple (10.6.22)	1·30	1·70
D104		400pf. purple	1·30	1·70
D105		500pf. purple	1·30	1·70
D106		800pf. purple (1.2.22)	1·30	1·70

(b) Value in 'marks' (numeral followed by 'M').

D107	**D20**	20m. purple (30.10.22)	1·30	1·70

See also Nos. D112/D122.

(Des E. Hellingrath. Typo J. Sauer)

1921 (16 Oct). Tuberculosis Week. W **14a**. Zigzag roulette (1.20m.) or Perf 14 (others).

93*b*	**20**	30pf. (+30pf.) green and orange	65	1·60
93*c*		60pf. (+60pf.) carmine and yellow	2·00	2·50
93*d*		1.20m. (+1.20m.) indigo and orange (25×29 mm)	3·25	3·75

(Des M. Buchholz. Typo J. Sauer)

1922. W **14a**. Zigzag roulette.

94	**21**	50m. red and gold	90·00	£180
		a. Wmk sideways	13·00	21·00
		b. Crimson and gold	3·25	10·50
		ba. Wmk sideways	3·25	8·50
95		100m. red and bronze-green	12·50	20·00
		a. Wmk sideways	5·25	9·00

The 50m. has a grey overprinted network. On the 100m. it is brown. The designs of the stamps differ in detail.

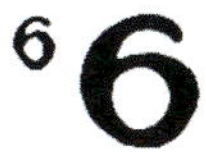

(O22)

(22)

(23)

1922. OFFICIAL. Optd with T **O22**.

O120	**19**	5m. green, black and red	6·50	17·00
		a. Wmk sideways	5·25	10·50

1922 (5 May–2 Oct). Surch as Type **22**/**23**. W **14a**.

96	**18**	6 on 3m. carmine (2.10)	50	90
		a. Surch double		
97		8 on 4m. indigo (R.) (15.5)	50	1·30
		a. Surch double	£120	£200
98		20 on 8m. pale blue (R.) (2.10)	50	90

1922 (1 Oct). OFFICIAL. No. 96 optd with T **O20**.

O121	**18**	6 on 3m. carmine	50	1·30
		a. Opt inverted	46·00	

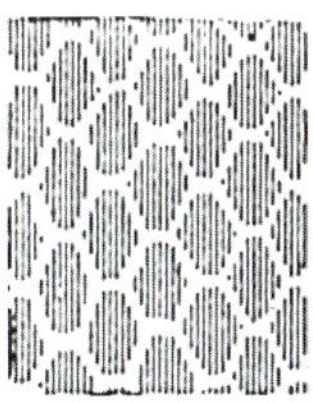

24 Small Honeycomb

25

25a

26

(Des M. Buchholz. Typo J. Sauer)

1922 (Nov)–**23** (Feb). W **24** (sideways). Perf 14

99	**25**	50m. red and pale blue (21.11.22)	25	65
		a. Wmk upright	80	1·30
100	**25a**	100m. red and deep olive (14.12.22)	25	65
		a. Wmk upright	1·60	1·30
101		150m. red and purple (23.1.23)	25	65
102	**26**	250m. red and purple (24.1.23)	65	65
103		500m. red and slate (24.1.23)	65	65
104		1000m. pink and black-brown (24.1.23)	65	65
105		5000m. pink and silver (27.2.23)	2·50	9·75

Nos. 99/105 have background of faint grey network.
See also Nos. 136/141.

1922 (Dec)–**23** (Sept). W **24** (sideways on 4m., 6m.). Perf 14

106	**18**	4m. indigo (16.12.22)	25	65
107		5m. deep green (1.23)	80	1·30
		a. Wmk sideways	25	65
107*b*		6m. carmine (9.23)	£3250	
108		10m. orange (1.23)	80	1·30
		a. Wmk sideways	25	65
109		20m. yellow-brown (1.23)	80	1·30
		a. Wmk sideways	25	65
110		40m. pale blue (15.5.23)	40	90
111		80m. scarlet (15.5.23)	40	90

Nos. 106/111 have background of faint grey network.

1922 (Dec)–**23** (Feb). OFFICIAL. Optd as T **O20**. W **24** (sideways on 4m.).

O122	**18**	4m. indigo (16.12.22)	40	1·00
O123		5m. deep green (1.23)	1·30	4·00
		a. Wmk sideways	40	1·30
O124		10m. orange (1.23)	1·30	4·00
		a. Wmk sideways	40	1·00
O125		20m. yellow-brown (1.23)		
		a. Wmk sideways	40	1·00
O126	**25**	50m. red and pale blue (10.1.23)	1·30	4·00
		a. Wmk sideways	40	1·00
O127	**25a**	100m. red and olive-green (21.2.23)	1·30	4·00
		a. Wmk sideways	40	1·00

See also Nos. O142/O147.

1923 (Jan–Apr). POSTAGE DUE. W **24** (sideways on 100m. to 400pf.). Perf 14

(a) Value in 'pfennig' (figures only).

D112	**D20**	100pf. purple	1·30	1·30
D113		200pf. purple	4·50	6·50
D114		300pf. purple	1·30	1·30
D115		400pf. purple	1·30	1·30
D116		500pf. purple	1·30	1·70
		a. Wmk sideways	1·30	1·30
D117		800pf. purple	2·20	6·50

(b) Value in 'marks'.

D118	**D20**	10m. purple	1·30	1·70
		a. Wmk sideways	1·30	1·30
D119		20m. purple	£180	
		a. Wmk sideways	1·30	1·30
D120		50m. purple	£100	
		a. Wmk sideways	1·30	1·30
D121		100m. purple	1·30	1·70
D122		500m. purple	1·30	1·70

Nos. D121/D122 have background of faint grey network.
Nos. D119 and D120 were prepared for the surcharges.
Remainders of these two stamps with upright watermark were placed on sale, but were not used by the post office.

27

1923 (Jan–Apr). AIR. Typo. W **24** (sideways). Zigzag roulette (5m., 10m., 20m.) or Perf 14 (others)

112	**15**	40pf. emerald (3.1)	90	3·25
113		60pf. dull purple (3.1)	90	3·25
114		1m. carmine (3.1)	90	3·25
115		2m. bistre-brown (3.1)	90	3·25
116	**16**	5m. blue-violet (3.1)	90	1·60
117		10m. olive-green (3.1)	90	1·60
118		20m. yellow-brown (10.1)	90	1·60
		a. Background omitted	26·00	20·00
119	**15**	25m. pale blue (5.2)	65	1·20
120	**27**	50m. orange (27.4)	65	1·20
		a. Background omitted	33·00	26·00
		b. Wmk upright	£100	
121		100m. scarlet (27.4)	65	1·20
		a. Background omitted	26·00	39·00
		b. Wmk upright	£100	95·00
122		250m. black-brown (27.4)	1·00	1·20
		a. Background omitted	26·00	39·00
123		500m. carmine (27.4)	1·00	1·20
		a. Background omitted	26·00	39·00
		b. Wmk upright	£100	95·00

Nos. 118 and 120/123 have background of faint grey network.

28

29

(Des Max Buchholz. Typo J. Sauer)

1923 (15 Mar). Poor People's Fund. W **24**. Perf 14.

123*c*	**28**	50+20m. lake	40	1·00
123*d*		100+30m. dull purple	40	1·00

Nos. 123*c*/123*d* have background of faint grey network.

1923 (Mar–Sept). Typo. W **24** (sideways except 3000m.). Perf 14

124	**29**	250m. scarlet and purple (15.5)	40	90
125		300m. scarlet and emerald (22.3)	40	65
126		500m. scarlet and slate (29.6)	40	90
		a. Wmk upright	£250	£400
127		1000m. brown (24.7)	25	65
128		1000m. scarlet and black-brown (30.7)	40	90
		a. Wmk upright	£400	£400
129		3000m. scarlet and violet (13.8)	40	90
130		5000m. pink (15.8)	25	65
131		20000m. pale blue (25.8)	25	65
132		50000m. green (1.9)	25	65
133		100000m. deep blue (6.9)	25	65
134		250000m. purple (11.9)	25	65
135		500000m. slate (16.9)	25	65

Nos. 124/135 have background of faint grey network.

1923 (July–Aug). W **24** (sideways on 200m. to 20000m.). Perf 14

136	**25**	50m. pale blue (20.7)	40	90
137	**25a**	100m. olive-green (29.7)	40	90
138	**25**	200m. orange (20.7)	40	90
139	**26**	10000m. scarlet and orange (8.8)	1·00	1·00
140		20000m. scarlet and pale blue (13.8)	1·00	1·70
141		50000m. scarlet and green (20.8)	1·00	1·70

Nos. 136/141 have background of faint grey network.

1923 (July). OFFICIAL. Optd as T **O20**. W **24** (sideways on Nos. O144/O147).

O142	**25**	50m. pale blue (21.7)	40	1·30
		a. Opt inverted	39·00	
O143	**25a**	100m. olive-green (29.7)	40	1·30
O144	**25**	200m. orange (21.7)	40	1·30
		a. Opt inverted	39·00	
O145	**29**	300m. scarlet and emerald (2.7)	40	1·00
O146		500m. scarlet and slate (21.7)	40	1·30
O147		1000m. scarlet and black-brown (29.7)	40	1·30

(30) T = Tausend (thousand)

(31)

(32)

(33)

(34) M = Million or Millionen

1923 (Aug–Oct). W **24**.

*(a) Surch as T **30**. Wmk sideways (except No. 145).*

142	**25**	40T. on 200m. orange (1.9)	1·30	3·25
		a. Surch double	£130	
143		100T. on 200m. orange (1.9)	1·30	3·25
144		250T. on 200m. orange (1.9)	9·75	22·00
145	**25a**	400T. on 100m. olive-green (24.9)	90	1·00
146	**29**	500T. on 50000m. green (8.9)	65	1·00

No. 145 has 'Tausend' in different type and a fleuron instead of bars. No. 146 has only one bar.

*(b) Surch as T **31**. Wmk sideways.*

147	**29**	1M. on 10000m. orange (13.9)	5·75	10·50
148		1M. on 10000m. carmine (19.9)	40	1·00
149		2M. on 10000m. carmine (19.9)	40	1·00
150		3M. on 10000m. carmine (23.9)	40	1·00
151		5M. on 10000m. carmine (23.9)	50	1·00
		a. Surch double	£130	
152		10M. on 10000m. lavender (15.10)	65	1·20
		a. Wmk upright	£140	
153		20M. on 10000m. lavender (15.10)	65	1·20
		a. Wmk upright	£140	
154		25M. on 10000m. lavender (15.10)	25	1·20
155		40M. on 10000m. lavender (22.10)	25	1·20
		a. Surch double	80·00	
156		50M. on 10000m. lavender (15.10)	25	1·20

*(c) Surch with Type **32** and **33**. Wmk sideways.*

157	**26**	100000 on 20000m. scarlet and pale blue (R.) (14.8)	1·30	9·75
158		10M. on 1000000m. orange (1.10)	65	2·00

No. 158 was not issued without the surcharge and has a background of faint grey network.

*(d) Surch as T **34**, in red. Wmk sideways.*

159	**29**	100M. on 10000m. lavender (22.10)	25	1·20
160		300M. on 10000m. lavender (23.10)	25	1·20
161		500M. on 10000m. lavender (23.10)	25	1·20

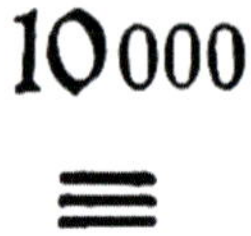
(D35)

35 Etrich/Rumpler Taube

(36)

1923 (1 Oct). POSTAGE DUE. Surch as T **D35**.

D162	**D20**	1000 on 100m. purple	£200	
D163		5000 on 50m. purple	65	1·30
D164		10000 on 20m. purple	65	1·30
D165		50000 on 500m. purple	65	1·30
D166		100000 on 20m. purple	1·30	2·50

(Des M. Buchholz. Typo J. Sauer)

1923 (18 Oct). AIR. W **24**. Perf 14.

162	**35**	250000m. scarlet (wmk sideways)	50	2·00
		a. Wmk upright	80·00	£325
		ab. Imperf	80·00	
163		500000m. scarlet (wmk sideways)	50	2·00
		a. Wmk upright	80·00	£325
		ab. Imperf	80·00	
164	**35**	2M. on 100000m. Surch as T **36**. scarlet (wmk sideways)	50	2·00
		a. Wmk upright	£160	£325
		ab. Error. Surch omitted	20·00	85·00
165		5M. on 50000m. scarlet (wmk sideways)	50	2·00
		a. Wmk upright	£180	£325
		ab. Error. Surch omitted	65·00	
		ac. Error. Stamp inscribed 10000m.	65·00	£250

No. 165ac exists on position 73 in the sheet of 100.

(37)

(38)

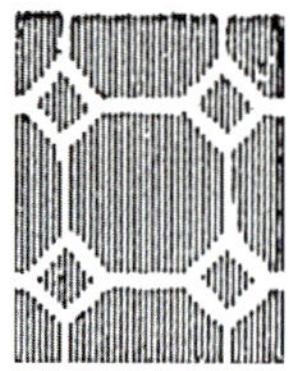
38a Octagonal Mesh

1923 (31 Oct–5 Nov). Surch as T **37** or T **38**. W **38a**.

166	**25**	5pf. on 50m. carmine	80	65
167		10pf. on 50m. carmine	80	65
168	**25a**	20pf. on 100m. carmine	80	65
169	**25**	25pf. on 50m. carmine	5·75	13·00
170		30pf. on 50m. carmine	5·75	3·25
171	**25a**	40pf. on 100m. carmine	3·75	3·25
172		50pf. on 100m. carmine	3·75	4·50
173		75pf. on 100m. carmine	13·00	26·00
174	**26**	1g. on 1000000m. carmine (5.11)	7·25	9·75
175		2g. on 1000000m. carmine (5.11)	20·00	26·00
176		3g. on 1000000m. carmine (5.11)	36·00	£100
177		5g. on 1000000m. carmine (5.11)	42·00	£100
166/177 *Set of* 12			£130	£250

D39

39

(O40)

1923 (24 Nov)–**27**. POSTAGE DUE. Typo. W **38a**. Perf 14.

D178	**D39**	5pf. blue and black	1·30	1·30
D179		10pf. blue and black	65	1·30
D180		15pf. blue and black (13.12.27)	2·00	2·50
D181		20pf. blue and black	2·10	3·25
D182		30pf. blue and black	13·00	3·25
D183		40pf. blue and black	3·75	5·25
D184		50pf. blue and black	3·75	4·00
D185		60pf. blue and black	20·00	31·00
D186		100pf. blue and black	29·00	17·00
D187		3g. blue and carmine (13.12.27)	14·50	80·00
D178/D187 *Set of* 10			80·00	£130

See also Nos. D263/D267.

(Des M. Buchholz. Typo)

1924 (19 Jan)–**38**. W **24** (sideways). Perf 14.

177*a*	**39**	3pf. brown (24.2.27)	4·00	3·25
		b. On pale yellow paper (10.35)	1·90	2·30
178		5pf. orange	26·00	3·50
		a. Interrupted perf (1932)	39·00	16·00

		b. On pale yellow paper (2.35)	4·50	90
		c. Wmk upright	£170	
		d. Pale yellow paper. Interrupted perf (10.35)	18·00	14·50
178*e*		7pf. yellow-green (27.4.33)	2·50	4·50
178*f*		8pf. yellow-green (14.8.37)	2·50	9·75
179		10pf. green	20·00	4·25
		a. Interrupted perf (1932)	46·00	20·00
		b. On pale yellow paper (3.35)	9·00	80
		c. Do. Interrupted perf (11.35)	26·00	17·00
179*d*		10pf. bright blue-green (24.6.37)	7·75	2·50
		e. Interrupted perf (24.8.37)	17·00	23·00
180		15pf. grey	6·50	1·00
180*a*		15pf. vermilion (20.8.25)	7·75	1·70
		b. On pale yellow paper (2.35)	3·25	1·70
181		20pf. red and carmine-red (26.1.24)	26·00	1·00
182		20pf. slate (20.6.35)	4·00	4·00
183		25pf. red and slate (12.3.24)	39·00	5·75
184		25pf. carmine-red (5.6.35)	26·00	2·50
185		30pf. red and deep green (12.3.24)	23·00	1·30
		a. Red and yellow-green	65·00	4·25
186		30pf. purple (21.8.35)	4·00	6·50
186*a*		35pf. blue (2110.25)	7·25	2·30
187		40pf. light blue and deep blue (14.2.24)	20·00	1·60
188		40pf. vermilion and brown (15.4.35)	10·50	20·00
189		40pf. deep blue (26.6.35)	4·00	5·75
190		50pf. red and deep blue (12.3.24)	26·00	13·00
		a. On pale yellow paper (3.38)	29·00	50·00
190*b*		55pf. vermilion and deep claret (4.37)	13·00	23·00
191		60pf. scarlet and bottle green (15.4.35)	10·50	29·00
192		70pf. vermilion and yellow-green (5.9.35)	4·00	11·50
193		75pf. red and purple (12.3.24)	16·00	13·00
		a. On pale yellow paper (1938)	13·00	46·00
194		80pf. vermilion and reddish brown (5.9.35)	4·00	11·50

1924 (1 Mar)–**25**. OFFICIAL. Optd with T **O40**.

O195	**39**	5pf. orange	3·25	5·25
O196		10pf. green	3·25	5·25
O197		15pf. grey	3·25	5·25
O198		15pf. vermilion (1925)	29·00	16·00
O199		20pf. red and carmine-red	3·25	3·25
O200		25pf. red and slate (12.3.24)	29·00	42·00
O201		30pf. red and yellow-green (12.3.24)	4·50	5·75
O202		35pf. blue (1925)	90·00	80·00
O203		40pf. light blue and deep blue	10·50	13·00
O204		50pf. red and deep blue (12.3.24)	33·00	65·00
O205		75pf. red and purple (12.3.24)	65·00	£180

Double overprints are fakes.

40 Etrich/ Rumpler Taube

41 Aeroplane

42 Oliva

(Des M. Buchholz. Typo J. Sauer)

1924 (5 June). AIR. No. 199 has network background. W **24** (upright). Perf 14.

195	**40**	10pf. vermilion	35·00	5·75
196		20pf. cerise	3·50	2·50
197		40pf. brown	5·00	3·25
198		1g. deep green	5·00	7·50
199	**41**	2½g. plum	29·00	55·00
		a. Without network background	£100	£325

All values exist imperforate.

(Des and eng E. Hellingrath. Recess Berlin State Ptg Works)

1924 (22 Sept–28 Nov). T **42** and similar designs. Wmk Lozenges (T **23** of Germany). Perf 14.

200		1g. black and yellow-green	33·00	70·00
201		2g. black and purple	70·00	£170
202		3g. black and blue (28.11)	7·75	7·75
203		5g. black and lake (28.11)	7·75	13·00
204		10g. black and brown (28.11)	33·00	£170
200/204 *Set of 5*			£140	£400

Designs: Horiz—1g. T **42**; 2g. Krantor and River Mottlau; 3g. Zoppot. Vert—5g. St Mary's Church; 10g. Town Hall and Langemarkt.

44 Fountain of Neptune

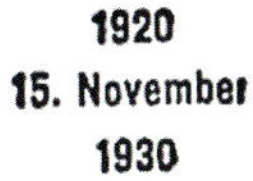

(45)

1925 (1 Jan)–**32**. As last, colours changed.

205		1g. black and orange	26·00	6·50
		a. Black and bright red-orange (5.32)	26·00	20·00
206		2g. black and carmine	5·75	13·00

See also No. 275.

(Recess Berlin State Ptg Works)

1929 (7 July). International Philatelic Exhibition. Various frames. Perf 14.

207	**44**	10pf. (+10pf.) black and green	4·00	7·75
208		15pf. (+15pf.) black and carmine	4·00	7·75
209		25pf. (+25pf.) black and blue	13·00	50·00
		a. Black and ultramarine	60·00	£275
207/209 *Set of 3*			19·00	60·00

1930 (15 Nov). Tenth Anniversary of Constitution of Free City of Danzig. Optd with T **45**.

210	**39**	5pf. orange	4·00	5·75
211		10pf. green (V.)	5·25	7·25
212		15pf. vermilion	9·00	17·00
213		20pf. red and carmine-red	4·50	9·00
214		25pf. red and slate	6·50	17·00
215		30pf. red and yellow-green	13·00	39·00
216		35pf. blue (R.)	50·00	£160
217		40pf. light blue and deep blue (R.)	17·00	60·00
218		50pf. red and deep blue	50·00	£130
219		75pf. vermilion and purple	50·00	£140
220	**42**	1g. black and orange (R.)	50·00	£130
210/220 *Set of 11*			£225	£650

(46)

(D47)

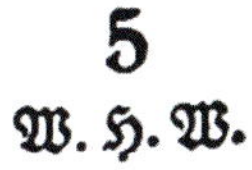

(47) ('Winterhilfswerk')

1932 (23 July). Danzig International Air Post Exhibition ('Luposta'). Nos. 200/204 surch as T **46**.

221		10pf.+10pf. on 1g. (G.)	14·50	41·00
222		15pf.+15pf. on 2g. (P.)	14·50	41·00
223		20pf.+20pf. on 3g. (B.)	14·50	41·00
224		25pf.+25pf. on 5g. (R.)	14·50	41·00
225		30pf.+30pf. on 10g. (Br.)	14·50	41·00
221/225 *Set of 5*			65·00	£180

On Nos. 222 and 224/225 the surcharge is in four lines; on Nos. 224/225 '1932' is the second line.

1932 (20 Dec). POSTAGE DUE. Surch as T **D47**. W **38a**. Perf 14.

D226	**D39**	5 on 40pf. blue and black (R.)	6·50	13·00
D227		10 on 60pf. blue and black (R.)	50·00	16·00
D228		20 on 100pf. blue and black (R.)	4·25	13·00
D226/D228 *Set of 3*			55·00	38·00

1934 (15 Jan). Winter Relief Work Charity stamps. Surch with T **47**.

226	**39**	5pf.+5pf. orange	14·50	33·00
227		10pf.+5pf. green	36·00	80·00
228		15pf.+5pf. vermilion	21·00	60·00
226/228 *Set of 3*			65·00	£160

(48)

(49)

1934 (28 Dec)–**36**. Nos. 178*e* and 186*a* surch.

229	**48**	6 on 7pf. yellow-green (R.)	1·30	2·50
230		8 on 7pf. yellow-green (B.) (5.6.35)	3·25	3·75
		a. Red surch (14.7.36)	2·00	4·00
		b. Green surch (23.12.36)	1·30	4·00
231	**49**	30 on 35pf. bright blue (B.)	16·00	39·00
229/231 *Set of 3 (cheapest)*			17·00	41·00

No. 232 is vacant.

50 Junkers F-13

51

52 Stockturm, 1346

(Des M. Buchholz. Typo Post Office Ptg Wks, Danzig)

1935 (25 Oct). AIR. W **24** (upright, except on 1g.). Perf 14.

233	**50**	10pf. salmon	2·50	1·30
		a. Error. 'DANZIO' instead of 'DANZIG' (pos. 3)	50·00	£180
		b. Error. 'STADL' instead of 'STADT' (pos. 4)	50·00	£180
234		15pf. orange-yellow	2·50	2·00
235		25pf. bottle green	2·50	2·50
236		50pf. blue	13·00	16·00
237	**51**	1g. bright purple	5·25	22·00
233/237 *Set of 5*			23·00	39·00

See also Nos. 263/266.

(Des M. Buchholz. Typo)

1935 (23 Dec). Winter Relief Fund. Designs inscr 'Für das Winterhilfswerk', as T **52**. W **24** (sideways on No. 239). Perf 14.

238	5pf.+5pf. orange	1·00	2·50
239	10pf.+5pf. green	1·80	4·00
240	15pf.+10pf. scarlet	4·25	5·75
238/240 *Set of 3*		6·25	11·00

Designs: Horiz—5pf. T **52**; 10pf. The Lege Tor. Vert—15pf. Georgshalle, 1487.

54 Brösen War Memorial

55 Frauentor and Observatory

56 'D(anziger) L(uftschutz) B(und)'

(Des M. Buchholz. Typo Post Office Ptg Wks, Danzig)

1936 (23 June). 125th Anniversary of Brösen. As T **54** (inscr '125 JAHRE OSTEEBAD BRÖSEN'). W **24** (sideways on horiz stamps). Perf 14.

241	-	10pf. deep green	1·60	2·00
242	-	25pf. carmine	2·10	3·75
243	**54**	40pf. light blue	3·75	7·25
241/243 *Set of 3*			6·75	11·50

Designs: Horiz—10pf. Brösen Beach; 25pf. Zoppot end of Brösen Beach.

1936 (25 Nov). Winter Relief Fund. As T **55** (inscr 'WINTERHILFE'). W **24** (sideways on horiz stamps). Perf 14.

244	10pf.+5pf. blue	2·50	7·75
245	15pf.+5pf. blue-green	2·50	10·50
246	25pf.+10pf. maroon	4·00	16·00
247	40pf.+20pf. brown and maroon	5·25	18·00
248	50pf.+20pf. pale blue and deep blue	9·00	26·00
244/248 *Set of 5*		21·00	70·00

Designs: Vert—10pf. Milchkannenturm; 15pf. T **55**; 25pf. Krantor. Horiz—40pf. Langgartertor; 50pf. Hohestor.

1937 (27 Mar). Air Defence League. Typo. W **24** (sideways). Perf 14.

249	**56**	10pf. deep blue	90	2·00
250		15pf. dull purple	2·50	4·00

57 Marienkirche, Danzig

57a Danziger Dorf, Magdeburg

(Des W. Lüdtcke. Typo)

1937 (6 June). First National Philatelic Exhibition, Danzig ('DAPOSTA'). Sheets 147×104 mm. W **24** (sideways). Perf 14.

(a) POSTAGE.

MS251 **57**	50pf. blue-green/*toned*	6·50	£200

(b) AIR.

MS252	50pf. blue/*toned*	6·50	£200

Design: No. **MS**252 Marienkirche and Junkers F-13.

(Des W. Brandt. Typo)

1937 (30 Oct). Foundation of Danzig Community, Magdeburg. T **57a** and similar type, inscr 'Danziger Dorf in Magdeburg'. W **24** (sideways on 25pf.). Perf 14.

253	25pf. (+25pf.) carmine	4·50	9·00
	a. Wmk upright	17·00	65·00
254	40pf. (+40pf.) vermilion and blue	4·50	9·00

Designs: Vert—25pf. T **57a**. Horiz—40pf. Village and Arms of Danzig and Magdeburg.

1937 (28 Nov). Danzig Productivity Show. Sheet 146×105 mm.

MS254*a*	Nos. 253/254 (*sold for* 1g.50)	80·00	£650

58 Madonna and Child

59 Schopenhauer

60 Yacht *Peter von Danzig* (1936)

(Des M. Buchholz. Typo)

1937 (13 Dec). Winter Relief Fund. As T **58** (statues inscr 'WINTERHILFSZUSCHLAG' or 'WINTERHILFE' (Nos. 258/259)). W **24**. Perf 14.

255	5pf.+5pf. violet	4·00	13·00
256	10pf.+5pf. brown	4·00	9·75
257	15pf.+5pf. orange and light blue	4·00	14·50
258	25pf.+10pf. green and blue-green	5·25	20·00
259	40pf.+25pf. blue and carmine	9·00	26·00
255/259 *Set of 5*		24·00	75·00

Designs: 5pf. T **58**; 10pf. Mercury; 15pf. The Golden Knight; 25pf. Fountain of Neptune; 40pf. St George and the Dragon.

(Des M. Buchholz, after J. Hamel (15pf.), L. S. Ruhl (25pf.) and Daguerre (40pf.). Photo State Ptg Wks, Berlin)

1938 (22 Feb). 150th Birth Anniversary of Schopenhauer (philosopher). As T **59** (portraits inscr 'Schopenhauer 1788–1860'). Perf 14.

260	-	15pf. blue	2·30	4·00
261	-	25pf. sepia	5·50	13·00
262	**59**	40pf. red	2·30	5·25
260/262 *Set of 3*			9·00	20·00

Portraits: 15pf. Schopenhauer as an old man; 25pf. Schopenhauer as a young man.

1938 (5 May)–**39**. POSTAGE DUE. W **97** of Germany (Swastikas). Perf 14.

D263	**D39**	10pf. blue and black (21.5.39)	2·00	£120
D264		30pf. blue and black	3·25	£100
D265		40pf. blue and black (21.5.39)	9·75	£200
D266		60pf. blue and black (21.5.39)	9·75	£200
D267		100pf. blue and black	16·00	£130
D263/D267 *Set of 5*			37·00	£650

1938–39. AIR. W **97** of Germany (Swastikas). Perf 14

263	**50**	10pf. salmon (7.38)	2·00	6·50
264		15pf. orange-yellow (8.7.38)	3·25	21·00
265		25pf. bottle green (7.38)	2·50	11·00
266		50pf. blue (13.2.39)	6·50	£100
263/266 *Set of 4*			13·00	£120

1938–39. W **97** of Germany (Swastikas). Perf 14

267	**39**	3pf. brown (28.9.38)	1·30	11·50
268		5pf. orange (23.7.38)	1·30	3·25
		a. Interrupted perf (24.8.38)	2·00	11·50
269		8pf. yellow-green (9.38)	6·50	50·00
270		10pf. green (10.38)	1·30	3·25
		a. Interrupted perf (18.7.38)	4·00	16·00
271		15pf. scarlet (28.9.38)	2·50	20·00
272		25pf. carmine (23.7.38)	2·00	10·50
273		40pf. indigo (19.7.38)	3·25	46·00
274		50pf. scarlet and blue (14.7.39)	3·25	£200
275	**42**	1g. black and orange (10.38)	10·50	£180
267/275 *Set of* 9			29·00	£475

(Des H. Gruber (Nos. 276/279), O. Lienau (No. 280). Photo State Ptg Wks, Berlin)

1938 (28 Nov). Winter Relief Fund. As T **60** (ship types inscr 'W H W'). No wmk. Perf 14.

276	5pf.+5pf. bottle green	2·20	2·75
277	10pf.+5pf. deep orange-brown	2·20	5·25
278	15pf.+10pf. olive-green	2·50	5·25
279	25pf.+10pf. deep blue	3·75	7·75
280	40pf.+15pf. purple-brown	5·25	11·50
276/280 *Set of* 5		14·50	29·00

Designs: 5pf. T **60**; 10pf. Dredger *Fu Shing*; 15pf. Liner *Columbus*; 25pf. Liner *Hansestadt Danzig*; 40pf. Sailing vessel *Peter von Danzig* (1472).

61 Teutonic Knights

62 Gregor Mendel

(Photo State Ptg Wks, Berlin)

1939 (7 Jan). 125th Anniversary of Prussian Annexation. As T **61** (historical designs). No wmk. Perf 14.

281	5pf. deep green	90	3·25
282	10pf. deep orange-brown	1·30	4·00
283	15pf. indigo	2·00	4·50
284	25pf. chocolate	2·50	6·50
281/284 *Set of* 4		6·00	16·00

Designs: 5pf. T **61**; 10pf. Danzig–Swedish treaty of neutrality, 1630; 15pf. Danzig united to Prussia, 2.1.1814; 25pf. Stephen Baton's defeat at Weichselmunde, 1577.

(Photo State Ptg Wks, Berlin)

1939 (29 Apr). Anti-Cancer Campaign. As T **62** (medical-scientists' portraits). No wmk. Perf 13×14½.

285	10pf. red-brown	1·00	1·30
286	15pf. black	1·00	3·25
287	25pf. olive-green	2·00	4·50
285/287 *Set of* 3		3·50	8·25

Portraits: 10pf. T **62**; 15pf. Robert Koch; 25pf. Wilhelm Konrad Röntgen.

On 1 September, 1939, Danzig was re-absorbed into Germany. Since 1945 it has been part of Poland.

STAMP BOOKLETS

The following checklist covers, in simplified form, booklets issued by Danzig. It is intended that it should be used in conjunction with the main listings and details of stamps and panes listed there are not repeated.

Booklets differing in the colour of cover or in the text on the front cover are separately priced. Booklets also occur with other differences, for example in the text on the inside covers; these are not covered by this list, but prices are generally the same for each version.

Prices are for complete booklets

SB1	10.25–26 Arms (T **39**) 1 pane, No. 178×6; 1 pane, No. 179×6; 1 pane, No. 180*a*×6 (1g.80)	
	(a). Grey cover	£9500
	(b). Pink cover (1.26)	£1100
SB2	4.28–34 Arms (T **39**) 1 pane, No. 178×10 1 pane No. 179×10; 1 pane, No. 180*a*×10 (3g.)	
	(a). Front cover inscr 'Post- und Telegraphenverwaltung...' brown cover	£8500
	(b). As a. but pink cover (4.30)	£10000
	(c). As a. but green cover (1.33)	£5000
	(d). Cover inscr 'Landespostdirektion...' pink cover (1.34)	
SB3	1.36 Arms (T **39**) 1 pane, No. 178*b*×10; 1 pane, No. 179*b*×10; 1 pane, No. 180*ab*×10 (3g.)	£17000
SB4	5.37 Arms (T **39**) 1 pane, No. 178*b*×10; 1 pane, No. 179*d*×10; 1 pane, No. 180*ab*×10 (3g.)	£11000
SB5	9.38 Arms (T **39**) 1 pane, No. 268×10; 1 pane, No. 270×10; 1 pane No. 271×10 (3g.)	£19000

POLISH POST IN DANZIG

The Poles operated a postal service in Danzig with a post office by the harbour.

100 Groszy = 1 Zloty

Stamps of Poland overprinted

(R1) (R2) (R3)

1925 (5 Jan). Nos. 218/228 (Arms) optd with T **R1**.

R1	**40**	1g. yellow-brown	65	3·75
R2		2g. grey-brown	65	8·75
R3		3g. orange	65	2·50
R4		5g. sage-green	19·00	12·50
R5		10g. blue-green	6·25	5·00
R6		15g. scarlet	35·00	12·50
R7		20g. light blue	1·90	2·50
R8		25g. claret	1·90	2·50
R9		30g. bright violet	1·90	2·50
R10		40g. slate	1·90	2·50
R11		50g. magenta	6·25	3·75
R1/R11 *Set of* 11			70·00	55·00

1926 (12 Apr). Nos. 244/245 optd with T **R1**.

R12	**44**	5g. green (Town Hall, Poznań)	55·00	65·00
R13		10g. violet (King Sigismund Monument. Warsaw)	15·00	25·00

1926–29. Optd with T **R2**.

R14	**44**	5g. green (No. 244a)	1·90	3·25
R15	**45**	10g. violet (No. 245a) (1927)	1·90	3·25
R16	**46**	15g. carmine (No. 246a) (Wawel Castle)	25·00	6·25
		a. Optd on No. 246	75·00	90·00
R17	**48**	20g. carmine (Ship) (15.2.28)	3·75	3·25
R18	**51**	25g. yellow-brown (Marshal Piłsudski)	6·25	7·50
R19	**57**	1z. slate-black/*cream* (President Mościcki) (30.11.29)	35·00	55·00
R14/R19 *Set of* 6			65·00	70·00

Inverted overprints of Nos. R14/R15, R17 and R24 are now believed to be private productions made from the original clichés.

1929 (28 May)–**30.** Optd with T **R3**.

R21	**61**	5g. violet (Arms)	1·90	3·25
R22		10g. green (1930)	1·90	3·25
R23	**59**	15g. deep blue (Sienkiewicz) (5.1.30)	5·00	9·50
R24	**61**	25g. red-brown	3·75	3·25
R21/R24 *Set of* 4			11·50	17·00

See note below No. R19.

(R4) (R5)

1933 (1 July). No. 273a (Mościcki) optd with T **R4**. Perf 11½.

R25	**57**	1z. slate-black/*cream* (V)	95·00	£225

1934 (22 Sept)–**35.** Nos. 284*a*/285*a* (Arms) optd with T **R3**.

R26	**65**	5g. violet	4·50	10·00
R27		10g. green (30.10.35)	44·00	£160
R28		15g. claret	4·50	10·00
R26/R28 *Set of* 3			48·00	£160

1936–37. Nos. 313, 315, 317, 319 and 321 optd as T **R5** in one or (Nos. R30 and R31) in two lines.

(a) Typo (August–September 1936).

R29	**79**	5g. violet-blue (Dog's Rock) (15.8.36) ..	3·75	38·00
R30		15g. greenish blue (MS *Piłsudski*) (10.9.36)	3·75	38·00
R31		5g. violet (Czestochowa) (25.10.37)	1·40	19·00

(b) Recess (September 1936–June 1937).

R32		15g. brown-lake (Lwòw University) (5.6.37)..	1·40	19·00
R33		25g. deep blue green (Belvedere Palace) (10.9.36)	3·75	12·50

R6 Port of Danzig

(Des W. Boratynski. Eng M. Dutczynskr. Recess Govt Ptg Wks, Warsaw)

1938 (11 Nov). 20th Anniversary of Polish Independence. Perf 12½×13.

R34	**R6**	5g. red-orange	65	31·00
R35		15g. red-brown	65	31·00
R36		25g. purple	65	31·00
R37		55g. bright blue	1·90	50·00
R34/R37 *Set of* 4			3·50	£130

Stamps inscribed 'GDANSK' showing a Crown surmounting two Maltese Crosses were issued by a Polish Defence organisation but they were not put on sale at the post office.

The Polish Post Office was closed on 1 September 1939 when Danzig was incorporated into Germany.

Marienwerder

100 Pfennig = 1 Mark

By the treaty of Versailles, 1919, a plebiscite was to be held to determine whether this district of West Prussia should belong to Germany or Poland and an Inter-allied Commission was appointed to supervise this.

1

(2)

(Recess Officine Grafiche Coen, Milan)

1920 (13 Mar–13 Apr). Inscr 'COMMISSION INTERALLIÉE' at top. Papermaker's wmk, O.B.M. and two Stars or P. & C.M. in sheet. Perf 11½.

1	**1**	5pf. green	1·00	4·00
2		10pf. red (13.4)	1·00	3·25
3		15pf. slate	1·00	4·50
4		20pf. orange-brown	1·00	3·25
5		25pf. blue	1·00	4·50
6		30pf. orange (13.4)	1·40	4·50
7		40pf. brown (13.4)	1·00	5·25
8		50pf. violet	1·00	4·00
9		60pf. red-brown (13.4)	6·50	6·50
10		75pf. chocolate (13.4)	1·40	4·00
11		1m. brown and green (13.4)	1·00	3·25
12		2m. purple (13.4)	3·25	7·75
13		3m. vermilion (13.4)	7·75	11·50
14		5m. blue and carmine (13.4)	46·00	33·00
1/14 *Set of* 14			65·00	90·00

Printings were made on thick bluish and greyish paper and on thin yellowish paper.

All values exist imperforate (*Price £55 each unused*).

1920 (27 Mar–11 May). Stamps of Germany (W **23**), optd as in T **2**.

15	**17**	5pf. green (8.5)	23·00	46·00
		a. Opt inverted	£200	£325
16		20pf. ultramarine (8.5)	11·50	46·00
		a. Opt inverted	£100	£225
		b. Opt double	£130	
17		50pf. black and purple/*buff* (9.4)	£600	£1300
		a. On cream (No. 90*a*) (11.5)	£1300	£4500
18		75pf. black and blue-green	7·75	16·00
		a. Opt inverted	£100	£225
19		80pf. black and carmine/*rose*	£120	£200
20	**18**	1m. carmine-red (No. 93B)	£130	£250
		a. Opt inverted	£650	
15/20 *Set of* 6			£800	£1700

An official proof sheet was made of the 1m. with the overprint in sans-serif capitals in black. This also exists with the overprint more widely spaced between the lines in serifed capitals, both in black and in red, whilst the 75pf. and 80pf. exist with the normal overprint in red but they were all private productions None of these was issued although copies have passed through the post.

1920 (21 Apr–11 May). Stamps of Germany (W **23**), surch as T **2**.

21	**24**	1m. on 2pf. grey	49·00	80·00
22		2m. on 2½pf. grey (11.5)	25·00	33·00
23	**17**	3m. on 3pf. brown (10.5)	25·00	33·00
24	**24**	5m. on 7½pf. orange (11.5)	25·00	33·00
21/24 *Set of* 4			£110	£160

There are minor varieties of lettering in T **2**, consisting of accented 'e' of different type in 'Interalliee', 'M' of 'Mark' or 'Marienwerder' with straight or slanting strokes, with or without serifs and two types of figures '2' and '5'.

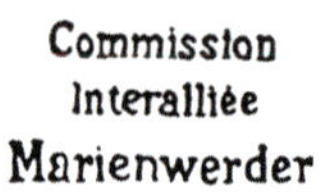

(3)

4

1920 (9–16 July). Stamps of Germany (offset ptg, W **23**) optd with T **3**.

25	**18**	1m. carmine-red (16.7)	4·00	11·50
26		1m.25 green	5·25	14·50
27		1m.50 brown	6·50	16·00
28	**20**	2m.50 claret (16.7)	4·00	14·50
25/28 *Set of* 4			18·00	50·00

1920 (11 July–3 Aug). Inscr 'PLEBISCITE' at top. Perf 11½.

29	**4**	5pf. green (3.8)	6·25	3·25
30		10pf. red(3.8)	6·25	3·25
31		15pf. slate (3.8)	23·00	22·00
32		20pf. orange-brown (3.8)	4·50	3·25
33		25pf. blue (3.8)	23·00	29·00
34		30pf. orange (3.8)	4·50	2·50
35		40pf. brown (3.8)	4·50	2·50
36		50pf. violet (3.8)	3·50	3·25
37		60pf. red-brown (3.8)	10·50	9·00
38		75pf. chocolate (3.8)	10·50	9·00
39		1m. brown and green (16.7)	4·50	2·50
40		2m. purple	4·50	2·50
41		3m. vermilion	4·50	3·25
42		5m. blue and carmine	6·75	4·50
29/42 *Set of* 14			£110	90·00

The plebiscite was held on 11 July 1920 and resulted in a vote of 92% in favour of remaining in Germany. Marienwerder was restored to Germany on 16 August 1920 and German stamps were used there until 1945, since when it has been administered by Poland under the name of Kwidzyn.

Upper Silesia

100 Pfennig = 1 Mark

By the Treaty of Versailles, 1919, a plebiscite was to be held in Upper Silesia, in Germany, to determine whether the inhabitants of part of the area wished to be included in Poland.

1

(Typo Govt Ptg Wks, Paris)

1920 (20 Feb). Perf 14×13½.

1	**1**	2½pf. slate	65	1·30
2		3pf. chocolate	65	2·00
3		5pf. green	40	1·30
4		10pf. chestnut	65	2·10
5		15pf. violet	40	1·30
6		20pf. blue	40	1·30
7		50pf. maroon	7·75	13·00
8		1m. pink	7·75	18·00
9		5m. orange	7·75	18·00
1/9 *Set of* 9			24·00	50·00

No. 10 is vacant.

5 Pf **(2)** 5 Pf. **(3)**

10 Pf. **(4)** 10 Pf **(5)**

50 Pf **(6)** 50 Pf **(7)** 50 Pf **(8)**

(Surch by Erdm. Raabe, Oppeln)

1920 (1 Mar). T **1** Surch.

11	**3**	5pf. on 15pf. violet	£250	£950
12	**2**	5pf. on 20pf. blue	1·80	5·25
13	**3**	5pf. on 20pf. blue	2·50	6·50
14	**4**	10pf. on 20pf. blue (R.)	1·80	5·25
15	**5**	10pf. on 20pf. blue (R.)	3·25	8·25
16	**6**	50pf. on 5m. orange	49·00	90·00
17	**7**	50pf. on 5m. orange	60·00	90·00
18	**8**	50pf. on 5m. orange	65·00	£140

No. 11 in violet was printed in error.

Other minor differences exist in the figures of Type **2** to **8**, but we only list the most prominent.

9

10 Coal Mine in Silesia

(Typo Govt Ptg Wks, Paris)

1920 (26 Mar). Perf 13½×14 (T **9**) or 14×13½ (T **10**).

19	**9**	2½pf. slate	50	1·30
20		3pf. dull maroon	90	1·30
21		5pf. green	50	1·30
22		10pf. red	90	1·30
23		15pf. violet	90	1·30
24		20pf. blue	1·30	3·25

25		25pf. grey-brown	1·70	3·50
26		30pf. orange-yellow	1·30	1·30
27		40pf. olive-green	1·30	1·70
28	**10**	50pf. slate	1·70	1·30
29		60pf. blue	90	2·50
30		75pf. green	2·50	3·25
31		80pf. maroon	2·50	1·70
32		1m. magenta	2·50	1·30
33		2m. grey-brown	2·50	1·30
34		3m. violet	2·10	1·30
35		5m. orange	6·50	9·00
19/35 *Set of* 17			27·00	34·00

(11)

(12)

(13)

1921 (20 Mar). Type **9** and **10** optd.

36	**11**	10pf. red	6·50	16·00
37		15pf. violet	6·50	16·00
38		20pf. blue	9·00	22·00
39		25pf. grey-brown (R.)	20·00	50·00
		a. Opt inverted		
40		30pf. orange-yellow	17·00	33·00
41		40pf. olive-green (R.)	17·00	33·00
42	**12**	50pf. slate (R.)	17·00	46·00
43		60pf. blue	20·00	39·00
44		75pf. green	20·00	46·00
		a. Opt inverted	£1300	
45		80pf. maroon	33·00	60·00
46		1m. magenta	39·00	£100
36/46 *Set of* 11			£180	£425

Double and inverted overprints exist, also numerous errors, including '1921' omitted.

1922 (1 Mar). Surch as T **13**.

47	**10**	4m. on 60pf. olive-green	1·30	3·25
48		10m. on 75pf. red	2·00	4·50
49		20m. on 80pf. orange	10·50	26·00
47/49 *Set of* 3			12·50	30·00

INTER-ALLIED COMMISSION

(O14)

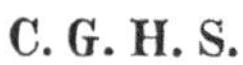

(O15)

1920 (14 Feb). Stamps of Germany handstamped with T **O14**, in blue.

(a) Postage stamps.

O1	**24**	2pf. yellowish grey		£5000
O2		2½pf. grey	£2750	£1200
O3	**17**	3pf. brown		£1100
O4		5pf. green	£1600	£800
O5	**24**	7½pf. orange	£2750	£1300
O6	**17**	10pf. carmine	£1000	£500
O7	**24**	15pf. slate-violet	£1000	£400
O8	**17**	20pf. violet-blue	£1000	£500
O9		25pf. black and red/*yellow*		£5000
O10		30pf. black and orange/*rose*	£1800	£425
O11	**24**	35pf. red-brown	£1800	£400
O12	**17**	40pf. black and carmine	£1200	£400
O13		50pf. black and purple/*rose*	£1200	£400
O14		60pf. rose-purple	£1800	£400
O15		75pf. black and blue-green	£1000	£400
O16		80pf. black and lake/*carmine*		£5000
O17	**18**	1m. carmine-red	£2750	£1200
O18	**20**	2m. deep blue		£5000

(b) War Charity. Nos. 105/106.

O19	**17**	10+5pf. carmine		
O20	**24**	15+5pf. slate-violet		

(c) National Assembly at Weimar. Nos. 107/110.

O21	**26**	10pf. carmine	£2000	£1600
O22	**27**	15pf. blue and chocolate		£1600
O23	**28**	25pf. scarlet and green		£8000
O24		30pf. scarlet and purple	£2000	£2000

Nos. O4, O7, O8, O10/O17 and O22 exist with red overprint. The above were in use between 14 and 19 February pending the arrival of Nos. 1/9.

1920–22. Official stamps of Germany optd with T **O15**, in black.

*(a) Types **O31** and **O32**, etc. (with figures '21') (April 1920).*

O25	5pf. green	50	5·00
O26	10pf. carmine	50	5·00
O27	15pf. chocolate	50	5·00
O28	20pf. deep blue	50	5·00
O29	30pf. orange/*buff*	50	5·00
O30	50pf. violet/*buff*	1·30	5·25
O31	1m. red/*buff*	10·50	21·00
O25/O31 *Set of* 7		13·00	46·00

*(b) Types **O31**, **O32**, etc but without figures (July 1920–1922).*

O32	5pf. green	1·30	13·00
O33	10pf. carmine	40	5·00
O34	15pf. brown-purple	40	5·00
O35	20pf. deep blue	40	5·00
O36	30pf. orange/*buff*	40	5·00
O37	40pf. carmine (10.20)	40	5·00
O38	50pf. violet/*buff*	40	5·00
O39	60pf. purple-brown (5.21)	40	5·00
O40	1m. red/*buff*	40	5·00
O41	1m.25 indigo/*yellow* (9.21)	40	5·25
O42	2m. blue (wmk Lozenges) (9.20)	13·00	20·00
O43	2m. blue (wmk Mesh) (2.22)	40	5·25
O44	5m. brown/*yellow*	40	5·25
O32/O44 *Set of* 13		17·00	80·00

Many stamps may be found with this overprint inverted, sideways, double, etc., but some of these are from printer's waste.

After the plebiscite of 20 March 1921, Upper Silesia was divided between Germany and Poland.

Stamp